AMERICAN SPEECHES:

THE REVOLUTION
TO THE CIVIL WAR

AMERICAN SPEECHES

POLITICAL ORATORY FROM
THE REVOLUTION TO THE CIVIL WAR

THE LIBRARY OF AMERICA

Some of the material in this volume is reprinted by
permission of the holders of copyright and publication rights.
Acknowledgments will be found on pages 751–55.

The paper used in this publication meets the
minimum requirements of the American National Standard for
Information Sciences—Permanence of Paper for Printed
Library Materials, ANSI Z39.48—1984.

Distributed to the trade in the United States
by Penguin Putnam Inc.
and in Canada by Penguin Books Canada Ltd.

Library of Congress Catalog Number: 2006040928
For cataloging information, see end of Index.
ISBN 978–1–931082–97–6
ISBN 1–931082–97–9

———

First Printing
The Library of America—166

Manufactured in the United States of America

TED WIDMER
IS THE EDITOR OF THIS VOLUME

American Speeches
is published with support from

THE ACHELIS FOUNDATION
and
THE BODMAN FOUNDATION

Contents

JAMES OTIS

Argument Against Writs of Assistance

Boston, February 24, 1761

May it please your Honours,
I was desired by one of the court to look into the books, and consider the question now before the court, concerning Writs of Assistance. I have accordingly considered it, and now appear not only in obedience to your order, but also in behalf of the inhabitants of this town, who have presented another petition, and out of regard to the liberties of the subject. And I take this opportunity to declare, that whether under a fee or not, (for in such a cause as this I despise a fee) I will to my dying day oppose, with all the powers and faculties God has given me, all such instruments of slavery on the one hand, and villainy on the other, as this writ of assistance is. It appears to me (may it please your honours) the worst instrument of arbitrary power, the most destructive of English liberty, and the fundamental principles of the constitution, that ever was found in an English law-book. I must therefore beg your honours patience and attention to the whole range of an argument, that may perhaps appear uncommon in many things, as well as points of learning, that are more remote and unusual, that the whole tendency of my design may the more easily be perceived, the conclusions better descend, and the force of them better felt.

I shall not think much of my pains in this cause as I engaged in it from principle. I was sollicited to engage on the other side. I was sollicited to argue this cause as Advocate-General, and because I would not, I have been charged with a desertion of my office; to this charge I can give a very sufficient answer, I renounced that office, and I argue this cause from the same principle; and I argue it with the greater pleasure as it is in favour of British liberty, at a time, when we hear the greatest monarch upon earth declaring from his throne, that he glories in the name of Briton, and that the privileges of his people are dearer to him than the most valuable prerogatives of his crown. And as it is in opposition to a kind of power, the exercise of which in former periods of English history, cost one King of England his head and another his throne. I have taken more pains in this cause, than I ever will take again: Although my engaging in this and another popular cause has raised much resentment; but I think I can sincerely declare, that I cheerfully submit myself to every odious name for conscience sake; and from my soul I despise all those whose guilt, malice or folly has made my foes. Let the consequences be what they will, I am determined to proceed. The only principles of public conduct that are worthy a gentleman, or a man are, to sacrifice estate, ease, health and applause, and even life itself to the sacred calls of his country. These manly sentiments in private life make the good citizen, in public life, the patriot and the hero.—I do not say, when brought to the test, I shall be invincible; I pray God I may never be brought to the melancholy trial; but if ever I should, it would be then known, how far I can reduce to practice principles I know founded in truth.—In the mean time I will proceed to the subject of the writ. In the first, may it please your Honours, I will admit, that writs of one kind, may be legal, that is, *special writs, directed to special officers*, and to search *certain houses*, &c. *especially set forth in the writ*, may be granted by the Court of Exchequer at home, *upon oath made before* the Lord Treasurer by the person, who asks, *that he suspects such goods to be concealed in* THOSE VERY PLACES HE DESIRES TO SEARCH. The Act of 14th Car. II. which Mr. Gridley mentions proves this. And in this light the writ appears like a warrant from a justice of peace to search for stolen goods. Your Honours will find in the old book, concerning the office of justice of peace, precedents of general warrants to search suspected houses. But in more modern books you will find only special warrants to search such and such houses specially named, in which the complainant has before sworn he suspects his goods are concealed; and you will find it adjudged *that special warrants only are legal*. In the same manner I rely on it, that the writ prayed for in this petition being general is illegal. It is a power that places the liberty of every man in the hands of every petty officer. I say I admit that *special* writs of assistance to search *special* houses, may be granted to certain persons on oath; but I deny that the writ now prayed for can be granted, for I beg leave to make some observations on the writ itself before I proceed to other Acts of Parliament.

In the first place the writ is UNIVERSAL, being directed "to all and singular justices, sheriffs, constables and all other officers and subjects, &c." So that in short it is directed to every subject in the king's dominions; every one with this writ may be a tyrant: If this commission is legal, a tyrant may, in a legal manner also, controul, imprison or murder any one within the realm.

In the next place, IT IS PERPETUAL; there's no return, a man is accountable to no person for his doings, every man may reign secure in his petty tyranny, and spread terror and desolation around him, until the trump of the arch angel shall excite different emotions in his soul.

In the third place, a person with this writ, IN THE DAY TIME may enter all houses, shops, &c. AT WILL, and command all to assist.

Fourth, by this not only deputies, &c. but even THEIR MENIAL SERVANTS ARE ALLOWED TO LORD IT OVER US—What is this but to have the curse of Canaan with a witness on us, to be the servant of servants, the most despicable of GOD'S creation. Now one of the most essential branches of English liberty, is the freedom of one's house. A man's house is his castle; and while he is quiet, he is as well guarded as a prince in his castle. This writ, if it should be declared legal, would totally annihilate this privilege. Custom house officers may enter our houses when they please—we are commanded to permit their entry—their menial servants may enter—may break locks, bars and every thing in their way—and whether they break through malice or revenge, no man, no court can inquire—bare suspicion without oath is sufficient. This wanton exercise of this power is no chimerical suggestion of a heated Brain—I will mention some facts. Mr. Pew had one of these writs, and when Mr. Ware succeeded him, he endorsed this writ over to Mr. Ware, so that THESE WRITS ARE NEGOTIABLE from one officer to another, and so your Honours have no opportunity of judging the persons to whom this vast power is delegated. Another instance is this.—Mr. Justice Wally had called this same Mr. Ware before him by a constable, to answer for a breach of the Sabbath day acts, or that of profane swearing. As soon as he had done, Mr. Ware asked him if he had done, he replied, yes. Well then, says he, I will shew you a little of my power—I command you to permit me to search your house for unaccustomed goods; and went on to search his house from the garret to the cellar, and then served the constable in the same manner. But to shew another absurdity in this writ, if it should be established, I insist upon it EVERY PERSON by 14th of Car. II. HAS THIS POWER as well as Custom-house officers; the words are, "it shall be lawful for any person or persons authorized, &c." What a scene does this open! Every man prompted by revenge, ill humour or wantonness to inspect the inside of his neighbour's house, may get a writ of assistance; others will ask it from self defence; one arbitrary exertion will provoke another, until society will be involved in tumult and in blood. Again these writs ARE NOT RETURNED. Writs in their nature are temporary things; when the purposes for which they are issued are answered, they exist no more; but these monsters in the law live forever, no one can be called to account. Thus reason and the constitution are both against this writ. Let us see what authority there is for it. No more than one instance can be found of it in all our law books, and that was in the zenith of arbitrary power, viz. In the reign of Car. II. when Star-chamber powers were pushed in extremity by some ignorant clerk of the Exchequer. But had this writ been in any book whatever it would have been illegal. ALL PRECEDENTS ARE UNDER THE CONTROUL OF THE PRINCIPLES OF THE LAW. Lord Talbot says, it is better to observe these than any precedents though in the House of Lords, the last resort of the subject. No Acts of Parliament can establish such a writ; Though it should be made in the very words of the petition it would be void, "AN ACT AGAINST THE CONSTITUTION IS VOID." Vid. Viner. But these prove no more than what I before observed, that *special* writs may be granted *on oath* and *probable suspicion*. The Act of 7th and 8th of William III. that the officers of the plantations shall have the same powers, &c. is confined to this sense, that an officer should show probable grounds, should take his oath on it, should do this before a magistrate, and that such magistrate, if he thinks proper should issue a *special warrant* to a constable to search the places. That of 6th of Anne can prove no more.

It is the business of this court to demolish this monster of oppression, and to tear into rags this remnant of Starchamber tyranny—&c.

The court suspended the absolute determination of this matter. I have omitted many authorities; also many fine touches in the order of reasoning, and numberless Rhetorical and popular flourishes.

JOHN HANCOCK

Oration on the Boston Massacre

Boston, March 5, 1774

MEN, BRETHREN, FATHERS AND FELLOW COUNTRYMEN!
The attentive gravity, the venerable appearance of this crouded audience, the dignity which I behold in the countenances of so many in this great Assembly, the solemnity of the occasion upon which we have met together, join'd to a consideration of the part I am to take in the important business of this day, fill me with an awe hitherto unknown; and heighten the sense which I have ever had, of my unworthiness to fill this sacred desk; but, allur'd by the call of some of my respected fellow-citizens, with whose request it is always my greatest pleasure to comply, I almost forgot my want of ability to perform what they required. In this situation, I find my only support, in assuring myself that a generous people will not severely censure what they know was well intended, though it's want of merit, should prevent their being able to applaud it. And I pray, that my sincere attachment to the interest of my country, and hearty detestation of every design formed against her liberties, may be admitted as some apology for my appearance in this place.

I have always from my earliest youth, rejoiced in the felicity of my Fellow-men, and have ever consider'd it as the indispensible duty of every member of society to promote, as far as in him lies, the prosperity of every individual, but more especially of the community to which he belongs; and also, as a faithful subject of the state, to use his utmost endeavours to detect, and having detected, strenuously to oppose every traiterous plot which its enemies may devise for its destruction. Security to the persons and properties of the governed, is so obviously the design and end of civil government, that to attempt a logical proof of it, would be like burning tapers at noon-day, to assist the sun in enlightening the world; and it cannot be either virtuous or honorable, to attempt to support a government, of which this is not the great and principal basis; and it is to the last degree vicious and infamous to attempt to support a government which manifestly tends to render the persons and properties of the governed insecure. Some boast of being *friends to government*; I am a friend to *righteous* government, to a government founded upon the principles of reason and justice; but I glory in publickly avowing my eternal enmity to tyranny. Is the present system which the British administration have adopted for the government of the colonies, a righteous government? Or is it tyranny?—Here suffer me to ask (and would to Heaven there could be an answer) What tenderness? What regard, respect or consideration has *Great-Britain* shewn in their late transactions for the security of the persons or properties of the inhabitants of the colonies? or rather, What have they omitted doing to destroy that security? They have declared that they have, ever had, and of right ought ever to have, full power to make laws of sufficient validity to bind the colonies in all cases whatever: They have exercised this pretended right by imposing a tax upon us without our consent; and lest we should shew some reluctance at parting with our property, her fleets and armies are sent to inforce their mad pretensions. The town of Boston, ever faithful to the British Crown, has been invested by a British fleet: The troops of George the Third have cross'd the wide atlantick, not to engage an enemy, but to assist a band of TRAITORS in trampling on the rights and liberties of his most loyal subjects in America,—those rights and liberties which as a father he ought ever to regard, and as a King he is bound in honour to defend from violations, even at the risque of his own life.

Let not the history of the illustrious house of Brunswick inform posterity, that a King descended from that glorious monarch George the second, once sent his British subjects to conquer and enslave his subjects in America; but be perpetual infamy entail'd upon that villain who dared to advise his Master to such execrable measures; for it was easy to foresee the consequences which so naturally followed upon sending troops into

America, to enforce obedience to acts of the British parliament, which neither God nor man ever empowered them to make. It was reasonable to expect that troops who knew the errand they were sent upon, would treat the people whom they were to subjugate, with a cruelty and haughtiness, which too often buries the honorable character of a *soldier*, in the disgraceful name of an *unfeeling ruffian*. The troops upon their first arrival took possession of our Senate House, and pointed their cannon against the Judgment-hall, and even continued them there whilst the Supreme Court of Judicature for this Province was actually sitting to decide upon the lives and fortunes of the King's subjects.—Our streets nightly resounded with the noise of riot and debauchery; our peaceful citizens were hourly exposed to shameful insults, and often felt the effects of their violence and outrage. But this was not all: As though they thought it not enough to violate our civil Rights, they endeavoured to deprive us of the enjoyment of our religious privileges, to viciate our morals, and thereby render us deserving of destruction. Hence the rude din of arms which broke in upon your solemn devotions in your temples, on that day hallowed by Heaven, and set apart by God himself for his peculiar worship. Hence, impious oaths and blasphemies so often tortur'd your unaccustomed ear. Hence, all the arts which idleness and luxury could invent, were used, to betray our youth of one sex into extravagance and effeminacy, and of the other to infamy and ruin; and did they not succeed but too well? Did not a reverence for religion sensibly decay? Did not our infants almost learn to lisp out curses before they knew their horrid import? Did not our youth forget they were Americans, and regardless of the admonitions of the wife and aged, servilely copy from their tyrants those vices which finally must overthrow the empire of Great-Britain? And must I be compelled to acknowledge, that even the noblest, fairest part of all the lower creation did not entirely escape the cursed snare? When virtue has once erected her throne within the female breast, it is upon so solid a basis that nothing is able to expel the heavenly inhabitant? But have there not been some, few indeed, I hope, whose youth and inexperience have render'd them a prey to wretches, whom upon the least reflection, they would have despised and hated as foes to God and their country? I fear there have been some such unhappy instances; or why have I seen an honest father cloathed with shame? or why a virtuous mother drowned in tears?

But I forbear, and come reluctantly to the transactions of that dismal night, when in such quick succession we felt the extremes of grief, astonishment and rage; when Heaven in anger, for a dreadful moment, suffer'd Hell to take the reins; when Satan with his chosen band open'd the sluices of New-England's blood, and sacrilegiously polluted our land with the dead bodies of her guiltless sons. Let this sad tale of death never be told without a tear; let not the heaving bosom cease to burn with a manly indignation at the barbarous story, thro' the long tracts of future time: Let every parent tell the shameful story to his listening children till tears of pity glisten in their eyes, and boiling passion shakes their tender frames; and whilst the anniversary of that ill-fated night is kept a jubilee in the grim court of pandæmonium, let all America join in one common prayer to Heaven, that, the inhuman, unprovok'd murders of the Fifth of March 1770, planned by Hillsborough, and a knot of treacherous knaves in Boston, and executed by the cruel hand of Preston and his sanguinary coadjutors, may ever stand on history without a parallel. But what, my countrymen, with-held the ready arm of vengeance from executing instant justice on the vile assassins? Perhaps you fear'd promiscuous carnage might ensue, and that the innocent might share the fate of those who had performed the infernal deed. But were not all guilty? Were you not too tender of the lives of those who came to fix a yoke on your necks? But I must not too severely blame a fault, which great souls only can commit. May that magnificence of spirit which scorns the low pursuits of malice, may that generous compassion which often preserves from ruin, even a guilty villain, forever actuate the noble bosoms of Americans!—But let not the miscreant host vainly imagine that we fear'd their arms. No; them we despis'd; we dread nothing but slavery. Death is the creature of a Poltroon's brains; 'tis immortality, to sacrifice ourselves for the salvation of our country. We fear not death. That gloomy night, the pale fac'd moon, and the affrighted stars that hurried through the sky, can witness that we fear not death.—Our hearts, which at the recollection glow with a rage that four revolving years have scarcely taught us to restrain, can witness that we fear not death; and happy 'tis for those who dared to insult us, that their naked bones are not now piled up an everlasting monument of Massachusetts' bravery. But they retir'd, they fled, and in that flight they found their only safety. We then expected that the hand of publick justice would soon inflict that punishment upon the murderers, which by the laws of God and man they had incurred. But let the unbiass'd pen of a Robinson, or perhaps of some equally fam'd American, conduct this trial before the great tribunal of succeeding generations. And though the murderers may escape the just resentment of an enraged people, though drowsy justice intoxicated by the poisonous draught prepared for her cup, still nods upon her rotten seat, yet be assured, such complicated crimes will meet their due reward. Tell me, ye bloody butchers, ye villains high and low, ye wretches who contrived, as well as you who executed the inhuman deed, do you not feel the goads and stings of conscious guilt pierce through your savage bosoms? Though some of you may think yourselves exalted to a heighth that bids defiance to the arms of human justice, and others shrowd yourselves beneath the mask of hypocrisy, and build your hopes of safety on the low arts of cunning, chicanery and falshood; yet, do you not sometimes feel the gnawings of that worm which never dies? Do not the injured shades of Maverick, Gray, Caldwell, Attucks and Carr, attend you in your solitary walks, arrest you even in the midst of your debaucheries, and fill even your dreams with terror? But if the unappeased manes of the dead should not disturb their murderers, yet sorely even your obdurate hearts must shrink, and your guilty blood must chill within your rigid veins, when you behold the miserable Monk, the wretched victim of your savage cruelty. Observe his tottering knees which scarce sustain his wasted body, look on his haggard eyes, mark well the deathlike paleness on his fallen cheek, and tell me, does not the sight plant daggers in your souls? Unhappy Monk! Cut off in the gay morn of manhood from all the joys which sweeten life, doom'd to drag on a pitiful existence without even a hope to taste the pleasures of returning health! Yet Monk, thou livest not in vain; thou livest a warning to thy country which sympathises with thee in thy sufferings;

thou livest an affecting, an alarming instance of the unbounded violence which lust of power, assisted by a standing army, can lead a traitor to commit.

For us he bled, and now languishes. The wounds by which he is tortur'd to a lingering death were aim'd at our country! Surely the meek-eyed charity can never behold such sufferings with indifference. Nor can her lenient hand forbear to pour oil and wine into these wounds; and to assuage at least, what it cannot heal.

Patriotism is ever united with humanity and compassion. This noble affection which impels us to sacrifice every thing dear, even life itself, to our country, involves in it a common sympathy and tenderness for every citizen, and must ever have a *particular feeling* for one who suffers in a publick cause. Thoroughly persuaded of this, I need not add a word to engage your compassion and bounty towards a fellow citizen, who with long protracted anguish falls a victim to the relentless rage of our common enemies.

Ye dark designing knaves, ye murderers, parricides! how dare you tread upon the earth, which has drank in the blood of slaughter'd innocents shed by your wicked hands? How dare you breathe that air which wafted to the ear of heaven the groans of those who fell a sacrifice to your accursed ambition? But if the labouring earth doth not expand her jaws, if the air you breathe is not commissioned to be the minister of death; yet, hear it, and tremble! the eye of Heaven penetrates the darkest chambers of the soul, traces the leading clue through all the labyrinths which your industrious folly has devised; and you, however you may have screen'd yourselves from human eyes, must be arraigned, must lift your hands, red with the blood of those whose death you have procur'd, at the tremendous bar of God.

But I gladly quit the gloomy theme of death, and leave you to improve the thought of that important day, when our naked Souls must stand before that Being, from whom nothing can be hid.—I would not dwell too long upon the horrid effects which have already follow'd from quartering regular troops in this town; let our misfortunes teach posterity to guard against such evils for the future. Standing armies are sometimes, (I would by no means say generally, much less universally) composed of persons who have render'd themselves unfit to live in civil society; who have no other motives of conduct than those which a desire of the present gratification of their passions suggests; who have no property in any country;—Men who have lost or given up their own liberties, and envy those who enjoy liberty; who are equally indifferent to the glory of a GEORGE or a Lewis; who for the addition of one peny a day to their wages would desert from the christian cross, and fight under the crescent of the Turkish Sultan; from such men as these, what has not a state to fear? With such as these, usurping Cæsar pass'd the Rubicon; with such as these he humbled mighty Rome, and forc'd the mistress of the world to own a master in a traitor. These are the men whom scepter'd robbers now employ to frustrate the designs of God, and render vain the bounties which his gracious hand pours indiscriminately upon his creatures. By these the miserable slaves in Turkey, Persia, and many other extensive countries, are render'd truly wretched, though their air is salubrious, and their soil luxuriously fertile.—By these France and Spain, tho' blessed by nature with all that administers to the convenience of life, have been reduc'd to that contemptible state in which they now appear; and by these Britain ——— But if I was possess'd of the gift of prophecy, I dare not, except by divine command, unfold the leaves on which the destiny of that once powerful kingdom is inscrib'd.

But since standing armies are so hurtful to a state, perhaps, my countrymen may demand some substitute, some other means of rendering us secure against the incursions of a foreign enemy. But can you be one moment at a loss? Will not a *well disciplin'd militia* afford you ample security against foreign foes? We want not courage; it is discipline alone in which we are exceeded by the most formidable troops that ever trod the earth. Surely our hearts flutter no more at the sound of war, than did those of the immortal band of Persia, the Macedonian phalanx, the invincible Roman legions, the Turkish Janissaries, the Gens des Armes of France, or the *well known Grena-diers of Britain*. A well disciplin'd militia is a safe, an honourable guard to a community like this, whose inhabitants are by nature brave, and are laudably tenacious of that freedom in which they were born. From a well regulated militia we have nothing to fear; their interest is the same with that of the state. When a country is invaded, the militia are ready to appear in it's defence; they march into the field with that fortitude which a consciousness of the justice of their cause inspires; they do not jeopard their lives for a master who considers them only as the instruments of his ambition, and whom they regard only as the daily dispenser of the scanty pittance of bread and water. No, they fight for their houses, their lands, for their wives, their children, for all who claim the tenderest names, and are held dearest in their hearts, they fight *pro aris & focis*, for their liberty, and for themselves, and for their God. And let it not offend if I say, that no militia ever appear'd in more flourishing condition, than that of this province now doth; and pardon me if I say,—of this town in particular.—I mean not to boast; I would not excite envy, but manly emulation. We have all one common cause; let it therefore be our only contest, who shall most contribute to the security of the liberties of America. And may the same kind providence which has watched over this country from her infant state, still enable us to defeat our enemies. I cannot here forbear noticing the signal manner in which the designs of those who wish not well to us have been discovered. The dark deeds of a treacherous Cabal, have been brought to publick view. You now know the serpents who, whilst cherished in your bosoms, were darting their invenom'd stings into the vitals of the constitution. But the Representatives of the people have fixed a mark on those ungrateful monsters, which, though it may not make them so secure as Cain of old, yet renders them at least as infamous. Indeed it would be affrontive to the tutelar deity of this country ever to despair of saving it from all the snares which human policy can lay.

True it is, that the British ministry have annexed a salary to the office of the Governor of this province, to be paid out of a revenue raised in America without our consent. They have attempted to render our Courts of Justice the instruments of extending the authority of acts of the British parliament over this colony, by making the Judges dependent on the British administration for their support. But this people will never be enslaved with their eyes open. The moment they knew that the Governor was not such a Governor as the charter of the province points out, he lost his power of hurting them. They were alarmed; they suspected him, have guarded against him, and he has found that a wise and a brave people, when they know their danger, are fruitful in expedients to escape it.

The Courts of Judicature also so far lost their dignity by being supposed to be under an undue influence, that our Representatives thought it absolutely necessary to Resolve, that they were bound to declare that they would not receive any other salary besides that which the General Court should grant them; and if they did not make this declaration, that it would be the duty of the House to Impeach them.

Great expectations were also formed from the artful scheme of allowing the East India company to export Tea to America upon their own account. This certainly, had it succeeded, would have effected the purpose of the contrivers, and gratified the most sanguine wishes of our adversaries. We soon should have found our trade in the hands of foreigners, and taxes imposed on every thing which we consumed; nor would it have been strange, if in a few years a company in London should have purchased an exclusive right of trading to America.—But their plot was soon discovered.—The people soon were aware of the poison which with so much craft and subtilty had been concealed: Loss and disgrace ensued: and perhaps this long-concerted, master-piece of policy, may issue in the total disuse of TEA in this country, which will eventually be the saving of the lives and the estates of thousands—Yet while we rejoice that the adversary has not hitherto prevailed against us, let us by no means put off the harness. Restless malice, and disappointed ambition will still suggest new measures to our inveterate *enemies.*—Therefore let *Us* also be ready to take the field whenever danger calls, let us be united and strengthen the hands of each other, by promoting a general union among us.—Much has been done by the Committees of Correspondence for this and the other towns of this province towards uniting the inhabitants; let them still go on and prosper. Much has been done by the Committees of Correspondence for the Houses of Assembly in this and our Sister Colonies, for uniting the Inhabitants of the whole Continent for the security of their common interest. May success ever attend their generous endeavours. But permit me here to suggest a general Congress of Deputies from the several Houses of Assembly on the Continent, as the most effectual method of establishing such an Union as the present posture of our affairs requires. At such a Congress, a firm foundation may be laid for the security of our Rights and Liberties; a system may be formed for our common safety, by a strict adherence to which we shall be able to frustrate any attempts to overthrow our constitution; restore peace and harmony to America, and secure honor and wealth to Great-Britain, even against the inclinations of her ministers, whose duty it is to study her welfare; and we shall also free ourselves from those unmannerly pillagers who impudently tell us, that they are licenced by an act of the British parliament to thrust their dirty hands into the pockets of every American. But I trust, the happy time will come, when with the besom of destruction, these noxious vermin will be swept for ever from the streets of Boston.

Surely you never will tamely suffer this country to be a den of thieves. Remember, my friends, from whom you sprang— Let not a meanness of spirit, unknown to those whom you boast of as your Fathers, excite a thought to the dishonour of your mothers. I conjure you by all that is dear, by all that is honourable, by all that is sacred, not only that ye pray, but that you act; that, if necessary, ye fight, and even die for the prosperity of our Jerusalem. Break in sunder, with noble disdain, the bonds with which the Philistines have bound you. Suffer not yourselves to be betrayed by the soft arts of luxury and effeminacy, into the Pit digged for your destruction. Despise the glare of wealth. That people who pay greater respect to a wealthy villain, than to an honest upright man in poverty, almost deserve to be enslaved; they plainly shew that wealth, however it may be acquired, is in their esteem, to be preferr'd to virtue.

But I thank GOD, that America abounds in men who are superior to all temptation, whom nothing can divert from a steady pursuit of the interest of their country; who are at once it's ornament and safe-guard. And sure I am, I should not incur your displeasure, if I paid a respect so justly due to their much honoured characters in this public place; but when I name an ADAMS, such a numerous host of Fellow-patriots rush upon my mind, that I fear it would take up too much of your time, should I attempt to call over the illustrious roll: But your grateful hearts will point you to the men; and their revered names, in all succeeding times, shall grace the annals of America. From them, let us, my friends, take example; from them let us catch the divine enthusiam; and feel, each for himself, the God-like pleasure of diffusing happiness on all around us; of delivering the oppressed from the iron grasp of tyranny; of changing the hoarse complaints and bitter moans of wretched slaves, into those cheerful songs, which freedom and contentment must inspire. There is a heart-felt satisfaction in reflecting on our exertions for the public weal, which all the sufferings an enraged tyrant can inflict, will never take away; which the ingratitude and reproaches of those whom we have sav'd from ruin cannot rob us of. The virtuous assertor of the Rights of mankind, merits a reward, which even a want of success in his endeavours to save his country, the heaviest misfortune which can befall a genuine Patriot, cannot entirely prevent him from receiving.

I have the most animating confidence that the present noble struggle for liberty, will terminate gloriously for America. And let us play the man for our God, and for the cities of our God; while we are using the means in our power, let us humbly commit our righteous cause to the great Lord of the universe, who loveth righteousness and hateth iniquity.—And having secured the approbation of our hearts, by a faithful and unwearied discharge of our duty to our country, let us joyfully leave her important concerns in the hands of HIM who raiseth up and putteth down the empires and kingdoms of the world as HE pleases; and with cheerful submission to HIS sovereign will, devoutly say,

> *"Although the Fig-Tree shall not Blossom, neither shall Fruit be in the Vines; the Labour of the Olive shall fail, and the Fields shall yield no Meat; the Flock shall be cut off from the Fold, and there shall be no Herd in the Stalls: Yet we will rejoice in the LORD, we will joy in the GOD of our Salvation."*

PATRICK HENRY

Speech in the Virginia Convention

Richmond, March 23, 1775

H E ROSE at this time with a majesty unusual to him in an exordium, and with all that self-possession by which he was so invariably distinguished. "No man," he said, "thought more highly than he did, of the patriotism, as well as abilities, of the very worthy gentlemen who had just addressed the house. But different men often saw the same subject in different lights; and therefore, he hoped it would not be thought disrespectful to those gentlemen, if, entertaining as he did, opinions of a character very opposite to theirs, he should speak forth *his* sentiments freely, and without reserve. This," he said, was no time for ceremony. The question before the house was one of awful moment to this country. For his own part, he considered it as nothing less than a question of freedom or slavery. And in proportion to the magnitude of the subject, ought to be the freedom of the debate. It was only in this way that they could hope to arrive at truth, and fulfil the great responsibility which they held to God and their country. Should he keep back his opinions, at such a time, through fear of giving offence, he should consider himself as guilty of treason towards his country, and of an act of disloyalty toward the majesty of Heaven, which he revered above all earthly kings."

"Mr. President," said he, "it is natural to man to indulge in the illusions of hope. We are apt to shut our eyes against a painful truth—and listen to the song of that syren, till she transforms us into beasts. Is it," he asked, "the part of wise men, engaged in a great and arduous struggle for liberty? Were we disposed to be of the number of those, who having eyes, see not, and having ears, hear not, the things which so nearly concern their temporal salvation? For his part, whatever anguish of spirit it might cost, *he* was willing to know the whole truth; to know the worst, and to provide for it."

"He had," he said, "but one lamp by which his feet were guided: and that was the lamp of experience. He knew of no way of judging of the future, but by the past. And judging by the past, he wished to know what there had been in the conduct of the British ministry for the last ten years, to justify those hopes with which gentlemen had been pleased to solace themselves and the house? Is it that insidious smile with which our petition has been lately received? Trust it not, sir; it will prove a snare to your feet. Suffer not yourselves to be betrayed with a kiss. Ask yourselves how this gracious reception of our petition, comports with those warlike preparations which cover our waters and darken our land? Are fleets and armies necessary to a work of love and reconciliation? Have we shown ourselves so unwilling to be reconciled, that force must be called in to win back our love? Let us not deceive ourselves, sir. These are the implements of war and subjugation—the last arguments to which kings resort. I ask gentlemen, sir, what means this martial array, if its purpose be not to force us to submission? Can gentlemen assign any other possible motive for it? Has Great Britain any enemy in this quarter of the world, to call for all this accumulation of navies and armies? No, sir: she has none. They are meant for us: they can be meant for no other. They are sent over to bind and rivet upon us those chains, which the British ministry have been so long forging. And what have we to oppose to them? Shall we try argument? Sir, we have been trying that for the last ten years. Have we any thing new to offer upon the subject? Nothing. We have held the subject up in every light of which it is capable; but it has been all in vain. Shall we resort to entreaty and humble supplication? What terms shall we find, which have not been already exhausted? Let us not, I beseech you, sir, deceive ourselves longer. Sir, we have done every thing that could be done, to avert the storm which is now coming on. We have petitioned—we have remonstrated—we have supplicated—we have prostrated ourselves before the throne, and have implored its interposition to arrest the tyrannical hands of the ministry and parliament. Our petitions have been slighted; our remonstrances have produced additional violence and insult; our supplications have been disregarded; and we have been spurned, with contempt, from the foot of the throne. In vain, after

these things, may we indulge the fond hope of peace and reconciliation. *There is no longer any room for hope.* If we wish to
be free—if we mean to preserve inviolate those inestimable
privileges for which we have been so long contending—if we
mean not basely to abandon the noble struggle in which we
have been so long engaged, and which we have pledged ourselves never to abandon, until the glorious object of our contest shall be obtained—we must fight!—I repeat it, sir, we must
fight!! An appeal to arms and to the God of Hosts, is all that is
left us!"

"They tell us, sir," continued Mr. Henry, "that we are
weak—unable to cope with so formidable an adversary. But
when shall we be stronger? Will it be the next week, or the
next year? Will it be when we are totally disarmed; and when a
British guard shall be stationed in every house? Shall we gather
strength by irresolution and inaction? Shall we acquire the
means of effectual resistance, by lying supinely on our backs,
and hugging the delusive phantom of hope, until our enemies
shall have bound us, hand and foot? Sir, we are not weak, if we
make a proper use of those means which the God of nature
hath placed in our power. Three millions of people, armed in
the holy cause of liberty, and in such a country as that which
we possess, are invincible by any force which our enemy can
send against us. Besides, sir, we shall not fight our battles
alone. There is a just God who presides over the destinies of
nations; and who will raise up friends to fight our battles for
us. The battle, sir, is not to the strong alone; it is to the vigi-
lant, the active, the brave. Besides, sir, we have no election. If
we were base enough to desire it, it is now too late to retire
from the contest. There is no retreat, but in submission and
slavery! Our chains are forged. Their clanking may be heard on
the plains of Boston! The war is inevitable—and let it come!! I
repeat it, sir, let it come!!!

"It is in vain, sir, to extenuate the matter. Gentlemen may cry,
peace, peace—but there is no peace. The war is actually begun!
The next gale that sweeps from the north, will bring to our
ears the clash of resounding arms! Our brethren are already in
the field! Why stand we here idle? What is it that gentlemen
wish? What would they have? Is life so dear, or peace so sweet,

as to be purchased at the price of chains, and slavery? Forbid it, Almighty God!—I know not what course others may take; but as for me," cried he, with both his arms extended aloft, his brows knit, every feature marked with the resolute purpose of his soul, and his voice swelled to its boldest note of exclamation—"give me liberty, or give me death!"

GEORGE WASHINGTON

Speech to Officers of the Continental Army

Newburgh, N.Y., March 15, 1783

GENTLEMEN: By an anonymous summons, an attempt has been made to convene you together; how inconsistent with the rules of propriety! how unmilitary! and how subversive of all order and discipline, let the good sense of the Army decide.

In the moment of this Summons, another anonymous production was sent into circulation, addressed more to the feelings and passions, than to the reason and judgment of the Army. The author of the piece, is entitled to much credit for the goodness of his Pen and I could wish he had as much credit for the rectitude of his Heart, for, as Men see thro' different Optics, and are induced by the reflecting faculties of the Mind, to use different means, to attain the same end, the Author of the Address, should have had more charity, than to mark for Suspicion, the Man who should recommend moderation and longer forbearance, or, in other words, who should not think as he thinks, and act as he advises. But he had another plan in view, in which candor and liberality of Sentiment, regard to justice, and love of Country, have no part; and he was right, to insinuate the darkest suspicion, to effect the blackest designs.

That the Address is drawn with great Art, and is designed to answer the most insidious purposes. That it is calculated to impress the Mind, with an idea of premeditated injustice in the Sovereign power of the United States, and rouse all those resentments which must unavoidably flow from such a belief. That the secret mover of this Scheme (whoever he may be) intended to take advantage of the passions, while they were warmed by the recollection of past distresses, without giving time for cool, deliberative thinking, and that composure of Mind which is so necessary to give dignity and stability to measures is rendered too obvious, by the mode of conducting the business, to need other proof than a reference to the proceeding.

Thus much, Gentlemen, I have thought it incumbent on me to observe to you, to shew upon what principles I opposed the irregular and hasty meeting which was proposed to have been held on Tuesday last: and not because I wanted a disposition to give you every opportunity consistent with your own honor, and the dignity of the Army, to make known your grievances. If my conduct heretofore, has not evinced to you, that I have been a faithful friend to the Army, my declaration of it at this time wd. be equally unavailing and improper. But as I was among the first who embarked in the cause of our common Country. As I have never left your side one moment, but when called from you on public duty. As I have been the constant companion and witness of your Distresses, and not among the last to feel, and acknowledge your Merits. As I have ever considered my own Military reputation as inseperably connected with that of the Army. As my Heart has ever expanded with joy, when I have heard its praises, and my indignation has arisen, when the mouth of detraction has been opened against it, it can *scarcely be supposed*, at this late stage of the War, that I am indifferent to its interests. But, how are they to be promoted? The way is plain, says the anonymous Addresser. If War continues, remove into the unsettled Country; there establish yourselves, and leave an ungrateful Country to defend itself. But who are they to defend? Our Wives, our Children, our Farms, and other property which we leave behind us. Or, in this state of hostile seperation, are we to take the two first (the latter cannot be removed), to perish in a Wilderness, with hunger, cold and nakedness? If Peace takes place, never sheath your Swords Says he untill you have obtained full and ample justice; this dreadful alternative, of either deserting our Country in the extremest hour of her distress, or turning our Arms against it, (which is the apparent object, unless Congress can be compelled into instant compliance) has something so shocking in it, that humanity revolts at the idea. My God! what can this writer have in view, by recommending such measures? Can he be a friend to the Army? Can he be a friend to this Country? Rather, is he not an insidious Foe? Some Emissary, perhaps, from New York, plotting the ruin of both, by sowing the seeds of discord and seperation between the Civil and Military powers of the Continent? And what a Compliment does he pay to our Understandings, when he recommends measures in either alternative, impracticable in their Nature?

But here, Gentlemen, I will drop the curtain, because it wd. be as imprudent in me to assign my reasons for this opinion, as it would be insulting to your conception, to suppose you stood in need of them. A moment's reflection will convince every dispassionate Mind of the physical impossibility of carrying either proposal into execution.

There might, Gentlemen, be an impropriety in my taking notice, in this Address to you, of an anonymous production, but the manner in which that performance has been introduced to the Army, the effect it was intended to have, together with some other circumstances, will amply justify my observations on the tendency of that Writing. With respect to the advice given by the Author, to suspect the Man, who shall recommend moderate measures and longer forbearance, I spurn it, as every Man, who regards that liberty, and reveres that justice for which we contend, undoubtedly must; for if Men are to be precluded from offering their Sentiments on a matter, which may involve the most serious and alarming consequences, that can invite the consideration of Mankind, reason is of no use to us; the freedom of Speech may be taken away, and, dumb and silent we may be led, like sheep, to the Slaughter.

I cannot, in justice to my own belief, and what I have great reason to conceive is the intention of Congress, conclude this Address, without giving it as my decided opinion, that that Honble Body, entertain exalted sentiments of the Services of the Army; and, from a full conviction of its merits and sufferings, will do it compleat justice. That their endeavors, to discover and establish funds for this purpose, have been unwearied, and will not cease, till they have succeeded, I have not a doubt. But, like all other large Bodies, where there is a variety of different Interests to reconcile, their deliberations are slow. Why then should we distrust them? and, in consequence of that distrust, adopt measures, which may cast a shade over that glory which, has been so justly acquired; and tarnish the reputation of an Army which is celebrated thro' all Europe, for its fortitude and Patriotism? and for what is this done? to bring the object we seek nearer? No! most certainly, in my opinion, it will cast it at a greater distance.

For myself (and I take no merit in giving the assurance, being induced to it from principles of gratitude, veracity and justice), a grateful sence of the confidence you have ever placed in me, a recollection of the chearful assistance, and prompt obedience I have experienced from you, under every vicissitude of Fortune, and the sincere affection I feel for an Army, I have so long had the honor to Command, will oblige me to declare, in this public and solemn manner, that, in the attainment of compleat justice for all your toils and dangers, and in the gratification of every wish, so far as may be done consistently with the great duty I owe my Country, and those powers we are bound to respect, you may freely command my Services to the utmost of my abilities.

While I give you these assurances, and pledge myself in the most unequivocal manner, to exert whatever ability I am possessed of, in your favor, let me entreat you, Gentlemen, on your part, not to take any measures, which, viewed in the calm light of reason, will lessen the dignity, and sully the glory you have hitherto maintained; let me request you to rely on the plighted faith of your Country, and place a full confidence in the purity of the intentions of Congress; that, previous to your dissolution as an Army they will cause all your Accts. to be fairly liquidated, as directed in their resolutions, which were published to you two days ago, and that they will adopt the most effectual measures in their power, to render ample justice to you, for your faithful and meritorious Services. And let me conjure you, in the name of our common Country, as you value your own sacred honor, as you respect the rights of humanity, and as you regard the Military and National character of America, to express your utmost horror and detestation of the Man who wishes, under any specious pretences, to overturn the liberties of our Country, and who wickedly attempts to open the flood Gates of Civil discord, and deluge our rising Empire in Blood. By thus determining, and thus acting, you will pursue the plain and direct road to the attainment of your wishes. You will defeat the insidious designs of our Enemies, who are compelled to resort from open force to secret Artifice.

You will give one more distinguished proof of unexampled patriotism and patient virtue, rising superior to the pressure of the most complicated sufferings; And you will, by the dignity of your Conduct, afford occasion for Posterity to say, when speaking of the glorious example you have exhibited to Mankind, "had this day been wanting, the World had never seen the last stage of perfection to which human nature is capable of attaining."

BENJAMIN FRANKLIN

Speech at the Conclusion
of the Constitutional Convention

Philadelphia, September 17, 1787

I CONFESS that I do not entirely approve of this Constitution at present, but Sir, I am not sure I shall never approve it: For having lived long, I have experienced many Instances of being oblig'd, by better Information or fuller Consideration, to change Opinions even on important Subjects, which I once thought right, but found to be otherwise. It is therefore that the older I grow the more apt I am to doubt my own Judgment and to pay more Respect to the Judgment of others. Most Men indeed as well as most Sects in Religion, think themselves in Possession of all Truth, and that wherever others differ from them it is so far Error. Steele, a Protestant, in a Dedication tells the Pope, that the only Difference between our two Churches in their Opinions of the Certainty of their Doctrine, is, the Romish Church is infallible, and the Church of England is never in the Wrong. But tho' many private Persons think almost as highly of their own Infallibility, as that of their Sect, few express it so naturally as a certain French lady, who in a little Dispute with her Sister, said, I don't know how it happens, Sister, but I meet with no body but myself that's *always* in the right. *Il n'y a que moi que a toujours raison.*

In these Sentiments, Sir, I agree to this Constitution, with all its Faults, if they are such: because I think a General Government necessary for us, and there is no *Form* of Government but what may be a Blessing to the People if well administred; and I believe farther that this is likely to be well administred for a Course of Years, and can only end in Despotism as other Forms have done before it, when the People shall become so corrupted as to need Despotic Government, being incapable of any other. I doubt too whether any other Convention we can obtain, may be able to make a better Constitution: For when you assemble a Number of Men to have the Advantage of their joint Wisdom, you inevitably assemble with those Men all their Prejudices, their Passions, their Errors of Opinion, their local Interests, and their selfish Views. From such an Assembly can a perfect Production be expected? It therefore astonishes me, Sir, to find this System approaching so near to Perfection as it does; and I think it will astonish our Enemies, who are waiting with Confidence to hear that our Councils are confounded, like those of the Builders of Babel, and that our States are on the Point of Separation, only to meet hereafter for the Purpose of cutting one another's Throats. Thus I consent, Sir, to this Constitution because I expect no better, and because I am not sure that it is not the best. The Opinions I have had of its Errors, I sacrifice to the Public Good. I have never whisper'd a Syllable of them abroad. Within these Walls they were born, & here they shall die. If every one of us in returning to our Constituents were to report the Objections he has had to it, and endeavour to gain Partizans in support of them, we might prevent its being generally received, and thereby lose all the salutary Effects & great Advantages resulting naturally in our favour among foreign Nations, as well as among ourselves, from our real or apparent Unanimity. Much of the Strength and Efficiency of any Government, in procuring & securing Happiness to the People depends on Opinion, on the general Opinion of the Goodness of that Government as well as of the Wisdom & Integrity of its Governors. I hope therefore that for our own Sakes, as a Part of the People, and for the Sake of our Posterity, we shall act heartily & unanimously in recommending this Constitution, wherever our Influence may extend, and turn our future Thoughts and Endeavours to the Means of having it well administred.—

On the whole, Sir, I cannot help expressing a Wish, that every Member of the Convention, who may still have Objections to it, would with me on this Occasion doubt a little of his own Infallibility, and to make *manifest* our *Unanimity*, put his Name to this Instrument.—

Then the Motion was made for adding the last Formula, viz Done in Convention by the unanimous Consent &c—which was agreed to and added—accordingly.

PATRICK HENRY

Speech in Virginia Ratifying Convention

Richmond, June 4, 1788

M R. CHAIRMAN.—The public mind, as well as my own, is extremely uneasy at the proposed change of Government. Give me leave to form one of the number of those who wish to be thoroughly acquainted with the reasons of this perilous and uneasy situation—and why we are brought hither to decide on this great national question. I consider myself as the servant of the people of this Commonwealth, as a centinel over their rights, liberty, and happiness. I represent their feelings when I say, that they are exceedingly uneasy, being brought from that state of full security, which they enjoyed, to the present delusive appearance of things. A year ago the minds of our citizens were at perfect repose. Before the meeting of the late Federal Convention at Philadelphia, a general peace, and an universal tranquillity prevailed in this country;—but since that period they are exceedingly uneasy and disquieted. When I wished for an appointment to this Convention, my mind was extremely agitated for the situation of public affairs. I conceive the republic to be in extreme danger. If our situation be thus uneasy, whence has arisen this fearful jeopardy? It arises from this fatal system—it arises from a proposal to change our government:—A proposal that goes to the utter annihilation of the most solemn engagements of the States. A proposal of establishing 9 States into a confederacy, to the eventual exclusion of 4 States. It goes to the annihilation of those solemn treaties we have formed with foreign nations. The present circumstances of France—the good offices rendered us by that kingdom, require our most faithful and most punctual adherence to our treaty with her. We are in alliance with the Spaniards, the Dutch, the Prussians: Those treaties bound us as thirteen States, confederated together—Yet, here is a proposal to sever that confederacy. Is it possible that we shall abandon all our treaties and national engagements?—And for what? I expected to have heard the reasons of an event so unexpected to my mind, and many others. Was our civil polity, or public justice, endangered or sapped? Was the real existence of the country threatened—or was this preceded by a mournful progression of events? This proposal of altering our Federal Government is of a most alarming nature: Make the best of this new Government—say it is composed by any thing but inspiration—you ought to be extremely cautious, watchful, jealous of your liberty; for instead of securing your rights you may lose them forever. If a wrong step be now made, the republic may be lost forever. If this new Government will not come up to the expectation of the people, and they should be disappointed—their liberty will be lost, and tyranny must and will arise. I repeat it again, and I beg Gentlemen to consider, that a wrong step made now will plunge us into misery, and our Republic will be lost. It will be necessary for this Convention to have a faithful historical detail of the facts, that preceded the session of the Federal Convention, and the reasons that actuated its members in proposing an entire alteration of Government—and to demonstrate the dangers that awaited us: If they were of such awful magnitude, as to warrant a proposal so extremely perilous as this, I must assert, that this Convention has an absolute right to a thorough discovery of every circumstance relative to this great event. And here I would make this enquiry of those worthy characters who composed a part of the late Federal Convention. I am sure they were fully impressed with the necessity of forming a great consolidated Government, instead of a confederation. That this is a consolidated Government is demonstrably clear, and the danger of such a Government, is, to my mind, very striking. I have the highest veneration for those Gentlemen,—but, Sir, give me leave to demand, what right had they to say, *We, the People*. My political curiosity, exclusive of my anxious solicitude for the public welfare, leads me to ask, who authorised them to speak the language of, *We, the People*, instead of *We, the States*? States are the characteristics, and the soul of a confederation. If the States be not the agents of this compact, it must be one great consolidated National Government of the people of all the States. I have the highest respect for those Gentlemen who formed the Convention, and were some of them not here, I would express some testimonial of my esteem for them. America had on a former occasion put the utmost confidence in them: A confidence which was well placed: And I am sure, Sir, I would give up any thing to them; I would chearfully confide in them as my Representatives. But, Sir, on this great occasion, I would demand the cause of their conduct.—Even from that illustrious man, who saved us by his valor, I would have a reason for his conduct—that liberty which he has given us by his valor, tells me to ask this reason,—and sure I am, were he here, he would give us that reason: But there are other Gentlemen here, who can give us this information. The people gave them no power to use their name. That they exceeded their power is perfectly clear. It is not mere curiosity that actuates me—I wish to hear the real actual existing danger, which should lead us to take those steps so dangerous in my conception. Disorders have arisen in other parts of America, but here, Sir, no dangers, no insurrection or tumult, has happened—every thing has been calm and tranquil. But notwithstanding this, we are wandering on the great ocean of human affairs. I see no landmark to guide us. We are running we know not whither. Difference in opinion has gone to a degree of inflammatory resentment in different parts of the country—which has been occasioned by this perilous innovation. The Federal Convention ought to have amended the old system—for this purpose they were solely delegated: The object of their mission extended to no other consideration. You must therefore forgive the solicitation of one unworthy member, to know what danger could have arisen under the present confederation, and what are the causes of this proposal to change our Government.

GEORGE WASHINGTON

First Inaugural Address

New York City, April 30, 1789

FELLOW CITIZENS of the Senate and of the House of Representatives

Among the vicissitudes incident to life, no event could have filled me with greater anxieties than that of which the notification was transmitted by your order, and received on the fourteenth day of the present month. On the one hand, I was summoned by my Country, whose voice I can never hear but with veneration and love, from a retreat which I had chosen with the fondest predilection, and, in my flattering hopes, with an immutable decision, as the asylum of my declining years: a retreat which was rendered every day more necessary as well as more dear to me, by the addition of habit to inclination, and of frequent interruptions in my health to the gradual waste committed on it by time. On the other hand, the magnitude and difficulty of the trust to which the voice of my Country called me, being sufficient to awaken in the wisest and most experienced of her citizens, a distrustful scrutiny into his qualifications, could not but overwhelm with despondence, one, who, inheriting inferior endowments from nature and unpractised in the duties of civil administration, ought to be peculiarly conscious of his own deficiencies. In this conflict of emotions, all I dare aver, is, that it has been my faithful study to collect my duty from a just appreciation of every circumstance, by which it might be affected. All I dare hope, is, that, if in executing this task I have been too much swayed by a grateful remembrance of former instances, or by an affectionate sensibility to this transcendent proof, of the confidence of my fellow-citizens; and have thence too little consulted my incapacity as well as disinclination for the weighty and untried cares before me; my *error* will be palliated by the motives which misled me, and its consequences be judged by my Country, with some share of the partiality in which they originated.

Such being the impressions under which I have, in obedience to the public summons, repaired to the present station; it would be peculiarly improper to omit in this first official Act, my fervent supplications to that Almighty Being who rules over the Universe, who presides in the Councils of Nations, and whose providential aids can supply every human defect, that his benediction may consecrate to the liberties and happiness of the People of the United States, a Government instituted by themselves for these essential purposes: and may enable every instrument employed in its administration, to execute with success, the functions allotted to his charge. In tendering this homage to the Great Author of every public and private good, I assure myself that it expresses your sentiments not less than my own; nor those of my fellow-citizens at large, less than either: No People can be bound to acknowledge and adore the invisible hand, which conducts the Affairs of men more than the People of the United States. Every step, by which they have advanced to the character of an independent nation, seems to have been distinguished by some token of providential agency. And in the important revolution just accomplished in the system of their United Government, the tranquil deliberations, and voluntary consent of so many distinct communities, from which the event has resulted, cannot be compared with the means by which most Governments have been established, without some return of pious gratitude along with an humble anticipation of the future blessings which the past seem to presage. These reflections, arising out of the present crisis, have forced themselves too strongly on my mind to be suppressed. You will join me I trust in thinking, that there are none under the influence of which, the proceedings of a new and free Government can more auspiciously commence.

By the article establishing the Executive Department, it is made the duty of the President "to recommend to your consideration, such measures as he shall judge necessary and expedient." The circumstances under which I now meet you, will acquit me from entering into that subject, farther than to refer to the Great Constitutional Charter under which you are assembled; and which, in defining your powers, designates the objects to which your attention is to be given. It will be more consistent with those circumstances, and far more congenial with the feelings which actuate me, to substitute, in place of a recommendation of particular measures, the tribute that is due to the talents, the rectitude, and the patriotism which adorn the characters selected to devise and adopt them. In these honorable qualifications, I behold the surest pledges, that as on one side, no local prejudices, or attachments; no seperate views, nor party animosities, will misdirect the comprehensive and equal eye which ought to watch over this great Assemblage of communities and interests: so, on another, that the foundations of our national policy, will be laid in the pure and immutable principles of private morality; and the pre-eminence of free Government, be exemplified by all the attributes which can win the affections of its Citizens, and command the respect of the world. I dwell on this prospect with every satisfaction which an ardent love for my Country can inspire: since there is no truth more thoroughly established, than that there exists in the œconomy and course of nature, an indissoluble union between virtue and happiness, between duty and advantage, between the genuine maxims of an honest and magnanimous policy, and the solid rewards of public prosperity and felicity: Since we ought to be no less persuaded that the propitious smiles of Heaven, can never be expected on a nation that disregards the eternal rules of order and right, which Heaven itself has ordained: And since the preservation of the sacred fire of liberty, and the destiny of the Republican model of Government, are justly considered as *deeply*, perhaps as *finally* staked, on the experiment entrusted to the hands of the American people.

Besides the ordinary objects submitted to your care, it will remain with your judgment to decide, how far an exercise of the occasional power delegated by the Fifth article of the Constitution is rendered expedient at the present juncture by the nature of objections which have been urged against the System, or by the degree of inquietude which has given birth to them. Instead of undertaking particular recommendations on this subject, in which I could be guided by no lights derived from official opportunities, I shall again give way to my entire confidence in your discernment and pursuit of the public good: For I assure myself that whilst you carefully avoid every alteration which might endanger the benefits of an United and effective Government, or which ought to await the future lessons of experience; a reverence for the characteristic rights of freemen, and a regard for the public harmony, will sufficiently influence your deliberations on the question how far the former can be more impregnably fortified, or the latter be safely and advantageously promoted.

To the preceding observations I have one to add, which will be most properly addressed to the House of Representatives. It concerns myself; and will therefore be as brief as possible. When I was first honoured with a call into the service of my Country, then on the eve of an arduous struggle for its liberties, the light in which I contemplated my duty required that I should renounce every pecuniary compensation. From this resolution I have in no instance departed—And being still under the impressions which produced it, I must decline as inapplicable to myself, any share in the personal emoluments, which may be indispensably included in a permanent provision for the Executive Department; and must accordingly pray that the pecuniary estimates for the Station in which I am placed, may, during my continuance in it, be limited to such actual expenditures as the public good may be thought to require.

Having thus imparted to you my sentiments, as they have been awakened by the occasion which brings us together, I shall take my present leave; but not without resorting once more to the benign Parent of the human race, in humble supplication that since he has been pleased to favour the American people, with opportunities for deliberating in perfect tranquility, and dispositions for deciding with unparellelled unanimity on a form of Government, for the security of their Union, and the advancement of their happiness; so this divine blessing may be equally *conspicuous* in the enlarged views—the temperate consultations, and the wise measures on which the success of this Government must depend.

RED JACKET

Reply to President Washington

Philadelphia, March 31, 1792

I NOW request the attention of the President of the United States, by his agent, Colonel Pickering, now present. A few days since, when the American chief had spoken to us, he gave us to understand that General Knox and Colonel Pickering should be the agents to negotiate with us on things which concern our welfare. Let me call for your compassion, as you can put all down upon paper, while we have to labor with our minds, to retain and digest what is spoken, to enable us to make an answer.

"BROTHER—whose attention I have called as the representative of the great chief of this Island:—when, the other day, he welcomed us to the great council-fire of the thirteen United States, he said it was from his very heart. He said it gave him pleasure to look around and see such numerous representatives of the Five Nations of Indians, and that it was at his special request we had been invited to the seat of the general government, to promote the happiness of our nation, in a friendly connection with the United States. He then told us that his love of peace did not terminate with the Five Nations, but extended to all the nations at the setting sun; and that it was his desire that universal peace might prevail in this island.

"BROTHER CON-NEH-SAUTY: I requested your compassion, on account of our different situations, by reason of which I should notice only a few of the principal things in the President's speech, delivered to us the other day. Three things I have mentioned of the introductory part of his speech. What other reply can we, your brothers of the Five Nations, make to that introductory part of the speech, than to thank him, and say that it has given a spring to every passion of our souls?

"BROTHER: The President again observed to us that he wished our minds might all be disposed to peace,—that a happy peace might be established between you and your brothers of the Five Nations, so firmly that nothing might move it; that it might be founded on a rock. This sentiment of your chief has given joy to our hearts,—to compare that peace to a *rock*, which is *immoveable*.

"The President further observed to us that by our continuing to walk in the path of peace, and hearkening to his counsel, we might share with you in all the blessings of civilized life. This also meets the approbation of our minds, and has the thanks of all your brothers of the Five Nations.

"He again observed to us that if we attended to his counsel in this matter, our children, and children's children, might partake in all the blessings which should rise out of this earth. This has taken hold of our minds, and even we who are grown up look forward, and anticipate its fulfilment.

"The President again observed to us that what he had spoken was in the sincerity of his heart, and that time and opportunities would give further evidence that what he said was true. And we believed it, because we saw the words come from his own lips,—and therefore they were lodged deep in our mind.

"The President of the Thirteen Fires, while continuing his speech, made also this remark, 'that in order to establish all his words for the best good of your nation and our's, we must forget all the evils that were past, and attend to what lies before us, and take such a course as shall cement our peace, that we may be as one.'

"The President again observed that it had come to his ears that the cause of the hostilities now prevailing with the Western Indians, was their persuasion that the United States had unjustly taken away their lands. But he assured us this was not the case. That it was not the mind of any of his chiefs to take any land on the whole island without agreeing for it. He then mentioned a treaty at Muskingum, and he concluded that what land was given up at that treaty was fairly obtained.

"He also observed to us that it was his opinion that the hostile Indians were in an error; that they had missed the true path; whatever evil spirit, or whatever lies had turned them aside, he wished they could be discovered, that they might be removed. He expressed a strong wish that those obstacles to the extending of peace to the westward might be discovered; and he would use all his exertions to remove them, that peace might be extended to the whole Island.—Toward the close of his speech the President informed us that there were many things which concerned the future happiness of the Five Nations, the concerting of which he should refer to you here present, and the Chief Warrior of the United States. And at the close he observed that our professions of friendship and regard were commonly witnessed by some token: therefore, in the name of the United States, he presented us with this white belt, which was to be handed down from one generation to another, as a confirmation of his words, and a witness of the friendly disposition of the United States, towards the peace and happiness of the five confederated Nations."

[Red-Jacket here laid aside the white belt received from the President, and taking up, a belt of their own, proceeded as follows:—]

"Now let the President of the United States possess his mind in peace. We have made but a short reply to his address to us the other day, for the belt he gave us is deposited with us; and we have taken fast hold of it. What more can we say than to return our united thanks for his address in welcoming us to the seat of the great council, and for the advice he gave us? And our pleasure is increased that you, Con-neh-sauty, are appointed to assist us in devising the means to promote and secure the happiness of the Five Nations.

"BROTHER! Now open your ears, as the Representative of the Great Council of the thirteen United States, in our present Council. Hear the words we may speak. And all here present, of the great Council, and our Brethren of the Five Nations, hear!—We consider ourselves in the presence of the Great Spirit, the proprietor of us all.

"The President, in effect, observed to us that we of the Five Nations were our own proprietors—were freemen, and might speak with freedom. This has gladdened our hearts, and removed a weight that was upon them. And therefore you will hear us patiently while we speak. The President has, in effect, told us that we were freemen; the sole proprietors of the soil on which we live. This is the source of the joy which we feel. How can two brothers speak freely together, unless they feel that they are upon equal ground?

"I observed to you, Brother, that our considering ourselves, by your own acknowledgment, as freemen, has given this joy to our hearts—that we might speak in character. Therefore, we join with the President in his wish that all the evils which have hitherto disturbed our peace may be buried in oblivion; and this wish proceeds from our hearts. Now we can speak our minds freely, as they are free from pressure.

"Now, Brother, while you continue to hear in behalf of the United States, let all here present also open their ears, while those of the Five Nations here present speak with one voice. We wish to see your words verified to our children, and children's children. You enjoy all the blessings of this life; to you, therefore, we look to make provision that the same may be enjoyed by our children. This wish comes from our heart; but we add that our happiness cannot be great if in the introduction of your ways we are put under too much constraint.

"BROTHER! Appointed agent to converse with us upon the affairs of our peace, continue to hear. We, your brothers of the Five Nations, believe that the Great Spirit let this island drop down from above. We also believe in his superintendency over this whole island. It is he who gives peace and prosperity, and he also sends evil. But prosperity has been yours. American Brethren—all the good which can spring out of this island you enjoy. We therefore wish that we and our children, and our children's children, may partake with you in that enjoyment.

"BROTHER! I observed that the Great Spirit might smile upon one people, and turn and frown upon another. This you have seen, who are of one color and one blood. The King of England and you Americans strove to advance your happiness by extending your possessions upon this island, which produces so many good things. And while you two great powers were thus contending for those good things, by which the whole island was shaken and violently agitated, is it strange that the peace of us, the Five Nations, was shaken and overturned?

"But, let me say no more of the trembling of our island. All is, in a measure, now quieted. Peace is now restored. The peace of us, the Five Nations, is now budding. But still there is some shaking among the original Americans, at the setting sun;— and you, the Thirteen Fires, and the King of England, know what is our situation, and the causes of this disturbance. Now, here you have an ambassador, as we are informed, from the King of England. Let him, in behalf of the King, and the Americans, adjust all their matters, according to their agreement, at the making of peace—and then you will soon see all things settled among the Indian Nations. Peace will be spread far and near. Let the President and the ambassador use all their exertions to bring about this settlement, (according to the peace,) and it will make us all glad, and we shall consider both as our real friends.

"BROTHER! Continue to hear! Be assured we have spoken from our very hearts, and not from our lips only. Let us therefore make this observation:—That when you Americans and the King made peace, he did not mention us, and showed us no compassion, notwithstanding all he said to us, and all we had suffered. This has been the occasion of great sorrow and pain, and great loss to us, the Five Nations. When you and he settled the peace between you two great nations, he never asked us for a delegation to attend to our interests. Had he done this, a settlement of peace among all the western nations might have been effected. But the neglecting of this, and passing us by unnoticed, has brought upon us great pain and trouble.

"BROTHER! It is evident that we of the Five Nations have suffered much in consequence of the strife between you and the King of England, who are of one color and one blood. Our chain of peace has been broken. Peace and friendship have been chased from us. But you Americans were determined not to treat us in the same manner as we had been treated by the King of England. You therefore desired us, at the reestablishment of peace, to sit down at our ancient fire-places, and again enjoy our lands. And had the peace between you and the King of England been completely accomplished, it would long before this time have extended far beyond the Five Nations.

"BROTHER CON-NEH-SAUTY: You are specially appointed with General Knox to confer with us on our peace and happiness. We have rejoiced in your appointment, and we hope that the great Warrior will remember that though a *Warrior*, he is to converse with us about *peace*; letting what concerns *war* sleep;—and the counselling part of his mind, while acting with us, be of *peace*.

"BROTHER! Have patience, and continue to listen. The President has assured us that *he* is not the cause of the hostilities now existing at the westward, but laments it. Brother, we wish you to point out to us of the Five Nations *what you think is the real cause.*

"BROTHER! Agent of the thirteen United States in the present council: We now publicly return our thanks to the President and all the Counsellors of the thirteen United States, for the words which he has spoken to us. They were good—without any mixture. Shall we observe that he wished that if the errors of the hostile Indians could be discovered, he would use his utmost exertions to remove them?

"BROTHER! You and the King of England are the two governing powers of this Island. What are we? You both are important and proud; and you cannot adjust your own affairs agreeably to your declarations of peace. Therefore the Western Indians are bewildered. One says one thing to them, and one says another. Were these things adjusted, it would be easy to diffuse peace every where.

"In confirmation of our words, we give this belt, which we wish the President to hold fast in remembrance of what we have now spoken."

HENRY LEE

Eulogy on George Washington

Philadelphia, December 26, 1799

I N obedience to your will, I rise your humble organ, with the hope of executing a part of the system of public mourning which you have been pleased to adopt, commemorative of the death of the most illustrious and most beloved personage this country has ever produced; and which, while it transmits to posterity your sense of the awful event, faintly represents your knowledge of the consummate excellence you so cordially honor.

Desperate indeed is any attempt on earth to meet correspondently this dispensation of Heaven: for, while with pious resignation we submit to the will of an all-gracious Providence, we can never cease lamenting in our finite view of Omnipotent Wisdom, the heart-rending privation for which our nation weeps. When the civilized world shakes to its centre; when every moment gives birth to strange and momentous changes; when our peaceful quarter of the globe, exempt as it happily has been from any share in the slaughter of the human race, may yet be compelled to abandon her pacific policy, and to risk the doleful casualties of war: What limit is there to the extent of our loss?—None within the reach of my words to express; none which your feelings will not disavow.

The founder of our fœderate republic—our bulwark in war, our guide in peace, is no more. Oh that this was but questionable! Hope, the comforter of the wretched, would pour into our agonized hearts its balmy dew. But, alas! there is no hope for us: our Washington is removed forever. Possessing the stoutest frame, and purest mind, he had passed nearly to his sixty-eighth year, in the enjoyment of high health, when, habituated by his care of us to neglect himself, a slight cold, disregarded, became inconvenient on Friday, oppressive on Saturday, and defying every medical interposition, before the morning of Sunday, put an end to the best of men. An end did I say—his fame survives! bounded only by the limits of the earth, and by the extent of the human mind. He survives in our hearts, in the growing knowledge of our children, in the affection of the good throughout the world; and when our monuments shall be done away; when nations now existing shall be no more; when even our young and far-spreading empire shall have perished, still will our Washington's glory unfaded shine, and die not, until love of virtue cease on earth, or earth itself sinks into chaos.

How, my fellow-citizens, shall I single to your grateful hearts his pre-eminent worth! Where shall I begin in opening to your view a character throughout sublime. Shall I speak of his war-like achievements, all springing from obedience to his country's will—all directed to his country's good?

Will you go with me to the Banks of the Monongahela, to see your youthful Washington, supporting, in the dismal hour of Indian victory, the ill-fated Braddock, and saving, by his judgment and by his valour, the remains of a defeated army, pressed by the conquering savage foe? Or, when oppressed America, nobly resolving to risk her all in defence of her violated rights, he was elevated by the unanimous voice of Congress to the command of her armies: Will you follow him to the high grounds of Boston, where to an undisciplined, courageous, and virtuous yeomanry, his presence gave the stability of system and infused the invincibility of love of country: Or shall I carry you to the painful scenes of Long-Island, York-Island and New-Jersey, when combating superior and gallant armies, aided by powerful fleets, and led by chiefs high in the roll of fame, he stood the bulwark of our safety; undismayed by disaster; unchanged by change of fortune. Or will you view him in the precarious fields of Trenton, where deep gloom unnerving every arm, reigned triumphant through our thinned, worn down unaided ranks: himself unmoved.—Dreadful was the night; it was about this time of winter—The storm raged—the Delaware rolling furiously with floating ice forbad the approach of man. Washington, self collected, viewed the tremendous scene—his country called; unappall'd by surrounding dangers, he passed to the hostile shore: he fought; he conquered. The morning sun cheered the American world. Our country rose on the event; and her dauntless Chief pursuing his blow, completed in the lawns of Princeton, what his vast soul had conceived on the shores of Delaware.

Thence to the strong grounds of Morris-Town he led his small but gallant band; and through an eventful winter, by the high efforts of his genius, whose matchless force was measurable only by the growth of difficulties, he held in check formidable hostile legions, conducted by a Chief experienced in the art of war, and famed for his valour on the ever-memorable heighths of Abraham, where fell Wolfe, Montcalm, and since our much lamented Montgomery; all covered with glory. In this fortunate interval, produced by his masterly conduct, our fathers, ourselves, animated by his resistless example, rallied around our country's standard and continued to follow her beloved Chief, through the various and trying scenes to which the destinies of our union led.

Who is there that has forgotten the vales of Brandywine—the fields of Germantown, or the plains of Monmouth; every where present, wants of every kind obstructing, numerous and valiant armies encountering, himself a host, he assuaged our sufferings, limited our privations, and upheld our tottering republic. Shall I display to you the spread of the fire of his soul, by rehearsing the praises of the hero of Saratoga, and his much lov'd compeer of the Carolina's? No; our Washington wears not borrowed glory: To Gates—to Green, he gave without reserve the applause due to their eminent merit; and long may the Chiefs of Saratoga, and of Eutaws, receive the grateful respect of a grateful people.

Moving in his own orbit, he imparted heat and light to his most distant satellites; and combining the physical and moral force of all within his sphere, with irresistable weight he took his course, commiserating folly, disdaining vice, dismaying treason and invigorating despondency, until the auspicious hour arrived, when, united with the intrepid forces of a potent and magnanimous ally, he brought to submission the since conqueror of India; thus finishing his long career of military glory with a lustre corresponding to his great name, and in this his last act of war affixing the seal of fate to our nation's birth.

To the horrid din of battle sweet peace succeeded, and our

virtuous chief, mindful only of the common good, in a moment tempting personal aggrandizement, hushed the discon-
tents of growing sedition, and surrendering his power into the
hands from which he had received it, converted his sword into
a ploughshare, teaching an admiring world that to be truly
great, you must be truly good.

Was I to stop here, the picture would be incomplete, and
the task imposed unfinished—Great as was our Washington in
war, and much as did that greatness contribute to produce the
American Republic, it is not in war alone his pre-eminence
stands conspicuous: his various talents combining all the capacities of a statesman with those of the soldier, fitted him alike
to guide the councils and the armies of our nation. Scarcely
had he rested from his martial toils, while his invaluable parental
advice was still sounding in our ears, when he who had been
our shield and our sword, was called forth to act a less splendid
but a more important part.

Possessing a clear and a penetrating mind, a strong and a
sound judgment, calmness and temper for deliberation, with
invincible firmness and perseverance in resolutions maturely
formed, drawing information from all, acting from himself,
with incorruptible integrity and unvarying patriotism: his own
superiority and the public confidence alike marked him as the
man designed by heaven to lead in the great political as well as
military events which have distinguished the æra of his life.

The finger of an overruling Providence, pointing at Washington, was neither mistaken nor unobserved; when to realize
the vast hopes to which our revolution had given birth, a
change of political system became indispensible.

How novel, how grand the spectacle, independent states
stretched over an immense territory, and known only by common difficulty, clinging to their union as the rock of their
safety, deciding by frank comparison of their relative condition, to rear on that rock, under the guidance of reason, a common government thro' whose commanding protection, liberty
and order, with their long train of blessings should be safe to
themselves, and the sure inheritance of their posterity.

This arduous task devolved on citizens selected by the
people, from knowledge of their wisdom and confidence in

their virtue. In this august assembly of sages and of patriots, Washington of course was found—and, as if acknowledged to be most wise, where all were wise, with one voice he was declared their chief. How well he merited this rare distinction, how faithful were the labours of himself and his compatriots, the work of their hands and our union, strength and prosperity, the fruits of that work, best attest.

But to have essentially aided in presenting to his country this consummation of her hopes, neither satisfied the claims of his fellow-citizens on his talents, nor those duties which the possession of those talents imposed. Heaven had not infused into his mind such an uncommon share of its ætherial spirit to remain unemployed, nor bestowed on him his genius unaccompanied with the corresponding duty of devoting it to the common good. To have framed a constitution, was shewing only, without realizing the general happiness. This great work remained to be done, and America, stedfast in her preference, with one voice summoned her beloved Washington, unpractised as he was in the duties of civil administration, to execute this last act in the completion of the national felicity. Obedient to her call, he assumed the high office with that self-distrust peculiar to his innate modesty, the constant attendant of preeminent virtue. What was the burst of joy thro' our anxious land on this exhilerating event is known to us all. The aged, the young, the brave, the fair, rivalled each other in demonstrations of their gratitude; and this high wrought delightful scene was heightened in its effect, by the singular contest between the zeal of the bestowers and the avoidance of the receiver of the honors bestowed. Commencing his administration, what heart is not charmed with the recollection of the pure and wise principles announced by himself, as the basis of his political life. He best understood the indissoluble union between virtue and happiness, between duty and advantage, between the genuine maxims of an honest and magnanimous policy, and the solid rewards of public prosperity and individual felicity: watching with an equal and comprehensive eye over this great assemblage of communities and interests, he laid the foundations of our national policy in the unerring immutable principles of morality, based on religion, exemplifying the pre-eminence of free government, by all the attributes which win the affections of its citizens or command the respect of the world.

"O fortunatos nimium, sua si bona norint!"

Leading thro' the complicated difficulties produced by previous obligations and conflicting interests, seconded by succeeding houses of Congress, enlightened and patriotic, he surmounted all original obstructions, and brightened the path of our national felicity.

The Presidential term expiring, his solicitude to exchange exaltation for humility returned, with a force encreased with increase of age, and he had prepared his farewell address to his countrymen, proclaiming his intention, when the united interposition of all around him, enforced by the eventful prospects of the epoch, produced a further sacrifice of inclination to duty. The election of President followed, and Washington, by the unanimous vote of the nation, was called to resume the chief magistracy: what a wonderful fixure of confidence! Which attracts most our admiration, a people so correct, or a citizen combining an assemblage of talents forbidding rivalry, and stifling even envy itself? Such a nation aught to be happy, such a chief must be forever revered.

War, long menaced by the Indian tribes, now broke out; and the terrible conflict deluging Europe with blood, began to shed its baneful influence over our happy land. To the first, outstretching his invincible arm, under the orders of the gallant Wayne, the American Eagle soared triumphant thro' distant forests. Peace followed victory, and the melioration of the condition of the enemy followed peace. Godlike virtue which uplifts even the subdued savage.

To the second he opposed himself. New and delicate was the conjuncture, and great was the stake.—Soon did his penetrating mind discern and seize the only course, continuing to us all, the felicity enjoyed. He issued his proclamation of neutrality. This index to his whole subsequent conduct, was sanctioned by the approbation of both houses of Congress, and by the approving voice of the people.

To this sublime policy he inviolably adhered, unmoved by foreign intrusion, unshaken by domestic turbulence.

> "Justum et tenacem propositi virum
> Non civium ardor prava jubentium,
> Non vultus instantis tyranni
> Mente quatit solida."

Maintaining his pacific system at the expence of no duty, America faithful to herself and unstained in her honour, continued to enjoy the delights of peace, while afflicted Europe mourns in every quarter, under the accumulated miseries of an unexampled war; miseries in which our happy country must have shared, had not our pre-eminent Washington been as firm in council as he was brave in the field.

Pursuing stedfastly his course, he held safe the public happiness, preventing foreign war, and quelling internal discord, till the revolving period of a third election approached, when he executed his interrupted but inextinguishable desire of returning to the humble walks of private life.

The promulgation of his fixed resolution, stopped the anxious wishes of an affecionate people, from adding a third unanimous testimonial of their unabated confidence in the man so long enthroned in their hearts. When, before, was affection like this exhibited on earth?—Turn over the records of antient Greece—Review the annals of mighty Rome,—examine the volumes of modern Europe; you search in vain. America and her Washington only afford the dignified exemplification.

The illustrious personage called by the national voice in succession to the arduous office of guiding a free people, had new difficulties to encounter: the amicable effort of settling our difficulties with France, begun by Washington, and pursued by his successor in virtue as in station, proving abortive, America took measures of self-defence. No sooner was the public mind roused by prospect of danger, than every eye was turned to the friend of all, though secluded from public view, and grey in public service: the virtuous veteran, following his plough, received the unexpected summons with mingled emotions of indignation at the unmerited ill-treatment of his country, and of a determination once more to risk his all in her defence.

The annunciation of these feelings, in his affecting letter to the President accepting the command of the army, concludes his official conduct.

First in war—first in peace—and first in the hearts of his countrymen, he was second to none in the humble and endearing scenes of private life; pious, just, humane, temperate and sincere; uniform, dignified and commanding, his example was as edifying to all around him, as were the effects of that example lasting.

To his equals he was condescending, to his inferiors kind, and to the dear object of his affections exemplarily tender: correct throughout, vice shuddered in his presence, and virtue always felt his fostering hand; the purity of his private character gave effulgence to his public virtues.

His last scene comported with the whole tenor of his life.—Although in extreme pain, not a sigh, not a groan escaped him; and with undisturbed serenity he closed his well spent life.—Such was the man America has lost—Such was the man for whom our nation mourns.

Methinks I see his august image, and hear falling from his venerable lips these deep sinking words:

"CEASE, Sons of America, lamenting our separation: go on, and confirm by your wisdom the fruits of our joint councils, joint efforts, and common dangers: Reverence religion, diffuse knowledge throughout your land, patronize the arts and sciences; let Liberty and Order be inseparable companions, controul party spirit, the bane of free governments; observe good faith to, and cultivate peace with all nations, shut up every avenue to foreign influence, contract rather than extend national connexion, rely on yourselves only: Be American in thought, word, and deed—Thus will you give immortality to that union, which was the constant object of my terrestrial labours; thus will you preserve undisturbed to the latest posterity, the felicity of a people to me most dear, and thus will you supply (if my happiness is now aught to you) the only vacancy in the round of pure bliss high Heaven bestows."

THOMAS JEFFERSON

First Inaugural Address

Washington, D.C., March 4, 1801

FRIENDS AND FELLOW-CITIZENS,

Called upon to undertake the duties of the first executive office of our country, I avail myself of the presence of that portion of my fellow-citizens which is here assembled to express my grateful thanks for the favor with which they have been pleased to look toward me, to declare a sincere consciousness that the task is above my talents, and that I approach it with those anxious and awful presentiments which the greatness of the charge and the weakness of my powers so justly inspire. A rising nation, spread over a wide and fruitful land, traversing all the seas with the rich productions of their industry, engaged in commerce with nations who feel power and forget right, advancing rapidly to destinies beyond the reach of mortal eye—when I contemplate these transcendent objects, and see the honor, the happiness, and the hopes of this beloved country committed to the issue and the auspices of this day, I shrink from the contemplation, and humble myself before the magnitude of the undertaking. Utterly, indeed, should I despair did not the presence of many whom I here see remind me that in the other high authorities provided by our Constitution I shall find resources of wisdom, of virtue, and of zeal on which to rely under all difficulties. To you, then, gentlemen, who are charged with the sovereign functions of legislation, and to those associated with you, I look with encouragement for that guidance and support which may enable us to steer with safety the vessel in which we are all embarked amidst the conflicting elements of a troubled world.

During the contest of opinion through which we have passed the animation of discussions and of exertions has sometimes worn an aspect which might impose on strangers unused to think freely and to speak and to write what they think; but this being now decided by the voice of the nation, announced according to the rules of the Constitution, all will, of course, arrange themselves under the will of the law, and unite in common efforts for the common good. All, too, will bear in mind this sacred principle, that though the will of the majority is in all cases to prevail, that will to be rightful must be reasonable; that the minority possess their equal rights, which equal law must protect, and to violate would be oppression. Let us, then, fellow-citizens, unite with one heart and one mind. Let us restore to social intercourse that harmony and affection without which liberty and even life itself are but dreary things. And let us reflect that, having banished from our land that religious intolerance under which mankind so long bled and suffered, we have yet gained little if we countenance a political intolerance as despotic, as wicked, and capable of as bitter and bloody persecutions. During the throes and convulsions of the ancient world, during the agonizing spasms of infuriated man, seeking through blood and slaughter his long-lost liberty, it was not wonderful that the agitation of the billows should reach even this distant and peaceful shore; that this should be more felt and feared by some and less by others, and should divide opinions as to measures of safety. But every difference of opinion is not a difference of principle. We have called by different names brethren of the same principle. We are all Republicans, we are all Federalists. If there be any among us who would wish to dissolve this Union or to change its republican form, let them stand undisturbed as monuments of the safety with which error of opinion may be tolerated where reason is left free to combat it. I know, indeed, that some honest men fear that a republican government can not be strong, that this Government is not strong enough; but would the honest patriot, in the full tide of successful experiment, abandon a government which has so far kept us free and firm on the theoretic and visionary fear that this Government, the world's best hope, may by possibility want energy to preserve itself? I trust not. I believe this, on the contrary, the strongest Government on earth. I believe it the only one where every man, at the call of the law, would fly to the standard of the law, and would meet invasions of the public order as his own personal concern. Sometimes it is said that man can not be trusted with the government of himself. Can he, then, be trusted with the government of others? Or have we found angels in the forms of kings to govern him? Let history answer this question.

Let us, then, with courage and confidence pursue our own Federal and Republican principles, our attachment to union and representative government. Kindly separated by nature and a wide ocean from the exterminating havoc of one quarter of the globe; too high-minded to endure the degradations of the others; possessing a chosen country, with room enough for our descendants to the thousandth and thousandth generation; entertaining a due sense of our equal right to the use of our own faculties, to the acquisitions of our own industry, to honor and confidence from our fellow-citizens, resulting not from birth, but from our actions and their sense of them; enlightened by a benign religion, professed, indeed, and practiced in various forms, yet all of them inculcating honesty, truth, temperance, gratitude, and the love of man; acknowledging and adoring an overruling Providence, which by all its dispensations proves that it delights in the happiness of man here and his greater happiness hereafter—with all these blessings, what more is necessary to make us a happy and a prosperous people? Still one thing more, fellow-citizens—a wise and frugal Government, which shall restrain men from injuring one another, shall leave them otherwise free to regulate their own pursuits of industry and improvement, and shall not take from the mouth of labor the bread it has earned. This is the sum of good government, and this is necessary to close the circle of our felicities.

About to enter, fellow-citizens, on the exercise of duties which comprehend everything dear and valuable to you, it is proper you should understand what I deem the essential principles of our Government, and consequently those which ought to shape its Administration. I will compress them within the narrowest compass they will bear, stating the general principle, but not all its limitations. Equal and exact justice to all men, of whatever state or persuasion, religious or political; peace, commerce, and honest friendship with all nations, entangling alliances with none; the support of the State governments in all their rights, as the most competent administrations for our domestic concerns and the surest bulwarks against antirepublican tendencies; the preservation of the General Government in its whole constitutional vigor, as the sheet anchor of our peace at home and safety abroad; a jealous care of the right of election by the people—a mild and safe corrective of abuses which are lopped by the sword of revolution where peaceable remedies are unprovided; absolute acquiescence in the decisions of the majority, the vital principle of republics, from which is no appeal but to force, the vital principle and immediate parent of despotism; a well-disciplined militia, our best reliance in peace and for the first moments of war till regulars may relieve them; the supremacy of the civil over the military authority; economy in the public expense, that labor may be lightly burthened; the honest payment of our debts and sacred preservation of the public faith; encouragement of agriculture, and of commerce as its handmaid; the diffusion of information and arraignment of all abuses at the bar of the public reason; freedom of religion; freedom of the press, and freedom of person under the protection of the habeas corpus, and trial by juries impartially selected. These principles form the bright constellation which has gone before us and guided our steps through an age of revolution and reformation. The wisdom of our sages and blood of our heroes have been devoted to their attainment. They should be the creed of our political faith, the text of civic instruction, the touchstone by which to try the services of those we trust; and should we wander from them in moments of error or of alarm, let us hasten to retrace our steps and to regain the road which alone leads to peace, liberty, and safety.

I repair, then, fellow-citizens, to the post you have assigned me. With experience enough in subordinate offices to have seen the difficulties of this the greatest of all, I have learnt to expect that it will rarely fall to the lot of imperfect man to retire from this station with the reputation and the favor which bring him into it. Without pretensions to that high confidence you reposed in our first and greatest revolutionary character, whose preeminent services had entitled him to the first place in his country's love and destined for him the fairest page in the volume of faithful history, I ask so much confidence only as may give firmness and effect to the legal administration of your affairs. I shall often go wrong through defect of judgment. When right, I shall often be thought wrong by those whose positions will not command a view of the whole ground. I ask your indulgence for my own errors, which will never be intentional, and your support against the errors of others, who may condemn what they would not if seen in all its parts. The approbation implied by your suffrage is a great consolation to me for the past, and my future solicitude will be to retain the good opinion of those who have bestowed it in advance, to conciliate that of others by doing them all the good in my power, and to be instrumental to the happiness and freedom of all.

Relying, then, on the patronage of your good will, I advance with obedience to the work, ready to retire from it whenever you become sensible how much better choice it is in your power to make. And may that Infinite Power which rules the destinies of the universe lead our councils to what is best, and give them a favorable issue for your peace and prosperity.

ALEXANDER HAMILTON

Remarks on the Repeal of the Judiciary Act

New York City, February 11, 1802

To these remarks General Hamilton rose again to reply—he remarked in substance that he had fostered the hope, that on this occasion, by cautiously avoiding to say any thing on the point of the constitutionality of the proposed repeal, and stating only the opinion of the New-York bar on that of its *inexpediency*, there would have been but one sentiment—He regretted, deeply regretted, that on this point there was a diversity of sentiment; he foresaw the unhappy effects that would hence result; he deplored them, not from any private or contracted view, but turning his eye inward on his heart, and looking to heaven as the witness of his motives, he declared he knew of none that influenced him but the sincerest attachment to the public good. So far as respected the unconstitutionality of the proposed repeal, he had no hesitation in avowing his own opinion. He considered it a most direct, and fatal violation of the most essential, the most *vital* principle of the constitution. The independence of the judges once destroyed, the constitution is gone, it is a dead letter; it is a vapor which the breath of faction in a moment may dissipate, and this boasted union the labor of true patriots, the hope of our country, which in the last 12 years has raised us to the most enviable height of prosperity, dissolves and dies.

He had cherished the idea, he said, that this part of the Constitution was the last that party violence would attack. That although certain extensions of executive authority, certain changes in the finances, or in diplomatic arrangements abroad might take place, yet that the essential rights of the judiciary in which foreigners and citizens, but more especially the mercantile interests of the U. States are so deeply concerned, would have been preserved inviolate. He had looked forward to many evils that he thought likely to flow from the known principles of the leading characters now in authority, but indeed, he had not calculated on such a rapid progression of evil. He had little hope that any thing that could now be *said* or done, would assist in averting the impending blow. He knew full well that the plan now going into effect had long been meditated and resolved on, and hence, his zeal was much abated, yet could any thing he could do have any effect in saving the constitution from the fatal blow that now menaced it, he would labor day and night; he would not give 'sleep to his eyes, nor slumber to his eye-lids,' while he had hope to support his exertions; nay, 'I would give a drop of my heart's blood,' said he, to save this *vital* principle of the constitution. There is no motive which induced me to put my life at hazard through our revolutionary war, that would not now as powerfully operate on me, to put it again in jeopardy, in defence of the independence of the judiciary; for remember what is said this night; if this fatal measure is not by *some means* arrested, if the *laws* are not suffered to controul the passions of individuals, thro the organs of an extended, firm and independent judiciary, the bayonet must. There is no alternative; we must be ruled by municipal law, or by—a military force: and I beg gentlemen to recollect what I now say, without aspiring to the character of a prophet, that if this rash unadvised repeal takes place, mutual confidence will be destroyed—the union will gradually crumble to pieces and in a few, very few years, the present confederation will either be parcelled out into separate territories, with clashing interests, and you will see the hand of brother, raised to shed a brother's blood, or you will see this country become the prey of a usurper, and sink into the calm of a military despotism. On those gentlemen, then, who truly value our republican government, I call, to banish for an instant, the influence of party-spirit, and to lend their aid in extinguishing a rising conflagration, which threatens to involve this devoted country in miseries incalculable. On the point of *expediency*, he observed, that he could, in no one point of view, consider the proposed repeal as defensible. Every gentleman present, who had been concerned in business depending in the circuit court of the United States, knew, without his going into details, the vices of the *old system*. Many of its defects were indeed removed by the present, which, however, was not to be considered as perfect. On this, certain improvements could be advantageously engrafted—which would render it a very eligible and convenient system. But he was surprised, greatly surprised indeed, to hear any gentleman who had any respect to his own character, risk an opinion, that the district courts, with the supreme court of the United States, were fully competent to all the business of the United States. The business of the former he said, from revenue and admiralty causes, and from what arose under the late bankrupt law, furnished full employ for the most industrious judge. Beside, if all suits were originally to be commenced in the district courts, no suitor would rest satisfied with the decision of a single man, but would remove the cause for a final hearing to the supreme court of the United States, in which case parties would be constantly obliged to travel with papers and vouchers from the extremities of the Union to the seat of government, there to retain new counsel, be at heavy expences, and far from their families, which would produce inconveniences that would not long be submitted to.

JOHN RANDOLPH

Speech in Congress Against Non-Importation

Washington, D.C., March 5, 1806

I AM extremely afraid, sir, that so far as it may depend on my acquaintance with details connected with the subject, I have very little right to address you, for in truth, I have not yet seen the documents from the Treasury, which were called for some time ago, to direct the judgment of this House in the decision of the question now before you; and, indeed after what I have this day heard, I no longer require that document or any other document—indeed I do not know that I ever should have required it—to vote on the resolution of the gentleman from Pennsylvania. If I had entertained any doubts they would have been removed by the style in which the friends of the resolution have this morning discussed it. I am perfectly aware, that on entering upon this subject, we go into it manacled, handcuffed, and tongue-tied; gentlemen know that our lips are sealed, on subjects of momentous foreign relations, which are indissolubly linked with the present question, and which would serve to throw a great light on it in every respect relevant to it. I will, however, endeavor to hobble over the subject, as well as my fettered limbs and palsied tongue will enable me to do it.

I am not surprised to hear this resolution discussed by its friends as a war measure. They say (it is true) that it is not a war measure; but they defend it on principles which would justify none but war measures, and seem pleased with the idea that it may prove the forerunner of war. If war is necessary—if we have reached this point—let us have war. But while I have life, I will never consent to these incipent war measures, which, in their commencement breathe nothing but peace, though they plunge at last into war. It has been well observed by the gentleman from Pennsylvania behind me (Mr. J. CLAY) that the situation of this nation in 1793, was in every respect different from that in which it finds itself in 1806. Let me ask, too, if the situation of England is not since materially changed? Gentlemen who, it would appear from their language, have not got beyond the horn-book of politics, talk of our ability to cope with the British navy, and tell us of the war of our Revolution. What was the situation of Great Britain then? She was then contending for the empire of the British channel, barely able to maintain a doubtful equality with her enemies, over whom she never gained the superiority until Rodney's victory of the twelfth of April. What is her present situation? The combined fleets of France, Spain, and Holland, are dissipated, they no longer exist. I am not surprised to hear men advocate these wild opinions, to see them goaded on by a spirit of mercantile avarice, straining their feeble strength to excite the nation to war, when they have reached this stage of infatuation, that we are an over-match for Great Britain on the ocean. It is mere waste of time to reason with such persons. They do not deserve anything like serious refutation. The proper arguments for such statesmen are a straight waistcoat, a dark room, water gruel, and depletion.

It has always appeared to me that there are three points to be considered, and maturely considered, before we can be prepared to vote for the resolution, of the gentleman from Pennsylvania: First. Our ability to contend with Great Britain for the question in dispute: Secondly. The policy of such a contest: Thirdly. In case both these shall be settled affirmatively, the manner in which we can, with the greatest effect, re-act upon and annoy our adversary.

Now the gentleman from Massachusetts (Mr. CROWNIN-SHIELD) has settled at a single sweep, to use one of his favorite expressions, not only that we are capable of contending with Great Britain on the ocean, but that we are actually her superior. Whence does the gentleman deduce this inference? Because, truly, at that time when Great Britain was not mistress of the ocean, when a North was her prime minister, a Sandwich the first lord of her admiralty, when she was governed by a counting-house administration, privateers of this country trespassed on her commerce! So, too, did the cruisers of Dunkirk; at that day Suffrein held the mastery of the Indian seas. But what is the case now? Do gentlemen remember the capture of Cornwallis on land, because De Grasse maintained the dominion of the ocean? To my mind no position is more clear, than that if we go to war with Great Britain, Charleston and Boston, the Chesapeake and the Hudson, will be invested by British squadrons. Will you call on the Count De Grasse to relieve them, or shall we apply to Admiral Gravina, or Admiral Villeneuve to raise the blockade? But you have not only a prospect of gathering glory, and what seems to the gentleman from Massachusetts, much dearer, profit, by privateering, but you will be able to make a conquest of Canada and Nova Scotia. Indeed! Then, sir, we shall catch a Tartar. I confess, however, I have no desire to see the Senators and Representatives of the Canadian French, or of the tories and refugees of Nova Scotia, sitting on this floor or that of the other House—to see them becoming members of the Union, and participating equally in our political rights. And on what other principle would the gentleman from Massachusetts be for incorporating those provinces with us? Or on what other principle could it be done under the Constitution? If the gentleman has no other bounty to offer us for going to war, than the incorporation of Canada and Nova Scotia with the United States. I am for remaining at peace.

What is the question in dispute? The carrying trade. What part of it? The fair, the honest, and the useful trade, that is engaged in carrying our own productions to foreign markets, and bringing back their productions in exchange? No, sir. It is that carrying trade which covers enemy's property, and carries the coffee, the sugar, and other West India products, to the mother country. No, sir, if this great agricultural nation is to be governed by Salem and Boston, New York and Phildelphia, and Baltimore and Norfolk and Charleston, let gentlemen come out and say so; and let a committee of public safety be appointed from those towns to carry on the Government. I, for one, will not mortgage my property and my liberty, to carry on this trade. The nation said so seven years ago—I said so then, and I say now. It is not for the honest carrying trade of America, but for this mushroom, this fungus of war—for a trade which, as soon as the nations of Europe are at peace, will no longer exist, it is for this that the spirit of avaricious traffic would plunge us into war.

I am forcibly struck on this occasion by the recollection of a remark made by one of the ablest (if not the honestest) Ministers that England ever produced. I mean Sir Robert Walpole, who said that the country gentlemen (poor meek souls!) came up every year to be sheared—that they laid mute and patient whilst their fleeces were taking off—but that if he touched a single bristle of the commercial interest, the whole stye was in an uproar. It was indeed shearing the hog—"great cry and little wool."

But we are asked, are we willing to bend the neck to England; to submit to her outrages? No, sir. I answer, that it will be time enough for us to vindicate the violation of our flag on the ocean, when they shall have told us what they have done in resentment of the violation of the actual territory of the United States by Spain—the true territory of the United States, not your new-fangled country over the Mississippi, but the good old United States—part of Georgia, of the old thirteen States—where citizens have been taken, not from our ships, but from our actual territory. When gentlemen have taken the padlock from our mouths, I shall be ready to tell them what I will do, relative to our dispute with Britain, on the law of nations, on contraband, and such stuff.

I have another objection to this course of proceeding. Great Britain, when she sees it, will say the American people have great cause of dissatisfaction with Spain. She will see by the documents furnished by the President, that Spain has outraged our territory, pirated upon our commerce, and imprisoned our citizens; and she will inquire what we have done? It is true, she will receive no answer, but she must know what we have not done. She will see that we have not repelled these outrages, nor made any addition to our army and navy—nor even classed the militia. No, sir not one of your militia generals in politics has marshalled a single brigade.

Although I have said it would be time enough to answer the question which gentlemen have put to me when they shall have answered mine, yet as I do not like long prorogations I will give them an answer now. I will never consent to go to war for that which I cannot protect. I deem it no sacrifice of dignity to say to the Leviathan of the deep—we are unable to contend with you in your own element, but if you come within our actual limits we will shed our last drop of blood in their defence. In such an event I would feel, not reason, and obey an impulse which never has, which never can deceive me.

France is at war with England—suppose her power on the continent of Europe no greater than it is on the ocean. How would she make her enemy feel it? There would be a perfect non-conductor between them. So with the United States and England—she scarcely presents to us a vulnerable point. Her commerce is now carried on for the most part in fleets—where in single ships they are stout and well armed—very different from the state of her trade during the American war, when her merchantmen became the prey of paltry privateers. Great Britain has been too long at war with the three most powerful maritime nations of Europe not to have learnt how to protect her trade. She can afford convoy to it all—she has eight hundred ships in commission, the navies of her enemies are annihilated. Thus this war has presented the new and curious political spectacle of a regular annual increase (and to an immense amount) of her imports and exports, and tonnage and revenue, and all the insignia of accumulating wealth, whilst in every former war, without exception, these have suffered a greater or less diminution. And wherefore? Because she has driven France, Spain, and Holland from the ocean. Their marine is no more. I verily believe that ten English ships-of-the-line would not decline a meeting with the combined fleets of those nations. I forewarn the gentleman from Massachusetts and his constituents of Salem, that all their golden hopes are vain. I forewarn them of the exposure of their trade beyond the Cape of Good Hope (or now doubling it) to capture and confiscation—of their unprotected seaport towns, exposed to contribution or bombardment. Are we to be legislated into war by a set of men, who in six weeks after its commencement may be compelled to take refuge with us up in the country? And for what? A mere fungus—a mushroom production of war in Europe, which will disappear with the first return of peace—an unfair trade. For is there a man so credulous as to believe that we possess a capital not only equal to what may be called our own proper trade, but large enough also to transmit to the respective parent States the vast and wealthy products of the French, Spanish and Dutch colonies? It is beyond the belief of any rational being. But this is not my only objection to entering upon this naval warfare; I am averse to a naval war with any nation whatever. I was opposed to the naval war of the last Administration, and I am as ready to oppose a naval war of the present Administration, should they meditate such a measure. What! shall this great mammoth of the American forest leave his native element and plunge into the water in a mad contest with the shark? Let him beware that his proboscis is not bitten off in the engagement. Let him stay on shore, and not be excited by the muscles and periwinkles on the strand, or political bears, in a boat to venture on the perils of the deep. Gentlemen say will you not protect your violated rights? and I say why take to water, where you can neither fight nor swim. Look at France—see her vessels stealing from port to port on her own coast—and remember that she is the first military Power of the earth, and as a naval people second only to England. Take away the British navy, and France to-morrow is the tyrant of the ocean.

This brings me to the second point. How far is it politic in the United States to throw their weight into the scale of France at this moment, from whatever motive—to aid the views of her gigantic ambition—to make her mistress of the sea and land—to jeopardize the liberties of mankind? Sir, you may help to crush Great Britain, you may assist in breaking down her naval dominion, but you cannot succeed to it. The iron sceptre of the ocean will pass into his hands who wears the iron crown of the land. You may then expect a new code of maritime law. Where will you look for redress? I can tell the gentlemen from Massachusetts that there is nothing in his rule of three that will save us, even although he should out-do himself, and exceed the financial ingenuity which he so memorably displayed on a recent occasion. No, sir, let the battle of Actium be once fought, and the whole line of seacoast will be at the mercy of the conqueror. The Atlantic, deep and wide as it is, will prove just as good a barrier against his ambition, if directed against you, as the Mediterranean to the power of the Cæsars. Do I mean (when I say so) to crouch to the invader? No! I will meet him at the water's edge, and fight every inch of ground from thence to the mountains—from the mountains to the

Mississippi. But after tamely submitting to an outrage on your domicil, will you bully and look big at an insult on your flag three thousand miles off?

But, sir, I have yet a more cogent reason against going to war, for the honor of the flag in the narrow seas, or any other maritime punctilio. It springs from my attachment to the Government under which I live. I declare, in the face of day, that this Government was not instituted for the purposes of offensive war. No! It was framed (to use its own language) "for the common defence and the general welfare," which are inconsistent with offensive war. I call that offensive war, which goes out of our jurisdiction and limits for the attainment or protection of objects, not within those limits, and that jurisdiction. As in 1798 I was opposed to this species of warfare, because I believed it would raze the Constitution to its very foundation—so, in 1806, I am opposed to it, and on the same grounds. No sooner do you put the Constitution to this use—to a test which it is by no means calculated to endure—than its incompetency becomes manifest, and apparent to all. I fear if you go into a foreign war, for a circuitous, unfair carrying trade, you will come out without your Constitution. Have not you contractors enough yet in this House? Or, do you want to be overrun and devoured by commissaries, and all the vermin of contract? I fear, sir, that what are called "the energy men" will rise up again—men who will burn the parchment. We shall be told that our Government is too free; or, as they would say, weak and inefficient. Much virtue, sir, in terms! That we must give the President power to call forth the resources of the nation. That is, to filch the last shilling from our pockets—to drain the last drop of blood from our veins. I am against giving this power to any man, be he who he may. The American people must either withhold this power, or resign their liberties. There is no other alternative. Nothing but the most imperious necessity will justify such a grant. And is there a powerful enemy at our doors? You may begin with a First Consul. From that chrysalis state he soon becomes an Emperor. You have your choice. It depends upon your election whether you will be a free, happy, and united people at home, or the light of your Executive Majesty shall beam across the Atlantic in one general blaze of the public liberty.

For my part, I will never go to war but in self-defence. I have no desire for conquests—no ambition to possess Nova Scotia. I hold the liberties of this people at a higher rate. Much more am I indisposed to war, when, among the first means for carrying it on, I see gentlemen propose the confiscation of debts due by Government to individuals. Does a *bona fide* creditor know who holds his paper? Dare any honest man ask himself the question? 'Tis hard to say whether such principles are more detestably dishonest, than they are weak and foolish. What, sir, will you go about with proposals for opening a loan in one hand, and a sponge for the national debt in the other? If, on a late occasion, you could not borrow at a less rate of interest than eight per cent., when the Government avowed that they would pay to the last shilling of the public ability, at what price do you expect to raise money with an avowal of these nefarious opinions? God help you, if these are your ways and means for carrying on war! if your finances are in the hands of such a Chancellor of the Exchequer. Because a man can take an observation, and keep a log-book and a reckoning; can navigate a cock-boat to the West Indies, or the East, shall he aspire to navigate the great vessel of State—to stand at the helm of public councils? *Ne sutor ultra crepidam.* What are you going to war for? For the carrying trade? Already you possess seven-eighths of it. What is the object in dispute? The fair, honest trade, that exchanges the product of our soil for foreign articles for home consumption? Not at all. You are called upon to sacrifice this necessary branch of your navigation, and the great agricultural interest—whose handmaid it is—to jeopardize your best interests for a circuitous commerce, for the fraudulent protection of belligerent property under your neutral flag. Will you be goaded, by the dreaming calculations of insatiate avarice, to stake your all for the protection of this trade? I do not speak of the probable effects of war on the price of our produce. Severely as we must feel, we may scuffle through it. I speak of its reaction on the Constitution. You may go to war for this excrescence of the carrying trade, and make peace at the expense of the Constitution. Your Executive will lord it over you, and you must make the best terms with the conqueror that you can. But the gentleman from Pennsylvania (Mr. GREGG) tells you that he is for acting in this, as in all

things, uninfluenced by the opinion of any Minister whatever—
foreign, or, I presume, domestic. On this point I am willing to
meet the gentleman—am unwilling to be dictated to by any
Minister, at home or abroad. Is he willing to act on the same
independent footing? I have before protested, and I again protest against secret, irresponsible, overruling influence. The first
question I asked when I saw the gentleman's resolution, was,
"Is this a measure of the Cabinet?" Not of an open declared
Cabinet; but, of an invisible, inscrutable, unconstitutional Cabinet, without responsibility, unknown to the Constitution. I
speak of back-stairs influence—of men who bring messages to
this House, which, although they do not appear on the Journals, govern its decisions. Sir, the first question that I asked on
the subject of British relations, was, What is the opinion of the
Cabinet? What measures will they recommend to Congress?—
(well knowing that whatever measures we might take, they
must execute them, and therefore, that we should have their
opinion on the subject.) My answer was, (and from a Cabinet
Minister too,) *There is no longer any Cabinet.* Subsequent
circumstances, sir, have given me a personal knowledge of the
fact. It needs no commentary.

But the gentleman has told you that we ought to go to war,
if for nothing else, for the fur trade. Now, sir, the people on
whose support he seems to calculate, follow, let me tell him, a
better business, and let me add, that whilst men are happy at
home reaping their own fields—the fruits of their labor and
industry—there is little danger of their being induced to go
sixteen or seventeen hundred miles in pursuit of beavers, rac-
coons, or opossums, much less of going to war for the privilege. They are better employed where they are. This trade, sir,
may be important to Britain, to nations who have exhausted
every resource of industry at home, bowed down by taxation
and wretchedness. Let them, in God's name, if they please,
follow the fur trade. They may, for me, catch every beaver in
North America. Yes, sir, our people have a better occupation—
a safe, profitable, honorable employment. While they should
be engaged in distant regions in hunting the beaver, they
dread lest those whose natural prey they are should begin to
hunt them, should pillage their property, and assassinate their
Constitution. Instead of these wild schemes, pay off your debt,

instead of prating about its confiscation. Do not, I beseech you, expose at once your knavery and your folly. You have more lands than you know what to do with, you have lately paid fifteen millions for yet more. Go and work them, and cease to alarm the people with the cry of wolf, until they become deaf to your voice, or at least laugh at you.

Mr. Chairman, if I felt less regard for what I deem the best interests of this nation than for my own reputation, I should not, on this day, have offered to address you, but would have waited to come out, bedecked with flowers and boquets of rhetoric, in a set speech. But, sir, I dreaded lest a tone might be given to the mind of the committee—they will pardon me, but I did fear, from all that I could see or hear, that they might be prejudiced by its advocates, (under pretence of protecting our commerce) in favor of this ridiculous and preposterous project; I rose, sir, for one, to plead guilty; to declare in the face of day that I will not go to war for this carrying trade. I will agree to pass for an idiot if this is not the public sentiment, and you will find it to your cost, begin the war when you will.

Gentlemen talk of 1793. They might as well go back to the Trojan war. What was your situation then? Then every heart beat high with sympathy for France, for *republican France!* I am not prepared to say, with my friend from Pennsylvania, that we were all ready to draw our swords in her cause, but I affirm that we were prepared to have gone great lengths. I am not ashamed to pay this compliment to the hearts of the American people, even at the expense of their understandings. It was a noble and generous sentiment, which nations like individuals are never the worse for having felt. They were, I repeat it, ready to make great sacrifices for France. And why ready? Because she was fighting the battles of the human race against the combined enemies of their liberty; because she was performing the part which Great Britain now, in fact, sustains, forming the only bulwark against universal dominion. Knock away her Navy, and where are you? Under the naval despotism of France, unchecked and unqualified by any antagonizing military power; at best but a change of masters. The tyrant of the ocean, and the tyrant of the land, is one and the same, lord of all, and who shall say him nay, or wherefore doest thou this thing? Give to the tiger the properties of the shark, and there is no longer safety for the beasts of the forest or the fishes of the sea. Where was this high anti-Britannic spirit of the gentleman from Pennsylvania, when his vote would have put an end to the British treaty, that pestilent source of evil to this country? and at a time, too, when it was not less the interest than the sentiment of this people to pull down Great Britain and exalt France. Then, when the gentleman might have acted with effect, he could not screw his courage to the sticking place. Then England was combined in what has proven a feeble, inefficient coalition, but which gave just cause of alarm to every friend of freedom. Now the liberties of the human race are threatened by a single Power, more formidable than the coalesced world, to whose utmost ambition, vast as it is, the naval force of Great Britain forms the only obstacle.

I am perfectly sensible and ashamed of the trespass I am making on the patience of the Committee; but as I know not whether it will be in my power to trouble them again on this subject, I must beg leave to continue my crude and desultory observations. I am not ashamed to confess that they are so. At the commencement of this session, we received a printed Message from the President of the United States, breathing a great deal of national honor, and indignation at the outrages we had endured, particularly from Spain. She was specially named and pointed at. She had pirated upon your commerce, imprisoned your citizens, violated your actual territory; invaded the very limits solemnly established between the two nations by the Treaty of San Lorenzo. Some of the State Legislatures, (among others the very State on which the gentleman from Pennsylvania relies for support,) sent forward resolutions pledging their lives, their fortunes, and their sacred honor, in support of any measures you might take in vindication of your injured rights. Well, sir, what have you done? You have had resolutions laid upon your table, gone to some expense of printing and stationery—mere pen, ink, and paper, that's all. Like true political quacks, you deal only in handbills and nostrums. Sir, I blush to see the record of our proceedings; they resemble nothing but the advertisements of patent medicines. Here you have "the worm-destroying lozenges," there, "Church's cough drops;" and, to crown the whole, "Sloan's vegetable specific," an infallible remedy for all nervous disorders and vertigoes of brain-sick politicians; each man earnestly adjuring you to give his medicine only a fair trial. If, indeed, these wonder-working nostrums could perform but one-half of what they promise, there is little danger of our dying a political death, at this time at least. But, sir, in politics as in physics, the doctor is ofttimes the most dangerous disease; and this I take to be our case at present.

But, sir, why do I talk of Spain? There are no longer Pyrenees. There exists no such nation, no such being as a Spanish King, or Minister. It is a mere juggle, played off for the benefit of those who put the mechanism into motion. You know, sir, that you have no differences with Spain; that she is the passive tool of a superior Power, to whom, at this moment, you are crouching. Are your differences, indeed, with Spain? And where are you going to send your political panacea, resolutions and handbills excepted, your sole arcanum of Government, your king cure all? To Madrid? No—you are not such quacks as not to know where the shoe pinches—to Paris. You know, at least, where the disease lies, and there you apply your remedy. When the nation anxiously demands the result of your deliberations, you hang your head and blush to tell. You are afraid to tell. Your mouth is hermetically sealed. Your honor has received a wound which must not take air. Gentlemen dare not come forward and avow their work, much less defend it in the presence of the nation. Give them all they ask, that Spain exists—and what then? After shrinking from the Spanish jackall, do you presume to bully the British lion? But here the secret comes out. Britain is your rival in trade, and governed as you are by counting-house politicians, you would sacrifice the paramount interests of the country, to wound that rival. For Spain and France you are carriers, and from good customers every indignity is to be endured. And what is the nature of this trade? Is it that carrying trade which sends abroad the flour, tobacco, cotton, beef, pork, fish, and lumber of this country, and brings back in return foreign articles necessary for our existence or comfort? No, sir, it is a trade carried on—the Lord knows where, or by whom; now doubling Cape Horn, now the Cape of Good Hope. I do not say that there is no profit in it—for it would not then be pursued—but it is a trade that tends to assimilate our manners and Government to those of the most corrupt countries of Europe. Yes, sir, and when a question of great national magnitude presents itself to you, it causes those who now prate about national honor and spirit to pocket any insult; to consider it as a mere matter of debit and credit; a business of profit and loss, and nothing else.

The first thing that struck my mind, when this resolution was laid on the table, was *unde derivatur?* A question always put to us at school. Whence comes it? Is this only the putative father of the bantling he is taxed to maintain, or, indeed, the actual parent, the real progenitor of the child? Or, is it the production of the Cabinet? But, I knew you had no Cabinet, no system. I had seen despatches relating to vital measures laid before you the day after your final decision on those measures, four weeks after they were received; not only their contents, but their very existence, all that time unsuspected and unknown to men whom the people fondly believe assist with their wisdom and experience at every important deliberation. Do you believe that this system, or rather this no-system, will do? I am free to answer it will not, it cannot last. I am not so afraid of the fair, open, Constitutional, responsible influence of Government, but I shrink intuitively from this left-handed, invisible, irresponsible influence, which defies the touch, but pervades and decides everything. Let the Executive come forward to the Legislature; let us see while we feel it. If we cannot rely on its wisdom, is it any disparagement to the gentleman from Pennsylvania to say that I cannot rely upon him? No, sir, he has mistaken his talent. He is not the Palinurus on whose skill the nation, at this trying moment, can repose their confidence. I will have nothing to do with his paper, much less will I endorse it, and make myself responsible for its goodness. I will not put my name to it. I assert that there is no Cabinet, no system, no plan; that which I believe in one place, I shall never hesitate to say in another. This is no time, no place, for mincing our steps. The people have a right to know; they shall know the state of their affairs; at least, as far as I am at liberty to communicate them. I speak from personal knowledge. Ten days ago there had been no consultation; there existed no opinion in your Executive department; at least, none that was avowed. On the contrary, there was an express disavowal of any opinion whatsoever, on the great subject before you; and I have good reason for saying that none has been formed since. Some time ago, a book was laid on our tables, which, like some other bantlings, did not bear the name of its father. Here I was taught to expect a solution of all doubts, an end to all our difficulties. If, sir, I were the foe—as I trust I am the friend of this nation—I would exclaim, "Oh, that mine enemy would write a book!" At the very outset, in the very first page, I believe, there is a complete abandonment of the principle in dispute. Has any gentleman got the work? [It was handed by one of the members.] The first position taken is the broad principle of the unlimited freedom of trade between nations at peace, which the writer endeavors to extend to the trade between a neutral and a belligerent Power, accompanied, however, by this acknowledgment: "But, inasmuch as the trade of a neutral with a belligerent nation, might, in certain special cases, affect the safety of its antagonist, usage, founded on the principle of necessity, has admitted a few exceptions to the general rule." Whence comes the doctrine of contraband, blockade, and enemy's property? Now, sir, for what does that celebrated pamphlet, "War in Disguise"—which is said to have been written under the eye of the British Prime Minister—contend, but this "principle of necessity?" And this is abandoned by this pamphleteer at the very threshold of the discussion. But, as if this were not enough, he goes on to assign as a reason for not referring to the authority of the ancients, "that the great change which has taken place in the state of manners, in the maxims of war, and in the course of commerce, make it pretty certain" (what degree of certainty is this?) "that either nothing will be found relating to the question, or nothing sufficiently applicable to deserve attention in deciding it." Here, sir, is an apology of the writer for not disclosing the whole extent of his learning, (which might have overwhelmed the reader,) is the admission that a change of circumstances, ("in the course of commerce,") has made (and, therefore, will now justify) a total change of the law of nations. What more could the most inveterate advocate of English usurpation demand? What else can they require to establish all, and even more than they contend for? Sir, there is a class of men—we know them very well—who, if you only permit them to lay the foundation, will build you up, step by step, and brick by brick, very neat and showy, if not tenable arguments. To detect them, it is only necessary to watch their premises, where you will often find the point at issue surrendered, as in this case it is.

Again: Is the *mare liberum* anywhere asserted in this book, that free ships make free goods? No, sir; the right of search is acknowledged; that enemy's property is lawful prize, is sealed and delivered. And, after abandoning these principles, what becomes of the doctrine that a mere shifting of the goods from one ship to another, the touching at another port, changes the property? Sir, give up this principle, and there is an end of the question. You lie at the mercy of the conscience of a Court of Admiralty. Is Spanish sugar, or French coffee, made American property, by the mere change of the cargo, or even by the landing and payment of the duties? Does this operation effect a change of property? And when those duties are drawn back, and the sugar and coffee re-exported, are they not (as enemy's property) liable to seizure upon the principles of the "Examination of the British doctrine," &c.? And, is there not the best reason to believe, that this operation is performed in many, if not in most cases, to give a neutral aspect and color to the merchandise?

I am prepared, sir, to be represented as willing to surrender important rights of this nation to a foreign Government. I have been told that this sentiment is already whispered in the dark, by time-servers and sycophants. But, if your Clerk dared to print them, I would appeal to your Journals. I would call for the reading of them, but that I know they are not for profane eyes to look upon. I confess that I am more ready to surrender to a naval Power a square league of ocean, than to a territorial one, a square inch of land within our limits; and I am ready to meet the friends of the resolution on this ground at any time.

Let them take off the injunction of secrecy. They dare not. They are ashamed and afraid to do it. They may give winks and nods, and pretend to be wise, but they dare not come out and tell the nation what they have done. Gentlemen may take notes if they please, but I will never, from any motive short of self-defence, enter upon war. I will never be instrumental to the ambitious schemes of Bonaparte, nor put into his hands what will enable him to wield the world, and on the very principle that I wished success to the French arms in 1793. And wherefore? Because the case is changed. Great Britain can never again see the year 1760. Her continental influence is gone forever. Let who will be uppermost on the continent of Europe, she must find more than a counterpoise for her strength. Her race is run. She can only be formidable as a maritime Power; and, even as such, perhaps not long. Are you going to justify the acts of the last Administration, for which they have been deprived of the Government at our instance? Are you going back to the ground of 1798–'9? I ask any man who now advocates a rupture with England to assign a single reason for his opinion, that would not have justified a French war in 1798? If injury and insult abroad would have justified it, we had them in abundance then. But what did the Republicans say at that day? That, under the cover of a war with France, the Executive would be armed with a patronage and power which might enable it to master our liberties. They deprecated foreign war and navies, and standing armies, and loans and taxes. The delirium passed away—the good sense of the people triumphed, and our differences were accommodated without a war. And what is there in the situation of England that invites to war with her? It is true she does not deal so largely in perfectability, but she supplies you with a much more useful commodity—with coarse woollens. With less profession indeed she occupies the place of France in 1793. She is the sole bulwark of the human race against universal dominion; no thanks to her for it. In protecting her own existence, she insures theirs. I care not who stands in this situation, whether England or Bonaparte. I practice the doctrines now that I professed in 1798. Gentlemen may hunt up the journals if they please; I voted against all such projects under the Administration of John Adams, and I will continue to do so under that of Thomas Jefferson. Are you not contented with being free and happy at home? Or will you surrender these blessings that your merchants may tread on Turkish and Persian carpets, and burn the perfumes of the East in their vaulted rooms? Gentlemen say it is but an annual million lost, and even if it were five times that amount, what is it compared with your neutral rights? Sir, let me tell them a hundred millions will be but a drop in the bucket, if once they launch without rudder or compass into this ocean of foreign warfare. Whom do they want to attack? England. They hope it is a popular thing, and talk about Bunker's Hill, and the gallant feats of our Revolution. But is Bunker's Hill to be the theatre of war? No, sir, you have selected the ocean, and the object of attack is that very navy which prevented the combined fleets of France and Spain from levying contribution upon you in your own seas; that very navy which, in the famous war of 1798, stood between you and danger. Whilst the fleets of the enemy were pent up in Toulon, or pinioned in Brest, we performed wonders to be sure; but, sir, if England had drawn off, France would have told you quite a different tale. You would have struck no medals. This is not the sort of conflict that you are to count upon, if you go to war with Great Britain. *Quem Deus vult perdere prius dementat.* And are you mad enough to take up the cudgels that have been struck from the nerveless hands of the three great maritime Powers of Europe? Shall the planter mortgage his little crop, and jeopardize the Constitution in support of commercial monopoly, in the vain hope of satisfying the insatiable greediness of trade? Administer the Constitution upon its own principles: for the general welfare, and not for the benefit of any particular class of men. Do you meditate war for the possession of Baton Rouge or Mobile, places which your own laws declare to be within your limits? Is it even for the fair trade that exchanges your surplus products for such foreign articles as you require? No, sir, it is for a circuitous trade—an ignis fatuus. And against whom? A nation from whom you have anything to fear?—I speak as to our liberties. No, sir, with a nation from whom you have nothing, or next to nothing, to fear; to the aggrandizement of one against which you have everything to dread. I look to their ability and interest, not to their disposition. When you rely on that the case is desperate. Is it to be inferred from all this that I would yield to Great Britain? No. I would act towards her now, as I was disposed to do towards France, in 1798–'9; treat with her, and for the same reason, on the same principles. Do I say I would treat with her? At this moment you have a negotiation pending with her Government. With her you have not tried negotiation and failed, totally failed, as you have done with Spain, or rather France; and wherefore, under such circumstances, this hostile spirit to the one, and this—I will not say what—to the other?

But a great deal is said about the laws of nations. What is national law but national power guided by national interest? You yourselves acknowledge and practice upon this principle where you can, or where you dare—with the Indian tribes for instance. I might give another and more forcible illustration. Will the learned lumber of your libraries add a ship to your fleet, or a shilling to your revenue? Will it pay or maintain a single soldier? And will you preach and prate of violations of your neutral rights when you tamely and meanly submit to the violation of your territory? Will you collar the stealer of your sheep, and let him escape that has invaded the repose of your fireside—has insulted your wife and children under your own roof? This is the heroism of truck and traffic—the public spirit of sordid avarice. Great Britain violates your flag on the high seas. What is her situation? Contending, not for the dismantling of Dunkirk, for Quebec, or Pondicherry, but for London and Westminster— for life. Her enemy violating at will the territories of other nations, acquiring thereby a colossal power that threatens the very existence of her rival. But she has one vulnerable point to the arms of her adversary, which she covers with the ensigns of neutrality; she draws the neutral flag over the heel of Achilles. And can you ask that adversary to respect it at the expense of her existence? and in favor of whom? An enemy that respects no neutral territory of Europe, and not even your own. I repeat that the insults of Spain towards this nation have been at the instigation of France; that there is no longer any Spain. Well, sir, because the French Government does not put this in the Moniteur, you choose to shut your eyes to it. None so blind as those who will not see. You shut your own eyes, and to blind those of other people, you go into conclave, and slink out again and say, "a great affair of State!"—*C'est une grande affaire d'Etat!* It seems that your sensibility is entirely confined to the extremities. You may be pulled by the nose and ears, and never feel it but let your strong box be attacked, and you are all nerve—"Let us go to war!" Sir, if they called upon me only for my little *peculium* to carry it on, perhaps I might give it; but my rights and liberties are involved in the grant, and I will never surrender them while I have life. The gentleman from Massachusetts (Mr. CROWNINSHIELD) is for sponging the debt. I can never consent to it; I will never bring the ways and means of fraudulent bankruptcy into your committee of supply.

Confiscation and swindling shall never be found among my estimates to meet the current expenditure of peace or war. No, sir, I have said with the doors closed, and I say so when the doors are open, "pay the public debt;" get rid of that dead weight upon your Government—that cramp upon all your measures—and then you may put the world at defiance. So long as it hangs upon you, you must have revenue, and to have revenue you must have commerce—commerce, peace. And shall these nefarious schemes be advised for lightening the public burdens; will you resort to these low and pitiful shifts; dare even to mention these dishonest artifices to eke out your expenses, when the public treasure is lavished on Turks and infidels, on singing boys and dancing girls, to furnish the means of beastiality to an African barbarian?

Gentlemen say that Great Britain will count upon our divisions. How? What does she know of them? Can they ever expect greater unanimity than prevailed at the last Presidential election? No, sir, it is the gentleman's own conscience that squeaks. But if she cannot calculate upon your divisions, at least she may reckon upon your pusillanimity. She may well despise the resentment that cannot be excited to honorable battle on its own ground; the mere effusion of mercantile cupidity. Gentlemen talk of repealing the British Treaty. The gentleman from Pennsylvania should have thought of that, before he voted to carry it into effect. And what is all this for? A point which Great Britain will not abandon to Russia, you expect her to yield to you—Russia! indisputably the second Power of Continental Europe; with not less than half a million of hardy troops; with sixty sail-of-the-line, thirty millions of subjects, and a territory more extensive even than our own—Russia, sir, the store-house of the British Navy, whom it is not more the policy and the interest than the sentiment of that Government to soothe and to conciliate—her sole hope of a diversion on the continent, and her only efficient ally. What this formidable Power cannot obtain with fleets and armies, you will command by writ—with pothooks and hangers. I am for no such policy. True honor is always the same. Before you enter into a contest, public or private, be sure you have fortitude enough to go through with it. If you mean war, say so, and prepare for it. Look on the other side; behold the respect in which France holds neutral rights on land; observe her conduct in regard to the Franconian estates of the King of Prussia. I say nothing of the petty Powers—of the Elector of Baden, or of the Swiss—I speak of a first rate Monarchy of Europe, and at a moment, too, when its neutrality was the object of all others nearest to the heart of the French Emperor. If you make him monarch of the ocean, you may bid adieu to it forever. You may take your leave, sir, of navigation— even of the Mississippi. What is the situation of New Orleans if attacked tomorrow? Filled with a discontented and repining people, whose language, manners, and religion, all incline them to the invader—a dissatisfied people, who despise the miserable Governor you have set over them—whose honest prejudices and basest passions alike take part against you. I draw my information from no dubious source; but from a native American, an enlightened member of that odious and imbecile Government. You have official information that the town and its dependencies are utterly defenceless and untenable. A firm belief that (apprized of this) Government would do something to put the place in a state of security, alone has kept the American portion of that community quiet. You have held that post, you now hold it, by the tenure of the naval predominance of England, and yet you are for a British naval war.

There are now but two great commercial nations—Great Britain is one, and the United States the other. When you consider the many points of contact between our interests, you may be surprised that there has been so little collision. Sir, to the other belligerent nations of Europe your navigation is a convenience, I might say, a necessary. If you do not carry for them they must starve, at least for the luxuries of life, which custom has rendered almost indispensable; and if you cannot act with some degree of spirit towards those who are dependent upon you as carriers, do you reckon to browbeat a jealous rival, who, the moment she lets slip the dogs of war, sweeps you at a blow from the ocean. And *cui bono?* for whose benefit? The planter? Nothing like it. The fair, honest, real American merchant? No, sir, for renegadoes; to-day American, to-morrow, Danes. Go to war when you will, the property, now covered by the American, will then pass under the Danish, or some other neutral flag. Gentlemen say that one English ship is worth three of ours; we shall therefore have the advantage in privateering. Did they ever know a nation to get rich by privateering? This is stuff, sir, for the nursery. Remember that your product are bulky, as has been stated; that they require a vast tonnage to transport them abroad, and that but two nations possess that tonnage. Take these carriers out of the market. What is the result? The manufactures of England, which (to use a finishing touch of the gentlemen's rhetoric) have received the finishing stroke of art, lie in small comparative compass. The neutral trade can carry them. Your produce rots in the warehouse. You go to Eustatia or St. Thomas and get a striped blanket for a joe, if you can raise one. Double freight, charges, and commission. Who receives the profit? The carrier. Who pays it? The consumer. All your produce that finds its way to England, must bear the same accumulated charges—with this difference, that *there* the burden falls on the home price. I appeal to the experience of the late war, which has been so often cited. What then was the price of produce, and of broadcloth?

But you are told England will not make war; that she has her hands full. Holland calculated in the same way in 1781. How did it turn out? You stand now in the place of Holland, then without her Navy, and unaided by the preponderating fleets of France and Spain, to say nothing of the Baltic Powers. Do you want to take up the cudgels where these great maritime States have been forced to drop them? to meet Great Britain on the ocean, and drive her off its face? If you are so far gone as this, every capital measure of your policy has hitherto been wrong. You should have nurtured the old, and devised new systems of taxation, and have cherished your navy. Begin this business when you may, land-taxes, stamp-acts, window-taxes, hearth-money, excise, in all its modifications of vexation and oppression, must precede or follow after. But, sir, as French is the fashion of the day, I may be asked for my *projet*. I can readily tell gentlemen what I will not do. I will not propitiate any foreign nation with money. I will not launch into a naval war with Gnat Britain, although I am ready to meet her at the Cowpens or on Bunker's Hill—and for this plain reason, we are a great land animal, and our business is on shore. I will send her money, sir, on no pretext whatever, much less on pretence of buying Labrador, or Botany Bay, when my real object was to secure limits, which she formally acknowledged at the peace of 1783. I go further: I would (if anything) have laid an embargo. This would have got our own property home, and our adversary's into our power. If there is any wisdom left among us, the first step towards hostility will always be an embargo. In six months all your mercantile megrims would vanish. As to us, although it would cut deep, we can stand it. Without such a precaution, go to war when you will, you go to the wall. As to debts, strike the balance to-morrow, and England is I believe in our debt.

I hope, sir, to be excused for proceeding in this desultory course. I flatter myself I shall not have occasion again to trouble you. I know not that I shall be able, certainly not willing, unless provoked in self-defence. I ask your attention to the character of the inhabitants of that Southern country, on whom gentlemen rely for support of their measure. Who and what are they? A simple, agricultural people, accustomed to travel in peace to market with the produce of their labor. Who takes it from us? Another people, devoted to manufactures—our sole source of supply. I have seen some stuff in the newspapers about manufactures in Saxony, and about a man who is no longer the chief of a dominant faction. The greatest man whom I ever knew—the immortal author of the letters of Curtius—has remarked the proneness of cunning people to wrap up and disguise in well-selected phrases doctrines too deformed and detestable to bear exposure in naked words; by a judicous choice of epithets to draw the attention from the lurking principle beneath, and perpetuate delusion. But a little while ago, and any man might have been proud to have been considered as the head of the Republican party. Now, it seems, it is reproachful to be deemed the chief of a dominant faction. Mark the magic of words. Head—*chief*. Republican party—*dominant faction*. But as to these Saxon manufactures. What became of their Dresden china? Why the Prussian bayonets have broken all the pots, and you are content with Worcestershire or Staffordshire ware. There are some other fine manufactures on the continent, but no supply, except perhaps of linens, the article we can best dispense with. A few individuals, sir, may have a coat of Louvier's cloth, or a service of Sevres china; but there is too little, and that little too dear, to furnish the nation. You must depend on the fur trade in earnest, and wear buffalo hides and bear skins.

Can any man who understands Europe pretend to say that a particular foreign policy is now right because it would have been expedient twenty, or even ten years ago, without abandoning all regard for common sense? Sir, it is the statesman's province to be guided by circumstances; to anticipate, to foresee them; to give them a course and a direction; to mould them to his purpose. It is the business of a counting-house clerk to peer into the day book and leger, to see no further than the spectacles on his nose, to feel not beyond the pen behind his ear; to chatter in coffee-houses, and be the oracle of clubs. From 1783 to 1793, and even later, (I dont stickle for dates,) France had a formidable marine—so had Holland—so had Spain. The two first possessed of thriving manufactures and a flourishing commerce. Great Britain, tremblingly alive to her manufacturing interests and carrying trade, would have felt to the heart any measure calculated to favor her rivals in these pursuits. She would have yielded then to her fears and her jealousy alone. What is the case now? She lays an export duty on her manufactures, and there ends the question. If Georgia shall (from whatever cause) so completely monopolize the culture of cotton as to be able to lay an export duty of three per cent. upon it, besides taxing its cultivators, in every other shape, that human or infernal ingenuity can devise, is Pennsylvania likely to rival her and take away the trade?

But, sir, it seems that we, who are opposed to this resolution, are men of no nerve, who trembled in the days of the British treaty—cowards (I presume) in the reign of terror? Is this true? Hunt up the journals; let our actions tell. We pursue our old unshaken course. We care not for the nations of Europe, but make foreign relations bend to our political principles and subserve our country's interest. We have no wish to see another Actium, or Pharsalia, or the lieutenants of a modern Alexander playing at piquet, or all-fours, for the empire of the world. It is poor comfort to us to be told that France has too decided a taste for luxurious things to meddle with us; that Egypt is her object, or the coast of Barbary, and, at the worst, we shall be the last devoured. We are enamored with neither nation; we would play their own game upon them, use them for our interest and convenience. But with all my abhorrence of the British Government, I should not hesitate between Westminster Hall and a

Middlesex jury, on the one hand, and the wood of Vincennes and a file of grenadiers on the other. That jury-trial, which walked with Horne Tooke and Hardy through the flames of ministerial persecution is, I confess, more to my taste than the trial of the Duke d'Enghein.

Mr. Chairman. I am sensible of having detained the Committee longer than I ought; certainly much longer than I intended. I am equally sensible of their politeness, and not less so, sir, of your patient attention. It is your own indulgence, sir, badly requited indeed, to which you owe this persecution. I might offer another apology for these undigested, desultory remarks—my never having seen the Treasury documents. Until I came into the House this morning I had been stretched on a sick bed. But when I behold the affairs of this nation instead of being where I hoped, and the people believed, they were, in the hands of responsible men committed to Tom, Dick, and Harry, to the refuse of the retail trade of politics, I do feel, I cannot help feeling, the most deep and serious concern. If the Executive government would step forward and say, "such is our plan, such is our opinion, and such are our reasons in support of it," I would meet it fairly, would openly oppose, or pledge myself to support it. But, without compass or polar star, I will not launch into an ocean of unexplored measures, which stand condemned by all the information to which I have access. The Constitution of the United States declares it to be the province and the duty of the President "to give to Congress, from time to time, information of the state of the Union, and recommend to their consideration such measures as he shall judge expedient and necessary." Has he done it? I know, sir, that we may say, and do say, that we are independent, (would it were true;) as free to give a direction to the Executive as to receive it from him. But do what you will, foreign relations, every measure short of war, and even the course of hostilities depends upon him. He stands at the helm, and must guide the vessel of State. You give him money to buy Florida, and he purchases Louisiana. You may furnish means; the application of those means rests with him. Let not the master and mate go below when the ship is in distress, and throw the responsibility upon the cook and the cabin-boy. I said so when your doors were shut; I scorn to say less now that they are open. Gentlemen may say what they please. They may put an insignificant individual to the ban of the Republic—I shall not alter my course. I blush with indignation at the misrepresentations which have gone forth in the public prints of our proceedings, public and private. Are the people of the United States, the real sovereigns of the country, unworthy of knowing what, there is too much reason to believe, has been communicated to the privileged spies of foreign Governments? I think our citizens just as well entitled to know what has passed as the Marquis Yrujo, who has bearded your President to his face, insulted your Government within its own peculiar jurisdiction, and outraged all decency. Do you mistake this diplomatic puppet for an automaton? He has orders for all he does. Take his instructions from his pocket to-morrow, they are signed "Charles Maurice Talleyrand." Let the nation know what they have to depend upon. Be true to them, and (trust me) they will prove true to themselves and to you. The people are honest—now at home at their ploughs, not dreaming of what you are about. But the spirit of inquiry, that has too long slept, will be, must be, awakened. Let them begin to think—not to say such things are proper because they have been done—of what has been done, and wherefore, and all will be right.

HENRY CLAY

Speech in Congress on the War of 1812

Washington, D.C., January 8–9, 1813

M<small>R.</small> H. C<small>LAY</small> (Speaker) said he was gratified yesterday by the recommitment of this bill to a committee of the whole House, from two considerations; one, since it afforded to him a slight relaxation from a most fatiguing situation; and the other, because it furnished him with an opportunity of presenting to the committee his sentiments upon the important topics which had been mingled in the debate. He regretted, however, that the necessity under which the chairman had been placed of putting the question, precluded him from an opportunity he had wished to have enjoyed of rendering more acceptable to the committee anything he might have to offer on the interesting points it was his duty to touch. Unprepared, however, as he was to speak on this day, of which he was the more sensible from the ill state of his health, he would solicit the attention of the committee for a few moments.

I was a little astonished, I confess, said Mr. C. when I found this bill permitted to pass silently through the committee of the whole, and that, not until the moment when the question was about to be put for its third reading, was it selected as that subject on which gentlemen in the opposition choose to lay before the House their views of the interesting attitude in which the nation stands. It did appear to me that the loan bill, which will soon come before us, would have afforded a much more proper occasion, it being more essential, as providing the ways and means for the prosecution of the war. But the gentlemen had the right of selection, and having exercised it, no matter how improperly, I am gratified, whatever I may think of the character of some part of the debate, at the latitude in which for once, they have indulged. I claim only, in return, of gentlemen on the other side of the House, and of the committee, a like indulgence in expressing, with the same unrestrained freedom, my sentiments. Perhaps in the course of the remarks which I may feel myself called upon to make, said he, gentlemen may apprehend that they assume too harsh an aspect: I have only now to say that I shall speak of parties, measures, and things, as they strike my moral sense, protesting against the imputation of any intention, on my part, to wound the feelings of any *gentleman*.

Considering the situation in which this country is now placed—in a state of actual war with one of the most powerful nations on the earth—it may not be useless to take a view of the past, of various parties which have at different times appeared in this country, and to attend to the manner by which we have been driven from a peaceful posture. Such an inquiry may assist in guiding us to that result, an honorable peace, which must be the sincere desire of every friend to America. The course of that opposition, by which the administration of the government had been unremittingly impeded for the last twelve years, was singular, and, I believe, unexampled in the history of any country. It has been alike the duty and the interest of the administration to preserve peace. Their duty, because it is necessary to the growth of an infant people, their genius, and their habits. Their interest, because a change of the condition of the nation brings along with it a danger of the loss of the affections of the people. The administration has not been forgetful of these solemn obligations. No art has been left unessayed; no experiment, promising a favorable result, left untried to maintain the peaceful relations of the country. When, some six or seven years ago, the affairs of the nation assumed a threatening aspect, a partial non-importation was adopted. As they grew more alarming, an embargo was imposed. It would have attained its purpose, but it was sacrificed upon the altar of conciliation. Vain and fruitless attempt to propitiate! Then came a law of non-intercourse; and a general non-importation followed in the train. In the meantime, any indications of a return to the public law and the path of justice, on the part of either belligerent, are seized with avidity by administration— the arrangement with Mr. Erskine is concluded. It is first applauded and then censured by the opposition. No matter with what unfeigned sincerity administration cultivates peace, the opposition will insist that it alone is culpable for any breach between the two countries. Because the President thought proper, in accepting the proffered reparation for the attack on a national vessel, to intimate that it would have better comported with the justice of the King (and who does not think so?) to punish the offending officer, the opposition, entering into the royal feelings, sees in that imaginary insult abundant cause for rejecting Mr. Erskine's arrangement. On another occasion, you cannot have forgotten the hypercritical ingenuity which they displayed to divest Mr. Jackson's correspondence of a premeditated insult to this country. If gentlemen would only reserve for their own government half the sensibility which is indulged for that of Great Britain, they would find much less to condemn. Restriction after restriction has been tried—negociation has been resorted to, until longer to have negociated would have been disgraceful. Whilst these peaceful experiments are undergoing a trial, what is the conduct of the opposition? They are the champions of war—the proud—the spirited—the sole repository of the nation's honor—the exclusive men of vigor and energy. The administration, on the contrary, is weak, feeble, and pusillanimous—"incapable of being kicked into a war." The maxim, "not a cent for tribute, millions for defence," is loudly proclaimed. Is the administration for negociation? The opposition is tired, sick, disgusted with negociation. They want to draw the sword and avenge the nation's wrongs. When, at length, foreign nations, perhaps, emboldened by the very opposition here made, refused to listen to the amicable appeals made, and repeated and reiterated by administration, to their justice and to their interests—when, in fact, war with one of them became identified with our independence and our sovereignty, and it was no longer possible to abstain from it, behold the opposition becoming the friends of peace and of commerce. They tell you of the calamities of war—its tragical events—the squandering away of your resources—the waste of the public treasure, and the spilling of innocent blood. They tell you that honor is an illusion! Now we see them exhibiting the terrific forms of the roaring king of the forest. Now the meekness and humility of the lamb! They are for war, and no restrictions, when the administration is for peace. They are for peace and restrictions, when the administration is for war. You find them, sir, tacking with every gale, displaying the colors of every party, and of all nations, steady only in one unalterable purpose, to steer, if possible, into the haven of power.

During all this time the parasites of opposition do not fail by cunning sarcasm or sly inuendo to throw out the idea of French influence, which is known to be false, which ought to be met in one manner only, and that is by the lie direct. The administration of this country devoted to foreign influence! The administration of this country subservient to France! Great God! how is it so influenced? By what ligament, on what basis, on what possible foundation does it rest? Is it on similarity of language? No! we speak different tongues, we speak the English language. On the resemblance of our laws? No! the sources of our jurisprudence spring from another and a different country. On commercial intercourse? No! we have comparatively none with France. Is it from the correspondence in the genius of the two governments? No! here alone is the liberty of man secure from the inexorable depotism which everywhere else tramples it under foot. Where then is the ground of such an influence? But, sir, I am insulting you by arguing on such a subject. Yet, preposterous and ridiculous as the insinuation is, it is propagated with so much industry, that there are persons found foolish and credulous enough to believe it. You will, no doubt, think it incredible (but I have nevertheless been told the fact), that an honorable member of this House, now in my eye, recently lost his election by the circulation of a story in his district, that he was the first cousin of the Emperor Napoleon. The proof of the charge was rested on a statement of facts which was undoubtedly true. The gentleman in question, it was alleged, had married a connexion of the lady of the President of the United States, who was the intimate friend of Thomas Jefferson, late President of the United States, who some years ago was in the habit of wearing red French breeches. Now, taking these premises as established, you, Mr. Chairman, are too good a logician not to see that the conclusion necessarily followed!

Throughout the period he had been speaking of, the opposition had been distinguished, amidst all its veerings and changes, by another inflexible feature—the application of every vile epithet which our rich language affords to Bonaparte. He has been compared to every hideous monster, and beast, from that of the revelations to the most insignificant quadruped. He has been called the scourge of mankind, the destroyer of Europe, the great robber, the infidel, and Heaven knows by what other names. Really, gentlemen remind me of an obscure lady in a city not very far off, who also took it into her head, in conversation with an accomplished French gentleman, to talk of the affairs of Europe. She, too, spoke of the destruction of the balance of power, stormed and raged about the insatiable ambition of the Emperor; called him the curse of mankind, the destroyer of Europe. The Frenchman listened to her with perfect patience, and when she had ceased, said to her, with ineffable politeness: Madam, it would give my master, the Emperor, infinite pain, if he knew how hardly you thought of him.

Sir, gentlemen appear to me to forget that they stand on American soil; that they are not in the British House of Commons, but in the chamber of the House of Representatives of the United States; that we have nothing to do with the affairs of Europe, the partition of territory and sovereignty there, except in so far as these things affect the interests of our own country. Gentlemen transform themselves into the Burkes, Chathams and Pitts, of another country, and forgetting from honest zeal the interests of America, engage with European sensibility in the discussion of European interests. If gentlemen ask me if I do not view with regret and horror the concentration of such vast power in the hands of Bonaparte? I reply that I do. I regret to see the Emperor of China holding such immense sway over the fortunes of millions of our species. I regret to see Great Britain possessing so uncontrolled a command over all the waters of our globe. And if I had the ability to distribute among the nations of Europe their several portions of power and of sovereignty, I would say that Holland should be resuscitated and given the weight she enjoyed in the days of her Dewitts. I would confine France within her natural boundaries, the Alps, the Pyrenees, and the Rhine, and make her a secondary naval power only. I would abridge the British maritime power, raise Prussia and Austria to first rate powers, and preserve the integrity of the empire of Russia. But these are speculations. I look at the political transactions of Europe, with the single exception of their possible bearing upon us, as I do the history of other countries or other times. I do not survey them with half the interest that I do the movements in South America. Our political relation is much less important than it is supposed to be. I have no fears of French or English subjugation. If we are united we are too powerful for the mightiest nation in Europe, or all Europe combined. If we are separated and torn asunder we shall become an easy prey to the weakest of them. In the latter dreadful contingency, our country will not be worth preserving.

Next to the notice which the opposition has found itself called upon to bestow upon the French Emperor, a distinguished citizen of Virginia, formerly President of the United States, has never for a moment failed to receive their kindest and most respectful attention. An honorable gentleman from Massachusetts (Mr. Quincy), of whom I am sorry to say it becomes necessary for me, in the course of my remarks, to take some notice, has alluded to him in a remarkable manner. Neither his retirement from public office, his eminent services, nor his advanced age, can exempt this patriot from the coarse assaults of party malevolence. No, sir, in 1801, he snatched from the rude hands of usurpation the violated constitution of his country, and *that* is his crime. He preserved that instrument in form, and substance, and spirit, a precious inheritance, for generations to come, and for *this* he can never be forgiven. How impotent is party rage directed against him! He is not more elevated by his lofty residence, upon the summit of his own favorite mountain, than he is lifted, by the serenity of his mind, and the consciousness of a well spent life, above the malignant passions and the turmoils of the day. No! his own beloved Monticello is not less moved by the storms that beat against its sides than he hears with composure, if he hears at all, the howlings of the whole British pack set loose from the Essex kennel! When the gentleman to whom I have been compelled to allude shall have mingled his dust with that of his abused ancestors, when he shall be consigned to oblivion, or if he lives at all, shall live only in the treasonable annals of a certain junto, the name of Jefferson will be hailed as the second founder of the liberties of this people, and the period of his administration will be looked back to as one of the happiest and brightest epochs in American history. I beg the gentleman's pardon; he has secured to himself a more imperishable fame. I think it was about this time four years ago that the gentleman submitted to the House of Representatives an initiative proposition for an impeachment of Mr. Jefferson. The House condescended to consider it. The gentleman debated it with his usual *temper, moderation and urbanity*. The House decided it in the most solemn manner, and although the gentleman had some how obtained a second, the final vote stood, one for the proposition, 117 against it! The same historic page that transmitted to posterity the virtues and the glory of Henry the Great of France, for their admiration and example, has preserved the infamous name of the fanatic assassin of that excellent monarch. The same sacred pen that pourtrayed the sufferings and crucifixion of the Saviour of mankind has recorded, for universal execration, the name of him who was guilty, not by betraying his country, but (a kindred crime) of betraying his God.

In one respect there is a remarkable difference between administration and the opposition—it is in a sacred regard for personal liberty. When out of power my political friends condemned the surrender of Jonathan Robbins; they opposed the violation of the freedom of the press, in the sedition law! they opposed the more insidious attack upon the freedom of the person under the imposing garb of an alien law. The party now in opposition, then in power, advocated the sacrifice of the unhappy Robbins, and passed those two laws. True to our principles, we are now struggling for the liberty of our seamen against foreign oppression. True to theirs, they oppose the war for this object. They have indeed lately affected a tender solicitude for the liberties of the people, and talk of the danger of standing armies, and the burden of taxes. But it is evident to you, Mr. Chairman, that they speak in a foreign idiom. Their brogue betrays that it is not their vernacular tongue. What, the opposition, who in 1798 and 1799, could raise an useless army to fight an enemy 3000 miles distant from us, alarmed at the existence of one raised for a known specified object—the attack of the adjoining provinces of the enemy. The gentleman from Massachusetts, who assisted by his vote to raise the army of 25,000, alarmed at the danger of our liberties from this very army!

I mean to speak of another subject, which I never think of but with the most awful considerations. The gentleman from

Massachusetts, in imitation of some of his predecessors of 1799, has entertained us with cabinet plots, presidential plots, which are conjured up in the gentleman's own perturbed imagination. I wish, sir, that another plot of a much more serious kind—a plot that aims at the dismemberment of our union, had only the same imaginary existence. But no man, who had paid any attention to the tone of certain prints, and to transactions in a particular quarter of the union for several years past, can doubt the existence of such a plot. It was far, very far from my intention to charge the opposition with such a design. No, he believed them generally incapable of it. He could not say as much for some who were unworthily associated with them in the quarter of the union to which he referred. The gentleman cannot have forgotten his own sentiment, uttered even on the floor of this House, 'peaceably if we can, FORCIBLY if we must;' in and about the same time Henry's mission to Boston was undertaken. The flagitiousness of that embassy had been attempted to be concealed by directing the public attention to the price which the gentleman says was given for the disclosure. As if any price could change the atrociousness of the attempt on the part of G. Britain, or could extenuate in the slightest degree the offence of those citizens, who entertained and deliberated upon the infamous proposition! There was a most remarkable coincidence between some of the things which that man states, and certain events in the quarter alluded to. In the contingency of war with G. Britain, it will be recollected that the neutrality and eventual separation of that section of the union was to be bro't about. How, sir, has it happened, since the declaration of war, that British officers in Canada have asserted to American officers that this very neutrality would take place? That they have so asserted can be established beyond controversy. The project is not brought forward openly, with a direct avowal of the intention. No, the stock of good sense and patriotism in that portion of the country is too great to be undisguisedly encountered. It is assailed from the masked batteries of friendship to peace and commerce on the one side, and by the groundless imputation of opposite propensities on the other. The affections of the people there are to be gradually undermined. The project is suggested or withdrawn; the diabolical parties, in this criminal tragedy, make their appearance or exit, as the audience to whom they address themselves are silent, applaud, or hiss. I was astonished, sir, to have lately read a letter, or pretended letter, published in a prominent print in that quarter, written not in the fervor of party zeal, but cooly and deliberately, in which the writer affects to reason about a separation, and attempts to demonstrate its advantages to different sections of the Union, deploring the existence now of what he terms prejudices against it, but hoping for the arrival of the period when they shall be eradicated. But, sir, I will quit this unpleasant subject; I will turn from one, whom no sense of decency or propriety could restrain from soiling the carpet on which he treads, to gentlemen who have not forgotten what is due to themselves, the place in which we are assembled, nor to those by whom they are opposed. The gentleman from North Carolina, (Mr. Pearson), from Connecticut, (Mr. Pitkin), and from New-York, (Mr. Bleecker), have, with their usual decorum, contended that the war would not have been declared, but for the duplicity of France, in withholding an authentic instrument of repeal of the decrees of Berlin and Milan; that upon the exhibition of such an instrument the revocation of the orders in council took place; that this main cause of the war, but for which it would not have been declared, being removed, the administration ought to seek for the restoration of peace; and that upon its sincerely doing so, terms compatible with the honor and interest of this country may be obtained. It is my purpose, said Mr. C. to examine, first, into the circumstances under which the war was declared; secondly, into the causes for continuing it; and lastly, into the means which have been taken or ought to be taken to procure peace. But, sir, I really am so exhausted that little as I am in the habit of asking of the House an indulgence of this kind, I feel that I must trespass on their goodness.

[Clay at this point sat down. The Committee reported progress, and was granted leave to meet again. On the following day, Clay continued his remarks.]

I am sensible, Mr. Chairman, that some part of the debate to which this bill has given rise, has been attended by circumstances much to be regretted, not usual in this House, and of which it is to be hoped there will be no repetition. The gentleman from

Boston had so absolved himself from every rule of decorum and propriety, had so outraged all decency, that I have found it impossible to suppress the feelings excited on the occasion. His colleague, whom I had the honor to follow (Mr. Wheaton), whatever else he might not have proven, in his very learned, ingenious, and original exposition of the powers of this government—an exposition in which he has sought, where nobody before him has looked, and nobody after him will examine, for a grant of our powers, the preamble to the constitution—has clearly shewn, to the satisfaction of all who *heard* him, that the power is conferred of defensive war. I claim the benefit of a similar principle, in behalf of my political friends, against the gentleman from Boston. I demand only the exercise of the right of repulsion. No one is more anxious than I am to preserve the dignity and the liberality of debate—no member more responsible for its abuse. And if, on this occasion, its just limits have been violated, let him, who has been the unprovoked cause, appropriate to himself exclusively the consequences.

I omitted yesterday, sir, when speaking of a very delicate and painful subject, to notice a powerful engine which the conspirators against the integrity of the Union employ to effect their nefarious purpose—I mean Southern influence. The true friend to his country, knowing that our constitution was the work of compromise, in which interests apparently conflicting were attempted to be reconciled, aims to extinguish or allay prejudices. But this patriotic exertion does not suit the views of those who are urged on by diabolical ambition. They find it convenient to imagine the existence of certain improper influences, and to propagate with their utmost industry a belief of them. Hence the idea of Southern preponderance—Virginia influence—the yoking of the respectable yeomanry of the north, with the negro slaves, to the car of southern nabobs. If Virginia really cherished a reprehensible ambition, and aimed to monopolize the chief magistracy of the country, how was such a purpose to be accomplished? Virginia, alone, cannot elect a President, whose elevation depends upon a plurality of electoral votes and a consequent concurrence of many states. Would Vermont, disinterested Pennsylvania, the Carolinas, independent Georgia, Kentucky, Tennessee, Ohio, Louisiana, all consent to become the tools of an inordinate ambition? But the present incumbent was designated to the office before his predecessor had retired. How? By public sentiment—public sentiment which grew out of his known virtues, his illustrious services, and his distinguished abilities. Would the gentleman crush this public sentiment—is he prepared to admit that he would arrest the progress of opinion?

The war was declared because Great Britain arrogated to herself the pretension of regulating our foreign trade under the delusive name of retaliatory orders in council—a pretension by which she undertook to proclaim to American enterprize— "Thus far shalt thou go, and no farther"—Orders which she refused to revoke after the alledged cause of their enactment had ceased; because she persisted in the practice of impressing American seamen; because she had instigated the Indians to commit hostilities against us; and because she refused indemnity for her past injuries upon our commerce. I throw out of the question other wrongs. The war in fact was announced, on our part, to meet the war which she was waging on her part. So undeniable were the causes of the war—so powerfully did they address themselves to the feelings of the whole American people, that when the bill was pending before this House, gentlemen in the opposition—although provoked to debate, would not, or could not, utter one syllable against it. It is true they wrapped themselves up in sullen silence, pretending that they did not choose to debate such a question in secret session. Whilst speaking of the proceedings on that occasion, I beg to be permitted to advert to another fact that transpired, an important fact, material for the nation to know, and which I have often regretted had not been spread upon our journals. My honorable colleague (Mr. M'Kee) moved, in committee of the whole, to comprehend France in the war; and when the question was taken upon the proposition, there appeared but ten votes in support of it, of whom seven belonged to this side of the House, and three only to the other!

It is said that we were inveigled into the war by the perfidy of France; and that had she furnished the document in time, which was first published in England, in May last, it would have been prevented. I will concede to gentlemen every thing they ask about the injustice of France towards this country. I wish to God that our ability was equal to our disposition to make her feel the sense we entertain of that injustice. The manner of the publication of the paper in question, was undoubtedly extremely exceptionable. But I maintain that, had it made its appearance earlier, it would not have had the effect supposed; and the proof lies in the unequivocal declarations of the British government. I will trouble you, sir, with going no further back than to the letters of the British minister, addressed to the Secretary of State, just before the expiration of his diplomatic functions. It will be recollected by the committee that he exhibited to this government a despatch from Lord Castlereagh, in which the principle was distinctly avowed, that to produce the effect of the repeal of the orders in council, the French decrees must be absolutely and entirely revoked as to all the world, and not as to America alone. A copy of that despatch was demanded of him, and he very awkwardly evaded it. But on the 10th of June, after the bill declaring war had actually passed this House, and was pending before the Senate (and which, I have no doubt, was known to him), in a letter to Mr. Monroe, he says: "I have no hesitation, sir, in saying that Great-Britain, as the case has hitherto stood, never did, nor ever *could* engage, without the greatest injustice to herself and her allies, as well as to other neutral nations, to repeal her orders as affecting America alone, leaving them in force against other states, upon condition that France would except singly and especially America from the operation of her decrees." On the 14th of the same month, the bill still pending before the Senate, he repeats: "I will now say, that I feel entirely authorised to assure you, that if you can at any time produce a *full and unconditional* repeal of the French decrees, as you have a right to demand it in your character of a neutral nation, and that it be disengaged from any question concerning our maritime rights, we shall be ready to meet you with a revocation of the orders in council. Previously to your producing *such* an instrument, which I am sorry to see you regard as unnecessary, you cannot expect of us to give up our orders in council." Thus, sir, you see that the British government would not be content with a repeal of the French decrees as to us only. But the French paper in question was such a repeal. It could not, therefore, satisfy the British government. It could not, therefore, have induced that government, had it been earlier promulgated, to repeal the orders in council. It could not, therefore, have averted the war. The withholding of it did not occasion the war, and the promulgation of it would not have prevented the war. But gentlemen have contended that, in point of fact, it did produce a repeal of the orders in council. This I deny. After it made its appearance in England, it was declared by one of the British ministry, in Parliament, not to be satisfactory. And all the world knows, that the repeal of the orders in council resulted from the inquiry, reluctantly acceded to by the ministry, into the effect upon their manufacturing establishments, of our non-importation law, or to the warlike attitude assumed by this government, or to both. But it is said, that the orders in council are done away, no matter from what cause; and that having been the sole motive for declaring the war, the relations of peace ought to be restored. This brings me into an examination of the grounds for continuing the war.

I am far from acknowledging that, had the orders in council been repealed, as they have been, before the war was declared, the declaration would have been prevented. In a body so numerous as this is, from which the declaration emanated, it is impossible to say with any degree of certainty what would have been the effect of such a repeal. Each member must answer for himself. I have no hesitation, then in saying, that I have always considered the impressment of American seamen as much the most serious aggression. But, sir, how have those orders at last been repealed? Great-Britain, it is true, has intimated a willingness to suspend their practical operation, but she still arrogates to herself the right to revive them upon certain contingencies, of which she constitutes herself the sole judge. She waives the temporary use of the rod, but she suspends it in terrorem over our heads. Supposing it was conceded to gentlemen that such a repeal of the orders in council, as took place on the 23d of June last, exceptionable as it is, being known before the war, would have prevented the war, does it follow that it ought to induce us to lay down our arms, without the redress of any other injury? Does it follow, in all cases, that that which would have prevented the war in the first instance, should terminate the war? By no means. It requires a great struggle for a nation, prone to peace as this is, to burst through its habits and encounter the difficulties of war. Such a nation ought but seldom to go to war. When it does, it should be for clear and essential rights alone, and it should firmly resolve to extort, at all hazards, their recognition. The war of the revolution is an example of a war began for one object and prosecuted for another. It was waged, in its commencement, against the right asserted by the parent country to tax the colonies. Then no one thought of absolute independence. The idea of independence was repelled. But the British government would have relinquished the principle of taxation. The founders of our liberties saw, however, that there was no security short of independence, and they achieved our independence. When nations are engaged in war, those rights in controversy, which are not acknowledged by the Treaty of Peace, are abandoned. And who is prepared to say that American seamen shall be surrendered, the victims to the British principle of impressment? And, sir, what is this principle? She contends that she has a right to the services of her own subjects; that, in the exercise of this right, she may lawfully impress them, even altho' she finds them in our vessels, upon the high seas, without her jurisdiction. Now, I deny that she has any right, without her jurisdiction, to come on board our vessels upon the high seas, for any other purpose but in pursuit of enemies, or their goods, or goods contraband of war. But she further contends, that her subjects cannot renounce their allegiance to her and contract a new obligation to other sovereigns. I do not mean to go into the general question of the right of expatriation. If, as is contended, all nations deny it, all nations at the same time admit and practise the right of naturalization. G. Britain herself does. Great-Britain, in the very case of foreign seamen, imposes, perhaps, fewer restraints upon naturalization than any other nation. Then, if subjects cannot break their original allegiance, they may, according to universal usage, contract a new allegiance. What is the effect of this double obligation? Undoubtedly, that the sovereign having the possession of the subject would have the right to the services of the subject. If he return within the jurisdiction of his primitive sovereign, he may resume his right to his services, of which the subject by his own act, could not divest himself. But his primitive sovereign can have no right to go in quest of him, out of his own jurisdiction, into the jurisdiction of another sovereign, or upon the high seas, where there exists either no jurisdiction, or it belongs to the nation owning the ship navigating them. But, sir, this discussion is altogether useless. It is not to the British principle, objectionable as it is, that we are alone to look;—it is to her practice—no matter what guise she puts on. It is in vain to assert the inviolability of the obligation of allegiance. It is in vain to set up the plea of necessity, and to allege that she cannot exist without the impressment of HER seamen. The naked truth is, she comes, by her press-gangs, on board of our vessels, seizes OUR native seamen, as well as naturalized, and drags them into her service. It is the case, then, of the assertion of an erroneous principle, and a practice not conformable to the principle—a principle which, if it were theoretically right, must be for ever practically wrong. We are told by gentlemen in the opposition, that government has not done all that was incumbent on it to do to avoid just cause of complaint on the part of Great-Britain—that, in particular, the certificates of protection, authorized by the act of 1796, are fraudulently used. Sir, government has done too much in granting those paper protections. I can never think of them without being shocked. They resemble the passes which the master grants to his negro slave, "Let the bearer, Mungo, pass and re-pass without molestation." What do they imply? That Great-Britain has a right to take all who are not provided with them. From their very nature they must be liable to abuse on both sides. If G. B. desires a mark by which she can know her own subjects, let her give them an ear mark. The colors that float from the mast head should be the credentials of our seamen. There is no safety to us, & the gentlemen have shewn it, but in the rule that all who sail under the flag (not being enemies) are protected by the flag. It is impossible that this country should ever abandon the gallant tars, who have won for us such splendid trophies. Let me suppose that the Genius of Columbia should visit one of them in his oppressor's prison and attempt to reconcile him to his wretched condition. She would say to him, in the language of gentlemen on the other side, 'Great Britain intends you no harm; she did not mean to impress you, but one of her own subjects; having taken you by mistake, I will remonstrate, and try to prevail upon her, by peaceable means, to release you, but I cannot, my son, fight for you.' If he did not consider this mockery, he would address her judgment and say, 'You owe me, my country, protection; I owe you, in return, obedience. I am no British subject, I am a native of old Massachusetts, where live my aged father, my wife, my children. I have faithfully discharged my duty. Will you refuse to do yours?' Appealing to her passions, he would continue, 'I lost this eye in fighting under Truxtun, with the Insurgente; I got this scar before Tripoli; I broke this leg on board the Constitution, when the Guerriere struck.' If she remained still unmoved, he would break out, in the accents of mingled distress and despair.

> *Hard, hard, is my fate! once I freedom enjoyed,*
> *Was as happy as happy could be!*
> *Oh! how hard is my fate, how galling these chains!*

I will not imagine the dreadful catastrophe to which he would be driven by an abandonment of him to his oppressor. It will not be, it cannot be, that his country will refuse him protection!

It is said, that Great Britain has been always willing to make a satisfactory arrangement of the subject of impressment; and that Mr. King had nearly concluded one prior to his departure from that country. Let us hear what that minister says upon his return to America. In his letter dated at New York in July, 1803, after giving an account of his attempt to form an arrangement for the protection of our seamen, and his interviews to this end with Lords Hawkesbury and St. Vincent; and stating that, when he had supposed the terms of a convention were agreed upon, a new pretension was set up (the *mare clausum*), he concludes: 'I regret not to have been able to put this business on a satisfactory footing, knowing as I do its very great importance to both parties; but I flatter myself that I have not misjudged the interests of our own country, in refusing to sanction a principle that might be productive of more extensive evils than those it was our aim to prevent.' The sequel of his negociation, on this affair, is more fully given in the recent conversation between Mr. Russell and Lord Castlereagh, communicated to Congress during its present session. Lord Castlereagh says to Mr. Russell:——

'Indeed there has evidently been much misapprehension on this subject, and an erroneous belief entertained that an arrangement, in regard to it, has been nearer an accomplishment than the facts will warrant. Even our friends in Congress, I mean those who were opposed to going to war with us, have been so confident in this mistake, that they have ascribed the failure of such an arrangement solely to the misconduct of the American government. This error probably originated with Mr. King, for being much esteemed here, and always well received by the persons in power, he seems to have misconstrued their readiness to listen to his representations, and their warm professions of a disposition to remove the complaints of America, in relation to impressment, into a supposed conviction on their part of the propriety of adopting the plan which he had proposed. But Lord St. Vincent, whom he might have thought he had brought over to his opinions, appears never for a moment to have ceased to regard all arrangement on the subject to be attended with formidable, if not insurmountable obstacles. This is obvious from a letter which his Lordship addressed to Sir William Scott at the time.' Here Lord Castlereagh read a letter, contained in the records before him, in which Lord St. Vincent states to Sir William Scott the zeal with which Mr. King had assailed him on the subject of impressment, confesses his own perplexity and total incompetency to discover any practical project for the safe discontinuance of that practice, and asks for counsel and advice. 'Thus you see,' proceeded Lord Castlereagh, 'that the confidence of Mr. King on this subject was entirely unfounded.'

Thus it is apparent, that, at no time, has the enemy been willing to place this subject on a satisfactory footing: I will speak hereafter of the overtures made by administration since the war.

The honorable gentleman from New York (Mr. Bleecker), in the very sensible speech with which he favored the committee, made one observation that did not comport with his usual liberal and enlarged views. It was that those who are most interested against the practice of impressment did not desire a continuance of the war on account of it, whilst those (the southern and western members) who had no interest in it, were the zealous advocates of the American seaman. It was a provincial sentiment unworthy of that gentleman. It was one which, in a change of condition, he would not express, because

I know he could not feel it. Does not that gentleman feel for the unhappy victims of the tomahawk in the Western country, although his quarter of the union may be exempted from similar barbarities? I am sure he does. If there be a description of rights which, more than any other, should unite all parties in all quarters of the Union, it is unquestionably the rights of the person. No matter what his vocation; whether he seeks subsistence amidst the dangers of the deep, or draws it from the bowels of the earth, or from the humblest occupations of mechanic life: whenever the sacred rights of an American freeman are assailed, all hearts ought to unite and every arm should be braced to vindicate his cause.

The gentleman from Delaware sees in Canada no object worthy of conquest. According to him, it is a cold, sterile, and inhospitable region. And yet, such are the allurements which it offers, that the same gentleman apprehends that, if it be annexed to the United States, already too much weakened by an extension of territory, the people of New England will rush over the line and depopulate that section of the Union! That gentleman considers it honest to hold Canada as a kind of hostage, to regard it as a sort of bond, for the good behaviour of the enemy. But he will not enforce the bond. The actual conquest of that country would, according to him, make no impression upon the enemy, and yet the very apprehension only of such a conquest would at all times have a powerful operation upon him! Other gentlemen consider the invasion of that country as wicked and unjustifiable. Its inhabitants are represented as unoffending, connected with those of the bordering states by a thousand tender ties, interchanging acts of kindness, and all the offices of good neighborhood; Canada, said Mr. C. innocent! Canada unoffending! Is it not in Canada that the tomahawk of the savage has been moulded into its death-like form? From Canadian magazines, Malden and others, that those supplies have been issued which nourish and sustain the Indian hostilities? Supplies which have enabled the savage hordes to butcher the garrison of Chicago, and to commit other horrible murders? Was it not by the joint cooperation of Canadians and Indians that a remote American fort, Michilimackinac, was fallen upon and reduced, while the garrison was in ignorance of a state of war? But, sir, how soon have the opposition changed. When administration was striving, by the operation of peaceful measures, to bring Great Britain back to a sense of justice, they were for old-fashioned war. And now that they have got old fashioned war, their sensibilities are cruelly shocked, and all their sympathies are lavished upon the harmless inhabitants of the adjoining provinces. What does a state of war present? The united energies of one people arrayed against the combined energies of another—a conflict in which each party aims to inflict all the injury it can, by sea and land, upon the territories, property and citizens of the other, subject only to the rules of mitigated war practised by civilized nations. The gentlemen would not touch the continental provinces of the enemy, nor, I presume, for the same reason, her possessions in the W. Indies. The same humane spirit would spare the seamen and soldiers of the enemy. The sacred person of his majesty must not be attacked, for the learned gentlemen, on the other side, are quite familiar with the maxim, that the king can do no wrong. Indeed, sir, I know of no person on whom we may make war, upon the principles of the honorable gentlemen, but Mr. Stephen, the celebrated author of the orders in council, or the board of admiralty, who authorise and regulate the practice of impressment!

The disasters of the war admonish us, we are told, of the necessity of terminating the contest. If our achievements upon the land have been less splendid than those of our intrepid seamen, it is not because the American soldier is less brave. On the one element organization, discipline, and a thorough knowledge of their duties exist, on the part of the officers and their men. On the other, almost every thing is yet to be acquired. We have however the consolation that our country abounds with the richest materials, and that in no instance when engaged in an action have our arms been tarnished. At Brownstown and at Queenstown the valor of veterans was displayed, and acts of the noblest heroism were performed. It is true, that the disgrace of Detroit remains to be wiped off. That is a subject on which I cannot trust my feelings, it is not fitting I should speak. But this much I will say, it was an event which no human foresight could have anticipated, and for which administration cannot be justly censured. It was the parent of all the misfortunes we have experienced on land. But for it the

Indian war would have been in a great measure prevented or terminated; the ascendency on lake Erie acquired, and the war pushed perhaps to Montreal. With the exception of that event, the war, even upon the land, has been attended by a series of the most brilliant exploits, which, whatever interest they may inspire on this side of the mountains, have given the greatest pleasure on the other. The expedition under the command of Gov. Edwards and Colonel Russell, to lake Pioria, on the Illinois, was completely successful. So was that of Captain Craig, who it is said ascended that river still higher. General Hopkins destroyed the Prophet's town. We have just received intelligence of the gallant enterprise of Colonel Campbell. In short, sir, the Indian towns have been swept from the mouth to source of the Wabash, and a hostile country has been penetrated far beyond the most daring incursions of any campaign during the former Indian war. Never was more cool deliberate bravery displayed than that by Newnan's party from Georgia. And the capture of the Detroit, and the destruction of the Caledonia, (whether placed to our maritime or land account) for judgment, skill, and courage on the part of Lieutenant Elliott, has never been surpassed.

It is alleged that the elections in England are in favor of the ministry, and that those in this country are against the war. If in such a cause (saying nothing of the impurity of their elections) the people of that country have rallied around their government, it affords a salutary lesson to the people here, who at all hazards ought to support theirs, struggling as it is to maintain our just rights. But the people here have not been false to themselves; a great majority approve the war, as is evinced by the recent reelection of the chief magistrate. Suppose it were even true, that an entire section of the Union were opposed to the war, that section being a minority, is the will of the majority to be relinquished? In that section the real strength of the opposition had been greatly exaggerated. Vermont has, by two successive expressions of her opinion, approved the declaration of war. In New-Hampshire, parties are so nearly equipoised that out of 30 or 35 thousand votes, those who approved, and are for supporting it, lost the election by only 1,000 or 1,500 votes. In Massachusetts alone have they obtained any considerable accession. If we come to New-York, we shall find that other and local causes have influenced her elections.

What cause, Mr. Chairman, which existed for declaring the war has been removed? We sought indemnity for the past and security for the future. The orders in council are suspended, not revoked; no compensation for spoliations, Indian hostilities, which were before secretly instigated, now openly encouraged; and the practice of impressment unremittingly persevered in and insisted upon. Yet administration has given the strongest demonstrations of its love of peace. On the 29th June, less than ten days after the declaration of war, the Secretary of State writes to Mr. Russell, authorising him to agree to an armistice, upon two conditions only, and what are they? That the orders in council should be repealed, and the practice of impressing American seamen cease, those already impressed being released. The proposition was for nothing more than a *real* truce; that the war should in fact cease on *both* sides. Again on the 27th July, one month later, anticipating a possible objection to these terms, reasonable as they are, Mr. Monroe empowers Mr. Russell to stipulate in general terms for an armistice, having only an informal understanding on these points. In return, the enemy is offered a prohibition of the employment of his seamen in our service, thus removing entirely all pretext for the practice of impressment. The very proposition which the gentleman from Connecticut (Mr. Pitkin) contends ought to be made has been made. How are these pacific advances met by the other party? Rejected as absolutely inadmissible, cavils are indulged about the inadequacy of Mr. Russell's powers, and the want of an act of Congress is intimated. And yet the constant usage of nations I believe is, where the legislation of one party is necessary to carry into effect a given stipulation, to leave it to the contracting party to provide the requisite laws. If he failed to do so, it is a breach of good faith, and a subject of subsequent remonstrance by the injured party. When Mr. Russell renews the overture, in what was intended as a more agreeable form to the British government, Lord Castlereagh is not content with a simple rejection, but clothes it in the langauge of insult. Afterwards, in conversation with Mr. Russell, the moderation of our government is misinterpreted and made the occasion of a sneer, that we are tired of the war. The proposition of Admiral Warren is submitted in a spirit not more pacific. He is instructed, he tells us, to propose that the government of the United States shall instantly recall their letters of marque and reprisal against British ships, together with all orders and instructions for any acts of hostility whatever against the territories of his Majesty or the persons or property of his subjects. That small affair being settled, he is further authorised to arrange as to the revocation of the laws which interdict the commerce and ships of war of his Majesty from the harbors and waters of the United States. This messenger of peace comes with one qualified concession in his pocket, not made to the justice of our demands, and is fully empowered to receive our homage, the contrite retraction of all our measures adopted against his master! And in default, he does not fail to assure us, the orders in council are to be forthwith revived. Administration, still anxious to terminate the war, suppresses the indignation which such a proposal ought to have created, and in its answer concludes by informing Admiral Warren, "that if there be no objection to an accommodation of the difference relating to impressment, in the mode proposed, other than the suspension of the British claim to impressment during the armistice, there can be none to proceeding, *without the armistice*, to an immediate discussion and arrangement of an article on that subject." Thus it has left the door of negotiation unclosed, and it remains to be seen if the enemy will accept the invitation tendered to him. The honorable gentleman from North Carolina (Mr. Pearson) supposes, that if Congress would pass a law, prohibiting the employment of British seamen in our service, upon condition of a like prohibition on their part, and repeal the act of non-importation, peace would immediately follow. Sir, I have no doubt if such a law were passed, with all the requisite solemnities, and the repeal to take place, Lord Castlereagh would laugh at our simplicity. No, sir, administration has erred in the steps which it has taken to restore peace, but its error has been not in doing too little but in betraying too great a solicitude for that event. An honorable peace is attainable only by an efficient war. My plan would be to call out the ample resources of the country, give them a judicious direction, prosecute the war with the utmost vigor, strike wherever we can reach the enemy, at sea or on land, and negotiate the terms of a peace at Quebec or Halifax. We are told that England is a proud and lofty nation that disdaining to wait for danger, meets it half way. Haughty as she is, we once triumphed over her, and if we do not listen to the councils of timidity and despair we shall again prevail. In such a cause, with the aid of Providence, we must come out crowned with success; but if we fail, let us fail like men, lash ourselves to our gallant tars, and expire together in one common struggle, fighting for "*seamen's rights and free trade.*"

DANIEL WEBSTER

Address at the Laying of the Cornerstone of the Bunker Hill Monument

Boston, June 17, 1825

THIS uncounted multitude before me, and around me, proves the feeling which the occasion has excited. These thousands of human faces, glowing with sympathy and joy, and, from the impulses of a common gratitude, turned reverently to heaven, in this spacious temple of the firmament, proclaim that the day, the place, and the purpose of our assembling have made a deep impression on our hearts.

If, indeed, there be any thing in local association fit to affect the mind of man, we need not strive to repress the emotions which agitate us here. We are among the sepulchres of our fathers. We are on ground, distinguished by their valor, their constancy, and the shedding of their blood. We are here, not to fix an uncertain date in our annals, nor to draw into notice an obscure and unknown spot. If our humble purpose had never been conceived, if we ourselves had never been born, the 17th of June 1775 would have been a day on which all subsequent history would have poured its light, and the eminence where we stand, a point of attraction to the eyes of successive generations. But we are Americans. We live in what may be called the early age of this great continent; and we know that our posterity, through all time, are here to suffer and enjoy the allotments of humanity. We see before us a probable train of great events; we know that our own fortunes have been happily cast; and it is natural, therefore, that we should be moved by the contemplation of occurrences which have guided our destiny before many of us were born, and settled the condition in which we should pass that portion of our existence, which God allows to men on earth.

We do not read even of the discovery of this continent, without feeling something of a personal interest in the event;

without being reminded how much it has affected our own fortunes, and our own existence. It is more impossible for us, therefore, than for others, to contemplate with unaffected minds that interesting, I may say, that most touching and pathetic scene, when the great Discoverer of America stood on the deck of his shattered bark, the shades of night falling on the sea, yet no man sleeping; tossed on the billows of an unknown ocean, yet the stronger billows of alternate hope and despair tossing his own troubled thoughts; extending forward his harassed frame, straining westward his anxious and eager eyes, till Heaven at last granted him a moment of rapture and ecstacy, in blessing his vision with the sight of the unknown world.

Nearer to our times, more closely connected with our fates, and therefore still more interesting to our feelings and affections, is the settlement of our own country by colonists from England. We cherish every memorial of these worthy ancestors; we celebrate their patience and fortitude; we admire their daring enterprise; we teach our children to venerate their piety; and we are justly proud of being descended from men, who have set the world an example of founding civil institutions on the great and united principles of human freedom and human knowledge. To us, their children, the story of their labors and sufferings can never be without its interest. We shall not stand unmoved on the shore of Plymouth, while the sea continues to wash it; nor will our brethren in another early and ancient colony, forget the place of its first establishment, till their river shall cease to flow by it. No vigor of youth, no maturity of manhood, will lead the nation to forget the spots where its infancy was cradled and defended.

But the great event, in the history of the continent, which we are now met here to commemorate; that prodigy of modern times, at once the wonder and the blessing of the world, is the American Revolution. In a day of extraordinary prosperity and happiness, of high national honor, distinction, and power, we are brought together, in this place, by our love of country, by our admiration of exalted character, by our gratitude for signal services and patriotic devotion.

The society, whose organ I am, was formed for the purpose of rearing some honorable and durable monument to the memory of the early friends of American Independence. They

have thought, that for this object no time could be more propitious, than the present prosperous and peaceful period; that
no place could claim preference over this memorable spot; and
that no day could be more auspicious to the undertaking, than
the anniversary of the battle which was here fought. The foundation of that monument we have now laid. With solemnities
suited to the occasion, with prayers to Almighty God for his
blessing, and in the midst of this cloud of witnesses, we have
begun the work. We trust it will be prosecuted; and that
springing from a broad foundation, rising high in massive
solidity and unadorned grandeur, it may remain, as long as
Heaven permits the works of man to last, a fit emblem, both of
the events in memory of which it is raised, and of the gratitude
of those who have reared it.

We know, indeed, that the record of illustrious actions is
most safely deposited in the universal remembrance of mankind. We know, that if we could cause this structure to ascend,
not only till it reached the skies, but till it pierced them, its
broad surfaces could still contain but part of that, which, in an
age of knowledge, hath already been spread over the earth,
and which history charges itself with making known to all future times. We know, that no inscription on entablatures less
broad than the earth itself, can carry information of the events
we commemorate, where it has not already gone; and that no
structure, which shall not outlive the duration of letters and
knowledge among men, can prolong the memorial. But our
object is, by this edifice to show our own deep sense of the
value and importance of the achievements of our ancestors;
and, by presenting this work of gratitude to the eye, to keep
alive similar sentiments, and to foster a constant regard for the
principles of the Revolution. Human beings are composed not
of reason only, but of imagination also, and sentiment; and that
is neither wasted nor misapplied which is appropriated to the
purpose of giving right direction to sentiments, and opening
proper springs of feeling in the heart. Let it not be supposed
that our object is to perpetuate national hostility, or even to
cherish a mere military spirit. It is higher, purer, nobler. We
consecrate our work to the spirit of national independence,
and we wish that the light of peace may rest upon it forever.
We rear a memorial of our conviction of that unmeasured

benefit, which has been conferred on our own land, and of the happy influences, which have been produced, by the same events, on the general interests of mankind. We come, as Americans, to mark a spot, which must forever be dear to us and our posterity. We wish, that whosoever, in all coming time, shall turn his eye hither, may behold that the place is not undistinguished, where the first great battle of the Revolution was fought. We wish, that this structure may proclaim the magnitude and importance of that event, to every class and every age. We wish, that infancy may learn the purpose of its erection from maternal lips, and that weary and withered age may behold it, and be solaced by the recollections which it suggests. We wish, that labor may look up here, and be proud, in the midst of its toil. We wish, that, in those days of disaster, which, as they come on all nations, must be expected to come on us also, desponding patriotism may turn its eyes hitherward, and be assured that the foundations of our national power still stand strong. We wish, that this column, rising towards heaven among the pointed spires of so many temples dedicated to God, may contribute also to produce, in all minds, a pious feeling of dependence and gratitude. We wish, finally, that the last object on the sight of him who leaves his native shore, and the first to gladden his who revisits it, may be something which shall remind him of the liberty and the glory of his country. Let it rise, till it meet the sun in his coming; let the earliest light of the morning gild it, and parting day linger and play on its summit.

We live in a most extraordinary age. Events so various and so important, that they might crowd and distinguish centuries, are, in our times, compressed within the compass of a single life. When has it happened that history has had so much to record, in the same term of years, as since the 17th of June 1775? Our own Revolution, which, under other circumstances, might itself have been expected to occasion a war of half a century, has been achieved; twenty-four sovereign and independent states erected; and a general government established over them, so safe, so wise, so free, so practical, that we might well wonder its establishment should have been accomplished so soon, were it not far the greater wonder that it should have been established at all. Two or three millions of people have been augmented to twelve; and the great forests of the West prostrated beneath the arm of successful industry; and the dwellers on the banks of the Ohio and the Mississippi, become the fellow citizens and neighbours of those who cultivate the hills of New England. We have a commerce, that leaves no sea unexplored; navies, which take no law from superior force; revenues, adequate to all the exigencies of government, almost without taxation; and peace with all nations, founded on equal rights and mutual respect.

Europe, within the same period, has been agitated by a mighty revolution, which, while it has been felt in the individual condition and happiness of almost every man, has shaken to the centre her political fabric, and dashed against one another thrones, which had stood tranquil for ages. On this, our continent, our own example has been followed; and colonies have sprung up to be nations. Unaccustomed sounds of liberty and free government have reached us from beyond the track of the sun; and at this moment the dominion of European power, in this continent, from the place where we stand to the south pole, is annihilated forever.

In the mean time, both in Europe and America, such has been the general progress of knowledge; such the improvements in legislation, in commerce, in the arts, in letters, and above all in liberal ideas, and the general spirit of the age, that the whole world seems changed.

Yet, notwithstanding that this is but a faint abstract of the things which have happened since the day of the battle of Bunker Hill, we are but fifty years removed from it; and we now stand here, to enjoy all the blessings of our own condition, and to look abroad on the brightened prospects of the world, while we hold still among us some of those, who were active agents in the scenes of 1775, and who are now here, from every quarter of New England, to visit, once more, and under circumstances so affecting, I had almost said so overwhelming, this renowned theatre of their courage and patriotism.

VENERABLE MEN! you have come down to us, from a former generation. Heaven has bounteously lengthened out your lives, that you might behold this joyous day. You are now, where you stood, fifty years ago, this very hour, with your brothers, and your neighbours, shoulder to shoulder, in the strife for your country. Behold, how altered! The same heavens are indeed over your heads; the same ocean rolls at your feet; but all else, how changed! You hear now no roar of hostile cannon, you see no mixed volumes of smoke and flame rising from burning Charlestown. The ground strewed with the dead and the dying; the impetuous charge; the steady and successful repulse; the loud call to repeated assault; the summoning of all that is manly to repeated resistance; a thousand bosoms freely and fearlessly bared in an instant to whatever of terror there may be in war and death;—all these you have witnessed, but you witness them no more. All is peace. The heights of yonder metropolis, its towers and roofs, which you then saw filled with wives and children and countrymen in distress and terror, and looking with unutterable emotions for the issue of the combat, have presented you to-day with the sight of its whole happy population, come out to welcome and greet you with an universal jubilee. Yonder proud ships, by a felicity of position appropriately lying at the foot of this mount, and seeming fondly to cling around it, are not means of annoyance to you, but your country's own means of distinction and defence. All is peace; and God has granted you this sight of your country's happiness, ere you slumber in the grave forever. He has allowed you to behold and to partake the reward of your patriotic toils; and he has allowed us, your sons and countrymen, to meet you here, and in the name of the present generation, in the name of your country, in the name of liberty, to thank you!

But, alas! you are not all here! Time and the sword have thinned your ranks. Prescott, Putnam, Stark, Brooks, Read, Pomeroy, Bridge! our eyes seek for you in vain amidst this broken band. You are gathered to your fathers, and live only to your country in her grateful remembrance, and your own bright example. But let us not too much grieve, that you have met the common fate of men. You lived, at least, long enough to know that your work had been nobly and successfully accomplished. You lived to see your country's independence established, and to sheathe your swords from war. On the light of Liberty you saw arise the light of Peace, like

'another morn,
Risen on mid-noon;'—

and the sky, on which you closed your eyes, was cloudless.

But—ah!—Him! the first great Martyr in this great cause! Him! the premature victim of his own self-devoting heart! Him! the head of our civil councils, and the destined leader of military bands; whom nothing brought hither, but the unquenchable fire of his own spirit; Him! cut off by Providence, in the hour of overwhelming anxiety and thick gloom; falling, ere he saw the star of his country rise; pouring out his generous blood, like water, before he knew whether it would fertilize a land of freedom or of bondage! how shall I struggle with the emotions, that stifle the utterance of thy name!—Our poor work may perish; but thine shall endure! This monument may moulder away; the solid ground it rests upon may sink down to a level with the sea; but thy memory shall not fail! Wheresoever among men a heart shall be found, that beats to the transports of patriotism and liberty, its aspirations shall be to claim kindred with thy spirt!

But the scene amidst which we stand does not permit us to confine our thoughts or our sympathies to those fearless spirits, who hazarded or lost their lives on this consecrated spot. We have the happiness to rejoice here in the presence of a most worthy representation of the survivors of the whole Revolutionary Army.

VETERANS! you are the remnant of many a well fought field. You bring with you marks of honor from Trenton and Monmouth, from Yorktown, Camden, Bennington, and Saratoga. VETERANS OF HALF A CENTURY! when in your youthful days, you put every thing at hazard in your country's cause, good as that cause was, and sanguine as youth is, still your fondest hopes did not stretch onward to an hour like this! At a period to which you could not reasonably have expected to arrive; at a moment of national prosperity, such as you could never have foreseen, you are now met, here, to enjoy the fellowship of old soldiers, and to receive the overflowings of an universal gratitude.

But your agitated countenances and your heaving breasts inform me that even this is not an unmixed joy. I perceive that a tumult of contending feelings rushes upon you. The images of the dead, as well as the persons of the living, throng to your embraces. The scene overwhelms you, and I turn from it. May the Father of all mercies smile upon your declining years, and bless them! And when you shall here have exchanged your embraces; when you shall once more have pressed the hands which have been so often extended to give succour in adversity, or grasped in the exultation of victory; then look abroad into this lovely land, which your young valor defended, and mark the happiness with which it is filled; yea, look abroad into the whole earth, and see what a name you have contributed to give to your country, and what a praise you have added to freedom, and then rejoice in the sympathy and gratitude, which beam upon your last days from the improved condition of mankind.

The occasion does not require of me any particular account of the battle of the 17th of June, nor any detailed narrative of the events which immediately preceded it. These are familiarly known to all. In the progress of the great and interesting controversy, Massachusetts and the town of Boston had become early and marked objects of the displeasure of the British Parliament. This had been manifested, in the Act for altering the Government of the Province, and in that for shutting up the Port of Boston. Nothing sheds more honor on our early history, and nothing better shows how little the feelings and sentiments of the colonies were known or regarded in England, than the impression which these measures every where produced in America. It had been anticipated, that while the other colonies would be terrified by the severity of the punishment inflicted on Massachusetts, the other seaports would be governed by a mere spirit of gain; and that, as Boston was now cut off from all commerce, the unexpected advantage, which this blow on her was calculated to confer on other towns, would be greedily enjoyed. How miserably such reasoners deceived themselves! How little they knew of the depth, and the strength, and the intenseness of that feeling of resistance to illegal acts of power, which possessed the whole American people! Every where the unworthy boon was rejected with scorn. The fortunate occasion was seized, every where, to show to the whole world, that the colonies were swayed by no local interest, no partial interest, no selfish interest. The temptation to profit by the punishment of Boston was strongest to our neighbours of Salem. Yet Salem was precisely the place, where this miserable proffer was spurned, in a tone of the most lofty self-respect, and the most indignant patriotism. 'We are deeply affected,' said its inhabitants, 'with the sense of our public calamities; but the miseries that are now rapidly hastening on our brethren in the capital of the Province, greatly excite our commiseration. By shutting up the port of Boston, some imagine that the course of trade might be turned hither and to our benefit; but we must be dead to every idea of justice, lost to all feelings of humanity, could we indulge a thought to seize on wealth, and raise our fortunes on the ruin of our suffering neighbours.' These noble sentiments were not confined to our immediate vicinity. In that day of general affection and brotherhood, the blow given to Boston smote on every patriotic heart, from one end of the country to the other. Virginia and the Carolinas, as well as Connecticut and New Hampshire, felt and proclaimed the cause to be their own. The Continental Congress, then holding its first session in Philadelphia, expressed its sympathy for the suffering inhabitants of Boston, and addresses were received from all quarters, assuring them that the cause was a common one, and should be met by common efforts and common sacrifices. The Congress of Massachusetts responded to these assurances; and in an address to the Congress at Philadelphia, bearing the official signature, perhaps among the last, of the immortal Warren, notwithstanding the severity of its suffering and the magnitude of the dangers which threatened it, it was declared, that this colony 'is ready, at all times, to spend and to be spent in the cause of America.'

But the hour drew nigh, which was to put professions to the proof, and to determine whether the authors of these mutual pledges were ready to seal them in blood. The tidings of Lexington and Concord had no sooner spread, than it was universally felt, that the time was at last come for action. A spirit pervaded all ranks, not transient, not boisterous, but deep, solemn, determined,

> 'totamque infusa per artus
> Mens agitat molem, et magno se corpore miscet.'

War, on their own soil and at their own doors, was, indeed, a strange work to the yeomanry of New England; but their consciences were convinced of its necessity, their country called them to it, and they did not withhold themselves from the perilous trial. The ordinary occupations of life were abandoned; the plough was staid in the unfinished furrow; wives gave up their husbands, and mothers gave up their sons, to the battles of a civil war. Death might come, in honor, on the field; it might come, in disgrace, on the scaffold. For either and for both they were prepared. The sentiment of Quincy was full in their hearts. 'Blandishments,' said that distinguished son of genius and patriotism, 'will not fascinate us, nor will threats of a halter intimidate; for, under God, we are determined, that wheresoever, whensoever, or howsoever we shall be called to make our exit, we will die free men.'

The 17th of June saw the four New England colonies standing here, side by side, to triumph or to fall together; and there was with them from that moment to the end of the war, what I hope will remain with them forever, one cause, one country, one heart.

The battle of Bunker Hill was attended with the most important effects beyond its immediate result as a military engagement. It created at once a state of open, public war. There could now be no longer a question of proceeding against individuals, as guilty of treason or rebellion. That fearful crisis was past. The appeal now lay to the sword, and the only question was, whether the spirit and the resources of the people would hold out, till the object should be accomplished. Nor were its general consequences confined to our own country. The previous proceedings of the colonies, their appeals, resolutions, and addresses, had made their cause known to Europe. Without boasting, we may say, that in no age or country, has the public cause been maintained with more force of argument, more power of illustration, or more of that persuasion which excited feeling and elevated principle can alone bestow, than the revolutionary state papers exhibit. These papers will forever deserve to be studied, not only for the spirit which they breathe, but for the ability with which they were written.

To this able vindication of their cause, the colonies had now added a practical and severe proof of their own true devotion to it, and evidence also of the power which they could bring to its support. All now saw, that if America fell, she would not fall without a struggle. Men felt sympathy and regard, as well as surprise, when they beheld these infant states, remote, unknown, unaided, encounter the power of England, and in the first considerable battle, leave more of their enemies dead on the field, in proportion to the number of combatants, than they had recently known in the wars of Europe.

Information of these events, circulating through Europe, at length reached the ears of one who now hears me. He has not forgotten the emotion, which the fame of Bunker Hill, and the name of Warren, excited in his youthful breast.

SIR, we are assembled to commemorate the establishment of great public principles of liberty, and to do honor to the distinguished dead. The occasion is too severe for eulogy to the living. But, sir, your interesting relation to this country, the peculiar circumstances which surround you and surround us, call on me to express the happiness which we derive from your presence and aid in this solemn commemoration.

Fortunate, fortunate man! with what measure of devotion will you not thank God, for the circumstances of your extraordinary life! You are connected with both hemispheres and with two generations. Heaven saw fit to ordain, that the electric spark of Liberty should be conducted, through you, from the new world to the old; and we, who are now here to perform this duty of patriotism, have all of us long ago received it in charge from our fathers to cherish your name and your virtues. You will account it an instance of your good fortune, sir, that you crossed the seas to visit us at a time which enables you to be present at this solemnity. You now behold the field, the renown of which reached you in the heart of France, and caused a thrill in your ardent bosom. You see the lines of the little redoubt thrown up by the incredible diligence of Prescott; defended, to the last extremity, by his lion-hearted valor; and within which the corner stone of our monument has now taken its position. You see where Warren fell, and where Parker, Gardner, McCleary, Moore, and other early patriots fell with him. Those who survived that day, and whose lives have been prolonged to the present hour, are now around you. Some of them you have known in the trying scenes of the war. Behold! they now stretch forth their feeble arms to embrace you. Behold! they raise their trembling voices to invoke the blessing of God on you, and yours, forever.

Sir, you have assisted us in laying the foundation of this

edifice. You have heard us rehearse, with our feeble commendation, the names of departed patriots. Sir, monuments and eulogy belong to the dead. We give them, this day, to Warren and his associates. On other occasions they have been given to your more immediate companions in arms, to Washington, to Greene, to Gates, Sullivan, and Lincoln. Sir, we have become reluctant to grant these, our highest and last honors, further. We would gladly hold them yet back from the little remnant of that immortal band. *Serus in cœlum redeas.* Illustrious as are your merits, yet far, oh, very far distant be the day, when any inscription shall bear your name, or any tongue pronounce its eulogy!

The leading reflection, to which this occasion seems to invite us, respects the great changes which have happened in the fifty years, since the battle of Bunker Hill was fought. And it peculiarly marks the character of the present age, that, in looking at these changes, and in estimating their effect on our condition, we are obliged to consider, not what has been done in our own country only, but in others also. In these interesting times, while nations are making separate and individual advances in improvement, they make, too, a common progress; like vessels on a common tide, propelled by the gales at different rates, according to their several structure and management, but all moved forward by one mighty current beneath, strong enough to bear onward whatever does not sink beneath it.

A chief distinction of the present day is a community of opinions and knowledge amongst men, in different nations, existing in a degree heretofore unknown. Knowledge has, in our time, triumphed, and is triumphing, over distance, over difference of languages, over diversity of habits, over prejudice, and over bigotry. The civilized and Christian world is fast learning the great lesson, that difference of nation does not imply necessary hostility, and that all contact need not be war. The whole world is becoming a common field for intellect to act in. Energy of mind, genius, power, wheresoever it exists, may speak out in any tongue, and the *world* will hear it. A great chord of sentiment and feeling runs through two continents, and vibrates over both. Every breeze wafts intelligence from country to country; every wave rolls it; all give it forth, and all in turn receive it. There is a vast commerce of ideas;

there are marts and exchanges for intellectual discoveries, and a wonderful fellowship of those individual intelligences which make up the mind and opinion of the age. Mind is the great lever of all things; human thought is the process by which human ends are ultimately answered; and the diffusion of knowledge, so astonishing in the last half century, has rendered innumerable minds, variously gifted by nature, competent to be competitors, or fellow-workers, on the theatre of intellectual operation.

From these causes, important improvements have taken place in the personal condition of individuals. Generally speaking, mankind are not only better fed, and better clothed, but they are able also to enjoy more leisure; they possess more refinement and more self-respect. A superior tone of education, manners, and habits prevails. This remark, most true in its application to our own country, is also partly true, when applied elsewhere. It is proved by the vastly augmented consumption of those articles of manufacture and of commerce, which contribute to the comforts and the decencies of life; an augmentation which has far outrun the progress of population. And while the unexampled and almost incredible use of machinery would seem to supply the place of labor, labor still finds its occupation and its reward; so wisely has Providence adjusted men's wants and desires to their condition and their capacity.

Any adequate survey, however, of the progress made in the last half century, in the polite and the mechanic arts, in machinery and manufactures, in commerce and agriculture, in letters and in science, would require volumes. I must abstain wholly from these subjects, and turn, for a moment, to the contemplation of what has been done on the great question of politics and government. This is the master topic of the age; and during the whole fifty years, it has intensely occupied the thoughts of men. The nature of civil government, its ends and uses, have been canvassed and investigated; ancient opinions attacked and defended; new ideas recommended and resisted, by whatever power the mind of man could bring to the controversy. From the closet and the public halls the debate has been transferred to the field; and the world has been shaken by wars of unexampled magnitude, and the greatest variety of fortune. A day of peace has at length succeeded; and now that the strife has subsided, and the smoke cleared away, we may begin to see what has actually been done, permanently changing the state and condition of human society. And without dwelling on particular circumstances, it is most apparent, that, from the beforementioned causes of augmented knowledge and improved individual condition, a real, substantial, and important change has taken place, and is taking place, greatly beneficial, on the whole, to human liberty and human happiness.

The great wheel of political revolution began to move in America. Here its rotation was guarded, regular, and safe. Transferred to the other continent, from unfortunate but natural causes, it received an irregular and violent impulse; it whirled along with a fearful celerity; till at length, like the chariot wheels in the races of antiquity, it took fire from the rapidity of its own motion, and blazed onward, spreading conflagration and terror around.

We learn from the result of this experiment, how fortunate was our own condition, and how admirably the character of our people was calculated for making the great example of popular governments. The possession of power did not turn the heads of the American people, for they had long been in the habit of exercising a great portion of self-control. Although the paramount authority of the parent state existed over them, yet a large field of legislation had always been open to our colonial assemblies. They were accustomed to representative bodies and the forms of free government; they understood the doctrine of the division of power among different branches, and the necessity of checks on each. The character of our countrymen, moreover, was sober, moral, and religious; and there was little in the change to shock their feelings of justice and humanity, or even to disturb an honest prejudice. We had no domestic throne to overturn, no privileged orders to cast down, no violent changes of property to encounter. In the American Revolution, no man sought or wished for more than to defend and enjoy his own. None hoped for plunder or for spoil. Rapacity was unknown to it; the axe was not among the instruments of its accomplishment; and we all know that it could not have lived a single day under any well founded imputation of possessing a tendency adverse to the Christian religion.

It need not surprise us, that, under circumstances less

auspicious, political revolutions elsewhere, even when well intended, have terminated differently. It is, indeed, a great achievement, it is the master work of the world, to establish governments entirely popular, on lasting foundations; nor is it easy, indeed, to introduce the popular principle at all, into governments to which it has been altogether a stranger. It cannot be doubted, however, that Europe has come out of the contest, in which she has been so long engaged, with greatly superior knowledge, and, in many respects, a highly improved condition. Whatever benefit has been acquired, is likely to be retained, for it consists mainly in the acquisition of more enlightened ideas. And although kingdoms and provinces may be wrested from the hands that hold them, in the same manner they were obtained; although ordinary and vulgar power may, in human affairs, be lost as it has been won; yet it is the glorious prerogative of the empire of knowledge, that what it gains it never loses. On the contrary, it increases by the multiple of its own power; all its ends become means; all its attainments, helps to new conquests. Its whole abundant harvest is but so much seed wheat, and nothing has ascertained, and nothing can ascertain, the amount of ultimate product.

Under the influence of this rapidly increasing knowledge, the people have begun, in all forms of government, to think, and to reason, on affairs of state. Regarding government as an institution for the public good, they demand a knowledge of its operations, and a participation in its exercise. A call for the Representative system, wherever it is not enjoyed, and where there is already intelligence enough to estimate its value, is perseveringly made. Where men may speak out, they demand it; where the bayonet is at their throats, they pray for it.

When Louis XIV. said, "I am the state," he expressed the essence of the doctrine of unlimited power. By the rules of that system, the people are disconnected from the state; they are its subjects; it is their lord. These ideas, founded in the love of power, and long supported by the excess and the abuse of it, are yielding, in our age, to other opinions; and the civilized world seems at last to be proceeding to the conviction of that fundamental and manifest truth, that the powers of government are but a trust, and that they cannot be lawfully exercised but for the good of the community. As knowledge is more and more extended, this conviction becomes more and more general. Knowledge, in truth, is the great sun in the firmament. Life and power are scattered with all its beams. The prayer of the Grecian combatant, when enveloped in unnatural clouds and darkness, is the appropriate political supplication for the people of every country not yet blessed with free institutions;

'Dispel this cloud, the light of heaven restore,
Give me TO SEE—and Ajax asks no more.'

We may hope, that the growing influence of enlightened sentiments will promote the permanent peace of the world. Wars, to maintain family alliances, to uphold or to cast down dynasties, to regulate successions to thrones, which have occupied so much room in the history of modern times, if not less likely to happen at all, will be less likely to become general and involve many nations, as the great principle shall be more and more established, that the interest of the world is peace, and its first great statute, that every nation possesses the power of establishing a government for itself. But public opinion has attained also an influence over governments, which do not admit the popular principle into their organization. A necessary respect for the judgment of the world operates, in some measure, as a control over the most unlimited forms of authority. It is owing, perhaps, to this truth, that the interesting struggle of the Greeks has been suffered to go on so long, without a direct interference, either to wrest that country from its present masters, and add it to other powers, or to execute the system of pacification by force, and, with united strength, lay the neck of christian and civilized Greece at the foot of the barbarian Turk. Let us thank God that we live in an age, when something has influence besides the bayonet, and when the sternest authority does not venture to encounter the scorching power of public reproach. Any attempt of the kind I have mentioned, should be met by one universal burst of indignation; the air of the civilized world ought to be made too warm to be comfortably breathed by any who would hazard it.

It is, indeed, a touching reflection, that while, in the fulness of our country's happiness, we rear this monument to her honor, we look for instruction, in our undertaking, to a country which is now in fearful contest, not for works of art or memorials of glory, but for her own existence. Let her be assured, that she is not forgotten in the world; that her efforts are applauded, and that constant prayers ascend for her success. And let us cherish a confident hope for her final triumph. If the true spark of religious and civil liberty be kindled, it will burn. Human agency cannot extinguish it. Like the earth's central fire it may be smothered for a time; the ocean may overwhelm it; mountains may press it down; but its inherent and unconquerable force will heave both the ocean and the land, and at some time or another, in some place or another, the volcano will break out and flame up to heaven.

Among the great events of the half century, we must reckon, certainly, the Revolution of South America; and we are not likely to overrate the importance of that Revolution, either to the people of the country itself or to the rest of the world. The late Spanish colonies, now independent states, under circumstances less favorable, doubtless, than attended our own Revolution, have yet successfully commenced their national existence. They have accomplished the great object of establishing their independence; they are known and acknowledged in the world; and although in regard to their systems of government, their sentiments on religious toleration, and their provisions for public instruction, they may have yet much to learn, it must be admitted that they have risen to the condition of settled and established states, more rapidly than could have been reasonably anticipated. They already furnish an exhilirating example of the difference between free governments and despotic misrule. Their commerce, at this moment, creates a new activity in all the great marts of the world. They show themselves able, by an exchange of commodities, to bear an useful part in the intercourse of nations. A new spirit of enterprise and industry begins to prevail; all the great interests of society receive a salutary impulse; and the progress of information not only testifies to an improved condition, but constitutes, itself, the highest and most essential improvement.

When the battle of Bunker Hill was fought, the existence of South America was scarcely felt in the civilized world. The thirteen little colonies of North America habitually called themselves the 'Continent.' Borne down by colonial subjugation, monopoly, and bigotry, these vast regions of the South were hardly visible above the horizon. But in our day there hath been, as it were, a new creation. The Southern Hemisphere emerges from the sea. Its lofty mountains begin to lift themselves into the light of heaven; its broad and fertile plains stretch out, in beauty, to the eye of civilized man, and at the mighty bidding of the voice of political liberty the waters of darkness retire.

And, now, let us indulge an honest exultation in the conviction of the benefit, which the example of our country has produced, and is likely to produce, on human freedom and human happiness. And let us endeavour to comprehend, in all its magnitude, and to feel, in all its importance, the part assigned to us in the great drama of human affairs. We are placed at the head of the system of representative and popular governments. Thus far our example shows, that such governments are compatible, not only with respectability and power, but with repose, with peace, with security of personal rights, with good laws, and a just administration.

We are not propagandists. Wherever other systems are preferred, either as being thought better in themselves, or as better suited to existing condition, we leave the preference to be enjoyed. Our history hitherto proves, however, that the popular form is practicable, and that with wisdom and knowledge men may govern themselves; and the duty incumbent on us is, to preserve the consistency of this cheering example, and take care that nothing may weaken its authority with the world. If, in our case, the Representative system ultimately fail, popular governments must be pronounced impossible. No combination of circumstances more favorable to the experiment can ever be expected to occur. The last hopes of mankind, therefore, rest with us; and if it should be proclaimed, that our example had become an argument against the experiment, the knell of popular liberty would be sounded throughout the earth.

These are excitements to duty; but they are not suggestions of doubt. Our history and our condition, all that is gone before us, and all that surrounds us, authorize the belief, that popular governments, though subject to occasional variations, perhaps not always for the better, in form, may yet, in their general character, be as durable and permanent as other systems. We know, indeed, that, in our country, any other is impossible. The *Principle* of Free Governments adheres to the American soil. It is bedded in it; immovable as its mountains.

And let the sacred obligations which have devolved on this generation, and on us, sink deep into our hearts. Those are daily dropping from among us, who established our liberty and our govenment. The great trust now descends to new hands. Let us apply ourselves to that which is presented to us, as our appropriate object. We can win no laurels in a war for Independence. Earlier and worthier hands have gathered them all. Nor are there places for us by the side of Solon, and Alfred, and other founders of states. Our fathers have filled them. But there remains to us a great duty of defence and preservation; and there is opened to us, also, a noble pursuit, to which the spirit of the times strongly invites us. Our proper business is improvement. Let our age be the age of improvement. In a day of peace, let us advance the arts of peace and the works of peace. Let us develop the resources of our land, call forth its powers, build up its institutions, promote all its great interests, and see whether we also, in our day and generation, may not perform something worthy to be remembered. Let us cultivate a true spirit of union and harmony. In pursuing the great objects, which our condition points out to us, let us act under a settled conviction, and an habitual feeling, that these twenty-four states are one country. Let our conceptions be enlarged to the circle of our duties. Let us extend our ideas over the whole of the vast field in which we are called to act. Let our object be, OUR COUNTRY, OUR WHOLE COUNTRY, AND NOTHING BUT OUR COUNTRY. And, by the blessing of God, may that country itself become a vast and splendid Monument, not of oppression and terror, but of Wisdom, of Peace, and of Liberty, upon which the world may gaze, with admiration, forever!

WILLIAM WIRT

Eulogy on John Adams and Thomas Jefferson

Washington, D.C., October 19, 1826

T HE SCENES which have been lately passing in our country, and of which this meeting is a continuance, are full of moral instruction. They hold up to the world a lesson of wisdom by which all may profit, if Heaven shall grant them the discretion to turn it to its use. The spectacle, in all its parts, has, indeed, been most solemn and impressive; and, though the first impulse be now past, the time has not yet come, and never will it come, when we can contemplate it, without renewed emotion.

In the structure of their characters; in the course of their action; in the striking coincidences which marked their high career; in the lives and in the deaths of the illustrious men, whose virtues and services we have met to commemorate—and in that voice of admiration and gratitude which has since burst, with one accord, from the twelve millions of freemen who people these States, there is a moral sublimity which overwhelms the mind, and hushes all its powers into silent amazement!

The European, who should have heard the *sound* without apprehending the cause, would be apt to inquire, "What is the meaning of all this? what had these men done to elicit this unanimous and splendid acclamation? Why has the whole American nation risen up, as one man, to do them honor, and offer to them this enthusiastic homage of the heart? Were they mighty warriors, and was the peal that we have heard, the shout of victory? Were they great commanders, returning from their distant conquests, surrounded with the spoils of war, and was this the sound of their triumphal procession? Were they covered with martial glory in any form, and was this 'the noisy wave of the multitude rolling back at their approach?'" Nothing of all this: No; they were peaceful and aged patriots, who, having served their country together, through their long and useful

lives, had now sunk together to the tomb. They had not
fought battles; but they had formed and moved the great machinery of which battles were only a small, and, comparatively,
trivial consequence. They had not commanded armies; but they
had commanded the master springs of the nation, on which all
its great political, as well as military movements depended. By
the wisdom and energy of their counsels, and by the potent
mastery of their spirits, they had contributed pre-eminently to
produce a mighty Revolution, which has changed the aspect of
the world. A Revolution which, in one-half of that world, has
already restored man to his "long lost liberty;" and government to its only legitimate object, the happiness of the People:
and, on the other hemisphere, has thrown a light so strong,
that even the darkness of despotism is beginning to recede.
Compared with the solid glory of an achievement like this,
what are battles, and what the pomp of war, but the poor and
fleeting pageants of a theatre? What were the selfish and petty
strides of Alexander, to conquer a little section of a savage
world, compared with this generous, this magnificent advance
towards the emancipation of the entire world!

And this, be it remembered, has been the fruit of intellectual
exertion! the triumph of mind! What a proud testimony does
it bear to the character of our nation, that they are able to
make a proper estimate of services like these! That while, in
other countries, the senseless mob fall down in stupid admiration, before the bloody wheels of the conqueror—even of the
conqueror by accident—in this, our People rise, with one accord, to pay *their* homage to intellect and virtue! What a
cheering pledge does it give of the stability of our institutions,
that while abroad, the yet benighted multitude are prostrating
themselves before the idols which their own hands have fashioned into Kings, here, in this land of the free, our People are
every where starting up, with one impulse, to follow with their
acclamations the ascending spirits of the great Fathers of the
Republic! This is a spectacle of which we may be permitted to
be proud. It honors our country no less than the illustrious
dead. And could those great Patriots speak to us from the tomb,
they would tell us that they have more pleasure in the testimony which these honors bear to the character of their country, than in that which they bear to their individual services.

They now see they as were seen, while in the body, and know the nature of the feeling from which these honors flow. It is love for love. It is the gratitude of an enlightened nation to the noblest order of benefactors. It is the only glory worth the aspiration of a generous spirit. Who would not prefer this living tomb in the hearts of his countrymen, to the proudest mausoleum that the Genius of Sculpture could erect!

Man has been said to be the creature of accidental position. The cast of his character has been thought to depend, materially, on the age, the country, and the circumstances, in which he has lived. To a considerable extent, the remark is, no doubt, true. Cromwell, had he been born in a Republic, might have been "guiltless of his country's blood;" and, but for those civil commotions which had wrought his great mind into tempest, even Milton might have rested "mute and inglorious." The occasion is, doubtless, necessary to develop the talent, whatsoever it may be; but the talent must exist, in embryo at least, or no occasion can quicken it into life. And it must exist, too, under the check of strong virtues; or the same occasion that quickens it into life, will be extremely apt to urge it on to crime. The hero who finished his career at St. Helena, extraordinary as he was, is a far more common character in the history of the world, than he who sleeps in our neighbourhood, embalmed in his country's tears—or than those whom we have now met to mourn and to honor.

Jefferson and Adams were great men by nature. Not great and eccentric minds "shot madly from their spheres" to affright the world and scatter pestilence in their course, but minds whose strong and steady light, restrained within their proper orbits by the happy poise of their characters, came to cheer and to gladden a world that had been buried for ages in political night. They were heaven-called avengers of degraded man. They came to lift him to the station for which God had formed him, and to put to flight those idiot superstitions with which tyrants had contrived to inthrall his reason and his liberty. And that Being who had sent them upon this mission, had fitted them, pre-eminently, for his glorious work. He filled their hearts with a love of country which burned strong within them, even in death. He gave them a power of understanding which no sophistry could baffle, no art elude; and a moral heroism which no dangers could appal. Careless of themselves, reckless, of all personal consequences, trampling under foot that petty ambition of office and honor which constitutes the master-passion of little minds, they bent all their mighty powers to the task for which they had been delegated—the freedom of their beloved country, and the restoration of fallen man. They felt that they were Apostles of *human liberty*; and well did they fulfil their high commission. They rested not until they had accomplished their work at home, and given such an impulse to the great ocean of mind, that they saw the waves rolling on the farthest shore, before they were called to their reward. And then left the world, hand in hand, exulting, as they rose, in the success of their labors.

From this glance at the consummation of their lives, it falls within the purpose that has drawn us together, to look back at the incidents by which these great men were prepared and led on to their destiny. The field is wide and tempting; and in this rich field, there is a double harvest to be gathered.—But the occasion is limited in point of time. With all the brevity, therefore, compatible with the subject, let us proceed to recall the more prominent incidents, leaving to their biographers those which we must reluctantly omit. And let me hope that the recapitulation, however devoid of interest in itself, will be endured, if not enjoyed, for the sake of those to whom it relates. The review will unavoidably carry us back to scenes of no pleasant nature, which once occurred between our country and a foreign nation with which we now maintain the happiest relations of peace and amity; towards which, at this day, we cherish no other feelings than those of the sincerest respect and good will; and with whose national glory, indeed, as the land of our forefathers, we feel ourselves, in a great measure, identified. If, therefore, there should be any one within the sound of my voice, to whom the language of this retrospect might otherwise seem harsh, I trust it will be borne in mind that we are Americans, assembled on a purely American occasion, and that we are speaking of things as they were, not as they are; for, in the language of our departed fathers, "though enemies in war, in peace we are friends."

The hand of Heaven was kindly manifested even in the place of birth assigned to our departed fathers. Their lots were cast in two distant States, forming links in the same extended chain of colonies. The one, to borrow the language of Isaiah, was called " from the North" and " the rising of the sun;" the other, from the South, where he shews his glory in the meridian. The colonies, though held together by their allegiance to a common crown, had separate local governments, separate local interests, and a strikingly contrasted cast of character. The intercourse between them had been rare; the sympathies consequently weak; and these sympathies still further weakened by certain rivalries, prejudices, and jealousies, the result of their mutual ignorance of each other, which were extremely unpropitious to that concerted action on which the success of the great work of Independence rested. To effect this work, it was necessary that men should arise in the different quarters of the Continent, with a reach of mind sufficiently extended to look over and beyond this field of prejudice, and mark the great point in which the interest of the whole united; and, with this reach of mind, that they should combine a moral power of sufficient force to make even the discordant materials around them harmoniously subservient to the great end to be accomplished. It pleased Heaven to give us such men, and so to plant them on the theatre of action, as to ensure the concert that the occasion demanded. And in that constellation of the great and the good, rose the two stars of first magnitude to which our attention is now to be confined.

Adams and Jefferson were born, the *first* in Massachusetts on the 19th of October, 1735; the *last* in Virginia, on the 2d of April, 1743. On the earliest opening of their characters, it was manifest that they were marked for distinction.—They both displayed that thirst for knowledge, that restless spirit of inquiry, that ferved sensibility, and that bold, fearless independence of thought, which are among the surest prognostics of exalted talent; and, fortunately for them, as well as for their country and mankind, the Universities in their respective neighborhoods opened to their use, all the fountains of ancient and modern learning. With what appetite they drank at these fountains, we need no testimony of witnesses to inform us. The living streams which afterwards flowed from their own lips and pens, are the best witnesses that can be called, of their youthful studies. They were, indeed, of that gifted order of minds, to which early instruction is of little other use than to inform them of their own powers, and to indicate the objects of human knowledge. Education was not with them, as with minor characters, an attempt to plant new talents and new qualities in a strange and reluctant soil. It was the development, merely of those which already existed. Thus, the pure and disinterested patriotism of Aristides, the firmness of Cato, and the devotion of Curtius, only awakened the principles that were sleeping in their young hearts, and touched the responding chords with which Heaven had attuned them. The statesman-like vigor of Pericles, and the spirit-stirring energy of Demosthenes, only roused their own lion powers and informed them of their strength. Aristotle, and Bacon and Sidney, and Locke, could do little more than to disclose to them their native capacity for the profound investigation and ascertainment of truth; and Newton taught their power to range among the stars. In short, every model to which they looked, and every great master to whom they appealed, only moved into life the scarcely dormant energies with which Heaven had endued them; and they came forth from the discipline, not decorated for pomp, but armed for battle.

From this first coincidence, in the character of their minds and studies, let us proceed to another. They both turned their attention to the same profession, the profession of the law; and they both took up the study of this profession on the same enlarged scale which was so conspicuous in all their other intellectual operations. They had been taught by Hooker to look with reverence upon the science of the law: for, he had told them that "her seat was the bosom of God, her voice the harmony of the world." Pursued in the spirit, on the extended plan, and with the noble aim, with which they pursued it, may it not be said, without the hazard of illiberal construction, that there was no profession in this country to which Heaven could have directed their choice, so well fitted to prepare them for the eventful struggle which was coming on.

Mr. Adams, we are told, commenced his legal studies, and passed through the initiatory course, under William Putnam, of Worcester; but, the crown of preparation was placed on his head by Jeremiah Gridley. Gridley was a man of first rate learning and vigor, and as good a judge of character as he was of law.

He had been the legal preceptor, also, some years before, of the celebrated James Otis: and, proud of his two pupils, he was wont to say of them at the bar, with playful affection, that "he had raised two young eagles who were one day or other to peck out his eyes." The two young eagles were never known to treat their professional father with irreverence; but how well they fulfilled his prediction of their future eminence, has been already well told by the elegant biographer of one, and remains to furnish a rich theme for that of the other.

It was in the commencement of his legal studies, and when he was yet but a boy, that Mr. Adams wrote that letter from Worcester which has been recently given to the world.—Considering the age of the writer, and the point of time at which it was written, that letter may be pronounced, without hyperbole, a mental phenomenon, and far better entitled to the character of a prophecy, than the celebrated passage from the Medea of Senaca, which Bacon has quoted as a prophecy of the discovery of America.

Before I call your attention more particularly to this letter, it is proper to remark, that Mr. Adams lived at a time, and among men, well fitted to evoke his youthful powers. Massachusetts had been, from its earliest settlement, a theatre of almost constant political contention. The spirit of liberty which had prompted the pilgrims to bid adieu to the land and tombs of their fathers, and to brave the horrors of an exile to the wilds of America, accompanied them to the forests which they came to subdue; and questions political right and power, between the parent country and the colony, were continually arising, to call that spirit into action, and to keep it bright and strong. These were a peculiar People, a stern and hardy race, the children of the storm; inured from the cradle to the most frightful hardships which they came to regard as their daily pastime, their minds, as well as their bodies, gathered new strength from the fearful elements that were warring around them, and whatever they dared to meditate as right, that they dared and never failed to accomplish. The robust character of the fathers descended upon their children, and with it, also, came the same invigorating contests. Violations of their charters, unconstitutional restraints upon their trade, and perpetual collisions with the royal Governors sent over to bend or to break them, had converted that province into an *arena*, in which the strength of mind had been tried against mind, for a century, before the tug of the Revolution came. And these were no puerile sports. They were the stern struggle of intellectual force, for power on the one hand, and liberty on the other. And from that discipline there came forth such men as such a struggle only seems capable of generating; rough, and strong, and bold, and daring; meeting their adversaries, foot to foot, on the field of argument, and beating them off that field by the superior vigor of their blows.

> Præcipitemque Daren, ardens agit æquore toto:
> Nunc dextra ingeminans ictus, nunc ille sinistra,
> Nec mora, nec requies.

From this school issued those men so well formed for the sturdy business of life and who shine so brightly in the annals of Massachusetts—Mayhew, and Hawley, and Thacher, and Otis, and Hancock, and a host of others, of the same strong stamp of character: men as stout of heart as of mind, and breathing around them an atmosphere of patriotic energy, which it was impossible to inhale without partaking of their spirit.

Such was the atmosphere which it was the fortune of John Adams to breathe, even from his infancy. Such were the high examples before him. From this proud eyry it was, that this young eagle first opened his eyes upon the sun and the ocean, and learned to plume his own wings for the daring flight.

His letter from Worcester bears date on the 12th of October, 1755. He was consequently then only in his twentieth year. At that time, remember, that no thought of a separation from the parent country had ever touched these shores. The conversations to which he alludes, were upon the topics of the day, and went no farther than to a discussion of the rights of the colony, considered as a colony of the British empire. These were the hints which set his young mind in motion, and this is the letter which they produced:

WORCESTER, *October 12, 1755*.

Soon after the Reformation, a few people came over into this New World for conscience' sake. Perhaps this apparently trivial incident may transfer the great seat of empire into America. It looks likely to me, if we can remove the turbulent Gallicks, our people, according to the exactest computations, will, in another century, become more numerous than England herself. Should this be the case, since we have, I may say, all the naval stores of the nation in our hands, it will be easy to obtain the mastery of the seas; and then the united force of all Europe will not be able to subdue us. [Here we see the first germ of the American Navy.] The only way to keep us from *setting up for ourselves*, is to disunite us. *Divide et impera.* Keep us in distinct colonies, and then some great men in each colony, desiring the monarchy of the whole, will destroy each other's influence, and keep the country in equilibrio. Be not surprised that I am turned politician; the whole town is immersed in politics. The interests of nations, and all the *dira* of war, make the subject of every conversation. I sit and hear, and, after having been led through a maze of sage observations, I sometimes retire, and, by laying things together, form some reflections pleasing to myself. The produce of one of these reveries you have read above.

Here we mark the political dawn of the mind of this great man. His country, her resources, her independence, her glory, were the first objects of his thoughts, as they were the last. Here, too, we see the earliest proof of that bold and adventurous turn for speculation, that sagacious flashing into futurity, and that sanguine anticipation, which became so conspicuous in his after life. He calls this letter *a reverie*; but, connecting it with his ardent character and his future career, there is reason to believe, that it was a reverie which produced in him all the effect of a prophetic vision, and opened to him a perspective which was never afterwards closed.

An incident soon occurred to give brighter tinting and stronger consistency to this dream of his youth; and this may be considered as among the most efficient of those means, devised by the wisdom of Providence, to shape the character and point the energies of this high-minded young man to the advancement of the great destiny that awaited his country. The famous question of *writs of assistance* was argued, in his presence, in Boston, in February, 1761. These writs were a kind of general search-warrants, transferable by manual delivery from one low tool of power to another, and without any return; which put at the mercy of these vulgar wretches, for an indefinite period, the domestic privacy, the peace and comfort, of the most respectable inhabitants in the colony; and even the sanctuary of female delicacy and devotion. The authority of the British tribunals in the province, themselves the instruments of a tyrant's will, to issue such writs, was the precise question to be discussed. The champion in opposition to the power was the great Otis. Of the character of his argument, and its effect upon Mr. Adams, we are not left to conjecture; he has given it to us, himself, in his own burning phraseology. "Otis was a flame of fire! With a promptitude of classical allusion, a depth of research, a rapid summary of historical events and dates, a profusion of legal authorities, a prophetic glance of his eyes into futurity, and a rapid torrent of impetuous eloquence, he hurried away all before him. *American Independence was then and there born.*" And he adds—"Every man of an immense crowded audience appeared to me to go away, as I did, ready to take arms against writs of assistance."

The "immense crowded audience," it is probable, left the hall with no impressions beyond the particular subject of debate. They were ready to take arms against *writs of assistance.* Not so with Mr. Adams. In him the "splendid conflagration of Otis" had set fire to a mind whose action it was not easy to restrain within narrow limits; a mind already looking out on the wide expanse of the future, and apparently waiting only for the occasion, to hold up to his countrymen the great revolving light of Independence, above the darkness of the coming storm. In *him* American Independence was then and there born: and, appealing to his own bosom, he was justified in saying, as he has done, on another occasion, in the most solemn terms, "that James Otis, then and there, first breathed into this nation the breath of life."

The flame thus given to his enthusiasm was never permitted to subside. The breach between the two countries grew wider and wider, until from being an excited spectator, he soon became a vigorous and most efficient actor. In his thirtieth year, he gave to his country, that powerful work "The Dissertation on the Canon and Feudal Law." It is but to read those extracts from this work which have been recently diffused among us from the North, to see that it was not limited in its purpose to the specific questions which had then arisen. The discussion travels far beyond these questions, and bears all the marks of a profound and comprehensive design, to prepare the country for a separation from Great Britain. It is a review of the whole system of the British institutions, and a most powerful assault upon those heresies, civil and religious, which constituted the outposts of that system. Besides the solid instruction which it conveys on the true theory of government, and the deep and impressive exhortation with which it urges the necessity of correct information to the People, it seems to have been the leading object of the work to disenchant his countrymen of that reverence for the institutions of the parent country which still lingered around their hearts, and to teach them to look upon these institutions, not only with indifference, but with aversion and contempt. Hence those burning sarcasms which he flings into every story of the citadel, until the whole edifice is wrapt in flames. It is, indeed, a work eminently fitted for the speedy regeneration of the country. The whole tone of the essay is so raised and bold, that it sounds like a trumpet-call to arms. And the haughty defiance which he hurls into the face of the oppressors of his country, is so brave and uncompromising, as to leave no doubt that, whatever might be the temper of the rest of the community, the author had already laid *his* hand upon the altar, and sworn that his country should be free.

All this fire, however, was tempered with judgment, and guided by the keenest and most discriminating sagacity; and if his character was marked with the stubborn firmness of the Pilgrim, it was because he was supported by the Pilgrim's conscious integrity. Another incident soon occurred to place *these* qualities in high relief. In the progress of the quarrel, Great Britain had quartered an army in Boston, to supply the place of argument, and enforce that submission which she could not command. The immediate consequence was, collision and affray between the soldiery and the citizens; and, in one of those affrays, on the 5th of November, 1770, the British captain, Preston, gave the fatal order to fire! Several were killed, and many more were wounded. It is easy to imagine the storm that instantly arose. The infuriated populace were, with great difficulty, restrained by the leading men of the town, from sating their vengeance upon the spot. Disappointed of this, they were loud, and even frantic, in their cry for the vengeance of law. Yet there was no murder in the case: for, in this instance it had happened that they were themselves the assailants. Preston was arrested for trial: and Mr. Adams then standing in the van of the profession, as well as that of the patriots, was called upon to undertake his defence. How was he to act? It is easy to know how a little, time-serving politician, or even a man of ordinary firmness, would have acted; the one would have thrown himself on the popular current, and the other would have been swept along by it, and joined in the public cry for the victim. But Adams belonged to a higher order of character. He was formed not only to impel and guide the torrent; but to head that torrent too, when it had taken a wrong direction, and "to roll it back upon its source." He was determined that the world should distinguish between a petty commotion of angry spirits, and the noble stand made by an enlightened nation in a just and noble cause. He was resolved that that pure and elevated cause should not be soiled and debased by an act of individual injustice. He undertook the defence, supported by his younger, but distinguished associate, Josiah Quincy; and, far from flattering the angry passions around him, he called upon the jury, in their presence, "*to be deaf, deaf as adders, to the clamors of the populace*;" and they were so. To their honor, a jury drawn from the excited people of Boston, acquitted the prisoner: and to their equal honor, that very populace, instead of resenting the language and conduct of his advocate, loaded him immediately with additional proofs of their confidence. These were the people, who, according to some European notions, are incapable of any agency in their own government. By their systems, deliberately planned for the purpose, they first degrade and brutalize their people, and then descant on their unfitness for self-rule. The man of America, it seems, is the only man fit for republican government! But man is every where the same, and requires only to be enlightened, to assert the native dignity of his character.

Mr. Adams was now among the most conspicuous champions of the colonial cause in Massachusetts. In the same year to which we have just adverted, 1770, he had been elected a member of the Provincial Legislature: and he thenceforth took a high and commanding part in every public measure; displaying, on every occasion, the same consistent character; the same sagacity to pierce the night of the future; the same bold and dauntless front; the same nerve of the Nemean lion.

The time had now come for concerted action among the Colonies: and, accordingly, on the 5th September, 1774, the first Continental Congress met at Philadelphia. With what emotions Mr. Adams witnessed this great movement of the nation, it is easy for those who know his ardent character, to imagine. Nor, are we left to our imaginations alone. He had been elected a member of that body; and immediately on his election, an incident occured which relieves us from the necessity of conjecturing the state of his feelings. His friend Sewall, the Attorney General, hearing of his election, sent for him, and he came; when Sewall, with all the solicitude and importunity of friendship, sought to divert him from his purpose of taking his seat in Congress: he represented to him that Great Britain was determined on her purpose: that her power was irresistible, and would be destructive to him and all who should persevere in opposition to her designs.—"I know," replied the dauntless and high-souled patriot, "that Great Britain has determined on her system; and that very determination, determines me on mine. You know that I have been constant and uniform in opposition to her designs. The die is now cast. I have passed the Rubicon. Sink or swim, live or die, survive or perish with my country, is my unalterable determination." He accordingly took his seat: and with what activity and effect he discharged its duties, the journals of the day sufficiently attest.

Of that august and venerable body, the old Continental Congress, what can be said that would not fall below the occasion? What that would not sound like a puerile and tumid effort, to exaggerate the praise of a body which was above all praise? Let me turn from any attempt at description to your own hearts, where that body lies entombed with all you hold most sacred. To that Congress, let future statesmen look and learn what it is to be a patriot. There was no self. No petty intrigue for power. No despicable faction for individual honors. None of those feuds, the fruit of an unhallowed ambition, which converted the Revolution of France into a mere contest for the command of the guillotine; and which have, now, nearly disarmed unhappy Greece, in the sacred war she is waging for

the tombs of her illustrious dead. No: of our Great Fathers we
may say with truth, what was said of the Romans in their golden
age; "with them the Republic was in all; for that alone they consulted; the only faction they formed was against the common
enemy: their minds, their bodies were exerted sincerely, and
greatly and nobly exerted, not for personal power, but for the
liberties, the honor, the glory of their country." May the time
never come, when an allusion to their virtues can give any other
feelings than those of pleasure and pride to their descendants.

Having in this imperfect manner, fellow-citizens, touched
rather than traced the incidents by which Mr. Adams was prepared and conducted into the scenes of the Revolution, let us
turn to the great luminary of the South.

Virginia, as you know, had been settled by other causes than
those which had peopled Massachusetts; and the Colonists
themselves were of a different character. The first attempts at
settlement in that quarter of the world had been conducted as
you remember, under the auspices of the gallant Raleigh, that
"man of wit and man of the sword," as Sir Edward Coke
tauntingly called him, and certainly one of the brightest flowers
in the courts of Elizabeth and James.—He did not live to make
a permanent establishment in Virginia; but, his genius seems,
nevertheless, to have presided over the State, and to have
stamped his own character on her distinguished sons. Virginia
had experienced none of those early and long continued conflicts which had contributed to form the robust character of
the North; on the contrary, during the century that Massachusetts had been buffeting with the storm, Virginia, resting on a
halcyon sea, had been cultivating the graces of science, and literature, and the genial elegancies of social life. But, her moral
and intellectual character was not less firm and vigorous than
that of her Northern sister: for the invader came, and Athens
as well as Sparta, was found ready to do her duty, and to do it
too, bravely, ably, heroically.

At the time of Mr. Jefferson's appearance, the society of Virginia was much diversified, and reflected, pretty distinctly, an
image of that of England. There was first, the landed aristocracy, shadowing forth the order of English nobility; then the
sturdy yeomanry, common to them both; and last, a *fæculum*

of beings, as they were called by Mr. Jefferson, corresponding with the mass of the English plebeians.

Mr. Jefferson, by birth, belonged to the aristociacy: but, the idle and voluptuous life which marked that order had no charms for a mind like his. He relished better the strong, unsophisticated, and racy character of the yeomanry, and attached himself, of choice, to that body. Born to an inheritance, then deemed immense, and with a decided taste for literature and science, it would not have been surprising if he had devoted himself, exclusively, to the luxury of his studies, and left the toils and the hazards of public action to others.—But he was naturally ardent, and fond of action, and of action too, on a great scale; and, so readily did he kindle in the feelings that were playing around him, that he could no more have stood still while his country was agitated, than the war horse can sleep under the sound of the trumpet.

He was a republican and a philanthropist from the earliest dawn of his character. He read with a sort of poetic illusion, which indentified him with every scene that his author spread before him. Enraptured with the brighter ages of republican Greece and Rome, he had followed, with an aching heart, the march of history which had told him of the desolation of those fairest portions of the earth; and had seen, with dismay and indignation, that swarm of monarchies, the progeny of the Scandinavian hive, under which genius and liberty were now every where crushed. He loved his own country with a passion not less intense, deep, and holy, than that of his great com-patriot: and with this love, he combined an expanded philanthropy which encircled the globe. From the working of the strong energies within him, there arose an early vision, too, which cheered his youth and accompanied him through life—the vision of emancipated man throughout the world. Nor was this a dream of the morning that passed away and was forgotten. On the contrary, like the Heaven-descended banner of Constantine, he hailed it as an omen of certain victory, and girded his loins for the onset, with the omnipotence of truth.

On his early studies we have already touched. The study of the law he pursued under George Wythe; a man of Roman stamp, in Rome's best age. Here he acquired that unrivaled neatness, system, and method in business, which, through all his future life, and in every office that he filled, gave him, in effect, the hundred hands of Briareus; here, too, following the giant step of his master, he travelled the whole round of the civil and common law. From the same example, he caught that untiring spirit of investigation which never left a subject till he had searched it to the bottom, and of which we have so noble a specimen in his correspondence with Mr. Hammond, on the subject of British debts. In short, Mr. Wythe performed for him, what Jeremiah Gridley had done for Mr. Adams; he placed on his head the crown of legal preparation: and well did it become him.—Permit me, here, to correct an error which seems to have prevailed. It has been thought that Mr. Jefferson made no figure at the bar: but the case was far otherwise. There are still extant, in his own fair and neat hand, in the manner of his master, a number of arguments which were delivered by him at the bar upon some of the most intricate questions of the law; which, if they shall ever see the light will vindicate his claim to the first honors of the profession. It is true he was not distinguished in popular debate; why he was not so, has often been matter of surprise to those who have seen his eloquence on paper and heard it in conversation. He had all the attributes of the mind, and the heart and the soul, which are essential to eloquence of the highest order. The only defect was a physical one: he wanted volume and compass of voice for a large deliberative assembly; and his voice, from the excess of his sensibilty, instead of rising with his feelings and conceptions, sunk under their pressure, and became guttural and inarticulate. The consciousness of this infirmity repressed any attempt in a large body in which he knew he must fail. But his voice was all sufficient for the purposes of judicial debate; and there is no reason to doubt that, if the service of his country had not called him away so soon from his profession, his fame as a lawyer would now have stood upon the same distinguished ground which he confessedly occupies as a statesman, an author, and a scholar.

It was not until 1764, when the Parliament of Great Britain passed its resolutions preparatory to the stamp act, that Virginia seems to have been thoroughly startled from her repose. Her Legislature was then in session; and her patriots, taking the alarm, remonstrated promptly and firmly against this assumed power. The remonstrance, however, was, as usual, disregarded, and the stamp act came. But it came to meet, on the floor of the House, an unlooked-for champion, whom Heaven had just raised up for the good of his country and of mankind. I speak of that untutored child of nature, Patrick Henry, who had now, for the first time, left his native forests to show the metal of which he was made, and "give the world assurance of a man."

The assembly met in the city of Williamsburg, where Mr. Jefferson was still pursuing the study of the law. Mr. Henry's celebrated resolutions against the stamp act were introduced in May, 1765. How they were resisted, and how maintained, has been already stated to the world, in terms that have been pronounced extravagant, by those who modestly consider themselves as furnishing a fair standard of Revolutionary excellence. The coldest glow-worm in the hedge, is about as fair a standard of the power of the sun.—To the present purpose, it is only necessary to remark, that Mr. Jefferson was present at this debate, and has left us an account of it, in his own words. He was then he says, but a student, and stood in the door of communication between the House and the lobby, where he heard the whole of this magnificent debate. The opposition to the last resolution was most vehement; the debate upon it, to use his own strong language, "most bloody:" but he adds, torrents of sublime eloquence from Henry, backed by the solid reasoning of Johnson, prevailed; and the resolution was carried by a single vote. I well remember, he continues, the cry of "treason," by the Speaker, echoed from every part of the House, against Mr. Henry: I well remember his pause, and the admirable address with which he recovered himself and baffled the charge thus vociferated.

He here alludes, as you must perceive, to that memorable exclamation of Mr. Henry, now become almost too familiar for quotation: "Cæsar had his Brutus, Charles the First his Cromwell, and George the Third ("Treason!" cried the Speaker. "Treason! treason!" echoed the House;)—may profit by their example. If this be treason, make the most of it."

While I am presenting to you this picture of Mr. Jefferson in his youth, listening to the almost super-human eloquence of

Henry on the great subject which formed the hinge of the American Revolution, are you not forcibly reminded of the parallel scene which had passed only four years before, in the Hall of Justice in Boston: Mr. Adams catching from Otis, "the breath of life?" How close the parallel, and how interesting the incident! Who can think of these two young men, destined themselves to make so great a figure in the future history of their country, thus lighting the fires of their own genius at the altars of Henry and of Otis, without being reminded of another picture, which has been exhibited to us by an historian of Rome: The younger Scipio Africanus, then in his military noviciate, standing a youthful spectator on a hill near Carthage, and looking down upon the battle-field on which those veteran generals, Hamilcar and Massanissa, were driving, with so much glory, the car of war! Whether Otis or Henry *first* breathed into this nation the breath of life, (a question merely for curious and friendly speculation,) it is very certain that they breathed into their two young hearers, that breath which has made them both immortal.

From this day, forth, Mr. Jefferson, young as he was, stood forward as a champion for his country. It was now in the fire of his youth, that he adopted those mottos for his seals, so well remembered in Virginia: "Ab eo libertas, a quo spiritus," and "Resistance to tyrants is obedience to God." He joined the band of the brave who were for the boldest measures: and by the light, the contagious spirit and vigor of his conversation, as well as by his enchanting and powerful pen, he contributed eminently to lift Virginia to that height which placed her by the side of her Northern sister. It is an historical fact well known to us all, that these two great States, then by far the most populous and powerful in the Union, led off, as it was natural and fit that they should do, all the strong measures that ended in the Declaration of Independence. Together, and stroke for stroke, they breasted the angry surge, and threw it aside "with hearts of controversy," until they reached that shore from which we now look back with so much pride and triumph.

It was in his thirtieth year, as you remember, that Mr. Adams gave to the world his first great work, the Dissertation on the Canon and Feudal Law; and it was about the same period of his life, that Mr. Jefferson produced his first great political work, "A Summary View of the Rights of British America." The history of this work is somewhat curious and interesting, and I give it to you on the authority of Mr. Jefferson himself. He had been elected a member of that State Convention of Virginia which, in August, 1774, appointed the first Delegates to the Continental Congress. Arrested by sickness on his way to Williamsburg, he sent forward, to be laid on the table, a draught of instructions to the Delegates whom Virginia should send. This was read by the members, and *they* published it, under the title of "A Summary View of the Rights of British America." A copy of this work having found its way to England, it received from the pen of the celebrated Burke such alterations as adapted it to the purposes of the opposition there, and it there re-appeared in a new edition; an honor which, as Mr. Jefferson afterwards learned, occasioned the insertion of his name in a bill of attainder, which, however, never saw the light. So far Mr. Jefferson. Let me add, that the old inhabitants of Williamsburg, a few years back, well remembered the effect of that work on Lord Dunmore, then the royal Governor of the State. His fury broke out in the most indecent and unmitigated language. Mr. Jefferson's name was marked high on his list of proscription, and the victim was only reprieved until the rebellion should be crushed; but that rebellion became revolution, and the high priest of the meditated sacrifice was sent to howl his disappointment to the hills and winds of his native Scotland.

In the next year, 1775, Mr. Jefferson, young as he was, was singled out by the Virginian Legislature, to answer Lord North's famous "conciliatory proposition," called, in the language of the day, his "olive branch." But it was an olive branch that hid the guileful serpent, or, in the language of Mr. Adams, "it was an asp in a basket of flowers." The answer stands upon the records of the country. Cool, calm, close, full of compressed energy and keen sagacity; while, at the same time it preserves the most perfect decorum, it is one of the most nervous and manly productions even of that age of men.

The second Congress met on the 10th of May, 1775. Mr. Adams was, of course, again, a member. Mr. Jefferson having been deputed, contingently, (to supply the place of Peyton Randolph,) did not take his seat at the commencement of the session. Of the political works of this Congress, as well as of the preceding, their petitions, memorials, remonstrances, to the Throne, to the Parliament, to the People of England, of Ireland, and of Canada, I have forborne to speak, because they are familiar to you all. Let it suffice to say, that, in the estimation of so great a judge as Lord Chatham, they were such as had never been surpassed even in the master States of the world, in ancient Greece and Rome; and, although they produced no good effect on the unhappy monarch of Britain; though Pharaoh's heart was hardened so that they moved not *him*, they moved all heaven and all earth besides, and opened a passage for our fathers through the great deep.

The plot of the awful drama now began to thicken. The sword had been drawn. The battles of Lexington and Concord had been fought; and Warren, the rose of American chivalry, had been cut down, in his bloom, on that hill which his death has hallowed. The blood which had been shed in Massachusetts cried from the ground in every quarter of the Union. Congress heard that cry, and resolved on war. Troops were ordered to be raised. A Commander-in-Chief came to be appointed, and General Ward of Massachusetts was put in nomination. Here we have an incident in the life of Mr. Adams most strikingly characteristic of the man. Giving to the winds all local prepossessions, and looking only to the cause that filled his soul, the cause of his country, *he* prompted and sustained the nomination of that patriot hero whom the Almighty, in his goodness, had formed for the occasion. Washington was elected, and the choice was ratified in Heaven. He accepted his commission on the very day on which the soul of Warren winged its flight from Bunker Hill, and well did he avenge the death of that youthful hero.

Five days after General Washington's appointment, Mr. Jefferson, for the first time, took his seat as a member of Congress; and here, for the first time, met the two illustrious men whom we are endeavouring to commemorate. They met, and at once became friends—to part no more, but for a short season, and then to be re-united, both for time and eternity.

There was now open war between Great Britain and her colonies. Yet the latter looked no farther than resistance to the specific power of the parent country to tax them at pleasure. A dissolution of the union had not yet been contemplated, either by Congress or the nation; and many of those who had voted for the war, would have voted, and did afterwards vote, against that dissolution.

Such was the state of things under which the Congress of 1776 assembled, when Adams and Jefferson again met. It was, as you know, in this Congress, that the question of American Independence came, for the first time, to be discussed; and never, certainly, has a more momentous question been discussed in any age or in any country; for, it was fraught, not only with the destinies of this wide extended continent, but, as the event has shown, and is still showing, with the destinies of man, all over the world.

How fearful that question then was, no one can tell but those who forgetting all that has since past, can transport themselves back to the time, and plant their feet on the ground which those patriots then occupied. "Shadows, clouds, and darkness" then covered all the future, and the present was full only of danger and terror. A more unequal contest never was proposed. It was, indeed, as it was then said to be, the shepherd boy of Israel going forth to battle against the giant of Gath; and there were yet among us, enough to tremble when they heard that giant say, "Come to me, and I will give thy flesh to the fowls of the air and the beasts of the field." But, there were those who never trembled—who knew that there was a God in Israel, and who were willing to commit their cause "to his even-handed justice," and his Almighty power. That their great trust was in Him, is manifest from the remarks that were continually breaking from the lips of the patriots. Thus, the patriot Hawley, when pressed upon the inequality of the contest, could only answer, "We must put to sea—Providence will bring us into port," and Patrick Henry, when urged upon the same topic, exclaimed, "True, true; but there is a God above, who rules and overrules the destinies of nations."

Amid this appalling array that surrounded them, the first to enter the breach, sword in hand, was John Adams—the vision of his youth at his heart, and his country in every nerve. On the sixth of May, he offered, in committee of the whole, the significant resolution, that the colonies should form governments independent of the crown. This was the harbinger of more important measures, and seems to have been put forward to feel the pulse of the House. The resolution, after a bloody struggle, was adopted on the 15th day of May following. On the 7th of June, by previous concert, Richard Henry Lee moved the great resolution of Independence, and was seconded by John Adams; and "then came the tug of war." The debate upon it was continued from the 7th to the 10th, when the further consideration of it was postponed to the 1st of July, and at the same time a committee of five was appointed to prepare, provisionally, a draught of a Declaration of Independence. At the head of this important committee, which was then appointed by a vote of the House, although he was probably the youngest member, and one of the youngest men in the House, (for he had served only part of the former session, and was but thirty-two years of age,) stands the name of Thomas Jefferson —Mr. Adams stands next. And these two gentlemen having been deputed a sub-committee to prepare the draught, that draught, at Mr. Adams' earnest importunity, was prepared by his more youthful friend. Of this transaction Mr. Adams is himself the historian, and the authorship of the Declaration, though once disputed, is thus placed forever beyond the reach of question.

The final debate on the resolution was postponed, as we have seen, for nearly a month. In the mean time, all who are conversant with the course of action of all deliberative bodies, know how much is done by conversation among the members. It is not often, indeed, that proselytes are made on great questions by public debate. On such questions, opinions are far more frequently formed in private, and so formed that debate is seldom known to change them. Hence the value of the out-of-door talent of chamber consultation where objections candidly stated are candidly, calmly, and mildly discussed; where neither pride, nor shame, nor anger, take part in the discussion, nor stand in the way of a correct conclusion: but where every thing being conducted frankly, delicately, respectfully, and kindly, the better cause and the better reasoner are almost always sure of success. In this kind of service, as well as in all that depended on the power of composition, Mr. Jefferson was as much a master-magician, as his eloquent friend Adams was in debate. They were, in truth, hemispheres of the same golden globe, and required only to be brought and put together, to prove that they were parts of the same heaven-formed whole.

On the present occasion, however, much still remained to be effected by debate. The first of July came, and the great debate on the resolution for Independence was resumed, with fresh spirit. The discussion was again protracted for two days, which, in addition to the former three, were sufficient, in that age, to call out all the speaking talent of the House. Botta, the Italian historian of our Revolution, has made Mr. Dickinson and Mr. Lee the principal speakers on the opposite sides of this question; and availing himself of that dramatic license of ancient historians, which the fidelity of modern history has exploded, he has drawn, from his own fancy, two orations, which he has put into the mouths of those distinguished men. With no disposition to touch, with a hostile hand, one leaf of the well-earned laurels of Mr. Lee, (which every American would feel far more pleasure in contributing to brighten and to cherish,) and with no feelings but those of reverence and gratitude for the memory of the other great patriots who assisted in that debate, may we not say, and are we not bound in justice to say, that Botta is mistaken in the relative prominency of one, at least, of his prolocutors? Mr. Jefferson has told us that "the *Colossus* of that Congress—the great pillar of support to the Declaration of Independence, and its ablest advocate and champion on the floor of the House, was John Adams." How he supported it, can now be only matter of imagination: for, the debate was conducted with closed doors, and there was no reporter on the floor to catch the strains living as they rose. I will not attempt what Mr. Adams himself, if he were alive, could not accomplish. He might recall the topics of argument: but with regard to those flashes of inspiration, those bursts of passion, which grew out of the awful feelings of the moment, they are gone for ever, with the reality of the occasion: and the happiest effort of fancy to supply their place, (by me, at least,) would bear no better resemblance to the original, than the petty cripitations of an artificial volcano, to the sublime explosions of thundering Ætna. Waiving, therefore, the example of Botta, let it suffice for us to know that in that moment of darkness, of terror, and of consternation, when the election was to be made between an attempt at liberty and Independence on the one hand, and defeat, subjugation, and death, on the other, the courage of Adams, in the true spirit of heroism, rose in proportion to the dangers that pressed around him; and that he poured forth that only genuine eloquence, the eloquence of the soul, which, in the language of Mr. Jefferson, "moved his hearers from their seats." The objections of his adversaries were seen no longer but in a state of wreck; floating, in broken fragments, on the billows of the storm: and over rocks, over breakers, and amid ingulphing whirlpools, that every where surrounded him, he brought the gallant ship of the nation safe into port.

It was on the evening of the day on which this great victory was achieved, (before which, in moral grandeur, the trophies of Marengo and the Nile fade away,) and while his mind was yet rolling with the agitation of the recent tempest, that he wrote that letter to the venerable partner of his bosom, which has now become matter of history; in which after announcing the adoption of the resolution, he foretells the future glories of his country, and the honors with which the returning anniversary of her Declaration of Independence would be hailed, till time should be no more. That which strikes us on the first perusal of this letter, is, the prophetic character with which it is stamped, and the exactness with which its predictions have been fulfilled. But, his biographer will remark in it another character: the deep political calculation of results, through which the mind of the writer, according to its habit, had flashed; and the firm and undoubting confidence with which, in spite of those appearances that alarmed and misled weaker minds, *he* looked to the triumphant close of the struggle.

The resolution having been carried, the draught of the Declaration came to be examined in detail; and, so faultless had it issued from the hands of its author, that it was adopted as he had prepared it, pruned only of a few of its brightest inherent beauties, through a prudent deference to some of the States. It was adopted about noon of the Fourth, and proclaimed to an exulting nation, on the evening of the same day.

That brave and animated band who signed it—where are they now? What heart does not sink at the question? One only survives: CHARLES CARROLL, of Carrollton—a noble specimen of the age that has gone by, and now the single object of that age, on whom the veneration and prayers of his country are concentrated. The rest have bequeathed to us the immortal record of their virtue and patriotism, and have ascended to a brighter reward than man can confer.

Of that instrument to which you listen with reverence on every returning anniversary of its adoption, "which forms the ornament of our halls, and the first political lesson of our children," it is needless to speak. You know that in its origin and object, it was a statement of the causes which had compelled our Fathers to separate themselves from Great Britain, and to declare these States free and independent. It was the voice of the American Nation addressing herself to the other Nations of the Earth: and the address is, in all respects, worthy of this noble personification. It is the great argument of America in vindication of her course; and as Mr. Adams had been the Colossus of the cause on the floor of Congress, his illustrious friend, the author of this instrument, may well be pronounced to have been its Colossus on the theatre of the World.

The decisive step which fixed the destiny of the nation had now been taken: and that step was irrevocable. "The die was now indeed, cast. The Rubicon had been crossed," effectually, finally, for ever. There was no return but to chains, to slavery, and death. No such backward step was meditated by the firm hearts that led on the march of the nation: but, confiding in the justice of Heaven, and the final triumph of truth, they moved forward in solid phalanx, and with martial step, regardless of the tempest that was breaking around them.

Their confidence in the favor and protection of Heaven, however, strong and unshaken as it was, did not dispose them to relax their own exertions, nor to neglect the earthly means of securing their triumph. They were not of the number of those who call upon Hercules, and put not their own shoulders to the wheel. Our adversary was one of the most powerful nations on earth. Our whole strength consisted of a few stout hearts and a good cause. But, we were wofully deficient in all the sinews of war: we wanted men, we wanted arms, we wanted money; and these could be procured only from abroad. But the intervening ocean was covered with the fleets of the enemy; and the patriot Laurens, one of their captives, was already a prisoner in the Tower of London.—Who was there to undertake this perilous service? He who was ever ready to peril any service in the cause of his country: John Adams. Congress knew their man, and did not hesitate on the choice. Appointed a minister to France, he promptly obeyed the sacred call, and, with a brave and fearless heart, he ran the gauntlet through the hostile fleet, and arrived in safety. Passing from Court to Court, he pleaded the cause of his country with all the resistless energy of truth; and availing himself, adroitly, of the selfish passions and interests of those Courts, he ceased not to ply his efforts, with matchless dexterity, until the objects of his mission were completely attained. With the exception of one short interval of a return home, in '79, when he aided in giving form to the Constitution of his native State, he remained abroad, in France, in Holland—wherever he could be most useful—in the strenuous, faithful and successful service of his country, receiving repeated votes of thanks from Congress, till the storm was over, and peace and liberty came to crown his felicity, and realize the cherished vision of his youth.

Mr. Jefferson, meanwhile, was not less strenuously and successfully engaged at home, in forwarding and confirming the great objects of the Revolution, and making it a revolution of mind, as well as of government. Marking, with that sagacity which distinguished him, the series of inventions by which tyranny had contrived to tutor the mind to subjection, and educate it in habits of servile subordination, he proceeded, in Virginia, with the aid of Pendleton and Wythe, to break off the manacles, one by one, and deliver the imprisoned intellect from this debasing sorcery. The law of entails, that feudal contrivance to foster and nourish a vicious aristocracy at the expense of the community, had, at a previous period, been broken up, on their suggestion; and property was left to circulate freely, and impart health and vigor to the operations of society. The law of primogeniture, that other feudal contrivance to create and keep up an artificial inequality among men whom their Creator had made equal, was now repealed, and the parent and his children were restored to their natural relation. And, above all, that daring usurpation on the rights of the Creator, as well as the creature, which presumes to dictate to man what he shall believe, and in what form he shall offer the worship of his heart, and this, too, for the vile purpose of strengthening the hands of a temporal tyrant, by feeding and pampering the tools of his power, was indignantly demolished, and the soul was restored to its free communion with the God who gave it.

The preamble to the bill establishing religious freedom in Virginia, is one of the most morally sublime of human productions. By its great author it was always esteemed as one of his happiest efforts, and the measure itself one of his best services, as the short and modest epitaph left by him attests. Higher praise cannot and need not be given to it, than to say, it is in all respects worthy of the pen which wrote the Declaration of Independence: that it breathes the same lofty and noble spirit; and is a fit companion for that immortal instrument.

The legislative enactments that have been mentioned, form a small part, only, of an entire revision of the laws of Virginia. The collection of bills passed by these great men, (one hundred and twenty-six in number,) presents a system of jurisprudence, so comprehensive, profound, and beautiful, so perfectly, so happily adapted to the new state of things, that, if its authors had never done any thing else, impartial history would have assigned them a place by the side of Solon and Lycurgus.

In 1779, Mr. Jefferson was called to assume the helm of government in Virginia, in succession to Patrick Henry.—He took that helm, at the moment when war, for the first time, had entered the limits of the Commonwealth. With what strength, fidelity and ability he held it, under the most trying circumstances, the highest testimonials now stand on the journals of Congress, as well as those of Virginia. It is true that a poor attempt was made, in after times, to wound the honor of his administration. But he bore a charmed character; and this, like every other blow that has ever been aimed at it, only recoiled to crush his accuser, and to leave him the brighter and stronger for the assault.

In 1781, his alert and active mind, which watched the rising character of his new-born country, with all the jealous vigilance of an anxious father, found a new occasion to call him into the intellectual field. Our country was yet but imperfectly known in Europe. Its face, its soil, its physical capacities, its animals, and even the men who inhabited it, were so little known, as to have furnished to philosophers abroad a theme of unfounded and degrading speculation. Those visionaries, dreaming over theories which they wanted the means or the inclination to confront with facts, had advanced, among others, the fantastic notion that even man degenerated by transplantation to America. To refute this insolent position, and to place his country before Europe and the world on the elevated ground she was entitled to hold, the Notes on Virginia were prepared and published. He there pointed to Washington, to Franklin, and to Rittenhouse, as being alone sufficient to exterminate this heresy; and we may now point to Jefferson and to Adams, as sufficient to annihilate it. This pure and proud offering on the altar of his country, "The Notes on Virginia," honored its author abroad not less than at home; and when shortly afterwards, the public service called him to Europe, it gave him a prompt and distinguished passport into the highest circles of science and literature.

Thus actively and usefully employed in guarding the fame, and advancing the honor and happiness of his country, the war of the Revolution came to its close; and, on the 19th of October, 1781, of which this day is the anniversary, Great Britain bowed to the ascendency of our cause. Her last effective army struck her standard on the heights of York, and peace and independence came to bless our land.

Mr. Adams was still abroad when this great consummation of his early hopes took place: and, although the war was over, a difficult task still remained to be performed. The terms of peace were yet to be arranged, and to be arranged under circumstances of the most complicated embarrassment. That the acknowledgment of our independence was to be its first and indispensable condition, was well understood; and Mr. Adams, then at the Hague, with that decision which always marked his character, refused to leave his post and take part in the negociation at Paris, until the powers of the British commissioner should be so enlarged as to authorize him to make that acknowledgment unequivocally. I will not detain you by a rehearsal of what you so well know, the difficulties and intricacies by which this negociation was protracted. Suffice it to say, that the firmness and skill of the American Commissioners triumphed on every point. The treaty of peace was executed; and the last seal was thus put to the independence of these States.

Thus closed the great drama of the American Revolution. And here for a moment let us pause. If the services of our departed fathers had closed at this point, as it did with many of their compatriots—with too many, if the wishes and prayers of their country could have averted it—what obligations, what honors, should we not owe to their memories! What would not the world owe to them! But, as if they had not already done enough, as if, indeed, they had done nothing, while any thing yet remained to be done, they were ready with renovated youth and elastic step, to take a new start in the career of their emancipated country.

The Federal Constitution was adopted, and a new leaf was turned in the history of man. With what characters the page should be inscribed—whether it should open a great æra of permanent good to the human family, or pass away like a portent of direful evil, was now to depend on the wisdom and virtue of America. At this time our two great patriots were both abroad in the public service: Mr. Adams in England, where, in 1787, he refuted, by his great work "The Defence of the American Constitutions," the wild theories of Turgot, De Mably, and Price; and Mr. Jefferson in France, where he was presenting in his own person a living and splendid refutation of the notion of degeneracy in the American man. On the adoption of the Federal Constitution, they were both called home, to lend the weight of their character and talents to this new and momentous experiment on the capacity of man for self-government. Mr. Adams was called to fill the second office under the new Government, the first having been justly conferred by the rule "*deter fortiori*:" and Mr. Jefferson, to take the direction of the highest Executive Department. The office of Vice President afforded, as you are aware, no scope for the public display of talent. But the leisure which it allowed, enabled Mr. Adams to pour out, from his full-fraught mind, another great political work, his Discourses on Davilla; and, while he presided over the Senate with unexceptionable dignity and propriety, President Washington always found in him an able and honest adviser, in whom his confidence was implicit and unbounded.

Mr. Jefferson had a theatre that called for action. The Department of State was now, for the first time to be organized.

Its operations were all to be moulded into system, and an intellectual character was to be given to it, as well as the Government to which it belonged, before this nation and before the world. The frequent calls made by Congress for reports on the most abtruse questions of science connected with Government, and on those vast and novel and multifarious subjects of political economy, peculiar to this wide extended and diversified continent: discussions with the ministers of foreign Governments, more especially with those of France and England and Spain, on those great and agitating questions of international law, which were then continually arising; and instructions to our own Ministers abroad, resident at the Courts of the great belligerent powers, and who had consequently the most delicate and discordant interests to manage: presented a series of labors for the mind, which few, *very few* men in this or any other country could have sustained with reputation. How Mr. Jefferson acquitted himself you all know. It is one of the peculiarities of his character to have discharged the duties of every office to which he was called, with such exact, appropriate, and felicitous ability, that he seemed, for the time, to have been born for that alone. As an evidence of the unanimous admiration of the matchless skill and talent with which he discharged the duties of this office, I hope it may be mentioned, without awaking any asperity of feeling, that when, at a subsequent period, he was put in nomination by his friends for the office of President, his adversaries publicly objected—"that Nature had made him only for a Secretary of State."

President Washington having set the great example, which has ingrafted on the Constitution as firmly as if it had formed one of its express provisions, the principle of retiring from the office of President at the end of eight years, Mr. Adams succeeded him, and Mr. Jefferson followed Mr. Adams in the office of Vice President.

Mr. Adams came into the office of President at a time of great commotion, produced chiefly by the progress of the revolution in France, and those strong sympathies which it naturally generated here. The spirit of party was high, and in the feverish excitement of the day much was said and done, on both sides, which the voice of impartial history, if it shall descend to such details, will unquestionably condemn, and which

the candid and the good on both sides lived, themselves, to regret. One incident I will mention, because it is equally honorable to both the great men whom we are uniting in these
obsequies. In Virginia, where the opposition ran high, the
younger politicians of the day, taking their tone from the public Journals, have, on more occasions than one, in the presence
of Mr. Jefferson, imputed to Mr. Adams a concealed design to
sap the foundations of the Republic, and to supply its place
with a Monarchy, on the British model. The uniform answer of
Mr. Jefferson to this charge will never be forgotten by those
who have heard it, and of whom (as I have recently had occasion to prove) there are many still living, besides the humble
individual who is now addressing you. It was this: "Gentlemen,
you do not know that man: there is not upon this earth a more
perfectly honest man than John Adams. Concealment is no part
of his character; of that he is utterly incapable: it is not in his
nature to meditate any thing that he would not publish to the
world. The measures of the General Government are a fair subject for difference of opinion. But do not found your opinions
on the notion, that there is the smallest spice of dishonesty,
moral or political, in the character of John Adams: for, I know
him *well*, and I repeat it, that a man more perfectly honest
never issued from the hands of his Creator." And such is now,
and has long been, the unanimous opinion of his countrymen.

Of the measures adopted during his administration you do
not expect me to speak. I should offend against your own sense
of propriety, were I to attempt it. We are here, to mingle together over the grave of the departed patriot, our feelings of
reverence and gratitude for services whose merit we all acknowledge: and cold must be the heart which does not see and
feel, in his life, enough to admire and to love, without striking
one string that could produce one unhallowed note. History
and biography will do ample justice to every part of his character, public and private; and impartial posterity will correct
whatever errors of opinion may have been committed to his
prejudice by his cotemporaries. Let it suffice for us, at this time,
to know, that he administered the Government with a pure,
and honest, and upright heart; and that whatever he advised,
flowed from the master passion of his breast, a holy and all-
absorbing love for the happiness and honor of his country.

Mr. Jefferson, holding the Vice Presidency, did not leave even that negative office, as, indeed, he never left any other, without marking its occupancy with some useful and permanent vestige. For, it was during this term, that he digested and compiled that able manual which now gives the law of proceeding, not only to the two Houses of Congress, but to all the Legislatures of the States throughout the Union.

On Mr. Adams' retirement, pursuing the destiny which seems to have tied them together, Mr. Jefferson again followed him in the office which he had vacated, the Presidency of the United States: and he had the good fortune to find, or to make, a smoother sea. The violence of the party storm gradually abated, and he was soon able to pursue his peaceful course without any material interruption. Having forborne, for the obvious reasons which have been suggested, to touch the particulars of Mr. Adams' administration, the same forbearance, for the same reasons, must be exercised with regard to Mr. Jefferson. But, forbearing details, it will be no departure from this rule to state in general the facts: that Mr. Jefferson continued at the helm for eight years, the term which the example of Washington had consecrated; that he so administered the Government as to meet the admiration and applause of a great majority of his countrymen, as the overwhelming suffrage at his second election attests: that by that majority he was thought to have presented a perfect model of a republican administration, on the true basis, and in the true spirit of the Constitution; and that, by them the measures of all the succeeding administrations have been continually brought to the standard of Mr. Jefferson's, as to an established and unquestionable test, and approved or condemned in proportion to their accordance with that standard. These are facts which are known to you all. Another fact I will mention, because it redounds so highly to the honor of his magnanimous and patriotic rival. It is this: that that part of Mr. Jefferson's administration, and of his successor treading in his steps, which was most violently opposed, the policy pursued towards the British Government subsequent to 1806, received the open, public, and powerful support of the pen, as well as the tongue, of the great sage of Quincy. The banished Aristides never gave a nobler proof of pure and disinterested patriotism. It was a genuine emanation from the altar of the Revolution, and in perfect accordance with the whole tenor of the life of our illustrious patriot sage.

Waving all comment on Mr. Jefferson's public measures, there is yet a minor subject, which, standing where we do, there seems to be a peculiar propriety in noticing; for, small as it is, it is strikingly characteristic of the man, and we have an immediate interest in the subject. It is this: the great objects of national concern, and the great measures which he was continually projecting and executing for the public good, on a new and vast scheme of policy wholly his own, and stamped with all the vigor and grandeur of his Olympic mind, although they were such as would not only have engrossed but overwhelmed almost any other man, did not even give full employment to him; but with that versatile and restless activity which was prone to busy itself usefully and efficaciously with all around him, he found time to amuse himself and to gratify his natural taste for the beautiful, by directing and over-looking in person, (as many of you can witness) the improvements and ornaments of this city of the nation: and it is to his taste and industry that we owe, among other things which it were needless to enumerate, this beautiful avenue, which he left in such order as to excite the admiration of all who approached us.

Having closed his administration, he was followed by the applause, the gratitude, and blessings of his country, into that retirement which no man was ever better fitted to grace and enjoy. And from this retirement, together with his precursor, the venerable patriarch of Quincy, could enjoy, that supreme of all earthly happiness, the retrospect of a life well and greatly spent in the service of his country and mankind. The successful warrior, who has desolated whole empires for his own aggrandizement, the successful usurper of his country's rights and liberties, may have their hours of swelling pride, in which they may look back with a barbarous joy upon the triumph of their talents, and feast upon the adulation of the sycophants that surround them; but, night and silence come; and conscience takes her turn. The bloody field rises upon the startled imagination. The shades of the slaughtered innocent stalk, in terrific procession before the couch. The agonizing cry of countless widows and orphans invades the ear. The bloody dagger of the assassin plays, in airy terror, before the vision.

Violated liberty lifts her avenging lance, and a down-trodden nation rises, before them, in all the majesty of its wrath. What, what are the hours of a splendid wretch like this, compared with those that shed their poppies and their roses upon the pillows of our peaceful and virtuous patriots! Every night bringing to them the balm and health of repose, and every morning offering to them "their history in a nation's eyes!" This, this it is to be greatly virtuous: and be this the only ambition that shall ever touch an American bosom!

Still unexhausted by such a life of service in the cause of his country, Mr. Jefferson found yet another and most appropriate employment for his old age: the erection of a seat of science in his native State. The University of Virginia is his work. His, the first conception: his, the whole impulse and direction; his, the varied and beautiful architecture, and the entire superintendence of its erection: the whole scheme of its studies, its organization, and government, are his. He is, therefore, indeed the father of the University of Virginia.—That it may fulfil to the full extent, the great and patriotic purposes and hopes of its founder, cannot fail to be the wish of every American bosom. This was the last and crowning labor of Mr. Jefferson's life: a crown so poetically appropriate, that fancy might well suppose it to have been wreathed and placed on his brow by the hand of the epic muse herself.

It is the remark of one of the most elegant writers of antiquity, in the beautiful essay which he has left us "on Old Age," that "to those who have not within themselves the resources of living well and happily, every age is oppressive; but that to those who have, nothing is an evil which the necessity of nature brings along with it." How rich our two patriots were in these internal resources, you all know. How lightly they bore the burthen of increasing years was apparent from the cheerfulness and vigor with which, after having survived the age to which they properly belonged, they continued to live among their posterity. How happy they were in their domestic relations, how beloved by their neighbors and friends, how revered and honored by their country and by the friends of liberty in every quarter of the world, is a matter of open and public notoriety. Their houses were the constant and thronged resort of the votaries of virtue, and science, and genius, and patriotism, from every portion of the civilized globe; and no one ever left them without confessing that his highest expectations had been realized, and even surpassed, in the interview.

Of "the chief of the Argonauts," as Mr. Jefferson so classically and so happily styled his illustrious friend of the North, it is my misfortune to be able to speak only by report. But every representation concurs, in drawing the same pleasing and affecting picture of the Roman simplicity in which that Father of his Country lived; of the frank, warm, cordial, and elegant reception that he gave to all who approached him; of the interesting kindness with which he disbursed the golden treasures of his experience, and shed around him the rays of his descending sun. His conversation was rich in anecdote and characters of the times that were past; rich in political and moral instruction; full of that best of wisdom, which is learnt from real life, and flowing from his heart with that warm and honest frankness, that fervor of feeling and force of diction, which so strikingly distinguished him in the meridian of his life. Many of us heard that simple and touching account given of a parting scene with him, by one of our eloquent divines: When he rose up from that little couch behind the door, on which he was wont to rest his aged and weary limbs, and with his silver locks hanging on each side of his honest face, stretched forth that pure hand, which was never soiled even by a suspicion, and gave his kind and parting benediction. Such was the blissful and honored retirement of the sage of Quincy. Happy the life which, verging upon a century, had met with but one serious political disappointment! and even for that, he had lived to receive a golden atonement, "even in that quarter in which he had garnered up his heart."

Let us now turn for a moment to the patriot of the South. The Roman moralist, in that great work which he has left for the government of man in all the offices of life, has descended even to prescribe the kind of habitation in which an honored and distinguished man should dwell. It should not, he says, be small, and mean, and sordid; nor, on the other hand extended with profuse and wanton extravagance. It should be large enough to receive and accommodate the visiters which such a man never fails to attract, and suited in its ornaments, as well as its dimensions, to the character and fortune of the individual.

Monticello has now lost its great charm. Those of you who have not already visited it, will not be very apt to visit it, hereafter: and, from the feelings which you cherish for its departed owner, I persuade myself that you will not be displeased with a brief and rapid sketch of that abode of domestic bliss, that temple of science. Nor is it, indeed, foreign to the express purpose of this meeting, which, in looking to "his life and character," naturally embraces his home and his domestic habits. Can any thing be indifferent to us, which was so dear to him, and which was a subject of such just admiration to the hundreds and thousands that were continually resorting to it, as to an object of pious pilgrimage?

The Mansion House at Monticello was built and furnished in the days of his prosperity. In its dimensions, its architecture, its arrangements, and ornaments, it is such a one as became the character and fortune of the man. It stands upon an elliptic plain, formed by cutting down the apex of a mountain; and, on the West, stretching away to the North and the South, it commands a view of the Blue Ridge for a hundred and fifty miles, and brings under the eye one of the boldest and most beautiful horizons in the world: while, on the East, it presents an extent of prospect, bounded only by the spherical form of the earth, in which nature seems to sleep in eternal repose, as if to form one of her finest contrasts with the rude and rolling grandeur on the West. In the wide prospect, and scattered to the North and South, are several detached mountains, which contribute to animate and diversify this enchanting landscape: and among them, to the South, Williss' Mountain, which is so interestingly depicted in his Notes. From this summit, the Philosopher was wont to enjoy that spectacle, among the sublimest of Nature's operations, the looming of the distant mountains; and to watch the motions of the planets, and the greater revolution of the celestial sphere. From this summit, too, the patriot could look down, with uninterrupted vision, upon the wide expanse of the world around, for which he considered himself born; and upward, to the open and vaulted Heavens which he seemed to approach, as if to keep him continually in mind of his high responsibility. It is indeed a prospect in which you see and feel, at once, that nothing mean or little could live. It is a scene fit to nourish those great and

high-souled principles which formed the elements of his character, and was a most noble and appropriate post, for such a
sentinel, over the rights and liberties of man.

Approaching the house on the East, the visiter instinctively
paused, to cast around one thrilling glance at this magnificent
panorama: and then passed to the vestibule, where, if he had
not been previously informed, he would immediately perceive
that he was entering the house of no common man. In the
spacious and lofty hall which opens before him, he marks no
tawdry and unmeaning ornaments: but before, on the right, on
the left, all around, the eye is struck and gratified with objects
of science and taste, so classed and arranged as to produce
their finest effect. On one side, specimens of sculpture set out,
in such order, as to exhibit at a *coup d'œil*, the historical progress of that art; from the first rude attempts of the aborigines
of our country, up to that exquisite and finished bust of the
great patriot himself, from the master hand of Caracci. On the
other side, the visiter sees displayed a vast collection of specimens of Indian art, their paintings, weapons, ornaments, and
manufactures; on another, an array of the fossil productions of
our country, mineral and animal; the polished remains of those
colossal monsters that once trod our forests, and are no more;
and a variegated display of the branching honors of those
"monarchs of the waste," that still people the wilds of the
American Continent.

From this hall he was ushered into a noble saloon, from
which the glorious landscape of the West again burst upon his
view; and which, within, is hung thick around with the finest
productions of the pencil—historical paintings of the most
striking subjects from all countries, and all ages; the portraits
of distinguished men and patriots, both of Europe and America, and medallions and engravings in endless profusion.

While the visiter was yet lost in the contemplation of these
treasures of the arts and sciences, he was startled by the approach of a strong and sprightly step, and turning with instinctive reverence to the door of entrance, he was met by the tall,
and animated, and stately figure of the patriot himself—his
countenance beaming with intelligence and benignity, and his
outstretched hand, with its strong and cordial pressure, confirming the courteous welcome of his lips. And then came that

charm of manner and conversation that passes all description
—so cheerful—so unassuming—so free, and easy, and frank,
and kind, and gay—that even the young, and overawed, and
embarrassed visiter at once forgot his fears, and felt himself by
the side of an old and familiar friend. There was no effort, no
ambition in the conversation of the philosopher. It was as simple and unpretending as nature itself. And while in this easy
manner he was pouring out instruction, like light from an inexhaustible solar fountain, he seemed continually to be asking,
instead of giving information. The visiter felt himself lifted by
the contact, into a new and nobler region of thought, and became surprised at his own buoyancy and vigor. He could not,
indeed, help being astounded, now and then, at those transcendant leaps of the mind, which he saw made without the slightest exertion, and the ease with which this wonderful man
played with subjects which he had been in the habit of considering among the *argumenta crucis* of the intellect. And then
there seemed to be no end to his knowledge. He was a thorough master of every subject that was touched. From the details of the humblest mechanic art, up to the highest summit of
science, he was perfectly at his ease, and, every where at home.
There seemed to be no longer any *terra incognita* of the human understanding: for, what the visiter had thought so, he
now found reduced to a familiar garden walk; and all this carried off so lightly, so playfully, so gracefully, so engagingly, that
he won every heart that approached him, as certainly as he astonished every mind.

Mr. Jefferson was wont to remark, that he never left the
conversation of Dr. Franklin without carrying away with him
something new and useful. How often, and how truly, has the
same remark been made of him. Nor is this wonderful, when
we reflect, that, that mind of matchless vigor and versatility
had been, all his life, intensely engaged in conversing with the
illustrious dead, or following the march of science in every
land, or bearing away, on its own steady and powerful wing,
into new and unexplored regions of thought.

Shall I follow him to the table of his elegant hospitality, and
show him to you in the bosom of his enchanting family? Alas!
those attic days are gone; that sparkling eye is quenched; that
voice of pure and delicate affection, which ran with such bril-

liancy and effect through the whole compass of colloquial music, now bright with wit, now melting with tenderness, is hushed forever in the grave! But let me leave a theme on which friendship and gratitude have, I fear, already been tempted to linger too long.

There was one solace of the declining years of both these great men, which must not be passed. It is that correspondence which arose between them, after their retirement from public life. That correspondence, it is to be hoped, will be given to the world. If it ever shall, I speak from knowledge when I say, it will be found to be one of the most interesting and affecting that the world has ever seen. That "cold cloud" which had hung for a time over their friendship, passed away with the conflict out of which it had grown, and the attachment of their early life returned in all its force. They had both now bid adieu, a final adieu, to all public employments, and were done with all the agitating passions of life. They were dead to the ambitious world; and this correspondence resembles, more than any thing else, one of those conversations in the Elysium of the ancients, which the shades of the departed great were supposed by them to hold, with regard to the affairs of the world they had left. There are the same playful allusions to the points of difference that had divided their parties: the same mutual, and light, and unimpassioned raillery on their own past misconceptions and mistakes; the same mutual and just admiration and respect for their many virtues and services to mankind. That correspondence was, to them both, one of the most genial employments of their old age: and it reads a lesson of wisdom on the bitterness of party spirit, by which the wise and the good will not fail to profit.

Besides this affectionate intercourse between them, you are aware of the extensive correspondence which they maintained with others, and of which some idea may be formed by those letters which, since their death, have already broken upon us through the press, from quarters so entirely unexpected. They were considered as the living historians of the Revolution and of the past age, as well as oracles of wisdom to all who consulted them. Their habit in this particular seems to have been the same; never to omit answering any respectful letter they received, no matter how obscure the individual, or how insignificant the subject. With Mr. Jefferson this was a sacred law, and as he always wrote at a polygraphic desk, copies have been preserved of every letter. His correspondence travelled far beyond his own country, and embraced within its circle many of the most distinguished men of his age in Europe. What a feast for the mind may we not expect from the published letters of these excellent men! They were both masters in this way, though somewhat contrasted. Mr. Adams, plain, nervous, and emphatic, the thought couched in the fewest and strongest words, and striking with a kind of epigrammatic force. Mr. Jefferson, flowing with easy and careless melody, the language at the same time pruned of every redundant word, and giving the thought with the happiest precision, the aptest words dropping unbidden and unsought into their places, as if they had fallen from the skies; and so beautiful, so felicitious, as to fill the mind with a succession of delightful surprises, while the judgment is, at the same time, made captive by the closely compacted energy of the argument. Mr. Jefferson's style is so easy and harmonious, as to have led superficial readers to remark, that he was deficient in strength: as if ruggedness and abruptness were essential to strength. Mr. Jefferson's strength was inherent in the thoughts and conceptions, though hidden by the light and graceful vestments which he threw over them. The internal divinity existed and was felt, though concealed under the finely harmonized form of the man; and if he did not exhibit himself in his compositions with the *insignia* of Hercules, the shaggy lion's skin and the knotted club; he bore the full quiver and the silver bow of Apollo; and every polished shaft that he loosened from the string, told with unerring and fatal precision:

Δεινὴ δὲ κλαγγὴ γένετ' ἀργυρέοιο βιοῖο

These two great men, so eminently distinguished among the patriots of the Revolution, and so illustrious by their subsequent services, became still more so, by having so long survived all that were most highly conspicuous among their coevals. All the stars of first magnitude, in the equatorial and tropical regions had long since gone down, and still they remained. Still they stood full in view, like those two resplendent constellations near the opposite poles, which never set to the inhabitants of the neighbouring zones.

But, they too were doomed at length to set: and such was their setting as no American bosom can ever forget!

In the midst of their fast decaying strength, and when it was seen that the approach of death was certain, their country and its glory still occupied their thoughts, and circulated with the last blood that was ebbing to their hearts. Those who surrounded the death-bed of Mr. Jefferson report, that in the few short intervals of delirium that occurred, his mind manifestly relapsed to the age of the Revolution. He talked, in broken sentences, of the Committees of Safety, and the rest of that great machinery which he imagined to be still in action. One of his exclamations was, "Warn the Committee to be on their guard;" and he instantly rose in his bed, with the help of his attendants, and went through the act of writing a hurried note. But these intervals were few and short. His reason was almost constantly upon her throne, and the only aspiration he was heard to breathe, was the prayer, that he might live to see the Fourth of July. When that day came, all that he was heard to whisper, was the repeated ejaculation,—"*Nunc Domine dimittas,*" Now, Lord, let thy servant depart in peace! And the prayer of the patriot was heard and answered.

The Patriarch of Quincy, too, with the same certainty of death before him, prayed only for the protraction of his life to the same day. His prayer was also heard: and when a messenger from the neighboring festivities, unapprized of his danger, was deputed to ask him for the honor of a toast, he showed the object on which his dying eyes were fixed, and exclaimed with energy, "Independence for ever!" His country first, his country last, his country always!

"O save my country—Heaven! he said—and died!"

Hitherto, Fellow citizens, the Fourth of July had been celebrated among us, only as the anniversary of our Independence, and its votaries had been merely human beings. But at its last recurrence—the great Jubilee of the nation—the anniversary, it may well be termed, of the liberty of man—Heaven, itself, mingled visibly in the celebration, and hallowed the day anew by a double apotheosis. Is there one among us to whom this language seems too strong? Let him recall his own feelings, and the objection will vanish. When the report first reached us, of the death of the great man whose residence was nearest, who among us was not struck with the circumstance that he should have been removed on the day of his own highest glory? And who, after the first shock of the intelligence, had passed, did not feel a thrill of mournful delight at the characteristic beauty of the close of such a life. But while our bosoms were yet swelling with admiration at this singularly beautiful coincidence, when the second report immediately followed, of the death of the great sage of Quincy, *on the same day*—I appeal to yourselves—is there a voice that was not hushed, is there a heart that did not quail, at this close manifestation of the hand of Heaven in our affairs! Philosophy, recovered of her supprise, may affect to treat the coincidence as fortuitous. But Philosophy herself was mute, at the moment, under the pressure of the feeling that these illustrious men had rather been translated, than had died. It is in vain to tell us that men die by thousands every day in the year, all over the world. The wonder is not that two men have died on the same day, but that two *such* men, after having performed so many and such splendid services in the cause of liberty—after the multitude of other coincidences which seem to have linked their destinies together—after having lived so long together, the objects of their country's joint veneration—after having been spared to witness the great triumph of their toils at home—and looked together from Pisgah's top on the sublime effect of that grand impulse which they had given to the same glorious cause throughout the world, should on this fiftieth anniversary of the day on which they had ushered that cause into light, be both caught up to Heaven, together, in the midst of their raptures! Is there a being, of heart so obdurate and sceptical, as not to feel the hand and hear the voice of Heaven in this wonderful dispensation? And may we not, with reverence, interpret its language? Is it not this? "These are my beloved servants, in whom I am well pleased. They have finished the work for which I sent them into the world: and are now called to their reward. *Go ye, and do likewise!*"

One circumstance, alone, remains to be noticed. In a *private* memorandum found among some other obituary papers and relics of Mr. Jefferson, is a suggestion, in case a memorial over him should ever be thought of, that a granite obelisk, of small dimensions, should be erected, with the following inscription:

HERE WAS BURIED
THOMAS JEFFERSON,
Author of the Declaration of Independence,
Of the Statutes of Virginia, for Religious Freedom,
And Father of the University of Virginia.

All the long catalogue of his great, and splendid, and glorious services, reduced to this brief and modest summary!

Thus lived and thus died our sainted Patriots! May their spirits still continue to hover over their countrymen, inspire all their counsels, and guide them in the same virtuous and noble path! And may that God, in whose hands are the issues of all things, confirm and perpetuate, to us, the inestimable boon which, through their agency, he has bestowed; and make our Columbia, the bright exemplar, for all the struggling sons of liberty around the globe!

FRANCES WRIGHT

Fourth of July Address

New Harmony, Indiana, July 4, 1828

THE CUSTOM which commemorates in rejoicing the anniversary of the national independence of these states, has its origin in a human feeling, amiable in its nature, and beneficial, under proper direction, in its indulgence.

From the era which dates the national existence of the American people, dates also a mighty step in the march of human knowledge. And it is consistent with that principle in our conformation which leads us to rejoice in the good which befals our species, and to sorrow for the evil, that our hearts should expand on this day;—on this day, which calls to memory the conquest achieved by knowledge over ignorance, willing cooperation over blind obedience, opinion over prejudice, new ways over old ways, when, fifty-two years ago, America declared her national independence, and associated it with her republican federation. Reasonable is it to rejoice on this day, and useful to reflect thereon; so that we rejoice for the real, and not any imaginary good, and reflect on the positive advantages obtained, and on those which it is ours farther to acquire.

Dating, as we justly may, a new era in the history of man from the Fourth of July, 1776, it would be well, that is, it would be useful, if on each anniversary we examined the progress made by our species in just knowledge and just practice. Each Fourth of July would then stand as a tide mark in the flood of time, by which to ascertain the advance of the human intellect, by which to note the rise and fall of each successive error, the discovery of each important truth, the gradual melioration in our public institutions, social arrangements, and, above all, in our moral feelings and mental views. Let such a review as this engage annually our attention, and sacred, doubly sacred, shall be this day; and that not to one nation only, but to all nations capable of reflection!

The political dismemberment of these once British colonies from the parent island, though involving a valuable principle, and many possible results, would scarcely merit a yearly commemoration, even in this country, had it not been accompanied by other occurrences more novel, and far more important. I allude to the seal then set to the system of representative government, till then imperfectly known in Europe, and insecurely practised in America, and to the crown then placed on this system by the novel experiment of political federation. The frame of federative government that sprung out of the articles signed in '76, is one of the most beautiful inventions of the human intellect. It has been in government what the steam engine has been in mechanics, and the printing press in the dissemination of knowledge.

But it needs not that we should now pause to analyse what all must have considered. It is to one particular feature in our political institutions that I would call attention, and this, because it is at once the most deserving of notice, and the least noticed. Are our institutions better than those of other countries? Upon fair examination most men will answer *yes*. But why will they so answer? Is it because they are republican, instead of monarchical? democratic, rather than aristocratic? In so far as the republican principle shall have been proved more conducive to the general good than the monarchical, and the democratic than the aristocratic—in so far will the reasons, be good. But there is another and a better reason than these. There is, in the institutions of this country, one principle, which, had they no other excellence, would secure to them the preference over those of all other countries. I mean—and some devout patriots will start—I mean the principle of *change*.

I have used a word to which is attached an obnoxious meaning. Speak of *change*, and the world is in alarm. And yet where do we not see change? What is there in the physical world *but* change? And what would there be in the moral world *without* change? The flower blossoms, the fruit ripens, the seed is received and germinates in the earth, and we behold the tree. The aliment we eat to satisfy our hunger incorporates with our frame, and the atoms composing our existence to-day, are exhaled to-morrow. In like manner our feelings and opinions are moulded by circumstance, and matured by observation and experience. All is change. Within and about us no one thing is as it was, or will be as it is. Strange, then, that we should start at a word used to signify a thing so familiar! Stranger yet that we should fail to appreciate a principle which, inherent in all matter, is no less inherent in ourselves; and which, as it has tracked our mental progress heretofore, so will it track our progress through time to come!

But will it be said *change* has a bad, as well as a good sense? It may be for the better, and it may be for the worse? In the physical world it can be neither the one nor the other. It can be simply such as it is. But in the moral world—that is, in the thoughts, and feelings, and inventions of men, change may certainly be either for the better or for the worse, or it may be for neither. Changes that are neither bad nor good can have regard *only* to trivial matters, and can be as little worthy of observation as of censure. Changes that are from better to worse can originate only in ignorance, and are ever amended so soon as experience has substantiated their mischief. Where men then are free to consult experience they will correct their practice, and make changes for the better. It follows, therefore, that the more free men are, the more changes they will make. In the beginning, possibly, for the worse; but most certainly in time for the better; until their knowledge enlarging by observation, and their judgment strengthening by exercise, they will find themselves in the straight, broad, fair road of improvement. Out of change, therefore, springs improvement; and the people who shall have imagined a peaceable mode of changing their institutions, hold a surety for their melioration. This surety is worth all other excellencies. Better were the prospects of a people under the influence of the worst government who should hold the power of changing it, than those of a people under the best who should hold no such power. Here, then, is the great beauty of American government. The simple machinery of representation carried through all its parts, gives facility for its being moulded at will to fit with the knowledge of the age. If imperfect in any or all of its parts, it bears within it a perfect principle—the principle of improvement. And, let us observe, that this principle is all that we can ever know of perfection. Knowledge, and all the blessings which spring out of

knowledge, can never be more than progressive; and whatsoever *sets open the door* does all for us—does every thing.

The clear sighted provision in the national constitution, as
in the constitutions of the different states, by which the frame
of government can be moulded at will by the public voice, and
so made to keep pace in progress with the public mind, is the
master-stroke in constitutional law. Were our institutions far
less enlightened and well digested than they are—were every
other regulation erroneous, every other ordinance defective—
nay, even tyrannous—this single provision would counter-
balance all. Let but the door be opened, and be fixed open, for
improvement to hold on her unimpeded course, and vices,
however flagrant, are but the evils of an hour. Once lanch the
animal man in the road of enquiry, and he *shall*—he *must*—
hold a forward career. He may be sometimes checked; he may
seem occasionally to retrograde; but his retreat is only that of
the receding wave in the inning tide. His master movement is
always in advance. By this do we distinguish man from all
other existences within the range of our observation. By this
does he stand pre-eminent over all known animals. By *this*—by
his capability of improvement: by his tendency to improve
whenever scope is allowed for the developement of his faculties. To hold him *still*, he must be chained. Snap the chain, and
he springs forward.

But will it be said, that the chains which bind him are more
than one? That political bonds are much, but not all; and that
when broken, we may still be slaves? I know not, my friends.
We tax our ingenuity to draw nice distinctions. We are told of
political liberty—of religious liberty—of moral liberty. Yet, after
all, is there more than one liberty; and these divisions, are they
not the more and the less of the same thing? The provision we
have referred to in our political institutions, as framed in accordance with the principle inherent in ourselves, insures to us
all of free action that statutes *can* insure. Supposing that our
laws, constitutional, civil, or penal, should in any thing cripple
us at the present, the power will be with us to amend or annul
them so soon (and how might it be sooner?) as our enlarged
knowledge shall enable us to see in what they err. All the liberty therefore that we yet lack will gradually spring up—*there,*

where our bondage is—in our minds. To be free we have but to see our chains. Are we disappointed—are we sometimes angry, because the crowd or any part of the crowd around us bows submissively to mischievous usages or unjust laws? Let us remember, that they do so in ignorance of their mischief and injustice, and that when they see these, as in the course of man's progressive state they must see them, these and other evils will be corrected.

Inappreciable is this advantage that we hold (unfortunately) above other nations! The great national and political revolution of '76 set the seal to the liberties of North America. And but for one evil, and that of immense magnitude, which the constitutional provision we have been considering does not fairly reach—I allude to negro slavery and the degradation of our colored citizens—we could foresee for the whole of this magnificent country a certain future of uniform and peaceful improvement. While other nations have still to win reform at the sword's point, we have only to will it. While in Europe men have still to fight, we have only to learn. While there they have to cope with ignorance armed cap-a-pee, encircled with armies and powerful with gold, we have only peacefully to collect knowledge, and to frame our institutions and actions in accordance with it.

It is true, that we have much knowledge to collect, and consequently much to amend in our opinions and our practice. It is also true that we are often ignorant of what has been done, and quite unaware that there is yet any thing to do. The very nature of the national institutions is frequently mistaken, and the devotion exhibited for them as frequently based on a wrong principle. Here, as in other countries, we hear of *patriotism*; that is, of love of country in an exclusive sense; of love of our countrymen in contradistinction to the love of our fellow-creatures; of love of the constitution, instead of love or appreciation of those principles upon which the constitution is, or ought to be, based, and upon which, if it should be found not to be based, it would merit no attachment at all.

The sentiment here adverted to involves much of importance to us in our double character of human beings and citizens. That double character it will be also useful that we examine, as much confusion prevails in the vulgar ideas on the subject.

It will be conceded, that we do not cease to be human beings when we become citizens; and farther, that our happy existence as human beings is of more importance to us than our artificial existence as members of a nation or subjects of a government. Indeed, the only rational purpose for which we can suppose men congregated into what are called nations, is the increase of happiness—the insuring of some advantage, real or imagined. The only rational purpose for which we can suppose governments organized, the same. If, upon examination, we should find the object not gained, the experiment, so far as it went, would have failed, and we should then act rationally to break up such national congregations, and to change or annul such governments. Our character as citizens, therefore, must ever depend upon our finding it for our interest as human beings to stand in that relation. What then is patriotism, or the fulfilment of our duties as citizens, but the acting consistently in that way which we conceive it for our interest that we should act? Or what reason might be offered for our consulting the interests of a government, unless its interests are in unison with our own?

The great error of the wisest known nations of antiquity, the Greeks and Romans, was the preference invariably given to the imagined interests of an imaginary existence called *the state* or *country*, and the real interests of the real existences, or human beings, upon whom, individually and collectively, their laws could alone operate. Another error was the opposition in which they invariably placed the interests of their own nation to the interests of all other nations; and a third and greater error, was the elevating into a virtue this selfish preference of their own national interests, under the name of patriotism. The moderns are growing a little wiser on these matters, but they are still very ignorant. The least ignorant are the people of this country; but they have much to learn. Americans no longer argue on the propriety of making all men soldiers, in order that their nation may be an object of terror to the rest of the world. They understand that the happiness of a people is the only rational object of a government, and the only object for which a people, free to choose, can have a government at all. They have, farther, almost excluded war as a profession, and reduced it from a system of robbery to one of simple defence. In so doing, they ought also to have laid aside all show of military parade, and all ideas of military glory. If they have not done so, it is that their reform in this matter is yet imperfect, and their ideas respecting it are confused.

Who among us but has heard, and, perhaps, echoed eulogiums on the patriotism of statesmen and soldiers—not because they have upheld some strict principle of justice, which should rather merit the name of virtue, but because they have flattered the vanity of their countrymen in a public speech, defended their own interests, and the national interests, in some foreign treaty, or their own possessions, and the national possessions, in a siege or a pitched battle? It is not that some of these actions may not be just and proper; but are they justly and properly estimated? Is it *virtuous* in a man if a pistol be presented to his breast, to knock down the assailant? The action is perfectly warrantable; but does it call forth admiration? Should the attack be made on another, and should he defend the life of that other at the risk of his own; the action, though not exceedingly meritorious, might excite a moderate admiration, as involving a forgetfulness of self in the service rendered.

Does not the defence of country afford a parallel case to the first supposition? Insomuch as it be ours, we defend our own. We do what it is fair and proper that we should do, but we do nothing more. What, then, is patriotism, of which we hear so much, and understand so little? If it mean only a proper attention to our own interests, and the interests of the people with whom we stand connected, and of the government instituted for our protection, it is a rational sentiment, and one appertaining to our organization. It is one, in short, with the love of self, and the principle of self-defence and self-preservation. Again; are we to understand by it an attachment to the soil we tread, because we tread it; the language we speak, because we speak it; the government that rules us, merely because it rules us? It means nothing, or it means nonsense. Again; are we to understand by patriotism a preference for the interests of our own nation under all circumstances, even to the sacrifice of those of other nations—it is a vice.

In continental Europe, of late years, the words patriotism and patriot have been used in a more enlarged sense than it is usual here to attribute to them, or than is attached to them in Great Britain. Since the political struggles of France, Italy, Spain, and Greece, the word patriotism has been employed, throughout continental Europe, to express a love of the public good; a preference for the interests of the many to those of the few; a desire for the emancipation of the human race from the thrall of despotism, religious and civil; in short, patriotism there is used rather to express the interest felt in the human race in general, than that felt for any country, or inhabitants of a country, in particular. And patriot, in like manner, is employed to signify a lover of human liberty and human improvement, rather than a mere lover of the country in which he lives, or the tribe to which he belongs. Used in this sense, patriotism is a virtue, and a patriot a virtuous man. With such an interpretation, a patriot is a useful member of society, capable of enlarging all minds, and bettering all hearts with which he comes in contact; a useful member of the human family, capable of establishing fundamental principles, and of merging his own interests, those of his associates, and those of his nation, in the interests of the human race. Laurels and statues are vain things, and mischievous as they are childish; but, could we imagine them of use, on *such* a patriot alone could they be with any reason bestowed.

> Is there a thought can fill the human mind
> More pure, more vast, more generous, more refin'd
> Than that which guides the enlightened patriot's toil:
> Not he, whose view is bounded by his soil:
> Not he, whose narrow heart can only shrine
> The land—the people that he calleth *mine*;
> Not he, who to set up that land on high,
> Will make whole nations bleed, whole nations die;
> Not he, who, calling that land's rights his pride,
> Trampleth the rights of all the earth beside;
> No!—He it is, the just, the generous soul!
> Who owneth brotherhood with either pole,
> Stretches from realm to realm his spacious mind,
> And guards the weal of all the human kind,
> Holds Freedom's banner o'er the earth unfurl'd,
> And stands the guardian patriot of a world!

If such a patriotism as we have last considered should seem likely to obtain in any country, it should be certainly in this. In this, which is truly the home of all nations, and in the veins of whose citizens flows the blood of every people on the globe. Patriotism, in the exclusive meaning, is surely not made for America. Mischievous every where, it were here both mischievous and absurd. The very origin of the people is opposed to it. The institutions, in their principle, militate against it. The day we are celebrating protests against it. It is for Americans, more especially, to nourish a nobler sentiment; one more consistent with their origin, and more conducive to their future improvement. It is for them more especially to know why they love their country, and to *feel* that they love it, not because it *is* their country, but because it is the palladium of human liberty —the favoured scene of human improvement. It is for them, more especially, to know why they honor their institutions, and to *feel* that they honor them because they are based on just principles. It is for them, more especially, to examine their institutions, because they have the means of improving them; to examine their laws, because at will they can alter them. It is for them to lay aside luxury, whose wealth is in industry; idle parade, whose strength is in knowledge; ambitious distinctions, whose principle is equality. It is for them not to rest satisfied with words, who can seize upon things; and to remember, that equality means, not the mere equality of political rights, however valuable, but equality of instruction, and equality in virtue; and that liberty means, not the mere voting at elections, but the free and fearless exercise of the mental faculties, and that self-possession which springs out of well-reasoned opinions and consistent practice. It is for them to honor principles rather than men—to commemorate events rather than days: when they rejoice, to know for what they rejoice, and to rejoice only for what has brought, and what brings, peace and happiness to men. The event we commemorate this day has procured much of both, and shall procure, in the onward course of human improvement, more than we can now conceive of. For this—for the good obtained, and yet in store for our race—let us rejoice! But let us rejoice as men, not as children—as human beings, rather than as Americans—as reasoning beings, not as ignorants. So shall we rejoice to good purpose, and in good feeling; so shall we improve the victory once on this day achieved, until all mankind hold with us the jubilee of independence.

ANDREW JACKSON

First Inaugural Address

Washington, D.C. March 4, 1829

FELLOW-CITIZENS: About to undertake the arduous duties that I have been appointed to perform by the choice of a free people, I avail myself of this customary and solemn occasion to express the gratitude which their confidence inspires and to acknowledge the accountability which my situation enjoins. While the magnitude of their interests convinces me that no thanks can be adequate to the honor they have conferred, it admonishes me that the best return I can make is the zealous dedication of my humble abilities to their service and their good.

As the instrument of the Federal Constitution it will devolve on me for a stated period to execute the laws of the United States, to superintend their foreign and their confederate relations, to manage their revenue, to command their forces, and, by communications to the Legislature, to watch over and to promote their interests generally. And the principles of action by which I shall endeavor to accomplish this circle of duties it is now proper for me briefly to explain.

In administering the laws of Congress I shall keep steadily in view the limitations as well as the extent of the Executive power, trusting thereby to discharge the functions of my office without transcending its authority. With foreign nations it will be my study to preserve peace and to cultivate friendship on fair and honorable terms, and in the adjustment of any differences that may exist or arise to exhibit the forbearance becoming a powerful nation rather than the sensibility belonging to a gallant people.

In such measures as I may be called on to pursue in regard to the rights of the separate States I hope to be animated by a proper respect for those sovereign members of our Union, taking care not to confound the powers they have reserved to themselves with those they have granted to the Confederacy.

The management of the public revenue—that searching operation in all governments—is among the most delicate and important trusts in ours, and it will, of course, demand no inconsiderable share of my official solicitude. Under every aspect in which it can be considered it would appear that advantage must result from the observance of a strict and faithful economy. This I shall aim at the more anxiously both because it will facilitate the extinguishment of the national debt, the unnecessary duration of which is incompatible with real independence, and because it will counteract that tendency to public and private profligacy which a profuse expenditure of money by the Government is but too apt to engender. Powerful auxiliaries to the attainment of this desirable end are to be found in the regulations provided by the wisdom of Congress for the specific appropriation of public money and the prompt accountability of public officers.

With regard to a proper selection of the subjects of impost with a view to revenue, it would seem to me that the spirit of equity, caution, and compromise in which the Constitution was formed requires that the great interests of agriculture, commerce, and manufactures should be equally favored, and that perhaps the only exception to this rule should consist in the peculiar encouragement of any products of either of them that may be found essential to our national independence.

Internal improvement and the diffusion of knowledge, so far as they can be promoted by the constitutional acts of the Federal Government, are of high importance.

Considering standing armies as dangerous to free governments in time of peace, I shall not seek to enlarge our present establishment, nor disregard that salutary lesson of political experience which teaches that the military should be held subordinate to the civil power. The gradual increase of our Navy, whose flag has displayed in distant climes our skill in navigation and our fame in arms; the preservation of our forts, arsenals, and dockyards, and the introduction of progressive improvements in the discipline and science of both branches of our military service are so plainly prescribed by prudence that

I should be excused for omitting their mention sooner than for enlarging on their importance. But the bulwark of our defense is the national militia, which in the present state of our intelligence and population must render us invincible. As long as our Government is administered for the good of the people, and is regulated by their will; as long as it secures to us the rights of person and of property, liberty of conscience and of the press, it will be worth defending; and so long as it is worth defending a patriotic militia will cover it with an impenetrable ægis. Partial injuries and occasional mortifications we may be subjected to, but a million of armed freemen, possessed of the means of war, can never be conquered by a foreign foe. To any just system, therefore, calculated to strengthen this natural safeguard of the country I shall cheerfully lend all the aid in my power.

It will be my sincere and constant desire to observe toward the Indian tribes within our limits a just and liberal policy, and to give that humane and considerate attention to their rights and their wants which is consistent with the habits of our Government and the feelings of our people.

The recent demonstration of public sentiment inscribes on the list of Executive duties, in characters too legible to be overlooked, the task of *reform*, which will require particularly the correction of those abuses that have brought the patronage of the Federal Government into conflict with the freedom of elections, and the counteraction of those causes which have disturbed the rightful course of appointment and have placed or continued power in unfaithful or incompetent hands.

In the performance of a task thus generally delineated I shall endeavor to select men whose diligence and talents will insure in their respective stations able and faithful cooperation, depending for the advancement of the public service more on the integrity and zeal of the public officers than on their numbers.

A diffidence, perhaps too just, in my own qualifications will teach me to look with reverence to the examples of public virtue left by my illustrious predecessors, and with veneration to the lights that flow from the mind that founded and the mind that reformed our system. The same diffidence induces me to hope for instruction and aid from the coordinate branches of the Government, and for the indulgence and support of my fellow-citizens generally. And a firm reliance on the goodness of that Power whose providence mercifully protected our national infancy, and has since upheld our liberties in various vicissitudes, encourages me to offer up my ardent supplications that He will continue to make our beloved country the object of His divine care and gracious benediction.

DANIEL WEBSTER

Second Reply to Hayne

Washington, D.C., January 26–27, 1830

M R. PRESIDENT,—When the mariner has been tossed for many days in thick weather, and on an unknown sea, he naturally avails himself of the first pause in the storm, the earliest glance of the sun, to take his latitude, and ascertain how far the elements have driven him from his true course. Let us imitate this prudence, and, before we float farther on the waves of this debate, refer to the point from which we departed, that we may at least be able to conjecture where we now are. I ask for the reading of the resolution before the Senate.

The Secretary read the resolution, as follows:—

Resolved, That the Committee on Public Lands be instructed to inquire and report the quantity of public lands remaining unsold within each State and Territory, and whether it be expedient to limit for a certain period the sales of the public lands to such lands only as have heretofore been offered for sale, and are now subject to entry at the minimum price. And, also, whether the office of Surveyor-General, and some of the land offices, may not be abolished without detriment to the public interest; or whether it be expedient to adopt measures to hasten the sales and extend more rapidly the surveys of the public lands.

We have thus heard, Sir, what the resolution is which is actually before us for consideration; and it will readily occur to every one, that it is almost the only subject about which something has not been said in the speech, running through two days, by which the Senate has been entertained by the gentleman from South Carolina. Every topic in the wide range of our public affairs, whether past or present,—every thing, general or local, whether belonging to national politics or party politics,—seems to have attracted more or less of the honorable member's attention, save only the resolution before the Senate. He has spoken of every thing but the public lands; they have escaped his notice. To that subject, in all his excursions, he has not paid even the cold respect of a passing glance.

When this debate, Sir, was to be resumed on Thursday morning, it so happened that it would have been convenient for me to be elsewhere. The honorable member, however, did not incline to put off the discussion to another day. He had a shot, he said, to return, and he wished to discharge it. That shot, Sir, which he thus kindly informed us was coming, that we might stand out of the way, or prepare ourselves to fall by it and die with decency, has now been received. Under all advantages, and with expectation awakened by the tone which preceded it, it has been discharged, and has spent its force. It may become me to say no more of its effect, than that, if nobody is found, after all, either killed or wounded, it is not the first time, in the history of human affairs, that the vigor and success of the war have not quite come up to the lofty and sounding phrase of the manifesto.

The gentleman, Sir, in declining to postpone the debate, told the Senate, with the emphasis of his hand upon his heart, that there was something rankling *here,* which he wished to relieve. [Mr. Hayne rose, and disclaimed having used the word *rankling.*] It would not, Mr. President, be safe for the honorable member to appeal to those around him, upon the question whether he did in fact make use of that word. But he may have been unconscious of it. At any rate, it is enough that he disclaims it. But still, with or without the use of that particular word, he had yet something *here,* he said, of which he wished to rid himself by an immediate reply. In this respect, Sir, I have a great advantage over the honorable gentleman. There is nothing *here,* Sir, which gives me the slightest uneasiness; neither fear, nor anger, nor that which is sometimes more troublesome than either, the consciousness of having been in the wrong. There is nothing, either originating *here,* or now received *here* by the gentleman's shot. Nothing originating here, for I had not the slightest feeling of unkindness towards the honorable member. Some passages, it is true, had occurred since our acquaintance in this body, which I could have wished might have been otherwise; but I had used philosophy and forgotten them. I paid the honorable member the attention of listening with respect to his first speech; and when he sat down, though surprised, and I must even say astonished, at some of his opinions, nothing was farther from my intention than to commence any personal warfare. Through the whole of the few remarks I made in answer, I avoided, studiously and carefully, every thing which I thought possible to be construed into disrespect. And, Sir, while there is thus nothing originating *here* which I have wished at any time, or now wish, to discharge, I must repeat, also, that nothing has been received *here* which *rankles,* or in any way gives me annoyance. I will not accuse the honorable member of violating the rules of civilized war; I will not say, that he poisoned his arrows. But whether his shafts were, or were not, dipped in that which would have caused rankling if they had reached their destination, there was not, as it happened, quite strength enough in the bow to bring them to their mark. If he wishes now to gather up those shafts, he must look for them elsewhere; they will not be found fixed and quivering in the object at which they were aimed.

The honorable member complained that I had slept on his speech. I must have slept on it, or not slept at all. The moment the honorable member sat down, his friend from Missouri rose, and, with much honeyed commendation of the speech, suggested that the impressions which it had produced were too charming and delightful to be disturbed by other sentiments or other sounds, and proposed that the Senate should adjourn. Would it have been quite amiable in me, Sir, to interrupt this excellent good feeling? Must I not have been absolutely malicious, if I could have thrust myself forward, to destroy sensations thus pleasing? Was it not much better and kinder, both to sleep upon them myself, and to allow others also the pleasure of sleeping upon them? But if it be meant, by sleeping upon his speech, that I took time to prepare a reply to it, it is quite a mistake. Owing to other engagements, I could not employ even the interval between the adjournment of the Senate and its meeting the next morning, in attention to the subject of this debate. Nevertheless, Sir, the mere matter of fact is undoubtedly true. I did sleep on the gentleman's speech, and slept soundly. And I slept equally well on his speech of yesterday, to which I am now replying. It is quite possible that in this respect, also, I possess some advantage over the honorable member, attributable, doubtless, to a cooler temperament on my part; for, in truth, I slept upon his speeches remarkably well.

But the gentleman inquires why *he* was made the object of such a reply. Why was *he* singled out? If an attack has been made on the East, he, he assures us, did not begin it; it was made by the gentleman from Missouri. Sir, I answered the gentleman's speech because I happened to hear it; and because, also, I chose to give an answer to that speech, which, if unanswered, I thought most likely to produce injurious impressions. I did not stop to inquire who was the original drawer of the bill. I found a responsible indorser before me, and it was my purpose to hold him liable, and to bring him to his just responsibility, without delay. But, Sir, this interrogatory of the honorable member was only introductory to another. He proceeded to ask me whether I had turned upon him, in this debate, from the consciousness that I should find an overmatch, if I ventured on a contest with his friend from Missouri. If, Sir, the honorable member, *modestiæ gratia*, had chosen thus to defer to his friend, and to pay him a compliment, without intentional disparagement to others, it would have been quite according to the friendly courtesies of debate, and not at all ungrateful to my own feelings. I am not one of those, Sir, who esteem any tribute of regard, whether light and occasional, or more serious and deliberate, which may be bestowed on others, as so much unjustly withholden from themselves. But the tone and manner of the gentleman's question forbid me thus to interpret it. I am not at liberty to consider it as nothing more than a civility to his friend. It had an air of taunt and disparagement, something of the loftiness of asserted superiority, which does not allow me to pass it over without notice. It was put as a question for me to answer, and so put as if it were difficult for me to answer, whether I deemed the member from Missouri an overmatch for myself, in debate here. It seems to me, Sir, that this is extraordinary language, and an extraordinary tone, for the discussions of this body.

Matches and overmatches! Those terms are more applicable elsewhere than here, and fitter for other assemblies than this. Sir, the gentleman seems to forget where and what we are. This is a Senate, a Senate of equals, of men of individual honor and personal character, and of absolute independence. We know no masters, we acknowledge no dictators. This is a hall for mutual consultation and discussion; not an arena for the exhibition of champions. I offer myself, Sir, as a match for no man; I throw the challenge of debate at no man's feet. But then, Sir, since the honorable member has put the question in a manner that calls for an answer, I will give him an answer; and I tell him, that, holding myself to be the humblest of the members here, I yet know nothing in the arm of his friend from Missouri, either alone or when aided by the arm of *his* friend from South Carolina, that need deter even me from espousing whatever opinions I may choose to espouse, from debating whenever I may choose to debate, or from speaking whatever I may see fit to say, on the floor of the Senate. Sir, when uttered as matter of commendation or compliment, I should dissent from nothing which the honorable member might say of his friend. Still less do I put forth any pretensions of my own. But when put to me as matter of taunt, I throw it back, and say to the gentleman, that he could possibly say nothing less likely than such a comparison to wound my pride of personal character. The anger of its tone rescued the remark from intentional irony, which otherwise, probably, would have been its general acceptation. But, Sir, if it be imagined that by this mutual quotation and commendation; if it be supposed that, by casting the characters of the drama, assigning to each his part, to one the attack, to another the cry of onset; or if it be thought that, by a loud and empty vaunt of anticipated victory, any laurels are to be won here; if it be imagined, especially, that any, or all these things will shake any purpose of mine, I can tell the honorable member, once for all, that he is greatly mistaken, and that he is dealing with one of whose temper and character he has yet much to learn. Sir, I shall not allow myself, on this occasion, I hope on no occasion, to be betrayed into any loss of temper; but if provoked, as I trust I never shall be, into crimination and recrimination, the honorable member may perhaps find that, in that contest, there will be blows to take as well as blows to give; that others can state comparisons as significant, at least, as his own, and that his impunity may possibly demand of him whatever powers of taunt and sarcasm he may possess. I commend him to a prudent husbandry of his resources.

But, Sir, the Coalition! The Coalition! Ay, "the murdered Coalition!" The gentleman asks, if I were led or frighted into this debate by the spectre of the Coalition. "Was it the ghost of the murdered Coalition," he exclaims, "which haunted the member from Massachusetts; and which, like the ghost of Banquo, would never down?" "The murdered Coalition!" Sir, this charge of a coalition, in reference to the late administration, is not original with the honorable member. It did not spring up in the Senate. Whether as a fact, as an argument, or as an embellishment, it is all borrowed. He adopts it, indeed, from a very low origin, and a still lower present condition. It is one of the thousand calumnies with which the press teemed, during an excited political canvass. It was a charge, of which there was not only no proof or probability, but which was in itself wholly impossible to be true. No man of common information ever believed a syllable of it. Yet it was of that class of falsehoods, which, by continued repetition, through all the organs of detraction and abuse, are capable of misleading those who are already far misled; and of further fanning passion already kindling into flame. Doubtless it served in its day, and in greater or less degree, the end designed by it. Having done that, it has sunk into the general mass of stale and loathed calumnies. It is the very cast-off slough of a polluted and shameless press. Incapable of further mischief, it lies in the sewer, lifeless and despised. It is not now, Sir, in the power of the honorable member to give it dignity or decency, by attempting to elevate it, and to introduce it into the Senate. He cannot change it from what it is, an object of general disgust and scorn. On the contrary, the contact, if he choose to touch it, is more likely to drag him down, down, to the place where it lies itself.

But, Sir, the honorable member was not, for other reasons, entirely happy in his allusion to the story of Banquo's murder and Banquo's ghost. It was not, I think, the friends, but the enemies of the murdered Banquo, at whose bidding his spirit would not *down*. The honorable gentleman is fresh in his reading of the English classics, and can put me right if I am wrong; but according to my poor recollection, it was at those who had begun with caresses and ended with foul and treacherous murder that the gory locks were shaken. The ghost of Banquo, like that of Hamlet, was an honest ghost. It disturbed no innocent man. It knew where its appearance would strike terror, and who would cry out, A ghost! It made itself visible in the right quarter, and compelled the guilty and the conscience-smitten, and none others, to start, with,

> "Pr'ythee, see there! behold!—look! lo
> If I stand here, I saw him!"

Their eyeballs were seared (was it not so, Sir?) who had thought to shield themselves by concealing their own hand, and laying the imputation of the crime on a low and hireling agency in wickedness; who had vainly attempted to stifle the workings of their own coward consciences by ejaculating through white lips and chattering teeth, "Thou canst not say I did it!" I have misread the great poet if those who had no way partaken in the deed of the death, either found that they were, or *feared that they should be,* pushed from their stools by the ghost of the slain, or exclaimed to a spectre created by their own fears and their own remorse, "Avaunt! and quit our sight!"

There is another particular, Sir, in which the honorable member's quick perception of resemblances might, I should think, have seen something in the story of Banquo, making it not altogether a subject of the most pleasant contemplation. Those who murdered Banquo, what did they win by it? Substantial good? Permanent power? Or disappointment, rather, and sore mortification; dust and ashes, the common fate of vaulting ambition overleaping itself? Did not even-handed justice ere long commend the poisoned chalice to their own lips? Did they not soon find that for another they had "filed their mind"? that their ambition, though apparently for the moment successful, had but put a barren sceptre in their grasp? Ay, Sir,

> "a barren sceptre in their gripe,
> *Thence to be wrenched with an unlineal hand,*
> *No son of theirs succeeding."*

Sir, I need pursue the allusion no farther. I leave the honorable gentleman to run it out at his leisure, and to derive from it all the gratification it is calculated to administer. If he finds himself pleased with the associations, and prepared to be quite satisfied, though the parallel should be entirely completed, I had almost said, I am satisfied also; but that I shall think of. Yes, Sir, I will think of that.

In the course of my observations the other day, Mr. President, I paid a passing tribute of respect to a very worthy man, Mr. Dane of Massachusetts. It so happened that he drew the Ordinance of 1787, for the government of the Northwestern Territory. A man of so much ability, and so little pretence; of so great a capacity to do good, and so unmixed a disposition to do it for its own sake; a gentleman who had acted an important part, forty years ago, in a measure the influence of which is still deeply felt in the very matter which was the subject of debate, might, I thought, receive from me a commendatory recognition. But the honorable member was inclined to be facetious on the subject. He was rather disposed to make it matter of ridicule, that I had introduced into the debate the name of one Nathan Dane, of whom he assures us he had never before heard. Sir, if the honorable member had never before heard of Mr. Dane, I am sorry for it. It shows him less acquainted with the public men of the country than I had supposed. Let me tell him, however, that a sneer from him at the mention of the name of Mr. Dane is in bad taste. It may well be a high mark of ambition, Sir, either with the honorable gentleman or myself, to accomplish as much to make our names known to advantage, and remembered with gratitude, as Mr. Dane has accomplished. But the truth is, Sir, I suspect, that Mr. Dane lives a little too far north. He is of Massachusetts, and too near the north star to be reached by the honorable gentleman's telescope. If his sphere had happened to range south of Mason and Dixon's line, he might, probably, have come within the scope of his vision.

I spoke, Sir, of the Ordinance of 1787, which prohibits slavery, in all future times, northwest of the Ohio, as a measure of great wisdom and foresight, and one which had been attended with highly beneficial and permanent consequences. I suppose that, on this point, no two gentlemen in the Senate could entertain different opinions. But the simple expression of this sentiment has led the gentleman, not only into a labored defence of slavery, in the abstract, and on principle, but also into a warm accusation against me, as having attacked the system of domestic slavery now existing in the Southern States. For all this, there was not the slightest foundation, in any thing said or intimated by me. I did not utter a single word which any ingenuity could torture into an attack on the slavery of the South. I said, only, that it was highly wise and useful, in legislating for the Northwestern country while it was yet a wilderness, to prohibit the introduction of slaves; and I added, that I presumed there was no reflecting and intelligent person, in the neighboring State of Kentucky, who would doubt that, if the same prohibition had been extended, at the same early period, over that commonwealth, her strength and population would, at this day, have been far greater than they are. If these opinions be thought doubtful, they are nevertheless, I trust, neither extraordinary nor disrespectful. They attack nobody and menace nobody. And yet, Sir, the gentleman's optics have discovered, even in the mere expression of this sentiment, what he calls the very spirit of the Missouri question! He represents me as making an onset on the whole South, and manifesting a spirit which would interfere with, and disturb, their domestic condition!

Sir, this injustice no otherwise surprises me, than as it is committed here, and committed without the slightest pretence of ground for it. I say it only surprises me as being done here; for I know full well, that it is, and has been, the settled policy of some persons in the South, for years, to represent the people of the North as disposed to interfere with them in their own exclusive and peculiar concerns. This is a delicate and sensitive point in Southern feeling; and of late years it has always been touched, and generally with effect, whenever the object has been to unite the whole South against Northern men or Northern measures. This feeling, always carefully kept alive, and maintained at too intense a heat to admit discrimination or reflection, is a lever of great power in our political machine. It moves vast bodies, and gives to them one and the same direction. But it is without adequate cause, and the suspicion which exists is wholly groundless. There is not, and never has been, a disposition in the North to interfere with these interests of the South. Such interference has never been supposed to be within the power of government; nor has it been in any way attempted. The slavery of the South has always been regarded as a matter of domestic policy, left with the States themselves, and with which the federal government had nothing to do. Certainly, Sir, I am, and ever have been, of that opinion. The gentleman, indeed, argues that slavery, in the abstract, is no evil. Most assuredly I need not say I differ with him, altogether and most widely, on that point. I regard domestic slavery as one of the greatest evils, both moral and political. But whether it be a malady, and whether it be curable, and if so, by what means; or, on the other hand, whether it be the *vulnus immedicabile* of the social system, I leave it to those whose right and duty it is to inquire and to decide. And this I believe, Sir, is, and uniformly has been, the sentiment of the North. Let us look a little at the history of this matter.

When the present Constitution was submitted for the ratification of the people, there were those who imagined that the powers of the government which it proposed to establish might, in some possible mode, be exerted in measures tending to the abolition of slavery. This suggestion would of course attract much attention in the Southern conventions. In that of Virginia, Governor Randolph said: —

I hope there is none here, who, considering the subject in the calm light of philosophy, will make an objection dishonorable to Virginia; that, at the moment they are securing the rights of their citizens, an objection is started, that there is a spark of hope that those unfortunate men now held in bondage may, by the operation of the general government, be made free.

At the very first Congress, petitions on the subject were presented, if I mistake not, from different States. The Pennsylvania society for promoting the abolition of slavery took a lead, and laid before Congress a memorial, praying Congress to promote the abolition by such powers as it possessed. This memorial was referred, in the House of Representatives, to a select committee, consisting of Mr. Foster, of New Hampshire, Mr. Gerry of Massachusetts, Mr. Huntington of Connecticut, Mr. Lawrence of New York, Mr. Sinnickson of New Jersey, Mr. Hartley of Pennsylvania, and Mr. Parker of Virginia; all of them, Sir, as you will observe, Northern men but the last. This committee made a report, which was referred to a committee of the whole House, and there considered and discussed for several days; and being amended, although without material alteration, it was made to express three distinct propositions, on the subject of slavery and the slave-trade. First, in the words of the Constitution, that Congress could not, prior to the year 1808, prohibit the migration or importation of such persons as any of the States then existing should think proper to admit; and secondly, that Congress had authority to restrain the citizens of the United States from carrying on the African slave-trade, for the purpose of supplying foreign countries. On this proposition, our early laws against those who engage in that traffic are founded. The third proposition, and that which bears on the present question, was expressed in the following terms:—

Resolved, That Congress have no authority to interfere in the emancipation of slaves, or in the treatment of them in any of the States; it remaining with the several States alone to provide rules and regulations therein which humanity and true policy may require.

This resolution received the sanction of the House of Representatives so early as March, 1790. And now, Sir, the honorable member will allow me to remind him, that not only were the select committee who reported the resolution, with a single exception, all Northern men, but also that, of the members then composing the House of Representatives, a large majority, I believe nearly two thirds, were Northern men also.

The House agreed to insert these resolutions in its journal, and from that day to this it has never been maintained or contended at the North, that Congress had any authority to regulate or interfere with the condition of slaves in the several States. No Northern gentleman, to my knowledge, has moved any such question in either House of Congress.

The fears of the South, whatever fears they might have entertained, were allayed and quieted by this early decision; and so remained till they were excited afresh, without cause, but for collateral and indirect purposes. When it became necessary, or was thought so, by some political persons, to find an unvarying ground for the exclusion of Northern men from confidence and from lead in the affairs of the republic, then, and not till then, the cry was raised, and the feeling industriously excited, that the influence of Northern men in the public counsels would endanger the relation of master and slave. For myself, I claim no other merit than that this gross and enormous injustice towards the whole North has not wrought upon me to change my opinions or my political conduct. I hope I am above violating my principles, even under the smart of injury and false imputations. Unjust suspicions and undeserved reproach, whatever pain I may experience from them, will not induce me, I trust, to overstep the limits of constitutional duty, or to encroach on the rights of others. The domestic slavery of the Southern States I leave where I find it,—in the hands of their own governments. It is their affair, not mine. Nor do I complain of the peculiar effect which the magnitude of that population has had in the distribution of power under this federal government. We know, Sir, that the representation of the States in the other house is not equal. We know that great advantage in that respect is enjoyed by the slave-holding States; and we know, too, that the intended equivalent for that advantage, that is to say, the imposition of direct taxes in the same ratio, has become merely nominal, the habit of the government being almost invariably to collect its revenue from other sources and in other modes. Nevertheless, I do not complain; nor would I countenance any movement to alter this arrangement of representation. It is the original bargain, the compact; let it stand; let the advantage of it be fully enjoyed. The Union itself is too full of benefit to be hazarded in propositions for changing its original basis. I go for the Constitution as it is, and for the Union as it is. But I am resolved not to submit in silence to accusations, either against myself individually or against the North, wholly unfounded and unjust; accusations which impute to us a disposition to evade the constitutional compact, and to extend the power of the government over the internal laws and domestic condition of the States. All such accusations, wherever and whenever made, all insinuations of the existence of any such purposes, I know and feel to be groundless and injurious. And we must confide in Southern gentlemen themselves; we must trust to those whose integrity of heart and magnanimity of feeling will lead them to a desire to maintain and disseminate truth, and who possess the means of its diffusion with the Southern public; we must leave it to them to disabuse that public of its prejudices. But in the mean time, for my own part, I shall continue to act justly, whether those towards whom justice is exercised receive it with candor or with contumely.

Having had occasion to recur to the Ordinance of 1787, in order to defend myself against the inferences which the honorable member has chosen to draw from my former observations on that subject, I am not willing now entirely to take leave of it without another remark. It need hardly be said, that that paper expresses just sentiments on the great subject of civil and religious liberty. Such sentiments were common, and abound in all our state papers of that day. But this Ordinance did that which was not so common, and which is not even now universal; that is, it set forth and declared it to be a high and binding duty of government itself to support schools and advance the means of education, on the plain reason that religion, morality, and knowledge are necessary to good government, and to the happiness of mankind. One observation further. The important provision incorporated into the Constitution of the United States, and into several of those of the States, and recently, as we have seen, adopted into the reformed constitution of Virginia, restraining legislative power in questions of private right, and from impairing the obligation of contracts, is first introduced and established, as far as I am informed, as matter of express written constitutional law, in this Ordinance of 1787. And I must add, also, in regard to the author of the Ordinance, who has not had the happiness to attract the gentleman's notice heretofore, nor to avoid his sarcasm now, that he was chairman of that select committee of the old Congress, whose report first expressed the strong sense of that body, that the old Confederation was not adequate to the exigencies of the country and recommended to the States to send delegates to the convention which formed the present Constitution.

An attempt has been made to transfer from the North to the South the honor of this exclusion of slavery from the Northwestern Territory. The journal, without argument or comment, refutes such attempts. The cession by Virginia was made in March, 1784. On the 19th of April following, a committee, consisting of Messrs. Jefferson, Chase, and Howell, reported a plan for a temporary government of the territory, in which was this article: "That, after the year 1800, there shall be neither slavery nor involuntary servitude in any of the said States, otherwise than in punishment of crimes, whereof the party shall have been convicted." Mr. Spaight of North Carolina moved to strike out this paragraph. The question was put, according to the form then practised, "Shall these words stand as a part of the plan?" New Hampshire, Massachusetts, Rhode Island, Connecticut, New York, New Jersey, and Pennsylvania, seven States, voted in the affirmative; Maryland, Virginia, and South Carolina, in the negative. North Carolina was divided. As the consent of nine States was necessary, the words could not stand, and were struck out accordingly. Mr. Jefferson voted for the clause, but was overruled by his colleagues.

In March of the next year (1785), Mr. King of Massachusetts, seconded by Mr. Ellery of Rhode Island, proposed the formerly rejected article, with this addition: "And that this regulation shall be an article of compact, and remain a fundamental principle of the constitutions between the thirteen original States, and each of the States described in the resolve." On this clause, which provided the adequate and thorough security, the eight Northern States at that time voted affirmatively, and the four Southern States negatively. The votes of nine States were not yet obtained, and thus the provision was again rejected by the Southern States. The perseverance of the North held out, and two years afterwards the object was attained. It is no derogation from the credit, whatever that may be, of drawing the Ordinance, that its principles had before been prepared and discussed, in the form of resolutions. If one should reason in that way, what would become of the distinguished honor of the author of the Declaration of Independence? There is not a sentiment in that paper which had not been voted and resolved in the assemblies, and other popular bodies in the country, over and over again.

But the honorable member has now found out that this gentleman, Mr. Dane, was a member of the Hartford Convention. However uninformed the honorable member may be of characters and occurrences at the North, it would seem that he has at his elbow, on this occasion, some high-minded and lofty spirit, some magnanimous and true-hearted monitor, possessing the means of local knowledge, and ready to supply the honorable member with every thing, down even to forgotten and moth-eaten two-penny pamphlets, which may be used to

the disadvantage of his own country. But as to the Hartford
Convention, Sir, allow me to say, that the proceedings of that
body seem now to be less read and studied in New England
than farther South. They appear to be looked to, not in New
England, but elsewhere, for the purpose of seeing how far they
may serve as a precedent. But they will not answer the purpose,
they are quite too tame. The latitude in which they originated
was too cold. Other conventions, of more recent existence,
have gone a whole bar's length beyond it. The learned doctors
of Colleton and Abbeville have pushed their commentaries
on the Hartford collect so far, that the original text-writers are
thrown entirely into the shade. I have nothing to do, Sir, with
the Hartford Convention. Its journal, which the gentleman
has quoted, I never read. So far as the honorable member may
discover in its proceedings a spirit in any degree resembling
that which was avowed and justified in those other conventions to which I have alluded, or so far as those proceedings
can be shown to be disloyal to the Constitution, or tending to
disunion, so far I shall be as ready as any one to bestow on
them reprehension and censure.

Having dwelt long on this convention, and other occurrences of that day, in the hope, probably, (which will not be
gratified,) that I should leave the course of this debate to follow him at length in those excursions, the honorable member
returned, and attempted another object. He referred to a
speech of mine in the other house, the same which I had occasion to allude to myself, the other day; and has quoted a passage or two from it, with a bold, though uneasy and laboring,
air of confidence, as if he had detected in me an inconsistency.
Judging from the gentleman's manner, a stranger to the course
of the debate and to the point in discussion would have imagined, from so triumphant a tone, that the honorable member
was about to overwhelm me with a manifest contradiction.
Any one who heard him, and who had not heard what I had,
in fact, previously said, must have thought me routed and discomfited, as the gentleman had promised. Sir, a breath blows
all this triumph away. There is not the slightest difference in
the purport of my remarks on the two occasions. What I said
here on Wednesday is in exact accordance with the opinion ex-

pressed by me in the other house in 1825. Though the gentleman had the metaphysics of Hudibras, though he were able

> "to sever and divide
> A hair twixt north and northwest side,"

he yet could not insert his metaphysical scissors between the
fair reading of my remarks in 1825, and what I said here last
week. There is not only no contradiction, no difference, but,
in truth, too exact a similarity, both in thought and language,
to be entirely in just taste. I had myself quoted the same
speech; had recurred to it, and spoke with it open before me;
and much of what I said was little more than a repetition from
it. In order to make finishing work with this alleged contradiction, permit me to recur to the origin of this debate, and review its course. This seems expedient, and may be done as well
now as at any time.

Well, then, its history is this. The honorable member from
Connecticut moved a resolution, which constitutes the first
branch of that which is now before us; that is to say, a resolution, instructing the committee on public lands to inquire into
the expediency of limiting, for a certain period, the sales of the
public lands, to such as have heretofore been offered for sale;
and whether sundry offices connected with the sales of the
lands might not be abolished without detriment to the public
service. In the progress of the discussion which arose on this
resolution, an honorable member from New Hampshire moved
to amend the resolution, so as entirely to reverse its object;
that is, to strike it all out, and insert a direction to the committee to inquire into the expediency of adopting measures to
hasten the sales, and extend more rapidly the surveys, of the
lands.

The honorable member from Maine suggested that both
those propositions might well enough go for consideration to
the committee; and in this state of the question, the member
from South Carolina addressed the Senate in his first speech.
He rose, he said, to give us his own free thoughts on the
public lands. I saw him rise with pleasure, and listened with expectation, though before he concluded I was filled with surprise. Certainly, I was never more surprised, than to find him

following up, to the extent he did, the sentiments and opinions which the gentleman from Missouri had put forth, and which it is known he has long entertained.

I need not repeat at large the general topics of the honorable gentleman's speech. When he said yesterday that he did not attack the Eastern States, he certainly must have forgotten, not only particular remarks, but the whole drift and tenor of his speech; unless he means by not attacking, that he did not commence hostilities, but that another had preceded him in the attack. He, in the first place, disapproved of the whole course of the government, for forty years, in regard to its disposition of the public lands; and then, turning northward and eastward, and fancying he had found a cause for alleged narrowness and niggardliness in the "accursed policy" of the tariff, to which he represented the people of New England as wedded, he went on for a full hour with remarks, the whole scope of which was to exhibit the results of this policy, in feelings and in measures unfavorable to the West. I thought his opinions unfounded and erroneous, as to the general course of the government, and ventured to reply to them.

The gentleman had remarked on the analogy of other cases, and quoted the conduct of European governments towards their own subjects settling on this continent, as in point, to show that we had been harsh and rigid in selling, when we should have given the public lands to settlers without price. I thought the honorable member had suffered his judgment to be betrayed by a false analogy; that he was struck with an appearance of resemblance where there was no real similitude. I think so still. The first settlers of North America were enterprising spirits, engaged in private adventure, or fleeing from tyranny at home. When arrived here, they were forgotten by the mother country, or remembered only to be oppressed. Carried away again by the appearance of analogy, or struck with the eloquence of the passage, the honorable member yesterday observed, that the conduct of government towards the Western emigrants, or my representation of it, brought to his mind a celebrated speech in the British Parliament. It was, Sir, the speech of Colonel Barre. On the question of the stamp act, or tea tax, I forget which, Colonel Barre had heard a member on the treasury bench argue, that the people of the United States, being British colonists, planted by the maternal care, nourished by the indulgence, and protected by the arms of England, would not grudge their mite to relieve the mother country from the heavy burden under which she groaned. The language of Colonel Barre, in reply to this, was,—"They planted by your care? Your oppression planted them in America. They fled from your tyranny, and grew by your neglect of them. So soon as you began to care for them, you showed your care by sending persons to spy out their liberties, misrepresent their character, prey upon them, and eat out their substance."

And how does the honorable gentleman mean to maintain, that language like this is applicable to the conduct of the government of the United States towards the Western emigrants, or to any representation given by me of that conduct? Were the settlers in the West driven thither by our oppression? Have they flourished only by our neglect of them? Has the government done nothing but prey upon them, and eat out their substance? Sir, this fervid eloquence of the British speaker, just when and where it was uttered, and fit to remain an exercise for the schools, is not a little out of place, when it is brought thence to be applied here, to the conduct of our own country towards her own citizens. From America to England, it may be true, from Americans to their own government, it would be strange language. Let us leave it, to be recited and declaimed by our boys against a foreign nation; not introduce it here, to recite and declaim ourselves against our own.

But I come to the point of the alleged contradiction. In my remarks on Wednesday, I contended that we could not give away gratuitously all the public lands; that we held them in trust; that the government had solemnly pledged itself to dispose of them as a common fund for the common benefit, and to sell and settle them as its discretion should dictate. Now, Sir, what contradiction does the gentleman find to this sentiment in the speech of 1825? He quotes me as having then said, that we ought not to hug these lands as a very great treasure. Very well, Sir, supposing me to be accurately reported in that expression, what is the contradiction? I have not now said, that we should hug these lands as a favorite source of pecuniary

income. No such thing. It is not my view. What I have said, and
what I do say, is, that they are a common fund, to be disposed
of for the common benefit, to be sold at low prices for the accommodation of settlers, keeping the object of settling the
lands as much in view as that of raising money from them. This
I say now, and this I have always said. Is this hugging them as a
favorite treasure? Is there no difference between hugging and
hoarding this fund, on the one hand, as a great treasure, and,
on the other, of disposing of it at low prices, placing the proceeds in the general treasury of the Union? My opinion is, that
as much is to be made of the land as fairly and reasonably may
be, selling it all the while at such rates as to give the fullest
effect to settlement. This is not giving it all away to the States,
as the gentleman would propose; nor is it hugging the fund
closely and tenaciously, as a favorite treasure; but it is, in my
judgment, a just and wise policy, perfectly according with all
the various duties which rest in government. So much for my
contradiction. And what is it? Where is the ground of the gentleman's triumph? What inconsistency in word or doctrine has
he been able to detect? Sir, if this be a sample of that discomfiture with which the honorable gentleman threatened me,
commend me to the word *discomfiture* for the rest of my life.

But, after all, this is not the point of the debate; and I must
now bring the gentleman back to what is the point.

The real question between me and him is, Has the doctrine
been advanced at the South or the East, that the population of
the West should be retarded, or at least need not be hastened,
on account of its effect to drain off the people from the Atlantic States? Is this doctrine, as has been alleged, of Eastern
origin? That is the question. Has the gentleman found any
thing by which he can make good his accusation? I submit to
the Senate, that he has entirely failed; and, as far as this debate
has shown, the only person who has advanced such sentiments
is a gentleman from South Carolina, and a friend of the honorable member himself. The honorable gentleman has given no
answer to this; there is none which can be given. The simple
fact, while it requires no comment to enforce it, defies all argument to refute it. I could refer to the speeches of another
Southern gentleman, in years before, of the same general character, and to the same effect, as that which has been quoted;

but I will not consume the time of the Senate by the reading of them.

So then, Sir, New England is guiltless of the policy of retarding Western population, and of all envy and jealousy of the growth of the new States. Whatever there be of that policy in the country, no part of it is hers. If it has a local habitation, the honorable member has probably seen by this time where to look for it; and if it now has received a name, he has himself christened it.

We approach, at length, Sir, to a more important part of the honorable gentleman's observations. Since it does not accord with my views of justice and policy to give away the public lands altogether, as a mere matter of gratuity, I am asked by the honorable gentleman on what ground it is that I consent to vote them away in particular instances. How, he inquires, do I reconcile with these professed sentiments, my support of measures appropriating portions of the lands to particular roads, particular canals, particular rivers, and particular institutions of education in the West? This leads, Sir, to the real and wide difference in political opinion between the honorable gentleman and myself. On my part, I look upon all these objects as connected with the common good, fairly embraced in its object and its terms; he, on the contrary, deems them all, if good at all, only local good. This is our difference. The interrogatory which he proceeded to put, at once explains this difference. "What interest," asks he, "has South Carolina in a canal in Ohio?" Sir, this very question is full of significance. It develops the gentleman's whole political system; and its answer expounds mine. Here we differ. I look upon a road over the Alleghanies, a canal round the falls of the Ohio, or a canal or railway from the Atlantic to the Western waters, as being an object large and extensive enough to be fairly said to be for the common benefit. The gentleman thinks otherwise, and this is the key to his construction of the powers of the government. He may well ask what interest has South Carolina in a canal in Ohio. On his system, it is true, she has no interest. On that system, Ohio and Carolina are different governments, and different countries; connected here, it is true, by some slight and ill-defined bond of union, but in all main respects separate and diverse. On that system, Carolina has no more interest in a canal in Ohio than in Mexico. The gentleman, therefore, only follows out his own principles; he does no more than arrive at the natural conclusions of his own doctrines; he only announces the true results of that creed which he has adopted himself, and would persuade others to adopt, when he thus declares that South Carolina has no interest in a public work in Ohio.

Sir, we narrow-minded people of New England do not reason thus. Our *notion* of things is entirely different. We look upon the States, not as separated, but as united. We love to dwell on that union, and on the mutual happiness which it has so much promoted, and the common renown which it has so greatly contributed to acquire. In our contemplation, Carolina and Ohio are parts of the same country; States, united under the same general government, having interests, common, associated, intermingled. In whatever is within the proper sphere of the constitutional power of this government, we look upon the States as one. We do not impose geographical limits to our patriotic feeling or regard; we do not follow rivers and mountains, and lines of latitude, to find boundaries, beyond which public improvements do not benefit us. We who come here, as agents and representatives of these narrow-minded and selfish men of New England, consider ourselves as bound to regard with an equal eye the good of the whole, in whatever is within our powers of legislation. Sir, if a railroad or canal, beginning in South Carolina and ending in South Carolina, appeared to me to be of national importance and national magnitude, believing, as I do that the power of government extends to the encouragement of works of that description, if I were to stand up here and ask, What interest has Massachusetts in a railroad in South Carolina? I should not be willing to face my constituents. These same narrow-minded men would tell me, that they had sent me to act for the whole country, and that one who possessed too little comprehension, either of intellect or feeling, one who was not large enough, both in mind and in heart, to embrace the whole, was not fit to be intrusted with the interest of any part.

Sir, I do not desire to enlarge the powers of the government by unjustifiable construction, nor to exercise any not within a fair interpretation. But when it is believed that a power does exist, then it is, in my judgment, to be exercised for the general benefit of the whole. So far as respects the exercise of such a power, the States are one. It was the very object of the Constitution to create unity of interests to the extent of the powers of the general government. In war and peace we are one; in commerce, one; because the authority of the general government reaches to war and peace, and to the regulation of commerce. I have never seen any more difficulty in erecting lighthouses on the lakes, than on the ocean; in improving the harbors of inland seas, than if they were within the ebb and flow of the tide; or in removing obstructions in the vast streams of the West, more than in any work to facilitate commerce on the Atlantic coast. If there be any power for one, there is power also for the other; and they are all and equally for the common good of the country.

There are other objects, apparently more local, or the benefit of which is less general, towards which, nevertheless, I have concurred with others, to give aid by donations of land. It is proposed to construct a road, in or through one of the new States, in which this government possesses large quantities of land. Have the United States no right, or, as a great and untaxed proprietor, are they under no obligation to contribute to an object thus calculated to promote the common good of all the proprietors, themselves included? And even with respect to education, which is the extreme case, let the question be considered. In the first place, as we have seen, it was made matter of compact with these States, that they should do their part to promote education. In the next place, our whole system of land laws proceeds on the idea that education is for the common good; because, in every division, a certain portion is uniformly reserved and appropriated for the use of schools. And, finally, have not these new States singularly strong claims, founded on the ground already stated, that the government is a great untaxed proprietor, in the ownership of the soil? It is a consideration of great importance, that probably there is in no part of the country, or of the world, so great call for the means of education, as in these new States, owing to the vast numbers of persons within those ages in which education and instruction are usually received, if received at all. This is the natural consequence of recency of settlement and rapid increase. The census of these States shows how great a proportion of the whole population occupies the classes between infancy and manhood. These are the wide fields, and here is the deep and quick soil for the seeds of knowledge and virtue; and this is the favored season, the very spring-time for sowing them. Let them be disseminated without stint. Let them be scattered with a bountiful hand, broadcast. Whatever the government can fairly do towards these objects, in my opinion, ought to be done.

These, Sir, are the grounds, succinctly stated, on which my votes for grants of lands for particular objects rest; while I maintain, at the same time, that it is all a common fund, for the common benefit. And reasons like these, I presume, have influenced the votes of other gentlemen from New England. Those who have a different view of the powers of the government, of course, come to different conclusions, on these, as on other questions. I observed, when speaking on this subject before, that if we looked to any measure, whether for a road, a canal, or any thing else, intended for the impovement of the West, it would be found that, if the New England *ayes* were struck out of the lists of votes, the Southern *noes* would always have rejected the measure. The truth of this has not been denied, and cannot be denied. In stating this, I thought it just to ascribe it to the constitutional scruples of the South, rather than to any other less favorable or less charitable cause. But no sooner had I done this, than the honorable gentleman asks if I reproach him and his friends with their constitutional scruples. Sir, I reproach nobody. I stated a fact, and gave the most respectful reason for it that occurred to me. The gentleman cannot deny the fact; he may, if he choose, disclaim the reason. It is not long since I had occasion, in presenting a petition from his own State, to account for its being intrusted to my hands, by saying, that the constitutional opinions of the gentleman and his worthy colleague prevented them from supporting it. Sir, did I state this as matter of reproach? Far from it. Did I attempt to find any other cause than an honest one for these scruples? Sir, I did not. It did not become me to doubt or to insinuate that the gentleman had either changed his sentiments, or that he had made up a set of constitutional opinions accommodated to any particular combination of political occurrences. Had I done so, I should have felt, that, while I was

entitled to little credit in thus questioning other people's motives, I justified the whole world in suspecting my own. But
how has the gentleman returned this respect for others' opinions? His own candor and justice, how have they been exhibited towards the motives of others, while he has been at so
much pains to maintain, what nobody has disputed, the purity
of his own? Why, Sir, he has asked *when*, and *how*, and *why*
New England votes were found going for measures favorable
to the West. He has demanded to be informed whether all this
did not begin in 1825, and while the election of President was
still pending.

Sir, to these questions retort would be justified; and it is
both cogent and at hand. Nevertheless, I will answer the inquiry, not by retort, but by facts. I will tell the gentleman
when, and *how*, and *why* New England has supported measures
favorable to the West. I have already referred to the early history of the government, to the first acquisition of the lands, to
the original laws for disposing of them, and for governing the
territories where they lie; and have shown the influence of New
England men and New England principles in all these leading
measures. I should not be pardoned were I to go over that
ground again. Coming to more recent times, and to measures
of a less general character, I have endeavored to prove that
every thing of this kind, designed for Western improvement,
has depended on the votes of New England; all this is true
beyond the power of contradiction. And now, Sir, there are
two measures to which I will refer, not so ancient as to belong
to the early history of the public lands, and not so recent as to
be on this side of the period when the gentleman charitably
imagines a new direction may have been given to New England feeling and New England votes. These measures, and
the New England votes in support of them, may be taken as
samples and specimens of all the rest.

In 1820 (observe, Mr. President, in 1820) the people of the
West besought Congress for a reduction in the price of lands.
In favor of that reduction, New England, with a delegation of
forty members in the other house, gave thirty-three votes, and
one only against it. The four Southern States, with more than
fifty members, gave thirty-two votes for it, and seven against it.
Again, in 1821 (observe again, Sir, the time), the law passed for

the relief of the purchasers of the public lands. This was a measure of vital importance to the West, and more especially to the
Southwest. It authorized the relinquishment of contracts for
lands which had been entered into at high prices, and a reduction in other cases of not less than thirty-seven and a half per
cent. on the purchase-money. Many millions of dollars, six or
seven, I believe, probably much more, were relinquished by
this law. On this bill, New England, with her forty members,
gave more affirmative votes than the four Southern States,
with their fifty-two or fifty-three members. These two are far
the most important general measures respecting the public
lands which have been adopted within the last twenty years.
They took place in 1820 and 1821. That is the time *when*.

As to the manner *how*, the gentleman already sees that it was
by voting in solid column for the required relief; and, lastly, as
to the cause *why*, I tell the gentleman it was because the members from New England thought the measures just and salutary; because they entertained towards the West neither envy,
hatred, nor malice; because they deemed it becoming them, as
just and enlightened public men, to meet the exigency which
had arisen in the West with the appropriate measure of relief;
because they felt it due to their own characters, and the characters of their New England predecessors in this government,
to act towards the new States in the spirit of a liberal, patron-
izing, magnanimous policy. So much, Sir, for the cause *why*; and
I hope that by this time, Sir, the honorable gentleman is satisfied; if not, I do not know *when*, or *how*, or *why* he ever
will be.

Having recurred to these two important measures, in answer to the gentleman's inquiries, I must now beg permission
to go back to a period somewhat earlier, for the purpose of still
further showing how much, or rather how little, reason there
is for the gentleman's insinuation that political hopes or fears,
or party associations, were the grounds of these New England
votes. And after what has been said, I hope it may be forgiven
me if I allude to some political opinions and votes of my own,
of very little public importance certainly, but which, from the
time at which they were given and expressed, may pass for good
witnesses on this occasion.

This government, Mr. President, from its origin to the peace of 1815, had been too much engrossed with various other important concerns to be able to turn its thoughts inward, and look to the development of its vast internal resources. In the early part of President Washington's administration, it was fully occupied with completing its own organization, providing for the public debt, defending the frontiers, and maintaining domestic peace. Before the termination of that administration, the fires of the French Revolution blazed forth, as from a new-opened volcano, and the whole breadth of the ocean did not secure us from its effects. The smoke and the cinders reached us, though not the burning lava. Difficult and agitating questions, embarrassing to government and dividing public opinion, sprung out of the new state of our foreign relations, and were succeeded by others, and yet again by others, equally embarrassing and equally exciting division and discord, through the long series of twenty years, till they finally issued in the war with England. Down to the close of that war, no distinct, marked, and deliberate attention had been given, or could have been given, to the internal condition of the country, its capacities of improvement, or the constitutional power of the government in regard to objects connected with such improvement.

The peace, Mr. President, brought about an entirely new and a most interesting state of things; it opened to us other prospects and suggested other duties. We ourselves were changed, and the whole world was changed. The pacification of Europe, after June, 1815, assumed a firm and permanent aspect. The nations evidently manifested that they were disposed for peace. Some agitation of the waves might be expected, even after the storm had subsided, but the tendency was, strongly and rapidly, towards settled repose.

It so happened, Sir, that I was at that time a member of Congress, and, like others, naturally, turned my thoughts to the contemplation of the recently altered condition of the country and of the world. It appeared plainly enough to me, as well as to wiser and more experienced men, that the policy of the government would naturally take a start in a new direction; because new directions would necessarily be given to the pursuits and occupations of the people. We had pushed our commerce far and fast, under the advantage of a neutral flag. But there were now no longer flags, either neutral or belligerent. The harvest of neutrality had been great, but we had gathered it all. With the peace of Europe, it was obvious there would spring up in her circle of nations a revived and invigorated spirit of trade, and a new activity in all the business and objects of civilized life. Hereafter, our commercial gains were to be earned only by success in a close and intense competition. Other nations would produce for themselves, and carry for themselves, and manufacture for themselves, to the full extent of their abilities. The crops of our plains would no longer sustain European armies, nor our ships longer supply those whom war had rendered unable to supply themselves. It was obvious, that, under these circumstances, the country would begin to survey itself, and to estimate its own capacity of improvement.

And this improvement,—how was it to be accomplished, and who was to accomplish it? We were ten or twelve millions of people, spread over almost half a world. We were more than twenty States, some stretching along the same seaboard, some along the same line of inland frontier, and others on opposite banks of the same vast rivers. Two considerations at once presented themselves with great force, in looking at this state of things. One was, that that great branch of improvement which consisted in furnishing new facilities of intercourse necessarily ran into different States in every leading instance, and would benefit the citizens of all such States. No one State, therefore, in such cases, would assume the whole expense, nor was the coöperation of several States to be expected. Take the instance of the Delaware breakwater. It will cost several millions of money. Would Pennsylvania alone ever have constructed it? Certainly never, while this Union lasts, because it is not for her sole benefit. Would Pennsylvania, New Jersey, and Delaware have united to accomplish it at their joint expense? Certainly not, for the same reason. It could not be done, therefore, but by the general government. The same may be said of the large inland undertakings, except that, in them, government, instead of bearing the whole expense, coöperates with others who bear a part. The other consideration is, that the United States have the means. They enjoy the revenues derived from commerce, and the States have no abundant and easy sources of public income. The custom-houses fill the general treasury, while the States have scanty resources, except by resort to heavy direct taxes.

Under this view of things, I thought it necessary to settle, at least for myself, some definite notions with respect to the powers of the government in regard to internal affairs. It may not savor too much of self-commendation to remark, that, with this object, I considered the Constitution, its judicial construction, its contemporaneous exposition, and the whole history of the legislation of Congress under it; and I arrived at the conclusion, that government had power to accomplish sundry objects, or aid in their accomplishment, which are now commonly spoken of as INTERNAL IMPROVEMENTS. That conclusion, Sir, may have been right, or it may have been wrong. I am not about to argue the grounds of it at large. I say only, that it was adopted and acted on even so early as in 1816. Yes, Mr. President, I made up my opinion, and determined on my intended course of political conduct, on these subjects, in the Fourteenth Congress, in 1816. And now, Mr. President, I have further to say, that I made up these opinions, and entered on this course of political conduct, *Teucro duce*. Yes, Sir, I pursued in all this a South Carolina track on the doctrines of internal improvement. South Carolina, as she was then represented in the other house, set forth in 1816 under a fresh and leading breeze, and I was among the followers. But if my leader sees new lights and turns a sharp corner, unless I see new lights also, I keep straight on in the same path. I repeat, that leading gentlemen from South Carolina were first and foremost in behalf of the doctrines of internal improvements, when those doctrines came first to be considered and acted upon in Congress. The debate on the bank question, on the tariff of 1816, and on the direct tax, will show who was who, and what was what, at that time.

The tariff of 1816, (one of the plain cases of oppression and usurpation, from which, if the government does not recede, individual States may justly secede from the government,) is, Sir, in truth, a South Carolina tariff, supported by South Carolina votes. But for those votes, it could not have passed in the form in which it did pass; whereas, if it had depended on Massachusetts votes, it would have been lost. Does not the honorable gentleman well know all this? There are certainly those who do, full well, know it all. I do not say this to reproach South Carolina. I only state the fact; and I think it will appear to be true, that among the earliest and boldest advocates of the tariff, as a measure of protection, and on the express ground of protection, were leading gentlemen of South Carolina in Congress. I did not then, and cannot now, understand their language in any other sense. While this tariff of 1816 was under discussion in the House of Representatives, an honorable gentleman from Georgia, now of this house, moved to reduce the proposed duty on cotton. He failed, by four votes, South Carolina giving three votes (enough to have turned the scale) against his motion. The act, Sir, then passed, and received on its passage the support of a majority of the Representatives of South Carolina present and voting. This act is the first in the order of those now denounced as plain usurpations. We see it daily in the list, by the side of those of 1824 and 1828, as a case of manifest oppression, justifying disunion. I put it home to the honorable member from South Carolina, that his own State was not only "art and part" in this measure, but the *causa causans*. Without her aid, this seminal principle of mischief, this root of Upas, could not have been planted. I have already said, and it is true, that this act proceeded on the ground of protection. It interfered directly with existing interests of great value and amount. It cut up the Calcutta cotton trade by the roots, but it passed, nevertheless, and it passed on the principle of protecting manufactures, on the principle against free trade, on the principle opposed to that *which lets us alone*.

Such, Mr. President, were the opinions of important and leading gentlemen from South Carolina, on the subject of internal improvement, in 1816. I went out of Congress the next year, and, returning again in 1823, thought I found South Carolina where I had left her. I really supposed that all things remained as they were, and that the South Carolina doctrine of internal improvements would be defended by the same eloquent voices, and the same strong arms, as formerly. In the lapse of these six years, it is true, political associations had assumed a new aspect and new divisions. A strong party had arisen in the South hostile to the doctrine of internal improvements. Anticonsolidation was the flag under which this party

fought; and its supporters inveighed against internal improvements, much after the manner in which the honorable gentleman has now inveighed against them, as part and parcel of the
system of consolidation. Whether this party arose in South
Carolina itself, or in the neighborhood, is more than I know. I
think the latter. However that may have been, there were those
found in South Carolina ready to make war upon it, and who
did make intrepid war upon it. Names being regarded as things
in such controversies, they bestowed on the anti-improvement
gentlemen the appellation of Radicals. Yes, Sir, the appellation
of Radicals, as a term of distinction applicable and applied to
those who denied the liberal doctrines of internal improvement, originated, according to the best of my recollection,
somewhere between North Carolina and Georgia. Well, Sir,
these mischievous Radicals were to be put down, and the strong
arm of South Carolina was stretched out to put them down.
About this time I returned to Congress. The battle with the
Radicals had been fought, and our South Carolina champions
of the doctrines of internal improvement had nobly maintained their ground, and were understood to have achieved a
victory. We looked upon them as conquerors. They had driven
back the enemy with discomfiture, a thing, by the way, Sir,
which is not always performed when it is promised. A gentleman to whom I have already referred in this debate had come
into Congress, during my absence from it, from South Carolina, and had brought with him a high reputation for ability.
He came from a school with which we had been acquainted, *et
noscitur a sociis*. I hold in my hand, Sir, a printed speech of this
distinguished gentleman, "ON INTERNAL IMPROVEMENTS,"
delivered about the period to which I now refer, and printed
with a few introductory remarks upon *consolidation*; in which,
Sir, I think he quite consolidated the arguments of his opponents, the Radicals, if to *crush* be to consolidate. I give you a
short but significant quotation from these remarks. He is
speaking of a pamphlet, then recently published, entitled "Consolidation"; and having alluded to the question of renewing
the charter of the former Bank of the United States, he says:—

Moreover, in the early history of parties, and when Mr. Crawford
advocated a renewal of the old charter, it was considered a Federal

measure; which internal improvement *never was*, as this author erroneously states. This latter measure originated in the administration of Mr. Jefferson, with the appropriation for the Cumberland Road; and was first proposed, *as a system*, by Mr. Calhoun, and carried through the House of Representatives by a large majority of the Republicans, including almost every one of the leading men who carried us through the late war.

So, then, internal improvement is not one of the Federal heresies. One paragraph more, Sir:—

The author in question, not content with denouncing as Federalists, General Jackson, Mr. Adams, Mr. Calhoun, and the majority of the South Carolina delegation in Congress, modestly extends the denunciation to Mr. Monroe and the whole Republican party. Here are his words:—'During the administration of Mr. Monroe much has passed which the Republican party would be glad to approve if they could!! But the principal feature, and that which has chiefly elicited these observations, is the renewal of the SYSTEM OF INTERNAL IMPROVEMENTS.' Now this measure was adopted by a vote of 115 to 86 of a Republican Congress, and sanctioned by a Republican President. Who, then, is this author, who assumes the high prerogative of denouncing, in the name of the Republican party, the Republican administration of the country? A denunciation including within its sweep *Calhoun*, *Lowndes*, and *Cheves*, men who will be regarded as the brightest ornaments of South Carolina, and the strongest pillars of the Republican party, as long as the late war shall be remembered, and talents and patriotism shall be regarded as the proper objects of the admiration and gratitude of a free people!!

Such are the opinions, Sir, which were maintained by South Carolina gentlemen, in the House of Representatives, on the subject of internal improvements, when I took my seat there as a member from Massachusetts in 1823. But this is not all. We had a bill before us, and passed it in that house, entitled, "An Act to procure the necessary surveys, plans, and estimates upon the subject of roads and canals." It authorized the President to cause surveys and estimates to be made of the routes of such roads and canals as he might deem of national importance in a commercial or military point of view, or for the transportation of the mail, and appropriated thirty thousand dollars out of the treasury to defray the expense. This act, though preliminary in its nature, covered the whole ground. It took for granted the complete power of internal improvement, as far as any of its advocates had ever contended for it. Having passed the other house, the bill came up to the Senate, and was here considered and debated in April, 1824. The honorable member from South Carolina was a member of the Senate at that time. While the bill was under consideration here, a motion was made to add the following proviso:—"*Provided*, That nothing herein contained shall be construed to affirm *or admit* a power in Congress, on their own authority, to make roads or canals within any of the States of the Union." The yeas and nays were taken on this proviso, and the honorable member voted *in the negative!* The proviso failed.

A motion was then made to add this proviso, viz. :—"*Provided*, That the faith of the United States is hereby pledged, that no money shall ever be expended for roads or canals, except it shall be among the several States, and in the same proportion as direct taxes are laid and assessed by the provisions of the Constitution." The honorable member voted *against this proviso* also, and it failed. The bill was then put on its passage, and the honorable member voted *for it*, and it passed, and became a law.

Now it strikes me, Sir, that there is no maintaining these votes, but upon the power of internal improvement, in its broadest sense. In truth, these bills for surveys and estimates have always been considered as test questions; they show who is for and who against internal improvement. This law itself went the whole length, and assumed the full and complete power. The gentleman's votes sustained that power, in every form in which the various propositions to amend presented it. He went for the entire and unrestrained authority, without consulting the States, and without agreeing to any proportionate distribution. And now suffer me to remind you, Mr. President, that it is this very same power, thus sanctioned, in every form, by the gentleman's own opinion, which is so plain and manifest a usurpation, that the State of South Carolina is supposed to be justified in refusing submission to any laws carrying the power into effect. Truly, Sir, is not this a little too hard? May we not crave some mercy, under favor and protection of the gentleman's own authority? Admitting that a road, or a canal, must be written down flat usurpation as was ever committed, may we find no mitigation in our respect for his place, and his vote, as one that knows the law?

The tariff, which South Carolina had an efficient hand in establishing, in 1816, and this asserted power of internal improvement, advanced by her in the same year, and, as we have seen, approved and sanctioned by her Representatives in 1824, these two measures are the great grounds on which she is now thought to be justified in breaking up the Union, if she sees fit to break it up!

I may now safely say, I think, that we have had the authority of leading and distinguished gentlemen from South Carolina in support of the doctrine of internal improvement. I repeat, that, up to 1824, I for one followed South Carolina; but when that star, in its ascension, veered off in an unexpected direction, I relied on its light no longer. [Here the Vice-President said, "Does the chair understand the gentleman from Massachusetts to say that the person now occupying the chair of the Senate has changed his opinions on the subject of internal improvements?"]

From nothing ever said to me, Sir, have I had reason to know of any change in the opinions of the person filling the chair of the Senate. If such change has taken place, I regret it. I speak generally of the State of South Carolina. Individuals we know there are, who hold opinions favorable to the power. An application for its exercise, in behalf of a public work in South Carolina itself, is now pending, I believe, in the other house, presented by members from that State.

I have thus, Sir, perhaps not without some tediousness of detail, shown, if I am in error on the subject of internal improvement, how, and in what company, I fell into that error. If I am wrong, it is apparent who misled me.

I go to other remarks of the honorable member; and I have to complain of an entire misapprehension of what I said on the subject of the national debt, though I can hardly perceive how any one could misunderstand me. What I said was, not that I wished to put off the payment of the debt, but, on the contrary, that I had always voted for every measure for its reduction, as uniformly as the gentleman himself. He seems to claim the exclusive merit of a disposition to reduce the public charge. I do not allow it to him. As a debt, I was, I am for paying it, because it is a charge on our finances, and on the industry of the country. But I observed, that I thought I perceived a morbid fervor on that subject, an excessive anxiety to pay off the debt, not so much because it is a debt simply, as because, while it lasts, it furnishes one objection to disunion. It is, while it continues, a tie of common interest. I did not impute such motives to the honorable member himself, but that there is such a feeling in existence I have not a particle of doubt. The most I said was, that if one effect of the debt was to strengthen our Union, that effect itself was not regretted by me, however much others might regret it. The gentleman has not seen how to reply to this, otherwise than by supposing me to have advanced the doctrine that a national debt is a national blessing. Others, I must hope, will find much less difficulty in understanding me. I distinctly and pointedly cautioned the honorable member not to understand me as expressing an opinion favorable to the continuance of the debt. I repeated this caution, and repeated it more than once; but it was thrown away.

On yet another point, I was still more unaccountably misunderstood. The gentleman had harangued against "consolidation." I told him, in reply, that there was one kind of consolidation to which I was attached, and that was the consolidation of our Union; that this was precisely that consolidation to which I feared others were not attached, and that such consolidation was the very end of the Constitution, the leading object, as they had informed us themselves, which its framers had kept in view. I turned to their communication, and read their very words, "the consolidation of the Union," and expressed my devotion to this sort of consolidation. I said, in terms, that I wished not in the slightest degree to augment the powers of this government; that my object was to preserve, not to enlarge; and that by consolidating the Union I understood no more than the strengthening of the Union, and perpetuating it. Having been thus explicit, having thus read from the printed book the precise words which I adopted, as expressing my own sentiments, it passes comprehension how any man could understand me as contending for an extension of the powers of the government, or for consolidation in that odious sense in which it means an accumulation, in the federal government, of the powers properly belonging to the States.

I repeat, Sir, that, in adopting the sentiment of the framers of the Constitution, I read their language audibly, and word for word; and I pointed out the distinction, just as fully as I have now done, between the consolidation of the Union and that other obnoxious consolidation which I disclaimed. And yet the honorable member misunderstood me. The gentleman had said that he wished for no fixed revenue,—not a shilling. If by a word he could convert the Capitol into gold, he would not do it. Why all this fear of revenue? Why, Sir, because, as the gentleman told us, it tends to consolidation. Now this can mean neither more nor less than that a common revenue is a common interest, and that all common interests tend to preserve the union of the States. I confess I like that tendency; if the gentleman dislikes it, he is right in deprecating a shilling of fixed revenue. So much, Sir, for consolidation.

As well as I recollect the course of his remarks, the honorable gentleman next recurred to the subject of the tariff. He did not doubt the word must be of unpleasant sound to me, and proceeded, with an effort neither new nor attended with new success, to involve me and my votes in inconsistency and contradiction. I am happy the honorable gentleman has furnished me an opportunity of a timely remark or two on that subject. I was glad he approached it, for it is a question I enter upon without fear from any body. The strenuous toil of the gentleman has been to raise an inconsistency between my dissent to the tariff in 1824, and my vote in 1828. It is labor lost. He pays undeserved compliment to my speech in 1824; but this is to raise me high, that my fall, as he would have it, in 1828, may be more signal. Sir, there was no fall. Between the ground I stood on in 1824 and that I took in 1828, there was not only no precipice, but no declivity. It was a change of position to meet new circumstances, but on the same level. A plain tale explains the whole matter. In 1816 I had not acquiesced in the tariff, then supported by South Carolina. To some parts of it, especially, I felt and expressed great repugnance. I held the same opinions in 1820, at the meeting in Faneuil Hall, to which the gentleman has alluded. I said then, and say now, that, as an original question, the authority of Congress to exercise the revenue power, with direct reference to the protection of manufactures, is a questionable authority, far more

questionable, in my judgment, than the power of internal improvements. I must confess, Sir, that in one respect some
impression has been made on my opinions lately. Mr. Madison's
publication has put the power in a very strong light. He has
placed it, I must acknowledge, upon grounds of construction
and argument which seem impregnable. But even if the power
were doubtful, on the face of the Constitution itself, it had
been assumed and asserted in the first revenue law ever passed
under that same Constitution; and on this ground, as a matter
settled by contemporaneous practice, I had refrained from expressing the opinion that the tariff laws transcended constitutional limits, as the gentleman supposes. What I did say at
Faneuil Hall, as far as I now remember, was, that this was originally matter of doubtful construction. The gentleman himself,
I suppose, thinks there is no doubt about it, and that the laws
are plainly against the Constitution. Mr. Madison's letters,
already referred to, contain, in my judgment, by far the most
able exposition extant of this part of the Constitution. He has
satisfied me, so far as the practice of the government had left it
an open question.

With a great majority of the Representatives of Massachusetts, I voted against the tariff of 1824. My reasons were then
given, and I will not now repeat them. But, notwithstanding
our dissent, the great States of New York, Pennsylvania, Ohio,
and Kentucky went for the bill, in almost unbroken column,
and it passed. Congress and the President sanctioned it, and it
became the law of the land. What, then, were we to do? Our
only option was, either to fall in with this settled course of public policy, and accommodate ourselves to it as well as we could,
or to embrace the South Carolina doctrine, and talk of nullifying the statute by State interference.

This last alternative did not suit our principles, and of course
we adopted the former. In 1827, the subject came again before
Congress, on a proposition to afford some relief to the branch
of wool and woollens. We looked upon the system of protection as being fixed and settled. The law of 1824 remained. It
had gone into full operation, and, in regard to some objects
intended by it, perhaps most of them, had produced all its expected effects. No man proposed to repeal it; no man attempted to renew the general contest on its principle. But,

owing to subsequent and unforeseen occurrences, the benefit intended by it to wool and woollen fabrics had not been realized. Events not known here when the law passed had taken place, which defeated its object in that particular respect. A measure was accordingly brought forward to meet this precise deficiency, to remedy this particular defect. It was limited to wool and woollens. Was ever any thing more reasonable? If the policy of the tariff laws had become established in principle, as the permanent policy of the government, should they not be revised and amended, and made equal, like other laws, as exigencies should arise, or justice require? Because we had doubted about adopting the system, were we to refuse to cure its manifest defects, after it had been adopted, and when no one attempted its repeal? And this, Sir, is the inconsistency so much bruited. I had voted against the tariff of 1824, but it passed; and in 1827 and 1828, I voted to amend it, in a point essential to the interest of my constituents. Where is the inconsistency? Could I do otherwise? Sir, does political consistency consist in always giving negative votes? Does it require of a public man to refuse to concur in amending laws, because they passed against his consent? Having voted against the tariff originally, does consistency demand that I should do all in my power to maintain an unequal tariff, burdensome to my own constituents in many respects, favorable in none? To consistency of that sort, I lay no claim. And there is another sort to which I lay as little, and that is, a kind of consistency by which persons feel themselves as much bound to oppose a proposition after it has become a law of the land as before.

The bill of 1827, limited, as I have said, to the single object in which the tariff of 1824 had manifestly failed in its effect, passed the House of Representatives, but was lost here. We had then the act of 1828. I need not recur to the history of a measure so recent. Its enemies spiced it with whatsoever they thought would render it distasteful; its friends took it, drugged as it was. Vast amounts of property, many millions, had been invested in manufactures, under the inducements of the act of 1824. Events called loudly, as I thought, for further regulation to secure the degree of protection intended by that act. I was disposed to vote for such regulation, and desired nothing more; but certainly was not to be bantered out of my purpose by a threatened augmentation of duty on molasses, put into the bill for the avowed purpose of making it obnoxious. The vote may have been right or wrong, wise or unwise; but it is little less than absurd to allege against it an inconsistency with opposition to the former law.

Sir, as to the general subject of the tariff, I have little now to say. Another opportunity may be presented. I remarked the other day, that this policy did not begin with us in New England; and yet, Sir, New England is charged with vehemence as being favorable, or charged with equal vehemence as being unfavorable, to the tariff policy, just as best suits the time, place, and occasion for making some charge against her. The credulity of the public has been put to its extreme capacity of false impression relative to her conduct in this particular. Through all the South, during the late contest, it was New England policy and a New England administration that were afflicting the country with a tariff beyond all endurance; while on the other side of the Alleghanies even the act of 1828 itself, the very sublimated essence of oppression, according to Southern opinions, was pronounced to be one of those blessings for which the West was indebted to the "generous South."

With large investments in manufacturing establishments, and many and various interests connected with and dependent on them, it is not to be expected that New England, any more than other portions of the country, will now consent to any measure destructive or highly dangerous. The duty of the government, at the present moment, would seem to be to preserve, not to destroy; to maintain the position which it has assumed; and, for one, I shall feel it an indispensable obligation to hold it steady, as far as in my power, to that degree of protection which it has undertaken to bestow. No more of the tariff.

Professing to be provoked by what he chose to consider a charge made by me against South Carolina, the honorable member, Mr. President, has taken up a new crusade against New England. Leaving altogether the subject of the public lands, in which his success, perhaps, had been neither distinguished nor satisfactory, and letting go, also, of the topic of the tariff, he sallied forth in a general assault on the opinions, politics, and parties of New England, as they have been exhibited in the last thirty years. This is natural. The "narrow policy" of the public lands had proved a legal settlement in South Carolina, and was not to be removed. The "accursed policy" of the tariff, also, had established the fact of its birth and parentage in the same State. No wonder, therefore, the gentleman wished to carry the war, as he expressed it, into the enemy's country. Prudently willing to quit these subjects, he was, doubtless, desirous of fastening on others, which could not be transferred south of Mason and Dixon's line. The politics of New England became his theme; and it was in this part of his speech, I think, that he menaced me with such sore discomfiture. Discomfiture! Why, Sir, when he attacks any thing which I maintain, and overthrows it, when he turns the right or left of any position which I take up, when he drives me from any ground I choose to occupy, he may then talk of discomfiture, but not till that distant day. What has he done? Has he maintained his own charges? Has he proved what he alleged? Has he sustained himself in his attack on the government, and on the history of the North, in the matter of the public lands? Has he disproved a fact, refuted a proposition, weakened an argument, maintained by me? Has he come within beat of drum of any position of mine? O, no; but he has "carried the war into the enemy's country"! Carried the war into the enemy's country! Yes, Sir, and what sort of a war has he made of it? Why, Sir, he has stretched a drag-net over the whole surface of perished pamphlets, indiscreet sermons, frothy paragraphs, and fuming popular addresses; over whatever the pulpit in its moments of alarm, the press in its heats, and parties in their extravagance, have severally thrown off in times of general excitement and violence. He has thus swept together a mass of such things as, but that they are now old and cold, the public health would have required him rather to leave in their state of dispersion. For a good long hour or two, we had the unbroken pleasure of listening to the honorable member, while he recited with his usual grace and spirit, and with evident high gusto, speeches, pamphlets, addresses, and all the *et cæteras* of the political press, such as warm heads produce in warm times; and such as it would be "discomfiture" indeed for any one, whose taste did not delight in that sort of reading, to be obliged to peruse. This is his war. This it is to carry war into the enemy's country.

It is in an invasion of this sort, that he flatters himself with the expectation of gaining laurels fit to adorn a Senator's brow!

Mr. President, I shall not, it will not, I trust, be expected that I should, either now or at any time, separate this farrago into parts, and answer and examine its components. I shall barely bestow upon it all a general remark or two. In the run of forty years, Sir, under this Constitution, we have experienced sundry successive violent party contests. Party arose, indeed, with the Constitution itself, and, in some form or other, has attended it through the greater part of its history. Whether any other constitution than the old Articles of Confederation was desirable, was itself a question on which parties divided; if a new constitution were framed, what powers should be given to it was another question; and when it had been formed, what was, in fact, the just extent of the powers actually conferred was a third. Parties, as we know, existed under the first administration, as distinctly marked as those which have manifested themselves at any subsequent period. The contest immediately preceding the political change in 1801, and that, again, which existed at the commencement of the late war, are other instances of party excitement, of something more than usual strength and intensity. In all these conflicts there was, no doubt, much of violence on both and all sides. It would be impossible, if one had a fancy for such employment, to adjust the relative *quantum* of violence between these contending parties. There was enough in each, as must always be expected in popular governments. With a great deal of popular and decorous discussion, there was mingled a great deal, also, of declamation, virulence, crimination, and abuse. In regard to any party, probably, at one of the leading epochs in the history of parties, enough may be found to make out another inflamed exhibition, not unlike that with which the honorable member has edified us. For myself, Sir, I shall not rake among the rubbish of bygone times, to see what I can find, or whether I cannot find something by which I can fix a blot on the escutcheon of any State, any party, or any part of the country. General Washington's administration was steadily and zealously maintained, as we all know, by New England. It was violently opposed elsewhere. We know in what quarter he had the most earnest, constant, and persevering support, in all his great and leading measures. We know where

his private and personal character was held in the highest degree of attachment and veneration; and we know, too, where
his measures were opposed, his services slighted, and his character vilified. We know, or we might know, if we turned to the
journals, who expressed respect, gratitude, and regret, when
he retired from the chief magistracy, and who refused to express either respect, gratitude, or regret. I shall not open those
journals. Publications more abusive or scurrilous never saw the
light, than were sent forth against Washington, and all his
leading measures, from presses south of New England. But I
shall not look them up. I employ no scavengers, no one is in
attendance on me, furnishing such means of retaliation; and
if there were, with an ass's load of them, with a bulk as huge as
that which the gentleman himself has produced, I would not
touch one of them. I see enough of the violence of our own
times, to be no way anxious to rescue from forgetfulness the
extravagances of times past.

Besides, what is all this to the present purpose? It has
nothing to do with the public lands, in regard to which the attack was begun; and it has nothing to do with those sentiments and opinions which, I have thought, tend to disunion,
and all of which the honorable member seems to have adopted
himself, and undertaken to defend. New England has, at times,
so argues the gentleman, held opinions as dangerous as those
which he now holds. Suppose this were so; why should *he*
therefore abuse New England? If he finds himself countenanced by acts of hers, how is it that, while he relies on these
acts, he covers, or seeks to cover, their authors with reproach?
But, Sir, if, in the course of forty years, there have been undue
effervescences of party in New England, has the same thing
happened nowhere else? Party animosity and party outrage,
not in New England, but elsewhere, denounced President
Washington, not only as a Federalist, but as a Tory, a British
agent, a man who in his high office sanctioned corruption. But
does the honorable member suppose, if I had a tender here
who should put such an effusion of wickedness and folly into
my hand, that I would stand up and read it against the South?
Parties ran into great heats again in 1799 and 1800. What was
said, Sir, or rather what was not said, in those years, against
John Adams, one of the committee that drafted the Declara-

tion of Independence, and its admitted ablest defender on the floor of Congress? If the gentleman wishes to increase his stores of party abuse and frothy violence, if he has a determined proclivity to such pursuits, there are treasures of that sort south of the Potomac, much to his taste, yet untouched. I shall not touch them.

The parties which divided the country at the commencement of the late war were violent. But then there was violence on both sides, and violence in every State. Minorities and majorities were equally violent. There was no more violence against the war in New England, than in other States; nor any more appearance of violence, except that, owing to a dense population, greater facility of assembling, and more presses, there may have been more in quantity spoken and printed there than in some other places. In the article of sermons, too, New England is somewhat more abundant than South Carolina; and for that reason the chance of finding here and there an exceptionable one may be greater. I hope, too, there are more good ones. Opposition may have been more formidable in New England, as it embraced a larger portion of the whole population; but it was no more unrestrained in principle, or violent in manner. The minorities dealt quite as harshly with their own State governments as the majorities dealt with the administration here. There were presses on both sides, popular meetings on both sides, ay, and pulpits on both sides also. The gentleman's purveyors have only catered for him among the productions of one side. I certainly shall not supply the deficiency by furnishing samples of the other. I leave to him, and to them, the whole concern.

It is enough for me to say, that if, in any part of this their grateful occupation, if, in all their researches, they find any thing in the history of Massachusetts, or New England, or in the proceedings of any legislative or other public body, disloyal to the Union, speaking slightingly of its value, proposing to break it up, or recommending non-intercourse with neighboring States, on account of difference of political opinion, then, Sir, I give them all up to the honorable gentleman's unrestrained rebuke; expecting, however, that he will extend his buffetings in like manner *to all similar proceedings, wherever else found*.

The gentleman, Sir, has spoken at large of former parties, now no longer in being, by their received appellations, and has undertaken to instruct us, not only in the knowledge of their principles, but of their respective pedigrees also. He has ascended to their origin, and run out their genealogies. With most exemplary modesty, he speaks of the party to which he professes to have himself belonged, as the true Pure, the only honest, patriotic party, derived by regular descent, from father to son, from the time of the virtuous Romans! Spreading before us the *family tree* of political parties, he takes especial care to show himself snugly perched on a popular bough! He is wakeful to the expediency of adopting such rules of descent as shall bring him in, to the exclusion of others, as an heir to the inheritance of all public virtue and all true political principle. His party and his opinions are sure to be orthodox; heterodoxy is confined to his opponents. He spoke, Sir, of the Federalists, and I thought I saw some eyes begin to open and stare a little, when he ventured on that ground. I expected he would draw his sketches rather lightly, when he looked on the circle round him, and especially if he should cast his thoughts to the high places out of the Senate. Nevertheless, he went back to Rome, *ad annum urbis conditæ*, and found the fathers of the Federalists in the primeval aristocrats of that renowned city! He traced the flow of Federal blood down through successive ages and centuries, till he brought it into the veins of the American Tories, of whom, by the way, there were twenty in the Carolinas for one in Massachusetts. From the Tories he followed it to the Federalists; and, as the Federal party was broken up, and there was no possibility of transmitting it further on this side the Atlantic, he seems to have discovered that it has gone off collaterally, though against all the canons of descent, into the Ultras of France, and finally become extinguished, like exploded gas, among the adherents of Don Miguel! This, Sir, is an abstract of the gentleman's history of Federalism. I am not about to controvert it. It is not, at present, worth the pains of refutation; because, Sir, if at this day any one feels the sin of Federalism lying heavily on his conscience, he can easily procure remission. He may even obtain an indulgence, if he be desirous of repeating the same transgression. It is an affair of no difficulty to get into this same

right line of patriotic descent. A man now-a-days is at liberty
to choose his political parentage. He may elect his own father.
Federalist or not, he may, if he choose, claim to belong to the
favored stock, and his claim will be allowed. He may carry
back his pretensions just as far as the honorable gentleman
himself; nay, he may make himself out the honorable gentleman's cousin, and prove, satisfactorily, that he is descended
from the same political great-grandfather. All this is allowable.
We all know a process, Sir, by which the whole Essex Junto
could, in one hour, be all washed white from their ancient
Federalism, and come out, every one of them, original Democrats, dyed in the wool! Some of them have actually undergone the operation, and they say it is quite easy. The only
inconvenience it occasions, as they tell us, is a slight tendency
of the blood to the face, a soft suffusion, which, however, is
very transient, since nothing is said by those whom they join
calculated to deepen the red on the cheek, but a prudent silence is observed in regard to all the past. Indeed, Sir, some
smiles of approbation have been bestowed, and some crumbs
of comfort have fallen, not a thousand miles from the door of
the Hartford Convention itself. And if the author of the Ordinance of 1787 possessed the other requisite qualifications, there
is no knowing, notwithstanding his Federalism, to what heights
of favor he might not yet attain.

Mr. President, in carrying his warfare, such as it is, into New
England, the honorable gentleman all along professes to be
acting on the defensive. He chooses to consider me as having
assailed South Carolina, and insists that he comes forth only as
her champion, and in her defence. Sir, I do not admit that I
made any attack whatever on South Carolina. Nothing like it.
The honorable member, in his first speech, expressed opinions,
in regard to revenue and some other topics, which I heard
both with pain and with surprise. I told the gentleman I was
aware that such sentiments were entertained *out* of the government, but had not expected to find them advanced in it; that I
knew there were persons in the South who speak of our Union
with indifference or doubt, taking pains to magnify its evils,
and to say nothing of its benefits; that the honorable member
himself, I was sure, could never be one of these; and I regretted
the expression of such opinions as he had avowed, because I

thought their obvious tendency was to encourage feelings of disrespect to the Union, and to impair its strength. This, Sir, is the sum and substance of all I said on the subject. And this constitutes the attack which called on the chivalry of the gentleman, in his own opinion, to harry us with such a foray among the party pamphlets and party proceedings of Massachusetts! If he means that I spoke with dissatisfaction or disrespect of the ebullitions of individuals in South Carolina, it is true. But if he means that I assailed the character of the State, her honor, or patriotism, that I reflected on her history or her conduct, he has not the slightest ground for any such assumption. I did not even refer, I think, in my observations, to any collection of individuals. I said nothing of the recent conventions. I spoke in the most guarded and careful manner, and only expressed my regret for the publication of opinions, which I presumed the honorable member disapproved as much as myself. In this, it seems, I was mistaken. I do not remember that the gentleman has disclaimed any sentiment, or any opinion, of a supposed anti-union tendency, which on all or any of the recent occasions has been expressed. The whole drift of his speech has been rather to prove, that, in divers times and manners, sentiments equally liable to my objection have been avowed in New England. And one would suppose that his object, in this reference to Massachusetts, was to find a precedent to justify proceedings in the South, were it not for the reproach and contumely with which he labors, all along, to load these his own chosen precedents. By way of defending South Carolina from what he chooses to think an attack on her, he first quotes the example of Massachusetts, and then denounces that example in good set terms. This twofold purpose, not very consistent, one would think, with itself, was exhibited more than once in the course of his speech. He referred, for instance, to the Hartford Convention. Did he do this for authority, or for a topic of reproach? Apparently for both, for he told us that he should find no fault with the mere fact of holding such a convention, and considering and discussing such questions as he supposes were then and there discussed; but what rendered it obnoxious was its being held at the time, and under the circumstances of the country then existing. We were in a war, he said, and the country needed all our aid; the hand of government required to be strengthened, not weakened; and patriotism should have postponed such proceedings to another day. The thing itself, then, is a precedent; the time and manner of it only, a subject of censure.

Now, Sir, I go much further, on this point, than the honorable member. Supposing, as the gentleman seems to do, that the Hartford Convention assembled for any such purpose as breaking up the Union, because they thought unconstitutional laws had been passed, or to consult on that subject, or *to calculate the value of the Union*; supposing this to be their purpose, or any part of it, then I say the meeting itself was disloyal, and was obnoxious to censure, whether held in time of peace or time of war, or under whatever circumstances. The material question is the *object*. Is dissolution the *object*? If it be, external circumstances may make it a more or less aggravated case, but cannot affect the principle. I do not hold, therefore, Sir, that the Hartford Convention was pardonable, even to the extent of the gentleman's admission, if its objects were really such as have been imputed to it. Sir, there never was a time, under any degree of excitement, in which the Hartford Convention, or any other convention, could have maintained itself one moment in New England, if assembled for any such purpose as the gentleman says would have been an allowable purpose. To hold conventions to decide constitutional law! To try the binding validity of statutes by votes in a convention! Sir, the Hartford Convention, I presume, would not desire that the honorable gentleman should be their defender or advocate, if he puts their case upon such untenable and extravagant grounds.

Then, Sir, the gentleman has no fault to find with these recently promulgated South Carolina opinions. And certainly he need have none; for his own sentiments, as now advanced, and advanced on reflection, as far as I have been able to comprehend them, go the full length of all these opinions. I propose, Sir, to say something on these, and to consider how far they are just and constitutional. Before doing that, however, let me observe that the eulogium pronounced by the honorable gentleman on the character of the State of South Carolina, for her Revolutionary and other merits, meets my hearty concurrence. I shall not acknowledge that the honorable member goes before me in regard for whatever of distinguished talent, or distinguished character, South Carolina has produced. I claim part of the honor, I partake in the pride, of her great names. I claim them for countrymen, one and all, the Laurenses, the Rutledges, the Pinckneys, the Sumpters, the Marions, Americans all, whose fame is no more to be hemmed in by State lines, than their talents and patriotism were capable of being circumscribed within the same narrow limits. In their day and generation, they served and honored the country, and the whole country; and their renown is of the treasures of the whole country. Him whose honored name the gentleman himself bears,—does he esteem me less capable of gratitude for his patriotism, or sympathy for his sufferings, than if his eyes had first opened upon the light of Massachusetts, instead of South Carolina? Sir, does he suppose it in his power to exhibit a Carolina name so bright, as to produce envy in my bosom? No, Sir, increased gratification and delight, rather. I thank God, that, if I am gifted with little of the spirit which is able to raise mortals to the skies, I have yet none, as I trust, of that other spirit, which would drag angels down. When I shall be found, Sir, in my place here in the Senate, or elsewhere, to sneer at public merit, because it happens to spring up beyond the little limits of my own State or neighborhood; when I refuse, for any such cause, or for any cause, the homage due to American talent, to elevated patriotism, to sincere devotion to liberty and the country; or, if I see an uncommon endowment of Heaven, if I see extraordinary capacity and virtue, in any of the South, and if, moved by local prejudice or gangrened by State jealousy, I get up here to abate the tithe of a hair from his just character and just fame, may my tongue cleave to the roof of my mouth!

Sir, let me recur to pleasing recollections; let me indulge in refreshing remembrance of the past; let me remind you that, in early times, no States cherished greater harmony, both of principle and feeling, than Massachusetts and South Carolina. Would to God that harmony might again return! Shoulder to shoulder they went through the Revolution, hand in hand they stood round the administration of Washington, and felt his own great arm lean on them for support. Unkind feeling, if it exist, alienation, and distrust are the growth, unnatural to such soils, of false principles since sown. They are weeds, the seeds of which that same great arm never scattered.

Mr. President, I shall enter on no encomium upon Massachusetts; she needs none. There she is. Behold her, and judge for yourselves. There is her history; the world knows it by heart. The past, at least, is secure. There is Boston, and Concord, and Lexington, and Bunker Hill; and there they will remain for ever. The bones of her sons, falling in the great struggle for Independence, now lie mingled with the soil of every State from New England to Georgia; and there they will lie for ever. And Sir, where American Liberty raised its first voice, and where its youth was nurtured and sustained, there it still lives, in the strength of its manhood and full of its original spirit. If discord and disunion shall wound it, if party strife and blind ambition shall hawk at and tear it, if folly and madness, if uneasiness under salutary and necessary restraint, shall succeed in separating it from that Union, by which alone its existence is made sure, it will stand, in the end, by the side of that cradle in which its infancy was rocked; it will stretch forth its arm with whatever of vigor it may still retain over the friends who gather round it; and it will fall at last, if fall it must, amidst the proudest monuments of its own glory, and on the very spot of its origin.

There yet remains to be performed, Mr. President, by far the most grave and important duty, which I feel to be devolved on me by this occasion. It is to state, and to defend, what I conceive to be the true principles of the Constitution under which we are here assembled. I might well have desired that so weighty a task should have fallen into other and abler hands. I could have wished that it should have been executed by those whose character and experience give weight and influence to their opinions, such as cannot possibly belong to mine. But, Sir, I have met the occasion, not sought it; and I shall proceed to state my own sentiments, without challenging for them any particular regard, with studied plainness, and as much precision as possible.

I understand the honorable gentleman from South Carolina to maintain, that it is a right of the State legislatures to interfere, whenever, in their judgment, this government transcends its constitutional limits, and to arrest the operation of its laws.

I understand him to maintain this right, as a right existing *under* the Constitution, not as a right to overthrow it on the ground of extreme necessity, such as would justify violent revolution.

I understand him to maintain an authority, on the part of the States, thus to interfere, for the purpose of correcting the exercise of power by the general government, of checking it, and of compelling it to conform to their opinion of the extent of its powers.

I understand him to maintain, that the ultimate power of judging of the constitutional extent of its own authority is not lodged exclusively in the general government, or any branch of it; but that, on the contrary, the States may lawfully decide for themselves, and each State for itself, whether, in a given case, the act of the general government transcends its power.

I understand him to insist, that, if the exigency of the case, in the opinion of any State government, require it, such State government may, by its own sovereign authority, annul an act of the general government which it deems plainly and palpably unconstitutional.

This is the sum of what I understand from him to be the South Carolina doctrine, and the doctrine which he maintains. I propose to consider it, and compare it with the Constitution. Allow me to say, as a preliminary remark, that I call this the South Carolina doctrine only because the gentleman himself has so denominated it. I do not feel at liberty to say that South Carolina, as a State, has ever advanced these sentiments. I hope she has not, and never may. That a great majority of her people are opposed to the tariff laws, is doubtless true. That a majority, somewhat less than that just mentioned, conscientiously believe these laws unconstitutional, may probably also be true. But that any majority holds to the right of direct State interference at State discretion, the right of nullifying acts of Congress by acts of State legislation, is more than I know, and what I shall be slow to believe.

That there are individuals besides the honorable gentleman who do maintain these opinions, is quite certain. I recollect the recent expression of a sentiment, which circumstances attending its utterance and publication justify us in supposing was not unpremeditated. "The sovereignty of the State,

—never to be controlled, construed, or decided on but by her own feelings of honorable justice."

[Mr. Hayne here rose and said, that, for the purpose of being clearly understood, he would state that his proposition was in the words of the Virginia resolution, as follows:—

[That this assembly doth explicitly and peremptorily declare, that it views the powers of the federal government, as resulting from the compact to which the States are parties, as limited by the plain sense and intention of the instrument constituting that compact, as no farther valid than they are authorized by the grants enumerated in that compact; and that, in case of a deliberate, palpable, and dangerous exercise of other powers, not granted by the said compact, the States who are parties thereto have the right, and are in duty bound, to interpose, for arresting the progress of the evil, and for maintaining within their respective limits the authorities, rights, and liberties appertaining to them.

[Mr. Webster resumed:—]

I am quite aware, Mr. President, of the existence of the resolution which the gentleman read, and has now repeated, and that he relies on it as his authority. I know the source, too, from which it is understood to have proceeded. I need not say that I have much respect for the constitutional opinions of Mr. Madison; they would weigh greatly with me always. But before the authority of his opinion be vouched for the gentleman's proposition, it will be proper to consider what is the fair interpretation of that resolution, to which Mr. Madison is understood to have given his sanction. As the gentleman construes it, it is an authority for him. Possibly, he may not have adopted the right construction. That resolution declares, that, *in the case of the dangerous exercise of powers not granted by the general government, the States may interpose to arrest the progress of the evil.* But how interpose, and what does this declaration purport? Does it mean no more than that there may be extreme cases, in which the people, in any mode of assembling, may resist usurpation, and relieve themselves from a tyrannical government? No one will deny this. Such resistance is not only acknowledged to be just in America, but in England also. Blackstone admits as much, in the theory, and practice, too, of the English constitution. We, Sir, who oppose the Carolina doctrine, do not deny that the people may, if they choose, throw off any government when it becomes oppressive and intolerable, and erect a better in its stead. We all know that civil institutions are established for the public benefit, and that when they cease to answer the ends of their existence they may be changed. But I do not understand the doctrine now contended for to be that, which, for the sake of distinction, we may call the right of revolution. I understand the gentleman to maintain, that, without revolution, without civil commotion, without rebellion, a remedy for supposed abuse and transgression of the powers of the general government lies in a direct appeal to the interference of the State governments.

[Mr. Hayne here rose and said: He did not contend for the mere right of revolution, but for the right of constitutional resistance. What he maintained was, that in case of a plain, palpable violation of the Constitution by the general government, a State may interpose; and that this interposition is constitutional.

Mr. Webster resumed:—]

So, Sir, I understood the gentleman, and am happy to find that I did not misunderstand him. What he contends for is, that it is constitutional to interrupt the administration of the Constitution itself, in the hands of those who are chosen and sworn to administer it, by the direct interference, in form of law, of the States, in virtue of their sovereign capacity. The inherent right in the people to reform their government I do not deny; and they have another right, and that is, to resist unconstitutional laws, without overturning the government. It is no doctrine of mine that unconstitutional laws bind the people. The great question is, Whose prerogative is it to decide on the constitutionality or unconstitutionality of the laws? On that, the main debate hinges. The proposition, that, in case of a supposed violation of the Constitution by Congress, the States have a constitutional right to interfere and annul the law of Congress, is the proposition of the gentleman. I do not admit it. If the gentleman had intended no more than to assert the right of revolution for justifiable cause, he would have said only what all agree to. But I cannot conceive that there can be a middle course, between submission to the laws, when regularly pronounced constitutional, on the one hand, and open resistance, which is revolution or rebellion, on the other. I say, the right of a State to annul a law of Congress cannot be maintained, but on the ground of the inalienable right of man to resist oppression; that is to say, upon the ground of revolution. I admit that there is an ultimate violent remedy, above the Constitution and in defiance of the Constitution, which may be resorted to when a revolution is to be justified. But I do not admit, that, under the Constitution and in conformity with it, there is any mode in which a State government, as a member of the Union, can interfere and stop the progress of the general government, by force of her own laws, under any circumstances whatever.

This leads us to inquire into the origin of this government and the source of its power. Whose agent is it? Is it the creature of the State legislatures, or the creature of the people? If the government of the United States be the agent of the State governments, then they may control it, provided they can agree in the manner of controlling it; if it be the agent of the people, then the people alone can control it, restrain it, modify, or reform it. It is observable enough, that the doctrine for which the honorable gentleman contends leads him to the necessity of maintaining, not only that this general government is the creature of the States, but that it is the creature of each of the States severally, so that each may assert the power for itself of determining whether it acts within the limits of its authority. It is the servant of four-and-twenty masters, of different wills and different purposes, and yet bound to obey all. This absurdity (for it seems no less) arises from a misconception as to the origin of this government and its true character. It is, Sir, the people's Constitution, the people's government, made for the people, made by the people, and answerable to the people. The people of the United States have declared that the Constitution shall be the supreme law. We must either admit the proposition, or dispute their authority. The States are, unquestionably, sovereign, so far as their sovereignty is not affected by this supreme law. But the State legislatures, as political bodies, however sovereign, are yet not sovereign over the people. So far as the people have given power to the general government, so far the grant is unquestionably good, and the government holds of the people, and not of the State governments. We are all agents of the same supreme power, the people. The general government and the State governments derive their authority from the same source. Neither can, in relation to the other, be called primary, though one is definite and restricted, and the other general and residuary. The national government possesses those powers which it can be shown the people have conferred on it, and no more. All the rest belongs to the State governments, or to the people themselves. So far as the people have restrained State sovereignty, by the expression of their will, in the Constitution of the United States, so far, it must be admitted, State sovereignty is effectually controlled. I do not contend that it is, or ought to be, controlled farther. The sentiment to which I have referred propounds that State sovereignty is only to be controlled by its own "feeling of justice"; that is to say, it is not to be controlled at all, for one who is to follow his own feelings is under no legal control. Now, however men may think this ought to be, the fact is, that the people of the United States have chosen to impose control on State sovereignties. There are those, doubtless, who wish they had been left without restraint; but the Constitution has ordered the matter differently. To make war, for instance, is an exercise of sovereignty; but the Constitution declares that no State shall make war. To coin money is another exercise of sovereign power, but no State is at liberty to coin money. Again, the Constitution says that no sovereign State shall be so sovereign as to make a treaty. These prohibitions, it must be confessed, are a control on the State sovereignty of South Carolina, as well as of the other States, which does not arise "from her own feelings of honorable justice." The opinion referred to, therefore, is in defiance of the plainest provisions of the Constitution.

There are other proceedings of public bodies which have already been alluded to, and to which I refer again, for the purpose of ascertaining more fully what is the length and breadth of that doctrine, denominated the Carolina doctrine, which the honorable member has now stood up on this floor to maintain. In one of them I find it resolved, that "the tariff of 1828, and every other tariff designed to promote one branch of industry at the expense of others, is contrary to the meaning and intention of the federal compact; and such a dangerous, palpable, and deliberate usurpation of power, by a determined majority, wielding the general government beyond the limits of its delegated powers, as calls upon the States which compose the suffering minority, in their sovereign capacity, to exercise the powers which, as sovereigns, necessarily devolve upon them, when their compact is violated."

Observe, Sir, that this resolution holds the tariff of 1828, and every other tariff designed to promote one branch of industry at the expense of another, to be such a dangerous, palpable, and deliberate usurpation of power, as calls upon the States, in their sovereign capacity, to interfere by their own authority. This denunciation, Mr. President, you will please to observe, includes our old tariff of 1816, as well as all others; because that was established to promote the interest of the manufacturers of cotton, to the manifest and admitted injury of the Calcutta cotton trade. Observe, again, that all the qualifications are here rehearsed and charged upon the tariff, which are necessary to bring the case within the gentleman's proposition. The tariff is a usurpation; it is a dangerous usurpation; it is a palpable usurpation; it is a deliberate usurpation. It is such a usurpation, therefore, as calls upon the States to exercise their right of interference. Here is a case, then, within the gentleman's principles, and all his qualifications of his principles. It is a case for action. The Constitution is plainly, dangerously, palpably, and deliberately violated; and the States must interpose their own authority to arrest the law. Let us suppose the State of South Carolina to express this same opinion, by the voice of her legislature. That would be very imposing; but what then? Is the voice of one State conclusive? It so happens that, at the very moment when South Carolina resolves that the tariff laws are unconstitutional, Pennsylvania and Kentucky resolve exactly the reverse. *They* hold those laws to be both highly proper and strictly constitutional. And now, Sir, how does the honorable member propose to deal with this case? How does he relieve us from this difficulty, upon any principle of his? His construction gets us into it; how does he propose to get us out?

In Carolina, the tariff is a palpable, deliberate usurpation; Carolina, therefore, may nullify it, and refuse to pay the duties. In Pennsylvania, it is both clearly constitutional and highly expedient; and there the duties are to be paid. And yet we live under a government of uniform laws, and under a Constitution too, which contains an express provision, as it happens, that all duties shall be equal in all the States. Does not this approach absurdity?

If there be no power to settle such questions, independent of either of the States, is not the whole Union a rope of sand? Are we not thrown back again, precisely, upon the old Confederation?

It is too plain to be argued. Four-and-twenty interpreters of constitutional law, each with a power to decide for itself, and none with authority to bind any body else, and this constitutional law the only bond of their union! What is such a state of things but a mere connection during pleasure, or, to use the phraseology of the times, *during feeling*? And that feeling, too, not the feeling of the people, who established the Constitution, but the feeling of the State governments.

In another of the South Carolina addresses, having premised that the crisis requires "all the concentrated energy of passion," an attitude of open resistance to the laws of the Union is advised. Open resistance to the laws, then, is the constitutional remedy, the conservative power of the State, which the South Carolina doctrines teach for the redress of political evils, real or imaginary. And its authors further say, that, appealing with confidence to the Constitution itself, to justify their opinions, they cannot consent to try their accuracy by the courts of justice. In one sense, indeed, Sir, this is assuming an attitude of open resistance in favor of liberty. But what sort of liberty? The liberty of establishing their own opinions, in defiance of the opinions of all others; the liberty of judging and of deciding exclusively themselves, in a matter in which others have as much right to judge and decide as they; the liberty of placing their own opinions above the judgment of all others, above the laws, and above the Constitution. This is their liberty, and this is the fair result of the proposition contended for by the honorable gentleman. Or, it may be more properly said, it is identical with it rather than a result from it.

In the same publication we find the following:—"Previously to our Revolution, when the arm of oppression was stretched over New England, where did our Northern brethren meet with a braver sympathy than that which sprung from the bosoms of Carolinians? We had no extortion, no oppression, no collision with the king's ministers, no navigation interests springing up, in envious rivalry of England."

This seems extraordinary language. South Carolina no collision with the king's ministers in 1775! No extortion! No oppression! But, Sir, it is also most significant language. Does any man doubt the purpose for which it was penned? Can any one fail to see that it was designed to raise in the reader's mind the question, whether, *at this time*,—that is to say, in 1828,—South Carolina has any collision with the king's ministers, any oppression, or extortion, to fear from England? whether, in short, England is not as naturally the friend of South Carolina as New England, with her navigation interests springing up in envious rivalry of England?

Is it not strange, Sir, that an intelligent man in South Carolina, in 1828, should thus labor to prove that, in 1775, there was no hostility, no cause of war, between South Carolina and England? That she had no occasion, in reference to her own interest, or from a regard to her own welfare, to take up arms in the Revolutionary contest? Can any one account for the expression of such strange sentiments, and their circulation through the State, otherwise than by supposing the object to be what I have already intimated, to raise the question, if they had no *"collision"* (mark the expression) with the ministers of King George the Third, in 1775, what *collision* have they, in 1828, with the ministers of King George the Fourth? What is there now in the existing state of things, to separate Carolina from *Old*, more, or rather, than from *New England*?

Resolutions, Sir, have been recently passed by the legislature of South Carolina. I need not refer to them; they go no farther than the honorable gentleman himself has gone, and I hope not so far. I content myself, therefore, with debating the matter with him.

And now, Sir, what I have first to say on this subject is, that at no time, and under no circumstances, has New England, or any State in New England, or any respectable body of persons in New England, or any public man of standing in New England, put forth such a doctrine as this Carolina doctrine.

The gentleman has found no case, he can find none, to support his own opinions by New England authority. New England has studied the Constitution in other schools, and under other teachers. She looks upon it with other regards, and deems more highly and reverently both of its just authority and its utility and excellence. The history of her legislative proceedings may be traced. The ephemeral effusions of temporary bodies, called together by the excitement of the occasion, may be hunted up; they have been hunted up. The opinions and votes of her public men, in and out of Congress, may be explored. It will all be in vain. The Carolina doctrine can derive from her neither countenance nor support. She rejects it now; she always did reject it; and till she loses her senses, she always will reject it. The honorable member has referred to expressions on the subject of the embargo law, made in this place, by an honorable and venerable gentleman, now favoring us with his presence. He quotes that distinguished Senator as saying, that, in his judgment, the embargo law was unconstitutional, and that therefore, in his opinion, the people were not bound to obey it. That, Sir, is perfectly constitutional language. An unconstitutional law is not binding; *but then it does not rest with a resolution or a law of a State legislature to decide whether an act of Congress be or be not constitutional.* An unconstitutional act of Congress would not bind the people of this District, although they have no legislature to interfere in their behalf; and, on the other hand, a constitutional law of Congress does bind the citizens of every State, although all their legislatures should undertake to annul it by act or resolution. The venerable Connecticut Senator is a constitutional lawyer, of sound principles and enlarged knowledge; a statesman practised and experienced, bred in the company of Washington, and holding just views upon the nature of our governments. He believed the embargo unconstitutional, and so did others; but what then? Who did he suppose was to decide that question? The State legislatures? Certainly not. No such sentiment ever escaped his lips.

Let us follow up, Sir, this New England opposition to the embargo laws; let us trace it, till we discern the principle which controlled and governed New England throughout the whole course of that opposition. We shall then see what similarity there is between the New England school of constitutional opinions, and this modern Carolina school. The gentleman, I think, read a petition from some single individual addressed to

the legislature of Massachusetts, asserting the Carolina doctrine; that is, the right of State interference to arrest the laws of
the Union. The fate of that petition shows the sentiment of the
legislature. It met no favor. The opinions of Massachusetts
were very different. They had been expressed in 1798, in answer
to the resolutions of Virginia, and she did not depart from
them, nor bend them to the times. Misgoverned, wronged, oppressed, as she felt herself to be, she still held fast her integrity
to the Union. The gentleman may find in her proceedings
much evidence of dissatisfaction with the measures of government, and great and deep dislike to the embargo; all this makes
the case so much the stronger for her; for, notwithstanding
all this dissatisfaction and dislike, she still claimed no right to
sever the bonds of the Union. There was heat, and there was
anger in her political feeling. Be it so; but neither her heat nor
her anger betrayed her into infidelity to the government. The
gentleman labors to prove that she disliked the embargo as
much as South Carolina dislikes the tariff, and expressed her
dislike as strongly. Be it so; but did she propose the Carolina
remedy? did she threaten to interfere, by State authority, to
annul the laws of the Union? That is the question for the gentleman's consideration.

No doubt, Sir, a great majority of the people of New England conscientiously believed the embargo law of 1807 unconstitutional; as conscientiously, certainly, as the people of South
Carolina hold that opinion of the tariff. They reasoned thus:
Congress has power to regulate commerce; but here is a law,
they said, stopping all commerce, and stopping it indefinitely.
The law is perpetual; that is, it is not limited in point of time,
and must of course continue until it shall be repealed by some
other law. It is as perpetual, therefore, as the law against treason
or murder. Now, is this regulating commerce, or destroying it?
Is it guiding, controlling, giving the rule to commerce, as a subsisting thing, or is it putting an end to it altogether? Nothing is
more certain, than that a majority in New England deemed
this law a violation of the Constitution. The very case required
by the gentleman to justify State interference had then arisen.
Massachusetts believed this law to be "a deliberate, palpable,
and dangerous exercise of a power not granted by the Constitution." Deliberate it was, for it was long continued; palpable

she thought it, as no words in the Constitution gave the power, and only a construction, in her opinion most violent, raised it; dangerous it was, since it threatened utter ruin to her most important interests. Here, then, was a Carolina case. How did Massachusetts deal with it? It was, as she thought, a plain, manifest, palpable violation of the Constitution, and it brought ruin to her doors. Thousands of families, and hundreds of thousands of individuals, were beggared by it. While she saw and felt all this, she saw and felt also, that, as a measure of national policy, it was perfectly futile; that the country was no way benefited by that which caused so much individual distress; that it was efficient only for the production of evil, and all that evil inflicted on ourselves. In such a case, under such circumstances, how did Massachusetts demean herself? Sir, she remonstrated, she memorialized, she addressed herself to the general government, not exactly "with the concentrated energy of passion," but with her own strong sense, and the energy of sober conviction. But she did not interpose the arm of her own power to arrest the law, and break the embargo. Far from it. Her principles bound her to two things; and she followed her principles, lead where they might. First, to submit to every constitutional law of Congress, and secondly, if the constitutional validity of the law be doubted, to refer that question to the decision of the proper tribunals. The first principle is vain and ineffectual without the second. A majority of us in New England believed the embargo law unconstitutional; but the great question was, and always will be in such cases, Who is to decide this? Who is to judge between the people and the government? And, Sir, it is quite plain, that the Constitution of the United States confers on the government itself, to be exercised by its appropriate department, and under its own responsibility to the people, this power of deciding ultimately and conclusively upon the just extent of its own authority. If this had not been done, we should not have advanced a single step beyond the old Confederation.

Being fully of opinion that the embargo law was unconstitutional, the people of New England were yet equally clear in the opinion, (it was a matter they did doubt upon,) that the question, after all, must be decided by the judicial tribunals of the United States. Before those tribunals, therefore, they brought

the question. Under the provisions of the law, they had given
bonds to millions in amount, and which were alleged to be for-
feited. They suffered the bonds to be sued, and thus raised the
question. In the old-fashioned way of settling disputes, they
went to law. The case came to hearing, and solemn argument;
and he who espoused their cause, and stood up for them against
the validity of the embargo act, was none other than that great
man, of whom the gentleman has made honorable mention,
Samuel Dexter. He was then, Sir, in the fulness of his knowledge, and the maturity of his strength. He had retired from
long and distinguished public service here, to the renewed pursuit of professional duties, carrying with him all that enlargement and expansion, all the new strength and force, which an
acquaintance with the more general subjects discussed in the
national councils is capable of adding to professional attainment, in a mind of true greatness and comprehension. He was a
lawyer, and he was also a statesman. He had studied the Constitution, when he filled public station, that he might defend it; he
had examined its principles that he might maintain them. More
than all men, or at least as much as any man, he was attached
to the general government and to the union of the States. His
feelings and opinions all ran in that direction. A question of
constitutional law, too, was, of all subjects, that one which was
best suited to his talents and learning. Aloof from technicality,
and unfettered by artificial rule, such a question gave opportunity for that deep and clear analysis, that mighty grasp of principle, which so much distinguished his higher efforts. His very
statement was argument; his inference seemed demonstration.
The earnestness of his own conviction wrought conviction in
others. One was convinced, and believed, and assented, because
it was gratifying, delightful, to think, and feel, and believe, in
unison with an intellect of such evident superiority.

Mr. Dexter, Sir, such as I have described him, argued the
New England cause. He put into his effort his whole heart, as
well as all the powers of his understanding; for he had avowed,
in the most public manner, his entire concurrence with his
neighbors on the point in dispute. He argued the cause; it was
lost, and New England submitted. The established tribunals
pronounced the law constitutional, and New England acquiesced. Now, Sir, is not this the exact opposite of the doctrine of

the gentleman from South Carolina? According to him, instead
of referring to the judicial tribunals, we should have broken up
the embargo by laws of our own; we should have repealed it,
quoad New England; for we had a strong, palpable, and oppressive case. Sir, we believed the embargo unconstitutional;
but still that was matter of opinion, and who was to decide it?
We thought it a clear case; but, nevertheless, we did not take
the law into our own hands, because we did not wish to bring
about a revolution, nor to break up the Union; for I maintain,
that between submission to the decision of the constituted tribunals, and revolution, or disunion, there is no middle ground;
there is no ambiguous condition, half allegiance and half rebellion. And, Sir, how futile, how very futile it is, to admit the
right of State interference, and then attempt to save it from the
character of unlawful resistance, by adding terms of qualification to the causes and occasions, leaving all these qualifications,
like the case itself, in the discretion of the State governments.
It must be a clear case, it is said, a deliberate case, a palpable
case, a dangerous case. But then the State is still left at liberty
to decide for herself what is clear, what is deliberate, what is
palpable, what is dangerous. Do adjectives and epithets avail
any thing?

Sir, the human mind is so constituted, that the merits of both
sides of a controversy appear very clear, and very palpable, to
those who respectively espouse them; and both sides usually
grow clearer as the controversy advances. South Carolina sees
unconstitutionality in the tariff; she sees oppression there also,
and she sees danger. Pennsylvania, with a vision not less sharp,
looks at the same tariff, and sees no such thing in it; she sees it
all constitutional, all useful, all safe. The faith of South Carolina is strengthened by opposition, and she now not only sees,
but *resolves*, that the tariff is palpably unconstitutional, oppressive, and dangerous; but Pennsylvania, not to be behind her
neighbors, and equally willing to strengthen her own faith by a
confident asseveration, *resolves*, also, and gives to every warm
affirmative of South Carolina, a plain, downright, Pennsylvania
negative. South Carolina, to show the strength and unity of her
opinion, brings her assembly to a unanimity, within seven
voices; Pennsylvania, not to be outdone in this respect any
more than in others, reduces her dissentient fraction to a single

vote. Now, Sir, again, I ask the gentleman, What is to be done? Are these States both right? Is he bound to consider them both right? If not, which is in the wrong? or rather, which has the best right to decide? And if he, and if I, are not to know what the Constitution means, and what it is, till those two State legislatures, and the twenty-two others, shall agree in its construction, what have we sworn to, when we have sworn to maintain it? I was forcibly struck, Sir, with one reflection, as the gentleman went on in his speech. He quoted Mr. Madison's resolutions, to prove that a State may interfere, in a case of deliberate, palpable, and dangerous exercise of a power not granted. The honorable member supposes the tariff law to be such an exercise of power; and that consequently a case has arisen in which the State may, if it see fit, interfere by its own law. Now it so happens, nevertheless, that Mr. Madison deems this same tariff law quite constitutional. Instead of a clear and palpable violation, it is, in his judgment, no violation at all. So that, while they use his authority for a hypothetical case, they reject it in the very case before them. All this, Sir, shows the inherent futility, I had almost used a stronger word, of conceding this power of interference to the State, and then attempting to secure it from abuse by imposing qualifications of which the States themselves are to judge. One of two things is true; either the laws of the Union are beyond the discretion and beyond the control of the States; or else we have no constitution of general government, and are thrust back again to the days of the Confederation.

Let me here say, Sir, that if the gentleman's doctrine had been received and acted upon in New England, in the times of the embargo and nonintercourse, we should probably not now have been here. The government would very likely have gone to pieces, and crumbled into dust. No stronger case can ever arise than existed under those laws; no States can ever entertain a clearer conviction than the New England States then entertained; and if they had been under the influence of that heresy of opinion, as I must call it, which the honorable member espouses, this Union would, in all probability, have been scattered to the four winds. I ask the gentleman, therefore, to apply his principles to that case; I ask him to come forth and declare, whether, in his opinion, the New England States would have been justified in interfering to break up the embargo system under the conscientious opinions which they held upon it? Had they a right to annul that law? Does he admit or deny? If what is thought palpably unconstitutional in South Carolina justifies that State in arresting the progress of the law, tell me whether that which was thought palpably unconstitutional also in Massachusetts would have justified her in doing the same thing. Sir, I deny the whole doctrine. It has not a foot of ground in the Constitution to stand on. No public man of reputation ever advanced it in Massachusetts in the warmest times, or could maintain himself upon it there at any time.

I wish now, Sir, to make a remark upon the Virginia resolutions of 1798. I cannot undertake to say how these resolutions were understood by those who passed them. Their language is not a little indefinite. In the case of the exercise by Congress of a dangerous power not granted to them, the resolutions assert the right, on the part of the State, to interfere and arrest the progress of the evil. This is susceptible of more than one interpretation. It may mean no more than that the States may interfere by complaint and remonstrance, or by proposing to the people an alteration of the Federal Constitution. This would all be quite unobjectionable. Or it may be that no more is meant than to assert the general right of revolution, as against all governments, in cases of intolerable oppression. This no one doubts, and this, in my opinion, is all that he who framed the resolutions could have meant by it; for I shall not readily believe that he was ever of opinion that a State, under the Constitution and in conformity with it, could, upon the ground of her own opinion of its unconstitutionality, however clear and palpable she might think the case, annul a law of Congress, so far as it should operate on herself, by her own legislative power.

I must now beg to ask, Sir, Whence is this supposed right of the States derived? Where do they find the power to interfere with the laws of the Union? Sir, the opinion which the honorable gentleman maintains is a notion founded in a total misapprehension, in my judgment, of the origin of this government, and of the foundation on which it stands. I hold it to be a popular government, erected by the people; those who administer it, responsible to the people; and itself capable of being amended and modified, just as the people may choose it should be. It is as popular, just as truly emanating from the people, as the State governments. It is created for one purpose; the State governments for another. It has its own powers; they have theirs. There is no more authority with them to arrest the operation of a law of Congress, than with Congress to arrest the operation of their laws. We are here to administer a Constitution emanating immediately from the people, and trusted by them to our administration. It is not the creature of the State governments. It is of no moment to the argument, that certain acts of the State legislatures are necessary to fill our seats in this body. That is not one of their original State powers, a part of the sovereignty of the State. It is a duty which the people, by the Constitution itself, have imposed on the State legislatures; and which they might have left to be performed elsewhere, if they had seen fit. So they have left the choice of President with electors; but all this does not affect the proposition that this whole government, President, Senate, and House of Representatives, is a popular government. It leaves it still all its popular character. The governor of a State (in some of the States) is chosen, not directly by the people, but by those who are chosen by the people, for the purpose of performing, among other duties, that of electing a governor. Is the government of the State, on that account, not a popular government? This government, Sir, is the independent offspring of the popular will. It is not the creature of State legislatures; nay, more, if the whole truth must be told, the people brought it into existence, established it, and have hitherto supported it, for the very purpose, amongst others, of imposing certain salutary restraints on State sovereignties. The States cannot now make war; they cannot contract alliances; they cannot make, each for itself, separate regulations of commerce; they cannot lay imposts; they cannot coin money. If this Constitution, Sir, be the creature of State legislatures, it must be admitted that it has obtained a strange control over the volitions of its creators.

The people, then, Sir, erected this government. They gave it a Constitution, and in that Constitution they have enumerated the powers which they bestow on it. They have made it a limited government. They have defined its authority. They have restrained it to the exercise of such powers as are granted; and all others, they declare, are reserved to the States or the people. But, Sir, they have not stopped here. If they had, they would have accomplished but half their work. No definition can be so clear, as to avoid possibility of doubt; no limitation so precise, as to exclude all uncertainty. Who, then, shall construe this grant of the people? Who shall interpret their will, where it may be supposed they have left it doubtful? With whom do they repose this ultimate right of deciding on the powers of the government? Sir, they have settled all this in the fullest manner. They have left it with the government itself, in its appropriate branches. Sir, the very chief end, the main design, for which the whole Constitution was framed and adopted, was to establish a government that should not be obliged to act through State agency, or depend on State opinion and State discretion. The people had had quite enough of that kind of government under the Confederation. Under that system, the legal action, the application of law to individuals, belonged exclusively to the States. Congress could only recommend; their acts were not of binding force, till the States had adopted and sanctioned them. Are we in that condition still? Are we yet at the mercy of State discretion and State construction? Sir, if we are, then vain will be our attempt to maintain the Constitution under which we sit.

But, Sir, the people have wisely provided, in the Constitution itself, a proper, suitable mode and tribunal for settling questions of constitutional law. There are in the Constitution grants of powers to Congress, and restrictions on these powers. There are, also, prohibitions on the States. Some authority must, therefore, necessarily exist, having the ultimate jurisdiction to fix and ascertain the interpretation of these grants, restrictions, and prohibitions. The Constitution has itself pointed out, ordained, and established that authority. How has it accomplished this great and essential end? By declaring, Sir, that *"the Constitution, and the laws of the United States made in pursuance thereof, shall be the supreme law of the land, any thing in the constitution or laws of any State to the contrary notwithstanding."*

This, Sir, was the first great step. By this the supremacy of the Constitution and laws of the United States is declared. The people so will it. No State law is to be valid which comes in conflict with the Constitution, or any law of the United States passed in pursuance of it. But who shall decide this question of interference? To whom lies the last appeal? This, Sir, the Constitution itself decides also, by declaring, "*that the judicial power shall extend to all cases arising under the Constitution and laws of the United States.*" These two provisions cover the whole ground. They are, in truth, the keystone of the arch! With these it is a government; without them it is a confederation. In pursuance of these clear and express provisions, Congress established, at its very first session, in the judicial act, a mode for carrying them into full effect, and for bringing all questions of constitutional power to the final decision of the Supreme Court. It then, Sir, became a government. It then had the means of self-protection; and but for this, it would, in all probability, have been now among things which are past. Having constituted the government, and declared its powers, the people have further said, that, since somebody must decide on the extent of these powers, the government shall itself decide; subject, always, like other popular governments, to its responsibility to the people. And now, Sir, I repeat, how is it that a State legislature acquires any power to interfere? Who, or what, gives them the right to say to the people, "We, who are your agents and servants for one purpose, will undertake to decide, that your other agents and servants, appointed by you for another purpose, have transcended the authority you gave them!" The reply would be, I think, not impertinent,—"Who made you a judge over another's servants? To their own masters they stand or fall."

Sir, I deny this power of State legislatures altogether. It cannot stand the test of examination. Gentlemen may say, that, in an extreme case, a State government might protect the people from intolerable oppression. Sir, in such a case, the people might protect themselves, without the aid of the State governments. Such a case warrants revolution. It must make, when it comes, a law for itself. A nullifying act of a State legislature cannot alter the case, nor make resistance any more lawful. In maintaining these sentiments, Sir, I am but asserting the rights of the people. I state what they have declared, and insist on their right to declare it. They have chosen to repose this power in the general government, and I think it my duty to support it, like other constitutional powers.

For myself, Sir, I do not admit the competency of South

Carolina, or any other State, to prescribe my constitutional duty; or to settle, between me and the people, the validity of laws of Congress, for which I have voted. I decline her umpirage. I have not sworn to support the Constitution according to her construction of its clauses. I have not stipulated, by my oath of office or otherwise, to come under any responsibility, except to the people, and those whom they have appointed to pass upon the question, whether laws, supported by my votes, conform to the Constitution of the country. And, Sir, if we look to the general nature of the case, could any thing have been more preposterous, than to make a government for the whole Union, and yet leave its powers subject, not to one interpretation, but to thirteen or twenty-four interpretations? Instead of one tribunal, established by all, responsible to all, with power to decide for all, shall constitutional questions be left to four-and-twenty popular bodies, each at liberty to decide for itself, and none bound to respect the decisions of others; and each at liberty, too, to give a new construction on every new election of its own members? Would any thing, with such a principle in it, or rather with such a destitution of all principle, be fit to be called a government? No, Sir. It should not be denominated a Constitution. It should be called, rather, a collection of topics for everlasting controversy; heads of debate for a disputatious people. It would not be a government. It would not be adequate to any practical good, or fit for any country to live under.

To avoid all possibility of being misunderstood, allow me to repeat again, in the fullest manner, that I claim no powers for the government by forced or unfair construction. I admit that it is a government of strictly limited powers; of enumerated, specified, and particularized powers; and that whatsoever is not granted, is withheld. But notwithstanding all this, and however the grant of powers may be expressed, its limit and extent may yet, in some cases, admit of doubt; and the general government would be good for nothing, it would be incapable of long existing, if some mode had not been provided in which those doubts, as they should arise, might be peaceably, but authoritatively, solved.

And now, Mr. President, let me run the honorable gentleman's doctrine a little into its practical application. Let us look at his probable *modus operandi*. If a thing can be done, an in-genious man can tell *how* it is to be done, and I wish to be in-formed *how* this State interference is to be put in practice, without violence, bloodshed, and rebellion. We will take the existing case of the tariff law. South Carolina is said to have made up her opinion upon it. If we do not repeal it (as we probably shall not), she will then apply to the case the remedy of her doctrine. She will, we must suppose, pass a law of her legislature, declaring the several acts of Congress, usually called the tariff laws, null and void, so far as they respect South Carolina, or the citizens thereof. So far, all is a paper transac-tion, and easy enough. But the collector at Charleston is col-lecting the duties imposed by these tariff laws. He, therefore, must be stopped. The collector will seize the goods if the tariff duties are not paid. The State authorities will undertake their rescue, the marshal, with his posse, will come to the collector's aid, and here the contest begins. The militia of the State will be called out to sustain the nullifying act. They will march, Sir, under a very gallant leader; for I believe the honorable mem-ber himself commands the militia of that part of the State. He will raise the NULLIFYING ACT on his standard, and spread it out as his banner! It will have a preamble, setting forth, that the tariff laws are palpable, deliberate, and dangerous viola-tions of the Constitution! He will proceed, with this banner flying, to the custom-house in Charleston,

"All the while,
Sonorous metal blowing martial sounds."

Arrived at the custom-house, he will tell the collector that he must collect no more duties under any of the tariff laws. This he will be somewhat puzzled to say, by the way, with a grave countenance, considering what hand South Carolina herself had in that of 1816. But, Sir, the collector would not, probably, desist, at his bidding. He would show him the law of Con-gress, the treasury instruction, and his own oath of office. He would say, he should perform his duty, come what come might.

Here would ensue a pause; for they say that a certain still-ness precedes the tempest. The trumpeter would hold his breath awhile, and before all this military array should fall on the custom-house, collector, clerks, and all, it is very probable some of those composing it would request of their gallant commander-in-chief to be informed a little upon the point of law; for they have, doubtless, a just respect for his opinions as a lawyer, as well as for his bravery as a soldier. They know he has read Blackstone and the Constitution, as well as Turenne and Vauban. They would ask him, therefore, something concerning their rights in this matter. They would inquire, whether it was not somewhat dangerous to resist a law of the United States. What would be the nature of their offence, they would wish to learn, if they, by military force and array, resisted the execution in Carolina of a law of the United States, and it should turn out, after all, that the law *was constitutional*? He would answer, of course, Treason. No lawyer could give any other answer. John Fries, he would tell them, had learned that, some years ago. How, then, they would ask, do you propose to defend us? We are not afraid of bullets, but treason has a way of taking people off that we do not much relish. How do you propose to defend us? "Look at my floating banner," he would reply; "see there the *nullifying law*!" Is it your opinion, gallant commander, they would then say, that, if we should be indicted for treason, that same floating banner of yours would make a good plea in bar? "South Carolina is a sovereign State," he would reply. That is true; but would the judge admit our plea? "These tariff laws," he would repeat, "are unconstitutional, palpably, deliberately, dangerously." That may all be so; but if the tribunal should not happen to be of that opinion, shall we swing for it? We are ready to die for our country, but it is rather an awkward business, this dying without touching the ground! After all, that is a sort of hemp tax worse than any part of the tariff.

Mr. President, the honorable gentleman would be in a dilemma, like that of another great general. He would have a knot before him which he could not untie. He must cut it with his sword. He must say to his followers, "Defend yourselves with your bayonets"; and this is war,—civil war.

Direct collision, therefore, between force and force, is the unavoidable result of that remedy for the revision of unconstitutional laws which the gentleman contends for. It must happen in the very first case to which it is applied. Is not this the plain result? To resist by force the execution of a law, generally, is treason. Can the courts of the United States take notice of the indulgence of a State to commit treason? The common saying, that a State cannot commit treason herself, is nothing to the purpose. Can she authorize others to do it? If John Fries had produced an act of Pennsylvania, annulling the law of Congress, would it have helped his case? Talk about it as we will, these doctrines go the length of revolution. They are incompatible with any peaceable administration of the government. They lead directly to disunion and civil commotion; and therefore it is, that at their commencement, when they are first found to be maintained by respectable men, and in a tangible form, I enter my public protest against them all.

The honorable gentleman argues, that if this government be the sole judge of the extent of its own powers, whether that right of judging be in Congress or the Supreme Court, it equally subverts State sovereignty. This the gentleman sees, or thinks he sees, although he cannot perceive how the right of judging, in this matter, if left to the exercise of State legislatures, has any tendency to subvert the government of the Union. The gentleman's opinion may be, that the right *ought not* to have been lodged with the general government; he may like better such a constitution as we should have under the right of State interference; but I ask him to meet me on the plain matter of fact. I ask him to meet me on the Constitution itself. I ask him if the power is not found there, clearly and visibly found there?

But, Sir, what is this danger, and what are the grounds of it? Let it be remembered, that the Constitution of the United States is not unalterable. It is to continue in its present form no longer than the people who established it shall choose to continue it. If they shall become convinced that they have made an injudicious or inexpedient partition and distribution of power between the State governments and the general government, they can alter that distribution at will.

If any thing be found in the national Constitution, either by original provision or subsequent interpretation, which ought not to be in it, the people know how to get rid of it. If any construction, unacceptable to them, be established, so as to become practically a part of the Constitution, they will amend it, at their own sovereign pleasure. But while the people choose to maintain it as it is, while they are satisfied with it, and refuse to change it, who has given, or who can give, to the State legislatures a right to alter it, either by interference, construction, or otherwise? Gentlemen do not seem to recollect that the people have any power to do any thing for themselves. They imagine there is no safety for them, any longer than they are under the close guardianship of the State legislatures. Sir, the people have not trusted their safety, in regard to the general Constitution, to these hands. They have required other security, and taken other bonds. They have chosen to trust themselves, first, to the plain words of the instrument, and to such construction as the government themselves, in doubtful cases, should put on their own powers, under their oaths of office, and subject to their responsibility to them; just as the people of a State trust their own State governments with a similar power. Secondly, they have reposed their trust in the efficacy of frequent elections, and in their own power to remove their own servants and agents whenever they see cause. Thirdly, they have reposed trust in the judicial power, which, in order that it might be trustworthy, they have made as respectable, as disinterested, and as independent as was practicable. Fourthly, they have seen fit to rely, in case of necessity, or high expediency, on their known and admitted power to alter or amend the Constitution, peaceably and quietly, whenever experience shall point out defects or imperfections. And, finally, the people of the United States have at no time, in no way, directly or indirectly, authorized any State legislature to construe or interpret *their* high instrument of government; much less, to interfere, by their own power, to arrest its course and operation.

If, Sir, the people in these respects had done otherwise than they have done, their constitution could neither have been preserved, nor would it have been worth preserving. And if its plain provisions shall now be disregarded, and these new doctrines interpolated in it, it will become as feeble and helpless a being as its enemies, whether early or more recent, could possibly desire. It will exist in every State but as a poor dependent on State permission. It must borrow leave to be; and will be, no longer than State pleasure, or State discretion, sees fit to grant the indulgence, and to prolong its poor existence.

But, Sir, although there are fears, there are hopes also. The people have preserved this, their own chosen Constitution, for forty years, and have seen their happiness, prosperity, and renown grow with its growth, and strengthen with its strength. They are now, generally strongly attached to it. Overthrown by direct assault, it cannot be; evaded, undermined, NULLI-FIED, it will not be, if we, and those who shall succeed us here, as agents and representatives of the people, shall conscientiously and vigilantly discharge the two great branches of our public trust, faithfully to preserve, and wisely to administer it.

Mr. President, I have thus stated the reasons of my dissent to the doctrines which have been advanced and maintained. I am conscious of having detained you and the Senate much too long. I was drawn into the debate with no previous deliberation, such as is suited to the discussion of so grave and important a subject. But it is a subject of which my heart is full, and I have not been willing to suppress the utterance of its spontaneous sentiments. I cannot, even now, persuade myself to relinquish it, without expressing once more my deep conviction, that since it respects nothing less than the Union of the States, it is of most vital and essential importance to the public happiness. I profess, Sir, in my career hitherto, to have kept steadily in view the prosperity and honor of the whole country, and the preservation of our Federal Union. It is to that Union we owe our safety at home, and our consideration and dignity abroad. It is to that Union that we are chiefly indebted for whatever makes us most proud of our country. That Union we reached only by the discipline of our virtues in the severe school of adversity. It had its origin in the necessities of disordered finance, prostrate commerce, and ruined credit. Under its benign influences, these great interests immediately awoke, as from the dead, and sprang forth with newness of life. Every year of its duration has teemed with fresh proofs of its utility and its blessings; and although our territory has stretched out wider and wider, and our population spread farther and farther, they have not outrun its protection or its benefits. It has been to us all a copious fountain of national, social, and personal happiness.

I have not allowed myself, Sir, to look beyond the Union, to see what might lie hidden in the dark recess behind. I have not coolly weighed the chances of preserving liberty when the bonds that unite us together shall be broken asunder. I have not accustomed myself to hang over the precipice of disunion, to see whether, with my short sight, I can fathom the depth of the abyss below; nor could I regard him as a safe counsellor in the affairs of this government, whose thoughts should be mainly bent on considering, not how the Union may be best preserved, but how tolerable might be the condition of the people when it should be broken up and destroyed. While the Union lasts, we have high, exciting, gratifying prospects spread out before us, for us and our children. Beyond that I seek not to penetrate the veil. God grant that in my day, at least, that curtain may not rise! God grant that on my vision never may be opened what lies behind! When my eyes shall be turned to behold for the last time the sun in heaven, may I not see him shining on the broken and dishonored fragments of a once glorious Union; on States dissevered, discordant, belligerent; on a land rent with civil feuds, or drenched, it may be, in fraternal blood! Let their last feeble and lingering glance rather behold the gorgeous ensign of the republic, now known and honored throughout the earth, still full high advanced, its arms and trophies streaming in their original lustre, not a stripe erased or polluted, nor a single star obscured, bearing for its motto, no such miserable interrogatory as "What is all this worth?" nor those other words of delusion and folly, "Liberty first and Union afterwards"; but everywhere, spread all over in characters of living light, blazing on all its ample folds, as they float over the sea and over the land, and in every wind under the whole heavens, that other sentiment, dear to every true American heart,—Liberty *and* Union, now and for ever, one and inseparable!

ANDREW JACKSON

Second Inaugural Address

Washington, D.C., March 4, 1833

F ELLOW CITIZENS: The will of the American people, expressed through their unsolicited suffrages, calls me before you to pass through the solemnities preparatory to taking upon myself the duties of President of the United States for another term. For their approbation of my public conduct through a period which has not been without its difficulties, and for this renewed expression of their confidence in my good intentions, I am at a loss for terms adequate to the expression of my gratitude. It shall be displayed to the extent of my humble abilities in continued efforts so to administer the Government as to preserve their liberty and promote their happiness.

So many events have occurred within the last four years which have necessarily called forth—sometimes under circumstances the most delicate and painful—my views of the principles and policy which ought to be pursued by the General Government that I need on this occasion but allude to a few leading considerations connected with some of them.

The foreign policy adopted by our Government soon after the formation of our present Constitution, and very generally pursued by successive Administrations, has been crowned with almost complete success, and has elevated our character among the nations of the earth. To do justice to all and to submit to wrong from none has been during my Administration its governing maxim, and so happy have been its results that we are not only at peace with all the world, but have few causes of controversy, and those of minor importance, remaining unadjusted.

In the domestic policy of this Government there are two objects which especially deserve the attention of the people and their representatives, and which have been and will continue to be the subjects of my increasing solicitude. They are the preservation of the rights of the several States and the integrity of the Union.

These great objects are necessarily connected, and can only be attained by an enlightened exercise of the powers of each within its appropriate sphere in conformity with the public will constitutionally expressed. To this end it becomes the duty of all to yield a ready and patriotic submission to the laws constitutionally enacted, and thereby promote and strengthen a proper confidence in those institutions of the several States and of the United States which the people themselves have ordained for their own government.

My experience in public concerns and the observation of a life somewhat advanced confirm the opinions long since imbibed by me, that the destruction of our State governments or the annihilation of their control over the local concerns of the people would lead directly to revolution and anarchy, and finally to despotism and military domination. In proportion, therefore, as the General Government encroaches upon the rights of the States, in the same proportion does it impair its own power and detract from its ability to fulfill the purposes of its creation. Solemnly impressed with these considerations, my countrymen will ever find me ready to exercise my constitutional powers in arresting measures which may directly or indirectly encroach upon the rights of the States or tend to consolidate all political power in the General Government. But of equal, and, indeed, of incalculable, importance is the union of these States, and the sacred duty of all to contribute to its preservation by a liberal support of the General Government in the exercise of its just powers. You have been wisely admonished to "accustom yourselves to think and speak of the Union as of the palladium of your political safety and prosperity, watching for its preservation with jealous anxiety, discountenancing whatever may suggest even a suspicion that it can in any event be abandoned, and indignantly frowning upon the first dawning of any attempt to alienate any portion of our country from the rest or to enfeeble the sacred ties which now link together the various parts." Without union our independence and liberty would never have been achieved; without union they never can be maintained. Divided into twenty-four, or even a smaller number, of separate communities, we shall see our internal trade burdened with numberless restraints and exactions; communication between distant points and sections obstructed or cut off; our sons made soldiers to deluge with blood the fields they now till in peace; the mass of our people borne down and impoverished by taxes to support armies and navies, and military leaders at the head of their victorious legions becoming our lawgivers and judges. The loss of liberty, of all good government, of peace, plenty, and happiness, must inevitably follow a dissolution of the Union. In supporting it, therefore, we support all that is dear to the freeman and the philanthropist.

The time at which I stand before you is full of interest. The eyes of all nations are fixed on our Republic. The event of the existing crisis will be decisive in the opinion of mankind of the practicability of our federal system of government. Great is the stake placed in our hands; great is the responsibility which must rest upon the people of the United States. Let us realize the importance of the attitude in which we stand before the world. Let us exercise forbearance and firmness. Let us extricate our country from the dangers which surround it and learn wisdom from the lessons they inculcate.

Deeply impressed with the truth of these observations, and under the obligation of that solemn oath which I am about to take, I shall continue to exert all my faculties to maintain the just powers of the Constitution and to transmit unimpaired to posterity the blessings of our Federal Union. At the same time, it will be my aim to inculcate by my official acts the necessity of exercising by the General Government those powers only that are clearly delegated; to encourage simplicity and economy in the expenditures of the Government; to raise no more money from the people than may be requisite for these objects, and in a manner that will best promote the interests of all classes of the community and of all portions of the Union. Constantly bearing in mind that in entering into society "individuals must give up a share of liberty to preserve the rest," it will be my desire so to discharge my duties as to foster with our brethren in all parts of the country a spirit of liberal concession and compromise, and, by reconciling our fellow-citizens to those partial sacrifices which they must unavoidably make for the preservation of a greater good, to recommend our invaluable Government and Union to the confidence and affections of the American people.

Finally, it is my most fervent prayer to that Almighty Being before whom I now stand, and who has kept us in His hands from the infancy of our Republic to the present day, that He will so overrule all my intentions and actions and inspire the hearts of my fellow-citizens that we may be preserved from dangers of all kinds and continue forever a united and happy people.

ELY MOORE

Address to the General Trades' Union

New York City, December 2, 1833

F ELLOW MECHANICS,

We have assembled, on the present occasion, for the purpose of publicly proclaiming the motives which induced us to organize a General Union of the various trades and arts in this city and its vicinity, as well as to defend the course, and to vindicate the measures we design to pursue. This is required of us by a due regard to the opinions of our fellow men.

We conceive it, then, to be a *truth*, enforced and illustrated by the concurrent testimony of history and daily observation, that man is disposed to avail himself of the possessions and services of his fellow man, without rendering an equivalent, and to prefer claims to that which of right belongs to another. This may be considered a hard saying; but we have only to turn our eyes inward, and examine ourselves, in order to admit, to the full extent, the truth of the proposition, that man, by nature, is selfish and aristocratic. *Self-love* is constitutional with man, and is displayed in every stage, and in all the diversities of life; in youth, and in manhood, in prosperity and in adversity. It not only discovers itself in the strifes and contentions of states and empires, but in the smallest fraternities—in the factory and the workshop—in the village school and the family circle. In fact, wherever society exists, however small the number, or rude the members, you will find *self-love* stimulating to a contest for power and dominion. This prevailing disposition of the human heart, so far from being an evil in itself, is one of the elements of life, and essential to the welfare of society. The *selfish* generate the *social* feelings. It is only pernicious in its tendency and operation, therefore, when it passes its true and natural bounds, and urges man to encroach upon the rights and immunities of man.

In order to mitigate the evils that ever flow from inordinate

desire and unrestricted selfishness; to restrain and chastise unlawful ambition; to protect the weak against the strong, and to
establish an equilibrium of power among nations and individuals, conventional compacts were formed. These confederate
associations, have never been fully able to stay the march of intolerance, of mercenary ambition, or of political despotism.
Even in this fair land of freedom, where liberty and equality
are guaranteed to all, and where our written constitutions have
so wisely provided limitations to power, and securities for
rights, the *twin fiends, intolerance* and *aristocracy*, presume to
rear their hateful crests! But we have no cause to marvel at this.
Wherever man exists, under whatever form of government, or
whatever be the structure or organization of society, this principle of his nature, selfishness, will appear, operating either for
evil or for good. To curb it sufficiently by legislative enactments
is impossible. Much *can* be done, however, towards restraining
it within proper limits, by unity of purpose, and concert of action, on the part of the *producing classes*. To contribute toward
the achievement of this great end, is one of the objects of the
"General Trades' Union." Wealth, we all know, constitutes the
aristocracy of this country. Happily no distinctions are known
among us save what wealth and worth confer. No legal barriers
are erected to protect exclusive privileges, or unmerited rank.
The law of primogeniture forms no part of American jurisprudence; and our revolution has converted all feudal tenures into
allodial rights. The greatest danger, therefore, which threatens
the stability of our government, and the liberty of the people,
is an undue accumulation and distribution of wealth. And I
do conceive, that *real danger* is to be apprehended from this
source, notwithstanding that tendency to distribution which
naturally grows out of the character of our statutes of conveyance, of inheritance, and descent of property; but, by securing
to the producing classes a fair, certain, and equitable compensation for their toil and skill, we insure a more just and equal
distribution of wealth than can ever be effected by statutory
law.

Unlike the septennial reversion of the Jews, or the Agrarian
law of Rome, the principle for which we contend holds out to
individuals proper motives for exertion and enterprise. We ask,
then, what better means can be devised for promoting a more

equal distribution of wealth, than for the producing classes to *claim*, and by virtue of union and concert, *secure their claims* to their respective portions? And why should not those who have the toil, have the enjoyment also? Or why should the sweat that flows from the brow of the labourer, be converted into a source of revenue for the support of the crafty or indolent?

It has been averred, with great truth, that all governments become cruel and aristocratical in their character and bearing, in proportion as one part of the community is elevated, and the other depressed; and that misery and degradation to the many, is the inevitable result of such a state of society. And we regard it to be equally true, that in proportion as the line of distinction between the employer and the employed is *widened*, the condition of the latter inevitably verges toward a state of vassalage, while that of the former as certainly approximates toward supremacy; and that whatever system is calculated to make the many dependent upon, or subject to, the few, not only tends to the subversion of the natural rights of man, but is hostile to the best interests of the community, as well as to the spirit and genius of our government. Fully persuaded that the foregoing positions are incontrovertible, WE, in order to guard against the encroachments of aristocracy, to preserve our natural and political rights, to elevate our moral and intellectual condition, to promote our pecuniary interests, to narrow the line of distinction between the journeyman and employer, to establish the honour and safety of our respective vocations upon a more secure and permanent basis, and to alleviate the distresses of those suffering from want of employment, have deemed it expedient to form ourselves into a "General Trades' Union."

It may be asked, how these desirable objects are to be achieved by a general union of trades? How the encroachments of aristocracy, for example, are to be arrested by our plan? We answer, by enabling the producer to enjoy the full benefit of his productions, and thus diffuse the streams of wealth more generally, and, consequently, more equally, throughout all the ramifications of society. This point conceded, and conceded it must be, it is not requisite, we conceive, that the line of investigation should be dropped very deep, in order to bring it up tinged with proof, that the verity of our other positions necessarily follow. But for the particular means by which the several objects just enumerated are to be attained, we beg leave to refer to our constitution, and to our general plan of organization.

There are, doubtless, many individuals who are resolved, right or wrong, to misrepresent our principles, impeach our measures, and impugn our motives. Be it so. They can harm us not. Let them, if they please, draw the vengeful bow to the very double, and let fly the barbed arrows—the temper and amplitude of the shield of the Union, we trust, will be found sufficient to ward off the stroke. Their shafts, though winged by hate, and hurled with their utmost strength, will scarcely reach the mark; but, like the spent javelin of aged Priam, fall to the ground without a blow. We have the consolation of knowing that all good men—all who love their country, and rejoice in the improvement of the condition of their fellow men—will acknowledge the policy of our views, and the purity of our motives. The residue, I trust, will not defame us with their approbation. Their censure we can endure, but their praise we should regard as an eternal disgrace. And why, let me ask, should the character of our union be obnoxious to censure? Wherefore is it wrong in principle? Which of its avowed objects reprehensible? What feature of it opposed to the public good? I defy the ingenuity of man to point to a single measure which it recognizes, that is wrong in itself, or in its tendency. What! is it wrong for men to unite for the purpose of resisting the encroachments of aristocracy? Wrong! to restrict the principle of selfishness to its proper and legitimate bounds and objects? Wrong! to oppose monopoly and mercenary ambition? Wrong! to consult the interests, and seek the welfare, of the producing classes? Wrong! to attempt the elevation of our moral and intellectual standing? Wrong! to establish the honour and safety of our respective vocations upon a more secure and permanent basis? I ask—in the name of heaven I ask—can it be wrong for men to attempt the melioration of their condition, and the preservation of their natural and political rights?

I am aware, that the charge of "illegal combination" is raised against us. The cry is as senseless, as 'tis stale and unprofitable. Why, I would inquire, have not journeymen the same right to ask their own price for their own property, or services, that employers have? or that merchants, physicians, and lawyers have? Is that equal justice, which makes it an offence for journeymen to combine for the purpose of maintaining their present prices, or raising their wages, while employers may combine with impunity for the purpose of lowering them? I admit that such is the common law. All will agree, however, that it is neither wise, just, nor politic, and that it is directly opposed to the spirit and genius of our free institutions, and ought, therefore, to be abrogated.

It is further alleged, that the "General Trades' Union" is calculated to encourage *strikes* and *turn-outs*. Now, the truth lies in the converse. Our constitution sets forth, that "Each trade or art may represent to the Convention, through their delegates, their grievances, who shall take cognizance thereof, and decide upon the same." And further, that "No trade or art shall strike for higher wages than they at present receive, without the sanction of the Convention." True, if the Convention shall, after due deliberation, decide that the members of any trade or art there represented are aggrieved, and that their demands are warrantable, then the Convention is pledged to sustain the members of such trade or art to the uttermost. Hence, employers will discover, that it is idle, altogether idle, to prolong a contest with journeymen, when they are backed by the Convention. And journeymen will perceive, that in order to obtain assistance from the Convention, in the event of a *strike*, or *turn-out*, that their claims must be founded in justice, and all their measures be so taken as not to invade the rights, or sacrifice the welfare, of employers. So far, then, from the Union encouraging strikes or turn-outs, it is destined, we conceive, to allay the jealousies, and abate the asperities, which now unhappily exist between employers and the employed.

We all know, that whenever journeymen stand out for higher wages, that the public are sufferers, as well as the parties more immediately concerned. The Trades' Union, we conceive, will have a tendency to correct this evil.

Again; it is alleged, that it is setting a dangerous precedent for journeymen to combine for the purpose of coercing a compliance with their terms. It may, indeed, be dangerous to aristocracy—dangerous to monopoly—dangerous to oppression—but not to the general good, or the public tranquillity.

Internal danger to a state is not to be apprehended from a general effort on the part of the people to improve and exalt their condition, but from an alliance of the crafty, designing, and intriguing few. What! tell us, in this enlightened age, that the welfare of the people will be endangered by a voluntary act of the people themselves? That the people will wantonly seek their own destruction? That the safety of the state will be plotted against by three fourths of the members comprising the state! O how worthless, how poor and pitiful, are all such arguments and objections!

MEMBERS OF THE "GENERAL TRADES' UNION!" permit me, at this time, and before I leave this part of my subject, to caution you against the wiles and perfidy of those individuals, who will approach you as friends, but who, in reality and in truth, are your secret enemies. You will know them by this sign: an attempt to excite your jealousy against certain individuals, who, peradventure, may stand somewhat conspicuous among you; by insinuations that these men have ulterior designs to accomplish; that political ambition lies at the root of the whole matter, and all that. This will be done, recollect, not so much to injure the individuals against whom the insinuations are ostensibly directed, as to abuse you, by impairing your confidence in the "Union." It is the heart of the Union at which these assassins aim the stroke! 'Tis the Union! your political safeguard, that they would prostrate! 'Tis the Union! the citadel of your hopes, that they would sack and destroy!! I entreat you, therefore, to shun such counsellors as you would the pestilence. Remember the tragedy in the garden of Eden, and hold no communion with the adversary. But why caution you thus, when your own good sense would so readily teach you, that the very attempt to deceive you was an insult to your understandings? Because, did they not presume upon your ignorance and credulity, they would never attempt to alienate your affections from the Union. Remember, then, fellow mechanics, that the man who attempts to seduce you from your duty to yourselves, to your families, and to your brother mechanics, by misrepresenting the objects of the Union, offers you not only an insult, but an *injury!* Remember! that those defamers would exult at your misfortunes—would "laugh at your calamity, and mock when your fear cometh." Aye, would trample down your liberties, and rejoice at beholding—

> "The seal of bondage on your brows—
> Its badge upon your breasts!"

You will not regard it as ill-timed, nor irrelevant to the present occasion, my friends, should I invite your attention for a moment to the important bearing which the useful arts have upon the welfare of society. In order to estimate their importance correctly, it is necessary to contemplate the condition of man as we find him in a state of nature, where the arts are unknown, and where the lights of civilization have never dawned upon his path. Wherever man is thus situated, we find him a creature of blind impulse, of passion, and of instinct—of grovelling hopes, and of low desires; and his wants, like those of the brute, supplied only by the spontaneous productions of nature—his only covering, a scanty supply of hair—his food, the acorn and the loathsome insect—the cavern his dwelling, the earth his couch, and the rock his pillow! The superiority of man's condition, therefore, over that of other animals, is attributable solely to the influence of the mechanic arts. Without their aid, the native powers of his mind, however great, could never have been developed; and the physical sciences, which he has been enabled to master, in a state of civilization, would have still been numbered among the secrets of nature. What progress, for example, could he have made in the science of astronomy, without the aid of a telescope? In chemistry, without the retort and receiver? In anatomy and surgery, without the knife and the tourniquet? In agriculture, without the hoe and the mattock, the spade and the plough, the scythe and the pruning hook?

Contrast *civilized*, with *savage* man. Compare, for example, the Boschmen of Southern Africa, whose chief supply of food consists of the locust and the ant; or the Esquimaux, who feast and fatten upon train oil and seals' blubber, with the inhabitants of those countries where the useful arts are known and cultivated, and you will be enabled to estimate more correctly their influence upon the welfare of man. The condition of the Esquimaux, although wretched and degraded, is far preferable to that of the Bosjesman. Physiologists tell us, that their physical structures and capacities are about the same. The comparative elevation, therefore, of the one, is ascribable, directly, to the fact of the arts having been partially introduced among them. The Esquimaux has been taught to construct the boat, to string the bow, and to fashion the spear. But the Boschmen are utterly ignorant of the arts, and, consequently, strangers to civilization and improvement; their moral and intellectual features, therefore, have been the same, through the succession of ages and the lapse of centuries! No improvement—no melioration in their condition have taken place; but, through the transition of generations, sires and sons have lived and died alike degraded!

Various philosophers have attributed the differences which exist between nations, to various causes. Hippocrates, for example, with regard to the Scythians; and Strabo, as respecting the Medes and Armenians, took it for granted, that *climate* alone causes the *distinctions*, or *similitudes*, whether *physical* or *moral*, which characterize various people. This ancient hypothesis has been adopted, to the full extent, by thousands, notwithstanding its manifest absurdity. La Mothe adopted the puerile and chimerical theory of natural *sympathies*, and *antipathies*, and contended, that to their influence was ascribable the difference which distinguishes one nation from another. While Bayle, with much more propriety and truth, attributed those differences to political interests and institutions of state. That climate and government exert great influence over the character and conduct of man, and create striking national distinctions, is admitted. It is a combination of those two causes which makes the Frenchman loquacious, gay, volatile; the Spaniard, taciturn, staid, and solemn; the Ottoman, dull, languid, and listless; the German, hardy, diligent, and contemplative. But, however opposite and distinctive the habits and principles which the influence of climate and government may generate, and however those causes operate upon the character and condition of man, yet they affect his happiness and welfare but remotely and partially indeed, when compared with the influence exercised by the mechanic arts. For, although men of different nations may be opposed in fundamental opinions, and the elements of their thoughts and actions be at variance, yet, where the arts are practised, man is *civilized*, and, therefore, comparatively blessed; but where the arts are unknown—no matter what be the climate, the form of government, or the circumstances that surround him—man is a *savage*, and degraded to the level of the brute that resembles him in form, and in habits. Civilized man, therefore, *is*, *what he is*, by means of the mechanic arts.

Who were the pioneers of the West? What class of society prepared the way for the agriculturist, the merchant, and the professional man? Were they not artificers? Was not the forest made to bow before the stroke of the *axe*? the stubborn glebe to yield to the *hoe* and the *ploughshare*? Was not the harvest gathered with the *rake* and the *reaping hook*? the grain converted into flour by the *mill* or the *mortar*? and the raw material into fabrics by the *wheel* and the *loom*, and fashioned into garments with the *shears* and the *needle*? The game of the forest, and of the prairie, secured with the *trap* and the *rifle*? The habitation, erected by means of the *trowel*, the *hammer*, and the *saw*? Unquestionably, without the agency of the arts, the adventurer must have returned disappointed, or perished in the enterprise. Place man, without a knowledge of the arts and their uses, in a country with a rigid climate, a stubborn and ungrateful soil, and want, starvation, and death, must be his destiny. No country can be cleared and settled, nor colony founded, without the aid of the mechanic arts. First settlers, therefore, are as much dependent upon the useful arts for their subsistence, comfort, and welfare, as are the plants of the field, for their life and growth, upon the life of the sun, and the dews of heaven!

I will no longer detain you on this part of my subject; but, in conclusion, will merely observe, that the culture of the mechanic arts are not only calculated to elicit, expand, and invigorate the inventive faculties of man—to strengthen his natural imbecility—inform his natural ignorance, and enrich his natural poverty; but, also, to advance his morals, refine his manners, and elevate his character.

My object in inviting you to a consideration of this subject at the present time, is to impress upon your minds the importance of the situation which you, in reality, ought to occupy in society. This you seem to have lost sight of in a very great degree; and, from some cause or other, have relinquished your claims to that consideration to which, as mechanics and as men, you are entitled. You have, most unfortunately for yourselves, and for the respectability of your vocations, become apparently unconscious of your own worth, and been led to regard your callings as humble and inferior, and your stations as too subordinate in life. And why?—why is it so? Why should the producer consider himself inferior to the consumer? Or why should the mechanic, who builds a house, consider himself less important than the owner or occupant? It is strange, indeed, and to me perfectly unaccountable, that the artificer, who prepares the accommodations, the comforts, and embellishments of life, should consider himself of less consequence than those to whose pleasure and convenience he ministers.

It was observed by some one of the olden time, that "A man's pretensions was the standard by which the world judged of his merits." Were you to be judged by this standard, my friends, your merits, I apprehend, would be somewhat difficult to find. Do not consider, from these observations, however, that I would urge you to put forth claims that are not well founded, or make pretensions to that which you are not entitled to. Far from it. I merely wish you to take a fair estimate of your worth and importance—but not to overrate yourselves or your callings. I would have you remember, however, that when a man sinks in his own estimation, he is sure to sink also in the estimation of the world. And just so in relation to any occupation or calling in life. If those who follow it, confess it to be degrading, the world is sure to consider it no *better*, but generally in a *worse* light.

In order to be convinced of the blessings conferred upon society by means of the useful arts, we have only to look around us for a moment. But, like all blessings familiar to us, they are not properly appreciated; and the services of those who practice them, like the services of all common benefactors, are vastly underrated. It is not my intention, as I have already intimated, to go into detail, or to attempt a comparison between the relative merits, or rather utility, of the various arts practised among us. Such a course would be neither gratifying, instructive, nor ingenuous. I will briefly allude, however, to some of those modem inventions and discoveries in mechanical philosophy, which I conceive to be of the greatest importance to the world.

The *art of printing* has, perhaps, contributed more essentially to the welfare of mankind, to the advancement of society, and to the promotion and diffusion of political, physical, and ethical truths, than all the arts beside. It is, in fact, an art that is "*preservative* of all arts." Wherever it is known and encouraged, the progressive improvement of society is certain, and the march of mind secure and unembarrassed. But where the press has never shed its light, or dispensed its intellectual treasures, the night of ignorance, and the gloom of superstition, rests upon the soul, and obscures the intellect of man; and should it be struck from existence, with its rich treasures of instruction, the world, ere long, would be merged in night and barbarism.

The invention of the *mariner's compass*, or, rather, the discovery of that mystic and incomprehensible law which gives polarity to the needle, claims to be ranked, on account of its importance, next to the press. The navigator is no longer compelled to keep the coast within view in order to steer his course aright, but now seeks the middle of the ocean with confidence and security; nor does it require a period of ten years, as in the days of Ulysses and Æneas, to make a voyage from Ilium to the island of Ithaca, or to the shores of Italy. Neither does the modern navigator require a PALINURUS, as did the pious Trojan of old, to stand at the helm, and observe the stars of heaven. He possesses, in the compass, a safer guide than either Orion or Arcturus. But for the compass, those geographical limits, which, from the dawn of creation had concealed one half of the world from the other, had never been passed; and America, perhaps, at this moment would have been a pathless world of woods, made vocal by the serpent's hiss, the panther's scream, and the wild man's terrific yell; and, perchance, here—even on this consecrated spot, where now stands the temple of the living God—the wild fox would have made his den, or the red man his habitation!

The *steam engine* next takes rank in point of importance. Its effects on the condition of society are of incalculable importance. In almost every branch of the arts it is hailed as an auxiliary. Its application to nautical purposes is of greater utility, and of deeper concernment to the world, than the world at present imagines. It is an agent, whose power and influence will be most beneficially felt in contributing toward the preservation of the American Union, by overcoming those physical barriers that have isolated one section of our country from the other. By means of its power, space is annihilated, and the inhabitants, from the extremes of the Union, are now brought into frequent and friendly intercourse. Let it be borne in mind, however, that neither the printing press, nor the mariner's compass, nor the steam engine, could have been produced without the aid of the common mechanic. The toil and skill of the artificers in wood, and iron, and steel, were requisite to their completion. The square and the compass, the axe and the plane, the hammer and the anvil, were all indispensable to their production.

Thus far I have combined my remarks chiefly to the mechanic arts; but we must not stop here; the field we have entered upon embraces a still wider range. We have only viewed the unadorned parts, and the furrow ground. The gardens and groves of flowers, and of beauty, we have yet to explore.

These later belong to genius and the fine arts—the former to the arts of want and of necessity; yet, in the progress of civilization and improvement, they become, in a thousand ways, so intimately blended, and so allied by their constant association, that their connexion remains fixed and inseparable; and it is difficult to treat of the one, without some reference to the other. A love and an admiration for the fine arts, and a due appreciation of their merits, tend to improve the mind, and beget in it the principles of good taste, order, and refinement, which soon exhibit their influence in the increasing excellence of every thing that we do, contrive, or execute. These help, also, when duly cultivated, to augment our pleasures and our happiness. It has been said, by an eminent writer, that the *essence* of a fine art is *expression*, and that its *end* is *pleasure*; and this is true. It is a truth which all within the hearing of my voice will feel and acknowledge, when we come to the illustration of its principles. For example: there is a painting on silk, representing the implements employed in our various pursuits, displayed in the form of a circle, and united by an oaken wreath. This design, as you all know, is emblematical of the Trades' Union. This, then, is *fine art*, (and a noble specimen it is too.) What, you will ask, is its utility, and how can it inspire pleasure? Can you, as mechanics and artists, look upon that *banner* without being reminded of your united strength? Can you contemplate that proud emblem of your union and your power, without feeling the secret emotions of pride and pleasure steal into your bosoms, and throb through your hearts? Can you witness the close alliance of your interests and your welfare, as there represented, and not feel your mutual sympathies, and friendship, and love, warmed, and elevated, and strengthened? And can you feel all this, and say that the picture is of no utility? that it imparts no pleasure? There, again, is a painting on canvass, representing the face of a good and amiable personage. This is also fine art. Now, what is its *essence*? Not flesh, nor bones—neither is it breath, nor life, nor spirit; and yet it has the *expression* of all these. What, then, is the *end*—the *use*—of all these presentations? Most assuredly it is pleasure; pleasure, too, of the noblest and most exalted character. Have you lost a relative or a friend whom you loved, and whose kind and generous look was always cheering and grateful to your soul?—and have you the painted or sculptured likeness of the parted one? What language shall describe the heartfelt pleasure you feel when you sit down in your own dwelling, and survey and contemplate the features of that portrait—the faithful expression of that form and face, endeared to you by so many kindred ties of your heart and nature? Yet this is but one item in an art that contributes more abundantly to the pleasures of this life than most people imagine, or can conceive at a single view.

We will now examine some of those branches of the fine arts which have a more intimate union and fellowship with the arts of trade and manufacture. When a temple, or other public edifice is to be erected, application is made to an architect for a design; and in proportion to his genius, his judgment, and his taste, do we place our confidence in him. He gives drawings of the plan, and elevations of the building, together with all its appropriate decorations, both for the exterior and interior; by these the workmen are guided. In most instances, the architect is employed to superintend the uprearing of the structure, and he goes hand in hand with the master builder, until every part of the work is complete. The carver and the stucco-worker are also worthy of mention, and come in for their share of praise in all that pertains to the art of enrichment and decoration. If niches or pedestals are reserved for statues, or for busts, an artist of a nobler branch is called in: the sculptor is applied to, and the breathing images from his chisel beautify, and give a richness and a glory to the whole edifice. See yonder valley of the dead! Behold, there, among the monuments to departed worth, we see the united labours of the sculptor and the stonecutter—there, the sacred images of religion, of piety, and of virtue, while they speak a language in veneration of the dead, awaken emotions of pure and holy joy in the bosoms of the living. Look again at the beautiful wares of gold, and of silver manufacture, and of porcelain and furnitures: In them we discover the combined skill of the artist and the artisan; while our eyes dwell with pleasure and delight upon the beautiful delineations of the pencil, or on the more bold reliefs thrown out by the ingenious hand of the *ornamentalist*.

In the productions of the loom, also, we behold this pleasing alliance of the two arts. The flowers and vines of ten thousand forms, so elegantly and gracefully displayed over the carpeting of our floors, on the upholstery of our windows and couch of sleep, and also upon the garments of our females; all—all attest the close and intimate connexion of the mechanic arts with the arts of design—the arts of usefulness and necessity with those of taste, elegance, and pleasure. I have dwelt the longer on this part of my subject, in order that you might be enabled to realize more fully the obligations that society is under to you, as artists and mechanics, as well as to impress upon your understandings, the fact of the mutual dependency of the various trades and arts upon each other. And, my friends, it is important for you to bear in mind, that your interests and welfare are as closely allied, as intimately blended, and as mutually dependent one upon another, as are your respective pursuits.

Once more, then, permit me to ask, why it is, that artists and mechanics have so far lost sight of the importance of their callings? Why is it that those who produce, prepare, and distribute the comforts, the pleasures, and conveniences of life, should not consider themselves (what they really are) the benefactors of mankind, and assume that station in society to which their callings and their worth so justly entitle them? Do you marvel at it? Do you think it strange and mysterious? You need not. A reason can be readily assigned why other classes of society regard you as their inferiors. *Know*, then, that you have, by your servility—by your want of self-respect—by your lack of confidence in yourselves, and in each other, courted your present standing. You alone have been instrumental in assigning yourselves the subordinate and humiliating station in society of which you now complain. You have long had the power to better your general condition, but you have either been too indolent, or too careless, to exercise it. I congratulate you—most sincerely do I congratulate you, upon your present prospects. Never did your affairs wear so cheering an aspect as at present. You have, at length, wisely concluded to throw yourselves upon your rights—to gather up your energies, and consolidate your strength. Only be true to yourselves, and faithful to each other, and the issue cannot be doubtful. All the circumstances that surround you are auspicious:—The general diffusion of knowledge—the rapid march of improvement—and especially the excellent plan of organization which you have recently adopted—all augur well for your future prosperity. But should you neglect to avail yourselves of the advantages that are now presented, you would not only *merit*, but *receive*, opprobrium and oppression. Beware, therefore, that you do not sacrifice your present advantages and prospects by folly or indolence, lest slavery and infamy be your portion, and your offspring, at some future day, drag their *inherited* chains across your graves, and load your memories with reproaches and imprecations!

I am aware we shall be told, that republican governments are unpropitious to the cultivation and encouragement of the arts—especially the fine arts. This has long been a fashionable doctrine; but it is as false as fashionable. It is a libel on popular governments. When we demand the evidence, we are confidently pointed to the page of history, and referred to the patronage and facilities afforded to artists by arbitrary governments—to the munificent pensions and donations granted by the Ptolemies of Egypt—the Augustuses of Rome, and the Louises of France. Well, I am quite willing that history should decide the question—that it should be the sole arbiter in the case. In what part of the world, then, at what period, and under what form of government, did the elegant and useful arts first spring up, and *flourish most*? Was it on the borders of the Nile, or the banks of the Euphrates—or under the Memphian or Babylonian despots? Not so—no, not so. But on the barren soil of Attica, the land of Codrus and of Miltiades—within the stormy republics of Greece!

When we inquire what discoveries and progress were made in the arts, by the millions and millions of thinking beings that lived and died anterior to the era of Grecian liberty, we are referred to the pyramids of Memphis, to the "Tower on Shinar's Plain," and to the temples of Thebes——*Monuments of folly, all!*

We date the decline of the arts in Greece from the decline of her liberty. For the proof, we invite you to compare the state of the arts of the Alexandrian with that of the Periclean age. When we come down to the Augustan age—the proud era of Mæcenas—'tis *imitation all*. Not an artist stands forth in the conscious pride of originality. All—all are content to *copy the Grecian masters*. It is true, the fine arts experienced a partial resuscitation under the princes of the Flavian house, but with *them* expired the arts of Rome; and when Constantine the Great wished to adorn an arch at Byzantium, he was obliged to tear down one of Trajan's, at Rome, for sculptures. But we are not confined to ancient history alone for proofs and illustrations. The history of our own country, and within the last half century, has furnished ample testimony, that not only mechanical genius, but the intellectual powers generally, are more universally developed in *free*, than in despotic governments. Where is the nation that can point to such illustrious names in war—in eloquence—in philosophy—in astronomy—in mechanics, and in painting, as those of Washington, and Henry, and Franklin, and Rittenhouse, and Fulton, and West?

The greatest efforts of the human mind have ever been made under the auspices of free governments. The patronage of the Macedonian, Alexanderian, and Pergamean princes, was unable to arouse in their subjects the intellectual energies that characterized the citizens of Athens in the days of her "fierce democracy." The fact is, a nation's freedom and its genius *rise* and *fall together*. And so with regard to the arts. They are fostered and cultivated in proportion as the government is free, and the people enlightened and happy. But when liberty declines, the arts decline with her, and they inevitably sink into one common grave!

So far as the government under which we live being unfavourable to our interests as artists and mechanics, it is, in every respect, *most propitious*! There never was a land under heaven, where the intellectual powers of man had so fine a field, and such fair play, as they have in our own country, and in our own times. If our march, therefore, is not *onward* to honour, competency, and *fame*, the fault is all our own.

Will you meet me with the excuse, that your early opportunities in life were limited?—that you have no time for improvement?—that it is too late to enter the lists for distinction? and that you must, therefore, be content to live and die in obscurity?——Such are the common apologies of the indolent, the spiritless, and the dissolute. Let no such pretexts, therefore, be made by members of the "Trades' Union." Would you have your ambition fired, your hopes elevated, or your resolution strengthened, by glorious example? Then contemplate, for a moment, the history of those illustrious men, whose names stand as "landmarks on the cliffs of fame"—who were the artificers of their own fortunes, and who, like yourselves, were mechanics and artists. FRANKLIN, who astonished and confounded the schoolmen of Europe, and with impunity *dallied with the lightnings of heaven*, was once an obscure *journeyman printer*! His elevation was the result of his own efforts. ROGER SHERMAN, one of the most extraordinary men in the extraordinary age in which he lived—and WILLIAM GIFFORD, the immortal author of the *Baviad and Mæviad*, were both *shoemakers*. GEORGE WALTON, the distinguished patriot and jurist of Georgia, acquired his education by *torch light*, during the term of his apprenticeship to a *carpenter*! General KNOX was a *bookbinder*—and General GREENE, (the second Washington,) a *blacksmith*. But we are not limited to the past for examples. Our distinguished townsman, FRAZEE, was a common *stone-mason*. As a sculptor, he now stands unequalled in this country—and as a *self-taught* artist, unsurpassed by any in the world.

Would you enjoy the fame of those illustrious men? Then follow their example, and imitate their virtues. Like them, be diligent—be honest—be firm—be indefatigable. Pursue knowledge with a diligence that never tires, and with a perseverance that never falters; and honour, and glory, and happiness, will be your reward! You have no longer an excuse why you should not prosper and flourish, both as a body, and as individuals. You know your rights, and, consequently, feel your strength. If mortification and defeat should attend you, blame not your fellow men—the cause will be found within yourselves. Neither blame your country—the fault will not be her's! No—Land of Genius—Land of Refuge—Land of the Brave and Free!—thy sons have no cause to reproach thee! All thy deserving children will find favour in thine eyes—support on thy arm, and protection in thy bosom!

THOMAS HART BENTON

Speech in the Senate on Expunging the Censure of President Jackson

Washington, D.C., January 12, 1837

M R. PRESIDENT, it is now near three years since the resolve was adopted by the Senate, which it is my present motion, to expunge from the journal. At the moment that this resolve was adopted, I gave notice of my intention to move to expunge it; and then expressed my confident belief that the motion would eventually prevail. That expression of confidence was not an ebullition of vanity, or a presumptuous calculation, intended to accelerate the event it affected to foretell. It was not a vain boast, or an idle assumption, but was the result of a deep conviction of the injustice done President Jackson, and a thorough reliance upon the justice of the American people. I felt that the President had been wronged; and my heart told me that this wrong would be redressed. The event proves that I was not mistaken. The question of expunging this resolution has been carried to the people, and their decision has been had upon it. They decide in favor of the expurgation; and their decision has been both made and manifested, and communicated to us in a great variety of ways. A great number of States have expressly instructed their Senators to vote for this expurgation. A very great majority of the States have elected Senators and Representatives to Congress, upon the express ground of favoring this expurgation. The Bank of the United States, which took the initiative in the accusation against the President, and furnished the material and worked the machinery which was used against him, and which was then so powerful on this floor, has become more and more odious to the public mind, and musters now but a slender phalanx of friends in the two Houses of Congress. The late presidential election furnishes additional evidence of public sentiment. The

candidate who was the friend of President Jackson, the supporter of his administration, and the avowed advocate for the
expurgation, has received a large majority of the suffrages of
the whole Union, and that after an express declaration of his
sentiments on this precise point. The evidence of the public
will, exhibited in all these forms, is too manifest to be mistaken,
too explicit to require illustration, and too imperative to be
disregarded. Omitting details and specific enumeration of
proofs, I refer to our own files for the instructions to expunge—
to the complexion of the two Houses for the temper of the
people—to the denationalized condition of the Bank of the
United States for the fate of the imperious accuser—and to
the issue of the presidential election for the answer of the
Union. All these are pregnant proofs of the public will; and the
last pre-eminently so—because both the question of the expurgation and the form of the process were directly put in
issue upon it. A representative of the people from the State of
Kentucky formally interrogated a prominent candidate for the
presidency on these points, and required from him a public answer, for the information of the public mind. The answer was
given, and published, and read by all the voters before the
election; and I deem it right to refer to that answer in this place,
not only as evidence of the points put in issue, but also for the
purpose of doing more ample justice to President Jackson, by
incorporating into the legislative history of this case the high
and honorable testimony in his favor of the eminent citizen
who has just been exalted to the lofty honors of the American
presidency:

"Your last question seeks to know 'my' opinion as to the
constitutional power of the Senate or House of Representatives
to expunge or obliterate from the journals the proceedings of
a previous session.

"You will, I am sure, be satisfied, upon further consideration,
that there are but few questions of a political character less connected with the duties of the office of President of the United
States, or that might not with equal propriety be put by an
elector to a candidate for that station, than this. With the journals of neither House of Congress can he properly have any
thing to do. But as your question has doubtless been induced
by the pendency of Colonel Benton's resolutions to expunge

from the journals of the Senate certain other resolutions touching the official conduct of President Jackson, I prefer to say that I regard the passage of Colonel Benton's preamble and resolutions to be an act of justice to a faithful and greatly injured public servant, not only constitutional in itself, but imperiously demanded by a proper respect for the well-known will of the people."

I do not propose, sir, to draw violent, unwarranted, or strained inferences. I do not assume to say that the question of this expurgation was a leading or a controlling point in the issue of this election. I do not assume to say, or insinuate, that every individual, and every voter, delivered his suffrage with reference to this question. Doubtless there were many exceptions. Still, the triumphant election of the candidate who had expressed himself in the terms just quoted, and who was, besides, the personal and political friend of President Jackson, and the avowed approver of his administration, must be admitted to a place among the proofs in this case, and ranked among the high concurring evidences of the public sentiment in favor of the motion which I make.

Assuming, then, that we have ascertained the will of the people on this great question, the inquiry presents itself, how far the expression of that will ought to be conclusive of our action here. I hold that it ought to be binding and obligatory upon us; and that, not only upon the principles of representative government, which require obedience to the known will of the people, but also in conformity to the principles upon which the proceeding against President Jackson was conducted, when the sentence against him was adopted. Then, every thing was done with especial reference to the will of the people. Their impulsion was assumed to be the sole motive to action, and to them the ultimate verdict was expressly referred. The whole machinery of alarm and pressure, every engine of political and moneyed power, was put in motion, and worked for many months, to excite the people against the President, and to stir up meetings, memorials, petitions, travelling committees, and distress deputations, against him; and each symptom of popular discontent was hailed as an evidence of public will, and quoted here as proof that the people demanded the condemnation of the President. Not only legislative assemblies, and memorials from large assemblies, were then produced here as evidence of public opinion, but the petitions of boys under age, the remonstrances of a few signers, and the results of the most inconsiderable elections, were ostentatiously paraded and magnified as the evidence of the sovereign will of our constituents. Thus, sir, the public voice was every thing, while that voice, partially obtained through political and pecuniary machinations, was adverse to the President. Then, the popular will was the shrine at which all worshipped. Now, when that will is regularly, soberly, repeatedly, and almost universally, expressed through the ballot-boxes, at the various elections, and turns out to be in favor of the President, certainly no one can disregard it, nor otherwise look at it than as the solemn verdict of the competent and ultimate tribunal, upon an issue fairly made up, fully argued, and duly submitted for decision. As such verdict, I receive it. As the deliberate verdict of the sovereign people, I bow to it. I am content. I do not mean to reopen the case, nor to recommence the argument. I leave that work to others, if any others choose to perform it. For myself, I am content; and, dispensing with further argument, I shall call for judgment, and ask to have execution done upon that unhappy journal, which the verdict of millions of freemen finds guilty of bearing on its face an untrue, illegal, and unconstitutional sentence of condemnation against the approved President of the republic.

But, while declining to reopen the argument of this question, and refusing to tread over again the ground already traversed, there is another and a different task to perform; one which the approaching termination of President Jackson's administration makes peculiarly proper at this time, and which it is my privilege, and perhaps my duty, to execute, as being the suitable conclusion to the arduous contest in which we have been so long engaged: I allude to the general tenor of his administration, and to its effect, for good or for evil, upon the condition of his country. This is the proper time for such a view to be taken. The political existence of this great man now draws to a close. In little more than forty days he ceases to be a public character. In a few brief weeks he ceases to be an object of political hope to any, and should cease to be an object of political hate, or envy, to all. Whatever of motive the servile and time-serving might have found in his exalted station for raising the altar of adulation, and burning the incense of praise before him, that motive can no longer exist. The dispenser of the patronage of an empire—the chief of this great confederacy of States—is soon to be a private individual, stripped of all power to reward or to punish. His own thoughts, as he has shown us in the concluding paragraph of that message which is to be the last of its kind that we shall ever receive from him, are directed to that beloved retirement from which he was drawn by the voice of millions of freemen, and to which he now looks for that interval of repose which age and infirmities require. Under these circumstances, he ceases to be a subject for the ebullition of the passions, and passes into a character for the contemplation of history. Historically, then, shall I view him; and, limiting this view to his civil administration, I demand where is there a chief magistrate of whom so much evil has been predicted, and from whom so much good has come? Never has any man entered upon the chief magistracy of a country under such appalling predictions of ruin and wo! never has any one been so pursued with direful prognostications! Never has any one been so beset and impeded by a powerful combination of political and moneyed confederates! Never has any one in any country, where the administration of justice has risen above the knife or the bow-string, been so lawlessly and shamelessly tried and condemned by rivals and enemies, without hearing, without defence, without the forms of law or justice! History has been ransacked to find examples of tyrants sufficiently odious to illustrate him by comparison. Language has been tortured to find epithets sufficiently strong to paint him in description. Imagination has been exhausted in her efforts to deck him with revolting and inhuman attributes. Tyrant, despot, usurper; destroyer of the liberties of his country; rash, ignorant, imbecile; endangering the public peace with all foreign nations; destroying domestic prosperity at home; ruining all industry, all commerce, all manufactories; annihilating confidence between man and man; delivering up the streets of populous cities to grass and weeds, and the wharves of commercial towns to the encumbrance of decaying vessels, depriving labor of all reward; depriving industry of all employment; destroying the currency; plunging an innocent and happy people from the summit of felicity to the depths of misery, want, and despair. Such is the faint outline, followed up by actual condemnation, of the appalling denunciations daily uttered against this one man, from the moment he became an object of political competition, down to the concluding moment of his political existence.

The sacred voice of inspiration has told us that there is a time for all things. There certainly has been a time for every evil that human nature admits of to be vaticinated of President Jackson's administration; equally certain, the time has now come for all rational and well-disposed people to compare the predictions with the facts, and to ask themselves if these calamitous prognostications have been verified by events? Have we peace, or war, with foreign nations? Certainly, we have peace! peace with all the world! peace with all its benign, and felicitous, and beneficent influences! Are we respected or despised abroad? Certainly the American name never was more honored throughout the four quarters of the globe, than in this very moment. Do we hear of indignity or outrage in any quarter? of merchants robbed in foreign ports? of vessels searched on the high seas? of American citizens impressed into foreign service? of the national flag insulted any where? On the contrary, we see former wrongs repaired; no new ones inflicted. France pays twenty-five millions of francs for spoliations committed thirty years ago; Naples pays two millions one hundred thousand ducats for wrongs of the same date; Denmark pays six hundred and fifty thousand rixdollars for wrongs done a quarter of a century ago; Spain engages to pay twelve millions of reals velon for injuries of fifteen years' date; and Portugal, the last in the list of former aggressors admits her liability, and only waits the adjustment of details to close her account by adequate indemnity. So far from war, insult, contempt, and spoliation, from abroad, this denounced administration has been the season of peace and good will, and the auspicious era of universal reparation. So far from suffering injury at the hands of foreign Powers, our merchants have received indemnities for all former injuries. It has been the day of accounting, of settlement, and of retribution. The long list of arrearages, extending through four successive previous administrations, has been closed and settled up. The wrongs done to commerce for thirty years back, and under so many different Presidents, and indemnities withheld from all, have been repaired and paid over under the beneficent and glorious administration of President Jackson. But one single instance of outrage has occurred, and that at the extremities of the world, and by a piratical horde, amenable to no law but the law of force. The Malays of Summatra committed a robbery and massacre upon an American vessel. Wretches! they did not then know that Jackson was President of the United States! and that no distance, no time, no idle ceremonial of treating with robbers and assassins, was to hold back the arm of justice. Commodore Downes went out. His cannon and his bayonets struck the outlaws in their den. They paid in terror and in blood for the outrage which was committed; and the great lesson was taught to these distant pirates—to our antipodes themselves—that not even the entire diameter of this globe could protect them! and that the name of American citizen, like that of Roman citizen in the great days of the republic and of the empire, was to be the inviolable passport of all that wore it throughout the whole extent of the habitable world.

At home the most gratifying picture presents itself to the view: the public debt paid off; taxes reduced one half; the completion of the public defences systematically commenced; the compact with Georgia, uncomplied with since 1802, now carried into effect, and her soil ready to be freed, as her jurisdiction has been delivered from the presence and encumbrance of an Indian population. Mississippi and Alabama, Georgia, Tennessee and North Carolina, Ohio, Indiana, Illinois, Missouri, and Arkansas, in a word, all the States encumbered with an Indian population, have been relieved from that encumbrance; and the Indians themselves have been transferred to new and permanent homes, every way better adapted to the enjoyment of their existence, the preservation of their rights, and the improvement of their condition.

The currency is not ruined! On the contrary, seventy-five millions of specie in the country is a spectacle never seen before, and is the barrier of the people against the designs of any banks which may attempt to suspend payments, and to force a dishonored paper currency upon the community. These seventy-five millions are the security of the people against the dangers of a depreciated and inconvertible paper money. Gold, after a disappearance of thirty years, is restored to our country. All Europe beholds with admiration the success of our efforts, in three years, to supply ourselves with the currency which our constitution guaranties, and which the example of France and Holland shows to be so easily attainable, and of such incalculable value to industry, morals, economy, and solid wealth. The success of these efforts is styled, in the best London papers, not merely a reformation, but a revolution in the currency! a revolution by which our America is now regaining from Europe the gold and silver which she has been sending to them for thirty years past.

Domestic industry is not paralyzed, confidence is not destroyed, factories are not stopped, workmen are not mendicants for bread and employment, credit is not extinguished, prices have not sunk, grass is not growing in the streets of populous cities, the wharves are not lumbered with decaying vessels, columns of curses, rising from the bosoms of a ruined and agonized people, are not ascending to heaven against the destroyer of a nation's felicity and prosperity. On the contrary, the reverse of all this is true! and true to a degree that astonishes and bewilders the senses. I know that all is not gold that glitters; that there is a difference between a specious and a solid prosperity. I know that a part of the present prosperity is apparent only, the effect of an increase of fifty millions of paper money forced into circulation by one thousand banks; but after making due allowance for this fictitious and delusive excess, the real prosperity of the country is still unprecedently and transcendently great. I know that every flow must be followed by its ebb, that every expansion must be followed by its contraction. I know that a revulsion in the paper system is inevitable; but I know, also, that these seventy-five millions of gold and silver is the bulwark of the country, and will enable every honest bank to meet its liabilities, and every prudent citizen to take care of himself.

Turning to some points in the civil administration of President Jackson, and how much do we not find to admire! The great cause of the constitution has been vindicated from an imputation of more than forty years' duration. He has demonstrated, by the fact itself, that a national bank is not "necessary" to the fiscal operations of the Federal Government, and in that demonstration he has upset the argument of General Hamilton, and the decision of the Supreme Court of the United States, and all that ever has been said in favor of the constitutionality of a national bank. All this argument and decision rested upon the single assumption of the "necessity" of that institution to the Federal Government. He has shown it is not "necessary;" that the currency of the constitution, and especially a gold currency, is all that the Federal Government wants, and that she can get that whenever she pleases. In this single act he has vindicated the constitution from an unjust imputation, and knocked from under the decision of the Supreme Court the assumed fact on which it rested. He has prepared the way for the reversal of that decision; and it is a question for lawyers to answer, whether the case is not ripe for the application of that writ of most remedial nature, as Lord Coke calls it, and which was invented lest in any case there should be an oppressive defect of justice—the venerable writ of *audita querela defendentis*—to ascertain the truth of a fact happening since the judgment, and upon the due finding of which the judgment will be vacated. Let the lawyers bring their books, and answer us if there is not a case here presented for the application of that ancient and most remedial writ.

From President Jackson the country has first learned the true theory and practical intent of the constitution, in giving to the Executive a qualified negative on the legislative power of Congress. Far from being an odious, dangerous, or kingly prerogative, this power, as vested in the President, is nothing but a qualified copy of the famous veto power vested in the tribunes of the people among the Romans, and intended to suspend the passage of a law until the people themselves should have time to consider it. The qualified veto of the President destroys nothing; it only delays the passage of a law, and refers it to the people for their consideration and decision. It is the reference of the law, not to a committee of the House, or of the whole House, but to the committee of the whole Union. It is a recommitment of the bill to the people, for them to examine and consider; and if, upon this examination, they are content to pass it, it will pass at the next session. The delay of a few months is the only effect of a veto in a case where the people shall ultimately approve a law; where they do not approve it, the interposition of the veto is the barrier which saves them the infliction of a law, the repeal of which might afterwards be almost impossible. The qualified negative is, therefore, a beneficent power, intended, as General Hamilton expressly declares in the Federalist, to protect, first, the executive department from the encroachments of the legislative department; and, secondly, to preserve the people from hasty, dangerous, or criminal legislation on the part of their representatives. This is the design and intention of the veto power; and the fear expressed by General Hamilton was, that Presidents, so far from exercising it too often, would not exercise it as often as the safety of the people required; that they might lack the moral courage to stake themselves in opposition to a favorite measure of the majority of the two Houses of Congress, and thus deprive the people, in many instances, of their right to pass upon a bill before it becomes a final law. The cases in which President Jackson has exercised the veto power has shown the soundness of these observations. No ordinary President would have staked himself against the Bank of the United States, and the two Houses of Congress, in 1832. It required President Jackson to confront that power—to stem that torrent—to stay the progress of that charter, and to refer it to the people for their decision. His moral courage was equal to the crisis. He arrested the charter until it could go to the people, and they have arrested it forever. Had he not done so, the charter would have become law, and its repeal almost impossible. The people of the whole Union would now have been in the condition of the people of Pennsylvania, bestrode by the monster, in daily conflict with him, and maintaining a doubtful contest for supremacy between the Government of a State and the directory of a moneyed corporation.

To detail specific acts which adorn the administration of President Jackson, and illustrate the intuitive sagacity of his intellect, the firmness of his mind, his disregard of personal popularity, and his entire devotion to the public good, would be inconsistent with this rapid sketch, intended merely to present general views, and not to detail single actions, howsoever worthy they may be of a splendid page in the volume of history. But how can we pass over the great measure of the removal of the public moneys from the Bank of the United States in the autumn of 1833? that wise, heroic, and masterly measure of prevention, which has rescued an empire from the fangs of a merciless, revengeful, greedy, insatiate, implacable, moneyed power! It is a remark for which I am indebted to the philosophic observation of my most esteemed colleague and friend, (pointing to Dr. LINN,) that, while it requires far greater talent to foresee an evil before it happens, and to arrest it by precautionary measures, than it requires to apply an adequate remedy to the same evil after it has happened, yet the applause bestowed by the world is always greatest in the latter case. Of this the removal of the public moneys from the Bank of the United States is an eminent instance. The veto of 1832, which arrested the charter which Congress had granted, immediately received the applause and approbation of a majority of the Union; the removal of the deposites, which prevented the bank from forcing a recharter, was disapproved by a large majority of the country, and even of his own friends; yet the veto would have been unavailing, and the bank would inevitably have been rechartered, if the deposites had not been removed. The immense sums of public money since accumulated would have enabled the bank, if she had retained the possession of it, to have coerced a recharter. Nothing but the removal could have prevented her from extorting a recharter from the sufferings and terrors of the people. If it had not been for that measure, the previous veto would have been unavailing; the bank would have been again installed in power, and this entire Federal Government would have been held as an appendage to that bank, and administered according to her directions, and by her nominees. That great measure of prevention, the removal of the deposites, though feebly and faintly supported by friends at first, has expelled the bank from the field, and driven her into abeyance under a State charter. She is not dead, but, holding her capital and stockholders together under a State charter, she has taken a position to watch events, and to profit by them. The royal tiger has gone into the jungle! and, crouched on his belly, he awaits the favorable moment for emerging from his cover, and springing on the body of the unsuspicious traveller!

The Treasury order for excluding paper money from the land offices is another wise measure, originating in an enlightened forecast, and preventing great mischiefs. The President fore-saw the evils of suffering a thousand streams of paper money, issuing from a thousand different banks, to discharge them-selves on the national domain. He foresaw that if these cur-rents were allowed to run their course, that the public lands would be swept away, the Treasury would be filled with irre-deemable paper, a vast number of banks must be broken by their folly, and the cry set up that nothing but a national bank could regulate the currency. He stopped the course of these streams of paper, and, in so doing, has saved the country from a great calamity, and excited anew the machinations of those whose schemes of gain and mischief have been disappointed, and who had counted on a new edition of panic and pressure, and again saluting Congress with the old story of confidence destroyed, currency ruined, prosperity annihilated, and distress produced, by the tyranny of one man. They began their lugu-brious song; but ridicule and contempt have proved too strong for money and insolence; and the panic letter of the ex-president of the denationalized bank, after limping about for a few days, has shrunk from the lash of public scorn, and disap-peared from the forum of public debate.

The difficulty with France: what an instance it presents of the superior sagacity of President Jackson over all the common-place politicians who beset and impede his administration at home! That difficulty, inflamed and aggravated by domestic fac-tion, wore, at one time, a portentous aspect; the skill, firmness, elevation of purpose, and manly frankness, of the President, avoided the danger, accomplished the object, commanded the admiration of Europe, and retained the friendship of France. He conducted the delicate affair to a successful and mutually honorable issue. All is amicably and happily terminated, leaving not a wound, nor even a scar, behind—leaving the Frenchman and American on the ground on which they have stood for fifty years, and should forever stand; the ground of friendship, respect, good will, and mutual wishes for the honor, happi-ness, and prosperity, of each other.

But why this specification? So beneficent and so glorious has been the administration of this President, that where to begin, and where to end, in the enumeration of great measures, would be the embarrassment of him who has his eulogy to make. He came into office the first of generals; he goes out the first of statesmen. His civil competitors have shared the fate of his military opponents; and Washington city has been to the American politicians who have assailed him, what New Orleans was to the British generals who attacked his lines. Repulsed! driven back! discomfited! crushed! has been the fate of all assailants, foreign and domestic, civil and military. At home and abroad, the impress of his genius and of his character is felt. He has impressed upon the age in which he lives the stamp of his arms, of his diplomacy, and of his domestic policy. In a word, so transcendent have been the merits of his administration, that they have operated a miracle upon the minds of his most inveterate opponents. He has expunged their objections to military chieftains! He has shown them that they were mistaken; that military men were not the dangerous rulers they had imagined, but safe and prosperous conductors of the vessel of state. He has changed their fear into love. With visible signs they admit their error, and, instead of deprecating, they now invoke the reign of chieftains. They labored hard to procure a military successor to the present incumbent; and if their love goes on increasing at the same rate, the republic may be put to the expense of periodical wars, to breed a perpetual succession of these chieftains to rule over them and their posterity forever.

To drop this irony, which the inconsistency of mad opponents has provoked, and to return to the plain delineations of historical painting, the mind instinctively dwells on the vast and unprecedented popularity of this President. Great is the influence, great the power, greater than any man ever before possessed in our America, which he has acquired over the public mind. And how has be acquired it? Not by the arts of intrigue, or the juggling tricks of diplomacy; not by undermining rivals, or sacrificing public interests for the gratification of classes or individuals. But he has acquired it, first, by the exercise of an intuitive sagacity which, leaving all book learning at an immeasurable distance behind, has always enabled him to adopt the right remedy, at the right time, and to conquer soonest when the men of forms and office thought him most near to ruin and despair. Next, by a moral courage which knew no fear when the public good beckoned him to go on. Last, and chiefest, he has acquired it by an open honesty of purpose, which knew no concealments; by a straight-forwardness of action, which disdained the forms of office and the arts of intrigue; by a disinterestedness of motive, which knew no selfish or sordid calculation; a devotedness of patriotism, which staked every thing personal on the issue of every measure which the public welfare required him to adopt. By these qualities, and these means, he has acquired his prodigious popularity and his transcendent influence over the public mind; and if there are any who envy that influence and popularity, let them envy, also, and emulate, if they can, the qualities and means by which they were acquired.

Great has been the opposition to President Jackson's administration; greater, perhaps, than ever has been exhibited against any Government, short of actual insurrection and forcible resistance. Revolution has been proclaimed! and every thing has been done that could be expected to produce revolution. The country has been alarmed, agitated, convulsed. From the Senate chamber to the village bar-room, from one end of the continent to the other, denunciation, agitation, excitement, has been the order of the day. For eight years the President of this republic has stood upon a volcano, vomiting fire and flames upon him, and threatening the country itself with ruin and desolation, if the people did not expel the usurper, despot, and tyrant, as he was called, from the high place to which the suffrages of millions of freemen had elevated him.

Great is the confidence which he has always reposed in the discernment and equity of the American people. I have been accustomed to see him for many years, and under many discouraging trials; but never saw him doubt, for an instant, the ultimate support of the people. It was my privilege to see him often, and during the most gloomy period of the panic conspiracy, when the whole earth seemed to be in commotion against him, and when many friends were faltering, and stout hearts were quailing, before the raging storm which bank machination, and senatorial denunciation, had conjured up to overwhelm him. I saw him in the darkest moments of this gloomy period; and never did I see his confidence in the ultimate support of his fellow-citizens forsake him for an instant. He always said the people would stand by those who stand by them; and nobly have they justified that confidence! That verdict, the voice of millions, which now demands the expurgation of that sentence which the Senate and the bank then pronounced upon him, is the magnificent response of the people's hearts to the implicit confidence which he then reposed in them. But it was not in the people only that he had confidence; there was another, and a far higher Power, to which he constantly looked to save the country, and its defenders, from every danger; and signal events prove that he did not look to that high Power in vain.

Sir, I think it right, in approaching the termination of this great question, to present this faint and rapid sketch of the brilliant, beneficent, and glorious administration of President Jackson. It is not for me to attempt to do it justice; it is not for ordinary men to attempt its history. His military life, resplendent with dazzling events, will demand the pen of a nervous writer; his civil administration, replete with scenes which have called into action so many and such various passions of the human heart, and which has given to native sagacity so many victories over practised politicians, will require the profound, luminous, and philosophical conceptions of a Livy, a Plutarch, or a Sallust. This history is not to be written in our day. The cotemporaries of such events are not the hands to describe them. Time must first do its office—must silence the passions, remove the actors, develop consequences, and canonize all that is sacred to honor, patriotism, and glory. In after ages the historic genius of our America shall produce the writers which the subject demands—men far removed from the contests of this day, who will know how to estimate this great epoch, and how to acquire an immortality for their own names by painting, with a master's hand, the immortal events of the patriot President's life.

And now, sir, I finish the task which, three years ago, I imposed on myself. Solitary and alone, and amidst the jeers and taunts of my opponents, I put this ball in motion. The people have taken it up, and rolled it forward, and I am no longer any thing but a unit in the vast mass which now propels it. In the name of that mass I speak. I demand the execution of the edict of the people; I demand the expurgation of that sentence which the voice of a few Senators, and the power of their confederate, the Bank of the United States, has caused to be placed on the journal of the Senate, and which the voice of millions of freemen has ordered to be expunged from it.

JOHN C. CALHOUN

Speech in the Senate on Antislavery Petitions

Washington, D.C., February 6, 1837

I F THE TIME of the Senate permitted, I would feel it to be my duty to call for the reading of the mass of petitions on the table, in order that we might know what language they hold towards the slave-holding States and their institutions; but as it will not, I have selected, indiscriminately from the pile, two: one from those in manuscript, and the other from the printed, and without knowing their contents will call for the reading of them, so that we may judge, by them, of the character of the whole.

(Here the Secretary, on the call of Mr. Calhoun, read the two petitions.)

Such, resumed Mr. C, is the language held towards us and ours. The peculiar institution of the South, that on the maintenance of which the very existence of the slave-holding States depends, is pronounced to be sinful and odious, in the sight of God and man; and this with a systematic design of rendering us hateful in the eyes of the world, with a view to a general crusade against us and our institutions. This too, in the legislative halls of the Union; created by these confederated States, for the better protection of their peace, their safety and their respective institutions; and yet we, the representatives of twelve of these sovereign States against whom this deadly war is waged, are expected to sit here in silence, hearing ourselves and our constituents day after day denounced, without uttering a word—if we but open our lips, the charge of agitation is re-sounded on all sides, and we are held up as seeking to aggra-vate the evil which we resist. Every reflecting mind must see in all this, a state of things deeply and dangerously diseased.

I do not belong, said Mr. C, to the school which holds that aggression is to be met by concession. Mine is the opposite creed, which teaches that encroachments must be met at the beginning, and that those who act on the opposite principle are prepared to become slaves. In this case in particular I hold concession or compromise to be fatal. If we concede an inch, concession would follow concession—compromise would follow compromise, until our ranks would be so broken that effectual resistance would be impossible. We must meet the enemy on the frontier, with a fixed determination of maintaining our position at every hazard. Consent to receive these insulting petitions, and the next demand will be that they be referred to a committee in order that they may be deliberated and acted upon. At the last session we were modestly asked to receive them simply to lay them on the table, without any view of ulterior action. I then told the Senator from Pennsylvania, (Mr. Buchanan) who strongly urged that course in the Senate, that it was a position that could not be maintained; as the argument in favor of acting on the petitions if we were bound to receive, could not be resisted. I then said that the next step would be to refer the petition to a committee, and I already see indications that such is now the intention. If we yield, that will be followed by another, and we would thus proceed step by step to the final consummation of the object of these petitions. We are now told that the most effectual mode of arresting the progress of Abolition is to reason it down, and with this view it is urged that the petitions ought to be referred to a committee. That is the very ground which was taken at the last session in the other House, but instead of arresting its progress it has since advanced more rapidly than ever. The most unquestionable right may be rendered doubtful, if once admitted to be a subject of controversy, and that would be the case in the present instance. The subject is beyond the jurisdiction of Congress—they have no right to touch it in any shape or form, or to make it the subject of deliberation or discussion.

In opposition to this view it is urged that Congress is bound by the Constitution to receive petitions in every case and on every subject, whether within its constitutional competency or not. I hold the doctrine to be absurd, and do solemnly believe, that it would be as easy to prove that it has the right to abolish slavery, as that it is bound to receive petitions for that purpose. The very existence of the rule that requires a question to be put on the reception of petitions, is conclusive to show, that there is no such obligation. It has been a standing rule from the commencement of the Government, and clearly shows the sense of those who formed the Constitution on this point. The question on the reception would be absurd, if as is contended we are bound to receive; but I do not intend to argue the question; I discussed it fully at the last session, and the arguments then advanced neither have nor can be answered.

As widely as this incendiary spirit has spread, it has not yet infected this body, or the great mass of the intelligent and business portion of the North; but unless it be speedily stopped, it will spread and work upwards till it brings the two great sections of the Union into deadly conflict. This is not a new impression with me. Several years since, in a discussion with one of the Senators from Massachusetts, (Mr. Webster,) before this fell spirit had showed itself, I then predicted that the doctrine of the proclamation and the force bill—that this Government had a right in the last resort to determine the extent of its own powers, and enforce it at the point of the bayonet, which was so warmly maintained by that Senator, would at no distant day arouse the dormant spirit of abolitionism; I told him that the doctrine was tantamount to the assumption of unlimited power on the part of the Government, and that such would be the impression on the public mind in a large portion of the Union. The consequence would be inevitable—a large portion of the Northern States believed slavery to be a sin, and would believe it to be an obligation of conscience to abolish it, if they should feel themselves in any degree responsible for its continuance, and that his doctrine would necessarily lead to the belief of such responsibility. I then predicted that it would commence as it has with this fanatical portion of society, and that they would begin their operation on the ignorant, the weak, the young, and the thoughtless, and would gradually extend upwards till they would become strong enough to obtain political control, when he and others holding the highest stations in society, would, however reluctant, be compelled to yield to their doctrine, or be driven into obscurity. But four years have since elapsed, and all this is already in a course of regular fulfilment.

Standing at the point of time at which we have now arrived, it will not be more difficult to trace the course of future events now than it was then. Those who imagine that the spirit now abroad in the North, will die away of itself without a shout or convulsion, have formed a very inadequate conception of its real character; it will continue to rise and spread, unless prompt and efficient measures, to stay its progress, be adopted. Already it has taken possession of the pulpit, of the schools, and to a considerable extent of the press; those great instruments by which the mind of the rising generation will be formed.

However sound the great body of the non-slaveholding States are at present, in the course of a few years they will be succeeded by those who will have been taught to hate the people and institutions of nearly one half of this Union, with a hatred more deadly than one hostile nation ever entertained towards another. It is easy to see the end. By the necessary course of events, if left to themselves, we must become, finally, two people. It is impossible under the deadly hatred which must spring up between the two great sections, if the present causes are permitted to operate unchecked, that we should continue under the same political system. The conflicting elements would burst the Union asunder as powerful as are the links which hold it together. Abolition and the Union cannot co-exist. As the friend of the Union I openly proclaim it, and the sooner it is known the better. The former may now be controlled, but in a short time it will be beyond the power of man to arrest the course of events. We of the South will not, can not surrender our institutions. To maintain the existing relations between the two races, inhabiting that section of the Union, is indispensable to the peace and happiness of both. It cannot be subverted without drenching the country in blood, and extirpating one or the other of the races. Be it good or bad, it has grown up with our society and institutions, and is so interwoven with them, that to destroy it would be to destroy us as a people. But let me not be understood as admitting even by implication that the existing relations between the two races in the slave-holding States is an evil—far otherwise; I hold it to be a good, as it has thus far proved itself to be to both, and will continue to prove so if not disturbed by the fell spirit of abolition. I appeal to facts. Never before has the black race of Central Africa, from the dawn of history to the present day, attained a condition so civilized and so improved, not only physically, but morally and intellectually. It came among us in a low, degraded, and savage condition, and in the course of a few generations it has grown up under the fostering care of our institutions, as reviled as they have been, to its present comparative civilized condition. This, with the rapid increase of numbers, is conclusive proof of the general happiness of the race in spite of all the exaggerated tales to the contrary.

In the mean time, the white or European race has not degenerated. It has kept pace with its brethren in other sections of the Union where slavery does not exist. It is odious to make comparison; but I appeal to all sides whether the South is not equal in virtue, intelligence, patriotism, courage, disinterestedness, and all the high qualities which adorn our nature. I ask whether we have not contributed our full share of talents and political wisdom in forming and sustaining this political fabric; and whether we have not constantly inclined most strongly to the side of liberty, and been the first to see and first to resist the encroachments of power. In one thing only are we inferior— the arts of gain; we acknowledge that we are less wealthy than the Northern section of the Union, but I trace this mainly to the fiscal action of this Government, which has extracted much from, and spent little among us. Had it been the reverse, if the exaction had been from the other section, and the expenditure with us, this point of superiority would not be against us now as it was not at the formation of this Government.

But I take higher ground. I hold that in the present state of civilization, where two races of different origin, and distinguished by color, and other physical differences, as well as intellectual, are brought together, the relation now existing in the slave-holding States between the two, is, instead of an evil, a good—a positive good. I feel myself called upon to speak freely upon the subject where the honor and interests of those I represent are involved. I hold then, that there never has yet existed a wealthy and civilized society in which one portion of the community did not, in point of fact, live on the labor of the other. Broad and general as is this assertion, it is fully borne out by history. This is not the proper occasion, but if it were, it would not be difficult to trace the various devices by which the wealth of all civilized communities has been so unequally divided, and to show by what means so small a share has been allotted to those by whose labor it was produced, and so large a share given to the non-producing classes. The devices are almost innumerable, from the brute force and gross superstition of ancient times, to the subtle and artful fiscal contrivances of modern. I might well challenge a comparison between them and the more direct, simple, and patriarchal mode by which the labor of the African race is among us commanded by the European. I may say with truth, that in few countries so much is left to the share of the laborer, and so little exacted from him, or where there is more kind attention to him in sickness or infirmities of age. Compare his condition with the tenants of the poor houses in the most civilized portions of Europe—look at the sick, and the old and infirm slave, on one hand, in the midst of his family and friends, under the kind superintending care of his master and mistress, and compare it with the forlorn and wretched condition of the pauper in the poor house. But I will not dwell on this aspect of the question; I turn to the political; and here I fearlessly assert that the existing relation between the two races in the South, against which these blind fanatics are waging war, forms the most solid and durable foundation on which to rear free and stable political institutions. It is useless to disguise the fact. There is and always has been in an advanced stage of wealth and civilization, a conflict between labor and capital. The condition of society in the South exempts us from the disorders and dangers resulting from this conflict; and which explains why it is that the political condition of the slave-holding States has been so much more stable and quiet than those of the North. The advantages of the former in this respect will become more and more manifest if left undisturbed by interference from without, as the country advances in wealth and numbers. We have in fact but just entered that condition of society where the strength and durability of our political institutions are to be tested; and I venture nothing in predicting that the experience of the next generation will fully test how vastly more favorable our condition of society is to that of other sections for free and stable institutions, provided we are not disturbed by the interference of others, or shall have sufficient intelligence and spirit to resist promptly and successfully such interference. It rests with ourselves to meet and repel them. I look not for aid to this Government, or to the other States; not but there are kind feelings towards us on the part of the great body of the non slave-holding States; but as kind as their feelings may be, we may rest assured that no political party in those States will risk their ascendancy for our safety. If we do not defend ourselves none will defend us; if we yield we will be more and more pressed as we recede; and if we submit we will be trampled under foot. Be assured that emancipation itself would not satisfy these fanatics—that gained, the next step would be to raise the negroes to a social and political equality with the whites; and that being effected, we would soon find the present condition of the two races reversed. They and their northern allies would be the masters, and we the slaves; the condition of the white race in the British West India Islands, bad as it is, would be happiness to ours;—there the mother country is interested in sustaining the supremacy of the European race. It is true that the authority of the former master is destroyed, but the African will there, still be a slave, not to individuals but to the community—forced to labor, not by the authority of the over-seer, but by the bayonet of the soldiery and the rod of the civil magistrate.

Surrounded as the slave-holding States are with such imminent perils, I rejoice to think that our means of defence are ample, if we shall prove to have the intelligence and spirit to see and apply them before it is too late. All we want is concert, to lay aside all party differences, and unite with zeal and energy in repelling approaching dangers. Let there be concert of action, and we shall find ample means of security without resorting to secession or disunion. I speak with full knowledge and a thorough examination of the subject, and for one see my way clearly. One thing alarms me—the eager pursuit of gain which overspreads the land, and which absorbs every faculty of the mind and every feeling of the heart. Of all passions avarice is the most blind and compromising—the last to see and the first to yield to danger. I dare not hope that any thing I can say will arouse the South to a due sense of danger; I fear it is beyond the power of mortal voice to awaken it in time from the fatal security into which it has fallen.

WENDELL PHILLIPS

The Murder of Lovejoy

Boston, December 8, 1837

M R. CHAIRMAN:—We have met for the freest discussion of these resolutions, and the events which gave rise to them. [Cries of "Question," "Hear him," "Go on," "No gagging," etc.] I hope I shall be permitted to express my surprise at the sentiments of the last speaker,—surprise not only at such sentiments from such a man, but at the applause they have received within these walls. A comparison has been drawn between the events of the Revolution and the tragedy at Alton. We have heard it asserted here, in Faneuil Hall, that Great Britain had a right to tax the Colonies, and we have heard the mob at Alton, the drunken murderers of Lovejoy, compared to those patriot fathers who threw the tea overboard! [Great applause.] Fellow-citizens, is this Faneuil Hall doctrine? ["No, no."] The mob at Alton were met to wrest from a citizen his just rights,—met to resist the laws. We have been told that our fathers did the same; and the glorious mantle of Revolutionary precedent has been thrown over the mobs of our day. To make out their title to such defence, the gentleman says that the British Parliament had a *right* to tax these Colonies. It is manifest, that, without this, his parallel falls to the ground; for Lovejoy had stationed himself within constitutional bulwarks. He was not only defending the freedom of the press, but he was under his own roof; in arms with the sanction of the civil authority. The men who assailed him went against and over the laws. The *mob*, as the gentleman terms it,—mob, forsooth! certainly we sons of the tea-spillers are a marvelously patient generation!—the "orderly mob" which assembled in the Old South to destroy the tea were met to resist, not the laws, but illegal exactions. Shame on the American who calls the tea-tax and stamp-act *laws*! Our fathers resisted, not the King's prerogative, but the Kings usurpation. To find any other account,

you must read our Revolutionary history upside down. Our
State archives are loaded with arguments of John Adams to
prove the taxes laid by the British Parliament unconstitutional,
—beyond its power. It was not till this was made out that the
men of New England rushed to arms. The arguments of the
Council Chamber and the House of Representatives preceded
and sanctioned the contest. To draw the conduct of our ancestors into a precedent for mobs, for a right to resist laws we
ourselves have enacted, is an insult to their memory. The difference between the excitements of those days and our own,
which the gentleman in kindness to the latter has overlooked,
is simply this: the men of that day went for the right, as secured by the laws. They were the people rising to sustain the
laws and constitution of the Province. The rioters of our day
go for their own wills, right or wrong. Sir, when I heard the
gentleman lay down principles which place the murderers of
Alton side by side with Otis and Hancock, with Quincy and
Adams, I thought those pictured lips [pointing to the portraits
in the Hall] would have broken into voice to rebuke the recreant American,—the slanderer of the dead. [Great applause and
counter applause.] The gentleman said that he should sink
into insignificance if he dared to gainsay the principles of these
resolutions. Sir, for the sentiments he has uttered, on soil consecrated by the prayers of Puritans and the blood of patriots,
the earth should have yawned and swallowed him up.

[Applause and hisses, with cries of "Take that back." The uproar
became so great that for a long time no one could be heard. At length
G. Bond, Esq., and Hon. W. Sturgis came to Mr. Phillips's side at the
front of the platform. They were met with cries of "Phillips or nobody," "Make him take back 'recreant,'" "He sha'n't go on till he
takes it back." When it was understood they meant to sustain, not to
interrupt Mr. Phillips, Mr. Sturgis was listened to, and said: "I did not
come here to take any part in this discussion, nor do I intend to; but
I do entreat you, fellow-citizens, by everything you hold sacred,—I
conjure you by every association connected with this Hall, consecrated by our fathers to freedom of discussion,—that you listen to
every man who addresses you in a decorous manner." Mr. Phillips
resumed.]

Fellow-citizens, I cannot take back my words. Surely the
Attorney-General, so long and well known here, needs not the

aid of your hisses against one so young as I am,—my voice never before heard within these walls!

Another ground has been taken to excuse the mob, and throw doubt and discredit on the conduct of Lovejoy and his associates. Allusion has been made to what lawyers understand very well,—the "conflict of laws." We are told that nothing but the Mississippi River rolls between St. Louis and Alton; and the conflict of laws somehow or other gives the citizens of the former a right to find fault with the defender of the press for publishing his opinions so near their limits. Will the gentleman venture that argument before lawyers? How the laws of the two States could be said to come into conflict in such circumstances I question whether any lawyer in this audience can explain or understand. No matter whether the line that divides one sovereign State from another be an imaginary one or ocean-wide, the moment you cross it the State you leave is blotted out of existence, so far as you are concerned. The Czar might as well claim to control the deliberations of Faneuil Hall, as the laws of Missouri demand reverence, or the shadow of obedience, from an inhabitant of Illinois.

I must find some fault with the statement which has been made of the events at Alton. It has been asked why Lovejoy and his friends did not appeal to the executive,—trust their defence to the police of the city. It has been hinted that, from hasty and ill-judged excitement, the men within the building provoked a quarrel, and that he fell in the course of it, one mob resisting another. Recollect, Sir, that they did act with the approbation and sanction of the Mayor. In strict truth, there was no executive to appeal to for protection. The Mayor acknowledged that he could not protect them. They asked him if it was lawful for them to defend themselves. He told them it was, and sanctioned their assembling in arms to do so. They were not, then, a mob; they were not merely citizens defending their own property; they were in some sense the *posse comitatus*, adopted for the occasion into the police of the city, acting under the order of a magistrate. It was civil authority resisting lawless violence. Where, then, was the imprudence? Is the doctrine to be sustained here, that it is *imprudent* for men to aid magistrates in executing the laws?

Men are continually asking each other, Had Lovejoy a right

to resist? Sir, I protest against the question, instead of answering it. Lovejoy did not resist, in the sense they mean. He did not throw himself back on the natural right of self-defence. He did not cry anarchy, and let slip the dogs of civil war, careless of the horrors which would follow.

Sir, as I understand this affair, it was not an individual protecting his property; it was not one body of armed men resisting another, and making the streets of a peaceful city run blood with their contentions. It did not bring back the scenes in some old Italian cities, where family met family, and faction met faction, and mutually trampled the laws under foot. No; the men in that house were regularly *enrolled*, under the sanction of the Mayor. There being no militia in Alton, about seventy men were enrolled with the approbation of the Mayor. These relieved each other every other night. About thirty men were in arms on the night of the sixth, when the press was landed. The next evening it was not thought necessary to summon more than half that number; among these was Lovejoy. It was, therefore, you perceive, Sir, the police of the city resisting rioters,—civil government breasting itself to the shock of lawless men.

Here is no question about the right of self-defence. It is in fact simply this: Has the civil magistrate a right to put down a riot?

Some persons seem to imagine that anarchy existed at Alton from the commencement of these disputes. Not at all. "No one of us," says an eyewitness and a comrade of Lovejoy, "has taken up arms during these disturbances but at the command of the Mayor." Anarchy did not settle down on that devoted city till Lovejoy breathed his last. Till then the law, represented in his person, sustained itself against its foes. When he fell, civil authority was trampled under foot. He had "planted himself on his constitutional rights,"—appealed to the laws,—claimed the protection of the civil authority,—taken refuge under "the broad shield of the Constitution. When through that he was pierced and fell, he fell but one sufferer in a common catastrophe." He took refuge under the banner of liberty,—amid its folds; and when he fell, its glorious stars and stripes, the emblem of free institutions, around which cluster so many heart-stirring memories, were blotted out in the martyr's blood.

It has been stated, perhaps inadvertently, that Lovejoy or his comrades fired first. This is denied by those who have the best means of knowing. Guns were first fired by the mob. After being twice fired on, those within the building consulted together and deliberately returned the fire. But suppose they did fire first. They had a right so to do; not only the right which every citizen has to defend himself, but the further right which every civil officer has to resist violence. Even if Lovejoy fired the first gun, it would not lessen his claim to our sympathy, or destroy his title to be considered a martyr in defence of a free press. The question now is, Did he act within the Constitution and the laws? The men who fell in State Street on the 5th of March, 1770, did more than Lovejoy is charged with. They were the *first* assailants. Upon some slight quarrel they pelted the troops with every missile within reach. Did this bate one jot of the eulogy with which Hancock and Warren hallowed their memory, hailing them as the first martyrs in the cause of American liberty?

If, Sir, I had adopted what are called Peace principles, I might lament the circumstances of this case. But all you who believe, as I do, in the right and duty of magistrates to execute the laws, join with me and brand as base hypocrisy the conduct of those who assemble year after year on the 4th of July, to fight over the battles of the Revolution, and yet "damn with faint praise," or load with obloquy, the memory of this man, who shed his blood in defence of life, liberty, property, and the freedom of the press!

Throughout that terrible night I find nothing to regret but this, that within the limits of our country, civil authority should have been so prostrated as to oblige a citizen to arm in his own defence, and to arm in vain. The gentleman says Lovejoy was presumptuous and imprudent,—he "died as the fool dieth." And a reverend clergyman of the city tells us that no citizen has a right to publish opinions disagreeable to the community! If any mob follows such publication, on *him* rests its guilt! He must wait, forsooth, till the people come up to it and agree with him! This libel on liberty goes on to say that the want of right to speak as we think is an evil inseparable from republican institutions! If this be so, what are they worth? Welcome the despotism of the Sultan, where one knows what he may publish and what he may not, rather than the tyranny of this many-headed monster, the mob, where we know not what we may do or say, till some fellow-citizen has tried it, and paid for the lesson with his life. This clerical absurdity chooses as a check for the abuses of the press, not the *law*, but the dread of a mob. By so doing, it deprives not only the individual and the minority of their rights, but the majority also, since the expression of *their* opinion may sometimes provoke disturbance from the minority. A few men may make a mob as well as many. The majority, then, have no right, as Christian men, to utter their sentiments, if by any possibility it may lead to a mob! Shades of Hugh Peters and John Cotton, save us from such pulpits!

Imprudent to defend the liberty of the press! Why? Because the defence was unsuccessful? Does success gild crime into patriotism, and the want of it change heroic self-devotion to imprudence? Was Hampden imprudent when he drew the sword and threw away the scabbard? Yet he, judged by that single hour, was unsuccessful. After a short exile, the race he hated sat again upon the throne.

Imagine yourself present when the first news of Bunker Hill battle reached a New England town. The tale would have run thus: "The patriots are routed,—the red-coats victorious,—Warren lies dead upon the field." With what scorn would that *Tory* have been received, who should have charged Warren with *imprudence*! who should have said that, bred a physician, he was "out of place" in that battle, and "died as the *fool dieth*"! [Great applause.] How would the intimation have been received, that Warren and his associates should have waited a better time? But if success be indeed the only criterion of prudence, *Respice finem*,—wait till the end.

Presumptuous to assert the freedom of the press on American ground! Is the assertion of such freedom before the age? So much before the age as to leave one no right to make it because it displeases the community? Who invents this libel on this country? It is this very thing which entitles Lovejoy to greater praise. The disputed right which provoked the Revolution—taxation without representation—is far beneath that for which he died. [Here there was a strong and general expression of disapprobation.] One word, gentlemen. As much as *thought* is better than money, so much is the cause in which Lovejoy died nobler than a mere question of taxes. James Otis thundered in this Hall when the King did but touch his *pocket*. Imagine, if you can, his indignant eloquence, had England offered to put a gag upon his lips. [Great applause.]

The question that stirred the Revolution touched our civil interests. *This* concerns us not only as citizens, but as immortal beings. Wrapped up in its fate, saved or lost with it, are not only the voice of the statesman, but the instructions of the pulpit, and the progress of our faith.

The clergy "marvellously out of place" where free speech is battled for,—liberty of speech on national sins? Does the gentleman remember that freedom to preach was first gained, dragging in its train freedom to print? I thank the clergy here present, as I reverence their predecessors, who did not so far forget their country in their immediate profession as to deem it duty to separate themselves from the struggle of '76,—the Mayhews and Coopers, who remembered they were citizens before they were clergymen.

Mr. Chairman, from the bottom of my heart I thank that brave little band at Alton for resisting. We must remember that Lovejoy had fled from city to city,—suffered the destruction of three presses patiently. At length he took counsel with friends, men of character, of tried integrity, of wide views, of Christian principle. They thought the crisis had come: it was full time to assert the laws. They saw around them, not a community like our own, of fixed habits, of character moulded and settled, but one "in the gristle, not yet hardened into the bone of manhood." The people there, children of our older States, seem to have forgotten the blood-tried principles of their fathers the moment they lost sight of our New England hills. Something was to be done to show them the priceless value of the freedom of the press, to bring back and set right their wandering and confused ideas. He and his advisers looked out on a community, staggering like a drunken man, indifferent to their rights and confused in their feelings. Deaf to argument, haply they might be stunned into sobriety. They saw that of which we cannot judge, the *necessity* of resistance. Insulted law called for it. Public opinion, fast hastening on the downward course, must be arrested.

Does not the event show they judged rightly? Absorbed in a

thousand trifles, how has the nation all at once come to a stand? Men begin, as in 1776 and 1640, to discuss principles, to weigh characters, to find out where they are. Haply we may awake before we are borne over the precipice.

I am glad, Sir, to see this crowded house. It is good for us to be here. When Liberty is in danger, Faneuil Hall has the right, it is her duty, to strike the key-note for these United States. I am glad, for one reason, that remarks such as those to which I have alluded have been uttered here. The passage of these resolutions, in spite of this opposition, led by the Attorney-General of the Commonwealth, will show more clearly, more decisively, the deep indignation with which Boston regards this outrage.

ANGELINA GRIMKÉ WELD

Antislavery Speech at Pennsylvania Hall

Philadelphia, May 16, 1838

M EN, brethren and fathers—mothers, daughters and sisters, what came ye out to see? A reed shaken with the wind? Is it curiosity merely, or a deep sympathy with the perishing slave, that has brought this large audience together? [A yell from the mob without the building.] Those voices without ought to awaken and call out our warmest sympathies. Deluded beings! "they know not what they do." They know not that they are undermining their own rights and their own happiness, temporal and eternal. Do you ask, "what has the North to do with slavery?" Hear it—hear it. Those voices without tell us that the spirit of slavery is *here*, and has been roused to wrath by our abolition speeches and conventions: for surely liberty would not foam and tear herself with rage, because her friends are multiplied daily, and meetings are held in quick succession to set forth her virtues and extend her peaceful kingdom. This opposition shows that slavery has done its deadliest work in the hearts of our citizens. Do you ask, then, "what has the North to do?" I answer, cast out first the spirit of slavery from your own hearts, and then lend your aid to convert the South. Each one present has a work to do, be his or her situation what it may, however limited their means, or insignificant their supposed influence. The great men of this country will not do this work; the church will never do it. A desire to please the world, to keep the favor of all parties and of all conditions, makes them dumb on this and every other unpopular subject. They have become worldly-wise, and therefore God, in his wisdom, employs them not to carry on his plans of reformation and salvation. He hath chosen the foolish things of the world to confound the wise, and the weak to overcome the mighty.

As a Southerner I feel that it is my duty to stand up here tonight and bear testimony against slavery. I have seen it—I have seen it. I know it has horrors that can never be described. I was brought up under its wing: I witnessed for many years its demoralizing influences, and its destructiveness to human happiness. It is admitted by some that the slave is not happy under the *worst* forms of slavery. But I have *never* seen a happy slave. I have seen him dance in his chains, it is true; but he was not happy. There is a wide difference between happiness and mirth. Man cannot enjoy the former while his manhood is destroyed, and that part of the being which is necessary to the making, and to the enjoyment of happiness, is completely blotted out. The slaves, however, may be, and sometimes are, mirthful. When hope is extinguished, they say, "let us eat and drink, for to-morrow we die." [Just then stones were thrown at the windows,—a great noise without, and commotion within.] What is a mob? What would the breaking of every window be? What would the levelling of this Hall be? Any evidence that we are wrong, or that slavery is a good and wholesome institution? What if the mob should now burst in upon us, break up our meeting and commit violence upon our persons—would this be anything compared with what the slaves endure? No, no: and we do not remember them "as bound with them," if we shrink in the time of peril, or feel unwilling to sacrifice ourselves, if need be, for their sake. [Great Noise.] I thank the Lord that there is yet left life enough to feel the truth, even though it rages at it—that conscience is not so completely seared as to be unmoved by the truth of the living God.

Many persons go to the South for a season, and are hospitably entertained in the parlor and at the table of the slaveholder. They never enter the huts of the slaves; they know nothing of the dark side of the picture, and they return home with praises on their lips of the generous character of those with whom they had tarried. Or if they have witnessed the cruelties of slavery, by remaining silent spectators they have naturally become callous—an insensibility has ensued which prepares them to apologize even for barbarity. Nothing but the corrupting influence of slavery on the hearts of the Northern people can induce them to apologize for it; and much will have been done for the destruction of Southern slavery when we have so reformed the North that no one here will be willing to risk his reputation by advocating or even excusing the holding of men as property. The South know it, and acknowledge that as fast as our principles prevail, the hold of the master must be relaxed. [Another outbreak of mobocratic spirit, and some confusion in the house.]

How wonderfully constituted is the human mind! How it resists, as long as it can, all efforts made to reclaim from error! I feel that all this disturbance is but an evidence that our efforts are the best that could have been adopted, or else the friends of slavery, would not care for what we say and do. The South know what we do. I am thankful that they are reached by our efforts. Many times have I wept in the land of my birth over the system of slavery. I knew of none who sympathized in my feelings—I was unaware that any efforts were made to deliver the oppressed—no voice in the wilderness was heard calling on the people to repent and do works meet for repentance—and my heart sickened within me. Oh, how should I have rejoiced to know that such efforts as these were being made. I only wonder that I had such feelings. I wonder when I reflect under what influence I was brought up, that my heart is not harder than the nether millstone. But in the midst of temptation, I was preserved, and my sympathy grew warmer, and my hatred of slavery more inveterate, until at last I have exiled myself from my native land because I could no longer endure to hear the wailing of the slave. I fled to the land of Penn; for here, thought I, sympathy for the slave will surely be found. But I found it not. The people were kind and hospitable, but the slave had no place in their thoughts. Whenever questions were put to me as to his condition, I felt that they were dictated by an idle curiosity, rather than by that deep feeling which would lead to effort for his rescue. I therefore shut up my grief in my own heart. I remembered that I was a Carolinian, from a state which framed this iniquity by law. I knew that throughout her territory was continued suffering, on the one part, and continual brutality and sin on the other. Every Southern breeze wafted to me the discordant tones of weeping and wailing, shrieks and groans, mingled with prayers and blasphemous curses. I thought there was no hope; that the wicked would go on his wickedness, until he had destroyed both himself and his country. My heart sunk within me at the abominations in the midst of which I had been born and educated. What will it avail, cried I in bitterness of spirit, to expose to the gaze of strangers the horrors and pollutions of slavery, when there is no ear to hear nor heart to feel and pray for the slave. The language of my soul was, "Oh tell it not in Gath, publish it not in the streets of Askelon." But how different do I feel now! Animated with hope, nay, with an assurance of the triumph of liberty and good will to man, I will lift up my voice like a trumpet, and show this people their transgression, their sins of omission towards the slave, and what they can do towards affecting Southern minds, and overthrowing Southern oppression.

We may talk of occupying neutral ground, but on this subject, in its present attitude, there is no such thing as neutral ground. He that is not for us is against us, and he that gathereth not with us, scattereth abroad. If you are on what you suppose to be neutral ground, the South look upon you as on the side of the oppressor. And is there one who loves his country willing to give his influence, even indirectly, in favor of slavery—that curse of nations? God swept Egypt with the besom of destruction, and punished Judea also with a sore punishment, because of slavery. And have we any reason to believe that he is less just now?—or that he will be more favorable to us than to his own "peculiar people"? [Shoutings, stones thrown against the windows, &c.]

There is nothing to be feared from those who would stop our mouths, but they themselves should fear and tremble. The current is even now setting fast against them. If the arm of the North had not caused the Bastille of slavery to totter to its foundations, you would not hear those cries. A few years ago, and the South felt secure, and with a contemptuous sneer asked, "Who are the abolitionists? The abolitionists are nothing"?—Ay, in one sense they were nothing, and they are nothing still. But in this we rejoice, that "God has chosen things that are not to bring to nought things that are." [Mob again disturbed the meeting.]

We often hear the question asked, "What shall we do?" Here is an opportunity for doing something now. Every man and every woman present may do something by showing that we fear not a mob, and, in the midst of threatenings and revilings, by opening our mouths for the dumb and pleading the cause of those who are ready to perish.

To work as we should in this cause, we must know what Slavery is. Let me urge you then to buy the books which have been written on this subject and read them, and then lend them to your neighbors. Give your money no longer for things which pander to pride and lust, but aid in scattering "the living coals of truth" upon the naked heart of this nation,—in circulating appeals to the sympathies of Christians in behalf of the outraged and suffering slave. But, it is said by some, our "books and papers do not speak the truth." Why, then, do they not contradict what we say? They cannot. Moreover the South has entreated, nay commanded us to be silent; and what greater evidence of the truth of our publications could be desired?

Women of Philadelphia! allow me as a Southern woman, with much attachment to the land of my birth, to entreat you to come up to this work. Especially let me urge you to petition. *Men* may settle this and other questions at the ballot-box, but you have no such right; it is only through petitions that you can reach the Legislature. It is therefore peculiarly *your* duty to petition. Do you say, "It does no good?" The South already turns pale at the number sent. They have read the reports of the proceedings of Congress, and there have seen that among other petitions were very many from the women of the North on the subject of slavery. This fact has called the attention of the South to the subject. How could we expect to have done more as yet? Men who hold the rod over slaves, rule in the councils of the nation: and they deny our right to petition and to remonstrate against abuses of our sex and of our kind. We have these rights, however, from our God. Only let us exercise them: and though often turned away unanswered, let us remember the influence of importunity upon the unjust judge, and act accordingly. The fact that the South look with jealousy upon our measures shows that they are effectual. There is, therefore, no cause for doubting or despair, but rather for rejoicing.

It was remarked in England that women did much to abolish Slavery in her colonies. Nor are they now idle. Numerous petitions from them have recently been presented to the Queen, to abolish the apprenticeship with its cruelties nearly equal to those of the system whose place it supplies. One petition two miles and a quarter long has been presented. And do you think these labors will be in vain? Let the history of the past answer. When the women of these States send up to Congress such a petition, our legislators will arise as did those of England, and say, "When all the maids and matrons of the land are knocking at our doors we must legislate." Let the zeal and love, the faith and works of our English sisters quicken ours— that while the slaves continue to suffer, and when they shout deliverance, we may feel that satisfaction of *having done what we could*.

HENRY HIGHLAND GARNET

Address to the Slaves of the United States of America

Buffalo, N.Y., August 21, 1843

B RETHREN AND FELLOW-CITIZENS:—Your brethren of the
North, East, and West have been accustomed to meet together in National Conventions, to sympathize with each other,
and to weep over your unhappy condition. In these meetings
we have addressed all classes of the free, but we have never,
until this time, sent a word of consolation and advice to you.
We have been contented in sitting still and mourning over
your sorrows, earnestly hoping that before this day your sacred
liberties would have been restored. But, we have hoped in
vain. Years have rolled on, and tens of thousands have been
borne on streams of blood and tears, to the shores of eternity.
While you have been oppressed, we have also been partakers
with you; nor can we be free while you are enslaved. We,
therefore, write to you as being bound with you.

Many of you are bound to us, not only by the ties of a common humanity, but we are connected by the more tender relations of parents, wives, husbands, children, brothers, and
sisters, and friends. As such we most affectionately address you.

Slavery has fixed a deep gulf between you and us, and while
it shuts out from you the relief and consolation which your
friends would willingly render, it afflicts and persecutes you
with a fierceness which we might not expect to see in the
fiends of hell. But still the Almighty Father of mercies has left
to us a glimmering ray of hope, which shines out like a lone
star in a cloudy sky. Mankind are becoming wiser, and better—
the oppressor's power is fading, and you, every day, are becoming better informed, and more numerous. Your grievances,
brethren, are many. We shall not attempt, in this short address,
to present to the world all the dark catalogue of this nation's
sins, which have been committed upon an innocent people.

Nor is it indeed necessary, for you feel them from day to day, and all the civilized world look upon them with amazement.

Two hundred and twenty-seven years ago, the first of our injured race were brought to the shores of America. They came not with glad spirits to select their homes in the New World. They came not with their own consent, to find an un-molested enjoyment of the blessings of this fruitful soil. The first dealings they had with men calling themselves Christians, exhibited to them the worst features of corrupt and sordid hearts: and convinced them that no cruelty is too great, no vil-lainy and no robbery too abhorrent for even enlightened men to perform, when influenced by avarice and lust. Neither did they come flying upon the wings of Liberty, to a land of free-dom. But they came with broken hearts, from their beloved native land, and were doomed to unrequited toil and deep degradation. Nor did the evil of their bondage end at their emancipation by death. Succeeding generations inherited their chains, and millions have come from eternity into time, and have returned again to the world of spirits, cursed and ruined by American slavery.

The propagators of the system, or their immediate ancestors, very soon discovered its growing evil, and its tremendous wickedness, and secret promises were made to destroy it. The gross inconsistency of a people holding slaves, who had them-selves "ferried o'er the wave" for freedom's sake, was too appar-ent to be entirely overlooked. The voice of Freedom cried, "Emancipate your slaves." Humanity supplicated with tears for the deliverance of the children of Africa. Wisdom urged her solemn plea. The bleeding, captive plead his innocence, and pointed to Christianity who stood weeping at the cross. Jeho-vah frowned upon the nefarious institution, and thunderbolts, red with vengeance, struggled to leap forth to blast the guilty wretches who maintained it. But all was vain. Slavery had stretched its dark wings of death over the land, the Church stood silently by—the priests prophesied falsely, and the people loved to have it so. Its throne is established, and now it reigns triumphant.

Nearly three millions of your fellow-citizens are prohibited by law and public opinion, (which in this country is stronger than law,) from reading the Book of Life. Your intellect has been destroyed as much as possible, and every ray of light they have attempted to shut out from your minds. The oppressors themselves have become involved in the ruin. They have become weak, sensual, and rapacious—they have cursed you—they have cursed themselves—they have cursed the earth which they have trod.

The colonists threw the blame upon England. They said that the mother country entailed the evil upon them, and that they would rid themselves of it if they could. The world thought they were sincere, and the philanthropic pitied them. But time soon tested their sincerity. In a few years the colonists grew strong, and severed themselves from the British Government. Their independence was declared, and they took their station among the sovereign powers of the earth. The declaration was a glorious document. Sages admired it, and the patriotic of every nation reverenced the God-like sentiments which it contained. When the power of Government returned to their hands, did they emancipate the slaves? No; they rather added new links to our chains. Were they ignorant of the principles of Liberty? Certainly they were not. The sentiments of their revolutionary orators fell in burning eloquence upon their hearts, and with one voice they cried, LIBERTY OR DEATH. Oh what a sentence was that! It ran from soul to soul like electric fire, and nerved the arm of thousands to fight in the holy cause of Freedom. Among the diversity of opinions that are entertained in regard to physical resistance, there are but a few found to gainsay that stern declaration. We are among those who do not.

SLAVERY! How much misery is comprehended in that single word. What mind is there that does not shrink from its direful effects? Unless the image of God be obliterated from the soul, all men cherish the love of Liberty. The nice discerning political economist does not regard the sacred right more than the untutored African who roams in the wilds of Congo. Nor has the one more right to the full enjoyment of his freedom than the other. In every man's mind the good seeds of liberty are planted, and he who brings his fellow down so low, as to make him contented with a condition of slavery, commits the highest crime against God and man. Brethren, your oppressors aim to do this. They endeavor to make you as much like brutes as possible. When they have blinded the eyes of your mind—when they have embittered the sweet waters of life—when they have shut out the light which shines from the word of God—then, and not till then, has American slavery done its perfect work.

TO SUCH DEGRADATION IT IS SINFUL IN THE EXTREME FOR YOU TO MAKE VOLUNTARY SUBMISSION. The divine commandments you are in duty bound to reverence and obey. If you do not obey them, you will surely meet with the displeasure of the Almighty. He requires you to love him supremely, and your neighbor as yourself—to keep the Sabbath day holy— to search the Scriptures—and bring up your children with respect for his laws, and to worship no other God but him. But slavery sets all these at nought, and hurls defiance in the face of Jehovah. The forlorn condition in which you are placed, does not destroy your moral obligation to God. You are not certain of heaven, because you suffer yourselves to remain in a state of slavery, where you cannot obey the commandments of the Sovereign of the universe. If the ignorance of slavery is a passport to heaven, then it is a blessing, and no curse, and you should rather desire its perpetuity than its abolition. God will not receive slavery, nor ignorance, nor any other state of mind, for love and obedience to him. Your condition does not absolve you from your moral obligation. The diabolical injustice by which your liberties are cloven down, NEITHER GOD, NOR ANGELS, OR JUST MEN, COMMAND YOU TO SUFFER FOR A SINGLE MOMENT. THEREFORE IT IS YOUR SOLEMN AND IMPERATIVE DUTY TO USE EVERY MEANS, BOTH MORAL, INTELLECTUAL, AND PHYSICAL, THAT PROMISES SUCCESS. If a band of heathen men should attempt to enslave a race of Christians, and to place their children under the influence of some false religion, surely, Heaven would frown upon the men who would not resist such aggression, even to death. If, on the other hand, a band of Christians should attempt to enslave a race of heathen men, and to entail slavery upon them, and to keep them in heathenism in the midst of Christianity, the God of heaven would smile upon every effort which the injured might make to disenthral themselves.

Brethren, it is as wrong for your lordly oppressors to keep you in slavery, as it was for the man thief to steal our ancestors from the coast of Africa. You should therefore now use the

same manner of resistance, as would have been just in our ancestors, when the bloody foot-prints of the first remorseless
soul-thief was placed upon the shores of our fatherland. The
humblest peasant is as free in the sight of God as the proudest
monarch that ever swayed a sceptre. Liberty is a spirit sent out
from God, and like its great Author, is no respecter of persons.

Brethren, the time has come when you must act for yourselves. It is an old and true saying that, "if hereditary bondmen
would be free, they must themselves strike the blow." You can
plead your own cause, and do the work of emancipation better
than any others. The nations of the old world are moving in
the great cause of universal freedom, and some of them at least
will, ere long, do you justice. The combined powers of Europe
have placed their broad seal of disapprobation upon the African
slave-trade. But in the slave-holding parts of the United States,
the trade is as brisk as ever. They buy and sell you as though
you were brute beasts. The North has done much—her opinion of slavery in the abstract is known. But in regard to the
South, we adopt the opinion of the *New York Evangelist*—
"We have advanced so far, that the cause apparently waits for a
more effectual door to be thrown open than has been yet." We
are about to point you to that more effectual door. Look
around you, and behold the bosoms of your loving wives
heaving with untold agonies! Hear the cries of your poor children! Remember the stripes your fathers bore. Think of the
torture and disgrace of your noble mothers. Think of your
wretched sisters, loving virtue and purity, as they are driven into
concubinage and are exposed to the unbridled lusts of incar-
nate devils. Think of the undying glory that hangs around the
ancient name of Africa:—and forget not that you are native-
born American citizens, and as such, you are justly entitled to
all the rights that are granted to the freest. Think how many
tears you have poured out upon the soil which you have cultivated with unrequited toil and enriched with your blood; and
then go to your lordly enslavers and tell them plainly, that you
are determined to be free. Appeal to their sense of justice, and
tell them that they have no more right to oppress you, than you
have to enslave them. Entreat them to remove the grievous
burdens which they have imposed upon you, and to remuner-
ate you for your labor. Promise them renewed diligence in the

cultivation of the soil, if they will render to you an equivalent for your services. Point them to the increase of happiness and prosperity in the British West-Indies since the Act of Emancipation. Tell them in language which they cannot misunderstand, of the exceeding sinfulness of slavery, and of a future judgment, and of the righteous retributions of an indignant God. Inform them that all you desire is FREEDOM, and that nothing else will suffice. Do this, and for ever after cease to toil for the heartless tyrants, who give you no other reward but stripes and abuse. If they then commence the work of death, they, and not you, will be responsible for the consequences. You had far better all die—*die immediately*, than live slaves, and entail your wretchedness upon your posterity. If you would be free in this generation, here is your only hope. However much you and all of us may desire it, there is not much hope of redemption without the shedding of blood. If you must bleed, let it all come at once—rather *die freemen, than live to be the slaves*. It is impossible, like the children of Israel, to make a grand exodus from the land of bondage. The Pharaohs are on both sides of the blood-red waters! You cannot move *en masse*, to the dominions of the British Queen—nor can you pass through Florida and overrun Texas, and at last find peace in Mexico. The propagators of American slavery are spending their blood and treasure, that they may plant the black flag in the heart of Mexico and riot in the halls of the Montezumas. In the language of the Rev. Robert Hall, when addressing the volunteers of Bristol, who were rushing forth to repel the invasion of Napoleon, who threatened to lay waste the fair homes of England, "Religion is too much interested in your behalf, not to shed over you her most gracious influences."

You will not be compelled to spend much time in order to become inured to hardships. From the first moment that you breathed the air of heaven, you have been accustomed to nothing else but hardships. The heroes of the American Revolution were never put upon harder fare than a peck of corn and a few herrings per week. You have not become enervated by the luxuries of life. Your sternest energies have been beaten out upon the anvil of severe trial. Slavery has done this, to make you subservient to its own purposes; but it has done more than this, it has prepared you for any emergency. If you receive good treatment, it is what you could hardly expect; if you meet with pain, sorrow, and even death, these are the common lot of the slaves.

Fellow-men! patient sufferers! behold your dearest rights crushed to the earth! See your sons murdered, and your wives, mothers and sisters doomed to prostitution. In the name of the merciful God, and by all that life is worth, let it no longer be a debatable question, whether it is better to choose *Liberty* or *death*.

In 1822, Denmark Veazie, of South Carolina, formed a plan for the liberation of his fellow-men. In the whole history of human efforts to overthrow slavery, a more complicated and tremendous plan was never formed. He was betrayed by the treachery of his own people, and died a martyr to freedom. Many a brave hero fell, but history, faithful to her high trust, will transcribe his name on the same monument with Moses, Hampden, Tell, Bruce and Wallace, Toussaint L'Ouverture, Lafayette and Washington. That tremendous movement shook the whole empire of slavery. The guilty soul-thieves were over-whelmed with fear. It is a matter of fact, that at that time, and in consequence of the threatened revolution, the slave States talked strongly of emancipation. But they blew but one blast of the trumpet of freedom, and then laid it aside. As these men became quiet, the slaveholders ceased to talk about emancipation: and now behold your condition to-day! Angels sigh over it, and humanity has long since exhausted her tears in weeping on your account!

The patriotic Nathaniel Turner followed Denmark Veazie. He was goaded to desperation by wrong and injustice. By despotism, his name has been recorded on the list of infamy, and future generations will remember him among the noble and brave.

Next arose the immortal Joseph Cinque, the hero of the Amistad. He was a native African, and by the help of God he emancipated a whole ship-load of his fellow men on the high seas. And he now sings of liberty on the sunny hills of Africa and beneath his native palm-trees, where he hears the lion roar and feels himself as free as that king of the forest.

Next arose Madison Washington, that bright star of freedom, and took his station in the constellation of true heroism.

He was a slave on board the brig Creole, of Richmond, bound to New Orleans, that great slave mart, with a hundred and four others. Nineteen struck for liberty or death. But one life was taken, and the whole were emancipated, and the vessel was carried into Nassau, New Providence.

Noble men! Those who have fallen in freedom's conflict, their memories will be cherished by the true-hearted and the God-fearing in all future generations; those who are living, their names are surrounded by a halo of glory.

Brethren, arise, arise! Strike for your lives and liberties. Now is the day and the hour. Let every slave throughout the land do this, and the days of slavery are numbered. You cannot be more oppressed than you have been—you cannot suffer greater cruelties than you have already. *Rather die freemen than live to be slaves.* Remember that you are FOUR MILLIONS!

It is in your power so to torment the God-cursed slave-holders, that they will be glad to let you go free. If the scale was turned, and black men were the masters and white men the slaves, every destructive agent and element would be employed to lay the oppressor low. Danger and death would hang over their heads day and night. Yes, the tyrants would meet with plagues more terrible than those of Pharaoh. But you are a patient people. You act as though you were made for the special use of these devils. You act as though your daughters were born to pamper the lusts of your masters and overseers. And worse than all, you tamely submit while your lords tear your wives from your embraces and defile them before your eyes. In the name of God, we ask, are you men? Where is the blood of your fathers? Has it all run out of your veins? Awake, awake; millions of voices are calling you! Your dead fathers speak to you from their graves. Heaven, as with a voice of thunder, calls on you to arise from the dust.

Let your motto be resistance! *resistance!* RESISTANCE! No oppressed people have ever secured their liberty without resistance. What kind of resistance you had better make, you must decide by the circumstances that surround you, and according to the suggestion of expediency. Brethren, adieu! Trust in the living God. Labor for the peace of the human race, and remember that you are FOUR MILLIONS.

ABRAHAM LINCOLN

Speech in Congress on the War with Mexico

Washington, D.C., January 12, 1848

M R. CHAIRMAN:
　　Some, if not all the gentlemen on, the other side of
the House, who have addressed the committee within the last
two days, have spoken rather complainingly, if I have rightly
understood them, of the vote given a week or ten days ago, declaring that the war with Mexico was unnecessarily and uncon-
stitutionally commenced by the President. I admit that such a
vote should not be given, in mere party wantonness, and that
the one given, is justly censurable, if it have no other, or better
foundation. I am one of those who joined in that vote; and I
did so under my best impression of the *truth* of the case. How
I got this impression, and how it may possibly be removed, I
will now try to show. When the war began, it was my opinion
that all those who, because of knowing too *little*, or because of
knowing too *much*, could not conscientiously approve the conduct of the President, in the beginning of it, should, nevertheless, as good citizens and patriots, remain silent on that point,
at least till the war should be ended. Some leading democrats,
including Ex President Van Buren, have taken this same view, as
I understand them; and I adhered to it, and acted upon it,
until since I took my seat here; and I think I should still adhere
to it, were it not that the President and his friends will not
allow it to be so. Besides the continual effort of the President
to argue every silent vote given for supplies, into an endorsement of the justice and wisdom of his conduct—besides that
singularly candid paragraph, in his late message in which he tells
us that Congress, with great unanimity, only two in the Senate
and fourteen in the House dissenting, had declared that, "by
the act of the Republic of Mexico, a state of war exists between
that Government and the United States," when the same journals that informed him of this, also informed him, that when

that declaration stood disconnected from the question of supplies, sixtyseven in the House, and not fourteen merely, voted
against it—besides this open attempt to prove, by telling the
truth, what he could not prove by telling the *whole truth*—
demanding of all who will not submit to be misrepresented, in
justice to themselves, to speak out—besides all this, one of my
colleagues (Mr. Richardson) at a very early day in the session
brought in a set of resolutions, expressly endorsing the original justice of the war on the part of the President. Upon these
resolutions, when they shall be put on their passage I shall be
compelled to vote; so that I can not be silent, if I would. Seeing
this, I went about preparing myself to give the vote understandingly when it should come. I carefully examined the President's messages, to ascertain what he himself had said and
proved upon the point. The result of this examination was to
make the impression, that taking for true, all the President
states as facts, he falls far short of proving his justification; and
that the President would have gone farther with his proof, if it
had not been for the small matter, that the *truth* would not
permit him. Under the impression thus made, I gave the vote
before mentioned. I propose now to give, concisely, the process of the examination I made, and how I reached the conclusion I did. The President, in his first war message of May 1846,
declares that the soil was *ours* on which hostilities were commenced by Mexico; and he repeats that declaration, almost in
the same language, in each successive annual message, thus
showing that he esteems that point, a highly essential one. In
the importance of that point, I entirely agree with the President. To my judgment, it is the *very point*, upon which he
should be justified, or condemned. In his message of Decr.
1846, it seems to have occurred to him, as is certainly true, that
title—ownership—to soil, or any thing else, is not a simple
fact; but is a conclusion following one or more simple facts;
and that it was incumbent upon him, to present the facts, from
which he concluded, the soil was ours, on which the first
blood of the war was shed.

Accordingly a little below the middle of page twelve in the
message last referred to, he enters upon that task; forming an
issue, and introducing testimony, extending the whole, to a
little below the middle of page fourteen. Now I propose to try

to show, that the whole of this,—issue and evidence—is, from beginning to end, the sheerest deception. The issue, as he presents it, is in these words "But there are those who, conceding all this to be true, assume the ground that the true western boundary of Texas is the Nueces, instead of the Rio Grande; and that, therefore, in marching our army to the east bank of the latter river, we passed the Texan line, and invaded the teritory of Mexico." Now this issue, is made up of two affirmatives and no negative. The main deception of it is, that it assumes as true, that *one* river or the *other* is necessarily the boundary; and cheats the superficial thinker entirely out of the idea, that *possibly* the boundary is somewhere *between* the two, and not actually at either. A further deception is, that it will let in *evidence*, which a true issue would exclude. A true issue, made by the President, would be about as follows "I say, the soil *was ours*, on which the first blood was shed; there are those who say it was not."

I now proceed to examine the Presidents evidence, as applicable to such an issue. When that evidence is analized, it is all included in the following propositions:

1. That the Rio Grande was the Western boundary of Louisiana as we purchased it of France in 1803.

2. That the Republic of Texas always *claimed* the Rio Grande, as her Western boundary.

3. That by various acts, she had claimed it *on paper*.

4. That Santa Anna, in his treaty with Texas, recognised the Rio Grande, as her boundary.

5. That Texas *before*, and the U. S. *after*, annexation had *exercised* jurisdiction *beyond* the Nueces—*between* the two rivers.

6. That our Congress, *understood* the boundary of Texas to extend beyond the Nueces.

Now for each of these in it's turn.

His first item is, that the Rio Grande was the Western boundary of Louisiana, as we purchased it of France in 1803; and seeming to expect this to be disputed, he argues over the amount of nearly a page, to prove it true; at the end of which he lets us know, that by the treaty of 1819, we sold to Spain the whole country from the Rio Grande eastward, to the Sabine. Now, admitting for the present, that the Rio Grande, was the boundary of Louisiana, what, under heaven, had that to do with the *present* boundary between us and Mexico? How, Mr. Chairman, the line, that once divided your land from mine, can *still* be the boundary between us, *after* I have sold my land to you, is, to me, beyond all comprehension. And how any man, with an honest purpose only, of proving the truth, could ever have *thought* of introducing such a fact to prove such an issue, is equally incomprehensible. His next piece of evidence is that "The Republic of Texas always *claimed* this river (Rio Grande) as her western boundary." That is not true, in fact. Texas *has* claimed it, but she has not *always* claimed it. There is, at least, one distinguished exception. Her state constitution,—the republic's most solemn, and well considered act—that which may, without impropriety, be called her last will and testament revoking all others—makes no such claim. But suppose she had always claimed it. Has not Mexico always claimed the contrary? so that there is but *claim* against *claim*, leaving nothing proved, until we get back of the claims, and find which has the better *foundation*. Though not in the order in which the President presents his evidence, I now consider that class of his statements, which are, in substance, nothing more than that Texas has, by various acts of her convention and congress, claimed the Rio Grande, as her boundary, *on paper*. I mean here what he says about the fixing of the Rio Grande as her boundary in her old constitution (not her state constitution) about forming congressional districts, counties &c &c. Now all of this is but naked *claim*; and what I have already said about claims is strictly applicable to this. If I should claim your land, by word of mouth, that certainly would not make it mine; and if I were to claim it by a deed which I had made myself, and with which, you had had nothing to do, the claim would be quite the same, in substance—or rather, in utter nothingness. I next consider the President's statement that Santa Anna in his *treaty* with Texas, recognised the Rio Grande, as the western boundary of Texas. Besides the position, so often taken that Santa Anna, while a prisoner of war—a captive—*could* not bind Mexico by a treaty, which I deem conclusive—besides this, I wish to say something in relation to this treaty, so called by the President, with Santa Anna. If any man would like to be amused by a sight of that *little* thing, which the President calls by that *big* name, he can have it, by turning to Niles' Register volume 50, page 336. And if any one should suppose that Niles' Register is a curious repository of so mighty a document, as a solemn treaty between nations, I can only say that I learned, to a tolerable degree of certainty, by enquiry at the State Department, that the President himself, never saw it any where else. By the way, I believe I should not err, if I were to declare, that during the first ten years of the existence of that document, it was never, by any body, *called* a treaty—that it was never so called, till the President, in his extremity, attempted, by so calling it, to wring something from it in justification of himself in connection with the Mexican war. It has none of the distinguishing features of a treaty. It does not call itself a treaty. Santa Anna does not therein, assume to bind Mexico; he assumes only to act as the President–Commander-in-chief of the Mexican Army and Navy; stipulates that the then present hostilities should cease, and that he would not *himself* take up arms, nor *influence* the Mexican people to take up arms, against Texas during the existence of the war of independence. He did not recognise the independence of Texas; he did not assume to put an end to the war; but clearly indicated his expectation of it's continuance; he did not say one word about boundary, and, most probably, never thought of it. It *is* stipulated therein that the Mexican forces should evacuate the teritory of Texas, *passing to the other side of the Rio Grande*; and in another article, it is stipulated that, to prevent collisions between the armies, the Texan army should not approach nearer than within five leagues—of *what* is not said—but clearly, from the object stated it is—of the Rio Grande. Now, if this is a treaty, recognising the Rio Grande, as the boundary of Texas, it contains the singular feature, of stipulating, that Texas shall not go within five leagues of *her own* boundary.

Next comes the evidence of Texas before annexation, and the United States, afterwards, *exercising* jurisdiction *beyond* the Nueces, and *between* the two rivers. This actual *exercise* of jurisdiction, is the very class or quality of evidence we want. It is excellent so far as it goes; but does it go far enough? He tells us it went *beyond* the Nueces; but he does not tell us it went *to* the Rio Grande. He tells us, jurisdiction was exercised *between* the two rivers, but he does not tell us it was exercised over *all* the teritory between them. Some simple minded people, think it is *possible*, to cross one river and go *beyond* it without going *all the way* to the next—that jurisdiction may be exercised *between* two rivers without covering *all* the country between them. I know a man, not very unlike myself, who exercises jurisdiction over a piece of land between the Wabash and the Mississippi; and yet so far is this from being *all* there is between those rivers, that it is just one hundred and fifty-two feet long by fifty wide, and no part of it much within a hundred miles of either. He has a neighbour between him and the Mississippi,—that is, just across the street, in that direction— whom, I am sure, he could neither *persuade* nor *force* to give up his habitation; but which nevertheless, he could certainly annex, if it were to be done, by merely standing on his own side of the street and *claiming* it, or even, sitting down, and writing a *deed* for it.

But next the President tells us, the Congress of the United States *understood* the state of Texas they admitted into the union, to extend *beyond* the Nueces. Well, I suppose they did. *I* certainly so understood it. But how *far* beyond? That Congress did *not* understand it to extend clear to the Rio Grande, is quite certain by the fact of their joint resolutions, for admission, expressly leaving all questions of boundary to future adjustment. And it may be added, that Texas herself, is proved to have had the same understanding of it, that our Congress had, by the fact of the exact conformity of her new constitution, to those resolutions.

I am now through the whole of the President's evidence; and it is a singular fact, that if any one should declare the President sent the army into the midst of a settlement of Mexican people, who had never submited, by consent or by force, to the authority of Texas or of the United States, and that *there*, and *thereby*, the first blood of the war was shed, there is not one word in all the President has said, which would either admit or deny the declaration. This strange omission, it does seem to me, could not have occurred but by design. My way of living leads me to be about the courts of justice; and there, I have sometimes seen a good lawyer, struggling for his client's neck, in a desparate case, employing every artifice to work round, befog, and cover up, with many words, some point arising in the case, which he *dared* not admit, and yet *could* not deny. Party bias may help to make it appear so; but with all the allowance I can make for such bias, it still does appear, to me, that just such, and from just such necessity, is the President's struggle in this case.

Some time after my colleague (Mr. Richardson) introduced the resolutions I have mentioned, I introduced a preamble, resolution, and interrogatories, intended to draw the President out, if possible, on this hitherto untrodden ground. To show their relevancy, I propose to state my understanding of the true rule for ascertaining the boundary between Texas and Mexico. It is, that *wherever* Texas was *exercising* jurisdiction, was hers; and *wherever* *Mexico* was exercising jurisdiction, was hers; and that *whatever* separated the actual exercise of jurisdiction of the one, from that of the other, was the true boundary between them. If, as is probably true, Texas was exercising jurisdiction along the western bank of the Nueces, and Mexico was exercising it along the eastern bank of the Rio Grande, then *neither* river was the boundary; but the uninhabited country between the two, was. The extent of our teritory in that region depended, not on any *treaty-fixed* boundary (for no treaty had attempted it) but on revolution. Any people anywhere, being inclined and having the power, have the *right* to rise up, and shake off the existing government, and form a new one that suits them better. This is a most valuable,—a most sacred right—a right, which we hope and believe, is to liberate the world. Nor is this right confined to cases in which the whole people of an existing government, may choose to exercise it. Any portion of such people that *can*, *may* revolutionize, and make their *own*, of so much of the teritory as they inhabit. More than this, a *majority* of any portion of such people may revolutionize, putting down a *minority*, intermingled with, or near about them, who may oppose their movement. Such minority, was precisely the case, of the tories of our own revolution. It is a quality of revolutions not to go by *old* lines, or *old* laws; but to break up both, and make new ones. As to the country now in question, we bought it of France in 1803, and sold it to Spain in 1819, according to the President's statements. After this, all Mexico, including Texas, revolutionized against Spain; and still later, Texas revolutionized against Mexico. In my view, just so far as she carried her revolution, by obtaining the *actual*, willing or unwilling, submission of the people, *so far*, the country was hers, and no farther. Now sir, for the purpose of obtaining the very best evidence, as to whether Texas had actually carried her revolution, to the place where the hostilities of the present war commenced, let the President answer the interrogatories, I proposed, as before mentioned, or some other similar ones. Let him answer, fully, fairly, and candidly. Let him answer with *facts*, and not with arguments. Let him remember he sits where Washington sat, and so remembering, let him answer, as Washington would answer. As a nation *should* not, and the Almighty *will* not, be evaded, so let him attempt no evasion—no equivocation. And if, so answering, he can show that the soil was ours, where the first blood of the war was shed—that it was not within an inhabited country, or, if within such, that the inhabitants had submitted themselves to the civil authority of Texas, or of the United States, and that the same is true of the site of Fort Brown, then I am with him for his justification. In that case I, shall be most happy to reverse the vote I gave the other day. I have a selfish motive for desiring that the President may do this. I expect to give some votes, in connection with the war, which, without his so doing, will be of doubtful propriety in my own judgment, but which will be free from the doubt if he does so. But if he *can* not, or *will* not do this—if on any pretence, or no pretence, he shall refuse or omit it, then I shall be fully convinced, of what I more than suspect already, that he is deeply conscious of being in the wrong—that he feels the blood of this war, like the blood of Abel, is crying to Heaven against him. That originally having some strong motive—what, I will not stop now to give my opinion concerning—to involve the two countries in a war, and trusting to escape scrutiny, by fixing the public gaze upon the exceeding brightness of military glory—that attractive rainbow, that rises in showers of blood—that serpent's eye, that charms to destroy—he plunged into it, and has swept, *on* and *on*, till, disappointed in his calculation of the ease with which Mexico might be subdued, he now finds himself, he knows not where. How like the half insane mumbling of a fever-dream, is the whole war part of his late message! At one time telling us that Mexico has nothing whatever, that we can get, but teritory; at another, showing us how we can support the war, by levying contributions on Mexico. At one time, urging the national honor, the security of the future, the prevention of foreign interference, and even, the good of Mexico herself, as among the objects of the war; at another, telling us, that "to reject indemnity, by refusing to accept a cession of teritory, would be to abandon all our just demands, and to wage the war, bearing all it's expenses, *without a purpose or definite object.*" So then, the national honor, security of the future, and every thing but teritorial indemnity, may be considered the *no-purposes*, and *indefinite*, objects of the war! But, having it now settled that teritorial indemnity is the only object, we are urged to seize, by legislation here, all that he was content to take, a few months ago, and the whole province of lower California to boot, and to still carry on the war—to take *all* we are fighting for, and *still* fight on. Again, the President is resolved, under all circumstances, to have full teritorial indemnity for the expenses of the war; but he forgets to tell us how we are to get the *excess*, after those expenses shall have surpassed the value of the *whole* of the Mexican teritory. So again, he insists that the separate national existence of Mexico, shall be maintained; but he does not tell us *how* this can be done, after we shall have taken *all* her teritory. Lest the questions, I here suggest, be considered speculative merely, let me be indulged a moment in trying to show they are not. The war has gone on some twenty months; for the expenses of which, together with an inconsiderable old score, the President now claims about one half of the Mexican teritory; and that, by far the better half, so far as concerns our ability to make any thing out of it. *It* is comparatively uninhabited; so that we could establish land offices in it, and raise some money in that way. But the other half is already inhabited, as I understand it, tolerably densely for the nature of the country; and all it's lands, or all that are valuable, already appropriated as private property. How then are we to make any thing out of these lands with this incumbrance on them? or how, remove the incumbrance? I suppose no one will say we should kill the people, or drive them out, or make slaves of them, or even confiscate their property. How then can we make much out of this part of the teritory? If the prossecution of the war has, in expenses, already equalled the *better* half of the country, how long it's future prosecution, will be in equalling, the less valuable half, is not a *speculative*, but a *practical* question, pressing closely upon us. And yet it is a question which the President seems to never have thought of. As to the mode of terminating the war, and securing peace, the President is equally wandering and indefinite. First, it is to be done by a more vigorous prossecution of the war in the vital parts of the enemies country; and, after apparently, talking himself tired, on this point, the President drops down into a half despairing tone, and tells us that "with a people distracted and divided by contending factions, and a government subject to constant changes, by successive revolutions, *the continued success of our arms may fail to secure a satisfactory peace*." Then he suggests the propriety of wheedling the Mexican people to desert the counsels of their own leaders, and trusting in our protection, to set up a government from which we can secure a satisfactory peace; telling us, that "*this may become the only mode of obtaining such a peace*." But soon he falls into doubt of this too; and then drops back on to the already half abandoned ground of "more vigorous prossecution." All this shows that the President is, in no wise, satisfied with his own positions. First he takes up one, and in attempting to argue us *into* it, he argues himself *out* of it; then seizes another, and goes through the same process; and then, confused at being able to think of nothing new, he snatches up the old one again, which he has some time before cast off. His mind, tasked beyond it's power, is running hither and thither, like some tortured creature, on a burning surface, finding no position, on which it can settle down, and be at ease.

Again, it is a singular omission in this message, that it, no where intimates *when* the President expects the war to terminate. At it's beginning, Genl. Scott was, by this same President, driven into disfavor, if not disgrace, for intimating that peace could not be conquered in less than three or four months. But now, at the end of about twenty months, during which time our arms have given us the most splendid successes— every department, and every part, land and water, officers and privates, regulars and volunteers, doing all that men *could* do, and hundreds of things which it had ever before been thought men could *not* do,—after all this, this same President gives us a long message, without showing us, that, *as to the end*, he himself, has, even an immaginary conception. As I have before said, he knows not where he is. He is a bewildered, confounded, and miserably perplexed man. God grant he may be able to show, there is not something about his conscience, more painful than all his mental perplexity!

ELIZABETH CADY STANTON

Address to Woman's Rights Convention

Seneca Falls, N.Y., July 19, 1848

I SHOULD FEEL exceedingly diffident to appear before you at this time, having never before spoken in public, were I not nerved by a sense of right and duty, did I not feel the time had fully come for the question of woman's wrongs to be laid before the public, did I not believe that woman herself must do this work; for woman alone can understand the height, the depth, the length, and the breadth of her own degradation. Man cannot speak for her, because he has been educated to believe that she differs from him so materially, that he cannot judge of her thoughts, feelings, and opinions by his own. Moral beings can only judge of others by themselves. The moment they assume a different nature for any of their own kind, they utterly fail. The drunkard was hopelessly lost until it was discovered that he was governed by the same laws of mind as the sober man. Then with what magic power, by kindness and love, was he raised from the slough of despond and placed rejoicing on high land.

Let a man once settle the question that a woman does not think and feel like himself, and he may as well undertake to judge of the amount of intellect and sensation of any of the animal creation as of woman's nature. He can know but little with certainty, and that but by observation.

Among the many important questions which have been brought before the public, there is none that more vitally affects the whole human family than that which is technically called Woman's Rights. Every allusion to the degraded and inferior position occupied by women all over the world has been met by scorn and abuse. From the man of highest mental cultivation to the most degraded wretch who staggers in the streets do we meet ridicule, and coarse jests, freely bestowed upon those who dare assert that woman stands by the side of man, his equal, placed here by her God, to enjoy with him the beautiful earth, which is her home as it is his, having the same sense of right and wrong, and looking to the same Being for guidance and support. So long has man exercised tyranny over her, injurious to himself and benumbing to her faculties, that few can nerve themselves to meet the storm; and so long has the chain been about her that she knows not there is a remedy.

The whole social, civil and religious condition of woman is a subject too vast to be brought within the limits of one short lecture. Suffice it to say, for the present, wherever we turn, the history of woman is sad and dark, without any alleviating circumstances, nothing from which we can draw consolation.

As the nations of the earth emerge from a state of barbarism, the sphere of woman gradually becomes wider, but not even under what is thought to be the full blaze of the sun of civilization is it what God designed it to be. In every country and clime does man assume the responsibility of marking out the path for her to tread. In every country does he regard her as a being inferior to himself, and one whom he is to guide and control. From the Arabian Kerek, whose wife is obliged to steal from her husband to supply the necessities of life; from the Mahometan who forbids pigs, dogs, women, and other impure animals, to enter a Mosque, and does not allow a fool, madman or woman to proclaim the hour of prayer; from the German who complacently smokes his meerschaum, while his wife, yoked with the ox, draws the plough through its furrow; from the delectable carpet-knight, who thinks an inferior style of conversation adapted to woman, to the legislator, who considers her incapable of saying what laws shall govern her, is the same feeling manifested.

In all eastern countries she is a mere slave, bought and sold at pleasure. There are many differences in habits, manners and customs among the heathen nations of the Old World, but there is little change for the better in woman's lot. She is either the drudge of man, to perform all the hard labor of the field, and all the menial duties of the hut, tent or house, or she is the idol of his lust, the mere creature of his varying whims and will. Truly has she herself said in her best estate,

I am a slave, a favored slave,
To share his pleasures and seem very blest,
When weary of these fleeting charms and me
There yawns the sack, and yonder the rolling sea,
What, am I then a toy for dotards play
To wear but till the gilding frets away?

In Christian countries, boasting a more advanced state of civilization and refinement, woman still holds a position infinitely inferior to man.

In France the Salic Law tells much, although it is said that woman there has ever had great influence in all political revolutions. In England she seems to have advanced a little, there she has a right to the throne, and is allowed to hold some other offices, and to vote on some questions. But in the United States of America, in a republic based on the theory that no just government can be formed without the consent of the governed, woman has no right either to hold office, or to the elective franchise. She stands at this moment unrepresented in this government, her rights and interests wholly overlooked.

There is a class of men who believe in their natural, inborn, inbred superiority, and their heaven-descended right to dominion over the fish of the sea, the fowl of the air, and last, though not least, the immortal being called woman. I would recommend this class to the attentive perusal of their Bibles— Gen., i. xxviii.; to historical research, to foreign travel, to a closer observation of the manisfestations of mind about them, and to a humble comparison of themselves with such women as Catharine of Russia, Elizabeth of England, distinguished for their statesmanlike qualities; Harriet Martineau and Madame De Stael, for their literary attainments; or Caroline Herschel and Mary Somerville for their scientific researches; or for physical equality, to that whole nation of famous women, the Amazons. We seldom find this class of objectors among liberally educated persons, who have the advantage of observing the race in different countries, climes and phases. But barbarians though they be, in entertaining such an opinion, they must be met and fairly vanquished. Let us consider, then, man's superiority, intellectually, morally, physically.

Man's intellectual superiority cannot be a question until

woman has had a fair trial. When we shall have had our freedom to find out our own sphere, when we shall have had our colleges, our professions, our trades, for a century, a comparison then may be justly instituted. When woman, instead of being taxed to endow colleges where she is forbidden to enter—instead of forming sewing societies to educate "poor, but pious," young men, shall first educate herself, when she shall be just to herself before she is generous to others; improving the talents God has given her, and leaving her neighbor to do the same for himself, we shall not then hear so much about this boasted superiority. How often, now, we see young men carelessly throwing away the intellectual food their sisters crave. A little music, that she may while an hour away pleasantly, a little French, a smattering of the sciences, and in rare instances, some slight classical knowledge, and woman is considered highly educated. She leaves her books and studies just as a young man is entering thoroughly into his. Then comes the gay routine of fashionable life, courtship and marriage, the perplexities of house and children, and she knows nothing beside. Her sphere is home. And whatever yearning her spirit may have felt for a higher existence, whatever may have been the capacity she well knew she possessed for more elevated enjoyments, enjoyments which would not conflict with those holy duties, but add new lustre to them, all, all is buried beneath the weight of these undivided cares.

Men, bless their innocence, are fond of representing themselves as beings of reason, of intellect, while women are mere creatures of the affections. There is a self-conceit that makes the possessor infinitely happy, and we would dislike to dispel the illusion if it were possible to endure it. But so far as we can observe, it is pretty much now-a-days as it was with Adam of old. No doubt you all recollect the account we have given us. A man and a woman were placed in a beautiful garden, with everything about them that could contribute to their enjoyment. Trees and shrubs, fruits and flowers, and gently murmuring streams made glad their hearts. Zephyrs freighted with delicious odors fanned their brows, and the serene stars looked down upon them with eyes of love. The Evil One saw their happiness, and it troubled him, and he set his wits to work to know how he should destroy it. He thought that man could be easily conquered through his affection for the woman, but the woman would require more management, she could be reached only through her intellectual nature. So he promised her the knowledge of good and evil. He told her the sphere of her reason should be enlarged. He promised to gratify the desires she felt for intellectual improvement. So he prevailed and she did eat. Did the Evil One judge rightly in regard to man? Eve took the apple, went to Adam, and said; "Dear Adam, taste this apple. If you love me, eat?" Adam stopped not so much as to ask if the apple were sweet or sour. He knew he was doing wrong, but his love for Eve prevailed, and he did eat. Which, I ask you, was the creature of the affections?

In consideration of man's claim to moral superiority, glance now at our theological seminaries, our divinity students, the long line of descendants from our Apostolic fathers, the immaculate priesthood, and what do we find here? Perfect moral rectitude in every relation of life, a devoted spirit of self-sacrifice, a perfect union of thought, opinion and feeling among those who profess to worship the one God, and whose laws they feel themselves called upon to declare to a fallen race? Far from it. These persons, all so thoroughly acquainted with the character of God, and of His designs, made manifest by His words and works, are greatly divided among themselves. Every sect has its God, every sect has its Bible, and there is as much bitterness, envy, hatred and malice between those contending sects, yea, even more, than in our political parties during the periods of their greatest excitement. Now the leaders of these sects are the priesthood, who are supposed to have passed their lives, almost, in the study of the Bible, in various languages and with various commentaries—in the contemplation of the infinite, the eternal, the glorious future open to the redeemed of earth. Are they distinguished among men for their holy aspirations, their virtue, purity and chastity? Do they keep themselves unspotted from the world? Is the moral and religious life of this class what we might expect from minds said to be fixed on such mighty themes? By no means. Not a year passes but we hear of some sad, soul-sickening deed, perpetrated by some of this class. If such be the state of the most holy, we need not pause now to consider those classes who claim of us less reverence and respect. The lamentable want of principle among our lawyers, generally, is too well known to need comment. The everlasting back-biting and bickering of our physicians is proverbial. The disgraceful riots at our polls, where man, in performing the highest duty of citizenship, and ought surely to be sober-minded, the perfect rowdyism that now characterizes the debates in our national Congress,—all these are great facts which rise up against man's claim for moral superiority. In my opinion, he is infinitely woman's inferior in every moral quality, not by nature, but made so by a false education. In carrying out his own selfishness, man has greatly improved woman's moral nature, but by an almost total shipwreck of his own. Woman has now the noble virtues of the martyr. She is early schooled to self-denial and suffering. But man is not so wholly buried in selfishness that he does not sometimes get a glimpse of the narrowness of his soul, as compared with woman. Then he says, by way of an excuse for his degradation, "God made woman more self-denying than man. It is her nature. It does not cost her as much to give up her wishes, her will, her life, even, as it does him. He is naturally selfish. God made him so."

No! think not that He who made the heavens and the earth, the whole planetary world, ever moving in such harmony and order, that He who so bountifully scattered through all nature so much that fills us with admiration and wonder, that He who made the mighty ocean, mountain and cataract, the bright birds and tender flowers, that He who made man in his own image, perfect, noble and pure, loving justice, mercy and truth,—oh say not that he has had any part in the production of that creeping, cringing, crawling, debased, selfish monster, now extant, claiming for himself the name of man. No! God's commands rest upon man as well as woman. It is as much his duty to be kind, self-denying and full of good works, as it is hers. As much his duty to absent himself from scenes of violence as it is hers. A place or position that would require the sacrifice of the delicacy and refinement of woman's nature is unfit for man, for these virtues should be as carefully guarded in him as in her. The false ideas that prevail with regard to the purity necessary to constitute the perfect character in woman, and that requisite for man, has done an infinite deal of mischief in the world. I would not have woman less pure, but I would have man more so. I would have the same code of morals for both. Delinquencies which exclude woman from the society of the true and the good, should assign to man the same place. Our laxity towards him has been the fruitful source of dissipation, drunkenness, debauchery and immorality of all kinds, It has not only affected woman injuriously, but he himself has been the greatest sufferer. It has destroyed the nobility of his character, the transparency of his soul, and all those finer qualities of our nature which raise us above the earth and give us a foretaste of the refined enjoyments of the world to come.

Let us now consider man's claim to physical superiority. Methinks I hear some say, surely, you will not contend for equality here. Yes, we must not give an inch, lest you take an ell. We cannot accord to man even this much, and he has no right to claim it until the fact has been fully demonstrated. Until the physical education of the boy and the girl shall have been the same for many years. If you claim the advantage of size, merely, why, it may be that under any course of training, in ever so perfect a development of physique in woman, man might still be the larger of the two, though we do not grant even this. But the perfection of the physique is great power combined with endurance. Now your strongest men are not always the tallest men, nor the broadest, nor the most corpulent, but very often the small, elastic man, who is well built, tightly put together, and possessed of an indomitable will. Bodily strength depends much on the power of the will. The sight of a small boy thoroughly thrashing a big one, is not rare. Now, would you say the big, fat boy whipped, was superior to the small active boy who conquered him? You do not say the horse is physically superior to man, for although he has more muscular power, yet the power of mind in man renders him his superior, and he guides him wherever he will. The power of mind seems to be in no way connected with the size and strength of body. Many men of herculean powers of mind have been small and weak in body. The late distinguished Dr. Channing, of Boston, was feeble in appearance and voice, yet he has moved the world by the eloquence of his pen. John Quincy Adams was a small man of little muscular power, yet we know he had more courage than all the Northern doughfaces, six feet high and well proportioned, that ever represented us at our capitol. Mental power depends far more on the temperament, than on the size of the head or the size of the body. I never heard that Daniel Lambert was distinguished for any great mental achievements. We cannot say what the woman might be physically, if the girl were allowed all the freedom of the boy in romping, climbing, swimming, playing whoop and ball. Among some of the Tartar tribes of the present day, women manage a horse, hurl a javelin, hunt wild animals, and fight an enemy as well as a man. The Indian women endure fatigues and carry burdens that some of our fair-faced, soft-handed, moustached young gentlemen would consider quite impossible for them to sustain. The Croatian and Wallachian women perform all the agricultural operations in addition to their domestic labors, and it is no uncommon sight in our cities, to see the German immigrant with his hands in his pockets, walking complacently by the side of his wife, whilst she bears the weight of some huge package or piece of furniture upon her head. Physically, as well as intellectually, it is use that produces growth and development.

But there is a class of objectors, who say they do not claim superiority, they merely assert a difference. But you will find by following them up closely, that they soon run this difference into the old groove of superiority. The phrenologist says that woman's head has just as many organs as man's, and that they are similarly situated. He says, too, that the organs most used are most prominent. They do not divide heads according to sex, but they call all the fine heads masculine, and the inferior feminine. When a woman presents a well-developed intellectual region, they say she has a masculine head, as if there could be nothing remarkable of the feminine gender. When a man has a small head, with little reasoning power, and the affections strongly developed, they say he has a woman's head, thus giving all reasoning power to the masculine gender.

> Some say our heads are less,
> Some men's are small, not they the least of men,
> For often fineness compensates for size,
> Besides the brain is like the hand, and grows with using.

We have met here to-day to discuss our rights and wrongs, civil and political, and not, as some have supposed, to go into the detail of social life alone. We do not propose to petition

the legislature to make our husbands just, generous and courteous, to seat every man at the head of a cradle, and to clothe
every woman in male attire. None of these points, however important they may be considered by leading men, will be
touched in this Convention. As to their costume, the gentlemen need feel no fear of our imitating that, for we think it in
violation of every principle of taste, beauty and dignity; notwithstanding all the contempt cast upon our loose, flowing
garments, we still admire the graceful folds, and consider our
costume far more artistic than theirs. Many of the nobler sex
seem to agree with us in this opinion, for the bishops, priests,
judges, barristers, and lord-mayors of the first nation on the
globe, and the Pope of Rome, with his Cardinals, too, all wear
the loose flowing robes, thus tacitly acknowledging that the
male attire is neither dignified nor imposing. No, we shall not
molest you in your philosophical experiments with stocks,
pants, high-heeled boots and Russian belts. Yours be the glory
to discover, by personal experience, how long the knee-pan can
resist the terrible strapping down which you impose, in how
short time the well developed muscles of the throat can be reduced to mere threads by the constant pressure of the stock,
how high the heel of a boot must be to make a short man tall,
and how tight the Russian belt may be drawn and yet have
wind enough left to sustain life. But we are assembled to protest
against a form of government, existing without the consent of
the governed—to declare our right to be free as man is free, to
be represented in the government which we are taxed to support, to have such disgraceful laws as give man the power to
chastise and imprison his wife, to take the wages which she
earns, the property which she inherits, and, in case of separation, the children of her love; laws which makes her the mere
dependent on his bounty. It is to protest against such unjust
laws as these that we are assembled to-day, and to have them,
if possible, forever erased from our statute-books, deeming
them a shame and a disgrace to a Christian republic in the
nineteenth century. We have met

> To uplift woman's fallen divinity
> Upon an even pedestal with man's.

And, strange as it may seem to many, we now demand our

right to vote according to the declaration of the government under which we live. This right no one pretends to deny. We need not prove ourselves equal to Daniel Webster to enjoy this privilege, for the ignorant Irishman in the ditch has all the civil rights he has. We need not prove our muscular power equal to this same Irishman to enjoy this privilege, for the most tiny, weak, ill-shaped stripling of twenty-one, has all the civil rights of the Irishman. We have no objection to discuss the question of equality, for we feel that the weight of argument lies wholly with us, but we wish the question of equality kept distinct from the question of rights, for the proof of the one does not determine the truth of the other. All white men in this country have the same rights, however they may differ in mind, body or estate. The right is ours. The question now is, how shall we get possession of what rightfully belongs to us. We should not feel so sorely grieved if no man who had not attained the full stature of a Webster, Clay, Van Buren, or Gerrit Smith could claim the right of the elective franchise. But to have drunkards, idiots, horse-racing, rumselling rowdies, ignorant foreigners and silly boys fully recognized, while we ourselves are thrust out from all the rights that belong to citizens, it is too grossly insulting to the dignity of woman to be longer quietly submitted to. The right is ours. Have it, we must. Use it, we will. The pens, the tongues, the fortunes, the indomitable wills of many women are already pledged to secure this right. The great truth, that no just government can be formed without the consent of the governed, we shall echo and re-echo in the ears of the unjust judge, until by continual coming we shall weary him.

But, say some, would you have woman vote? What, refined, delicate women at the polls, mingling in such scenes of violence and vulgarity? Most certainly. Where there is so much to be feared for the pure, the innocent, the noble, the mother surely should be there, to watch and guard her sons who must encounter such stormy, dangerous scenes at the tender age of twenty-one. Much is said of woman's influence, might not her presence do much toward softening down this violence, refining this vulgarity? Depend upon it, the places that, by their impure atmosphere, are unfit for women, cannot but be dangerous to her sires and sons.

But, if woman claims all the rights of a citizen, will she

buckle on her armor and fight in defence of her country? Has not woman already often shown herself as courageous in the field, as wise and patriotic in counsel as man? But for myself, I think all war sinful. I believe in Christ. I believe that command, "resist not evil," to be divine. "Vengeance is mine, and I will repay, saith the Lord." Let frail man, who cannot foresee the consequences of an action, walk humbly with his God, loving his enemies, blessing them who curse him, and always returning good for evil. This is the highest kind of courage that mortal man can attain to. And this moral warfare with our own bad passions requires no physical power to achieve. I would not have man go to war. I can see no glory in fighting with such weapons as guns and swords, whilst man has in his possession the infinitely superior ones of righteousness and truth.

But what would woman gain by voting? Men must know the advantages of voting, for they all seem very tenacious about the right. Think you, if woman had a voice in this government, that all those laws affecting her interests would so entirely violate every principle of right and justice? Had woman a vote to give, might not the office-holders and seekers propose some change in her condition? Might not Woman's Rights become as great a question as free soil?

"But are you not already represented by your fathers, husbands, brothers and sons?" Let your statute books answer the question. We have had enough of such representation. In nothing is woman's true happiness consulted. Men like to call her an angel—to feed her on what they think sweet food—nourishing her vanity; to make her believe that her organization is so much finer than theirs, that she is not fitted to struggle with the tempests of public life, but needs their care and protection!! Care and protection—such as the wolf gives the lamb—such as the eagle the hare he carries to his eyrie!! Most cunningly he entraps her, and then takes from her all those rights which are dearer to him than life itself—rights which have been baptized in blood—and the maintenance of which is even now rocking to their foundations the kingdoms of the Old World.

The most discouraging, the most lamentable aspect our cause wears is the indifference, indeed, the contempt with which women themselves regard the movement. Where the subject is introduced, among those even who claim to be intelligent and educated, it is met by the scornful curl of the lip, and by expression of ridicule and disgust. But we shall hope better things of them when they are enlightened in regard to their present position. When women know the laws and constitutions under which they live, they will not publish their degradation, by declaring themselves satisfied, nor their ignorance, by declaring they have all the rights they want. They are not the only class of beings who glory in their bondage. In the Turkish harem, in those Seraglios, where intellect and soul are buried beneath the sensualism and brutality which are the inevitable results of woman's degradation, even there, she declares herself not only satisfied with her position, but glories in it. Miss Martineau, in her "Travels in the East," recently published, says, refering to the inmates of the harems: "Everywhere they pitied us European women heartily, that we had to go about travelling, and appearing in the streets without being properly taken care of, that is, watched." They think us strangely neglected in being left so free, and boast of their spy system and imprisonment as tokens of the value in which they are held. Can woman here, although her spiritual and intellectual nature is recognized to a somewhat greater degree than among the Turks, and she is allowed the privilege of being in her nursery and kitchen, and although the Christian promises her the ascendency in heaven as man has it here, while the Mahometan closes the gates of the celestial city tight against her, can she be content, notwithstanding these good things, to be denied the pure enjoyments arising from a full cultivation of her mind, and an admission into all the rights and privileges which are hers? She must and will, ere long, when her spirit awakens, and she learns to care less for the

> Barren verbiage, current among men,
> Light coin, the tinsel clink of compliment.

She must and will demand everywhere

> Two heads in council—two beside the hearth,
> Two in the tangled business of the world.
> Two in the liberal offices of life,
> Two plummets dropped to sound the abyss
> Of science, and the secrets of the mind.

Let woman live as she should. Let her feel her accountability to her Maker. Let her know that her spirit is fitted for as high a sphere as man's, and that her soul requires food as pure and exalted as his. Let her live *first* for God, and she will not make imperfect man an object of reverence and awe. Teach her her responsibility as a being of conscience and reason, that all earthly support is weak and unstable, that her only safe dependence is the arm of omnipotence, and that true happiness springs from duty accomplished. Thus will she learn the lesson of individual responsibility for time and eternity. That neither father, husband, brother or son, however willing they may be, can discharge her high duties of life, or stand in her stead when called into the presence of the great Searcher of Hearts at the last day. Methinks I hear some woman say, "Must we not obey our husbands? Does not the Bible so command us?" No, you have not rightly read your Bible. At the creation of our first parents, God called their name Adam, and gave them dominion over the fish of the sea, the fowls of the air, and every living thing that moved upon the earth, but he says nothing to them of obedience to each other. After the fall, after Noah came out of the ark, he addressed them in like manner. The chief support that man finds for this authority over woman in the Bible, he gets from St. Paul. It needs but little consideration to see how limited this command of St. Paul must be, even if you give it all the weight which is usually claimed. "Wives, obey your husbands in the Lord." Now as the command is given to me, I am of course to be the judge of what is "in the Lord," and this opens a wide field of escape from any troublesome commands. There can be no subordination where the one to whom a command is given is allowed to sit in judgment on the character of the command. The Bible argument on this subject would of itself afford sufficient material for an entire lecture. I shall not, therefore, attempt to go into it at this time, enough to say that that best of Books is ever on the side of freedom, and we shrink not from pleading our cause on its principles of universal justice and love.

Let me here notice one of the greatest humbugs of the day, which has long found for itself the most valuable tool in woman—"The Education Society." The idea, to me, is simply absurd, for women, in their present degradation and ignorance, to form sewing societies for the education of young men for the ministry. An order of beings above themselves, claiming to be gifted with superior powers, having all the avenues to learning, wealth and distinction thrown freely open to them, who, if they had but the energy to avail themselves of all these advantages, could easily secure an education for themselves, while woman herself, poor, friendless, robbed of all her rights, oppressed on all sides, civilly, religiously and socially, must needs go ignorant herself. Now, is not the idea preposterous, for such a being to educate a great, strong, lazy man, by working day and night with her needle, stitch, stitch, and the poor widow always throws in her mite, being taught to believe that all she gives for the decoration of churches and their black-coated gentry, is given unto the Lord. I think a man, who, under such conditions, has the moral hardihood to take an education at the hands of woman, and at such an expense to her, should, as soon as he graduates, with all his honors thick upon him, take the first ship for Turkey, and there pass his days in earnest efforts to rouse the inmates of the harems to a true sense of their degradation, and not, as is his custom, immediately enter our pulpits to tell us of his superiority to us, "weaker vessels"—his prerogative to command, ours to obey—his duty to preach, ours to keep silence. Oh, for the generous promptings of the days of chivalry. Oh, for the poetry of romantic gallantry. May they shine on us once more. Then may we hope that these pious young men, who profess to believe in the golden rule, will clothe and educate themselves and encourage woman to do the same for herself; or perhaps they might conceive the happy thought of reciprocating the benefits so long enjoyed by them. There is something painfully affecting in the self-sacrifice and generosity of women, who can neither read nor write their own language with correctness, going about begging money for the education of men. The last time when an appeal of this kind was made to me, I told the young girl that I would send her to school a year, if she would go, but I would never again give one red cent to the Education Society. And I do hope that every Christian woman, who has the least regard for her sex, will make the same resolve. We have worked long enough for man, and at a most unjust and unwarrantable sacrifice of self, yet he gives no evidence of gratitude, but has, thus far, treated his benefactors with scorn, ridicule and neglect. But, say they, you do not need an education as we do. We expect to shine in the great world. Our education is our living. What, let me ask, is the real object of education. Just in proportion as the faculties which God hath given us are harmoniously developed, do we attain our highest happiness. And has not woman an equal right to happiness here as well as hereafter? And should she not have equal facilities with him for making an honest living while on this footstool?

One common objection to this movement is, that if the principles of freedom and equality which we advocate were put into practice, it would destroy all harmony in the domestic circle. Here let me ask, how many truly harmonious households have we now? Look round your circle of friends: on the one hand you will find the meek, sad-looking, thoroughly subdued wife, with no freedom of thought or action, her days passed in the dull routine of household cares, and her nights perchance in making tattered garments whole, and the other half in slumbers oft disturbed by sick and restless children. She knows nothing of the great world without; she has no time to read, and her husband finds more pleasure in discussing politics with men in groceries, taverns, or depots, than he could in reading or telling his wife the news, whilst she sits mending his stockings and shirts through many a lonely evening; nor dreams he, selfish being, that he owes any duty to the perishing soul by his side, beyond providing a house to cover her head, with food and raiment. As to her little "heaven ordained" world within, she finds not much comfort there, for her will and wishes, should she have any, must be in subjection to that of her tyrant. The comfort of wife, children, servants, one and all, must be given up, wholly disregarded, until the great head of the house has all his wants supplied. No matter what the case may be, he must have his hot dinner. If wife or children are sick, they must look elsewhere for care; he cannot be disturbed at night; it does not agree with him to have his slumbers broken, it gives him the headache and renders him unfit for business; and, worse than all, how often woman's very soul is tortured by the harsh, brutal treatment of fathers toward their children. What mother cannot bear me witness to anguish of this sort. Oh! women, how sadly you have learned your duty to your children, to the holy promptings of your own hearts, to the God that gave you that merciful love for them in all their wanderings, when you stand silent witnesses of the cruel infliction of blows and stripes from angry fathers on the trembling forms of helpless infancy. It is a mother's sacred duty to shield her children from violence, from whatever source it may come. It is woman's mission to resist oppression wherever she may find it, whether at her own fireside, or on a Southern plantation, by every moral power within her reach. Many men, well known for their philanthropy, who hate oppression in the outer world, can play the tyrant right well at home. It is a much easier matter to denounce all the crying sins of the day, most eloquently, too, under the inspiration of applauding thousands, than to endure alone, for an hour, the peevish moaning of a sick child. To know whether a man is truly great and good, you must not judge by his actions in the great world, but follow him to his home, where all restraints are laid aside, and there you see the true man, his virtues and his vices, too.

On the other hand, in these "harmonious households," you sometimes find the so-called "hen-pecked husband" oftimes a kind, generous, noble-minded man, who hates contention and is willing to do anything for peace. He having unwarily caught a Tartar, tries to make the best of her. He can think his own thoughts, tell them, too, when he feels quite sure that she is not at hand. He can absent himself from home, as much as possible, but he does not feel like a free man. The detail of his suffering I can neither describe or imagine, never having been the confident of one of these unfortunate beings; but are not his sorrows all written in the book of the immortal Caudle, written by his own hand, that all may read and pity the poor man, though feeling all through that the hapless Mrs. Caudle had, after all, many reasons for her continual wail for substantial grief. Now, in the ordinary households we see there may be no open rupture; they may seemingly glide on without a ripple over the surface; the aggrieved parties having resigned themselves to suffer all things with Christian fortitude, with stern philosophy, but there can be no harmony or happiness there. The only happy households we now see are those in which husband and wife share equally in counsel and government. There can be no true dignity or independence where there is subordination to the absolute will of another, no happiness without freedom. Let us then have no fears that this movement will disturb what is seldom found a truly united and happy family.

Is it not strange that man—with the pages of history all spread out before him—is so slow to admit the intellectual power, the moral heroism of woman, and her identity with himself. That there have been comparatively a greater number of good queens than of good kings is a fact stated by several historians. Zenobia, the celebrated queen of the East, is not exceeded by any king on record for talent, courage and daring ambition. The Emperor Aurelian, while beseiging her beautiful city of Palmes, writes thus: "The Roman people speak with contempt of the war I am waging with a woman, but they are ignorant both of the character and power of Zenobia." She was possessed of attainments very unusual in that age, and was a liberal patron of literature and science. No contemporary sovereign is represented as capable of such high pursuits. Margaret, Queen of Denmark, Norway and Sweden, justly called the Semiramis of the North, by her talent, energy, firmness and foresight, raised herself to a degree of power and grandeur then unequalled in Europe. No monarch has ever rivalled Isabella of Spain, in bravery, sagacity, political wisdom, and a proud sense of honor. Yet these characteristics were united with the purest modesty and the warmest feminine affections. Ferdinand, her husband, was her inferior in mind, heart and nobility of character. As a wife and a mother she seems to have been as perfect a model as of a queen. Her treaty with the Queen of Portugal is probably the only one in history of which it could be said: "The fair negotiators experienced none of the embarrassments usually incident to such deliberations, growing out of jealousy, distrust and a mutual desire to overreach. They were conducted in perfect good faith, and a sincere desire on both sides to establish a cordial reconciliation." Austria has produced no wiser or better sovereign than Maria Theresa, to whose strength of character her nobles paid involuntary homage when they unanimously exclaimed, "We will die for our King Maria Theresa." She, too, was an affectionate wife and mother. In England it was common to hear the people talk of King Elizabeth and Queen James. Catharine of Russia bears honorable comparison with Peter the Great. The annals of Africa furnish no example of a monarch equal to the brave, intelligent and proud hearted Tinga, the negro Queen of Angola. Blanche of Castile evinced great ability in administering the government of France, during the minority of her son, and similar praise is due to Caroline of England during the absence of her husband. What did woman not do? what did she not suffer in our revolutionary struggle? In all great national difficulties, her heart has ever been found to beat in the right place. She has been loyal alike to her country and her tyrants. "He said it, and it must be right," was the remark of Josephine in her happy days, when her own judgment suggested a change of course from the one marked out to her by Napoleon, but she lived long enough to learn that he might both do and say much that was not right. It has happened more than once that in a crisis of national affairs woman has been appealed to for her aid. Hannah Moore, one of the great minds of her day, at a time when French revolutionary and atheistical opinions were spreading, was earnestly besought by many leading men to write something to counteract these destructive influences. Her style was so popular, and she had shown so intimate a knowledge of human nature that they hoped much from her influence. Her Village Politics by Will Chip, written in a few hours, showed that she merited the opinion entertained of her powers upon all classes of mind. It had, as was expected, great effect. The tact and intelligence of this woman completely turned the tide of opinion, and many say prevented a revolution. Whether she did old England's poor any essential service by warding off, for a time, what must surely come, is a question; however, she did it, and the wise ones of her day gloried in her success. Where was the spirit found to sustain that mighty discoverer, Christopher Columbus, in the dark hours of his despair? Isabella of Arragon may be truly said to be the mother of this western world. She was the constant friend and protector of Columbus during her life; and although assailed at all sides, yet she steadily and firmly rejected the advice of narrow-minded, timid counsellors, and generously bestowed her patronage upon that heroic adventurer. In all those things in which the priests had no interest, consequently did not influence her mind, she was ever the noble woman, loving justice; the Christian, loving mercy. The persecution of the Jews, and the establishment of the Inquisition cannot be said to have been countenanced by her, they were the results of priestly cruelty and impudence. Torquemada, the Confessor of the Queen, did not more fatally mislead her then, than do the priests of our day mislead us; the cry of heretic was not more potent in her day than that of infidel in ours. They burned and tortured the bodies of all who rejected the popular faith, we consign their souls to hell-fire and their lives to misrepresentation and persecution. The feeling of aversion so often expressed at seeing woman in places of publicity is merely the effect of custom, very like that prejudice against color, so truly American. White men make no objections to women or negroes to serve or amuse them in public, but the claim of equality is what chagrins the tyrant. Man never rejects the aid of either, when they serve him in the accomplishment of his work. What man or woman has a feeling of disapproval in reading the history of Joan of Arc. The sympathies of every heart are at once enlisted in the success of that extraordinary girl. Her historian tells us that when all human power seemed unavailing, the French no longer despised the supernatural aid of the damsel of Domremy. The last stronghold of the Dauphin Charles was beseiged; the discouraged French were about to abandon it when the coming of this simple girl paralyzed the English, and inspired the followers of Charles with the utmost courage. Her success was philosophical, in accordance with the laws of mind. She had a full faith in herself and inspired all those who saw her with the same. Let us cultivate like faith, like enthusiasm, and we, too, shall impress all who see and hear us with the same confidence we ourselves feel in our final success. There seems now to be a kind of moral stagnation in our midst. Philanthropists have done their utmost to rouse the nation to a sense of its sins. War, slavery, drunkenness, licentiousness, gluttony, have been dragged naked before the people, and all their abominations and deformities fully brought to light, yet with idiotic laugh we hug those monsters to our breasts and rush on to destruction. Our churches are multiplying on all sides, our missionary societies, Sunday schools, and prayer meetings and innumerable charitable and reform organizations are all in operation, but still the tide of vice is swelling, and threatens the destruction of everything, and the battlements of righteousness are weak against the raging elements of sin and death. Verily, the world waits the coming of some new element, some purifying power, some spirit of mercy and love. The voice of woman has been silenced in the state, the church, and the home, but man cannot fulfill his destiny alone, he cannot redeem his race unaided. There are deep and tender chords of sympathy and love in the hearts of the down-fallen and oppressed that woman can touch more skillfully than man. The world has never yet seen a truly great and virtuous nation, because in the degradation of woman the very fountains of life are poisoned at their source. It is vain to look for silver and gold from mines of copper and lead. It is the wise mother that has the wise son. So long as your women are slaves you may throw your colleges and churches to the winds. You can't have scholars and saints so long as your mothers are ground to powder between the upper and nether millstone of tyranny and lust. How seldom, now, is a father's pride gratified, his fond hopes realized, in the budding genius of his son. The wife is degraded, made the mere creature of caprice, and the foolish son is heaviness to his heart. Truly are the sins of the fathers visited upon the children to the third and fourth generation. God, in his wisdom, has so linked the whole human family together, that any violence done at one end of the chain is felt throughout its length, and here, too, is the law of restoration, as in woman all have fallen, so in her elevation shall the race be recreated. "Voices" were the visitors and advisers of Joan of Arc. Do not "voices" come to us daily from the haunts of poverty, sorrow, degradation and despair, already too long unheeded. Now is the time for the women of this country, if they would save our free institutions, to defend the right, to buckle on the armor that can best resist the keenest weapons of the enemy—contempt and ridicule. The same religious enthusiasm that nerved Joan of Arc to her work nerves us to ours. In every generation God calls some men and women for the utterance of truth, a heroic action, and our work to-day is the fulfilling of what has long since been foretold by the Prophet—Joel, ii., xxviii: "And it shall come to pass afterward, that I will pour out my spirit upon all flesh, and your sons and your daughters shall prophecy." We do not expect our path will be strewn with the flowers of popular applause, but over the thorns of bigotry and prejudice will be our way, and on our banners will beat the dark storm-clouds of opposition from those who have entrenched themselves behind the stormy bulwarks of custom and authority, and who have fortified their position by every means, holy and unholy. But we will steadfastly abide the result. Unmoved we will bear it aloft. Undauntedly we will unfurl it to the gale, for we know that the storm cannot rend from it a shred, that the electric flash will but more clearly show to us the glorious words inscribed upon it, "Equality of Rights."

> Then fear not thou to wind thy horn,
> Though elf and gnome thy courage scorn.
> Ask for the Castle's King and Queen,
> Though rabble rout may rush between,
> Beat thee senseless to the ground
> And in the dark beset thee round,
> Persist to ask and it will come;
> Seek not for rest in humbler home,
> So shalt thou see what few have seen;
> The palace home of King and Queen.

THEODORE PARKER

The Political Destination of America and the Signs of the Times

1848

EVERY NATION has a peculiar character, in which it differs from all others that have been, that are, and possibly from all that are to come; for it does not yet appear that the Divine Father of the nations ever repeats himself and creates either two nations or two men exactly alike. However, as nations, like men, agree in more things than they differ, and in obvious things too, the special peculiarity of any one tribe does not always appear at first sight. But if we look through the history of some nation which has passed off from the stage of action, we find certain prevailing traits which continually reappear in the language and laws thereof; in its arts, literature, manners, modes of religion—in short, in the whole life of the people. The most prominent thing in the history of the Hebrews is their continual trust in God, and this marks them from their first appearance to the present day. They have accordingly done little for art, science, philosophy, little for commerce and the useful arts of life, but much for religion; and the psalms they sung two or three thousand years ago are at this day the hymns and prayers of the whole Christian world. Three great historical forms of religion, Judaism, Christianity, and Mahometanism, all have proceeded from them.

He that looks at the Ionian Greeks finds in their story always the same prominent characteristic, a devotion to what is beautiful. This appears often to the neglect of what is true, right, and therefore holy. Hence, while they have done little for religion, their literature, architecture, sculpture, furnish us with models never surpassed, and perhaps not equalled. Yet they lack the ideal aspiration after religion that appears in the literature and art, and even language of some other people, quite inferior to the Greeks in elegance and refinement. Science, also, is most largely indebted to these beauty-loving Greeks, for truth is one form of loveliness.

If we take the Romans, from Romulus their first king, to Augustulus the last of the Cæsars, the same traits of national character appear, only the complexion and dress thereof changed by circumstances. There is always the same hardness and materialism, the same skill in organizing men, the same turn for affairs and genius for legislation. Rome borrowed her theology and liturgical forms; her art, science, literature, philosophy, and eloquence; even her art of war was an imitation. But law sprung up indigenous in her soil; her laws are the best gift she offers to the human race,—the "monument more lasting than brass," which she has left behind her.

We may take another nation, which has by no means completed its history, the Saxon race, from Hengist and Horsa to Sir Robert Peel: there also is a permanent peculiarity in the tribe. They are yet the same bold, handy, practical people as when their bark first touched the savage shores of Britain; not over religious; less pious than moral; not so much upright before God, as downright before men; servants of the understanding more than children of reason; not following the guidance of an intuition, and the light of an idea, but rather trusting to experiment, facts, precedents, and usages; not philosophical, but commercial; warlike through strength and courage, not from love of war or its glory; material, obstinate, and grasping, with the same admiration of horses, dogs, oxen, and strong drink; the same willingness to tread down any obstacle, material, human or divine, which stands in their way; the same impatient lust of wealth and power; the same disposition to colonize and reannex other lands; the same love of liberty and love of law; the same readiness in forming political confederations.

In each of these four instances, the Hebrews, the Ionians, the Romans, and the Anglo-Saxon race, have had a nationality so strong, that while they have mingled with other nations in commerce and in war, as victors and vanquished, they have stoutly held their character through all; they have thus modified feebler nations joined with them. To take the last, neither the Britons nor the Danes affected very much the character of the Anglo-Saxons; they never turned it out of its course. The Normans gave the Saxon manners, refinement, letters, elegance.

The Anglo-Saxon bishop of the eleventh century, dressed in untanned sheep-skins, "the woolly side out and the fleshy side in;" he ate cheese and flesh, drank milk and mead. The Norman taught him to wear cloth, to eat also bread and roots, to drink wine. But in other respects the Norman left him as he found him. England has received her kings and her nobles from Normandy, Anjou, the Provence, Scotland, Holland, Hanover, often seeing a foreigner ascend her throne; yet the sturdy Anglo-Saxon character held its own, spite of the new element infused into its blood: change the ministries, change the dynasties often as they will, John Bull is obstinate as ever, and himself changes not; no philosophy or religion makes him less material. No nation but the English could have produced a Hobbes, a Hume, a Paley, or a Bentham; they are all instantial and not exceptional men in that race.

Now this idiosyncrasy of a nation is a sacred gift; like the genius of a Burns, a Thorwaldsen, a Franklin, or a Bowditch, it is given for some divine purpose, to be sacredly cherished and patiently unfolded. The cause of the peculiarities of a nation or an individual man we cannot fully determine as yet, and so we refer it to the chain of causes which we call Providence. But the national persistency in a common type is easily explained. The qualities of father and mother are commonly transmitted to their children, but not always, for peculiarities may lie latent in a family for generations, and reappear in the genius or the folly of a child—often in the complexion and features: and besides, father and mother are often no match. But such exceptions are rare, and the qualities of a race are always thus reproduced, the deficiency of one man getting counterbalanced by the redundancy of the next: the marriages of a whole tribe are not far from normal.

Some nations, it seems, perish through defect of this national character, as individuals fail of success through excess or deficiency in their character. Thus the Celts, that great flood of a nation which once swept over Germany, France, England, and, casting its spray far over the Alps, at one time threatened destruction to Rome itself, seem to have been so filled with love of individual independence that they could never accept a minute organization of human rights and duties, and so their children would not group themselves into a city, as other races, and submit to a strong central power, which should curb individual will enough to insure national unity of action. Perhaps this was once the excellence of the Celts, and thereby they broke the trammels and escaped from the theocratic or despotic traditions of earlier and more savage times, developing the power of the individual for a time, and the energy of a nation loosely bound; but when they came in contact with the Romans, Franks and Saxons, they melted away as snow in April— only, like that, remnants thereof yet lingering in the mountains and islands of Europe. No external pressure of famine or political oppression now holds the Celts in Ireland together, or gives them national unity of action enough to resist the Saxon foe. Doubtless in other days this very peculiarity of the Irish has done the world some service. Nations succeed each other as races of animals in the geological epochs, and like them, also, perish when their work is done.

The peculiar character of a nation does not appear nakedly, without relief and shadow. As the waters of the Rhone, in coming from the mountains, have caught a stain from the soils they have traversed which mars the cerulean tinge of the mountain snow that gave them birth, so the peculiarities of each nation become modified by the circumstances to which it is exposed, though the fundamental character of a nation, it seems, has never been changed. Only when the blood of the nation is changed by additions from another stock is the idiosyncrasy altered.

Now, while each nation has its peculiar genius or character which does not change, it has also and accordingly a particular work to perform in the economy of the world, a certain fundamental idea to unfold and develop. This is its national task, for in God's world, as in a shop, there is a regular division of labor. Sometimes it is a limited work, and when it is done the nation may be dismissed, and go to its repose. *Non omnia possumus omnes* is as true of nations as of men; one has a genius for one thing, another for something different, and the idea of each nation and its special work will depend on the genius of the nation. Men do not gather grapes of thorns.

In addition to this specific genius of the nation and its corresponding work, there are also various accidental or subordinate

qualities, which change with circumstances, and so vary the
nation's aspect that its peculiar genius and peculiar duty are
often hid from its own consciousness, and even obscured to
that of the philosophic looker-on. These subordinate peculiarities will depend first on the peculiar genius, idea and work of
the nation, and next on the transient circumstances, geographical, climactic, historical and secular, to which the nation has
been exposed. The past helped form the circumstances of the
present age, and they the character of the men now living.
Thus new modifications of the national type continually take
place; new variations are played, but on the same old strings
and of the same old tune. Once circumstances made the Hebrews entirely pastoral, now as completely commercial; but the
same trust in God, the same national exclusiveness appear, as
of old. As one looks at the history of the Ionians, Romans,
Saxons, he sees unity of national character, a continuity of idea
and of work; but it appears in the midst of variety, for while
these remained ever the same to complete the economy of
the world, subordinate qualities—sentiments, ideas, actions—
changed to suit the passing hour. The nation's *course* was laid
towards a certain point, but they stood to the right hand or
the left, they sailed with much canvas or little, and swift or slow,
as the winds and waves compelled: nay, sometimes the national
ship "heaves to," and lies with her "head to the wind," regardless of her destination; but when the storm is overblown re-
sumes her course. Men will carelessly think the ship has no
certain aim, but only drifts.

The most marked characteristic of the American nation is
Love of Freedom; of man's natural rights. This is so plain to a
student of American history, or of American politics, that the
point requires no arguing. We have a genius for liberty: the
American idea is freedom, natural rights. Accordingly, the work
providentially laid out for us to do seems this,—to organize
the rights of man. This is a problem hitherto unattempted on
a national scale, in human history. Often enough attempts have
been made to organize the powers of priests, kings, nobles, in
a theocracy, monarchy, oligarchy, powers which had no foundation in human duties or human rights, but solely in the selfishness of strong men. Often enough have the mights of men

been organized, but not the rights of man. Surely there has never been an attempt made on a national scale to organize the rights of man as man; rights resting on the nature of things; rights derived from no conventional compact of men with men; not inherited from past generations, nor received from parliaments and kings, nor secured by their parchments; but rights that are derived straightway from God, the Author of Duty and the Source of Right, and which are secured in the great charter of our being.

At first view it will be said, the peculiar genius of America is not such, nor such her fundamental idea, nor that her destined work. It is true that much of the national conduct seems exceptional when measured by that standard, and the nation's course as crooked as the Rio Grande; it is true that America sometimes seems to spurn liberty, and sells the freedom of three million men for less than three million annual bales of cotton; true, she often tramples, knowingly, consciously, tramples on the most unquestionable and sacred rights. Yet, when one looks through the whole character and history of America, spite of the exceptions, nothing comes out with such relief as this love of freedom, this idea of liberty, this attempt to organize right. There are numerous subordinate qualities which conflict with the nation's idea and work, coming from our circumstances, not our soul, as well as many others which help the nation perform her providential work. They are signs of the times, and it is important to look carefully among the most prominent of them, where, indeed, one finds striking contradictions.

The first is an impatience of authority. Every thing must render its reason, and show cause for its being. We will not be commanded, at least only by such as we choose to obey. Does some one say, "Thou shalt," or "Thou shalt not," we ask, "Who are you!" Hence comes a seeming irreverence. The shovel hat, the symbol of authority, which awed our fathers, is not respected unless it covers a man, and then it is the man we honor, and no longer the shovel hat. "I will complain of you to the government!" said a Prussian nobleman to a Yankee stage-driver, who uncivilly threw the nobleman's trunk to the top of the coach. "Tell the government to go to the devil!" was the symbolical reply.

Old precedents will not suffice us, for we want something anterior to all precedents; we go beyond what is written, asking the cause of the precedent and the reason of the writing. "Our fathers did so," says some one. "What of that?" say we. "Our fathers—they were giants, were they? Not at all, only great boys, and we are not only taller than they, but mounted on their shoulders to boot, and see twice as far. My dear wise man, or wiseacre, it is we that are the ancients, and have forgotten more than all our fathers knew. We will take their wisdom joyfully, and thank God for it, but not their authority, we know better; and of their nonsense not a word. It was very well that they lived, and it is very well that they are dead. Let them keep decently buried, for respectable dead men never walk."

Tradition does not satisfy us. The American scholar has no folios in his library. The antiquary unrolls his codex, hid for eighteen hundred years in the ashes of Herculaneum, deciphers its fossil wisdom, telling us what great men thought in the bay of Naples, and two thousand years ago. "What do you tell of that for?" is the answer to his learning. "What has Pythagoras to do with the price of cotton? You may be a very learned man; you can read the hieroglyphics of Egypt, I dare say, and know so much about the Pharaohs, it is a pity you had not lived in their time, when you might have been good for something; but you are too old-fashioned for our business, and may return to your dust." An eminent American, a student of Egyptian history, with a scholarly indignation declared, "There is not a man who cares to know whether Shoophoo lived one thousand years before Christ, or three."

The example of other and ancient States does not terrify or instruct us. If slavery were a curse to Athens, the corruption of Corinth, the undoing of Rome, and all history shows it was so, we will learn no lesson from that experience, for we say, "We are not Athenians, men of Corinth, nor pagan Romans, thank God, but free republicans, Christians of America. We live in the nineteenth century, and though slavery worked all that mischief then and there, we know how to make money out of it, twelve hundred millions of dollars, as Mr. Clay counts the cash."

The example of contemporary nations furnishes us little

warning or guidance. We will set our own precedents, and do not like to be told that the Prussians or the Dutch have learned some things in the education of the people before us, which we shall do well to learn after them. So when a good man tells us of their schools and their colleges, "patriotic" school-masters exclaim, "It is not true; our schools are the best in the world! But if it were true, it is unpatriotic to say so; it aids and comforts the enemy." Jonathan knows little of war; he has heard his grandfather talk of Lexington and Saratoga; he thinks he should like to have a little touch of battle on his own account: so when there is difficulty in setting up the fence betwixt his estate and his neighbors, he blusters for awhile, talks big, and threatens to strike his father; but, not having quite the stomach for that experiment, falls to beating his other neighbor, who happens to be poor, weak, and of a sickly constitution; and when he beats her at every step,—

> "For 't is no war, as each one knows,
>   When only one side deals the blows,
>   And t' other bears 'em,"—

Jonathan thinks he has covered himself, "with imperishable honors," and sets up his general for a great king. Poor Jonathan—he does not know the misery, the tears, the blood, the shame, the wickedness, and the sin he has set a-going, and which one day he is to account for with God who forgets nothing!

Yet while we are so unwilling to accept the good principles, to be warned by the fate, or guided by the success, of other nations, we gladly and servilely copy their faults, their follies, their vice and sin. Like all upstarts, we pique ourselves on our imitation of aristocratic ways. How many a blusterer in Congress,— for there are two denominations of blusterers, differing only in degree, your great blusterer in Congress and your little blusterer in a bar-room,—has roared away hours long against aristocratic influence, in favor of the "pure democracy," while he played the oligarch in his native village, the tyrant over his hired help, and though no man knows who his grandfather was, spite of the herald's office, conjures up some trumpery coat of arms! Like a clown, who by pinching his appetite, has bought a gaudy cloak for Sabbath wearing, we chuckle inwardly at our brave

apery of foreign absurdities, hoping that strangers will be astonished at us—which, sure enough, comes to pass. Jonathan
is as vain as he is conceited, and expects that the Fiddlers, and
the Trollopes, and others, who visit us periodically as the swal-
lows, and likewise for what they can catch, shall only extol, or
at least stand aghast at the brave spectacle we offer, of "the
freest and most enlightened nation in the world;" and if they
tell us that we are an ill-mannered set, raw and clownish, that
we pick our teeth with a fork, loll back in our chairs and make
our countenance hateful with tobacco, and that with all our
excellences we are a nation of "rowdies,"—why, we are offended, and our feelings are hurt. There was an African chief,
long ago, who ruled over a few miserable cabins, and one day
received a French traveller from Paris, under a tree. With the
exception of a pair of shoes, our chief was as naked as a pestle,
but with great complacency he asked the traveller, "What do
they say of me at Paris?"

Such is our dread of authority, that we like not old things;
hence we are always a-changing. Our house must be new, and
our book, and even our church. So we choose a material that
soon wears out, though it often outlasts our patience. The
wooden house is an apt emblem of this sign of the times. But
this love of change appears not less in important matters. We
think "Of old things all are over old, of new things none are
new enough." So the age asks of all institutions their right to
be: What right has the government to existence? Who gave the
majority a right to control the minority, to restrict trade, levy
taxes, make laws, and all that? If the nation goes into a committee of the whole and makes laws some little man goes into a
committee of one and passes his counter resolves. The State of
South Carolina is a nice example of this self-reliance, and this
questioning of all authority. That little brazen State, which
contains only about half so many free white inhabitants as the
single city of New York, but which none the less claims to have
monopolized most of the chivalry of the nation, and its patriotism, as well as political wisdom—that chivalrous little State
says, "If the nation does not make laws to suit us; if it does not
allow us to imprison all black seamen from the North; if it
prevents the extension of Slavery wherever we wish to carry

it—then the State of South Carolina will nullify, and leave the other nine-and-twenty States to go to ruin!"

Men ask what right have the churches to the shadow of authority which clings to them—to make creeds, and to bind and to loose! So it is a thing which has happened, that when a church excommunicates a young stripling for heresy, he turns round, fulminates his edict, and excommunicates the church. Said a sly Jesuit to an American Protestant at Rome, "But the rites and customs and doctrines of the Catholic church go back to the second century, the age after the apostles!" "No doubt of it," said the American, who had also read the Fathers, "they go back to the times of the apostles themselves; but that proves nothing, for there were as great fools in the first century as the last. A fool or a folly is no better because it is an old folly or an old fool. There are fools enough now, in all conscience. Pray don't go back to prove their apostolical succession."

There are always some men who are born out of due season, men of past ages, stragglers of former generations, who ought to have been born before Dr. Faustus invented printing, but who are unfortunately born now, or, if born long ago, have been fraudulently and illegally concealed by their mothers, and are now, for the first time, brought to light. The age lifts such aged juveniles from the ground, and bids them live, but they are sadly to seek in this day; they are old-fashioned boys; their authority is called in question; their traditions and old wives' fables are laughed at, at any rate disbelieved; they get profanely elbowed in the crowd—men not knowing their great age and consequent venerableness; the shovel hat, though apparently born on their head, is treated with disrespect. The very boys laugh pertly in their face when they speak, and even old men can scarce forbear a smile, though it may be a smile of pity. The age affords such men a place, for it is a catholic age, large-minded and tolerant,—such a place as it gives to ancient armor, Indian Bibles, and fossil bones of the mastodon; it puts them by in some room seldom used, with other old furniture, and allows them to mumble their anilities by themselves; now and then takes off its hat; looks in, charitably, to keep the mediæval relics in good heart, and pretends to listen, as they discourse of what comes of nothing and goes to it; but in matters which the age cares about, commerce, manufactures, politics, which it cares much for, even in education, which it cares far too little about, it trusts no such counsellors, nor tolerates, nor ever affects to listen.

Then there is a philosophical tendency, distinctly visible; a groping after ultimate facts, first principles, and universal ideas. We wish to know first the fact, next the law of that fact, and then the reason of the law. A sign of this tendency is noticeable in the titles of books; we have no longer "treatises" on the eye, the ear, sleep, and so forth, but in their place we find works professing to treat of the "philosophy" of vision, of sound, of sleep. Even in the pulpits, men speak about the "philosophy" of religion; we have philosophical lectures, delivered to men of little culture, which would have amazed our grandfathers, who thought a shoemaker should never go beyond his last, even to seek for the philosophy of shoes. "What a pity," said a grave Scotchman, in the beginning of this century, "to teach the beautiful science of geometry to weavers and cobblers." Here nothing is too good or high for any one tall and good enough to get hold of it. What audiences attend the Lowell lectures in Boston—two or three thousand men, listening to twelve lectures on the philosophy of fish! It would not bring a dollar or a vote, only thought to their minds! Young ladies are well versed in the philosophy of the affections, and understand the theory of attraction, while their grandmothers, good easy souls, were satisfied with the possession of the fact. The circumstance, that philosophical lectures get delivered by men like Walker, Agassiz, Emerson, and their coadjutors, men who do not spare abstruseness, get listened to, and even understood, in town and village, by large crowds of men, of only the most common culture; this indicates a philosophical tendency, unknown in any other land or age. Our circle of professed scholars, men of culture and learning, is a very small one, while our circle of thinking men is disproportionately large. The best thought of France and Germany finds a readier welcome here than in our parent land: nay, the newest and the best thought of England, finds its earliest and warmest welcome in America. It was a little remarkable, that Bacon and Newton should be reprinted here, and La Place should have found his translator and expositor coming out of an insurance office in Salem! Men

of no great pretensions object to an accomplished and eloquent politician: "That is all very well; he made us cry and
laugh, but the discourse was not philosophical; he never tells
us the reason of the thing; he seems not only not to know it,
but not to know that there *is* a reason for the thing, and if not,
what is the use of this bobbing on the surface?" Young maid-
ens complain of the minister, that he has no philosophy in his
sermons, nothing but precepts, which they could read in the
Bible as well as he; perhaps in heathen Seneca. He does not
feed their souls.

One finds this tendency where it is least expected: there is a
philosophical party in politics, a very small party it may be, but
an actual one. They aim to get at everlasting ideas and universal laws, not made by man, but by God, and for man, who only
finds them; and from them they aim to deduce all particular
enactments, so that each statute in the code shall represent a
fact in the universe; a point of thought in God; so, indeed, that
legislation shall be divine in the same sense that a true system
of astronomy is divine—or the Christian religion—the law corresponding to a fact. Men of this party, in New England, have
more ideas than precedents, are spontaneous more than logical; have intuitions, rather than intellectual convictions, arrived
at by the process of reasoning. They think it is not philosophical to take a young scoundrel and shut him up with a party of
old ones, for his amendment; not philosophical to leave children with no culture, intellectual, moral, or religious, exposed
to the temptations of a high and corrupt civilization, and then,
when they go astray—as such barbarians needs must, in such
temptations—to hang them by the neck for the example's sake.
They doubt if war is a more philosophical mode of getting
justice between two nations, than blows to settle a quarrel between two men. In either case, they do not see how it follows,
that he who can strike the hardest blow is always in the right.
In short, they think that judicial murder, which is hanging,
and national murder, which is war, are not more philosophical
than homicide, which one man commits on his own private
account.

Theological sects are always the last to feel any popular movement. Yet all of them, from the Episcopalians to the Quakers,
have each a philosophical party, which bids fair to outgrow the

party which rests on precedent and usage, to overshadow and destroy it. The Catholic church itself, though far astern of all the sects, in regard to the great movements of the age, shares this spirit, and abroad, if not here, is wellnigh rent asunder by the potent medicine which this new Daniel of philosophy has put into its mouth. Everywhere in the American churches there are signs of a tendency to drop all that rests merely on tradition and hearsay, to cling only to such facts as bide the test of critical search, and such doctrines as can be verified in human consciousness here and to-day. Doctors of divinity destroy the faith they once preached.

True, there are antagonistic tendencies, for, soon as one pole is developed, the other appears; objections are made to philosophy, the old cry is raised—"Infidelity," "Denial," "Freethinking." It is said that philosophy will corrupt the young men, will spoil the old ones, and deceive the very elect. "Authority and tradition," say some, "are all we need consult; reason must be put down, or she will soon ask terrible questions." There is good cause for these men warring against reason and philosophy; it is purely in self-defence. But this counsel and that cry come from those quarters before mentioned, where the men of past ages have their place, where the forgotten is re-collected, the obsolete preserved, and the useless held in esteem. The counsel is not dangerous; the bird of night, who overstays his hour, is only troublesome to himself, and was never known to hurt a dovelet or a mouseling after sunrise. In the night only is the owl destructive. Some of those who thus cry out against this tendency, are excellent men in their way, and highly useful, valuable as conveyancers of opinions. So long as there are men who take opinions as real estate, "to have and to hold for themselves and their heirs forever," why should there not be such conveyancers of opinions, as well as of land? And as it is not the duty of the latter functionary to ascertain the quality or the value of the land, but only its metes and bounds, its appurtenances and the title thereto; to see if the grantor is regularly seized and possessed thereof, and has good right to convey and devise the same, and to make sure that the whole conveyance is regularly made out,—so is it with these conveyancers of opinion; so should it be, and they are valuable men. It is a good thing to know that we hold under

Scotus, and Ramus, and Albertus Magnus, who were regularly seized of this or that opinion. It gives an absurdity the dignity of a relic. Sometimes these worthies, who thus oppose reason and her kin, seem to have a good deal in them, and, when one examines, he finds more than he looked for. They are like a nest of boxes from Hingham and Nuremburg, you open one, and behold another; that, and lo! a third. So you go on, opening and opening, and finding and finding, till at last you come to the heart of the matter, and then you find a box that is very little, and entirely empty.

Yet, with all this tendency—and it is now so strong that it cannot be put down, nor even howled down, much as it may be howled over—there is a lamentable want of first principles, well known and established; we have rejected the authority of tradition, but not yet accepted the authority of truth and justice. We will not be treated as striplings, and are not old enough to go alone as men. Accordingly, nothing seems fixed. There is a perpetual see-sawing of opposite principles. Somebody said ministers ought to be ordained on horseback, because they are to remain so short a time in one place. It would be as emblematic to inaugurate American politicians, by swearing them on a weathercock. The great men of the land have as many turns in their course as the Euripus or the Missouri. Even the facts given in the spiritual nature of man are called in question. An eminent Unitarian divine regards the existence of God as a matter of opinion, thinks it cannot be demonstrated, and publicly declares that it is "not a certainty." Some American Protestants no longer take the Bible as the standard of ultimate appeal, yet venture not to set up in that place reason, conscience, the soul getting help of God; others, who affect to accept the Scripture as the last authority, yet, when questioned as to their belief in the miraculous and divine birth of Jesus of Nazareth, are found unable to say yes or no, not having made up their minds.

In politics, it is not yet decided whether it is best to leave men to buy where they can buy cheapest, and sell where they can sell dearest, or to restrict that matter.

It was a clear case to our fathers, in '76, that all men were "created equal," each with "Unalienable Rights." That seemed

so clear, that reasoning would not make it appear more reasonable; it was taken for granted, as a self-evident proposition.
The whole nation said so. Now, it is no strange thing to find it
said that negroes are not "created equal" in unalienable rights
with white men. Nay, in the Senate of the United States, a
famous man declares all this talk a dangerous mistake. The
practical decision of the nation looks the same way. So, to
make our theory accord with our practice, we ought to recom-
mit the Declaration to the hands which drafted that great
State-paper, and instruct Mr. Jefferson to amend the document, and declare that "All men are created equal, and endowed by their Creator with certain unalienable rights, if born
of white mothers; but if not, not."

In this lack of first principles, it is not settled in the popular
consciousness, that there is such a thing as an absolute right, a
great law of God, which we are to keep, come what will come.
So the nation is not upright, but goes stooping. Hence, in private affairs, law takes the place of conscience, and, in public,
might of right. So the bankrupt pays his shilling in the pound,
and gets his discharge, but afterwards, becoming rich, does
not think of paying the other nineteen shillings. He will tell
you the law is his conscience; if that be satisfied, so is he. But
you will yet find him letting money at one or two per cent. a
month, contrary to law; and then he will tell you that paying
a debt is a matter of law, while letting money is only a matter
of conscience. So he rides either indifferently—now the public hack, and now his own private nag, according as it serves
his turn.

So a rich State borrows money and "repudiates" the debt,
satisfying its political conscience, as the bankrupt his commercial conscience, with the notion that there is no absolute right;
that expediency is the only justice, and that King People can
do no wrong. No calm voice of indignation cries out from the
pulpit and the press and the heart of the people, to shame the
repudiators into decent morals; because it is not settled in
the popular mind that there is any absolute right. Then, because we are strong and the Mexicans weak, because we want
their land for a slave-pasture and they cannot keep us out of it,
we think that is reason enough for waging an infamous war of
plunder. Grave men do not ask about "the natural justice" of

such an undertaking, only about its cost. Have we not seen an American Congress vote a plain lie, with only sixteen dissenting voices in the whole body; has not the head of the nation continually repeated that lie; and do not both parties, even at this day, sustain the vote?

Now and then there rises up an honest man, with a great Christian heart in his bosom, and sets free a score or two of slaves inherited from his father; watches over and tends them in their new-found freedom: or another, who, when legally released from payment of his debts, restores the uttermost farthing. We talk of this and praise it, as an extraordinary thing. Indeed it is so; justice is an unusual thing, and such men deserve the honor they thus win. But such praise shows that such honesty is a rare honesty. The northern man, born on the battle-ground of freedom, goes to the South and becomes the most tyrannical of slave-drivers. The son of the Puritan, bred up in austere ways, is sent to Congress to stand up for truth and right, but he turns out a "dough-face," and betrays the duty he went to serve. Yet he does not lose his place, for every dough-faced representative has a dough-faced constituency to back him.

It is a great mischief that comes from lacking first principles, and the worst part of it comes from lacking first principles in morals. Thereby our eyes are holden so that we see not the great social evils all about as. We attempt to justify slavery, even to do it in the name of Jesus Christ. The whig party of the North loves slavery; the democratic party does not even seek to conceal its affection therefor. A great politician declares the Mexican war wicked, and then urges men to go and fight it; he thinks a famous general not fit to be nominated for President, but then invites men to elect him. Politics are national morals, the morals of Thomas and Jeremiah, multiplied by millions. But it is not decided yet that honesty is the best policy for a politician; it is thought that the best policy is honesty, at least as near it as the times will allow. Many politicians seem undecided how to turn, and so sit on the fence between honesty and dishonesty. Mr. Facing-both-ways is a popular politician in America just now, sitting on the fence between honesty and dishonesty, and, like the blank leaf between the Old and New Testaments, belonging to neither dispensation. It is a little amusing to a trifler to hear a man's fitness for the Presidency defended on the ground that he has no definite convictions or ideas!

There was once a man who said he always told a lie when it would serve his special turn. It is a pity he went to his own place long ago. He seemed born for a party politician in America. He would have had a large party, for he made a great many converts before he died, and left a numerous kindred busy in the editing of newspapers, writing addresses for the people, and passing "resolutions."

It must strike a stranger as a little odd, that a republic should have a slave-holder for President five sixths of the time, and most of the important offices be monopolized by other slave-holders; a little surprising that all the pulpits and most of the presses should be in favor of slavery, at least not against it. But such is the fact. Everybody knows the character of the American government for some years past, and of the American parties in politics. "Like master, like man," used to be a true proverb in old England, and "Like people, like ruler," is a true proverb in America; true now. Did a decided people ever choose dough-faces?—a people that loved God and man, choose representatives that cared for neither truth nor justice? Now and then, for dust gets into the brightest eyes; but did they ever choose such men continually? The people are always fairly represented; our representatives do actually re-present us, and in more senses than they are paid for. Congress and the Cabinet are only two thermometers hung up in the capital, to show the temperature of the national morals.

But amid this general uncertainty there are two capital maxims which prevail amongst our huxters of politics. To love your party better than your country, and yourself better than your party. There are, it is true, real statesmen amongst us, men who love justice and do the right, but they seem lost in the mob of vulgar politicians and the dust of party editors.

Since the nation loves freedom above all things, the name democracy is a favorite name. No party could live a twelve-month that should declare itself anti-democratic. Saint and sinner, statesman and politician, alike love the name. So it comes to pass that there are two things which bear that name; each has its type and its motto. The motto of one is, "You are as good as I, and let us help one another." That represents the democracy of the Declaration of Independence, and of the New Testament; its type is a free school, where children of all ranks meet under the guidance of intelligent and Christian men, to be educated in mind, and heart, and soul. The other has for its motto, "I am as good as you, so get out of my way." Its type is the bar-room of a tavern—dirty, offensive, stained with tobacco, and full of drunken, noisy, quarrelsome "rowdies," just returned from the Mexican war, and ready for a "buffalo hunt," for privateering, or to go and plunder any one who is better off than themselves, especially if also better. That is not exactly the democracy of the Declaration, or of the New Testament; but of—no matter whom.

Then, again, there is a great intensity of life and purpose. This displays itself in our actions and speeches; in our speculations; in the "revivals" of the more serious sects; in the excitements of trade; in the general character of the people. All that we do we overdo. It appears in our hopefulness; we are the most aspiring of nations. Not content with half the continent, we wish the other half. We have this characteristic of genius: we are dissatisfied with all that we have done. Somebody once said we were too vain to be proud. It is not wholly so; the national idea is so far above us that any achievement seems little and low. The American soul passes away from its work soon as it is finished. So the soul of each great artist refuses to dwell in his finished work, for that seems little to his dream. Our fathers deemed the Revolution a great work; it was once thought a surprising thing to found that little colony on the shores of New England; but young America looks to other revolutions, and thinks she has many a Plymouth colony in her bosom. If other nations wonder at our achievements, we are a disappointment to ourselves, and wonder we have not done more. Our national idea out-travels our experience, and all experience. We began our national career by setting all history at defiance—for that said, "A republic on a large scale cannot exist." Our progress since has shown that we were right in refusing to be limited by the past. The political ideas of the nation are transcendant, not empirical. Human history could not justify the

Declaration of Independence and its large statements of the new idea: the nation went behind human history and appealed to human nature.

We are more spontaneous than logical; we have ideas, rather than facts or precedents. We dream more than we remember, and so have many orators and poets, or poetasters, with but few antiquaries and general scholars. We are not so reflective as forecasting. We are the most intuitive of modern nations. The very party in politics which has the least culture, is richest in ideas which will one day become facts. Great truths—political, philosophical, religious—lie a-burning in many a young heart which cannot legitimate nor prove them true, but none the less feels, and feels them true. A man full of new truths finds a ready audience with us. Many things which come disguised as truths under such circumstances pass current for a time, but by and by their bray discovers them. The hope which comes from this intensity of life and intuition of truths is a national characteristic. It gives courage, enterprise, and strength. They can who think they can. We are confident in our star; other nations may see it or not, we know it is there above the clouds. We do not hesitate at rash experiments—sending fifty thousand soldiers to conquer a nation with eight or nine millions of people. We are up to every thing, and think ourselves a match for any thing. The young man is rash, for he only hopes, having little to remember; he is excitable, and loves excitement; change of work is his repose; he is hot and noisy, sanguine and fearless, with the courage that comes from warm blood and ignorance of dangers; does not know what a hard, tough, sour old world he is born into. We are a nation of young men. We talked of annexing Texas and northern Mexico, and did both; now we grasp at Cuba, Central America,—all the continent,—and speak of a railroad to the Pacific as a trifle for us to accomplish. Our national deeds are certainly great, but our hope and promise far outbrags them all.

If this intensity of life and hope have its good side, it has also its evil; with much of the excellence of youth we have its faults— rashness, haste, and superficiality. Our work is seldom well done. In English manufactures there is a certain solid honesty of performance; in the French a certain air of elegance and refinement: one misses both these in American works. It is said

America invents the most machines, but England builds them best. We lack the phlegmatic patience of older nations. We are always in a hurry, morning, noon and night. We are impatient of the process, but greedy of the result; so that we make short experiments but long reports, and talk much though we say little. We forget that a sober method is a short way of coming to the end, and that he who, before he sets out, ascertains where he is going and the way thither, ends his journey more prosperously than one who settles these matters by the way. Quickness is a great desideratum with us. It is said an American ship is known far off at sea by the quantity of canvas she carries. Rough and ready is a popular attribute. Quick and off would be a symbolic motto for the nation at this day, representing one phase of our character. We are sudden in deliberation; the "one-hour rule" works well in Congress. A committee of the British Parliament spends twice or thrice our time in collecting facts, understanding and making them intelligible, but less than our time in speech-making after the report; speeches there commonly being for the purpose of facilitating the business, while here one sometimes is half ready to think, notwithstanding our earnestness, that the business is to facilitate the speaking. A State revises her statutes with a rapidity that astonishes a European. Yet each revision brings some amendment, and what is found good in the constitution or laws of one State gets speedily imitated by the rest; each new State of the North becoming more democratic than its predecessor.

We are so intent on our purpose that we have no time for amusement. We have but one or two festivals in the year, and even then we are serious and reformatory. Jonathan thinks it a very solemn thing to be merry. A Frenchman said we have but two amusements in America—Theology for the women and politics for the men; preaching and voting. If this be true, it may help to explain the fact that most men take their theology from their wives, and women politics from their husbands. No nation ever tried the experiment of such abstinence from amusement. We have no time for sport, and so lose much of the poetry of life. All work and no play does not always make a dull boy, but it commonly makes a hard man.

We rush from school into business early; we hurry while in business; we aim to be rich quickly, making a fortune at a stroke, making or losing it twice or thrice in a lifetime. "Soft and fair, goes safe and far," is no proverb to our taste. We are the most restless of people. How we crowd into cars and steamboats; a locomotive would well typify our fuming, fizzing spirit. In our large towns life seems to be only a scamper. Not satisfied with bustling about all day, when night comes we cannot sit still, but alone of all nations have added rockers to our chairs.

All is haste, from the tanning of leather to the education of a boy, and the old saw holds its edge good as ever—"the more haste the worse speed." The young stripling, innocent of all manner of lore, whom a judicious father has barrelled down in a college, or law-school, or theological seminary, till his beard be grown, mourns over the few years he must spend there awaiting that operation. His rule is, "to make a spoon or spoil a horn;" he longs to be out in the world "making a fortune," or "doing good," as he calls what his father better names "making noisy work for repentance, and doing mischief." So he rushes into life not fitted, and would fly towards heaven, this young Icarus, his wings not half fledged. There seems little taste for thoroughness. In our schools as our farms, we pass over much ground but pass over it poorly.

In education the aim is not to get the most we can, but the least we can get along with. A ship with over-much canvas and over-little ballast were no bad emblem of many amongst us. In no country is it so easy to get a reputation for learning— accumulated thought, because so few devote themselves to that accumulation. In this respect our standard is low. So a man of one attainment is sure to be honored, but a man of many and varied abilities is in danger of being undervalued. A Spurzheim would be warmly welcomed, while a Humboldt would be suspected of superficiality, as we have not the standard to judge him by. Yet in no country in the world is it so difficult to get a reputation for eloquence, as many speak and that well. It is surprising with what natural strength and beauty the young American addresses himself to speak. Some hatter's apprentice, or shoemaker's journeyman, at a temperance or anti-slavery meeting, will speak words like the blows of an axe, that cut clean and deep. The country swarms with orators, more abundantly where education is least esteemed—in the West or South.

We have secured national unity of action for the white

citizens, without much curtailing individual variety of action, so we have at the North pretty well solved that problem which other nations have so often boggled over; we have balanced the centripetal power, the government and laws, with the centrifugal power, the mass of individuals, into harmonious proportions. If one were to leave out of sight the three million slaves, one sixth part of the population, the problem might be regarded as very happily solved. As the consequences of this, in no country is there more talent, or so much awake and active. In the South this unity is attained by sacrificing all the rights of three million slaves, and almost all the rights of the other colored population. In despotic countries this unity is brought about by the sacrifice of freedom, individual variety of action, in all except the despot and his favorites; so, much of the nation's energy is stifled in the chains of the State, while here it is friendly to institutions which are friendly to it, goes to its work, and approves itself in the vast increase of wealth and comfort throughout the North, where there is no class of men which is so oppressed that it cannot rise. One is amazed at the amount of ready skill and general ability which he finds in all the North, where each man has a little culture, takes his newspaper, manages his own business, and talks with some intelligence of many things—especially of politics and theology. In respect to this general intellectual ability and power of self-help, the mass of people seem far in advance of any other nation. But at the same time our scholars, who always represent the nation's higher modes of consciousness, will not bear comparison with the scholars of England, France, and Germany, men thoroughly furnished for their work. This is a great reproach and mischief to us, for we need most accomplished leaders, who by their thought can direct this national intensity of life. Our literature does not furnish them; we have no great men there; Irving, Channing, Cooper, are not names to conjure with in literature. One reads thick volumes devoted to the poets of America, or her prose writers, and finds many names which he wonders he never heard of before, but when he turns over their works, he finds consolation and recovers his composure.

American literature may be divided into two departments: the permanent literature, which gets printed in books, that sometimes reach more than one edition; and the evanescent literature, which appears only in the form of speeches, pamphlets, reviews, newspaper articles, and the like extempore productions. Now our permanent literature, as a general thing, is superficial, tame, and weak; it is not American; it has not our ideas, our contempt of authority, our philosophical turn, nor even our uncertainty as to first principles, still less our national intensity, our hope, and fresh intuitive perceptions of truth. It is a miserable imitation. Love of freedom is not there. The real national literature is found almost wholly in speeches, pamphlets, and newspapers. The latter are pretty thoroughly American; mirrors in which we see no very flattering likeness of our morals or our manners. Yet the picture is true: that vulgarity, that rant, that bragging violence, that recklessness of truth and justice, that disregard of right and duty, are a part of the nation's everyday life. Our newspapers are low and "wicked to a fault;" only in this weakness are they un-American. Yet they exhibit, and abundantly, the four qualities we have mentioned as belonging to the signs of our times. As a general rule, our orators are also American, with our good and ill. Now and then one rises who has studied Demosthenes in Leland or Francis, and got a second-hand acquaintance with old models: a man who uses literary commonplaces, and thinks himself original and classic because he can quote a line or so of Horace, in a Western House of Representatives, without getting so many words wrong as his reporter; but such men are rare, and after making due abatement for them, our orators all over the land are pretty thoroughly American, a little turgid, hot, sometimes brilliant, hopeful, intuitive, abounding in half truths, full of great ideas; often inconsequent; sometimes coarse; patriotic, vain, self-confident, rash, strong, and young-mannish. Of course the most of our speeches are vulgar, ranting, and worthless, but we have produced some magnificent specimens of oratory, which are fresh, original, American and brand new.

The more studied, polished, and elegant literature is not so; that is mainly an imitation. It seems not a thing of native growth. Sometimes, as in Channing, the thought and the hope are American, but the form and the coloring old and foreign. We dare not be original; our American pine must be cut to the trim pattern of the English yew, though the pine bleed at every clip. This poet tunes his lyre at the harp of Goethe, Milton,

Pope, or Tennyson. His songs might be better sung on the Rhine than the Kennebec. They are not American in form or feeling; they have not the breath of our air; the smell of our ground is not in them. Hence our poet seems cold and poor. He loves the old mythology; talks about Pluto—the Greek devil, the fates and furies—witches of old time in Greece, but would blush to use our mythology, or breathe the name in verse of our devil, or our own witches, lest he should be thought to believe what he wrote. The mother and sisters, who with many a pinch and pain sent the hopeful boy to college, must turn over the classical dictionary before they can find out what the youth would be at in his rhymes. Our poet is not deep enough to see that Aphrodite came from the ordinary waters, that Homer only hitched into rhythm and furnished the accomplishment of verse to street-talk, nursery tales, and old men's gossip in the Ionian towns; he thinks what is common is unclean. So he sings of Corinth and Athens, which he never saw, but has not a word to say of Boston, and Fall River, and Baltimore, and New York, which are just as meet for song. He raves of Thermopylæ and Marathon, with never a word for Lexington and Bunker-hill, for Cowpens, and Lundy's Lane, and Bemis's Heights. He loves to tell of the Ilyssus, of "smooth-sliding Mincius, crowned with vocal reeds," yet sings not of the Petapsco, the Susquehanna, the Aroostook, and the Willimantick. He prates of the narcissus and the daisy, never of American dandelions and blue-eyed grass; he dwells on the lark and the nightingale, but has not a thought for the brown thrasher and the bobolink, who every morning in June rain down such showers of melody on his affected head. What a lesson Burns teaches us, addressing his "rough bur-thistle," his daisy, "wee crimson tippit thing," and finding marvelous poetry in the mouse whose nest his plough turned over! Nay, how beautifully has even our sweet poet sung of our own Green river, our waterfowl, of the blue and fringed gentian, the glory of autumnal days.

Hitherto, spite of the great reading public, we have no permanent literature which corresponds to the American idea. Perhaps it is not time for that; it must be organized in deeds before it becomes classic in words; but as yet we have no such literature which reflects even the surface of American life, certainly nothing which portrays our intensity of life, our hope, or even our daily doings and drivings, as the Odyssey paints old Greek life, or Don Quixote and Gil Blas portray Spanish life. Literary men are commonly timid; ours know they are but poorly fledged as yet, so dare not fly away from the parent tree, but hop timidly from branch to branch. Our writers love to creep about in the shadow of some old renown, not venturing to soar away into the unwinged air, to sing of things here and now, making our life classic. So, without the grace of high culture, and the energy of American thought, they become weak, cold, and poor; are "curious, not knowing, not exact, but nice." Too fastidious to be wise, too unlettered to be elegant, too critical to create, they prefer a dull saying that is old to a novel form of speech, or a natural expression of a new truth. In a single American work,—and a famous one too,—there are over sixty similes, not one original, and all poor. A few men, conscious of this defect, this sin against the Holy Spirit of Literature, go to the opposite extreme, and are American-mad; they wilfully talk rude, write in-numerous verse, and play their harps all jangling, out of tune. A yet fewer few are American without madness. One such must not here be passed by, alike philosopher and bard, in whose writings "ancient wisdom shines with new-born beauty," and who has enriched a genius thoroughly American in the best sense, with a cosmopolitan culture and literary skill, which were wonderful in any land. But of American literature in general, and of him in special, more shall be said at another time.

Another remarkable feature is our excessive love of material things. This is more than a Utilitarianism, a preference of the useful over the beautiful. The Puritan at Plymouth had a cornfield, a cabbage-garden, and a patch for potatoes, a school-house, and a church, before he sat down to play the fiddle. He would have been a fool to reverse this process. It were poor economy and worse taste to have painters, sculptors, and musicians, while the rude wants of the body are uncared for. But our fault in this respect is, that we place too much the charm of life in mere material things,—houses, lands, well-spread tables, and elegant furniture,—not enough in man, in virtue, wisdom, genius, religion, greatness of soul, and nobleness of life. We mistake a perfection of the means of manliness for the end—manhood itself. Yet the housekeeping of a Shakspeare, Milton, Franklin, had only one thing worth boasting of. Strange to say, that was the master of the house. A rich and vulgar man once sported a coach and four, and at its first turn-out rode into the great commercial street of a large town in New England. "How fine you must feel with your new coach and four," said one of his old friends, though not quite so rich. "Yes," was the reply, "as fine as a beetle in a gold snuff-box." All of his kindred are not so nice and discriminating in their self-consciousness.

This practical materialism is a great affliction to us. We think a man cannot be poor and great also. So we see a great man sell himself for a little money, and it is thought "a good operation." A conspicuous man, in praise of a certain painter, summed up his judgment with this: "Why, Sir, he has made twenty thousand dollars by his pictures." "A good deal more than Michael Angelo, Leonardo, and Raphael together," might have been the reply. But it is easier to weigh purses than artistic skill. It was a characteristic praise bestowed in Boston on a distinguished American writer, that his book brought him more money than any man had ever realized for an original work in this country. "Commerce," said Mr. Pitt, "having got into both houses of Parliament, privilege must be done away,"—the privilege of wit and genius, not less than rank. Clergymen estimate their own and their brothers' importance, not by their apostolical gifts, or even apostolic succession, but by the value of the living.

All other nations have this same fault, it may be said. But there is this difference: in other nations the things of a man are put before the man himself; so a materialism which exalts the accidents of the man—rank, wealth, birth, and the like—above the man, is not inconsistent with the general idea of England or Austria. In America it is a contradiction. Besides, in most civilized countries, there is a class of men living on inherited wealth, who devote their lives to politics, art, science, letters, and so are above the mere material elegance which surrounds them. That class has often inflicted a deep wound on society, which festers long and leads to serious trouble in the system, but at the same time it redeems a nation from the reproach of mere material vulgarity; it has been the source of refinement, and has warmed into life much of the wisdom and beauty which have thence spread over all the world. In America there is no such class. Young men inheriting wealth very rarely turn to any thing noble; they either convert their talents into gold, or their gold into furniture, wines, and confectionary. A young man of wealth does not know what to do with himself or it; a rich young woman seems to have no resource but marriage! Yet it must be confessed, that at least in one part of the United States wealth flows freely for the support of public institutions of education.

Here it is difficult for a man of science to live by his thought. Was Bowditch one of the first mathematicians of his age? He must be at the head of an annuity office. If Socrates should set up as a dealer in money, and outwit the brokers as formerly the Sophists, and shave notes as skilfully as of old, we should think him a great man. But if he adopted his old plan, what should we say of him?

Manliness is postponed and wealth preferred. "What a fine house is this," one often says; "what furniture; what feasting. But the master of the house!—why every stone out of the wall laughs at him. He spent all of himself in getting this pretty show together, and now it is empty, and mocks its owner. He is the emblematic coffin at the Egyptian feast." "Oh, man!" says the looker-on, "why not furnish thyself with a mind, and conscience, a heart and a soul, before getting all this brass and mahogany together; this beef and these wines?" The poor wight would answer,—"Why, Sir, there were none such in the market!"—The young man does not say, "I will first of all things be a man, and so being will have this thing and the other," putting the agreeable after the essential. But he says, "First of all, by hook or by crook, I will have money, the manhood may take care of itself." He has it,—for tough and hard as the old world is, it is somewhat fluid before a strong man who resolutely grapples with difficulty and will swim through; it can be made to serve his turn. He has money, but the man has evaporated in the process; when you look he is not there. True, other nations have done the same thing, and we only repeat their experiment. The old devil of conformity says to our American Adam and Eve, "Do this and you shall be as gods," a promise as likely to hold good as the devil's did in the beginning. A man was meant for something more than a tassel to a large estate, and a woman to be more than a rich housekeeper.

With this offensive materialism we copy the vices of feudal aristocracy abroad, making our vulgarity still more ridiculous. We are ambitious or proud of wealth, which is but labor stored up, and at the same time are ashamed of labor which is wealth in process. With all our talk about democracy, labor is thought less honorable in Boston than in Berlin and Leipsic. Thriving men are afraid their children will be shoemakers, or ply some such honorable and useful craft. Yet little pains are taken to elevate the condition or improve the manners and morals of those who do all the manual work of society. The strong man takes care that his children and himself escape that condition. We do not believe that all stations are alike honorable if honorably filled; we have little desire to equalize the burdens of life, so that there shall be no degraded class; none cursed with work, none with idleness. It is popular to endow a college; vulgar to take an interest in common schools. Liberty is a fact, equality a word, and fraternity, we do not think of yet.

In this struggle for material wealth and the social rank which is based thereon, it is amusing to see the shifting of the scenes; the social aspirations of one and the contempt with which another rebuts the aspirant. An old man can remember when the most exclusive of men, and the most golden, had scarce a penny in their purse, and grumbled at not finding a place where they would. Now the successful man is ashamed of the steps he rose by. The gentleman who came to Boston half a century ago, with all his worldly goods tied up in a cotton handkerchief, and that not of so large a pattern as are made now-a-days, is ashamed to recollect that his father was a currier, or a blacksmith, or a skipper at Barnstable or Beverly; ashamed, also, of his forty or fifty country cousins, remarkable for nothing but their large hands and their excellent memory. Nay, he is ashamed of his own humble beginnings, and sneers at men starting as he once started. The generation of English "Snobs" came in with the Conqueror, and migrated to America at an early day, where they continue to thrive marvellously—the chief "conservative party" in the land.

Through this contempt for labor, a certain affectation runs

through a good deal of American society, and makes our aristocracy vulgar and contemptible. What if Burns had been ashamed of his plough, and Franklin had lost his recollection of the candle-moulds and the composing stick? Mr. Chubbs, who got rich to-day, imitates Mr. Swipes, who got rich yesterday, buys the same furniture, gives similar entertainments, and counts himself "as good a man as Swipes, any day." Nay, he goes a little beyond him, puts his servants in livery, with the "Chubbs arms" on the button; but the new-found family arms are not descriptive of the character of the Chubbses, or of their origin and history—only of their vanity. Then Mr. Swipes looks down on poor Chubbs, and curls his lip with scorn; calls him a "parvenu," "an upstart," "a plebeian;" speaks of him as one of "that sort of people," "one of your ordinary men;" "thrifty and well off in the world, but a little vulgar." At the same time Mr. Swipes looks up to Mr. Bung, who got rich the day before yesterday, as a gentleman of old family and quite distinguished, and receives from that quarter the same treatment he bestows on his left-hand neighbor. The real gentleman is the same all the world over. Such are by no means lacking here, while the pretended gentlemen swarm in America. Chaucer said a good word long ago:

> "—This is not mine intendément
> To clepen no wight in no age
> Only gentle for his lineáge;
> But whoso that is virtuous,
> And in his port not outragéous:
> When such one thou see'st thee beforn,
> Though he be not gentle born,
> Thou mayest well see this in soth,
> That he is gentle, because he doth
> As 'longeth to a gentleman;
> Of them none other deem I can;
> For certainly withouten drede,
> A churl is deeméd by his deed,
> Of high or low, as ye may see,
> Or of what kindred that he be."

It is no wonder vulgar men, who travel here and eat our dinners, laugh at this form of vulgarity. Wiser men see its cause, and prophesy its speedy decay. Every nation has its aristocracy, or controlling class; in some lands it is permanent, an aristocracy of blood; men that are descended from distinguished warriors, from the pirates and freebooters of a rude age. The nobility of England are proud of their fathers' deeds, and emblazon the symbols thereof in their family arms, emblems of barbarism. Ours is an aristocracy of wealth, not got by plunder, but by toil, thrift, enterprise; of course it is a movable aristocracy: the first families of the last century are now forgot, and their successors will give place to new names. Now earning is nobler than robbing, and work is before war; but we are ashamed of both, and seek to conceal the noble source of our wealth. An aristocracy of gold is far preferable to the old and immovable nobility of blood, but it has also its peculiar vices: it has the effrontery of an upstart, despises its own ladder, is heartless and lacks noble principle, vulgar and cursing. This lust of wealth, however, does us a service, and gives the whole nation a stimulus which it needs, and, low as the motive is, drives us to continual advancement. It is a great merit for a nation to secure the largest amount of useful and comfortable and beautiful things which can be honestly earned, and used with profit to the body and soul of man. Only when wealth becomes an idol, and material abundance is made the end, not the means, does the love of it become an evil. No nation was ever too rich, or overthrifty, though many a nation has lost its soul by living wholly for the senses.

Now and then we see noble men living apart from this vulgarity and scramble; some rich, some poor, but both content to live for noble aims, to pinch and spare for virtue, religion, for truth and right. Such men never fail from any age or land, but everywhere they are the exceptional men. Still they serve to keep alive the sacred fire in the hearts of young men, rising amid the common mob as oaks surpass the brambles or the fern.

In these secondary qualities of the people which mark the special signs of the times, there are many contradictions, quality contending with quality; all by no means balanced into harmonious relations. Here are great faults not less than great virtues. Can the national faults be corrected? Most certainly;

they are but accidental, coming from our circumstances, our history, our position as a people—heterogeneous, new, and placed on a new and untamed continent They come not from the nation's soul; they do not belong to our fundamental idea, but are hostile to it. One day our impatience of authority, our philosophical tendency, will lead us to a right method, that to fixed principles, and then we shall have a continuity of national action. Considering the pains taken by the fathers of the better portion of America to promote religion here, remembering how dear is Christianity to the heart of all, conservative and radical—though men often name as Christian what is not— and seeing how truth and right are sure to win at last,—it becomes pretty plain that we shall arrive at true principles, laws of the universe, ideas of God; then we shall be in unison also with it and Him. When that great defect—lack of first principles—is corrected, our intensity of life, with the hope and confidence it inspires, will do a great work for us. We have already secured an abundance of material comforts hitherto unknown; no land was ever so full of corn and cattle, clothing, comfortable houses, and all things needed for the flesh. The desire of those things, even the excessive desire thereof, performs an important part in the divine economy of the human race; nowhere is its good effect more conspicuous than in America, where in two generations the wild Irishman becomes a decent citizen, orderly, temperate, and intelligent. This done or even a-doing, as it is now, we shall go forth to realize our great national idea, and accomplish the great work of organizing into institutions the unalienable rights of man. The great obstacle in the way of that is African slavery—the great exception in the nation's history; the national sin. When that is removed, as soon it must be, lesser but kindred evils will easily be done away; the truth which the land-reformers, which the associationists, the free-traders, and others, have seen, dimly or clearly, can readily be carried out. But while this monster vice continues, there is little hope of any great and permanent national reform. The positive things which we chiefly need for this work, are first, education, next, education, and then education, a vigorous development of the mind, conscience, affections, religious power of the whole nation. The method and the means for that I shall not now discuss.

The organization of human rights, the performance of human duties, is an unlimited work. If there shall ever be a time when it is all done, then the race will have finished its course. Shall the American nation go on in this work, or pause, turn off, fall, and perish? To me it seems almost treason to doubt that a glorious future awaits us. Young as we are, and wicked, we have yet done something which the world will not let perish. One day we shall attend more emphatically to the rights of the hand, and organize labor and skill; then to the rights of the head, looking after education, science, literature, and art; and again to the rights of the heart, building up the State with its laws, society with its families, the church with its goodness and piety. One day we shall see that it is a shame, and a loss, and a wrong, to have a criminal, or an ignorant man, or a pauper, or an idler, in the land; that the jail, and the gallows, and the almshouse are a reproach, which need not be. Out of new sentiments and ideas, not seen as yet, new forms of society will come, free from the antagonism of races, classes, men—representing the American idea in its length, breadth, depth, and height, its beauty and its truth, and then the old civilization of our time shall seem barbarous and even savage. There will be an American art commensurate with our idea and akin to this great continent; not an imitation, but a fresh, new growth. An American literature also must come with democratic freedom, democratic thought, democratic power—for we are not always to be pensioners of other lands, doing nothing but import and quote; a literature with all of German philosophic depth, with English solid sense, with French vivacity and wit, Italian fire of sentiment and soul, with all of Grecian elegance of form, and more than Hebrew piety and faith in God. We must not look for the maiden's ringlets on the baby's brow; we are yet but a girl; the nameless grace of maturity, and womanhood's majestic charm, are still to come. At length we must have a system of education, which shall uplift the humblest, rudest, worst born child in all the land; which shall bring forth and bring up noble men.

An American State is a thing that must also be; a State of free men who give over brawling, resting on industry, justice, love, not on war, cunning, and violence,—a State where liberty, equality, and fraternity are deeds as well as words. In its time the American Church must also appear, with liberty, holiness, and love for its watchwords, cultivating reason, conscience, affection, faith, and leading the world's way in justice, peace, and love. The Roman Church has been all men know what and how; the American Church, with freedom for the mind, freedom for the heart, freedom for the soul, is yet to be, sundering no chord of the human harp, but tuning all to harmony. This also must come; but hitherto no one has risen with genius fit to plan its holy walls, conceive its columns, project its towers, or lay its corner-stone. Is it too much to hope all this? Look at the arena before us—look at our past history. Hark! there is the sound of many million men, the trampling of their freeborn feet, the murmuring of their voice; a nation born of this land that God reserved so long a virgin earth, in a high day married to the human race,—rising, and swelling, and rolling on, strong and certain as the Atlantic tide; they come numerous as ocean waves when east winds blow, their destination commensurate with the continent, with ideas vast as the Mississippi, strong as the Alleghanies, and awful as Niagara; they come murmuring little of the past, but, moving in the brightness of their great idea, and casting its light far on to other lands and distant days—come to the world's great work, to organize the rights of man.

HENRY CLAY

Speech in the Senate on Compromise Resolutions

Washington, D.C., February 5–6, 1850

M R. PRESIDENT, never, on any former occasion, have I
risen under feelings of such deep solicitude. I have witnessed many periods of great anxiety, of peril, and of danger
even to the country; but I have never before arisen to address any
assembly so oppressed, so appalled, so anxious. And, sir, I hope
it will not be out of place to do here what again and again I have
done in my private chamber—to implore of Him who holds
the destinies of nations and individuals in his hands to bestow
upon our country his blessings—to bestow upon our people all
his blessings—to calm the violence and rage of party—to still
passion—to allow reason once more to resume its empire.
And may I not ask of Him, to bestow upon his humble servant,
now before Him, the blessings of his smiles, of strength, and of
ability, to perform the work which lies before him.

Sir, I have said that I have witnessed other anxious periods
in the history of our country; and if I were to mention—to trace
to their original source—the cause of all our present dangers
and difficulties, I should ascribe them to the violence and intemperance of party spirit. We have had testimony of this in the
progress of this session, and Senators, however they may differ
in other matters, concur in acknowledging the existence of
that cause in originating the unhappy differences which prevail
throughout the country upon this subject of the institution of
slavery. Parties, in their endeavors to obtain the one the ascendency over the other, catch at every passing and floating plank,
in order to add strength and power to themselves. We have
been told by two honorable Senators, [Mr. HALE and Mr.
PHELPS,] that the parties at the North have each in its turn,
wooed and endeavored to obtain the assistance of a small party
called Abolitionists, in order that the scale in its favor might

preponderate over its adversaries. Let us look wherever we may, we see too many indications of the existence of the spirit and intemperance of party. I might go to other legislative bodies besides our own. I might draw from the Legislatures all the melancholy truth upon which I am dwelling; but, sir, I need not pass out of this Capitol itself—I say it with all deference and respect to that portion of Congress assembled in the other wing of the Capitol. But what have we seen there during this very session? One whole week—I think it was an entire week—exhausted in the vain endeavor to elect a Doorkeeper of the House!

[Much confusion prevailed in the lobbies and the avenues leading to the Senate chamber.]

Mr. CASS. Will the honorable Senator pause a few moments, until order is restored here?

The VICE PRESIDENT. The Sergeant-at Arms will see that the avenues to the galleries and this chamber are closed, and that a sufficient number withdraw from them to give room for those who are in, and to restore order.

Mr. FOOTE. Let all the disorderly be taken out.

Mr. BADGER. There are persons in the ante-rooms that, because they cannot hear themselves, will not let others hear. I would suggest the propriety of extending the order to their case also.

Mr. CASS. Is the Sergeant-at-Arms in the chamber.

The VICE PRESIDENT. He is discharging his duty in restoring order.

Mr. BADGER. Let the ante-rooms be entirely closed.

Order having at length been restored,

Mr. CLAY resumed. Mr. President, what was the question in this struggle to elect a Doorkeeper? It was not as regarded the man or the qualifications of the man, best adapted to the situation. It was, whether the Doorkeeper entertained opinions upon certain great national measures coincident with those of this or that side of the House! That was the sole question that prevented the election of that officer for about the period of a week. I make no reproaches, sir—none, to either portion of the House. I state the fact; and I state that fact to draw from it the conclusion, and to express the hope that there will be an endeavor to check this violence of party.

What vicissitudes do we not pass through in this short mortal existence of ours. Eight years ago, I took my leave finally, and—as I supposed—forever of this body. At that time I did not conceive of the possibility of being again returned to it; and if my private wishes and particular inclinations, and the desire during the short remnant of my days to remain in repose and quiet, could have prevailed, you would never have seen me, sir, occupying the seat which I now do upon this floor. The Legislature of the State to which I belong, unsolicited by me, chose to designate me to represent them in this Senate; and I have come here in obedience to a sense of stern duty, with no personal objects—no private views now or hereafter to gratify. I know, sir, the jealousies, fears, and apprehensions which are engendered by the spirit of party to which I have referred; and if there be any in my hearing now—if there be in or out of this Capitol—any one who is running the race for honor, and for elevation—for higher honor, for higher elevation, than that which he may enjoy—I beg him to believe that I at least will never jostle him in the pursuit of these honors or that elevation. I beg him to be persuaded that, if my wishes prevail, my name shall never be used in competition with his. I beg leave to assure him, that when my services are terminated in this body—and I hope that before the expiration of my present term they may be—my mission, so far as respects the public affairs of this world and upon earth, is closed, and closed, if my wishes prevail, forever.

But, it is impossible for us to be blind to the facts which are daily transpiring before us. It is impossible for us not to perceive that party spirit and future elevation mix more or less in all our affairs, in all our deliberations. At a moment when the White House itself is in danger of conflagration, instead of all hands uniting to extinguish the flames, we are contending about who shall be its next occupant. When a dreadful *crevasse* has occurred, which threatens inundation and destruction to all around it, we are contesting and disputing about the profits of the estate which is threatened with total submersion.

Mr. President, it is passion, passion—party, party—and intemperance; that is all I dread in the adjustment of the great questions which unhappily at this time divide our distracted country. At this moment, we have in the legislative bodies of this capitol, and in the States, twenty-odd furnaces in full blast in generating heat, and passion, and intemperance, and diffusing them throughout the whole extent of this broad land. Two months ago, all was calm in comparison with the present moment. All now is uproar, confusion, menace to the existence of the Union and to the happiness and safety of this people. I implore Senators—I entreat them, by all that they expect hereafter, and by all that is dear to them here below, to repress the ardor of these passions, to look at their country at this crisis—to listen to the voice of reason, not as it shall be attempted to be uttered by me, for I am not so presumptuous as to indulge the hope that anything I can say shall deserve the attention I have desired, but to listen to their own reason, their own judgment, their own good sense, in determining what is best to be done for our country in the actual posture in which we find it. To this great object have my efforts been directed during this whole session. I have cut myself off from all the usual enjoyments of social life, I have confined myself almost exclusively, with very few exceptions, to my own chamber, and from the beginning of the session up to this time, my thoughts have been anxiously directed to the object of finding some plan, of proposing some mode of accommodation, which should once more restore the blessings of concord, harmony, and peace to this great country. I am not vain enough to suppose that I have been successful in the accomplishment of this object. But I have presented a scheme; and allow me to say to honorable Senators, that if they find in that plan anything which is defective—if they find in it anything which is worthy of acceptance, but is susceptible of improvement by amendment, it seems to me that the true and patriotic course for them to pursue is, not to denounce it, but to improve it; not to reject, without examination, any project of accommodation, having for its object the restoration of harmony in this country, but to look at it, and see if it be susceptible of alteration or improvement, so as to accomplish the object which I indulge the hope is common to all and every one of us, to restore peace, and quiet, and harmony, and happiness to this country.

When I came to consider this subject, there were two or three general purposes which seemed to me most desirable, if possible, to accomplish. The one was to settle all the controverted questions arising out of the subject of slavery; and it seamed to me to be doing very little if we settled one question and left other disturbing questions unadjusted. It seemed to me to be doing but little if we stopped one leak only in the ship of State, and left other leaks capable of producing danger, if not destruction, to the vessel. I therefore turned my attention to every subject connected with the institution of slavery, and out of which controverted questions have sprung, to see if it were possible or practicable to accommodate and adjust the whole of them.

Another principal object which attracted my attention was, to endeavor to frame such a scheme of accommodation as that neither of the two classes of States into which our country is unhappily divided should make a sacrifice of any great principle. I believe, sir, that the series of resolutions which I have had the honor of presenting to the Senate accomplishes that object.

Another purpose, sir, which I had in view was this: I was aware of the difference of opinion prevailing between these two classes of States. I was aware that while a portion of the Union was pushing matters, as it seemed to me, to a dangerous extremity, another portion of the Union was pushing them to an opposite, and perhaps to a no less dangerous extremity. It appeared to me, then, that if any arrangement, any satisfactory adjustment could be made of the controverted questions between the two classes of States, that adjustment, that arrangement, could only be successful and effectual by exacting from both parties some concession—not of principle, not of principle at all, but of feeling, of opinion, in relation to the matters in controversy between them. I believe that the resolutions which I have prepared fulfill that object. I believe that you will find upon that careful, rational, and attentive examination of them which I think they deserve, that by them, neither party makes any concession of principle at all, though the concessions of forbearance are ample.

In the next place, in respect to the slaveholding States, there are resolutions making concessions to them by the class of opposite States, without any compensation whatever being rendered by them to the non-slaveholding States.

I think every one of these characteristics which I have

assigned to the measures which I propose is susceptible of clear, satisfactory demonstration, by an attentive perusal and critical examination of the resolutions themselves. Let us take up the first, sir.

The first resolution, Mr. President, as you are aware, relates to California; and it declares that California, with suitable limits, ought to be admitted as a member of this Union, without the imposition of any restriction, either to interdict or to introduce slavery within her limits. Now, is there any concession in this resolution by either party to the other? I know that gentlemen who come from the slaveholding States say that the North gets all that it desires; but by whom does it get it? Does it get it by any action of Congress? If slavery be interdicted in California, it is done by Congress, by this Government? No, sir; the interdiction is imposed by California herself. And has it not been the doctrine of all parties, that when a State is about to be admitted into the Union, that State has a right to decide for itself whether it will or will not have within its limits slavery? The great principle which was in contest upon the memorable occasion of the introduction of Missouri into the Union was, whether it was competent or was not competent for Congress to impose any restriction which should exist after she became a member of the Union? We, who were in favor of the admission of Missouri, contended that, by the Constitution, no such restriction could be imposed. We contended that, whenever she was once admitted into the Union, she had all the rights and privileges of any preexisting State of the Union; and that of these rights and privileges, one was to decide for herself whether slavery should or should not exist within her limits—that she had as much a right to decide upon the introduction of slavery, or upon its abolition, as New York had a right to decide upon the introduction or abolition of slavery; and that she stood among her peers equal, and invested with all the privileges that any one of the original thirteen States, and those subsequently admitted, had a right to enjoy.

And so I thought that those who have been contending with so much earnestness and with so much perseverance for the Wilmot proviso ought to reflect that, even if they could carry their object and adopt the Wilmot proviso, it would cease the moment any State to whose territory it was applicable came to be admitted as a member of the Union. No one contends now—no one believes—that with regard to the northwestern States, to which the ordinance of 1787 was applied—Ohio, Indiana, Illinois, and Michigan—no one now believes that any one of those States, if they thought proper to do it, has not just as much a right to introduce slavery within her borders as Virginia has a right to maintain the existence of slavery within hers.

Then, if in this struggle of power and empire between the two classes of States a decision of California has taken place adverse to the wishes of the southern States, it is a decision not made by the General Government; it is a decision respecting which they cannot complain to the General Government. It is a decision made by California herself, and which California had incontestibly a right to make under the Constitution of the United States. There is, then, in that first resolution, according to the observation which I made some time ago, a case where neither party concedes; where the question of slavery, either of its introduction or interdiction, is silent as respects the action of this Government; and if it has been decided, it has been decided by a different body—by a different power—by California herself, who had a right to make that decision.

Mr. President, the next resolution of the series which I have offered, I beg gentlemen candidly now to look at. I was aware, perfectly aware, of the perseverance with which the Wilmot proviso was insisted upon. I knew that every one of the free States of this Union—I believe without exception—had, by its legislative bodies, passed resolutions instructing its Senators and requesting its Representatives to get that restriction incorporated into any territorial bill that might be offered under the auspices of Congress. I knew how much—although I regretted how much—the free States had—if I may say so—put their hearts upon the adoption of this measure. In this second resolution I call upon them to waive persisting in it. I ask them, for the sake of peace, and in a spirit of mutual forbearance to other members of the Union, to give up, and to no longer insist upon it—to see, as they must see, if their eyes are open, the dangers which lie under it, if they persevere in insisting upon it,

Well, when I called upon them in that resolution to do this, was I not bound to offer, for the surrender of that favorite measure of theirs, some compensation—not an equivalent by any means, but some compensation—as that spirit of mutual forbearance which animates the one side, ought at the same time to animate the other side? What is it that is offered them? It is a declaration of what I characterize and must style, with great deference to all those who entertain the opposite opinion —I will not say incontestible, but to me clear, and I think they ought to be regarded as—indisputable truths. And what are they? The first is, that by law slavery no longer exists in any portion of the acquisition made by us from the Republic of Mexico; and the other is, that in our opinion, according to all the probabilities of the case, slavery never will be introduced into any portion of the territories so acquired from Mexico.

Now, I have heard it said that this declaration of what I call these two truths is equivalent to the enactment of the Wilmot proviso. I have heard this asserted, but is that the case? If the Wilmot proviso were adopted in territorial governments established in these countries acquired from Mexico, it would be a positive enactment, a prohibition, an interdiction as to the introduction of slavery within them. But with regard to those truths, I had hoped, and still indulge the hope, that those who represent the free States will be inclined not to insist that we shall give—and indeed it would be extremely difficult to give to these declarations—the form of a positive enactment. I had hoped that they would be satisfied with the simple expression of the opinion of Congress, leaving it upon the basis of that opinion, without asking for what seems to be almost impracticable, if not impossible—for any subsequent enactments to be introduced into the bill by which territorial governments shall be established. I can only say that that second resolution, even without the declaration of these two truths, would be more acceptable to me than with them. But I could not forget that I was proposing a scheme of arrangement and compromise, and I could not, therefore, depart from the duty, which the preparation of the scheme seemed to me to impose, while we ask upon the one side a surrender of their favorite measure, of offering upon the other side some compensation for that surrender or sacrifice.

Mr. President, the first of these truths is, that by law slavery does not exist within the territories ceded to us by the Republic of Mexico. It is a misfortune in the various weighty and important topics which are connected with the subject that I am now addressing you upon, that any one of the five or six embraced in these resolutions would of itself furnish a theme for a lengthened speech, and I am therefore reduced to the necessity, I think, at least in this stage of the discussion of limiting myself rather to the expression of opinion, than to going at any great length into the discussion of all these various topics. Now with respect to the opinion here asserted, that slavery does not exist in the territories ceded to the United States by Mexico, I can only refer to the fact of the passage of a law by the supreme Government of Mexico abolishing it, I think in the year 1824, and the subsequent passage of a law by the legislative body of Mexico—I forget in what year—by which they propose—what, it is true, they never yet carried into full effect—a compensation to the owners of slaves for the property of which they were deprived by the act of abolition. I can only refer to the acquiescence of Mexico in the abolition of slavery, from the time of this extinction down to the time of the treaty by which we acquired those countries. All Mexico, so far as I know, acquiesced in the non-existence of slavery. Gentlemen, I am aware, talk about the irregularity of the acts by which slavery was abolished; but does it become us, a foreign power, to look into the modes by which an act was accomplished by a foreign power, when she herself is satisfied with what is done, and when she, too, is exclusively the judge whether the object, then local, municipal in Mexico, has or has not been abolished in conformity with her fundamental law? Mexico, upon this subject, showed to the last moment her anxiety. In the documents which were laid before the country upon the subject of the negotiation of the treaty by Mr. Trist, you will find this passage contained in one of his dispatches:

"Among the points which came under discussion was the exclusion of slavery from all territory which should pass from Mexico. In the course of their remarks on the subject, I was told that if it were proposed to the people of the United States to part with a portion of their territory, in order that the *inquisition* should be therein established, the proposal could not excite stronger feelings of abhorrence than those awakened in Mexico by the prospect of the introduction of slavery in any territory parted with by her. Our conversation on this topic was perfectly frank, and no less friendly; and the more effective upon their minds, inasmuch as I was enabled to say, with perfect security, that, although their impressions respecting the practical fact of slavery, as it existed in the United States, were, I had no doubt, entirely erroneous, yet there was probably no difference between my individual views and sentiments on slavery, considered in itself, and those which they entertained. I concluded by assuring them that the bare *mention* of the subject in any treaty to which the United Sates were a party, was an absolute impossibility; that no President of the United States would dare to present any such treaty to the Senate; and that if it were in their power to offer me the whole territory described in our projet, increased tenfold in value, and, in addition to that, covered a foot thick all over with pure gold, upon the single condition that slavery should be excluded therefrom, I could not entertain the offer for a moment, nor think even of communicating it to Washington. The matter ended in their being fully satisfied that this topic was one not to be touched, and it was dropped, with good feeling on both sides."

Thus you find that, in the very act of negotiation by which the treaty was concluded, which ceded to us the country in question, the diplomatic representatives of the Mexican Republic urged the abhorrence with which Mexico would view the introduction of slavery into any portion of the territory which she was about to cede to the United States. But a prohibition of its introduction was not inserted, in consequence of the firm ground taken by Mr. Trist, and his declaration that it was an utter impossibility even to mention the subject. I take it then, for granted,—availing myself of the benefit of the discussions which took place upon this topic at a former session, which I think have left the whole country under the impression of the non-existence of slavery in the ceded territories—I take it for granted that what I have said will satisfy the Senate of that first truth—that slavery does not exist there by law, unless slavery was carried there the moment the treaty was ratified by the two parties to the treaty, under the operation of the Constitution of the United States.

Now, really, I must say, that the idea that *eo instanti*, upon the consummation of the treaty the Constitution of the United States spread itself over the acquired country, and carried along with it the institution of slavery, is so irreconcilable with any comprehension or any reason which I possess, that I hardly know how to meet it. Why, sir, these United States consist of thirty States. In fifteen of them, there was slavery; in fifteen, slavery did not exist. How can it be argued that the fifteen slave States, by the operation of the Constitution of the United States, carried into the ceded country their institution of slavery, any more than it can be argued, upon the other side, that by the operation of the same Constitution, the fifteen free States carried into the ceded territories the principle of freedom, which they, from policy, have chosen to adopt within their limits? Let me suppose a case. Let me imagine that Mexico had never abolished slavery there at all. Let me suppose that it was existing there, by virtue of law, from the shores of the Pacific to those of the Gulf of Mexico, at the moment of the cession of those countries to us by the treaty in question. With what patience would gentlemen, coming from the slaveholding States, listen to an argument which should be urged by the free States, that, notwithstanding the existence of slavery within those territories, the Constitution of the United States, the moment it operated upon and took effect within the ceded territories, abolished slavery and rendered them free? Well, is there not just as much ground to contend, where a moiety of the States are free and the other moiety are slaveholding States, that the principle of freedom which prevails in the one class shall operate as the principle of slavery which prevails in the other class of States shall operate? Can you, amidst this conflict of interests, of principles, and of legislation, which prevails in the two parts of the Union—can you come to any other conclusion than that which I understand to be the conclusion of the public law of the world, of reason, and of justice, that the *status* of law, as it existed at the moment of the conquest or acquisition, remains unchanged until it is altered by the sovereign authority of the conquering or acquiring power? That is a great principle, and you can scarcely turn over a page of the public law where you will not find it recognized. The laws of Mexico, as they existed at the moment of the cession of the ceded territories to this country, remained their laws still, unless they were altered by that new sovereign power which this people and these territories came under in consequence of the treaty of cession to the United States. I think then, Mr. President—without trespassing further, or exhausting the little stock of strength which I have, and for which I shall find ample occasion in the progress of the argument—that I may leave that part of the subject with two or three observations only upon the general power which I think appertains to this Government upon the subject of slavery within those territories.

But, before I approach that subject, allow me to say that, in my humble judgment, the institution of slavery presents two questions totally distinct, and resting upon entirely different grounds—slavery within the States, and slavery without the States. Congress, the General Government, has no power, under the Constitution of the United States, to touch slavery within the States, except in the three specified particulars in that instrument; to adjust the subject of representation, to impose taxes on slaves when a system of direct taxation is made, and to perform the duty of surrendering, or causing to be delivered up, fugitive slaves when they escape from the service which they owe in the slave States, and take refuge in the free States. And I am ready to say that if Congress were to attack within the States the institution of slavery, with the purpose of the overthrow or the extinction of slavery, then, Mr. President, "my voice would be for war." Then would be made a case which would justify in the sight of God, and in the presence of the nations of the earth, resistance on the part of the slave States to such an unconstitutional usurped attempt as would be made under the supposition I have stated. Then we should be acting in defence of our rights, of our domicils, of our property, of our safety, of our lives. Then I think would be furnished a case in which the slave States would be justified, by all the considerations which pertain to the happiness or security of man, to employ every instrument which God or nature has placed in our hands, to resist such an attempt upon the part of this Government. Then if, unfortunately, civil war should break out, we should present to the nations of the earth the spectacle of one portion of this Union endeavoring to subvert an institution of another portion, in violation of the Constitution and the most sacred obligations. We should present a spectacle in which we should have the sympathy and good wishes, and desire for our success, of all men who love justice and truth.

Far different would, I fear, be our case, if, unhappily, we should be led into war, into civil war—if the two parts of this country should be placed in a hostile position towards each other in order to carry slavery into new territories acquired from Mexico. Mr. President, we have heard—all of us have read—of the efforts of France to propagate—what, on the continent of Europe? Not slavery, sir, not slavery, but the rights of man; and we know the fate of her efforts of propagandism of that kind. But if, unhappily, we should be involved in war, in civil war, between the two parts of this Confederacy, in which the effort upon the one side should be to restrain the introduction of slavery into the new territories, and upon the other side to force its introduction there, what a spectacle should we present to the astonishment of mankind, in an effort, not to propagate rights, but—I must say it, though I trust it will be understood to be said with no design to excite feeling—a war to propagate wrongs in the territories thus acquired from Mexico. It would be a war in which we should have no sympathies, no good wishes; in which all mankind would be against us; in which our own history itself would be against us; for, from the commencement of the Revolution down to the present time, we have constantly reproached our British ancestors for the introduction of slavery into this country. And allow me to say that, in my opinion, it is one of the best defences which can be made to preserve the institution of slavery in this country, that it was forced upon us against the wishes of our ancestors—of our own American colonial ancestors—and by the cupidity of our British commercial ancestors.

The power, then, Mr. President, in my opinion—and I extend it to the introduction as well as to the prohibition of slavery in the new territories—does exist in Congress; and I think there is this important distinction between slavery outside of the States and slavery inside of the States; that all outside of the States is debatable, and all inside of the States is not debatable. The Government has no right to attack the institution within the States; but whether she has, and to what extent she has or has not, the right to attack slavery outside of the States, is a debatable question—one upon which men may honorably and fairly differ; and however it may be decided, furnishes, I trust, no just occasion for breaking up this glorious Union of ours.

I am not going to take up that part of the subject which relates to the power of Congress to legislate on slavery—I shall have occasion to make some observations upon that subject in the course of my remarks—whether in this District of Columbia or in the Territories; but I must say, in a few words, that I think there are two sources of power, either of which is sufficient, in my judgment, to authorize the exercise of the power either to introduce or keep out slavery, outside of the States and within the Territories. Mr. President, I shall not take up time, of which so much has been consumed already, to show that the clause which gives to Congress the power to make needful rules and regulations respecting the territory and other property of the United States conveys the power to legislate for the Territories. I cannot concur with my worthy friend—and I use the term in its best and most emphatic sense—my friend from Michigan, [Mr. Cass]—for I believe we have known each other longer than I have known, and longer than he has known, any other Senator in this hall—I say I cannot concur with that honorable Senator, though I entertain the most profound respect for the opinion which he has advanced adverse to my own; but I must say, that when a point is settled by all the elementary authorities, and by the uniform interpretation and action of every department of our Government,—legislative, executive, and judicial—and when that point has been settled during a period of fifty years, and never was seriously disturbed until recently, I think that if we are to regard anything as fixed and settled under the administration of this Constitution of ours, it is the question which has been thus invariably and uniformly settled. Or, are we to come to the conclusion that nothing—nothing upon earth is settled under this Constitution, but the principle that everything is unsettled?

Mr. President, we are to recollect that it is very possible—that it is, indeed, quite likely—that when that Constitution was formed, the application of it to such Territories as Louisiana, Florida, California, and New Mexico was never within the contemplation of the framers of that instrument. It will be recollected that, when that Constitution was formed, the whole country northwest of the Ohio was unpeopled; and it must be recollected, also, that the exercise of the power to make governments for Territories in their infant state is, in the nature of the power, temporary, and such as must terminate whenever they have acquired a population competent to self-government. Sixty thousand is the number specified in the ordinance of 1787.

Now, sir, recollect that when this Constitution was adopted, that territory was unpeopled; and how was it possible that Congress, to whom it had been ceded, for the common benefit of the ceding States and the other States of the Union, had no power whatever to declare what description of settlers should occupy the public lands? Suppose that Congress had taken up the notion that slavery would enhance the value of the land, and, with a view to replenish the public treasury and augment the revenue from that source, that the introduction of slavery there would be more advantageous than its exclusion, would they not have had the right, under that clause which authorizes Congress to make the necessary "rules and regulations respecting the territory and other property belonging to the United States"—would they have no right, discretion, or authority— whatever you may choose to call it—to say that anybody who chose to bring his slaves and settle upon the land and improve it should do so? It might be said that it would enhance the value of the property; it would give importance to the country; it would build up towns and villages; and in fine we may suppose that Congress might think that a greater amount of revenue might be derived from the waste lands by the introduction of slavery, than could be secured by its exclusion; and will it be contended, if they so thought, that they would have no right to make such rule? Why, sir, remember how those settlements were made. They began with very few persons. Marietta was, I think, the first place settled in the Northwest Territory. My friend now before me [Mr. CORWIN] will correct me if I am wrong. It was a small settlement, made by some two or three hundred persons from New England. Cincinnati was the next, and was settled by a handful of persons from New Jersey, perhaps, or some other of the States. Had those few settlers the right, from the moment they arrived there—a mere handful of men, who may have planted themselves at Marietta or Cincinnati—to govern and dispose of the territories, or to govern themselves as a sovereign community? or was it not in the mean time right and proper, and within the contemplation of the Constitution, that Congress, who owned the soil, acting under the authority therein contained, should regulate the settlement of the soil, and govern the settlers in those infant colonies until they should reach a sufficient degree of consideration, in respect of numbers and capacity for self-government, to be constituted into more regular municipal organizations, and be allowed to govern themselves?

I will not further dwell upon this part of the subject; but I have said there is another source of power equally satisfactory in my mind—equally conclusive as that which relates specifically to the Territories. This is the treaty-making power—the acquiring power. Now, I put it to gentlemen, is there not at this moment a power somewhere existing either to admit or exclude slavery from the territories acquired from Mexico? It is not an annihilated power. That is impossible. It is a substantive, actual, existing power. And where does it exist? It existed—no one, I presume, denies—in Mexico, prior to the cession of those territories. Mexico could have abolished slavery or have introduced slavery either in California or New Mexico. Now, that power must have been ceded. Who will deny that? Mexico has parted with the territory, and with it the sovereignty over the territory; and to whom did she transfer it? She transferred the territory and the sovereignty over the territory to the Government of the United States. The Government of the United States then acquired all the territory and all the sovereignty over that territory which Mexico held in California and New Mexico prior to the cession of these territories. Sir, dispute that who can. The power exists, or it does not exist. No one will contend for its annihilation. It existed in Mexico. No one, I think, can deny that Mexico alienates her sovereignty over the territory to the Government of the United Sates. The Government of the United States, therefore, possess all the powers which Mexico possessed over those territories; and the Government of the United States can do with reference to them— within, I admit, certain limits of the Constitution—whatever Mexico could have done. There are prohibitions upon the power of Congress within the Constitution, which prohibitions, I admit, must apply to Congress whenever it legislates, whether for the old States or the new Territories; but within the scope of those prohibitions—and none of them restrain the exercise of the power of Congress upon the subject of slavery— the powers of Congress are coextensive and coequal with the powers of Mexico prior to the cession.

Sir, with regard to this treaty-making power, all who have

had any occasion to examine into its character, and into the possible extent to which it may be carried, know that it is unlimited in its nature, except in so far as any limitations may be found within the Constitution of the United States; but upon this subject there is no limitation which prescribes the extent to which the power shall be exercised.

I know, that it is argued that there is no grant of power in express terms, in the Constitution over the subject of slavery. But there is no grant in the Constitution, specifically, over a vast variety of subjects upon which the powers of Congress are unquestionable. The major includes the minor. The general grant of power comprehends all the particulars of which that power consists. The power of acquisition by treaty draws with it the power to govern all the territory acquired. If there be a power to acquire, there must be a power to govern, and I think, therefore, without at present dwelling further upon this part of the subject, that from the two sources of authority in Congress to which I have referred may be traced the power of the Government of the United States to act upon the territories in general.

I come now to the question of the extent of the power. I think it is a power adequate either to introduce or to exclude slavery. I admit the argument in both its forms of application. I admit that, if the power exists of excluding, the power must also exist of introducing or tolerating slavery within the territories. But I have been drawn off so far from the second resolution, which I have now under consideration, that I have almost lost it out of view. In order, therefore, that we may come back understandingly to the subject, I will again read it:

Resolved, That as slavery does not exist by law, and is not likely to be introduced into any of the territory acquired by the United States from the Republic of Mexico, it is inexpedient for Congress to provide by law either for its introduction into or exclusion from any part of the said territory; and that appropriate territorial governments ought to be established by Congress in all of the said territory not assigned as the boundaries of the proposed State of California, without the adoption of any restriction or condition on the subject or slavery.

The other truth, as I respectfully and with great deference submit, is this: I propose to admit and announce that slavery is not likely to be introduced into any of those territories. Well, is not that the fact? Is there a member of this body who doubts it? What has occurred within the last three months? In California, more than in any other portion of the ceded territories, was it most probable, if slavery was adapted to the industrial habits of the people, that slavery would be introduced; yet, within the last three months, slavery has been excluded by the vote—the unanimous vote—of the Convention, against its introduction— a vote, as I observed on a former occasion, not confined to men from the non-slaveholding States. There were men from the slaveholding States as well, who concurred in that declaration; and that declaration has been responded to by the people of California of all classes and from all parts of the United States, and from foreign countries. Well, if we come down to those mountainous ridges which abound in New Mexico, the nature of its soil, its barrenness, its unproductive character, everything that we know, everything that we hear of it, must necessarily lead to the conclusion which I have mentioned, that slavery is not likely to be introduced there.

If it be true, then, that by law slavery does not now exist in the territories—if it is not likely to be introduced into the territories—if you, Senators, here, or a majority of you, believe these truths, as I am persuaded a large majority of you do— where is the difficulty in your announcing it to the whole world? Why hesitate or falter in the declaration of these indisputable truths? On the other hand, with regard to the Senators from the free States, allow me to make a reference to California in one or two other observations. When this feeling within the limits of your States was gotten up—when the Wilmot proviso was disseminated through them—did you not fear, whatever may have been the state of the facts—did you not at that time apprehend the introduction of slavery there? You did not know much in relation to the country or its inhabitants. They were far distant from you, and you were truly apprehensive that slavery might be introduced there, and you felt that the Wilmot proviso was a necessary measure of prevention. It was in this state of want of information that the whole North blazed up in behalf of this Wilmot proviso. It was in the apprehension that slavery might be introduced there that you left your constituents when you came here; for at the time you left your respective residences, you did not know the fact, which has reached us since the commencement of the session of Congress —you did not know the fact that a constitution had been unanimously adopted by the people of California, excluding slavery.

Well, now, let me suppose that two years ago it had been known in the free States that such a Constitution would be adopted; let me suppose that it had been believed that in no other part of the territory did slavery exist by law, and that it could not be introduced except by a positive enactment; suppose that, in relation to this whole subject—the solicitude in relation slavery—the people of the North had supposed that there was no danger; let me also suppose that they had foreseen the excitement, the danger, the irritation, the resolutions which have been adopted by southern Legislatures, and the manifestations of the people of the slave States—let me suppose all this had been known at the North at the time the agitation was being excited upon the subject of this Wilmot proviso, do you believe that it would ever have reached the height to which it has since risen? Do any of you believe it? And if, prior to your departure from your respective homes, you had had the opportunity of conversing with your constituents upon this great, controlling, and important fact of the adoption of a constitution excluding slavery in California, do you believe, Senators and Representatives coming from the free States, that if you had had the aid of this fact in a calm, serious, fireside conversation, your constituents would not have told you to come here and settle all these questions without danger to the Union? What do you want?—what do you want?—you who reside in the free States. Do you want that there shall be no slavery introduced into the territories acquired by the war with Mexico? Have you not your desire in California? And in all human probability you will have it in New Mexico also. What more do you want? You have got what is worth more than a thousand Wilmot provisos. You have nature on your side—facts upon your side—and this truth staring you in the face, that there is no slavery in those territories. If you are not infuriated, if you can elevate yourselves from the mud and mire of mere party contentions, to the purer regions of patriotism, what will you not do? Look at the fact as it exists. You will see that this fact was unknown to the great majority of the people; you will see that they acted upon one state of facts, while we have another and far different state of facts before us; and we will act as patriots—as responsible men, and as lovers of liberty, and lovers, above all, of this Union. We will act upon this altered state of facts which were unknown to our constituents, and appeal to their justice and magnanimity to concur with us in this action for peace, concord, and harmony.

I think, entertaining these views, that there is nothing extravagant in the hope which I indulged at the time resolutions were proposed—nothing extravagant in the hope that the North might content itself even with striking out these two declarations. They are unnecessary for any purpose which the free States have in view. At all events, if they should insist upon Congress expressing the opinions which are here asserted, they might even limit their wishes to the simple assertion of that, without insisting on their being incorporated in any territorial government which might be devised for the territories in question.

I pass from the second resolution to the third and fourth, which relate to the Texas question. But allow me to say, Mr. President, that I approach the subject with a full knowledge of all its difficulties; and of all the questions connected with or growing out of this institution of slavery, which Congress is called upon to pass upon at this time, there are none so difficult and troublesome as this which relates to Texas; because Texas has the question of boundary to settle. The question of slavery, or the feeling connected with the institution of slavery, runs into the question of the boundary of Texas. The North are, perhaps, anxious to contract Texas within the narrowest possible limits, in order to exclude all beyond them, and to make it free territory. The South, on the contrary, are anxious to extend their limits to the source of the Rio Grande, for the purpose of obtaining an additional theatre for slavery; and it is this question of the limits of Texas, and the proper settlement of her boundaries, which embarrass all others. You will perceive that these difficulties of the boundary question meet us at every step we take, in which there is a third question also adding to the difficulty. By the resolution of annexation, all territory north of 36° 30′ was interdicted from slavery. But of New Mexico, all that which lies north of 36° 30′ embraces about one-third of the whole of New Mexico east of the Rio Grande; so that free and slave territory, slavery and non-slavery, are mixed up together. All these difficulties are to be met. And allow me to say, that among the considerations which induced me to think that it was necessary to settle all these questions, was the state of things that now exists in New Mexico, and a state of things to be apprehended both here and in the territories. Why, sir, at this moment—and I think I shall have the concurrence of the two Senators from that State when I mention the fact—there is a feeling approximating to abhorrence, on the part of the people New Mexico of any union with Texas.

Mr. RUSK. Only on the part of office-holders, office-seekers, and those they could influence.

Mr. CLAY. Well, that may be, and I am afraid that New Mexico is not the only place where office-holders and office-seekers compose the majority of the population of the country. [Laughter.] They are a terribly large class, I assure you, sir. Now, if the questions are not settled which relate to Texas, her boundaries, &c., and which relate to the territory not claimed by Texas and included in New Mexico, all these questions being left open, will but tend to agitation, confusion, disorder and anarchy there, and agitation here. There will be, I have no doubt, parties at the North crying out for the imposition of the Wilmot proviso, or some other restriction upon the subject of slavery. And in my opinion, we absolutely do nothing, or next to nothing, if we do not provide against these difficulties, and the recurrence of these dangers. With respect to the state of things in New Mexico, allow me to call the attention of the Senate to what I consider as the highest authority I could offer as to the state of things there existing. I mean the act of their Convention, unless that Convention happened to be composed of office-seekers and office-holders, &c. I will call your attention to what they say of their situation, if my colleague will be so kind as to read for me.

Mr. UNDERWOOD read as follows:

"We, the people of New Mexico, in convention assembled, having elected a delegate to represent this Territory in the Congress of the United States, and to urge upon the Supreme Government a redress of our grievances, and the protection due to us as citizens of our common country, under the Constitution, instruct him as follows: That whereas, for the last three years we have suffered under the paralyzing effects of a government undefined and doubtful in its character, inefficient to protect the rights of the people, or to discharge the high and absolute duty of every government, the enforcement and regular administration of its own laws, in consequence of which, industry and enterprise are paralyzed, and discontent and confusion prevail throughout the land. The want of proper protection against the various barbarous tribes of Indians that surround us on every side, has prevented the extension of settlements upon our valuable public domain, and rendered utterly futile every attempt to explore or develop the great resources of the Territory. Surrounded by the Utahs, Camanches, and Apaches on the north, east, and south, by the Navejos on the west, with Jicarillas within our limits, and without any adequate protection against their hostile inroads, our flocks and herds are driven off by thousands, our fellow-citizens, men, women, and children, are murdered or carried into captivity. Many of our citizens, of all ages and sexes, are at this moment suffering all the horrors of barbarian bondage, and it is utterly out of our power to obtain their release from a condition to which death would be preferable. The wealth of our Territory is being diminished. We have neither the means nor any adopted plan by government for the education of the rising generation. In fine, with a government temporary, doubtful, uncertain, and inefficient in character and in operation, surrounded and despoiled by barbarous foes, ruin appears inevitable before us, unless speedy and effectual protection be extended to us by the Congress of the United States."

Mr. CLAY. Now, sir, there is a vivid and faithful exhibition of the actual condition of things there, and if we go beyond the Rio Grande, to that part not claimed by Texas, we, I apprehend, shall find no better state of things. In fact, I cannot for a moment reconcile it to my sense of duty to suffer Congress to adjourn without an effort at least being made to extend the benefits and blessings of government to those people who have recently been acquired by us. With regard to that portion of New Mexico which lies east of the Rio Grande, undoubtedly if it were conceded to Texas, there would be two incongruous, if not hostile populations thrown together, endangering public peace and tranquillity. And all beyond, including New Mexico, Deseret, and north of California, beyond the Rio Grande, would be still open to all the consequences of disorder, confusion, and anarchy, without some stable government emanating from the authority of that nation of which they form now a part, and with which they are but little acquainted. I think, therefore, that all these questions, difficult and troublesome as they may be, ought to be met in a spirit of candor and calmness, and decided upon as a matter of duty. Now, sir, the resolutions which I have immediately under consideration propose a decision of these questions. I have said that there is scarcely a resolution in the series I have offered that did not contain some mutual concession, or evidence of mutual forbearance; that the concession was not altogether from the non-slaveholding States, or the slaveholding States. These resolutions propose a boundary to Texas. What is it? We know the diversity of opinion which exists in the country upon the subject of that boundary. We know that a very large portion of the people of the United States have supposed that the western limit of Texas was the Nueces—that it did not extend to the Rio Grande. We know that the question of what is the western limit and the northern limit of Texas, was an open question—has been all along an open question—was an open question when the boundary was run in virtue of the act of 1838 marking the boundary between the United States and Texas. At that time, the boundary authorized by that act of 1838 was to begin at the mouth of the Sabine, run up to its head to the Red river, and thence westwardly, with that river, to the 100° of longitude. Well, that did not go as far as Texas now claims, and why? Because it was an open question. War was waging between Texas and Mexico, and it was at that time impossible to say what might ultimately be established as the western and northern limits of Texas. But when we come to the question of what was done at the time of her annexation, the whole resolution which relates to boundaries, from beginning to end, assumes an open, unascertained, and unfixed boundary to Texas on the west. What is the first part of the resolution? It is "that Congress doth consent that the territory properly included within and rightfully belonging to Texas may be erected into a new State." "Properly included"—"rightfully belonging." It specifies no boundaries—it could specify no boundary. It assumes the state of uncertainty which in point of fact we know existed.

Now, sir, what does the resolution further provide? Why, "first, said State to be formed, subject to the adjustment by this Government of all questions of boundary that may arise with other Governments." These boundaries at the west and north, it was asserted, the Government of the United States retained to itself the power to settle with any foreign power.

It is impossible for me to go into the whole question. I mean to express rather my opinion than to go into the whole extent of the argument. The western boundary of Texas being unsettled, and Congress retaining to itself the power to settle it, I ask, suppose that power had been exercised, and that no cession of territory to the United States had ensued, and that the negotiations between the two countries had been limited to the settlement of the western and northern limits of Texas, could it not have been done by the United States and Mexico conjointly? Suppose that a treaty of limits of Texas had been concluded between Mexico and the United States, fixing the Nueces as the boundary, would not Texas have been bound by it? Or suppose it had been the Rio Grande, Colorado, or any other point, whatever limit had been fixed upon by the joint act of the two Powers, would it not have been obligatory upon Texas, by the express terms of the resolution by which it was annexed?

Well now, if Mexico and the United States conjointly, by treaty, might have fixed upon the western and northern limits of Texas, and if the United States have acquired all the territory on which the two Powers acting together must have established the limits of Texas, have not the United States, in virtue of that cession to them, become solely and exclusively possessed of all the power which they jointly had prior to the cession? It seems to me, that the conclusion and reasoning are perfectly irresistible. If Mexico and the United States could have fixed upon any western limits for Texas, and did not do it, and if the United States have acquired to themselves by the treaty any extent of the territory upon which the western limit was to be fixed, and must be fixed, it seems to me that no one can resist the logical conclusion that the United States now has the power to do what the United States and Mexico conjointly could have done. I admit that it is a delicate power—an extremely delicate power. I admit that it ought to be exercised with a spirit of justice, generosity, and liberality, towards this youngest member of the great American family.

Possibly if the United States fixes it in a way contrary to the desire and rights of Texas, she might bring it before the Supreme Court of the United States, and have the question again decided. I say possibly, because I am not of that class of politicians who believe that every question is a proper question for the Supreme Court of the United States. There are questions too large for any tribunal of that kind to decide—great political, national, and territorial questions, which transcend their limits, and to which they are utterly incompetent. Whether this is one or not, I will not decide; but I will maintain that the United States are now invested solely and exclusively with that power which was in both nations—to fix, ascertain, and settle the western and northern limits of Texas.

Sir, the other day my honorable friend who represents so well the State of Texas, [Mr. RUSK,] said that we had no more right to touch the limits of Texas than we have to touch the limits of Kentucky; that the State is one and indivisible, and that the Federal Government has no right to separate it. I agree with him that, when the limits are certain and ascertained, they are undisputed and indisputable. The General Government has no right or power to interfere with the limits of a State whose boundaries are fixed, known, ascertained, and recognized—no power, at least, to interfere with it voluntarily. An extreme case may be put—one which I trust in God never will happen to this Union—of a conquered nation, and of a constitution adapting itself to the state of subjugation and conquest to which it has been reduced; and the giving up of whole States, as well as parts of the State, in order to save what remains from the conquering arm of the successful invader. I say such a power may possibly exist for a case or extremity such as this; and I admit that, short of such an extremity, voluntarily, the General Government has no right to separate a State, or to take any portion of its territory from it, or to regard it otherwise than an integer—one and indivisible.

But then I assume—what does not exist in the State of Texas—that this boundary was known, ascertained, and indisputable. On the contrary, it was open—it was unfixed, and remains unfixed to this moment, with respect to her western limits and north of the head of the Nueces. Why, sir, we gave fifteen millions of dollars for these territories that we bought—and God knows what a costly bargain to this country that was! We gave fifteen millions of dollars for the territories ceded by Mexico to us, and can Texas justly, fairly, and honorably claim all she has asserted a right to, without paying any portion of that fifteen millions of dollars? She talks, indeed, about the United States being her agent—her trustee. Why, sir, she was no more her agent or trustee than she was the agent or trustee of any other part of the United States.

Texas involved the United States in a war with Mexico; I make no reproaches—none—none. Texas brought them into the war; but when they got into it, it was not a war of Texas and Mexico—it was a war of the whole thirty States with Mexico—a war in which the Government of the United States conducted the hostilities, and was as much the trustee and agent of the twenty-nine other States composing this Union as she was the trustee and agent of Texas. With respect to all circumstances on which Texas relies to make out a title to New Mexico, such as the map annexed to the recent treaty with Mexico, and the opinions of individuals, highly respectable and eminently elevated individuals, as was the lamented Mr. Polk, late President of the United States, I must say it was his individual opinion, that he had no right, as President of the United States, or in any other character, otherwise than as negotiating with Mexico—and then the Senate had to act in concurrence with him—to fix a boundary. In respect to that map, which is attached to the treaty, it is sufficient to say that the treaty itself is silent, from beginning to end, upon the limits of Texas; and the annexing of the map to the treaty no more confirms the truth of anything delineated upon that map in relation to Texas than it does in relation to any other geographical subject which composes the map.

Mr. President, I have said that I thought the power has been concentrated in the United States to fix upon the limits of Texas. I have said that this power ought to be exercised in a spirit of great liberality and justice, and I put it to you, to say, upon this second resolution of mine, whether that liberality and justice have not been displayed in the resolution. What is proposed? To confine her to the Nueces? No, sir. To extend it from the Sabine to the mouth of the Rio Grande—and thence up the Rio Grande to the southern limits of New Mexico, and thence, with that limit, to the boundary between the United States and Spain, as marked out under the treaty of 1819. Why, sir, here is a vast country. I have made no estimate about it, but I believe it is equal in amount of acres—of square miles—to what Texas east of the Nueces and extending to the Sabine had before. But who is there that can say, with truth and justice, that there is no reciprocity, no concession, in these resolutions made to Texas, even with reference to the question of boundary line? They give her a vast country, equal in amount nearly, I repeat, to what she indisputably possessed before—a country sufficiently large, with her consent hereafter, to carve out of it some two or three additional States, when the condition and number of the population may render it expedient to make new States. Well, sir, is not that concession, liberality, and justice?

But, sir, that is not all we propose to give. The second resolution proposes to pay a certain amount of the debt of Texas. A blank is left because I have not hitherto been able to ascertain the amount.

Mr. FOOTE. Will the honorable Senator allow me to make a motion that we now go into Executive session, in order to enable him to finish his remarks to-morrow?

Mr. CLAY. I do not think it will be possible for me to conclude to-day, although I wished to go through as much as possible.

Mr. FOOTE. I will make the motion at any time that the Senator may feel disposed to give way.

Mr. CLAY. If the Senate will allow me, I will merely conclude what I have to say in relation to Texas, and then I will give way it the Senator desires.

Mr. President, I was about to remark, independent of the most liberal and generous boundary tendered to Texas, we propose to offer by this second resolution a sum which the worthy Senator from Texas, in my eye, thinks will not be less than about three millions of dollars—the exact amount neither he nor I yet possesses the requisite materials to ascertain. Well, you get this large boundary and three millions of your debt paid. I shall not repeat the argument I offered upon a former occasion as to the obligation of the United States to pay that debt, but

I was struck upon reading the treaty of limits, first between the United States and Mexico, then the treaty of limits between the United States and Texas, to find, in the preamble of both these treaties, a direct recognition of the principles, out of which, I think, spring our obligations to pay the debt for which the duties of foreign imports were pledged while Texas was an independent State.

The principle asserted in the treaties of limits with Mexico is, that whereas, by the treaty of 1819, between Spain and the United States, a limit was fixed between Mexico and the United States, Mexico composing then a portion of the possessions of the Spanish Crown, although Mexico was, at the date of the treaty with her, severed from the crown of Spain, yet she was bound, as having been a part of the crown of Spain when the treaty of 1819 was made—she was bound by that treaty as much as if it was made with herself instead of Spain. In other words, that preamble asserts that the severance of any part of a common empire cannot exonerate either portion of that empire from the obligations which are created when the empire was entire and unsevered. So the same principle is asserted in the treaty of 1838 between Texas and the United States; the principle asserted being that the treaty of 1828 between Mexico and the United States having been made when Texas was a part of Mexico, and now Texas being dissevered from Mexico, she nevertheless remains bound by that treaty as if no such severance had taken place. In other words, the principle is this: that when an independent Power creates an obligation or duty, no subsequent political misfortune—no subsequent political severance of the territory of that Power—can exonerate it from the obligations which were created while it was an independent Power. In other words, to bring it down and apply it to this specific case: Texas being an independent Power, and having a right to take loans and to make pledges, having taken loans, and having pledged the specific imports arising from the customs to the public creditor, the public creditor became vested with a right to that fund, of which he could not be divested by any other act but his own consent—by no political changes which Texas might subsequently think proper to make. In the absorption or merging of Texas in the United States, the creditor, being no party to the treaty by which that operation was performed, did not lose his rights, but retained his rights to demand the fulfillment of the pledge and the appropriation of the fund, just as if there had never been any annexation of Texas to the United States.

That was the foundation upon which I arrived at the conclusion embraced in that resolution. The United States, having appropriated to themselves the duties arising from imports which have been pledged to the creditor by Texas, as an honorable and just Power, ought now to pay the debt for which these duties were solemnly pledged by a Power independent and competent to make the pledge.

Well, sir, I think that were you to give to Texas the large boundary that is assigned to her, when you take into view the abhorrence—for I think I am warranted in using that expression—with which the people of New Mexico, east of the Rio Grande, would look upon any political connection with Texas, and when you take into view the large amount of money, liberating and exonerating Texas from a portion of her public debts, equal to that amount—when you take all these circumstances into consideration, I think they present a case, with regard to which, I confess, I should be greatly surprised, if the people of Texas themselves, when they come to deliberate upon this seriously, should hesitate a moment to accede.

I have finished my remarks upon this resolution, and if the Senator wishes it, I will give way to an adjournment.

Mr. FOOTE moved that the Senate proceed to the consideration of executive business, but gave way to

Mr. MANGUM, who moved an adjournment; which was agreed to, and

The Senate thereupon adjourned.

———

SECOND DAY.—Wednesday, *February 6, 1850*.

Mr. CLAY resumed, and concluded his speech, as follows:

He said: Mr. President, if there be in this vast assemblage of beauty, grace, elegance, and intelligence, any who have come here under the expectation that the humble individual who now addresses you means to attempt any display, or to use any ambitious language, any extraordinary ornaments or decorations of speech, they will be utterly disappointed. The season of the year, and my own season of life, both admonish me to abstain from the use of any unnecessary ornaments; but, above all, Mr. President, the grave and momentous subject upon which it is my duty to address the Senate and the country forbids my saying anything but what appertains strictly to that subject; and my sole desire is to make myself, with seriousness, soberness, and plainness, understood by you and by those who think proper to listen to me.

When, yesterday, the adjournment of the Senate took place, at that stage of the discussion of the resolutions which I have submitted which related to Texas and her boundaries, I thought I had concluded the whole subject; but I was reminded by a friend that perhaps I was not sufficiently explicit upon a single point, and that is, the relation of Texas to the Government of the United States, in regard to that portion of the debts of Texas for which I think a responsibility exists upon the part of the Government of the United States. It was said that it might perhaps be understood, that in the proposed grant of three millions—or whatever may be the sum when it may be ascertained—to Texas, in consideration of her surrender of her title to New Mexico, on this side of the Rio Grande, in that grant we merely discharge the obligation which exist upon the part of the Government of the United States in consequence of the appropriation of the imports receivable in the ports of Texas while she was an independent Power. But that is not my understanding, Mr. President, of the subject as between Texas and the United States. The obligation on the part of Texas to pay the portion the debt referred to, is complete and uncancelled; and there is, as between these two parties, no obligation on the part of the United States to discharge one dollar of the public debt of Texas. On the contrary, by an express declaration in the resolution of admission, it is declared and provided that in no event are the United States to be liable to or charged with any portion of the debt or liabilities of Texas. It is not, therefore, from any responsibility which exists to the State of Texas on the part of the Government of the United States, that I think provision ought to be made for that debt. No such thing. As between these two parties, the responsibility upon the part of Texas is complete to pay the debt, and there is no responsibility upon the part of the United States to pay one cent of it. But then there is a third party, no party to the annexation whatever—that is to say, the creditor of Texas, who advanced his money upon the credit and faith of a solemn pledge made by Texas to him to reimburse the loan, and by the appropriation of the duties receivable upon foreign imports. The last is the party to whom we are bound, according to the view I presented upon the subject. Nor, sir, can the other creditors of Texas complain that a provision is made for a particular portion of the debt, leaving the residue unprovided for by the United States; because in so far as we may extinguish any portion of the debt of Texas, under which she is now bound, in so far we shall contribute to the benefit of the residue of the creditors of Texas by leaving the funds of the public lands held by Texas, and what other sources she may have applicable to the payment of those other debts with more effect than if the entire debt, including the pledged portion of it, as well as the unpledged, was obligatory upon her, and she stood bound by it.

Nor can those creditors complain, for another reason. Texas has all the resources which she had when an independent Power; with the exception of the duties receivable in her ports upon foreign imports; and she is exempted from certain charges, expenditures and responsibilities which she would have had to encounter if she had remained a separate and independent Power. For example, she would have had to provide for a certain amount of naval force, in order to protect herself against Mexico or against any foreign enemy whatever; but, by her annexation to the United States she becomes liberated from all those charges, and of course those entire revenues my be applied to the payment of her debts, except those only which are applicable to the support of the Government of Texas. But, if the United States should discharge that portion of the debt of Texas for which the duties on foreign imports were pledged, Texas would become the debtor of the United States to the extent of the extinguished debt. With this explanation of that part of the subject, I pass to the next resolution in the series which I had the honor to submit. It relates, if I am not mistaken, to this District:

5th. *Resolved*, That it is inexpedient to abolish slavery in the District of Columbia, whilst that institution continues to exist in the State of

Maryland, without the consent of that State, without the consent of the people of the District, and without just compensation to the owners of slaves within the District.

Mr. President, an objection was made to this resolution by some honorable Senators upon the other side of this body, that it did not contain an assertion of the unconstitutionality of the exercise of the power of abolition upon the part of Congress, with regard to this District. I said then, as I have uniformly maintained in this body, as I contended in 1838, and ever have done, that the power to abolish slavery in the District of Columbia has been vested in Congress by language too clear and explicit to admit, in my judgment, of any rational question whatever.

What is the language of the Constitution? Congress shall have power "To exercise exclusive legislation in all cases whatsoever, over such District, not exceeding ten miles square, as may, by cession of particular States, and the acceptance of Congress, become the seat of the Government of the United States."

Congress, by this grant of power, is invested with all legislation whatsoever over the District. Not only is it here invested, but it is exclusively invested with all legislation whatsoever over the District. Now, can we conceive of any language more particular and comprehensive than that which invests a legislative body with exclusive power, in all cases whatsoever, of legislation over a given district of territory or country? Let me ask, is there any power to abolish slavery in this District? Let me suppose, in addition to what I suggested the other day, that slavery had been abolished in Maryland and Virginia; let me add to that supposition that it was abolished in all the States in the Union, is there power then to abolish slavery within the District of Columbia, or is slavery planted here to all eternity, without the possibility of the exercise of any legislative power for its abolition? It cannot be invested in Maryland, because the power with which Congress is invested is exclusive. Maryland, therefore, is excluded, as all the other States of the Union are excluded. It is here, or it is nowhere.

This was the view which I took in 1838, and I think there is nothing in the resolution which I offered upon that occasion incompatible with the view which I now present, and which this resolution contains. While I admitted the power to exist in Congress, and exclusively in Congress, to legislate in all cases whatsoever—and consequently in the case of the abolition of slavery within this District, if it deemed it proper to do so—I admitted upon that occasion, as I contend now, that it was a power which Congress cannot, in conscience and good faith, exercise while the institution of slavery continues within the State of Maryland. The question is a good deal altered now from what it was twelve years ago, when the resolution to which I allude was adopted by the Senate. Upon that occasion Virginia and Maryland were both concerned in the exercise of the power; but, in the retrocession of the portion of the District which lies south of the Potomac, Virginia has become no more interested in the question of the abolition of slavery in the rest of the District than any other slaveholding State in the Union is interested in its abolition. The question now is confined to Maryland. I said upon that occasion, that, although the power was complete and perfect to abolish slavery, yet that it was a thing which never could have entered into the conception of Maryland or Virginia that slavery would be abolished here while slavery continued to exist in either of those two ceding States. I said, moreover, what the granting of the power itself indicates, that, although exclusive legislation in all cases over the District was invested by Congress within the ten miles square, it was to make it the seat of government of the United States. That was the great, paramount, substantial object of the grant. And, in exercising all the powers with which we are invested, complete and full as they may be, yet the great purpose of the concession having been to create a suitable seat of government, that ought to be the leading and controlling idea with Congress in the exercise of this power. And inasmuch as it is not necessary, in order to render it a proper and suitable seat of government of the United States, that slavery should be abolished within the limits of the ten miles square; and inasmuch as, at the time of the cession, in a spirit of generosity, immediately after the formation of this Constitution, when all was peace, and harmony, and concord—when brotherly affection, fraternal feeling, prevailed throughout this whole Union— when Maryland and Virginia, in a moment of generous impulse, and with feelings of high regard towards the principles of this Union, chose to make this grant—neither party could have suspected that at some distant and future period, after the agitation of this unfortunate subject, their generous grant, without equivalent, was to be turned against them, and the sword was to be lifted, as it were within their own bosom, to strike at their own hearts. This implied faith, this honorable obligation, this honesty and propriety of keeping in constant view the object of the cession—these were the considerations which, in 1838, urged me, as they now influence me, in the preparation of the resolution which I have submitted for your consideration. Now, as then, I do think that Congress, as an honorable body, acting in good faith, according to the nature and purpose, and objects of the cession at the time it was made, and looking at the condition of the ceding States at this time—Congress cannot, without forfeiture of all those obligations of honor which men of honor, and nations of honor, will respect as much as if they were found literally, in so many words, in the bond itself, interfere with the institution of slavery in this District, without a violation of those obligations, not, in my opinion, less sacred or less binding than if they had been inserted in the constitutional instrument itself.

Well, what does the resolution propose? The resolution, neither affirms nor disaffirms the constitutionality of the exercise of the power of abolition in the District. It is silent upon the subject. It says that it is inexpedient to do it but upon certain conditions. And what are those conditions? Why, first, that the State of Maryland shall give its consent; in other words, that the State of Maryland shall release the United States from the obligation of that implied faith which I contend is connected with the act of cession by Maryland to the Untied States. Well, if Maryland, the only State now that ceded any portion of the territory which remains to us, will consent; in other words, if she releases Congress from the obligation growing out of the cession with regard to slavery, I consider that that would remove one of the obstacles to the exercise of the power, if it were deemed expedient to exercise it; but it is only removing one of them. There are two other conditions which are inserted in this resolution. The first is the consent of the people of the District.

Mr. President, the condition of the people of this District is anomalous—a condition in violation of the great principle which lies at the bottom of our own free institutions, and of all free institutions, because it is the case of a people who are acted upon by legislative authority, and taxed by legislative authority, without having any voice in the administration of affairs. The Government of the United States, in respect to the people of the District, is a tyranny, an absolute Government—not exercised hitherto, I admit, and I hope it will never be so exercised, tyrannically or arbitrarily; but it is in the nature of all arbitrary power; for if I were to give a definition of arbitrary authority, I would say it is that power which is exercised by an authority over a people who have no voice nor influence in the enactment of laws, or the imposition of taxes; and that is the precise condition of the people to whom I have referred.

Well, that being their condition, and this question of the abolition of slavery affecting them in all the relations of life which we can imagine—of property, society, comfort, peace— I think we should require, as another of the conditions upon which alone this power should be exercised, the consent of the people of the District of Columbia. And I have not stopped there. This resolution requires still a third condition, and that is, that slavery shall not be abolished within the District of Columbia, although Maryland consents, and although the people of the District itself consent, without the third condition—that of making compensation to the owners of the slaves within the District. And, sir, it is immaterial to me upon what basis this obligation to compensate the slaveholders in the District for such slaves as may be liberated under the authority of Congress is placed. There is a clause, an amendment of the Constitution of the United States, which provides that no property—no private property—shall be taken for public use, without just compensation to the owners of such property. Well, I think, that in a just and liberal interpretation of that clause, we are restrained from taking the property of the people of the District of Columbia in slaves, in consideration of any public policy, without full and complete compensation. But if there be no constitutional restriction, such as is contained in the amendment I have referred to, upon principles of eternal justice it is wrong to deprive those who have property in slaves in this District of that property without compensation.

No one of the European powers—Great Britain, France, nor any other of the powers which have undertaken to abolish slavery in their colonies—have ever ventured to do it without making compensation to the owners. They were under no such constitutional obligation as I have referred to; but they were under that obligation to which all men ought to bow— that obligation of eternal justice, which declares that no man ought to be deprived of his property without full and just compensation for its value. Whether under the constitutional provision or not, the case is the same. I know, sir, that it has been argued that this clause of the Constitution which requires compensation to be made for property, when taken by the Government for the public use, would not apply to the case of the abolition of slavery, because the property is not taken by the Government *for* the public use. Perhaps literally it would not be taken for the use of the public; but it would be taken in consideration of a policy and a purpose adopted by the Government for the good of the public, or one which it was deemed expedient to carry into full effect and operation. By a liberal interpretation of the clause, it seems to me, however, that slave property would be so far regarded—that it *ought* to be so far regarded—as taken for the use of the public, or at the instance of the public, as to entitle the owners of the slaves so taken to a compensation, under and by virtue of the clause itself, to the full extent of the value of the slaves liberated. It appears to me that this is an effectual and constitutional restriction upon the power of Congress over the subject of slavery within this District. If this be not so, then the power is unrestricted—I mean unrestricted by any constitutional injunction or inhibition. But the restriction imposed by the obligation of justice remains; and I contend that that would be sufficient to render it oppressive and tyrannical to use the power, without at the same time making the compensation. I put it to gentlemen whether that would not be a better condition for the slave-holders of the District, than to assume the rigid application of the amendment of the Constitution to which I have referred? It would always be an equitable, and, I doubt not, a sufficient cause for exacting from Congress a full and just compensation for the value of the property taken.

Mr. President, I said on yesterday that there was no one of these resolutions, except the first, which contained any concession by either party, that did not either contain some mutual concession by the two parties, or did not contain concessions altogether from the North to the South. Now, with respect to the resolution under consideration; the North has contended that the power exists under the Constitution to abolish slavery here. I am aware that the South, or a greater portion of the South, have contended for the opposite doctrine. What does this resolution ask? It asks of both parties to forbear urging their respective opinions the one to the exclusion of the other. But it concedes to the South all that the South, it appears to me, ought in reason to demand, inasmuch as it requires such conditions as amount to an absolute security for the property in slaves within the District—such conditions as will make the existence of slavery in the District coeval and coextensive with its existence in any of the States out of or beyond the District. The second clause of this resolution provides that it is expedient to prohibit within the District the trade in slaves brought into it.

Mr. President, if it be conceded that Congress has the power of legislation—exclusive legislation—in all cases whatsoever, how can it be doubted that Congress has the power to prohibit what is called the slave trade within the District of Columbia? My interpretation of the Constitution is this: that with regard to all those portions of jurisdiction which operate upon the States, Congress can exercise no power which is not granted, or not a necessary implication from a granted power. Such is the rule for the action of Congress in relation to its legislation upon the States. But in relation to its legislation upon this District, the reverse, I take it, is the true rule—that Congress has all power which is not prohibited by some provision of the Constitution of the United States. In other words, Congress has a power within the District equivalent to and coextensive with the power which any State itself possesses within its own limits. Well, can any one doubt the power and right of any State in this Union—of any slaveholding State—to forbid the introduction as merchandise of slaves within its own limits? Why almost every slaveholding State in the Union has exercised its power to prohibit the introduction of slaves as merchandise. It is in the constitution of my own State; and after all the agitation and excitement upon the subject of slavery which has existed in the State of Kentucky during the last year, the same principle is incorporated in the new constitution. It is in the constitution, I know, of Mississippi also. That State prohibits the introduction of slaves within its limits as merchandise. I believe it to be in the constitution or in the laws of Maryland and Virginia, and in the laws of most of the slaveholding States. It is true, that the policy of the several slaveholding States has vacillated from time to time upon this subject—sometimes tolerating and sometimes excluding the trade; but there has never been the slightest diversity of opinion as to the right—no departure from the great principle that every one of them has the power and authority to prohibit the introduction of slaves within their respective limits, if they choose to exercise it.

Well, then, I really do not think that this resolution, which proposes to abolish that trade, ought to be considered as a concession by either class of States to the other class. I think it should be regarded as an object, acceptable to both, conformable to the wishes and feelings of both; and yet, sir, in these times of fearful and alarming excitement—in these times when every night that I go to sleep, and every morning when I awake, it is with the apprehension of some new and terrible tidings upon this agitating subject—I have seen, sir, that in one of the neighboring States, amongst the various contingencies which are enumerated, upon the happening of any one of which, delegates are to be sent to a famous Convention, to assemble in Nashville in June next—amongst the substantive causes for which delegates are to be sent to the Convention to which I refer, one is, if Congress abolishes the slave trade within the District of Columbia. That is to be the cause for assembling in convention—in other words, cause for considering whether this Union ought to be dissolved or not. Is it possible to contemplate a greater extent of wildness and extravagance to which men can be carried by the indulgence of their passions? Why, sir, there has been no time in my public life—in which statement I concur with what was said the other day by the honorable Senator from Alabama [Mr. KING]—there has been no time in my public life that I was not willing, for one, to coöperate in any steps for the abolition of the slave trade in the District of Columbia. I was willing to do so while the other portion of the District south of the Potomac remained attached; and there is still less ground for objection now that a large portion of the District has been retroceded to Virginia, and when the motive or reason for concentrating slaves here in depôt, for the purpose of transporting them to distant foreign markets is lessened to the extent of the diminution of the territory by the act of retrocession. Why should the slave traders who buy their slaves in Maryland or Virginia, come here with them, in order to transport them to New Orleans or other southern markets? Why not transport them from the States in which they are purchased? Why should the feelings of those who are outraged by the scenes that are exhibited, by the *corteges* which pass along our avenues of manacled human beings—not collected in our own District, nor in our own neighborhood, but brought from distant portions of the neighboring States—why should the feelings of those who are outraged by such scenes—who are unable to contemplate such a spectacle without horror—why should they be thus outraged by the continuance of a trade so exceptionable, so repugnant, as this? Sir, it is a concession, I repeat, neither from one class of the States nor the other. It is an object upon which both of them, it seems to me, should readily unite, and which one set of States as well as the other should rejoice to adopt, inasmuch as it lessens by one the causes of irritation and discontent which exist as connected with this subject.

Abolish the slave trade within the District of Columbia; re-assert the doctrine of the resolution of 1838, that by an implied obligation, on the part of Congress, slavery ought not to be abolished within the District of Columbia so long as it remains in the State of Maryland—re-assert the principle of that resolution, and adopt the other measures proposed in these resolutions, or some other similar measures—for I am not attached to anything as the production of my own mind, and am quite willing to adopt instead the better suggestions of anybody else—adopt these or similar measures, and I venture to predict that, instead of the distractions and anxieties which now prevail, we shall have peace and quiet for thirty years hereafter, such as followed the disposition of the same exciting and unhappy subject after the Missouri compromise.

The next resolution is as follows:

7th. *Resolved*, That more effectual provision ought to be made by law, according to the requirement of the Constitution, for the restitution and delivery of persons bound to service or labor in any State, who may escape into any other State or Territory of this Union.

Well, Mr. President, upon this subject, I go with him who goes furthest in the interpretation of that clause in the Constitution which relates to this subject. In my humble opinion, that is a requirement by the Constitution of the United States which is not limited in its operation to the Congress of the United States, but which extends to every State in the Union and to the officers of every State in the Union. And I go one step further. It extends to every *man* in the Union, and devolves upon him the obligation to assist in the recovery of a fugitive slave from labor, who takes refuge in or escapes into one of the free States. And I maintain all this by a fair interpretation of the Constitution. The clause is as follows:

"That no person held to service or labor in one State under the laws thereof, escaping into another, shall, in consequence of any law or regulation therein, be discharged from such service or labor, but shall be delivered up on claim of the party to whom such service or labor may be due."

It will be observed, Mr. President, that this clause in the Constitution is not amongst the enumerated powers granted to Congress—where, if it had been placed, it might have been argued that Congress alone can legislate and carry it into effect—but it is one of the general powers, or one of the general rights secured by this constitution or instrument, and it addresses itself to all who are bound by the Constitution of the United States. Now, the officers of the General Government are bound to take an oath to support the Constitution of the United States. All State officers are required by the Constitution to take an oath to support it, and all men who love their country, and are obedient to its laws, are bound to assist in the execution of those laws, whether fundamental or derivative. I do not say that a private individual is obliged to make the tour of his whole State, in order to assist the owner of a slave to recover his property; but I do say, if he is present when the owner of a slave is about to assert his rights and regain possession of his property, that he, that every man present, whether officer or agent of the State Governments, or private individual, is bound to assist in the execution of the laws of their country. What is the provision? It is that such fugitive "shall be delivered up on claim of the party to whom such service or labor may be due." It has been already remarked, in course of debate upon the bill which is now pending upon this subject, that the terms used in regard to fugitives from criminal offences and fugitives from labor are precisely the same. The fugitive from justice is to be delivered up, and removed to the State having jurisdiction. The fugitive from labor is to be delivered up on claim of the party to whom such service is due. Well, sir, has it ever been contended by any State that she is not bound to surrender a fugitive from justice upon the demand of the State from which he has fled? I think there have been some exceptions to the performance of this duty enjoined in the Constitution, but they have not denied the general right; and if they have refused in any instance to give up the persons demanded, it has been upon some technical or legal ground, not at all as questioning the general right to have the fugitive surrendered on the application to deliver him up, as enjoined by the Constitution.

I think, Mr. President, that with regard to the object of this provision there can be no doubt. It imposes an obligation upon the States—free or slaveholding—it imposes an obligation upon the officers of Government, State or Federal—and I add upon the people of the United States, under particular circumstances —to assist in the recovery and surrender of fugitive slaves from their masters. There has been some confusion, and I think misconception, upon the subject, in consequence of a recent decision of the Supreme Court of the United States. I think that decision has been entirely misapprehended. There is a vast difference between imposing impediments, and affording facilities in the way of recovering the fugitive slave. The Supreme Court of the United States have only decided that the laws of impediments are unconstitutional. I know, sir, there are some general expressions in the opinions to which I have referred—the case of Maryland and Pennsylvania—that would seem to import otherwise; but I think that when you come to attentively read the whole opinions pronounced by the judges, and take the trouble that I have taken to converse with the judges themselves, you will find that the whole extent of the principle which they intended to adopt was, that any laws of impediment enacted by the States were laws forbidden by the provision of the Constitution to which I have referred, and that the General Government had no right to impose obligations upon the State officers that were not imposed by the authority of their own constitutional laws. Why, it is impossible! If the decision had been otherwise, it would have been extrajudicial. The court had no right to decide whether the laws of facility were or were not unconstitutional. The only question before the court was upon the laws of impediment passed by the Legislature of Pennsylvania. If they have gone beyond the case before them to decide upon a case not before them, the decision is what lawyers call "*obiter dictum*," and is not binding upon that court itself, or upon any other tribunal. I say it is utterly impossible for that court with the case before them of the passage of a law by a State Legislature, affording aid and assistance to the owner of the slave to get back his property again; it is utterly impossible that that or any other tribunal should pronounce the decision that such aid and assistance rendered by the authorities of the State under this provision of the Constitution of the United States was unconstitutional and void. The court has not said so; and even if they had said so, they would have transcended their authority, and gone beyond the case which was before them.

The laws passed by States in order to assist the General Government, so far from being laws repugnant to the Constitution, are rather to be regarded as laws carrying out, enforcing, and fulfilling the constitutional duties which are created by that instrument. Why, sir, as well might it be contended that if Congress were to declare war—and no one will doubt that the power to declare war is vested exclusively in Congress, and that no State has a right to it—no one will contend that after the declaration of war it would be unconstitutional on the part of any State to lend its aid and assistance for the vigorous and effectual prosecution of that war. And yet it would be just as unconstitutional to lend their aid to a successful and glorious termination of that war in which we might be engaged, as it would be unconstitutional for them to assist in the performance of a high duty which presents itself to all the States and to all the people in all the States. Then, Mr. President, I think that the whole class of legislation, beginning in the northern States, and extending to some of the western States, by which obstructions and impediments have been thrown in the way of the recovery of fugitive slaves, are unconstitutional, and have originated in a spirit which I trust will correct itself when these States come to consider calmly upon the nature of their duty. Of all the States in this Union, unless it be the State of Virginia, the State of which I am a citizen suffers most by the escape of slaves to adjoining States. I have but little doubt that the loss of Kentucky, in consequence of the escape of her slaves, is greater, in proportion to the total number of slaves which are held in that Commonwealth than it is in the State of Virginia; and I know too well, and so do the honorable Senators from Ohio know, that it is at the utmost hazard and insecurity of life itself, that a Kentuckian can cross the river and go into the interior and take back the fugitive slave to the State from which he has fled. A recent example occurred in the city of Cincinnati. One of our most respectable citizens having visited—not Ohio at all—but having visited Covington, on the opposite side of the river, a little slave of his escaped over to Cincinnati. He pursued it, recovered it—having found it in a house where he was concealed—took it out; but it was rescued by the violence and force of a negro mob from his possession—the police of the city standing by, and either unwilling or unable to afford assistance to him.

Upon this subject I do think we have just and serious cause of complaint against the free States. I think that they have failed in fulfilling a great obligation, and the failure is precisely upon one of those subjects which in its nature is most irritating and inflammatory to those who live in slave States. Why, sir, I think it is a mark of no good brotherhood, of no kindness, of no courtesy, that a man from a slave State cannot now, in any degree of safety, travel in a free State with his servant, although he has no purpose of stopping there any longer than a short time. Upon this subject, the Legislatures of the free States have altered for the worse in the course of the last twenty or thirty years. Most of those States, until during the period of the last twenty or thirty years, had laws for the benefit of "sojourners," as they were called, passing through or abiding for a time in the free States with their servants. I recollect a case that occurred during the war, of my friend, Mr. Cheeves, from South Carolina. Instead of going home during the vacation, he went to Philadelphia, taking his family and his family servant with him. Some of the abolitionists of that day sued out a *habeas corpus* for the slave, and the question was brought before the Supreme Court of the State of Pennsylvania. It was argued for days; and it was necessary, during the progress of the argument, to refer to a great variety of statutes passed from time to time by the State of Pennsylvania in behalf of the sojourners, guarantying and securing to them the possession of their property during their temporary passage or abode in the Commonwealth. Finally, the court gave their opinion *seriatim*, each judge delivering his separate opinion, until it came to Judge Breckenridge who was the youngest judge upon the bench, to deliver his. During the delivery of their opinions they had frequent occasions to refer to those acts passed for the benefit of sojourners; and each of the judges who preceded Judge Breckenridge always pronounced the word "sudjourner." When it came to Judge Breckenridge to deliver his opinion, he said, "I agree in all my learned brethren have pronounced upon this occasion, except their pronunciation of the word 'sojourner.' They pronounced it 'sudjourner;' and I think it should be pronounced 'sojourner.'" [Laughter.] Now, sir, all these laws in behalf of sojourners in the free States are swept away, I believe, in all the States except Rhode Island.

Mr. DAYTON. And New Jersey.

Mr. CLAY. And in New Jersey, I am happy to hear. But in most of the free States these laws have been abolished, showing a progressive tendency to a bad neighborhood and unkind action upon the part of the free States towards the slaveholding States. Well, sir, I do not mean to contest the ground; I am not going to argue the question whether if a man voluntarily carries his slave into a free State, he is or is not entitled to his freedom. I am not going to argue that question. I know what its decision has been in the North. What I mean to say is, that it is unkind, unneighborly, it is not in the spirit of that fraternal connection existing between all parts of this Confederacy. But as to the exact and legal principle in the way suggested, even supposing the right is here, it is but proper, when there is no purpose of a permanent abode—of settling finally and conclusively—of planting his slaves in the Commonwealth—it is but the right of good neighborhood, and kind and friendly feeling, to allow the owner of the slave to pass with his property unmolested.

Allow me to say upon this subject, that, of all the instances in which the power is exercised to seduce slaves from their owners, there is no instance in which it is exercised so unjustly as in the case of the seduction of family servants from the service of their owners. Servants in the families are treated with all the kindness with which the children of the family are treated. Everything they want for their comfort is given to them with the most liberal indulgence. I have known more instances than one, where, by this practice of seduction of family servants from their owners into free States, they have been rendered wretched and unhappy. In an instance in my own family, the seduced slave addressed her mistress, begging and imploring her to furnish her the means of getting back from the state of freedom into which she had been seduced, into the state of slavery, in which she was much more happy. She returned to the State of Kentucky and to her mistress from whom she had been seduced.

Now, Mr. President, I think that the existing laws for the recovery of fugitive slaves, and the restoration and delivering of them to their owners, being often inadequate and ineffective, it is incumbent upon Congress—(and I hope that hereafter, when a better state of feeling, when more harmony and good-will prevails among the various parts of this Confederacy—I hope it will be regarded by the free States themselves as a part of their duty)—to assist in allaying this subject, so irritating and disturbing to the peace of this Union. At all events, whether they do it or not, it is our duty to do it. It is our duty to make the laws more effective; and I will go with the furthest Senator from the South in this body to make penal laws, to impose the heaviest sanctions upon the recovery of fugitive slaves, and the restoration of them to their owners.

While upon this part of the subject, however, allow me to make one observation or two. I do not think that States, as States, are to be held responsible for all the misconduct of particular individuals within those States. I think States are to be held responsible only when they act in their sovereign capacity. If there are a few persons indiscreet—mad, if you choose—fanatics, if you choose to call them so—who are for dissolving the Union—(and we know there are some at the North who are for dissolving it, in consequence of the connection which exists between the free and slaveholding States,)—I do not think that any State ought to be held responsible for the doctrines which they propagate, unless the State, itself adopts those doctrines.

There have been, perhaps, mutual causes of complaint. I know—at least I have heard—that Massachusetts, in apology for some of her unfriendly laws upon the subject of the recovery of fugitive slaves, urges the treatment which a certain minister of hers received in Charleston, South Carolina, some years ago. A most respectable, venerable, and worthy man, (Mr. Hoar,) was sent by Massachusetts to South Carolina to take care of the free negroes of Massachusetts that might pass to Charleston in any of the vessels of Massachusetts. I think it was a mission hardly worthy for Massachusetts to have created. I think she might as well have omitted to send Mr. Hoar upon any such mission as that. She thought it her right, however, and sent him upon that mission. He went for the purpose merely, as it was said, to ascertain the rights of the free people of color before the courts of justice—to test the validity of certain laws of South Carolina in regard to the prohibition of free negroes coming into her ports. I believe that was the object— that was the purpose of his mission. He went there, and created no disturbance, as I understand, except so far as asserting these rights and privileges in the sense that Massachusetts had understood them—except so far as her people of color might create disturbance. Well, he was virtually driven out of Charleston, as I believe some other emissary of the same character was driven out of New Orleans. I do not mean to say whether it was right or wrong to expel him from that city; but I do mean to say that Massachusetts, for the treatment towards those whom she chose to consider as citizens of the State of

Massachusetts, on the part of South Carolina, determined upon that course of legislation by which she has withdrawn all aid and assistance, and interposed obstacles to the recovery of fugitive slaves. She gives this as her apology; but I think that it furnished her with no sufficient apology. If South Carolina treated her ill it was no reason why she in turn should treat Virginia, Kentucky, and other States ill. But she thought so. I mention the case of the expulsion from Charleston, and the passage of the laws by Massachusetts—or rather the spirit in which they were passed—not by way of reproach, but to show Senators that there have been, unhappily, mutual causes of irritation, furnished, perhaps, by one class of the States as well as the other, though I admit not in the same degree by slave States as by free States. I admit, also, that the free States have much less cause for any solicitude and inquietude upon this whole subject of slavery than the slave States have, and that far more extensive excuses, if not justification, ought to be extended to the slave States than to the free States, on account of the difference in the condition of the respective parties.

Mr. President, in passing from that resolution, I will add, that when the time comes for final action, I will vote most cordially and willingly for the most stringent measures that can be devised to secure the execution of the consitutional provision it alludes to.

Mr. DAVIS, of Massachusetts, (interposing.) I am unwilling to interrupt the honorable Senator; but if he will permit me, I will say one word in behalf of my State.

Mr. CLAY. Certainly, sir; certainly.

Mr. DAVIS. I have never heard any apology which was offered by Massachusetts for passing the laws to which reference has been made. On the contrary, I have always understood that the laws that Massachusetts had passed for restoring fugitive slaves were repealed because the courts, as they understood them, had pronounced them to be unconstitutional. That is the ground they took. Whether they were wise in the legislation which they adopted, I will not undertake to say. But I wish to add one word in regard to the mission, as it is termed by the honorable Senator from Kentucky, to South Carolina. If I call the facts to my recollection aright, they are these: We are the owners of much shipping; we employ many sailors;

among them we employ free people of color, who are acknowledged in Massachusetts to be citizens of the United States, citizens of the Commonwealth, entitled to the rights of citizens.
These citizens were taken from our vessels when they arrived
in South Carolina, and held in custody until the vessel sailed
again. This our citizens complained of, whether justly or unjustly; they felt that it was an infringement, in the first place, of
the rights of the citizens, and, in the next place, it was a great
inconvenience to men engaged in this trade. If I remember
correctly, and I think I do, the people of the State of Massachusetts authorized their government to propose, at the expense of the State, some proper individual to go to the State of
South Carolina, to contest the right of that State to hold these
citizens in custody in this way, in the courts of the United
States. If I remember, that was the complaint of our citizens;
and the mission to which the honorable Senator refers was
then instituted, and the termination of it I believe he has correctly stated. And I wish it to be understood that Massachusetts had no aggressive purpose whatever, but simply desired
the judicial tribunal to settle the question. They wanted
nothing more—they asked nothing more.

Mr. CLAY. I hear with much pleasure, Mr. President, this
explanation; but I have been informed by an eminent citizen of
Massachusetts, whose name it is not necessary to mention—
not a member of this body—that the motive for the repeal of
those laws of restoration—or the passage of those laws of obstruction—that one of the motives was, the treatment of Mr.
Hoar in Charleston. I am glad to hear that it proceeded from
another cause—from what I conceive to be a misconception of
the decision of the Supreme Court of the United States. When
the true exposition of the opinion comes to be known in Massachusetts, I trust that she will restore all those laws for the recovery of those fugitive slaves that she repealed from a
misconception of that decision.

Mr. President, I have a great deal more to say; but I shall
pass from that resolution with the observation that I believe I
partly made before, that the most stringent provisions upon
this subject that can be devised will meet with my hearty concurrence and coöperation in the passage of the bill under consideration.

The last resolution declares—

"That Congress has no power to prohibit or obstruct the trade in slaves between the slaveholding States; but that the admission or exclusion of slaves brought from one into another or them depends exclusively upon their own particular laws."

This is a concession—not, I admit, of any real constitutional provision, but a concession—of what is understood, I believe, by a great number at the North to be a constitutional provision—from the North to the South, if the resolution be adopted. Take away the decisions of the Supreme Court of the United States on that subject, and I know there is a great deal that might be said on both sides of the subject in relation to the right of Congress to regulate the trade between the States. But I believe the decision of the Supreme Court has been founded upon correct principles; and I hope it will forever put an end to the question whether Congress has or has not the power to regulate the slave trade between the different States.

Such, Mr. President, is the series of resolutions which, with an earnest and anxious desire to present the olive-branch to both parts of this distracted, and at this moment, unhappy country, I thought it my duty to offer. Of all men upon earth, am I the least attached to any productions of my own mind. No man upon earth is more ready than I am to surrender anything which I have proposed, and to accept, in lieu of it, anything which is better. But I put it to the candor of honorable Senators upon the other side, and upon all sides of the Chamber, whether their duty will be performed by simply limiting themselves to objections to any one or two of the series of resolutions which I have offered. If my plan of peace, and accommodation, and harmony, is not right, present us your plan. Let us see a *contre projet*. Let us see how all the questions that have arisen out of this unhappy subject of slavery can be better settled, more fairly and justly settled, to all quarters of the Union, than is proposed in the resolutions which I have offered. Present me such a scheme, and I hail it with pleasure, and will accept it without the slightest feeling of regret that my own is abandoned.

Sir, while I was engaged in anxious consideration upon this subject, the idea of the Missouri compromise, as it has been termed, came under my review, was considered by me, and finally rejected, as in my judgment less worthy of the common acceptance of both parties of this Union than the project which I offer to your consideration.

Mr. President, before I enter into a particular examination, however, of that Missouri compromise, I beg to be allowed to correct a great error, not merely in the Senate, but throughout the whole country, in respect to my agency in regard to the Missouri compromise, or rather the line of 36° 30′, established by the agency of Congress. I do not know whether anything has excited more surprise in my mind as to the rapidity with which important historical transactions are obliterated and pass out of memory, than has the knowledge of the fact that I was everywhere considered the author of the tune of 36° 30′, which was established upon the occasion of the admission of Missouri into the Union.

It would take up too much time to go over the whole of that important era in the public affairs of this country. I shall not attempt it; although I have ample materials before me, derived from a careful and particular examination of the journals of both Houses. I will not occupy your time by going into any detailed account of the whole transaction; but I will content myself with stating that, so far from my having presented as a proposition the line of 36° 30′, upon the occasion of considering whether Missouri ought to be admitted into the Union or not, it did not originate in the House of which I was a member. It originated in this body. Those who will cast their recollection back—and I am sure the honorable Senator from Missouri, [Mr. BENTON,] more correctly perhaps than anybody else—must bring to recollection the fact, that at the first Congress, when the proposition was made to admit Missouri— or rather to permit her to hold a convention and to form a constitution, as preliminary to deciding whether she should be admitted into this Union—the bill failed by a disagreement between the two Houses; the House of Representatives insisting upon, and the Senate dissenting from, the provision contained in the ordinance of 1787; the House insisting upon the interdiction of slavery, and the Senate rejecting the proposition for the interdiction of slavery. The bill failed. It did not pass that session of Congress.

At the next session it was renewed; and at the time of its renewal, Maine was knocking at our door, also, to be admitted into the Union. In the House there was a majority for a restriction of the admission of slavery; in the Senate a majority was opposed to any such restriction. In the Senate, therefore, in order to carry Missouri through, a bill, or provision for her admission—or rather authorizing her to determine the question of her admission, was coupled with the bill for the admission of Maine. They were connected together, and the Senate said to the House, "You want the bill for the admission of Maine passed; you shall not have it, unless you take along with it the bill for the admission of Missouri also." There was a majority—not a very large one, but a very firm and decided majority—in the Senate for coupling them together. Well, the bill went through all the usual stages of disagreement, and of committees of conference, for there were two committees of conference upon the occasion before the matter was finally decided. It was finally settled to disconnect the two bills; to admit Maine separately, without any connection with Missouri, and to insert in the Missouri bill a clause—which was inserted in the Senate of the United States—a clause which was proposed by Mr. Thomas, of Illinois, in the Senate, restricting the admission of slavery north of 36° 30′, and leaving the question open south of 36° 30′, either to admit or not to admit slavery. The bill was finally passed. The committees of conference of the two Houses recommended the detachment of the two bills, and the passage of the Missouri bill with the clause 36° 30′ in it. So it passed. So it went to Missouri. So, for a moment, it quieted the country. But the clause 36° 30′, I repeat, you will find, sir, if you will take the trouble to look into the journals, was, upon three or four different occasions offered. Mr. Thomas, acting in every instance, presented the proposition of 36° 30′, and it was finally agreed to. But I take the occasion to say, that among those who agreed to that line were a majority of southern members. My friend from Alabama, in the Senate, [Mr. KING,] Mr. Pinkney, from Maryland, and a majority of the southern Senators in this body voted in favor of the line 36° 30′; and a majority of the southern members in the other House, at the head of whom was Mr. Lowndes himself, voted also for that line. I have no doubt that I did also; but as I was

Speaker of the House, and as the journal does not show which way the Speaker votes, except in the cases of a tie, I am not able to tell with certainty, how I actually did vote; but I have no earthly doubt that I voted, in common with my other southern friends, for the adoption of the line 36° 30′.

So the matter ended in 1820. During that year Missouri held a convention, adopted a constitution, sent her constitution by her members to Congress, to be admitted into the Union; but she had inadvertently inserted into that constitution a provision to prevent the migration of free people of color into that State. She came here with the constitution containing that provision; and immediately northern members took exception to it. The flame which had been repressed at the previous session now burst out with redoubled force and violence throughout the whole Union. Legislative bodies all got in motion to keep out Missouri, from the Union, in consequence of her interdiction of the admission of free people of color within her limits.

I did not arrive at Washington at that session until January; and when I got here I found both bodies completely paralyzed, by the excitement which had been produced in the struggle to admit or to exclude Missouri from the Union in consequence of that prohibition. Well, I made an effort, first, in the House of Representatives to settle it. I asked for a committee of thirteen, and a committee of thirteen was granted to me, representing all the old States of the Union. That committee met. I presented to the committee a resolution, which was adopted by it, and reported to the House, not unlike the one to which I will presently call the attention of the Senate. We should have carried it through the House but for the votes of Mr. Randolph of Virginia, Mr. Edwards of North Carolina, and Mr. Burton of North Carolina—two, I think, of the three, no longer living. Those three southern votes were all cast against the compromise proposed to the committee of thirteen by myself, as chairman of that committee, and they defeated it.

In that manner things remained for several days. The greatest anxiety prevailed. The country was unsettled; men were unhappy. There was a large majority in the House then—as I hope and trust there is now a large majority in Congress—in favor of the equitable accommodation and settlement of the question. I could have any collateral question passed which I pleased, except that when it came to the vote, by ayes and noes, unfortunately—more unfortunately then than now, I hope, should there be occasion for it—there were but few Curtius's and Leonidas's, ready to risk themselves for the safety and honor of the country. But I endeavored to avail myself, as much as I could of the good feeling that prevailed; and after some days had elapsed, I brought forward another proposition, and a new one, perfectly unpractised upon in the country, before or since, so far as I know. I proposed a joint committee of the two Houses; that of the House consisted of twenty-three members; that of the Senate of—I do not recollect precisely how many, but of a proper number, to meet the committee of the House; and that this committee be appointed by ballot. At that time, Mr. Taylor, of New York, was in the chair; and Mr. Taylor had been the very man who had first proposed the restriction upon Missouri that she should only be admitted under the provisions of the ordinance of 1787. I proposed, therefore, that the committee should be chosen by ballot. Well, sir, my motion was carried by a large majority, and members came to me from all quarters of the House asking—who, Mr. Clay, do you want to serve with you upon that committee? I named my selection; and I venture to say that there happened upon that occasion what would hardly happen again; eighteen of the twenty-three were elected upon the first ballot, and the remaining five, having the largest number of votes, but not a majority, were appointed upon my list. I moved to dispense with further balloting, and to take those five gentlemen who had received the greatest number of votes, with the eighteen actually elected, to compose the Committee of twenty-three. One or two gentlemen—Mr. Livermore, of New Hampshire, and one or two other gentlemen—declined, and very much to my regret, and somewhat to my annoyance, the lamented Mr. Randolph and one other gentleman were placed in their situation. I forget whether it was done by ballot or by the Speaker. The Senate immediately agreed to the proposition, and appointed its committee.

We met. It was in this hall, upon the Sabbath day, within two or three days of the close of the session, when the whole nation was listening with breathless anxiety for some final and healing measure upon that distracting subject. We met here,

and upon that day. The moment we met, Mr. Randolph made
a suggestion which I knew would be attended with the greatest embarrassment and difficulty. He contended that when the
two committees of the two Houses met together, the chairman of the committee of the House, who was myself, had a
right to preside. He was about insisting at some length upon
that proposition, that the chairman of the committee of the
House should preside over both committees when blended
together—should be the presiding officer of both. I instantly
opposed, however, this plan, and stated that I did not consider
this the proper mode, but I thought that the chairman of the
committee of each House should preside over his own committee, and when the committee of either branch had adopted
a proposition, it should be submitted to the committee of the
other branch, and if they also agreed in it, then it should be reported back to the two Houses with the recommendation of
both committees. That mode was agreed upon, and Mr.
Holmes, I think it was, from Maine, presided over the committee of the Senate. I—if I could be said to preside at all, when
I took a more active part in the chair than I could have well
taken out of it; and when, as at this session, I was thought to
manifest a desire rather to take too much lead—presided over
the committee of the House. I brought forward the proposition which I will read presently, and I appealed to the members
of the committee, if I may use the expression. Now, gentlemen,
said I, we do not want a proposition carried here by a small
majority, thereupon reported to the House, and rejected. I am
for something practical, something conclusive, something decisive upon the question. How will you vote, Mr. A.? How will
you vote, Mr. B.? How will you vote, Mr. C.? I appealed in that
way to the gentlemen of the North. To my very great happiness, a sufficient number of them responded affirmatively to my
question whether they would vote for this proposition, to enable me to be confident that, if they continued to vote in that
way—of which I had not a particle of doubt—in the House we
should carry the proposition. Accordingly, that proposition
having been agreed upon by both committees, was reported
by us to our respective Houses, where it was finally adopted,
and here it is.

[Mr. C. here commenced reading a resolution but discontinued, stating that it was not that to which he referred. A messenger went in search of the volume containing the resolution, and Mr. CLAY proceeded.]

That resolution, I said, was finally adopted. Probably I can state, without reading it, what its provisions are. It declares that if there be any provisions in the constitution of Missouri incompatible with the Constitution of the United States, the State of Missouri shall forbear to enforce that repugnant provision in that constitution, and that she shall by some solemn and authentic act, declare that she will not enforce any provision in her constitution incompatible with the Constitution of the United States; and upon the passage of such a solemn and authentic act, the President of the United States—who was Mr. Monroe at that time—shall make a proclamation of the fact, and thereupon, and without any further legislation of Congress, Missouri shall be admitted into the Union.

Now, sir, I want to call your attention to this period of our history, and to the transactions during the progress of this discussion in Congress. During the discussion in the House, from day to day and from night to night—for they frequently ran into the night—we, who were for admitting Missouri into the Union, said to our brethren from the North, why, gentlemen, if there be any provision in that constitution of Missouri which is repugnant to the Constitution of the United States, it is a nullity. The Constitution of the United States, by virtue of its own operation, vindicates itself. There is not a tribunal upon earth, if the question should be brought before them, but would pronounce the Constitution of the United States paramount, and must pronounce as invalid any repugnant provision of the constitution of Missouri. Sir, that argument was turned and twisted, and used in every possible variety of form; but all was in vain. An inflexible majority stuck out to the last against the admission of Missouri, until the resolution was offered and passed.

Mr. UNDERWOOD, at the request of Mr. CLAY, here read the resolution as follows:

Resolution providing for the admission of the State of Missouri into the Union on a certain condition.

Resolved by the Senate and House of Representatives of the United States of America in Congress assembled, That Missouri shall be admitted into this Union on an equal footing with the original States in all respects whatever, upon the fundamental condition that the fourth clause of the 26th section of the third article of the constitution, submitted on the part of said State to Congress, shall never be construed to authorize the passage of any law, and that no law shall be passed in conformity thereto, by which any citizen of either of the states in this Union shall be excluded from the enjoyment of any of the privileges and immunities to which such citizen is entitled under the Constitution of the United States: *Provided,* That the Legislature of the said State, by a solemn public act, shall declare the assent of the said State to the said fundamental condition, and shall transmit to the President of the United States, on or before the fourth Monday in November next, an authentic copy of the said act; upon the receipt whereof, the President, by proclamation, shall announce the fact; whereupon, and without any further proceeding on the part of Congress, the admission of the said State into this Union shall be considered as complete.

[Approved, March 2, 1821.

Mr. CLAY resumed. There is the resolution, sir, and you see it is precisely as I stated. After all this excitement throughout the country had reached to such an alarming point, that the Union itself was supposed to be in the most imminent peril and danger, all parties were satisfied with a declaration of an incontestable principle of constitutional law, that when the constitution of a State is violative, in its provisions, of the Constitution of the United States, the Constitution of the United States is to be paramount, and the constitution of the State in that particular is a nullity and void. That was all. They wanted something for a justification of the course which they took. There is a great deal of language there of a high-sounding character; it shall be a "fundamental" act—it shall be a "solemn and an authentic" act; but at last, when you come to strip it of all its verbiage, it is nothing more than the principle I have announced of the paramount character of the Constitution of the United States over any local constitution of any one of the States of this Union.

Mr. President, we may draw from these transactions in our history this moral, I hope. Now, as then, if we will only suffer our reason to have its scope and sway, and if we will still and hush the passion and excitement which have been created by the occasion, difficulties will be more than half removed in the settlement, upon just and amicable principles, of the question which unhappily divides us at this moment.

But, I wish to contrast the plan of accommodation which is proposed by me with that which is offered by the Missouri line, to be extended to the Pacific ocean, and to ask gentlemen from the South and from the North, too, which is most proper, which most just, to which is there the least cause of objection? What was done, sir, by the Missouri line? Slavery was positively interdicted north of that line. The question of the admission or exclusion of slavery south of that line was not settled. There was no provision that slavery should be admitted south of that line. In point of fact, it existed there. In all the territory south of 36° 30', embraced in Arkansas and Louisiana, slavery was then existing. It was not necessary, it is true, to insert a clause admitting slavery at that time. But, if there is a power to interdict, there is a power to admit; and I put it to gentlemen from the South, are they prepared to be satisfied with the line of 36° 30', interdicting slavery north of that line, and giving them no security for the admission of slavery south of that line? The Senator from Mississippi [Mr. DAVIS] told us, the other day, that he was not prepared to be satisfied with anything short of the positive introduction of slavery.

A SENATOR. Recognition.

Mr. CLAY. A positive recognition of slavery south of the line of 36° 30'. Is there anybody who believes that you can get twenty votes in this body, or a proportionate number in the other House, to declare in favor of the recognition of slavery south of the line of 36° 30'? It is impossible. All that you can get—all that you can expect to get—all that was proposed at the last session—is action north of that line, and non-action as regards slavery south of that line. It is interdiction upon the one side, with no corresponding provision for its admission on the other side of the line of 36° 30'.

When I came to consider the subject, and to compare the provisions of the line of 36° 30'—the Missouri compromise line —with the plan which I have proposed for the accommodation of this question, said I to myself, if I offer the line of 36° 30', to interdict the question of slavery north of it, and to leave it unsettled and open south of it, I offer that which is illusory to the South—I offer that which will deceive them, if they suppose that slavery will be received south of that line. It is better for them—I said to myself—it is better for the South, that there should be non-action as to slavery both north and south of the line—far better that there should be non-action both sides of the line, than that there should be action by the interdiction on the one side, without action for the admission upon the other side of the line. Is it not so? What is there gained by the South, if the Missouri line is extended to the Pacific, with the interdiction of slavery north of it? Why, the very argument which has been most often and most seriously urged by the South has been this: we do not want Congress to legislate upon the subject of slavery at all; you ought not to touch it. You have no power over it. I do not concur, as is well known from what I have said upon that question, in this view of the subject; but that is the southern argument. We do not want you, say they, to legislate upon the subject of slavery. But if you adopt the Missouri line and thus interdict slavery north of that line, you do legislate upon the subject of slavery, and you legislate for its restriction without a corresponding equivalent of legislation south of that line for its admission; for I insist that if there be legislation interdicting slavery north of the line, then the principles of equality would require that there should be legislation admitting slavery south of the line.

I have said that I never could vote for it myself, and I repeat that I never can, and never will vote, and no earthly power will ever make me vote, to spread slavery over territory where it does not exist. Still, if there be a majority who are for interdicting slavery north of the line, there ought to be a majority, if justice is done to the South, to admit slavery south of the line. And if there be a majority to accomplish both of these purposes, although I cannot concur in their action, yet I shall be one of the last to create any disturbance; I shall be one of the first to acquiesce in that legislation, although it is contrary to my own judgment and to my own conscience.

I hope then to keep the whole of these matters untouched by any legislation of Congress upon the subject of slavery, leaving it open and undecided. Non-action by Congress is best for the South, and best for all the views which the South have disclosed to us from time to time as corresponding to their wishes. I know it has been said with regard to the territories, and especially has it been said with regard to California, that non-legislation upon the part of Congress implies the same thing as the exclusion of slavery. That we cannot help. That Congress is not responsible for. If nature has pronounced the doom of slavery in these territories—if she has declared, by her immutable laws, that slavery cannot and shall not be introduced there—who can you reproach but nature and nature's God? Congress you cannot. Congress abstains. Congress is passive. Congress is non-acting, south and north of the line; or rather if Congress agrees to the plan which I propose, extending no line, it leaves the entire theatre of the whole cession of these territories untouched by legislative enactments, either to exclude or admit slavery. Well, I ask again, if you will listen to the voice of calm and dispassionate reason—I ask of any man of the South, to rise and tell me if it is not better for that section of the Union, that Congress should remain passive upon both sides of the ideal line, rather than that we should interdict slavery upon the one side of that line and be passive upon the other side of that line?

I am taxing both the physical and intellectual powers which a kind Providence has bestowed upon me too much, and I will endeavor soon to conclude; for I do not desire to trespass upon the time and patience of the Senate.

Mr. MANGUM having offered to make a motion to adjourn,

Mr. CLAY said: No, sir; no sir; if the Senate will bear with me, I think I can go through with it better to-day than I could to-morrow.

Mr. President, this Union is threatened with subversion. I desire to take a very rapid glance at the course of public measures in this Union presently. I wanted, however, before I did that, to ask the Senate to look back upon the career which this country has run from the adoption of the Constitution down to the present day. Was there ever a nation upon which the sun of heaven has shone which has exhibited so much of prosperity as our own? At the commencement of this Government, our population amounted to about four millions. It has now reached upwards of twenty millions. Our territory was limited chiefly and principally to that bordering upon the Atlantic ocean, and that which includes the southern shores of the interior lakes of our country. Our territory now extends from the northern provinces of Great Britain to the Rio Grande and the Gulf of Mexico; from the Atlantic ocean on the one side, to the Pacific on the other; the largest extent of territory under one Government existing upon earth, with only two solitary exceptions. Our tonnage, from being nothing, has risen to a magnitude and amount to rival that of the nation which has been proudly called the mistress of the ocean. We have gone through many wars; one with that very nation from whom in 1776, we broke off, as weak and feeble colonies, when we asserted our independence as a member of the family of nations. And, sir, we came out of that struggle—unequal as it was, armed as she was at all points, in consequence of the long struggles of Europe, and unarmed as we were at all points, in consequence of the habits and nature of our country and its institutions—we came out of that war without the loss of any honor whatever; we emerged from it gloriously. In every Indian war—we have been engaged in many of them—our arms have been triumphant. And without speaking at all as to the causes of the recent war with Mexico, whether they were right or wrong, and abstaining from the expression of any opinion as to the justice or propriety of the war when it commenced, all must unite in respect to the gallantry of our arms, and the glory of our triumphs. There is no page—there are no pages of history which record more brilliant successes. With respect to the one in command of an important portion of our army, I need say nothing in praise of him who has been borne by the voice of his country to the highest station in it, mainly on account of his glorious military career. But of another military commander, less fortunate in other respects, I must take the opportunity of saying, that for skill—for science—for strategy— for bold and daring fighting—for chivalry of individuals and of masses—that portion of the Mexican war which was conducted by the gallant Scott as chief commander, stands unrivaled either by the deeds of Cortes himself, or by those of any other commander in ancient or modern times.

Our prosperity is unbounded. Nay, Mr. President, I sometimes fear that it is the very wantonness of our prosperity that leads us to these threatening ills of the moment, that restlessness and these erratic schemes throughout the whole country, some of which have even found their way into legislative halls.

We want, I fear, the chastising wand of Heaven to bring us back to a sense of the immeasurable benefits and blessings which have been bestowed upon us by Providence. At this moment, with the exception of here and there a particular department in the manufacturing business of the country, all is prosperous and happy—both the rich and poor. Our nation has grown to a magnitude in power and in greatness, to command the respect, if it does not call for the apprehensions of all the powers of the earth with which we can come in contact. Sir, do I depict with colors too lively the prosperity which has resulted to us from the operation of the Constitution under which we live? Have I exaggerated in any degree?

Now, let me go a little into detail as to the sway in the councils of the nation, whether of the North or of the South, during the sixty years of unparalleled prosperity that we enjoy. During the first twelve years of the administration of the Government, northern counsels rather prevailed; and out of them sprung the Bank of the United States; the assumption of the State debts; bounties to the fisheries; protection to the domestic manufactures—I allude to the act of 1789; neutrality in the wars with Europe; Jay's treaty; alien and sedition laws; and a *quasi* war with France. I do not say, sir, that those leading and prominent measures which were adopted during the administration of Washington and the elder Adams were carried exclusively by northern counsels. They could not have been, but were carried mainly by the sway which northern counsels had obtained in the affairs of the country.

So, also, with the latter party, for the last fifty years. I do not mean to say that southern counsels alone have carried the measures which I am about to enumerate. I know they could not exclusively have carried them; but I say they have been carried by their preponderating influence, with coöperation, it is true, and large coöperation, in some instances, from the northern section of the Union.

And what are those measures during the fifty years that southern counsels have preponderated? The embargo and other commercial restrictions of non-intercourse and non-importation; war with Great Britain; the Bank of the United States overthrown; protection to domestic manufactures enlarged and extended; (I allude to the passage of the act of 1815 or 1816;) the Bank of the United States reëstablished; the same bank put down; reëstablished by southern counsels and put down by southern counsels; Louisiana acquired; Florida bought; Texas annexed; war with Mexico; California and other Territories acquired from Mexico by conquest and purchase; protection superseded and free trade established; Indians removed west of the Missouri; fifteen new States admitted into the Union. I may very possibly have omitted some of the important measures which have been adopted during the later period or time to which I have referred—the last fifty years; but these I believe are the most prominent.

I do not deduce from the enumeration of the acts of the one side or the other, any just cause of reproach to the one side or the other, although one side or the other has predominated in the two periods to which I have referred. It has been at least the work of both, and neither need justly reproach the other. But I must say, in all candor and sincerity, that least of all ought the South to reproach the North, when we look at the long list of measures we have had under our sway in the councils of the nation, and which have been adopted as the policy of the Government; when we reflect that even opposite doctrines have been prominently advanced by the South and carried at different times. A Bank of the United States was established under the administration of Mr. Madison, with the coöperation of the South. I do not, when I speak of the South or the North, speak of the entire South or North. I speak of the prominent and larger proportion of the South or North. It was during Mr. Madison's administration that the Bank of the United States was established. The friend [Mr. CALHOUN] whose sickness I again deplore, as it prevents us from having his attendance here upon this occasion, was the chairman of the committee of the House of Representatives, and carried the measure through Congress. I voted for it with all my heart, although I had been instrumental in putting down the old Bank of the United States. I had changed my mind; and I coöperated in the establishment of the bank of 1816. That same bank was again put down by southern counsels, with General Jackson at their head, at a later period. Then, with respect to the policy of protection: the South in 1815—I mean the prominent and leading men of the South, Lowndes, Calhoun, and others—united in extending a certain measure of protection to the domestic manufactures of the South, as well as of the North. You find, a few years afterwards, that the South opposes the most serious objection to this policy, at least one member of the Union staking upon that objection the dissolution of the Union.

Let us take another view; and of these several views no one is brought forward in any spirit of reproach, but in a spirit of conciliation—not to provoke or exasperate, but to quiet and produce harmony and repose, if possible. What have been the territorial acquisitions made by this country, and to what interests have they conduced? Florida, where slavery exists, has been introduced. All the most valuable parts of Louisiana have also added to the extent and consideration of the slaveholding portion of the Union; for although there is a large extent of that territory north of 36° 30′, yet, in point of intrinsic value and importance, I would not give the single State of Louisiana for the whole of it. All Louisiana, with the exception of what lies north of 36° 30′, including Oregon, to which we obtained title mainly on the ground of its being a part of the acquisition of Louisiana; all Texas, all the territories which have been acquired by the Government of the United States during sixty years of the operation of that Government, have been slave territories— theatres of slavery—with the exception I have mentioned lying north of the line of 36° 30′. But how was it in the case of a war made essentially by the South, growing out of the annexation of Texas, which was a measure pressed by the South upon the councils of the country, and which led to the war with Mexico? I do not say of the whole South; but a major portion of the South pressed the annexation of Texas upon the country, and that led to a war with Mexico, and to the ultimate acquisition of these territories, which now constitute the bone of contention between the members of the Confederacy. And now, when, for the first time, any free territory—after these great acquisitions in Florida, Louisiana, and Texas, had been made and redounded to the benefit of the South—now, when, for the first time, free territories are attempted to be introduced—territories without the institution of slavery, I put it to the hearts of my countrymen of the South, if it is right to press matters to the disastrous consequences that have been intimated no longer ago than this very morning, upon the presentation of the resolutions from North Carolina.

A SENATOR here offered to move an adjournment.

Mr. CLAY. Mr. President, I hope the Senate will only have the goodness—if I don't tire out their patience, to permit me to go on. I would prefer concluding to-day. I begin to see land. I shall pretty soon arrive at the end. I had much rather occupy half an hour now than leave what I have to say for to-morrow— to trespass upon the patience of the Senate another day.

Such is the Union, and such are its glorious fruits. We are told now, and it is rung throughout this entire county, that the Union is threatened with subversion and destruction. Well, the first question which naturally arises is, supposing the Union to be dissolved—having all the causes of grievances which are complained of—how far will a dissolution furnish a remedy for those grievances? If the Union is to be dissolved for any existing causes, it will be dissolved because slavery is interdicted or not allowed to be introduced into the ceded territories; because slavery is threatened to be abolished in the District of Columbia, and because fugitive slaves are not returned, as in my opinion they ought to be, restored to their masters. These I believe will be the causes, if there be any causes, which can lead to the direful event to which I have referred.

Well, now, let us suppose that the Union has been dissolved. What remedy does it furnish for the grievances complained of in its united condition? Will you be able to push slavery into the ceded territories? How are you to do it, supposing the North—all the States north of the Potomac, and which are opposed to it—in possession of the navy and army of the United States? Can you expect, if there is a dissolution of the Union, that you can carry slavery into California and New Mexico? You cannot dream of such a purpose. If it were abolished in the District of Columbia, and the Union was dissolved, would the dissolution of the Union restore slavery in the District of Columbia? Are you safer in the recovery of your fugitive slaves in a state of dissolution or of severance of the Union, than you are in the Union itself? Why, what is the state of the fact *in* the Union? You lose *some* slaves. You recover some others. Let me advert to a fact which I ought to have introduced before, because it is highly creditable to the courts and juries of the free

States. In every case, so far as my information extends, where an appeal has been made to the courts of justice for the recovery of fugitives, or for the recovery of penalties inflicted upon persons who have assisted in decoying slaves from their masters and aiding them in escaping from their masters—as far as I am informed, the courts have asserted the rights of the owner, and the juries have promptly returned adequate verdicts in favor of the owner. Well, this is some remedy. What would you have if the Union were dissevered? Why, sir, then the severed parts would be independent of each other—foreign countries! Slaves taken from the one into the other would be there like slaves now escaping from the United States into Canada. There would be no right of extradition—no right to demand your slaves—no right to appeal to the courts of justice to demand your slaves which escape, or the penalties for decoying them. Where one slave escapes now, by running away from his owner, hundreds and thousands would escape if the Union were severed in parts—I care not where nor how you run the line, if independent sovereignties were established.

Well, finally, will you, in a state of dissolution of the Union, be safer with your slaves within the bosom of the States than you are now? Mr. President, that they will escape much more frequently from the border States, no one will doubt.

But, I must take the occasion to say that, in my opinion, there is no right on the part of one or more of the States to secede from the Union. War and the dissolution of the Union are identical and inseparable. There can be no dissolution of the Union, except by consent or by war. No one can expect, in the existing state of things, that that consent would be given, and war is the only alternative by which a dissolution could be accomplished. And, Mr. President, if consent were given—if possibly we were to separate by mutual agreement and by a given line, in less than sixty days after such an agreement had been executed, war would break out between the free and slaveholding portions of this Union—between the two independent portions into which it would be erected in virtue of the act of separation. Yes, sir, sixty days—in *less* time than sixty days, I believe, our slaves from Kentucky would be fleeing over in numbers to the other side of the river, would be pursued by their owners, and the excitable and ardent spirits who would engage in the pursuit would be restrained by no sense of the rights which appertain to the independence of the other side of the river, supposing it, then, to be the line of separation. They would pursue their slaves; they would be repelled, and war would break out. In less than sixty days, war would be blazing forth in every part of this now happy and peaceable land.

But how are you going to separate them? In my humble opinion, Mr. President, we should begin at least with three Confederacies—the Confederacy of the North, the Confederacy of the Atlantic southern States, (the slaveholding States,) and the Confederacy of the Valley of the Mississippi. My life upon it, sir, that vast population that has already concentrated, and will concentrate, upon the head-waters and tributaries of the Mississippi, will never consent that the mouth of that river shall be held subject to the power of any foreign State whatever. Such I believe would be the consequences of a dissolution of the Union. But other Confederacies would spring up, from time to time, as dissatisfaction and discontent were disseminated over the country. There would be the Confederacy of the Lakes—perhaps the Confederacy of New England, and of the middle States.

But, sir, the veil which covers these sad and disastrous events that lie beyond a possible rupture of this Union is too thick to be penetrated or lifted by any mortal eye or hand.

Mr. President, I am directly opposed to any purpose of secession, of separation. I am for staying within the Union, and defying any portion of this Union to expel or drive me out of the Union. I am for staying within the Union, and fighting for my rights—if necessary, with the sword—within the bounds and under the safeguard of the Union. I am for vindicating these rights; but not by being driven out of the Union rashly and unceremoniously by any portion of this Confederacy. Here I am within it, and here I mean to stand and die; as far as my individual purposes or wishes can go—within it to protect myself, and to defy all power upon earth to expel me or drive me from the situation in which I am placed. Will there not be more safety in fighting within the Union than without it?

Suppose your rights to be violated; suppose wrongs to be done you, aggressions to be perpetrated upon you, cannot you better fight and vindicate them, if you have occasion to resort to that last necessity of the sword, within the Union, and with the sympathies of a large portion of the population of the Union of these States differently constituted from you, than you can fight and vindicate your rights, expelled from the Union, and driven from it without ceremony and without authority?

I said that I thought that there was no right on the part of one or more of the States to secede from this Union. I think that the Constitution of the thirteen States was made, not merely for the generation which then existed, but for posterity, undefined, unlimited, permanent and perpetual—for their posterity, and for every subsequent State which might come into the Union, binding themselves by that indissoluble bond. It is to remain for that posterity now and forever. Like another of the great relations of private life, it was a marriage that no human authority can dissolve or divorce the parties from; and, if I may be allowed to refer to this same example in private life, let us say what man and wife say to each other: We have mutual faults, nothing in the form of human beings can be perfect; let us, then, be kind to each other, forbearing, conceding; let us live in happiness and peace.

Mr. President, I have said what I solemnly believe—that the dissolution of the Union and war are identical and inseparable; that they are convertible terms.

Such a war, too, as that would be, following the dissolution of the Union! Sir, we may search the pages of history, and none so furious, so bloody, so implacable, so exterminating, from the wars of Greece down, including those of the Commonwealth of England, and the revolution of France—none, none of them raged with such violence, or was ever conducted with such bloodshed and enormities as will that war which shall follow that disastrous event—if that event ever happens—of dissolution.

And what would be its termination? Standing armies and navies, to an extent draining the revenues of each portion of the dissevered empire, would be created; exterminating wars would follow—not a war of two or three years, but of interminable duration—an exterminating war would follow, until some Philip or Alexander, some Cæsar or Napoleon, would rise to cut the Gordian knot, and solve the problem of the capacity of man for self-government, and crush the liberties of both the dissevered portions of this Union. Can you doubt it? Look at history—consult the pages of all history, ancient or modern: look at human nature—look at the character of the contest in which you would be engaged in the supposition of a war following the dissolution of the Union, such as I have suggested—and I ask you if it is possible for you to doubt that the final but perhaps distant termination of the whole will be some despot treading down the liberties of the people?—that the final result will be the extinction of this last and glorious light which is leading all mankind, who are gazing upon it, to cherish hope and anxious expectation that the liberty which prevails here will sooner or later be advanced throughout the civilized world? Can you, Mr. President, lightly contemplate the consequences? Can you yield yourself to a torrent of passion, amidst dangers which I have depicted in colors far short of what would be the reality, if the event should ever happen? I conjure gentlemen—whether from the South or the North, by all they hold dear in this world—by all their love of liberty—by all their veneration for their ancestors—by all their regard for posterity—by all their gratitude to Him who has bestowed upon them such unnumbered blessings—by all the duties which they owe to mankind, and all the duties they owe to themselves—by all these considerations I implore them to pause—solemnly to pause—at the edge of the precipice, before the fearful and disastrous leap is taken in the yawning abyss below, which will inevitably lead to certain and irretrievable destruction.

And, finally, Mr. President, I implore, as the best blessing which Heaven can bestow upon me upon earth, that if the direful and sad event of the dissolution of the Union shall happen, I may not survive to behold the sad and heart-rending spectacle.

JOHN C. CALHOUN

Speech in the Senate on Compromise Resolutions

Washington, D.C., March 4, 1850

As much indisposed as I have been, Mr. President and Senators, I have felt it to be my duty to express to you my sentiments upon the great question which has agitated the country and occupied your attention. And I am under peculiar obligations to the Senate for the very courteous manner in which they have afforded me an opportunity of being heard to-day.

I had hoped that it would have been in my power during the last week to have delivered my views in relation to this all-engrossing subject, but I was prevented from doing so by being attacked by a cold which is at this time so prevalent, and which has retarded the recovery of my strength.

Acting under the advice of my friends, and apprehending that it might not be in my power to deliver my sentiments before the termination of the debate, I have reduced to writing what I intended to say. And, without further remark, I will ask the favor of my friend, the Senator behind me to read it.

MR. MASON. It affords me great pleasure to comply with the request of the honorable Senator, and to read his remarks.

The honorable gentleman then read Mr. Calhoun's remarks as follows:

I have, Senators, believed from the first that the agitation of the subject of slavery would, if not prevented by some timely and effective measure, end in disunion. Entertaining this opinion, I have, on all proper occasions, endeavored to call the attention of both of the two great parties which divide the country to adopt some measure to prevent so great a disaster, but without success. The agitation has been permitted to proceed, with almost no attempt to resist it, until it has reached a period when it can no longer be disguised or denied that the

Union is in danger. You have thus had forced upon you the greatest and the gravest question that can ever come under your consideration—How can the Union be preserved?

To give a satisfactory answer to this mighty question, it is indispensable to have an accurate and thorough knowledge of the nature and the character of the cause by which the Union is endangered. Without such knowledge it is impossible to pronounce, with any certainty, by what measure it can be saved; just as it would be impossible for a physician to pronounce in the case of some dangerous disease, with any certainty, by what remedy the patient could be saved, without similar knowledge of the nature and character of the cause of the disease. The first question, then, presented for consideration, in the investigation I propose to make, in order to obtain such knowledge, is—What is it that has endangered the Union?

To this question there can be but one answer; that the immediate cause is the almost universal discontent which pervades all the States composing the Southern section of the Union. This widely extended discontent is not of recent origin. It commenced with the agitation of the slavery question, and has been increasing ever since. The next question, going one step further back, is—What has caused this widely diffused and almost universal discontent?

It is a great mistake to suppose, as is by some, that it originated with demagogues, who excited the discontent with the intention of aiding their personal advancement, or with the disappointed ambition of certain politicians, who resorted to it as the means of retrieving their fortunes. On the contrary, all the great political influences of the section were arrayed against excitement, and exerted to the utmost to keep the people quiet. The great mass of the people of the South were divided, as in the other section, into Whigs and Democrats. The leaders and the presses of both parties in the South were very solicitous to prevent excitement and to preserve quiet; because it was seen that the effects of the former would necessarily tend to weaken, if not destroy, the political ties which united them with their respective parties in the other section. Those who know the strength of party ties will readily appreciate the immense force which this cause exerted against agitation and in favor of preserving quiet. But, as great as it was, it was not sufficient to prevent the wide-spread discontent which now pervades the section. No; some cause, far deeper and more powerful than the one supposed, must exist, to account for discontent so wide and deep. The question, then, recurs—What is the cause of this discontent? It will be found in the belief of the people of the Southern States, as prevalent as the discontent itself, that they cannot remain, as things now are, consistently with honor and safety, in the Union. The next question to be considered is, what has caused this belief?

One of the causes is, undoubtedly, to be traced to the long-continued agitation of the slave question on the part of the North, and the many aggressions which they have made on the rights of the South during the time. I will not enumerate them at present, as it will be done hereafter in its proper place.

There is another lying back of it, with which this is intimately connected, that may be regarded as the great and primary cause. That is to be found in the fact that the equilibrium between the two sections in the Government, as it stood when the Constitution was ratified and the Government put in action, has been destroyed. At that time there was nearly a perfect equilibrium between the two, which afforded ample means to each to protect itself against the aggression of the other; but, as it now stands, one section has the exclusive power of controlling the Government, which leaves the other without any adequate means of protecting itself against its encroachment and oppression. To place this subject distinctly before you, I have, Senators, prepared a brief statistical statement, showing the relative weight of the two sections in the Government under the first census of 1790 and the last census of 1840.

According to the former, the population of the United States, including Vermont, Kentucky, and Tennessee, which then were in their incipient condition of becoming States, but were not actually admitted, amounted to 3,929,827. Of this number the Northern States had 1,977,899, and the Southern 1,952,072—making a difference of only 25,827 in favor of the former States. The number of States, including Vermont, Kentucky, and Tennessee, were sixteen; of which eight, including Vermont, belonged to the Northern section, and eight, including Kentucky and Tennessee, to the Southern, making an equal division of the States between the two sections under the first census. There was a small preponderance in the House of Representatives, and in the electoral college, in favor of the Northern, owing to the fact that, according to the provisions of the Constitution, in estimating federal numbers, five slaves count but three; but it was too small to affect sensibly the perfect equilibrium, which, with that exception, existed at the time. Such was the equality of the two sections when the States composing them agreed to enter into a Federal Union. Since then the equilibrium between them has been greatly disturbed.

According to the last census the aggregate population of the United States amounted to 17,063,357, of which the Northern section contained 9,728,920, and the Southern 7,334,437, making a difference, in round numbers, of 2,400,000. The number of States had increased from sixteen to twenty-six, making an addition of ten States. In the mean time the position of Delaware had become doubtful as to which section she properly belongs. Considering her as neutral, the Northern States will have thirteen and the Southern States twelve, making a difference in the Senate of two Senators in favor of the former. According to the apportionment under the census of 1840, there were 223 members of the House of Representatives, of which the Northern States had 135, and the Southern States (considering Delaware as neutral) 87, making a difference in favor of the former in the House of Representatives of 48. The difference in the Senate of two members added to this, gives to the North in the electoral college, a majority of 50. Since the census of 1840, four States have been added to the Union: Iowa, Wisconsin, Florida, and Texas. They leave the difference in the Senate as it stood when the census was taken; but add two to the side of the North in the House, making the present majority in the House in its favor of 50, and in the electoral college of 52.

The result of the whole is to give the Northern section a predominance in every department of the Government, and thereby concentrate in it the two elements which constitute the Federal Government; majority of States, and a majority of their population, estimated in federal numbers. Whatever section concentrates the two in itself possesses the control of the entire Government.

But we are just at the close of the sixth decade, and the commencement of the seventh. The census is to be taken this year, which must add greatly to the decided preponderance of the North in House of Representatives and in the electoral college. The prospect is, also, that a great increase will be added to its present preponderance in the Senate during the period of the decade by the addition of new States. Two Territories, Oregon and Minesota, are already in progress, and strenuous efforts are making to bring in three additional States from the territory recently conquered from Mexico; which, if successful, will add three other States in a short time to the Northern section, making five States; and increasing the present number of its States from fifteen to twenty, and of its Senators from thirty to forty. On the contrary, there is not a single Territory in progress in the Southern section, and no certainty that any additional State will be added to it during the decade. The prospect then is, that the two sections in the Senate, should the efforts now made to exclude the South from the newly acquired Territories succeed, will stand, before the end of the decade, twenty Northern States to fourteen Southern, (considering Delaware as neutral,) and forty Northern Senators to twenty-eight Southern. This great increase of Senators, added to the great increase of members of the House of Representatives and electoral college on the part of the North, which must take place under the next decade, will effectually and irretrievably destroy the equilibrium which existed when the Government commenced.

Had this destruction been the operation of time, without the interference of Government, the South would have had no reason to complain; but such was not the fact. It was caused by the legislation of this Government, which was appointed, as the common agent of all, and charged with the protection of the interests and security of all. The legislation by which it has been effected may be classed under three heads. The first is, that series of acts by which the South has been excluded from the common territory belonging to all of the States, as the members of the Federal Union, and which have had the effect of extending vastly the portion allotted to the Northern section, and restricting within narrow limits, the portion left to the South. The next consists in adopting a system of revenue and disbursements, by which an undue proportion of the burden of taxation has been imposed upon the South, and an undue proportion of its proceeds appropriated to the North; and the last is a system of political measures, by which the original character of the Government has been radically changed. I propose to bestow upon each of these, in the order they stand, a few remarks, with the view of showing that it is owing to the action of this Government that the equilibrium between the two sections has been destroyed, and the whole powers of the system centered in a sectional majority.

The first of the series of acts by which the South was deprived of its due share of the Territories, originated with the Confederacy which preceded the existence of this Government. It is to be found in the provision of the ordinance of 1787. Its effect was to exclude the South entirely from that vast and fertile region which lies between the Ohio and the Mississippi rivers, now embracing five States and one Territory. The next of the series is the Missouri compromise, which excluded the South from that large portion of Louisiana which lies north of 36° 30′, excepting what is included in the State of Missouri. The last of the series excluded the South from the whole of the Oregon Territory. All these, in the slang of the day, were what are called slave territories, and not free soil; that is, territories belonging to slaveholding powers and open to the emigration of masters with their slaves. By these several acts, the South was excluded from 1,238,025 square miles, an extent of country considerably exceeding the entire valley of the Mississippi. To the South was left the portion of the Territory of Louisiana lying south of 36° 30′, and the portion north of it included in the State of Missouri. The portion lying south of 36° 30′, including the States of Louisiana and Arkansas, and the territory lying west of the latter and south of 36° 30′, called the Indian country. These, with the Territory of Florida, now the State, makes in the whole, 283,503 square miles. To this must be added the territory acquired with Texas. If the whole should be added to the Southern section, it would make an increase of 325,520, which would make the whole left to the South, 609,023. But a large part of Texas is still in contest between the two sections, which leaves it uncertain what will be the real extent of the portion of territory that may be left to the South.

I have not included the territory recently acquired by the treaty with Mexico. The North is making the most strenuous efforts to appropriate the whole to herself, by excluding the South from every foot of it. If she should succeed, it will add to that from which the South has already been excluded 526,078 square miles, and would increase the whole which the North has appropriated to herself to 1,764,023, not including the portion that she may succeed in excluding us from in Texas. To sum up the whole, the United States since they declared their independence, have acquired 2,373,046 square miles of territory, from which the North will have excluded the South, if she should succeed in monopolizing the newly-acquired territories, about three-fourths of the whole, leaving to the South but about one-fourth.

Such is the first and great cause that has destroyed the equilibrium between the two sections in the Government.

The next is the system of revenue and disbursements which has been adopted by the Government. It is well known that the Government has derived its revenue mainly from duties on imports. I shall not undertake to show that such duties must necessarily fall mainly on the exporting States, and that the South, as the great exporting portion of the Union, has in reality paid vastly more than her due proportion of the revenue; because I deem it unnecessary, as the subject has on so many occasions been fully discussed. Nor shall I, for the same reason, undertake to show that a far greater portion of the revenue has been disbursed at the North, than its due share; and that the joint effect of these causes has been, to transfer a vast amount from South to North, which, under an equal system of revenue and disbursements, would not have been lost to her. If, to this be added, that many of the duties were imposed, not for revenue, but for protection—that is, intended to put money, not in the treasury, but directly into the pocket of the manufacturers, some conception may be formed of the immense amount which, in the long course of sixty years, have been transferred from South to North. There are no data by which it can be estimated with any certainty; but it is safe to say, that it amounts to hundreds of millions of dollars. Under the most moderate estimate, it would be sufficient to add greatly to the wealth of the North, and thus greatly increase her population by attracting emigration from all quarters to that section.

This, combined with the great and primary cause, amply explains why the North has acquired a preponderance over every department of the Government by its disproportionate increase of population and States. The former, as has been shown, has increased in fifty years 2,400,000 over that of the South. This increase of population, during so long a period, is satisfactorily accounted for, by the number of emigrants, and the increase of their descendants, which have been attracted to the Northern section from Europe and the South, in consequence of the advantages derived from the causes assigned. If they had not existed—if the South had retained all the capital which has been extracted from her by the fiscal action of the Government; and, if it had not been excluded by the ordinance of '87 and the Missouri compromise, from the region lying between the Ohio and the Mississippi rivers, and between the Mississippi and the Rocky mountains north of 36° 30'—it scarcely admits of a doubt, that it would have divided the emigration with the North, and by retaining her own people, would have at least equalled the North in population under the census of 1840, and probably under that about to be taken. She would also, if she had retained her equal rights in those territories, have maintained an equality in the number of States with the North, and have preserved the equilibrium between the two sections that existed at the commencement of the Government. The loss then of the equilibrium is to be attributed to the action of this Government.

But while these measures were destroying the equilibrium between the two sections, the action of the Government was leading to a radical change in its character, by concentrating all the power of the system in itself. The occasion will not permit me to trace the measures by which this great change has been consummated. If it did, it would not be difficult to show that the process commenced at an early period of the Government; that it proceeded, almost without interruption, step by step, until it absorbed virtually its entire powers; but without going through the whole process to establish the fact, it may be done satisfactorily by a very short statement.

That the Government claims, and practically maintains, the right to decide in the last resort, as to the extent of its powers, will scarcely be denied by any one conversant with the political history of the country. That it also claims the right to resort to force to maintain whatever power she claims, against all opposition, is equally certain. Indeed it is apparent, from what we daily hear, that this has become the prevailing and fixed opinion of a great majority of the community. Now, I ask, what limitation can possibly be placed upon the powers of a government claiming and exercising such rights? And, if none can be, how can the separate governments of the States maintain and protect the powers reserved to them by the Constitution, or the people of the several States maintain those, which are reserved to them, and among others, the sovereign powers by which they ordained and established, not only their separate State Constitutions and Governments, but also the Constitution and Government of the United States? But, if they have no constitutional means of maintaining them against the right claimed by this Government, it necessarily follows, that they hold them at its pleasure and discretion, and that all the powers of the system are in reality concentrated in it. It also follows, that the character of the Government has been changed in consequence, from a federal Republic, as it originally came from the hands of its framers, into a great national consolidated Democracy. It has indeed, at present, all the characteristics of the latter and not one of the former, although it still retains its outward form.

The result of the whole of these causes combined is, that the North has acquired a decided ascendancy over every department of this Government, and through it a control over all the powers of the system. A single section governed by the will of the numerical majority, has now, in fact, the control of the Government and the entire powers of the system. What was once a constitutional federal Republic, is now converted, in reality, into one as absolute as that of the Autocrat of Russia, and as despotic in its tendency, as any absolute government that ever existed.

As then, the North has the absolute control over the Government, it is manifest, that on all questions between it and the South, where there is a diversity of interests, the interest of the latter will be sacrificed to the former, however oppressive the effects may be, as the South possesses no means by which it can resist, through the action of the Government. But if there was no question of vital importance to the South, in reference to which there was a diversity of views between the two sections, this state of things might be endured, without the hazard of destruction to the South. But such is not the fact. There is a question of vital importance to the Southern section, in reference to which the views and feelings of the two sections are as opposite and hostile as they can possibly be.

I refer to the relation between the two races in the Southern section, which constitutes a vital portion of her social organization. Every portion of the North entertains views and feelings more or less hostile to it. Those most opposed and hostile, regard it as a sin, and consider themselves under the most sacred obligation to use every effort to destroy it. Indeed to the extent that they conceive they have power, they regard themselves as implicated in the sin, and responsible for suppressing it, by the use of all and every means. Those less opposed and hostile, regard it as a crime—an offence against humanity, as they call it; and although not so fanatical, feel themselves bound to use all efforts to effect the same object, while those who are least opposed and hostile, regard it as a blot and a stain on the character, of what they call the Nation, and feel themselves accordingly bound to give it no countenance or support. On the contrary, the Southern section regards the relation as one which cannot be destroyed without subjecting the two races to the greatest calamity, and the section to poverty, desolation, and wretchedness; and accordingly they feel bound, by every consideration of interest and safety, to defend it.

This hostile feeling on the part of the North towards the social organization of the South, long lay dormant, but it only required some cause to act on those who felt most intensely that they were responsible for its continuance, to call it into action. The increasing power of this Government, and of the control of the Northern section over all its departments, furnished the cause. It was this which made an impression on the minds of many, that there was little, or no restraint, to prevent the Government from doing whatever it might choose to do. This was sufficient of itself to put the most fanatical portion of the North in action for the purpose of destroying the existing relation between the two races in the South.

The first organized movement towards it commenced in 1835. Then, for the first time, societies were organized, presses established, lecturers sent forth to excite the people of the North, and incendiary publications scattered over the whole South, through the mail. The South was thoroughly aroused. Meetings were held everywhere, and resolutions adopted, calling upon the North to apply a remedy to arrest the threatened evil, and pledging themselves to adopt measures for their own protection, if it was not arrested. At the meeting of Congress petitions poured in from the North, calling upon Congress to abolish slavery in the District of Columbia, and to prohibit what they called the internal slave trade between the States, announcing at the same time, that their ultimate object was to abolish slavery, not only in the District, but in the States and throughout the Union. At this period, the number engaged in the agitation was small, and possessed little or no personal influence.

Neither party in Congress had, at that time, any sympathy with them, or their cause. The members of each party presented their petitions with great reluctance. Nevertheless, as small and contemptible as the party then was, both of the great parties of the North dreaded them. They felt, that though small, they were organized in reference to a subject which had a great and a commanding influence over the Northern mind. Each party, on that account, feared to oppose their petitions, lest the opposite party should take advantage of the one who might do so, by favoring their petitions. The effect was that both united in insisting that the petitions should be received, and that Congress should take jurisdiction of the subject for which they prayed. To justify their course, they took the extraordinary ground, that Congress was bound to receive petitions on every subject, however objectionable it might be, and whether they had or had not jurisdiction over the subject. These views prevailed in the House of Representatives, and partially in the Senate, and thus the party succeeded in their first movements in gaining what they proposed—a position in Congress, from which agitation could be extended over the whole Union. This was the commencement of the agitation, which has ever since continued, and which, as is now acknowledged, has endangered the Union itself.

As for myself, I believed at that early period, if the party who got up the petitions should succeed in getting Congress to take jurisdiction, that agitation would follow, and that it would in the end, if not arrested, destroy the Union. I then so expressed myself in debate, and called upon both parties to take grounds against assuming jurisdiction, but in vain. Had my voice been heeded, and had Congress refused to take jurisdiction, by the united votes of all parties, the agitation which followed would have been prevented, and the fanatical zeal that gives impulse to the agitation, and which has brought us to our present perilous condition, would have become extinguished from the want of fuel to feed the flame. *That* was the time for the North to show her devotion to the Union; but unfortunately both of the great parties of that section were so intent on obtaining or retaining party ascendency, that all other considerations were overlooked or forgotten.

What has since followed are but the natural consequences. With the success of their first movement, this small fanatical party began to acquire strength; and with that, to become an object of courtship to both the great parties. The necessary consequence was, a further increase of power, and a gradual tainting of the opinions of both of the other parties with their doctrines, until the infection has extended over both; and the great mass of the population of the North, who, whatever may be their opinion of the original abolition party, which still preserves its distinctive organization, hardly ever fail, when it comes to acting, to co-operate in carrying out their measures. With the increase of their influence, they extended the sphere of their action. In a short time after the commencement of their first movement, they had acquired sufficient influence to induce the Legislatures of most of the Northern States to pass acts, which in effect abrogated the provision of the Constitution that provides for the delivery up of fugitive slaves. Not long after, petitions followed to abolish slavery in forts, magazines, and dockyards, and all other places where Congress had exclusive power of legislation. This was followed by petitions and resolutions of Legislatures of the Northern States and popular meetings, to exclude the Southern States from all Territories acquired, or to be acquired, and to prevent the admission of any State hereafter into the Union, which, by its Constitution, does not prohibit slavery. And Congress is invoked to do all this expressly with the view of the final abolition of slavery in the States. That has been avowed to be the ultimate object from the beginning of the agitation until the present time; and yet the great body of both parties of the North, with the full knowledge of the fact, although disavowing the abolitionists, have co-operated with them in almost all their measures.

Such is a brief history of the agitation, as far as it has yet advanced. Now I ask, Senators, what is there to prevent its further progress, until it fulfils the ultimate end proposed, unless some decisive measure should be adopted to prevent it? Has any one of the causes, which has added to its increase from its original small and contemptible beginning until it has attained its present magnitude, diminished in force? Is the original cause of the movement, that slavery is a sin, and ought to be suppressed, weaker now than at the commencement? Or is the Abolition party less numerous or influential, or have they less influence over, or control over the two great parties of the North in elections? Or has the South greater means of influencing or controlling the movements of this Government now, than it had when the agitation commenced? To all these questions but one answer can be given: no, no, no. The very reverse is true. Instead of being weaker, all the elements in favor of agitation are stronger now than they were in 1835, when it first commenced, while all the elements of influence on the part of the South are weaker. Unless something decisive is done, I again ask, what is to stop this agitation, before the great and final object at which it aims—the abolition of slavery in the States—is consummated? Is it, then, not certain that if something decisive is not now done to arrest it, the South will be forced to choose between abolition and secession? Indeed, as events are now moving, it will not require the South to secede to dissolve the Union. Agitation will of itself effect it, of which its past history furnishes abundant proof, as I shall next proceed to show.

It is a great mistake to suppose that disunion can be effected by a single blow. The cords which bound these States together in one common Union are far too numerous and powerful for that. Disunion must be the work of time. It is only through a long process, and successively, that the cords can be snapped, until the whole fabric falls asunder. Already the agitation of the slavery question has snapped some of the most important, and has greatly weakened all the others, as I shall proceed to show.

The cords that bind the States together are not only many, but various in character. Some are spiritual or ecclesiastical; some political; others social. Some appertain to the benefit conferred by the Union, and others to the feeling of duty and obligation.

The strongest of those of a spiritual and ecclesiastical nature consisted in the unity of the great religious denominations, all of which originally embraced the whole Union. All these denominations, with the exception, perhaps, of the Catholics, were organized very much upon the principle of our political institutions; beginning with smaller meetings corresponding with the political divisions of the country, their organization terminated in one great central assemblage, corresponding very much with the character of Congress. At these meetings the principal clergymen and lay members of the respective denominations from all parts of the Union met to transact business relating to their common concerns. It was not confined to what appertained to the doctrines and discipline of the respective denominations, but extended to plans for disseminating the Bible, establishing missionaries, distributing tracts, and of establishing presses for the publication of tracts, newspapers, and periodicals, with a view of diffusing religious information, and for the support of the doctrines and creeds of the denomination. All this combined contributed greatly to strengthen the bonds of the Union. The strong ties which held each denomination together formed a strong chord to hold the whole Union together; but, as powerful as they were, they have not been able to resist the explosive effect of slavery agitation.

The first of these cords which snapped, under its explosive force, was that of the powerful Methodist Episcopal Church. The numerous and strong ties which held it together are all broke, and its unity gone. They now form separate churches; and, instead of that feeling of attachment and devotion to the interests of the whole church which was formerly felt, they are now arrayed into two hostile bodies, engaged in litigation about what was formerly their common property.

The next cord that snapped was that of the Baptists, one of the largest and most respectable of the denominations. That of the Presbyterian is not entirely snapped, but some of its strands have given away. That of the Episcopal Church is the only one of the four great Protestant denominations which remains unbroken and entire.

The strongest cord, of a political character, consists of the many and strong ties that have held together the two great parties which have, with some modifications, existed from the beginning of the Government. They both extended to every portion of the Union, and strongly contributed to hold all its parts together. But this powerful cord has fared no better than the spiritual. It resisted for a long time the explosive tendency of the agitation, but has finally snapped under its force—if not entirely, in a great measure. Nor is there one of the remaining cords which has not been greatly weakened. To this extent the Union has already been destroyed by agitation, in the only way it can be, by snapping asunder and weakening the cords which bind it together.

If the agitation goes on, the same force, acting with increased intensity, as has been shown, will finally snap every cord, when nothing will be left to hold the States together except force. But, surely, that can, with no propriety of language, be called a Union when the only means by which the weaker is held connected with the stronger portion is *force*. It may, indeed, keep them connected; but the connexion will partake much more of the character of subjugation, on the part of the weaker to the stronger, than the union of free, independent, and sovereign States, in one confederation, as they stood in the early stages of the Government, and which only is worthy of the sacred name of Union.

Having now, Senators, explained what it is that endangers the Union, and traced it to its cause, and explained its nature and character, the question again recurs—How can the Union be saved? To this I answer, there is but one way by which it can be, and that is by adopting such measures as will satisfy the States belonging to the Southern section that they can remain in the Union consistently with their honor and their safety. There is, again, only one way by which that can be effected, and that is by removing the causes by which this belief has been produced. Do *that*, and discontent will cease, harmony and kind feelings between the sections be restored, and every apprehension of danger to the Union removed. The question, then, is—By what can this be done? But, before I undertake to answer this question, I propose to show by what the Union cannot be saved.

It cannot, then, be saved by eulogies on the Union, however splendid or numerous. The cry of "Union, Union—the glorious Union!" can no more prevent disunion than the cry of "Health, health—glorious health!" on the part of the physician, can save a patient lying dangerously ill. So long as the Union, instead of being regarded as a protector, is regarded in the opposite character, by not much less than a majority of the States, it will be in vain to attempt to conciliate them by pronouncing eulogies on it.

Besides, this cry of Union comes commonly from those who we cannot believe to be sincere. It usually comes from our assailants. But we cannot believe them to be sincere; for, if they loved the Union, they would necessarily be devoted to the Constitution. It made the Union, and to destroy the Constitution would be to destroy the Union. But the only reliable and certain evidence of devotion to the Constitution is, to abstain, on the one hand, from violating it, and to repel, on the other, all attempts to violate it. It is only by faithfully performing these high duties that the Constitution can be preserved, and with it the Union.

But how stands the profession of devotion to the Union by our assailants, when brought to this test? Have they abstained from violating the Constitution? Let the many acts passed by the Northern States to set aside and annul the clause of the Constitution providing for the delivery up of fugitive slaves answer. I cite this, not that it is the only instance, (for there are many others,) but because the violation in this particular is too notorious and palpable to be denied. Again: have they stood forth faithfully to repel violations of the Constitution? Let their course in reference to the agitation of the slavery question, which was commenced and has been carried on for fifteen years, avowedly for the purpose of abolishing slavery in the States—an object all acknowledged to be unconstitutional—answer. Let them show a single instance, during this long period, in which they have denounced the agitators or their attempts to effect what is admitted to be unconstitutional, or a single measure which they have brought forward for that purpose. How can we, with all these facts before us, believe that they are sincere in their profession of devotion to the Union, or avoid believing their profession is but intended to increase the vigor of their assaults and to weaken the force of our resistance?

Nor can we regard the profession of devotion to the Union, on the part of those who are not our assailants, as sincere, when they pronounce eulogies upon the Union, evidently with the intent of charging us with disunion, without uttering one word of denunciation against our assailants. If friends of the Union, their course should be to unite with us in repelling these assaults, and denouncing the authors as enemies of the Union. Why they avoid this, and pursue the course they do, it is for them to explain.

Nor can the Union be saved by invoking the name of the illustrious Southerner whose mortal remains repose on the western bank of the Potomac. He was one of us—a slaveholder and a planter. We have studied his history, and find nothing in it to justify submission to wrong. On the contrary, his great fame rests on the solid foundation, that, while he was careful to avoid doing wrong to others, he was prompt and decided in repelling wrong. I trust that, in this respect, we profited by his example.

Nor can we find any thing in his history to deter us from seceding from the Union, should it fail to fulfil the objects for which it was instituted, by being permanently and hopelessly converted into the means of oppressing instead of protecting us. On the contrary, we find much in his example to encourage us, should we be forced to the extremity of deciding between submission and disunion.

There existed then, as well as now, a union—that between parent country and her then colonies. It was a union that had much to endear it to the people of the colonies. Under its protecting and superintending care, the colonies were planted and grew up and prospered, through a long course of years, until they became populous and wealthy. Its benefits were not limited to them. Their extensive agricultural and other productions, gave birth to a flourishing commerce, which richly rewarded the parent country for the trouble and expense of establishing and protecting them. Washington was born and grew up to manhood under that union. He acquired his early distinction in its service, and there is every reason to believe that he was devotedly attached to it. But his devotion was a rational one. He was attached to it, not as an end, but as a means to an end. When it failed to fulfil its end, and, instead of affording protection, was converted into the means of oppressing the colonies, he did not hesitate to draw his sword, and head the great movement by which that union was forever severed, and the independence of these States established. This was the great and crowning glory of his life, which has spread his fame over the whole globe, and will transmit it to the latest posterity.

Nor can the plan proposed by the distinguished Senator from Kentucky, nor that of the Administration, save the Union. I shall pass by, without remark, the plan proposed by the Senator, and proceed directly to the consideration of that of the Administration. I however assure the distinguished and able Senator, that in taking this course, no disrespect whatever is intended to him or his plan. I have adopted it, because so many Senators of distinguished abilities, who were present when he delivered his speech, and explained his plan, and who were fully capable to do justice to the side they support, have replied to him.

The plan of the Administration cannot save the Union, because it can have no effect whatever towards satisfying the States composing the Southern section of the Union, that they can, consistently with safety and honor, remain in the Union. It is in fact but a modification of the Wilmot proviso. It proposes to effect the same object, to exclude the South from all territory acquired by the Mexican treaty. It is well known that the South is united against the Wilmot proviso, and has committed itself by solemn resolutions, to resist, should it be adopted. Its opposition *is not to the name*, but that which it *proposes to effect*. That the Southern States hold to be unconstitutional, unjust, inconsistent with their equality as members of the common Union, and calculated to destroy irretrievably, the equilibrium between the two sections. These objections equally apply to what, for brevity, I will call the Executive proviso. There is no difference between it and the Wilmot, except in the mode of effecting the object, and in that respect I must say, that the latter is much the least objectionable. It goes to its object, openly, boldly, and distinctly. It claims for Congress unlimited power over the Territories, and proposes to assert it over the Territories acquired from Mexico, by a positive prohibition of slavery. Not so the Executive proviso. It takes an indirect course, and in order to elude the Wilmot proviso, and thereby avoid encountering the united and determined resistance of the South, it denies, by implication, the authority of Congress to legislate for the Territories, and claims the right as belonging exclusively to the inhabitants of the Territories. But to effect the object of excluding the South, it takes care, in the mean time, to let in emigrants freely from the Northern States and all other quarters, except from the South, which it takes special care to exclude by holding up to them the danger of having their slaves liberated under the Mexican laws. The necessary consequence is to exclude the South from the Territory, just as effectually as would the Wilmot proviso. The only difference in this respect is, that what one proposes to effect directly and openly, the other proposes to effect indirectly and covertly.

But the Executive proviso is more objectionable than the Wilmot, in another and more important particular. The latter, to effect its object, inflicts a dangerous wound upon the Constitution, by depriving the Southern States, as joint partners and owners of the Territories, of their rights in them; but it inflicts no greater wound than is absolutely necessary to effect its object. The former, on the contrary, while it inflicts the same wound, inflicts others equally great, and, if possible, greater, as I shall next proceed to explain.

In claiming the right for the inhabitants, instead of Congress, to legislate for the Territories, the Executive proviso, assumes that the sovereignty over the Territories, is vested in the former; or to express it in the language used in a resolution offered by one of the Senators from Texas, (General Houston, now absent,) they have "the same inherent right of self-government as the people in the States." The assumption is utterly unfounded, unconstitutional, without example, and contrary to the entire practice of the Government, from its commencement to the present time, as I shall proceed to show.

The recent movement of individuals in California to form a constitution and a State government, and to appoint Senators and Representatives is the first fruit of this monstrous assumption. If the individuals, who made this movement, had gone into California as adventurers, and if, as such, they had conquered the Territory and established their independence, the sovereignty of the country would have been vested in them, as a separate and independent community. In that case, they would have had the right to form a constitution, and to establish a government for themselves; and, if afterwards, they thought proper to apply to Congress for admission into the Union as a sovereign and independent State, all this would have been regular, and according to established principles. But such is not the case. It was the United States who conquered California, and finally acquired it by treaty. The sovereignty, of course, is invested in them, and not in the individuals who have attempted to form a constitution and a State, without their consent. All this is clear, beyond controversy, unless it can be shown that they have since lost or been divested of their sovereignty.

Nor is it less clear, that the power of legislating over the acquired territory is vested in Congress, and not, as is assumed, in the inhabitants of the Territories. None can deny that the Government of the United States have the power to acquire Territories, either by war or treaty; but if the power to acquire exists, it belongs to Congress to carry it into execution. On this point there can be no doubt, for the Constitution expressly provides, that Congress shall have power "to make all laws which shall be necessary and proper to carry into execution the foregoing powers," (those vested in Congress,) "and all other powers vested by this Constitution in *the Government* of the United States, or in *any department* or *office* thereof." It matters not, then, where the power is vested; for, if vested at all in the Government of the United States, or any of its departments, or officers, the power of carrying it into execution is clearly vested in Congress. But this important provision, while it gives to Congress the power of legislating over Territories, imposes important restrictions on its exercise, by restricting Congress to passing laws necessary and proper for carrying the power into execution. The prohibition extends, not only to all laws not suitable or appropriate to the object of the power, but also to all that are unjust, unequal, or unfair, for all such laws would be unnecessary and improper, and, therefore, unconstitutional.

Having now established, beyond controversy, that the sovereignty over the Territories is vested in the United States— that is in the several States composing the Union—and that the power of legislating over them is expressly vested in Congress, it follows, that the individuals in California who have undertaken to form a constitution and a State, and to exercise the power of legislating without the consent of Congress, have usurped the sovereignty of the State and the authority of Congress, and have acted in open defiance of both. In other words, what they have done is revolutionary and rebellious in its character, anarchical in its tendency, and calculated to lead to the most dangerous consequences. Had they acted from premeditation and design, it would have been, in fact, actual rebellion; but such is not the case. The blame lies much less upon them than upon those who have induced them to take a course so unconstitutional and dangerous. They have been led into it by language held here, and the course pursued by the Executive branch of the Government.

I have not seen the answer of the Executive to the calls made by the two Houses of Congress for information as to the course which it took, or the part which it acted, in reference to what was done in California. I understand the answers have not yet been printed. But there is enough known to justify the assertion, that those who profess to represent and act under the authority of the Executive, have advised, aided, and encouraged the movement, which terminated in forming what they call a Constitution and a State. General Riley, who professed to act as civil Governor, called the Convention, determined on the number and distribution of the delegates, appointed the time and place of its meeting, was present during the session, and gave its proceedings his approbation and sanction. If he acted without authority, he ought to have been tried, or at least reprimanded and disavowed. Neither having been done, the presumption is, that his course has been approved. This of itself is sufficient to identify the Executive with his acts, and to make it responsible for them. I touch not the question, whether General Riley was appointed or received the instructions under which he professed to act from the present Executive, or its predecessor. If from the former, it would implicate the preceding as well as the present Administration. If not, the responsibility rests exclusively on the present.

It is manifest from this statement, that the Executive Department has undertaken to perform acts preparatory to the meeting of the individuals to form their so-called Constitution and Government, which appertain exclusively to Congress. Indeed, they are identical in many respects, with the provisions adopted by Congress, when it gives permission to a Territory to form a constitution and government, in order to be admitted as a State into the Union.

Having now shown that the assumption upon which the Executive and the individuals in California acted throughout this whole affair, is unfounded, unconstitutional, and dangerous, it remains to make a few remarks, in order to show that what has been done is contrary to the entire practice of the Government from its commencement to the present time.

From its commencement until the time that Michigan was admitted, the practice was uniform. Territorial Governments were first organized by Congress. The Government of the United States appointed the Governors, Judges, Secretaries, Marshals, and other officers, and the inhabitants of the Territory were represented by legislative bodies, whose acts were subject to the revisions of Congress. This state of things continued until the government of a Territory applied to Congress to permit its inhabitants to form a constitution and government, preparatory to admission into the Union. The preliminary act to giving permission was, to ascertain whether the inhabitants were sufficiently numerous to authorize them to be formed into a State. This was done by taking a census. That being done, and the number proving sufficient, permission was granted. The act granting it fixed all the preliminaries—the

time and place of holding the convention; the qualification of
the voters; establishment of its boundaries, and all other measures necessary to be settled previous to admission. The act
giving permission necessarily withdraws the sovereignty of the
United States, and leaves the inhabitants of the incipient State
as free to form their constitution and government, as were
the original States of the Union after they had declared their
independence. At this stage, the inhabitants of the Territory
became for the first time a people, in legal and constitutional
language. Prior to this, they were, by the old acts of Congress;
called inhabitants, and not people. All this is perfectly consistent with the sovereignty of the United States, with the powers
of Congress, and with the right of a people to self government.

Michigan was the first case in which there was any departure
from the uniform rule of acting. Hers was a very slight departure from established usage. The ordinance of '87 secured to
her the right of becoming a State, when she should have
60,000 inhabitants. Owing to some neglect, Congress delayed
taking the census. In the mean time her population increased,
until it clearly exceeded more than twice the number which
entitled her to admission. At this stage she formed a constitution and government without the census being taken by the
United States, and Congress waived the omission, as there was
no doubt she had more than a sufficient number to entitle her
to admission. She was not admitted at the first session she
applied, owing to some difficulty respecting the boundary between her and Ohio. The great irregularity, as to her admission, took place at the next session, but on a point which can
have no possible connexion with the case of California.

The irregularities in all other cases that have since occurred
are of a similar nature. In all, there existed territorial governments established by Congress, with officers appointed by the
United States. In all, the territorial government took the lead
in calling conventions, and fixing the preliminaries preparatory
to the formation of a constitution and admission into the
Union. They all recognized the sovereignty of the United
States, and the authority of Congress over the Territories; and
wherever there was any departure from established usage, it
was done on the presumed consent of Congress, and not in

defiance of its authority, or the sovereignty of the United States over the Territories. In this respect California stands alone, without usage, or a single example to cover her case.

It belongs now, Senators, for you to decide what part you will act in reference to this unprecedented transaction. The Executive has laid the paper purporting to be the Constitution of California before you, and asks you to admit her into the Union as a State; and the question is, will you or will you not admit her? It is a grave question, and there rests upon you a heavy responsibility. Much, very much, will depend upon your decision. If you admit her, you endorse and give your sanction to all that has been done. Are you prepared to do so? Are you prepared to surrender your power of legislation for the Territories—a power expressly vested in Congress by the Constitution, as has been fully established? Can you, consistently with your oath to support the Constitution, surrender the power? Are you prepared to admit that the inhabitants of the Territories possess the sovereignty over them, and that any number, more or less, may claim any extent of Territory they please; may form a Constitution and Government, and erect it into a State, without asking your permission? Are you prepared to surrender the sovereignty of the United States over whatever territory may be hereafter acquired to the first adventurers who may rush into it? Are you prepared to surrender virtually to the Executive Department, all the powers which you have heretofore exercised over the Territories? If not, how can you consistently with your duty and your oaths to support the Constitution, give your assent to the admission of California as a State, under a pretended constitution and government? Again, can you believe that the project of a constitution which they have adopted, has the least validity? Can you believe that there is such a State in reality as the State of California? No; there is no such State. It has no legal or constitutional existence. It has no validity, and can have none, without your sanction. How, then, can you admit it as *a State*, when according to the provision of the Constitution, your power is limited to admitting new *States*. To be admitted, it must be a State, an existing State, independent of your sanction, before you can admit it. When you give your permission to the inhabitants of a Territory to form a constitution and a State, the constitution and State they form, derive their authority from the people, and not from you. The State before admitted is actually a State, and does not become so by the *act of admission*, as would be the case with California, should you admit her contrary to constitutional provisions and established usage heretofore.

The Senators on the other side of the Chamber must permit me to make a few remarks in this connection particularly applicable to them, with the exception of a few Senators from the South, sitting on that side of the Chamber, when the Oregon question was before this body, not two years since. You took (if I mistake not) universally the ground, that Congress had the sole and absolute power of legislating for the Territories. How then, can you now, after the short interval which has elapsed, abandon the ground which you took, and thereby virtually admit that the power of legislating, instead of being in Congress, is in the inhabitants of the Territories? How can you justify and sanction by your votes, the acts of the Executive, which are in direct derogation of what you then contended for? But to approach still nearer to the present time, how can you, after condemning, little more than a year since, the grounds taken by the party which you defeated at the last election, wheel round and support by your votes the grounds which, as explained recently on this floor by the candidate of the party in the last election, are identical with those on which the Executive has acted in reference to California? What are we to understand by all this? Must we conclude that there is no sincerity, no faith in the acts and declarations of public men, and that all is mere acting or hollow profession? Or are we to conclude that the exclusion of the South from the territory acquired from Mexico is an object of so paramount a character in your estimation, that Right, Justice, Constitution, and Consistency, must all yield, when they stand in the way of our exclusion?

But, it may be asked, what is to be done with California, should she not be admitted? I answer, remand her back to the territorial condition, as was done in the case of Tennessee, in the early stage of the Government. Congress, in her case, had established a territorial government in the usual form, with a Governor, Judges, and other officers, appointed by the United States. She was entitled, under the deed of cession, to be admitted into the Union as a State as soon as she had sixty thousand inhabitants. The Territorial Government, believing it had that number, took a census, by which it appeared it exceeded it. She then formed a Constitution, and applied for admission. Congress refused to admit her, on the ground that the census should be taken by the United States, and that Congress had not determined whether the territory should be formed into one or two States, as it was authorized to do under the cession. She returned quietly to her territorial condition. An act was passed to take a census by the United States, containing a provision that the Territory should form one State. All afterwards was regularly conducted, and the Territory admitted as a State in due form. The irregularities in the case of California are immeasurably greater, and offer much stronger reasons for pursuing the same course. But, it may be said, California may not submit. That is not probable; but if she should not, when she refuses, it will then be time for us to decide what is to be done.

Having now shown what cannot save the Union, I return to the question with which I commenced, How can the Union be saved? There is but one way by which it can with any certainty, and that is, by a full and final settlement, on the principle of justice, of all the questions at issue between the two sections. The South asks for justice, simple justice, and less she ought not to take. She has no compromise to offer, but the Constitution; and no concession or surrender to make. She has already surrendered so much that she has little left to surrender. Such a settlement would go to the root of the evil, and remove all cause of discontent, by satisfying the South, she could remain honorably and safely in the Union, and thereby restore the harmony and fraternal feelings between the sections, which existed anterior to the Missouri agitation. Nothing else can, with any certainty, finally and forever settle the questions at issue, terminate agitation, and save the Union.

But can this be done. Yes, easily; not by the weaker party, for it can of itself do nothing—not even protect itself—but by the stronger. The North has only to will it to accomplish it—to do justice by conceding to the South an equal right in the acquired Territory, and to do her duty by causing the stipulations relative to fugitive slaves to be faithfully fulfilled—to cease the agitation of the slave question, and to provide for the insertion of a provision in the Constitution, by an amendment, which will restore to the South in substance the power she possessed of protecting herself, before the equilibrium between the sections was destroyed by the action of this Government. There will be no difficulty in devising such a provision—one that will protect the South, and which, at the same time, will improve and strengthen the Government, instead of impairing and weakening it.

But will the North agree to do this? It is for her to answer this question. But, I will say, she cannot refuse, if she has half the love of the Union which she professes to have, or without justly exposing herself to the charge that her love of power and aggrandizement is far greater than her love of the Union. At all events, the responsibility of saving the Union rests on the North, and not the South. The South cannot save it by any act of hers, and the North may save it without any sacrifice whatever, unless to do justice, and to perform her duties under the Constitution, should be regarded by her as a sacrifice.

It is time, Senators, that there should be an open and manly avowal on all sides, as to what is intended to be done. If the question is not now settled, it is uncertain whether it ever can hereafter be; and we, as the representatives of the States of this Union, regarded as Governments, should come to a distinct understanding as to our respective views, in order to ascertain whether the great questions at issue can be settled or not. If you, who represent the stronger portion, cannot agree to settle them on the broad principle of justice and duty, say so; and let the States we both represent agree to separate and part in peace. If you are unwilling we should part in peace, tell us so, and we shall know what to do, when you reduce the question to submission or resistance. If you remain silent, you will compel us to infer by your acts what you intend. In that case, California will become the test question. If you admit her, under all the difficulties that oppose her admission, you compel us to infer that you intend to exclude us from the whole of the acquired Territories, with the intention of destroying irretrievably the equilibrium between the two sections. We would be blind not to perceive in that case, that your real objects are power and aggrandizement, and infatuated not to act accordingly.

I have now, Senators, done my duty in expressing my opinions fully, freely, and candidly, on this solemn occasion. In doing so, I have been governed by the motives which have governed me in all the stages of the agitation of the slavery question since its commencement. I have exerted myself, during the whole period, to arrest it, with the intention of saving the Union, if it could be done; and if it could not, to save the section where it has pleased Providence to cast my lot, and which I sincerely believe has justice and the Constitution on its side. Having faithfully done my duty to the best of my ability, both to the Union and my section, throughout this agitation, I shall have the consolation, let what will come, that I am free from all responsibility.

DANIEL WEBSTER

Speech in the Senate on Compromise Resolutions

Washington, D.C., March 7, 1850

Mr. President, I wish to speak to-day, not as a Massachusetts man, nor as a northern man, but as an American, and a member of the Senate of the United States. It is fortunate that there is a Senate of the United States; a body not yet moved from its propriety, not lost to a just sense of its own dignity, and its own high responsibilities, and a body to which the country looks with confidence, for wise, moderate, patriotic, and healing counsels. It is not to be denied that we live in the midst of strong agitations, and are surrounded by very considerable dangers to our institutions of government. The imprisoned winds are let loose. The East, the West, the North, and the stormy South, all combine to throw the whole ocean into commotion, to toss its billows to the skies, and to disclose its profoundest depths. I do not affect to regard myself, Mr. President, as holding, or as fit to hold, the helm in this combat of the political elements; but I have a duty to perform, and I mean to perform it with fidelity—not without a sense of surrounding dangers, but not without hope. I have a part to act, not for my own security or safety, for I am looking out for no fragment upon which to float away from the wreck, if wreck there must be, but for the good of the whole, and the preservation of the whole, and there is that which will keep me to my duty during this struggle, whether the sun and the stars shall appear, or shall not appear, for many days. I speak to-day for the preservation of the Union. "Hear me for my cause." I speak to-day, out of a solicitous and anxious heart, for the restoration to the country of that quiet and that harmony which make the blessings of this Union so rich and so dear to us all. These are the topics that I propose to myself to discuss; these are the motives, and the sole motives, that influence me in the wish to communicate my opinions to the Senate and the country; and if I can do anything, however little, for the promotion of these ends, I shall have accomplished all that I desire.

Mr. President, it may not be amiss to recur very briefly to the events which, equally sudden and extraordinary, have brought the political condition of the country to what it now is. In May, 1846, the United States declared war against Mexico. Her armies, then on the frontiers, entered the provinces of that Republic, met and defeated all her troops, penetrated her mountain passes, and occupied her capital. The marine force of the United States took possession of her forts and her towns on the Atlantic and on the Pacific. In less than two years a treaty was negotiated, by which Mexico ceded to the United States a vast territory, extending seven or eight hundred miles along the shores of the Pacific, and reaching back over the mountains, and across the desert, until it joined the frontier of the State of Texas. It so happened, that, in the distracted and feeble state of the Mexican Government, before the declaration of war by the United States against Mexico had become known in California, the people of California, under the lead of American officers, overthrew the existing Provincial Government of California, the Mexican authorities, and ran up an independent flag. When the news arrived at San Francisco, that war had been declared by the United States against Mexico, this independent flag was pulled down, and the stars and stripes of this Union hoisted in its stead. So, sir, before the war was over, the powers of the United States, military and naval, had possession of San Francisco and Upper California, and a great rush of emigrants, from various parts of the world, took place into California, in 1846 and 1847. But now, behold another wonder.

In January of 1848, the Mormons, it is said, or some of them, made a discovery of an extraordinarily rich mine of gold; or, rather, of a very great quantity of gold, hardly fit to be called a mine, for it was spread near the surface—on the lower part of the south or American branch of the Sacramento. They seem to have attempted to conceal their discovery for some time; but soon another discovery, perhaps of greater importance, was made, of gold in another part of the American branch of the Sacramento, and near Sutter's fort, as it is called. The fame of these discoveries spread far and wide. They excited more and more the spirit of emigration toward California, which had already been excited; and persons crowded in hundreds, and flocked toward the Bay of San Francisco. This, as I have said, took place in the winter and spring of 1848. The digging commenced in the spring of that year; and from that time to this, the work of searching for gold has been prosecuted with a success not heretofore known in the history of this globe. We all know, sir, how incredulous the American public was at the accounts which reached us at first of these discoveries; but we all know now that these accounts received, and continue to receive, daily confirmation; and down to the present moment, I suppose the assurances are as strong, after the experience of these several months, of mines of gold, apparently inexhaustible in the regions near San Francisco, in California, as they were at any period of the earlier dates of the accounts. It so happened, sir, that although in the time of peace it became a very important subject for legislative consideration and legislative decision, to provide a proper territorial government for California, yet, differences of opinion in the counsels of the Government prevented the establishment of any such territorial government for California, at the last session of Congress. Under this state of things, the inhabitants of San Francisco and California—then amounting to a great number of people—in the summer of last year, thought it to be their duty to establish a local government. Under the proclamation of General Riley, the people chose delegates to a convention. That convention met at Monterey. They formed a constitution for the State of California, and it was adopted by the people of California in their primary assemblages. Desirous of immediate connection with the United States, its Senators were appointed and Representatives chosen, who have come hither, bringing with them the authentic constitution of the State of California; and they now present themselves, asking in behalf of their State, that the State may be admitted into this Union as one of the United States. This constitution, sir, contains an express prohibition against slavery, or involuntary servitude, in the State of California. It is said, and I suppose truly, that of the members who composed that convention, some sixteen were natives, and had been residents of the slaveholding States, and about twenty-two were from the non-slaveholding States, and the remaining ten members were either native Californians, or old settlers in that country. This prohibition against slavery, it is said was inserted with entire unanimity.

Mr. HALE. Will the Senator give way until order is restored?

The VICE PRESIDENT. The Sergeant-at-Arms will see that order is restored, and no more persons admitted to the floor.

Mr. CASS. I trust the scene of the other day will not be repeated. The Sergeant-at-Arms must display more energy in suppressing this disorder.

Mr. HALE. The noise is outside of the door.

Mr. WEBSTER. And it is this circumstance, sir, the prohibition of slavery by that convention, which has contributed to raise—I do not say it has wholly raised—the dispute as to the propriety of the admission of California into the Union under this constitution. It is not to be denied, Mr. President—nobody thinks of denying—that, whatever reasons were assigned at the commencement of the late war with Mexico, it was prosecuted for the purpose of the acquisition of territory, and under the alleged argument that the cession of territory was the only form in which proper compensation could be made to the United States, by Mexico, for the various claims and demands which the people of this country had against that Government. At any rate, it will be found that President Polk's message at the commencement of the session of December, 1847, avowed, that the war was to be prosecuted until some acquisition of territory was made. And, as the acquisition was to be south of the line of the United States, in warm climates and countries, it was naturally, I suppose, expected by the South, that whatever acquisitions were made in that region, would be added to the slaveholding portion of the United States. Events have turned out as was not expected, and that expectation has not been realized; and therefore some degree of disappointment and surprise has resulted, of course. In other words, it is obvious that the question which has so long harassed the country, and at times very seriously alarmed the minds of wise and good men, has come upon us for afresh discussion—the question of slavery in these United States.

Now, sir, I propose—perhaps at the expense of some detail and consequent detention of the Senate—to review, historically, this question of slavery, which—partly in consequence of its own merits, and partly, perhaps mostly, in the manner it is discussed, in one and the other portion of the country—has been a source of so much alienation and unkind feeling between the different portions of the Union. We all know, sir, that slavery has existed in the world from time immemorial. There was slavery, in the earliest periods of history, in the Oriental nations. There was slavery among the Jews—the theocratic government of that people made no injunction against it. There was slavery among the Greeks; and the ingenious philosophy of the Greeks found, or sought to find, a justification for it, exactly upon the grounds which have been assumed, for such a justification, in this country; that is, a natural and original difference among the races of mankind—the inferiority of the black or colored race, to the white. The Greeks justified their system of slavery upon that ground precisely. They held the African, and in some parts, the Asiatic tribes, to be inferior to the white race; but they did not show, I think, by any close process of logic, that, if this were true, the more intelligent and the stronger, had therefore a right to subjugate the weaker.

The more manly philosophy, and jurisprudence of the Romans, placed the justification of slavery on entirely different grounds.

The Roman jurists, from the first, and down to the fall of the empire, admitted that slavery was against the natural law, by which, as they maintained, all men, of whatsoever clime, color or capacity, were equal; but they justified slavery—first, upon the ground and authority of the law of nations—arguing, and arguing truly, that at that day the conventional law of nations admitted, that captives in war, whose lives, according to the notions of the times, were at the absolute disposal of the captors, might, in exchange for exemption from death, be made slaves for life, and that such servitude might descend to their posterity. The jurists of Rome also maintained that, by the civil law, there might be servitude—slavery, personal and hereditary—first, by the voluntary act of an individual who might sell himself into slavery; second, by his being received into a state of slavery, by his creditors, in satisfaction of a debt; and, thirdly, by being placed in a state of servitude, or slavery, for crime. At the introduction of Christianity into the world, the Roman world was full of slaves, and I suppose there is to be found no injunction against that relation between man and man in the teachings of the Gospel of Jesus Christ, or of any of his Apostles. The object of the instruction, imparted to mankind, by the Founder of Christianity, was to touch the heart, purify the soul, and improve the lives of individual men. That object went directly to the first fountain of all political and all social relations of the human race—the individual heart and mind of man.

Now, sir, upon the general nature, and character, and influence of slavery, there exists a wide difference between the northern portion of this country and the southern. It is said, on the one side, that if not the subject of any injunction or direct prohibition in the New Testament, slavery is a wrong; that it is founded merely in the right of the strongest; and that it is an oppression, like all unjust wars—like all those conflicts by which a mighty nation subjects a weaker nation to their will; and that slavery, in its nature, whatever may be said of it in the modifications which have taken place, is not in fact according to the meek spirit of the Gospel. It is not kindly affectioned, it does not "seek another's, and not its own." It does not "let the oppressed go free." These are sentiments that are cherished, and recently with greatly augmented force, among the people of the northern States. It has taken hold of the religious sentiment of that part of the country, as it has more or less taken hold of the religious feelings of a considerable portion of mankind. The South, upon the other side, having been accustomed to this relation between the two races all their lives, from their birth; having been taught in general to treat the subjects of this bondage with care and kindness—and I believe, in general, feeling for them great care and kindness—have yet not taken this view of the subject which I have mentioned. There are thousands of religious men, with consciences as tender as any of their brethren at the North, who do not see the unlawfulness of slavery; and there are more thousands, perhaps, that, whatsoever they may think of it in its origin, and as a matter depending upon natural right, yet take things as they are, and, finding slavery to be an established relation of the society in which they live, can see no way in which—let their opinions on the abstract question be what they may—it is in the power of the present generation to relieve themselves from this relation. And, in this respect, candor obliges me to say, that I believe they are just as conscientious, many of them—and of the religious people, all of them—as they are in the North, in holding different opinions.

Why, sir, the honorable Senator from South Carolina, the other day, alluded to the great separation of that great religious community, the Methodist Episcopal Church. That separation was brought about by differences of opinion upon this peculiar subject of slavery. I felt great concern, as that dispute went on, about the result; and I was in hopes that the difference of opinion might be adjusted, because I looked upon that religious denomination as one of the great props of religion and morals, throughout the whole country, from Maine to Georgia. The result was against my wishes and against my hopes. I have read all their proceedings, and all their arguments, but I have never yet been able to come to the conclusion, that there was any real ground for that separation; in other words, that no good could be produced by that separation. I must say, I think there was some want of candor and charity. Sir, when a question of this kind takes hold of the religious sentiments of mankind, and comes to be discussed in religious assemblies of the clergy and laity, there is always to be expected, or always to be feared, a great degree of excitement. It is in the nature of man, manifested by his whole history, that religious disputes are apt to become warm, and men's strength of conviction is proportionate to their views of the magnitude of the questions. In all such disputes, there will sometimes be men found with whom everything is absolute—absolutely wrong, or absolutely right. They see the right clearly; they think others ought so to see it, and they are disposed to establish a broad line of distinction between what is right, and what is wrong. And they are not seldom willing to establish that line upon their own convictions of the truth and the justice of their own opinions; and are willing to mark and guard that line, by placing along it a series of dogmas, as lines of boundary are marked by posts and stones. There are men, who, with clear perceptions, as they think, of their own duty, do not see how too hot a pursuit of one duty may involve them in the violation of another, or how too warm an embracement of one truth may lead to a disregard of other truths equally important. As I heard it stated strongly, not many days ago, these persons are disposed to mount upon some particular duty as upon a war horse, and to drive furiously on, and upon, and over all other duties, that may stand in the way. There are men, who, in times of that sort, and disputes of that sort, are of opinion, that human duties may be ascertained with the exactness of mathematics. They deal with morals as with mathematics, and they think what is right, may be distinguished from what is wrong, with the precision of an algebraic equation. They have, therefore, none too much charity toward others who differ with them. They are apt, too, to think that nothing is good but what is perfect, and that there are no compromises or modifications to be made in submission to difference of opinion, or in deference to other men's judgment. If their perspicacious vision enables them to detect a spot on the face of the sun, they think that a good reason why the sun should be struck down from Heaven. They prefer the chance of running into utter darkness, to living in heavenly light, if that heavenly light be not absolutely without any imperfection. There are impatient men—too impatient always to give heed to the admonition of St. Paul, "that we are not to do evil that good may come"—too impatient to wait for the slow progress of moral causes in the improvement of mankind. They do not remember, that the doctrines and the miracles of Jesus Christ have, in eighteen hundred years, converted only a small portion of the human race; and among the nations that are converted to Christianity, they forget how many vices and crimes, public and private, still prevail, and that many of them—public crimes especially, which are offenses against the Christian religion—pass without exciting particular regret or indignation. Thus wars are waged, and unjust wars. I do not deny that there may be just wars. There certainly are; but it was the remark of an eminent person, not many years ago, on the other side of the Atlantic, that it was one of the greatest reproaches to human nature, that wars were sometimes necessary. The defense of nations sometimes causes a war against the injustice of other nations.

Now, sir, in this state of sentiment, upon the general nature of slavery, lies the cause of a great portion of those unhappy divisions, exasperations, and reproaches, which find vent and support in different parts of the Union. Slavery does exist in the United States. It did exist in the States before the adoption of this Constitution, and at that time.

And now let us consider, sir, for a moment, what was the state of sentiment, North and South, in regard to slavery at the time this Constitution was adopted. A remarkable change has taken place since, but what did the wise and great men of all parts of the country then think of slavery? In what estimation did they hold it in 1787, when this Constitution was adopted? Now, it will be found, sir, if we will carry ourselves by historical research back to that day, and ascertain men's opinions by authentic records still existing among us, that there was no great diversity of opinion between the North and the South upon the subject of slavery; and it will be found that both parts of the country held it equally an evil, a moral and political evil. It will not be found, that either at the North or at the South, there was much, though there was some, invective against slavery as inhuman and cruel. The great ground of objection to it was political; that it weakened the social fabric; that, taking the place of free labor, society was less strong, and labor was less productive; and, therefore, we find, from all the eminent men of the time, the clearest expression of their opinion that slavery was an evil. And they ascribed its existence here, not without truth, and not without some acerbity of temper and force of language, to the injurious policy of the mother country, who, to favor the navigator, had entailed these evils upon the colonies. I need hardly refer, sir, to the publications of the day. They are matters of history on the record. The eminent men, the most eminent men, and nearly all the conspicuous politicians of the South, held the same sentimerits, that slavery was an "evil," a "blight," a "blast," a "mildew," a "scourge," and a "curse." There are no terms of reprobation of slavery so vehement in the North of that day as in the South. The North was not so much excited against it as the South, and the reason is, I suppose, because there was much less at the North; and the people did not see, or think they saw, the evils so prominently as they were seen, or thought to be seen, at the South.

Then, sir, when this constitution was framed, this was the light in which the Convention viewed it. The Convention reflected the judgment and sentiments of the great men of the

South. A member of the other house, whom I have not the
honor to know, in a recent speech, has collected extracts from
these public documents. They prove the truth of what I am
saying, and the question then was, how to deal with it, and
how to deal with it as an evil? Well, they came to this general
result. They thought that slavery could not be continued in the
country if the importation of slaves were made to cease, and
therefore they provided, that after a certain period, the importation might be prevented by the act of the new Government.
Twenty years was proposed by some gentleman—a northern
gentleman, I think—and many of the southern gentlemen opposed it as being too long. Mr. Madison, especially, was something warm against it. He said it would bring too much of this
mischief into the country to allow the importation of slaves for
such a period, because we must take along with us, in the
whole of this discussion, when we are considering the sentiments and opinions in which this constitutional provision
originated, that the conviction of all men was, that if the importation of slaves ceased, the white race would multiply faster
than the black race, and that slavery would therefore gradually
wear out and expire. It may not be improper here to allude to
that, I had almost said celebrated, opinion of Mr. Madison.
You observe, sir, that the term "slave," or " slavery," is not
used in the Constitution. The Constitution does not require
that "fugitive slaves" shall be delivered up. It requires that
"persons bound to service in one State, and escaping into
another, shall be delivered up." Mr. Madison opposed the introduction of the term slave, or slavery, into the Constitution;
for he said, that he did not wish to see it recognized by the
Constitution of the United States of America, that there could
be property in men. Now, sir, all this took place at the Convention in 1787; but connected with this—concurrent and
contemporaneous—is another important transaction, not sufficiently attended to. The Convention, for framing this Constitution, assembled in Philadelphia in May, and sat until
September, 1787. During all that time, the Congress of the
United States was in session at New York. It was a matter of
design, as we know, that the Convention should not assemble
in the same city where Congress was holding its sessions. Almost all the public men of the country, therefore, of distinc-

tion and eminence, were in one or the other of these two assemblies; and I think it happened in some instances, that the same gentlemen were members of both. If I mistake not, such was the case of Mr. Rufus King, then a member of Congress from Massachusetts, and at the same time a member of the Convention to frame the Constitution, from that State. Now, it was in the summer of 1787, the very time when the Convention in Philadelphia was framing this Constitution, that the Congress in New York was framing the ordinance of 1787. They passed that ordinance on the 13th July, 1787, at New York, the very month—perhaps the very day—on which these questions about the importation of slaves, and the character of slavery, were debated in the Convention at Philadelphia. And, so far as we can now learn, there was a perfect concurrence of opinion between these respectives bodies; and it resulted in this ordinance of 1787, excluding slavery, as applied to all the territory over which the Congress of the United States had jurisdiction, and that was, all the territory northwest of the Ohio. Three years before, Virginia and other States had made a cession of that great territory to the United States. And a most magnificent act it was. I never reflect upon it without a disposition to do honor and justice—and justice would be the highest honor—to Virginia for that act of cession of her northwestern territory. I will say, sir, it is one of her fairest claims to the respect and gratitude of the United States, and that perhaps it is only second to that other claim which attaches to her, that from her counsels, and from the intelligence and patriotism of her leading statesmen, proceeded the first idea, put into practice, for the formation of a general Constitution of the United States. Now, sir, the ordinance of 1787 applied thus to the whole territory over which the Congress of the United States had jurisdiction. It was adopted nearly three years before the Constitution of the United States went into operation; because the ordinance took effect immediately on its passage, while the Constitution of the United States, having been framed, was to be sent to the States to be adopted by their Conventions; and then a Government had to be organized under it. This ordinance, then, was in operation and force when the Constitution was adopted, and this Government put in motion, in April, 1789.

Mr. President, three things are quite clear as historical truths.

One is, that there was an expectation that on the ceasing of the importation of slaves from Africa, slavery would begin to run out. That was hoped and expected. Another is, that as far as there was any power in Congress to prevent the spread of slavery in the United States, that power was executed in the most absolute manner and to the fullest extent. An honorable member whose health does not allow him to be here to-day——

A SENATOR. He is here. (Referring to Mr. CALHOUN.)

Mr. WEBSTER. I am very happy to hear that he is—may he long be in health and the enjoyment of it to serve his country—said the other day, that he considered this ordinance as the first in the series of measures calculated to enfeeble the South, and deprive them of their just participation in the benefits and privileges of this Government. He says, very properly, that it was done under the old Confederation, and before this Constitution went into effect; but, my present purpose is only to say, Mr. President, that it was done with the entire and unanimous concurrence of the whole South. Why, there it stands! The vote of every State in the Union was unanimous in favor of the ordinance, with the exception of a single individual vote, and that individual was a northern man. But, sir, the ordinance abolishing or rather prohibiting slavery northwest of the Ohio, has the hand and seal of every southern member in Congress.

The other and third clear historical truth is, that the Convention meant to leave slavery, in the States, as they found it, entirely under the authority and control of the States.

This was the state of things, sir, and this the state of opinion, under which those very important matters were arranged, and those important things done; that is, the establishment of the Constitution, with a recognition of slavery as it existed in the States, and the establishment of the ordinance prohibiting, to the full extent of all territory owned by the United States, the introduction of slavery into those territories, and the leaving to the States all power over slavery, in their own limits. And here, sir, we may pause. We may reflect for a moment upon the entire coincidence and concurrence of sentiment between the North and the South upon these questions, at the period of the adoption of the Constitution. But opinions, sir, have changed— greatly changed—changed North and changed South. Slavery is not regarded in the South now as it was then. I see an honorable member of this body paying me the honor of listening to my remarks; he brings to me, sir, freshly and vividly the sentiments of his great ancestor, so much distinguished in his day and generation, so worthy to be succeeded by so worthy a grandson, with all the sentiments he expressed in the Convention in Philadelphia.

Here we may pause. There was a general concurrence of sentiment, if not an entire unanimity, running through the whole community, and especially entertained by the eminent men of all portions of the country. But soon a change began at the North and the South, and a severance of opinion showed itself—the North growing much more warm and strong against slavery, and the South growing much more warm and strong in its support. Sir, there is no generation of mankind whose opinions are not subject to be influenced by what appears to them to be their present, emergent, and exigent interest. I impute to the South no particularly selfish view, in the change which has come over her. I impute to her certainly no dishonest view. All that has happened has been natural. It has followed those causes which always influence the human mind and operate upon it. What, then, have been the causes which have created so new a feeling in favor of slavery in the South—which have changed the whole nomenclature of the South on the subject—and from being thought of and described in the terms I have mentioned, but will not repeat, it has now become an "institution," a "cherished institution," in that quarter; no evil, no scourge, but a great religious, social, and moral blessing, as I think I have heard it laterly described? I suppose this, sir, is owing to the sudden uprising and rapid growth of the cotton plantations of the South. So far as any motive of honor, justice, and general judgment could act, it was the cotton interest that gave a new desire to promote slavery, to spread it and to use its labor. I again say that that was produced by the causes, which we must always expect to produce like effects; their whole interests became connected with it. If we look back to the history of the commerce of this country, in the early years of this Government, what were our exports? Cotton was hardly, or but to a very limited extent, known. The tables will show that the exports of cotton for the years 1790 and '91, were not more than forty or fifty thousand dollars a year. It has gone on increasing rapidly until it may now, perhaps, in a season of great product and high prices, amount to a hundred millions of dollars. In the years I have mentioned, there was more of wax, more of indigo, more of rice, more of almost every article of export from the South, than of cotton. I think I have heard it said, when Mr. Jay negotiated the treaty of 1794 with England, he did not know that cotton was exported at all from the United States; and I have heard it said, that after the treaty, which gave to the United States the right to carry their own commodities to England in their own ships, the custom-house in London refused to admit cotton, upon an allegation that it could not be an American production, there being, as they supposed, no cotton raised in America. They would hardly think so now!

Well, sir, we know what followed. The age of cotton became a golden age for our southern brethren. It gratified their desire for improvement and accumulation, at the same time that it excited it. The desire grew by what it fed upon, and there soon came to be an eagerness for other territory—a new area or new areas for the cultivation of the cotton crop; and measures leading to this result, were brought about somewhat rapidly, one after another, under the lead of southern men at the head of the Government, they having a majority in both branches, to accomplish their ends. The honorable member from Carolina observed, that there has been a majority all along in favor of the North. If that be true, sir, the North has acted either very liberally and kindly, or very weakly; for they never exercised that majority five times in the history of the Government. Never. Whether they were out-generalled, or whether it was owing to other causes, I shall not stop to consider, but no man acquainted with the history of the country can deny, that the general lead in the politics of the country, for three-fourths of the period that has elapsed since the adoption of the Constitution, has been a southern lead. In 1802, in pursuit of the idea of opening a new cotton region, the United States obtained a cession from Georgia of the whole of her western territory, now embracing the rich and growing State of Alabama. In 1803 Louisiana was purchased from France, out of which the States of Louisiana, Arkansas, and Missouri have been framed, as slaveholding States. In 1819 the cession of Florida was made, bringing another cession of slaveholding property and territory. Sir, the honorable member from South Carolina thought he saw in certain operations of the Government, such as the manner of collecting the revenue and the tendency of those measures to promote emigration into the country, what accounts for the more rapid growth of the North than the South. He thinks that more rapid growth was not the operation of time, but of the system of Government established under this Constitution. That is a matter of opinion. To a certain extent, it may be so; but it does seem to me, that if any operation of the Government could be shown in any degree to have promoted the population, and growth, and wealth of the North, it is much more sure that there are sundry important and distinct operations of the Government, about which no man can doubt, tending to promote, and which absolutely have promoted, the increase of the slave interest, and the slave territory, of the South. Allow me to say, that it was not time that brought in Louisiana; it was the act of men. It was not time that brought in Florida; it was the act of men. And lastly, sir, to complete those acts of men, which have contributed so much to enlarge the area and the sphere of the institution of slavery, Texas—great, and vast, and illimitable Texas—was added to the Union, as a slave State, in 1845; and that, sir, pretty much closed the whole chapter and settled the whole account. That closed the whole chapter—that settled the whole account— because the annexation of Texas, upon the conditions and under the guarantees upon which she was admitted, did not leave an acre of land, capable of being cultivated by slave labor, between this Capitol and the Rio Grande, or the Nueces, or whatever is the proper boundary of Texas—not an acre, not one. From that moment, the whole country from this place to the western boundary of Texas, was fixed, pledged, fastened, decided, to be slave territory forever, by the solemn guaranties of law. And I now say, sir, as the proposition upon which I stand this day, and upon the truth and firmness of which I intend to act until it is overthrown, that there is not, at this moment, within the United States, or any territory of the United States, a single foot of land, the character of which, in regard to its being free-soil territory or slave territory, is not fixed by

some law, and some irrepealable law, beyond the power of the
action of this Government. Now, is it not so with respect to
Texas? Why, it is most manifestly so. The honorable Senator
from South Carolina, at the time of the admission of Texas,
held an important post in the Executive Department of the
Government; he was Secretary of State. Another eminent person, of great activity and adroitness in affairs—I mean the late
Secretary of the Treasury, (Mr. Walker)—was a leading member of this body, and took the lead in the business of annexation; and I must say that they did their business faithfully and
thoroughly; there was no botch left in it. They rounded it off,
and made as close joiner-work as ever was put together. Resolutions of annexation were brought into Congress fitly joined
together—compact, firm, efficient, conclusive upon the great
object which they had in view, and those resolutions passed.

Allow me to read the resolution. It is the third clause of the
second section of the resolution of the 1st March, 1845, for the
admission of Texas, which applies to this part of the case. That
clause reads in these words:

"New States, of convenient size, not exceeding four in number, in
addition to said State of Texas, and having sufficient population, may
hereafter, by the consent of said State, be formed out of the territory
thereof, which shall be entitled to admission under the provisions of
the Federal Constitution. And such States as may be formed out of that
portion of said territory lying south of 36° 30′ north latitude, commonly known as the Missouri compromise line, shall be admitted into
the Union, with or without slavery, as the people of each State, asking
admission, may desire; and in such State or States as shall be formed
out of said territory north of said Missouri compromise line, slavery
or involuntary servitude (except for crime) shall be prohibited."

Now what is here stipulated, enacted, secured? It is, that all
Texas south of 36° 30′, which is nearly the whole of it, shall be
admitted into the Union as a slave State. It was a slave State,
and therefore came in as a slave State—and the guaranty is,
that new States shall be made out of it; and that such States as
are formed out of that portion of Texas lying south of 36° 30′,
may come in as slave States, to the number of four, in addition
to the State then in existence, and admitted at that time by
these resolutions. I know no mode of legislation which can
strengthen that. I know no form of recognition that can add a

tittle of weight to it. I listened respectfully to the resolutions of my honorable friend from Tennessee, [Mr. BELL.] He proposed to recognize that stipulation with Texas. But any additional recognition would weaken the force of it, because it stands here on the ground of a contract, a thing done, for a consideration. It is a law founded on a contract with Texas, and designed to carry that contract into effect. A recognition founded not on any consideration, or any contract, would not be so strong as it now stands on the face of the resolution. Now, I know no way, I candidly confess, in which this Government, acting in good faith, as I trust it always will, can relieve itself from that stipulation and pledge, by any honest course of legislation whatever. And, therefore, I say again, that so far as Texas is concerned—the whole of Texas south of 36° 30′, which I suppose embraces all the slave territory—there is no land, not an acre, the character of which is not established by law—a law which cannot be repealed without the violation of a contract, and plain disregard of the public faith.

I hope, sir, it is now apparent, that my proposition, so far as Texas is concerned, has been maintained; and the provision in this article—and it has been well suggested by my friend from Rhode Island, that that part of Texas which lies north of thirty-four degrees of north latitude may be formed into free States—is dependent, in like manner, upon the consent of Texas, herself a slave State.

Well, now, sir, how came this?—how came it, that within these walls, where it is said by the honorable member from South Carolina, the free States have a majority—that this resolution of annexation, such as I have described it, found a majority in both Houses of Congress? Why, sir, it found that majority by the great addition of northern votes added to the entire southern vote, or, at least, nearly the whole of the southern votes. That majority was made up of northern as well as of southern votes. In the House of Representatives it stood, I think, about eighty southern votes for the admission of Texas, and about fifty northern votes for the admission of Texas. In the Senate the vote stood for the admission of Texas twenty-seven, and twenty-five against it; and of those twenty-seven votes, constituting a majority for the admission of Texas, in this body, no less than thirteen of them came from the free States—four of them were from New England. The whole of these thirteen Senators, from the free States—within a fraction, you see, of one-half of all the votes in this body for the admission of Texas, with its immeasurable extent of slave territory—were sent here by the votes of free States.

Sir, there is not so remarkable a chapter in our history of political events, political parties, and political men, as is afforded by this measure for the admission of Texas, with this immense territory, over which a bird can not fly in a week. [Laughter.] Sir, New England, with some of her votes, supported this measure. Three-fourths of the votes of liberty-loving Connecticut went for it in the other House, and one-half here. There was one vote for it in Maine, but I am happy to say, not the vote of the honorable member who addressed the Senate the day before yesterday, [Mr. HAMLIN,] and who was then a Representative from Maine in the other House; but there was a vote or two from Maine—ay, and there was one vote for it in Massachusetts, the gentleman then representing, and now living in, the district in which the prevalence of free-soil sentiment for a couple of years or so, has defeated the choice of any member to represent it in Congress. Sir, that body of northern and eastern men, who gave those votes at that time, are now seen taking upon themselves, in the nomenclature of politics, the appellation of the northern Democracy. They undertook to wield the destinies of this empire—if I may call a republic an empire—and their policy was, and they persisted in it, to bring into this country all the territory they could. They did it under pledges—absolute pledges to the slave interest in the case of Texas, and afterward they lent their aid in bringing in these new conquests. My honorable friend from Georgia, in March, 1847, moved the Senate to declare that the war ought not be prosecuted for acquisition, for conquest, for the dismemberment of Mexico. The same northern Democracy entirely voted against it. He did not get a vote from them. It suited the views, the patriotism, the elevated sentiments of the northern Democracy, to bring in a world here, among the mountains and valleys of California and New Mexico, or any other part of Mexico, and then quarrel about it—to bring it in, and then endeavor to put upon it the saving grace of the Wilmot proviso. There were two eminent and highly respectable gentlemen from the north and east, then leading gentlemen in the Senate—I refer, and I do so with entire respect, for I entertain for both of those gentlemen in general, high regard, to Mr. Dix of New York, and Mr. Niles of Connecticut, who voted for the admission of Texas. They would not have that vote any other way than as it stood; and they would have it as it did stand. I speak of the vote upon the annexation of Texas. Those two gentlemen would have the resolution of annexation just as it is, and they voted for it just as it is, and their eyes were all open to it. My honorable friend, the member who addressed us the other day from South Carolina, was then Secretary of State. His correspondence with Mr. Murphy, the chargé d'affaires of the United States in Texas, had been published. That correspondence was all before those gentlemen, and the Secretary had the boldness and candor to avow in that correspondence, that the great object sought by the annexation of Texas was to strengthen the slave interest of the South. Why, sir, he said, in so many words——

Mr. CALHOUN. Will the honorable Senator permit me to interrupt him for a moment?

Mr. WEBSTER. Certainly.

Mr. CALHOUN. I am very reluctant to interrupt the honorable gentleman; but, upon a point of so much importance, I deem it right to put myself *rectus*. I did not put it upon the ground assumed by the Senator. I put it upon this ground: that Great Britain had announced to this country, in so many words, that her object was to abolish slavery in Texas, and through Texas, to accomplish the abolishment of slavery in the United States and the world. The ground I put it on was, that it would make an exposed frontier, and, if Great Britain succeeded in her object, it would be impossible that that frontier could be secured against the aggression of the Abolitionists; and that this Government was bound, under the guaranties of the Constitution, to protect us against such a state of things.

Mr. WEBSTER. That comes, I suppose, sir, to exactly the same thing. It was, that Texas must be obtained for the security of the slave interest of the South.

Mr. CALHOUN. Another view is very distinctly given.

Mr. WEBSTER. That was the object set forth in the correspondence of a worthy gentleman not now living, who preceded

the honorable member from South Carolina in that office.
There repose on the files of the Department of State, as I have
occasion to know, strong letters from Mr. Upshur to the United
States Minister in England, and I believe there are some to the
same minister from the honorable Senator himself, asserting
to this effect the sentiments of this Government; that Great
Britain was expected not to interfere to take Texas out of the
hands of its then existing government, and make it a free
country. But my argument, my suggestion is this; that those
gentlemen who composed the northern Democracy, when
Texas was brought into the Union, saw, with all their eyes, that
it was brought in as a slave country, and brought in for the
purpose of being maintained, as slave territory, to the Greek
Kalends. I rather think the honorable gentleman, who was then
Secretary of State, might, in some of his correspondence with
Mr. Murphy, have suggested that it was not expedient to say
too much about this object, that it might create some alarm.
At any rate, Mr. Murphy wrote to him, that England was anxious to get rid of the constitution of Texas, because it was a
constitution, establishing slavery; and that what the United
States had to do, was to aid the people of Texas in upholding
their constitution; but that nothing should be said which should
offend the fanatical men of the North. But, sir, the honorable
member did avow this object, himself, openly, boldly and manfully; he did not disguise his conduct or his motives.

Mr. CALHOUN. Never, never.

Mr. WEBSTER. What he means he is very apt to say.

Mr. CALHOUN. Always, always.

Mr. WEBSTER. And I honor him for it. This admission of
Texas was in 1845. Then, in 1847, *flagrante bello* between the
United States and Mexico, the proposition I have mentioned,
was brought forward by my friend from Georgia, and the
northern Democracy voted straight ahead against it. Their
remedy was to apply to the acquisitions, after they should come
in, the Wilmot proviso. What follows? These two gentlemen,
worthy and honorable, and influential men—and if they had
not been, they could not have carried the measure—these two
gentlemen, members of this body, brought in Texas, and by
their votes they also prevented the passage of the resolution of

the honorable member from Georgia, and then they went home and took the lead in the Free-Soil party. And there they stand, sir! They leave us here, bound in honor and conscience by the resolutions of annexation; they leave us here to take the odium of fulfilling the obligations, in favor of slavery, which they voted us into, or else the greater odium of violating those obligations, while they are at home making rousing and capital speeches for free soil and no slavery. [Laughter.] And therefore I say, sir, that there is not a chapter in our history, respecting public measures and public men, more full of what should create surprise, more full of what does create, in my mind, extreme mortification, than that of the conduct of this northern Democracy.

Mr. President, sometimes, when a man is found in a new relation to things around him, and to other men, he says that the world has changed, and that he has not changed. I believe, sir, that our self-respect leads us often to make this declaration in regard to ourselves, when it is not exactly true. An individual is more apt to change, perhaps, than all the world around him. But, under the present circumstances, and under the responsibility which I know I incur by what I am now stating here, I feel at liberty to recur to the various expressions and statements, made at various times, of my own opinions and resolutions respecting the admission of Texas, and all that has followed. Sir, as early as 1836, or in the earlier part of 1837, a matter of conversation and correspondence between myself and some private friends, was this project of annexing Texas to the United States; and an honorable gentleman, with whom I have had a long acquaintance, a friend of mine, now perhaps in this chamber—I mean Gen. Hamilton, of South Carolina—was knowing to that correspondence. I had voted for the recognition of Texan independence, because I believed it was an existing fact, surprising and astonishing as it was, and I wished well to the new Republic; but I manifested from the first utter opposition to bringing her, with her territory, into the Union. I had occasion, sir, in 1837, to meet friends in New York, on some political occasion, and I then stated my sentiments upon the subject. It was the first time that I had occasion to advert to it; and I will ask a friend near me to do me the favor to read an extract from the speech, for the Senate may find it rather tedious to listen to the whole of it. It was delivered in Niblo's Garden in 1837.

Mr. GREENE then read the following extract from the speech of the honorable Senator, to which he referred:

"Gentleman, we all see that, by whomsoever possessed, Texas is likely to be a slaveholding country; and I frankly avow my entire unwillingness to do anything which shall extend the slavery of the African race on this continent, or add other slaveholding States to the Union.

"When I say that I regard slavery in itself as a great moral, social, and political evil, I only use language which has been adopted by distinguished men, themselves citizens of slaveholding States.

"I shall do nothing, therefore, to favor or encourage its further extension. We have slavery already among us. The Constitution found it among us; it recognized it, and gave it solemn guaranties.

"To the full extent of these guaranties, we are all bound in honor, in justice, and by the Constitution. All the stipulations contained in the Constitution in favor of the slaveholding States, which are already in the Union, ought to be fulfilled, and, so far as depends on me, shall be fulfilled in the fullness of their spirit, and to the exactness of their letter. Slavery, as it exists in the States, is beyond the reach of Congress. It is a concern of the States themselves. They have never submitted it to Congress, and Congress has no rightful power over it.

"I shall concur, therefore, in no act, no measure, no menace, no indication of purpose which shall interfere or threaten to interfere with the exclusive authority of the several States over the subject of slavery, as it exists within their respective limits. All this appears to me to be matter of plain and imperative duty.

"But when we come to speak of admitting new States, the subject assumes an entirely different aspect. Our rights and our duties are then both different.   *   *   *

"I see, therefore, no political necessity for the annexation of Texas to the Union—no advantages to be derived from it; and objections to it of a strong, and, in my judgment, of a decisive character."

Mr. WEBSTER. I have nothing, sir, to add to, nor to take back, from those sentiments. That, the Senate will perceive, was in 1837. The purpose of immediately annexing Texas, at that time, was abandoned or postponed, and it was not revived, with any vigor, for some years. In the mean time, it had so happenened, that I had become a member of the Executive Administration, and was, for a short period, in the Department of

State. The annexation of Texas was a subject of conversation—
not confidential—with the President and heads of Departments, as well as with other public men. No serious attempt
was then made, however, to bring it about. I left the Department of State in May, 1843, and shortly after, I learned, though
no way connected with official information, that a design had
been taken up, of bringing in Texas, with her slave territory
and population, into the United States. I was here, in Washington, at the time; and persons are now here who will remember,
that we had an arranged meeting for conversation upon it. I
went home, to Massachusetts, and proclaimed the existence of
that purpose; but I could get no audience, and but little attention. Some did not believe it, and some were too much engaged in their own pursuits to give it any heed. They had gone
to their farms, or to their merchandise, and it was impossible
to arouse any sentiment in New England or in Massachusetts
that should combine the two great political parties against this
annexation; and, indeed, there was no hope of bringing the
northern Democracy into that view, for the leaning was all the
other way. But, sir, even with Whigs, and leading Whigs, I am
ashamed to say, there was a great indifference toward the admission of Texas, with slave territory, into this Union. It went
on. I was then out of Congress. The annexation resolution
passed the 1st of March, 1845. The Legislature of Texas complied with the conditions, and accepted the guaranties; for the
phraseology of the language of the resolution is, that Texas is
to come in "upon the conditions, and under the guaranties,
herein prescribed." I happened to be returned to the Senate in
March, 1845, and was here in December, 1845, when the acceptance by Texas, of the conditions proposed by Congress, were
laid before us by the President; and an act, for the consummation of the connection, was laid before the two Houses. The
connection was not completed. A final law, doing the deed of
annexation ultimately, had not been passed; and when it was
upon its final passage here, I expressed my opposition to it,
and recorded my vote in the negative; and there that vote
stands, with the observations that I made upon that occasion.
It has happened, that between 1837 and this time, on various
occasions and opportunities, I have expressed my entire opposition to the admission of slave States, or the acquisition of

new slave territories, to be added to the United States. I know, sir, no change in my own sentiments, or my own purposes, in that respect. I will now, again, ask my friend from Rhode Island, to read another extract from a speech of mine, made at a Whig Convention, in Springfield, Massachusetts, in the month of September, 1847.

Mr. GREENE here read the following extract from the speech:

"We hear much just now of a *panacea* for the dangers and evils of slavery and slave annexation, which they call the *'Wilmot Proviso.'* That certainly is a just sentiment, but it is not a sentiment to found any new party upon. It is not a sentiment on which Massachusetts Whigs differ. There is not a man in this hall who holds to it more firmly than I do, nor one who adheres to it more than another.

"I feel some little interest in this matter, sir. Did not I commit myself in 1838 to the whole doctrine, fully, entirely? And I must be permitted to say, that I cannot quite consent that more recent discoverers should claim the merit and take out a patent.

"I deny the priority of their invention. Allow me to say, sir, it is not their thunder.   *   *   *

"We are to use the first, and last, and every occasion which offers, to oppose the extension of slave power.

"But I speak of it here, as in Congress, as a political question—a question for statesmen to act upon. We must so regard it. I certainly do not mean to say that it is less important in a moral point of view— that it is not more important in many other points of view; but, as a legislator, or in any official capacity, I must look at it, consider it, and decide it, as a matter of political action."

Mr. WEBSTER. On other occasions, in debates here, I have expressed my determination to vote for no acquisition, or cession, or annexation, North or South, East or West. My opinion has been, that we have territory enough, and that we should follow the Spartan maxim, "Improve, adorn what you have, seek no farther." I think that it was in some observations that I made here on the three million loan bill, that I avowed that sentiment. In short, sir, the sentiment has been avowed quite as often, in as many places, and before as many assemblages, as any humble sentiments of mine ought to be avowed.

But now that, under certain conditions, Texas is in, with all her territories, as a slave State, with a solemn pledge that if she is divided into many States, those States may come in as slave

States south of 36° 30′, how are we to deal with this subject? I know no way of honorable legislation, when the proper time comes for the enactment, but to carry into effect all that we have stipulated to do. I do not entirely agree with my honorable friend from Tennessee, [Mr. BELL,] that, as soon as the time comes when she is entitled to another Representative, we should create a new State. The rule in regard to it I take to be this: that when we have created new States out of territories, we have generally gone upon the idea, that when there is population enough to form a State—sixty thousand, or some such thing—we would create a State; but it is quite a different thing when a State is divided, and two or more States made out of it. It does not follow, in such a case, that the same rule of apportionment should be applied. That, however, is a matter for the consideration and discretion of Congress, when the proper time arrives. I may not then be here—I may have no vote to give on the occasion; but I wish it to be distinctly understood, to-day, that according to my view of the matter, this Government is solemnly pledged, by law and contract, to create new States out of Texas, with her consent, when her population shall justify such a proceeding, and so far as such States are formed out of Texan territory lying south of 36° 30′, to let them come in as slave States. The time of admission, and requisite population, must depend, of course, on the discretion of Congress. But when new States shall be formed out of Texas, they have a fixed right to come into the Union as slave States. That is the meaning of the resolution which our friends, the northern Democracy, have left us to fulfill; and I, for one, mean to fulfill it, because I will not violate the faith of the Government.

Now, as to California and New Mexico, I hold slavery to be excluded from those territories by a law even superior to that which admits and sanctions it in Texas—I mean the law of nature—of physical geography—the law of the formation of the earth. That law settles forever, with a strength beyond all terms of human enactment, that slavery cannot exist in California or New Mexico. Understand me, sir—I mean slavery as we regard it; slaves in gross, or the colored race, transferable by sale and delivery, like other property. I shall not discuss the point, but leave it to the learned gentlemen who have undertaken to discuss it; but I suppose there is no slave of that description in

California now. I understand that *peonism*, a sort of penal servitude, exists there; or, rather, a voluntary sale of a man and his offspring for debt, as it is arranged and exists in some parts of California and New Mexico. But what I mean to say is, that African slavery, as we see it among us, is as utterly impossible to find itself, or to be found in Mexico, as any other natural impossibility. California and New Mexico are Asiatic, in their formation and scenery. They are composed of vast ridges of mountains, of enormous height, with broken ridges and deep valleys. The sides of these mountains are barren—entirely barren—their tops capped by perennial snow. There may be in California, now made free by its constitution—and no doubt there are—some tracts of valuable land. But it is not so in New Mexico. Pray, what is the evidence which every gentleman must have obtained on this subject, from information sought by himself or communicated by others? I have inquired, and read all I could find, in order to obtain information on this important question. What is there in New Mexico that could by any possibility induce anybody to go there with slaves? There are some narrow strips of tillable land on the borders of the rivers; but the rivers themselves dry up before mid-summer is gone. All that the people can do, is to raise some little articles—some little wheat for their tortillas—and all that by irrigation. And who expects to see a hundred black men cultivating tobacco, corn, cotton, rice, or anything else, on lands in New Mexico, made fertile only by irrigation? I look upon it, therefore, as a fixed fact, to use an expression current at this day, that both California and New Mexico are destined to be free, so far as they are settled at all, which I believe, especially in regard to New Mexico, will be very little for a great length of time—free by the arrangement of things by the Power above us. I have therefore to say, in this respect also, that this country is fixed for freedom, to as many persons as shall ever live there, by as irrepealable and a more irrepealable law, than the law that attaches to the right of holding slaves in Texas; and I will say further, that if a resolution, or a law, were now before us, to provide a territorial government for New Mexico, I would not vote to put any prohibition into it whatever. The use of such a prohibition would be idle, as it respects any effect it would have upon the territory; and I would not take pains to reaffirm an ordinance of nature, nor to reënact the will of God. And I would put in no Wilmot proviso, for the purpose of a taunt or a reproach. I would put into it no evidence of the votes of superior power, to wound the pride, even whether a just pride, a rational pride, or an irrational pride—to wound the pride of the gentlemen who belong to the southern States. I have no such object—no such purpose. They would think it a taunt—an indignity. They would think it to be an act taking away from them what they regard a proper equality of privilege; and whether they expect to realize any benefit from it or not, they would think it a theoretic wrong—that something more or less derogatory to their character and their rights had taken place. I propose to inflict no such wound upon any body, unless something essentially important to the country, and efficient to the preservation of liberty and freedom, is to be effected. Therefore, I repeat, sir—and I repeat it because I wish it to be understood—that I do not propose to address the Senate often on this subject. I desire to pour out all my heart in as plain a manner as possible; and I say again, that if a proposition were now here for a government for New Mexico, and it was moved to insert a provision for a prohibition of slavery, I would not vote for it.

Now, Mr. President, I have established, so far as I proposed to go into any line of observation to establish, the proposition with which I set out, and upon which I propose to stand or fall; and that is, that the whole territory of the States in the United States, or in the newly-acquired territory of the United States, has a fixed and settled character, now fixed and settled by law, which can not be repealed in the case of Texas, without a violation of public faith, and can not be repealed by any human power in regard to California or New Mexico; that, under one or other of these laws, every foot of territory in the States, or in the Territories, has now received a fixed and decided character.

Sir, it we were now making a Government for New Mexico, and any body should propose a Wilmot proviso, I should treat it exactly as Mr. Polk treated that provision for excluding slavery from Oregon. Mr. Polk was known in be in opinion decidedly averse to the Wilmot proviso; but he felt the necessity of establishing a government for the Territory of Oregon, and, though the proviso was there, he knew it would be entirely nugatory; and, since it must be entirely nugatory, since it took away no right, no describable, no estimable, no weighable, or tangible right of the South, he said he would sign the bill for the sake of enacting a law to form a Government in that Territory, and let that entirely useless, and, in that connection, entirely senseless, proviso remain. For myself, I will say that we hear much of the annexation of Canada; and if there be any man, any of the northern Democracy, or any one of the Free-Soil party, who supposes it necessary to insert a Wilmot proviso in a Territorial Government for New Mexico, that man will of course be of opinion that it is necessary to protect the everlasting snows of Canada from the foot of slavery, by the same overpowering wing of an act of Congress. Sir, where-ever there is a particular good to be done—where-ever there is a foot of land to be staid back from becoming slave territory—I am ready to assert the principle of the exclusion of slavery. I am pledged to it from the year 1837; I have been pledged to it again and again; and I will perform those pledges; but I will not do a thing unnecessary, that wounds the feelings of others, or that does disgrace to my own understanding.

Mr. President, in the excited times in which we live, there is found to exist a state of crimination and recrimination between the North and the South. There are lists of grievances produced by each; and those grievances, real or supposed, alienate the minds of one portion of the country from the other, exasperate the feelings, subdue the sense of fraternal connection, and patriotic love, and mutual regard. I shall bestow a little attention, sir, upon these various grievances, produced on the one side and on the other. I begin with the complaints of the South: I will not answer, farther than I have, the general statements of the honorable Senator from South Carolina, that the North has grown upon the South in consequence of the manner of administering this Government, in the collecting of its revenues, and so forth. These are disputed topics, and I have no inclination to enter into them. But I will state these complaints, especially one complaint of the South, which has in my opinion just foundation; and that is, that there has been found at the North, among individuals and among the Legislatures of the North, a disinclination to perform, fully, their constitutional duties, in regard to the return of persons bound to service, who have escaped into the free States. In that respect, it is my judgment that the South is right, and the North is wrong. Every member of every northern Legislature is bound, by oath, like every other officer in the country, to support the Constitution of the United States; and this article of the Constitution, which says to these States, they shall deliver up fugitives from service, is as binding in honor and conscience as any other article. No man fulfills his duty in any Legislature who sets himself to find excuses, evasions, escapes from this constitutional obligation. I have always thought that the Constitution addressed itself to the Legislatures of the States themselves, or to the States themselves. It says, that those persons escaping to other States, shall be delivered up, and I confess I have always been of the opinion, that it was an injunction upon the States themselves. When it is said that a person escaping into another State, and becoming therefore within the jurisdiction of that State, shall be delivered up, it seems to me the import of the passage is, that the State itself, in obedience to the Constitution, shall cause him to be delivered up. That is my judgment. I have always entertained that opinion, and I entertain it now. But when the subject, some years ago, was before the Supreme Court of the United States, the majority of the judges held that the power, to cause fugitives from service to be delivered up, was a power to be exercised under the authority of this Government. I do not know, on the whole, that it may not have been a fortunate decision. My habit is to respect the result of judicial deliberations and the solemnity of judicial decisions. But, as it now stands, the business of seeing that these fugitives are delivered up, resides in the power of Congress, and the national judicature, and my friend at the head of the Judiciary Committee has a bill on the subject, now before the Senate, with some amendments to it, which I propose to support, with all its provisions, to the fullest extent. And I desire to call the attention of all sober-minded men, of all conscientious men, in the North, of all men who are not carried away by any fanatical idea, or by any false idea whatever, to their constitutional obligations. I put it to all the sober and sound minds at the North, as a question of morals and a question of consience, What right have they, in all their legislative capacity, or any other, to endeavor to get round this Constitution, to embarrass the free exercise of the rights secured by the Constitution, to the persons whose slaves escape from them? None at all—none at all. Neither in the forum of conscience, nor before the face of the Constitution, are they justified, in my opinion. Of course, it is a matter for their consideration. They probably, in the turmoil of the times, have not stopped to consider of this; they have followed what seemed to be the current of thought and of motives as the occasion arose, and neglected to investigate fully the real question, and to consider their constitutional obligations, as I am sure, if they did consider, they would fulfill them with alacrity. Therefore, I repeat, sir, that here is a ground of complaint against the North, well founded, which ought to be removed—which it is now in the power of the different departments of this Government to remove— which calls for the enactment of proper laws, authorizing the judicature of this Government, in the several States, to do all that is necessary for the recapture of fugitive slaves, and for the restoration of them to those who claim them. Wherever I go, and whenever I speak on the subject—and when I speak here, I desire to speak to the whole North—I say that the South has been injured in this respect, and has a right to complain; and the North has been too careless of what I think the Constitution peremptorily and emphatically enjoins upon it as a duty.

Complaint has been made against certain resolutions that emanate from Legislatures at the North, and are sent here to us, not only on the subject of slavery in this District, but sometimes recommending Congress to consider the means of abolishing slavery in the States. I should be sorry to be called upon to present any resolutions here which could not be referable to any committee or any power in Congress, and, therefore, I should be unwilling to receive from the Legislature of Massachusetts any instructions to present resolutions expressive of any opinion whatever on the subject of slavery, as it exists at the present moment in the States, for two reasons; because— first, I do not consider that the Legislature of Massachusetts has anything to do with it; and next, I do not consider that I, as her representative here, have anything to do with it. Sir, it has become, in my opinion, quite too common; and if the Legislatures of the States do not like that opinion, they have a great deal more power to put it down, than I have to uphold it. It has become, in my opinion, quite too common a practice for the State Legislatures to present resolutions here on all subjects, and to instruct us here on all subjects. There is no public man that requires instruction more than I do, or who requires information more than I do, or desires it more heartily; but I do not like to have it come in too imperative a shape. I took notice, with pleasure, of some remarks upon this subject made the other day in the Senate of Massachusetts, by a young man of talent and character, from whom the best hopes may be entertained. I mean Mr. Hilliard. He told the Senate of Massachusetts that he would vote for no instructions whatever to be forwarded to members of Congress, nor for any resolutions to be offered, expressive of the sense of Massachusetts, as to what their members of Congress ought to do. He said that he saw no propriety in one set of public servants giving instructions and reading lectures to another set of public servants. To their own master, all of them must stand or fall, and that master is their constituents. I wish these sentiments could become more common—a great deal more common. I have never entered into the question, and never shall, about the binding force of instructions. I will, however, simply say this: if there be any matter of interest pending in this body, while I am a member of it, in which Massachusetts has an interest of her own not adverse to the general interest of the country, I shall pursue her instructions with gladness of heart, and with all the efficiency which I can bring to the occasion. But if the question be one which affects her interest, and at the same time affects the interests of all other States, I shall no more regard her political wishes or instructions, than I would regard the wishes of a man who might appoint me an arbitrator or referee, to decide some question of important private right, and who might *instruct* me to decide in his favor. If ever there was a government upon earth, it is this Government; if ever there was a body upon earth, it is this body, which should consider itself as composed by agreement of all, appointed by some, but organized by the general consent of all, sitting here under the solemn obligations of oath and conscience, to do that which they think is best for the good of the whole.

Then, sir, there are those abolition societies, of which I am unwilling to speak, but in regard to which I have very clear notions and opinions. I do not think them useful. I think their operations for the last twenty years have produced nothing good or valuable. At the same time, I know thousands of them are honest and good men; perfectly well-meaning men. They have excited feelings; they think they must do something for the cause of liberty; and in their sphere of action, they do not see what else they can do, than to contribute to an abolition press, or an abolition society, or to pay an abolition lecturer. I do not mean to impute gross motives even to the leaders of these societies, but I am not blind to the consequences. I cannot but see what mischiefs their interference with the South has produced. And is it not plain to every man? Let any gentleman who doubts of that, recur to the debates in the Virginia House of Delegates in 1832, and he will see with what freedom a proposition, made by Mr. Randolph for the gradual abolition of slavery, was discussed in that body. Every one spoke of slavery as he thought; very ignominious and disparaging names and epithets were applied to it. The debates in the House of Delegates on that occasion, I believe, were all published. They were read by every colored man who could read, and if there were any who could not read, those debates were read to them by others. At that time Virginia was not unwilling nor afraid to discuss this question, and to let that part of her population know as much of it as they could learn. That was in 1832. As has been said by the honorable member from Carolina, these abolition societies commenced their course of action in 1835. It is said—I do not know how true it may be—that they sent incendiary publications into the slave States; at any event, they attempted to arouse, and did arouse, a very strong feeling; in other words, they created great agitation in the North against southern slavery. Well, what was the result? The bonds of the slaves were bound more firmly than before; their rivets were more strongly fastened. Public opinion, which in Virginia had begun to be exhibited against slavery, and was opening out for the discussion of the question, drew back and shut itself up in its castle. I wish to know whether any body in Virginia can, now, talk as Mr. Randolph, Gov. McDowell, and others talked there, openly, and sent their remarks to the press, in 1832. We all know the fact, and we all know the cause, and everything that this agitating people have done, has been, not to enlarge, but to restrain, not to set free, but to bind faster, the slave population of the South. That is my judgment. Sir, as I have said, I know many Abolitionists in my own neighborhood, very honest good people, misled, as I think, by strange enthusiasm; but they wish to do something, and they are called on to contribute, and they do contribute; and it is my firm opinion this day, that within the last twenty years, as much money has been collected and paid to the abolition societies, abolition presses, and abolition lecturers, as would purchase the freedom of every slave, man, woman, and child in the State of Maryland, and send them all to Liberia. I have no doubt of it. But I have yet to learn that the benevolence of these abolition societies has at any time taken that particular turn. [Laughter.]

Again, sir, the violence of the press is complained of. The press violent! Why, sir, the press is violent everywhere. There are outrageous reproaches in the North against the South, and there are reproaches in not much better taste in the South against the North. Sir, the extremists of both parts of this country are violent; they mistake loud and violent talk for eloquence and for reason. They think that he who talks loudest, reasons the best. And this we must expect, when the press is free, as it is here—and I trust always will be—for, with all its licentiousness, and all its evil, the entire and absolute freedom of the press is essential to the preservation of government, on the basis of a free constitution. Wherever it exists, there will be foolish paragraphs, and violent paragraphs, in the press, as there are, I am sorry to say, foolish speeches and violent speeches in both Houses of Congress. In truth, sir, I must say that, in my opinion, the vernacular tongue of the country has become greatly vitiated, depraved, and corrupted, by the style of our congressional debates. [Laughter.] And if it were possible for our debates in Congress to vitiate the principles of the people as much as they have depraved their taste, I should cry out, "God save the Republic."

Well, in all this I see no solid grievance—no grievance presented by the South, within the redress of the Government, but the single one to which I have referred; and that is, the want of a proper regard to the injunction of the Constitution, for the delivery of fugitive slaves.

There are also complaints of the North against the South. I need not go over them particularly. The first and gravest is, that, the North adopted the Constitution, recognizing the existence of slavery in the States, and recognizing the right, to a certain extent, of representation of the slaves in Congress, under a state of sentiment and expectation which do not now exist; and that, by events, by circumstances, by the eagerness of the South to acquire territory, and extend their slave population, the North finds itself, in regard to the influence of the South and the North, of the free States and the slave States, where it never did expect to find itself when they entered the compact of the Constitution. They complain, therefore, that, instead of slavery being regarded as an evil, as it was then, an evil, which all hoped would be extinguished gradually, it is now regarded by the South as an institution to be cherished, and preserved, and extended—an institution which the South has already extended to the utmost of her power by the acquisition of new territory. Well, then, passing from that, everybody in the North reads; and everybody reads whatsoever the newspapers contain; and the newspapers, some of them—especially those presses to which I have alluded—are careful to spread about among the people every reproachful sentiment uttered by any southern man bearing at all against the North—everything that is calculated to exasperate, to alienate; and there are many such things, as everybody will admit, from the South, or some portion of it, which are spread abroad among the reading people; and they do exasperate, and alienate, and produce a most mischievous effect upon the public mind at the North. Sir, I would not notice things of this sort appearing in obscure quarters; but one thing has occurred in this debate which struck me very forcibly. An honorable member from Louisiana addressed us the other day on this subject. I suppose there is not a more amiable and worthy gentleman in this chamber, nor a gentleman who would be more slow to give offence to anybody, and he did not mean in his remarks to give offense. But what did he say? Why, sir, he took pains to run a contrast between the slaves of the South and the laboring people of the North, giving the preference in all points of condition, and comfort, and happiness, to the slaves of the South. The honorable member doubtless did not suppose that he gave any offense, or did any injustice. He was merely expressing his opinion. But does he know how remarks of that sort will be received by the laboring people of the North? Why, who are the laboring people of the North? They are the North. They are the people who cultivate their own farms with their own hands—freeholders, educated men, independent men. Let me say, sir, that five sixths of the whole property of the North, is in the hands of the laborers of the North; they cultivate their farms, they educate their children, they provide the means of independence; if they are not freeholders, they earn wages; these wages accumulate, are turned into capital, into new freeholds; and small capitalists are created. That is the case, and such the course of things, with us, among the industrious, and frugal. And what can these people think when so respectable and worthy a gentleman as the member from Louisiana, undertakes to prove that the absolute ignorance, and the abject slavery of the South, is more in conformity with the high purposes and destinies of immortal, rational, human beings, than the educated, the independent free laborers of the North?

There is a more tangible, and irritating cause of grievance, at the North. Free blacks are constantly employed in the vessels of the North, generally as cooks or stewards. When the vessel arrives, these free colored men, are taken on shore, by the police or municipal authority, imprisoned, and kept in prison, till the vessel is again ready to sail. This is not only irritating, but exceedingly inconvenient in practice, and seems altogether unjustifiable, and oppressive. Mr. Hoar's mission, some time ago, to South Carolina, was a well-intended effort to remove this cause of complaint. The North thinks such imprisonment illegal, and unconstitutional; as the cases occur constantly and frequently, they think it a great grievance.

Now, sir, so far as any of these grievances have their foundation in matters of law, they can be redressed, and ought to be redressed; and so far as they have foundation in matters of opinion, in sentiment, in mutual crimination and recrimination, all that we can do is, to endeavor to allay the agitation, and cultivate a better feeling and more fraternal sentiments between the South and the North.

Mr. President, I should much prefer to have heard, from every member on this floor, declarations of opinion that this

Union should never be dissolved, than the declaration of opinion that in any case, under the pressure of any circumstances, such a dissolution was possible. I hear with pain, and anguish, and distress, the word secession, especially when it falls from the lips of those who are eminently patriotic, and known to the country, and known all over the world, for their political services. Secession! Peaceable secession! Sir, your eyes and mine are never destined to see that miracle. The dismemberment of this vast country without convulsion! The breaking up of the fountains of the great deep without ruffling the surface! Who is so foolish—I beg everybody's pardon—as to expect to see any such thing? Sir, he who sees these States, now revolving in harmony around a common centre, and expects to see them quit their places and fly off without convulsion, may look the next hour to see the heavenly bodies rush from their spheres, and jostle against each other in the realms of space, without producing the crush of the universe. There can be no such thing as a peaceable secession. Peaceable secession is an utter impossibility. Is the great Constitution under which we live here—covering this whole country—is it to be thawed and melted away by secession, as the snows on the mountain melt under the influence of a vernal sun—disappear almost unobserved, and die off? No, sir! no, sir! I will not state what might produce the disruption of the States; but, sir, I see it as plainly as I see the sun in heaven—I see that disruption must produce such a war as I will not describe, in its twofold characters.

Peaceable secession! peaceable secession! The concurrent agreement of all the members of this great Republic to separate! A voluntary separation, with alimony on one side and on the other. Why, what would be the result? Where is the line to be drawn? What States are to secede? What is to remain American? What am I to be?—an American no longer? Where is the flag of the Republic to remain? Where is the eagle still to tower? or is he to cower, and shrink, and fall to the ground? Why, sir, our ancestors—our fathers, and our grandfathers, those of them that are yet living among us with prolonged lives—would rebuke and reproach us; and our children, and our grandchildren, would cry out, Shame upon us! if we, of this generation, should dishonor these ensigns of the power of the Government, and the harmony of the Union, which is every day felt among us with so much joy and gratitude. What is to become of the army? What is to become of the navy? What is to become of the public lands? How is each of the thirty States to defend itself? I know, although the idea has not been stated distinctly, there is to be a southern Confederacy. I do not mean, when I allude to this statement, that any one seriously contemplates such a state of things. I do not mean to say that it is true, but I have heard it suggested elsewhere, that that idea has originated in a design to separate. I am sorry, sir, that it has ever been thought of, talked of, or dreamed of, in the wildest flights of human imagination. But the idea must be of a separation, including the slave States upon one side, and the free States on the other. Sir, there is not—I may express myself too strongly perhaps—but some things, some moral things, are almost as impossible, as other natural or physical things; and I hold the idea of a separation of these States—those that are free to form one government, and those that are slaveholding to form another—as a moral impossibility. We could not separate the States by any such line, if we were to draw it. We could not sit down here to-day, and draw a line of separation, that would satisfy any five men in the country. There are natural causes that would keep and tie us together, and there are social and domestic relations which we could not break, if we would, and which we should not, if we could. Sir, nobody can look over the face of this country at the present moment—nobody can see where its population is the most dense and growing—without being ready to admit, and compelled to admit, that, ere long, America will be in the valley of the Mississippi.

Well, now, sir, I beg to inquire what the wildest enthusiast has to say, on the possibility of cutting off that river, and leaving free States at its source and its branches, and slave States down near its mouth? Pray, sir—pray, sir, let me say to the people of this country, that these things are worthy of their pondering and of their consideration. Here, sir, are five millions of freemen in the free States north of the river Ohio: can anybody suppose that this population can be severed by a line that divides them from the territory of a foreign and an alien government, down somewhere, the Lord knows where, upon the lower banks of the Mississippi? What will become of Missouri? Will she join the arrondissement of the slave States? Shall the man from the Yellow Stone and the Platte be connected in the new Republic with the man who lives on the southern extremity of the Cape of Florida? Sir, I am ashamed to pursue this line of remark. I dislike it—I have an utter disgust for it. I would rather hear of natural blasts and mildews, war, pestilence, and famine, than to hear gentlemen talk of secession. To break up! to break up this great Government! to dismember this great country! to astonish Europe with an act of folly, such as Europe for two centuries has never beheld in any government! No, sir! no, sir! There will be no secession. Gentlemen are not serious when they talk of secession.

Sir, I hear there is to be a Convention held at Nashville. I am bound to believe that if worthy gentlemen meet at Nashville in Convention, their object will be to adopt counsels conciliatory—to advise the South to forbearance and moderation, and to advise the North to forbearance and moderation, and to inculcate principles of brotherly love, and affection, and attachment to the Constitution of the country, as it now is. I believe, if the Convention meet at all, it will be for this purpose; for certainly, if they meet for any purpose hostile to the Union, they have been singularly inappropriate in their selection of a place. I remember, sir, that when the treaty was concluded between France and England, at the peace of Amiens, a stern old Englishman and an orator, who disliked the terms of the peace as ignominious to England, said in the House of Commons, that if King William could know the terms of that treaty, he would turn in his coffin. Let me commend this saying of Mr. Windham, in all its emphasis and in all its force, to any persons who shall meet at Nashville for the purpose of concerting measures for the overthrow of the Union of this country, over the bones of Andrew Jackson.

Sir, I wish to make two remarks, and hasten to a conclusion. I wish to say, in regard to Texas, that if it should be hereafter at any time the pleasure of the Government of Texas to cede to the United States a portion, larger or smaller, of her territory which lies adjacent to New Mexico and north of the 34° of north latitude, to be formed into free States, for a fair equivalent in money, or in the payment of her debt, I think it an object well worthy the consideration of Congress, and I shall be happy to concur in it myself, if I should be in the public counsels of the country at the time.

I have one other remark to make: In my observations upon slavery as it has existed in the country, and as it now exists, I have expressed no opinion of the mode of its extinguishment or melioration. I will say, however, though I have nothing to propose on that subject, because I do not deem myself so competent as other gentlemen to consider it, that if any gentleman from the South shall propose a scheme of colonization, to be carried on by this government upon a large scale, for the transportation of free colored people to any colony or any place in the world, I should be quite disposed to incur almost any degree of expense to accomplish that object. Nay, sir, following an example set here more than twenty years ago, by a great man, then a Senator from New York, I would return to Virginia, and through her for the benefit of the whole South, the money received from the lands and territories ceded by her to this Government, for any such purpose as to relieve, in whole or in part, or in any way, to diminish or deal beneficially with, the free colored population of the southern States. I have said that I honor Virginia for her cession of this territory. There have been received into the treasury of the United States eighty millions of dollars, the proceeds of the sales of the public lands ceded by Virginia. If the residue should be sold at the same rate, the whole aggregate will exceed two hundred millions of dollars. If Virginia and the South see fit to adopt any proposition to relieve themselves from the free people of color among them, they have my free consent that the Government shall pay them any sum of money out of its proceeds which may be adequate to the purpose.

And now, Mr. President, I draw these observations to a close. I have spoken freely, and I meant to do so. I have sought to make no display; I have sought to enliven the occasion by no animated discussion; nor have I attempted any train of elaborate argument. I have sought only to speak my sentiments, fully and at large, being desirous, once and for all, to let the Senate know, and to let the country know, the opinions and sentiments which I entertain on all these subjects. These opinions are not likely to be suddenly changed. If there be any future service that I can render to the country, consistently with these sentiments and opinions, I shall cheerfully render it. If there be not, I shall still be glad to have had an opportunity to disburden my conscience from the bottom of my heart, and to make known every political sentiment that therein exists.

And now, Mr. President, instead of speaking of the possibility or utility of secession, instead of dwelling in these caverns of darkness, instead of groping with those ideas so full of all that is horrid and horrible, let us come out into the light of day; let us enjoy the fresh air of liberty and union; let us cherish those hopes which belong to us; let us devote ourselves to those great objects that are fit for our consideration and our action; let us raise our conceptions to the magnitude and the importance of the duties that devolve upon us; let our comprehension be as broad as the country for which we act, our aspirations as high as its certain destiny; let us not be pigmies in a case that calls for men. Never did there devolve, on any generation of men, higher trusts than now devolve upon us for the preservation of this Constitution, and the harmony and peace of all who are destined to live under it. Let us make our generation one of the strongest, and the brightest link, in that golden chain which is destined, I fully believe, to grapple the people of all the States to this Constitution, for ages to come. It is a great popular Constitutional Government, guarded by legislation, by law, by judicature, and defended by the whole affections of the people. No monarchical throne presses these States together; no iron chain of despotic power encircles them; they live and stand upon a Government popular in its form, representative in its character, founded upon principles of equality, and calculated, we hope, to last forever. In all its history, it has been beneficent; it has trodden down no man's liberty; it has crushed no State. Its daily respiration, is liberty and patriotism; its yet youthful veins are full of enterprise, courage, and honorable love of glory and renown. It has received a vast addition of territory. Large before, the country has now, by recent events, become vastly larger. This Republic now extends, with a vast breadth, across the whole continent. The two great seas of the world wash the one and the other shore. We realize on a mighty scale, the beautiful description of the ornamental edging of the buckler of Achilles—

> "Now the broad shield complete the artist crowned,
> With his last hand, and poured the ocean round;
> In living silver seemed the waves to roll,
> And beat the buckler's verge, and bound the whole."

SOJOUNER TRUTH

Speech to Woman's Rights Convention

Akron, Ohio, May 29, 1851

WELL, chillen, whar dar's so much racket dar must be som'ting out o' kilter. I tink dat, 'twixt de niggers of de South and de women of de Norf, all a-talking 'bout rights, de white men will be in a fix pretty soon. But what's all this here talking 'bout? Dat man ober dar say dat woman needs to be helped into carriages, and lifted over ditches, and to have de best place eberywhar. Nobody eber helps me into carriages, or ober mud-puddles, or gives me any best place"; and, raising herself to her full height, and her voice to a pitch like rolling thunder, she asked "And ar'n't I a woman? Look at me. Look at my arm," and she bared her right arm to the shoulder, showing its tremendous muscular power. "I have plowed and planted and gathered into barns, and no man could head me— and ar'n't I a woman? I could work as much and eat as much as a man (when I could get it), and bear de lash as well—and ar'n't I a woman? I have borne thirteen chillen, and seen 'em mos' all sold off into slavery, and when I cried out with a mother's grief, none but Jesus heard—and ar'n't I a woman? Den dey talks 'bout dis ting in the head. What dis dey call it?" "Intellect," whispered some one near. "Dat's it, honey. What's dat got to do with woman's rights or niggers' rights? If my cup won't hold but a pint and yourn holds a quart, wouldn't ye be mean not to let me have my little half-measure full?" and she pointed her significant finger and sent a keen glance at the minister who had made the argument. The cheering was long and loud. "Den dat little man in black dar, he say woman can't have as much right as man 'cause Christ wa'n'nt a woman. *Whar did your Christ come from?*"

Rolling thunder could not have stilled that crowd as did those deep, wonderful tones, as she stood there with outstretched arms and eye of fire. Raising her voice still louder, she repeated—

"Whar did your Christ come from? From God and a woman. Man had not'ing to do with him." Oh! what a rebuke she gave the little man. Turning again to another objector, she took up the defence of Mother Eve. I cannot follow her through it all. It was pointed and witty and solemn, eliciting at almost every sentence deafening applause; and she ended by asserting "that if de fust woman God ever made was strong enough to turn de world upside down all her one lone, all dese togeder," and she glanced her eye over us, "ought to be able to turn it back and git it right side up again, and now dey is asking to, de men better let 'em" (long continued cheering). "'Bleeged to ye for hearin' on me, and now ole Sojourner ha'n't got nothin' more to say."

FREDERICK DOUGLASS

What to the Slave Is the 4th of July?

Rochester, N.Y., July 5, 1852

M R. PRESIDENT, FRIENDS AND FELLOW CITIZENS: He who could address this audience without a quailing sensation, has stronger nerves than I have. I do not remember ever to have appeared as a speaker before any assembly more shrinkingly, nor with greater distrust of my ability, than I do this day. A feeling has crept over me, quite unfavorable to the exercise of my limited powers of speech. The task before me is one which requires much previous thought and study for its proper performance. I know that apologies of this sort are generally considered flat and unmeaning. I trust, however, that mine will not be so considered. Should I seem at ease, my appearance would much misrepresent me. The little experience I have had in addressing public meetings, in country school houses, avails me nothing on the present occasion.

The papers and placards say, that I am to deliver a 4th of July oration. This certainly sounds large, and out of the common way, for me. It is true that I have often had the privilege to speak in this beautiful Hall, and to address many who now honor me with their presence. But neither their familiar faces, nor the perfect gage I think I have of Corinthian Hall, seems to free me from embarrassment.

The fact is, ladies and gentlemen, the distance between this platform and the slave plantation, from which I escaped, is considerable—and the difficulties to be overcome in getting from the latter to the former, are by no means slight. That I am here to-day is, to me, a matter of astonishment as well as of gratitude. You will not, therefore, be surprised, if in what I have to say, I evince no elaborate preparation, nor grace my speech with any high sounding exordium. With little experience and with less learning, I have been able to throw my thoughts hastily and imperfectly together; and trusting to your patient and generous indulgence, I will proceed to lay them before you.

This, for the purpose of this celebration, is the 4th of July. It is the birthday of your National Independence, and of your political freedom. This, to you, is what the Passover was to the emancipated people of God. It carries your minds back to the day, and to the act of your great deliverance; and to the signs, and to the wonders, associated with that act, and that day. This celebration also marks the beginning of another year of your national life; and reminds you that the Republic of America is now 76 years old. I am glad, fellow-citizens, that your nation is so young. Seventy-six years, though a good old age for a man, is but a mere speck in the life of a nation. Three score years and ten is the allotted time for individual men; but nations number their years by thousands. According to this fact, you are, even now, only in the beginning of your national career, still lingering in the period of childhood. I repeat, I am glad this is so. There is hope in the thought, and hope is much needed, under the dark clouds which lower above the horizon. The eye of the reformer is met with angry flashes, portending disastrous times; but his heart may well beat lighter at the thought that America is young, and that she is still in the impressible stage of her existence. May he not hope that high lessons of wisdom, of justice and of truth, will yet give direction to her destiny? Were the nation older, the patriot's heart might be sadder, and the reformer's brow heavier. Its future might be shrouded in gloom, and the hope of its prophets go out in sorrow. There is consolation in the thought that America is young. Great streams are not easily turned from channels, worn deep in the course of ages. They may sometimes rise in quiet and stately majesty, and inundate the land, refreshing and fertilizing the earth with their mysterious properties. They may also rise in wrath and fury, and bear away, on their angry waves, the accumulated wealth of years of toil and hardship. They, however, gradually flow back to the same old channel, and flow on as serenely as ever. But, while the river may not be turned aside, it may dry up, and leave nothing behind but the withered branch, and the unsightly rock, to howl in the abyss-sweeping wind, the sad tale of departed glory. As with rivers so with nations.

Fellow-citizens, I shall not presume to dwell at length on

the associations that cluster about this day. The simple story of it is that, 76 years ago, the people of this country were British subjects. The style and title of your "sovereign people" (in which you now glory) was not then born. You were under the British Crown. Your fathers esteemed the English Government as the home government; and England as the fatherland. This home government, you know, although a considerable distance from your home, did, in the exercise of its parental prerogatives, impose upon its colonial children, such restraints, burdens and limitations, as, in its mature judgement, it deemed wise, right and proper.

But, your fathers, who had not adopted the fashionable idea of this day, of the infallibility of government, and the absolute character of its acts, presumed to differ from the home government in respect to the wisdom and the justice of some of those burdens and restraints. They went so far in their excitement as to pronounce the measures of government unjust, unreasonable, and oppressive, and altogether such as ought not to be quietly submitted to. I scarcely need say, fellow-citizens, that my opinion of those measures fully accords with that of your fathers. Such a declaration of agreement on my part would not be worth much to anybody. It would, certainly, prove nothing, as to what part I might have taken, had I lived during the great controversy of 1776. To say *now* that America was right, and England wrong, is exceedingly easy. Everybody can say it; the dastard, not less than the noble brave, can flippantly discant on the tyranny of England towards the American Colonies. It is fashionable to do so; but there was a time when to pronounce against England, and in favor of the cause of the colonies, tried men's souls. They who did so were accounted in their day, plotters of mischief, agitators and rebels, dangerous men. To side with the right, against the wrong, with the weak against the strong, and with the oppressed against the oppressor! *here* lies the merit, and the one which, of all others, seems unfashionable in our day. The cause of liberty may be stabbed by the men who glory in the deeds of your fathers. But, to proceed.

Feeling themselves harshly and unjustly treated by the home government, your fathers, like men of honesty, and men of spirit, earnestly sought redress. They petitioned and remonstrated; they did so in a decorous, respectful, and loyal manner. Their conduct was wholly unexceptionable. This, however, did not answer the purpose. They saw themselves treated with sovereign indifference, coldness and scorn. Yet they persevered. They were not the men to look back.

As the sheet anchor takes a firmer hold, when the ship is tossed by the storm, so did the cause of your fathers grow stronger, as it breasted the chilling blasts of kingly displeasure. The greatest and best of British statesmen admitted its justice, and the loftiest eloquence of the British Senate came to its support. But, with that blindness which seems to be the unvarying characteristic of tyrants, since Pharoah and his hosts were drowned in the Red Sea, the British Government persisted in the exactions complained of.

The madness of this course, we believe, is admitted now, even by England; but we fear the lesson is wholly lost on our present rulers.

Oppression makes a wise man mad. Your fathers were wise men, and if they did not go mad, they became restive under this treatment. They felt themselves the victims of grievous wrongs, wholly incurable in their colonial capacity. With brave men there is always a remedy for oppression. Just here, the idea of a total separation of the colonies from the crown was born! It was a startling idea, much more so, than we, at this distance of time, regard it. The timid and the prudent (as has been intimated) of that day, were, of course, shocked and alarmed by it.

Such people lived then, had lived before, and will, probably, ever have a place on this planet; and their course, in respect to any great change, (no matter how great the good to be attained, or the wrong to be redressed by it), may be calculated with as much precision as can be the course of the stars. They hate all changes, but silver, gold and copper change! Of this sort of change they are always strongly in favor.

These people were called tories in the days of your fathers; and the appellation, probably, conveyed the same idea that is meant by a more modern, though a somewhat less euphonious term, which we often find in our papers, applied to some of our old politicians.

Their opposition to the then dangerous thought was earnest

and powerful; but, amid all their terror and affrighted vociferations against it, the alarming and revolutionary idea moved on, and the country with it.

On the 2d of July, 1776, the old Continental Congress, to the dismay of the lovers of ease, and the worshippers of property, clothed that dreadful idea with all the authority of national sanction. They did so in the form of a resolution; and as we seldom hit upon resolutions, drawn up in our day, whose transparency is at all equal to this, it may refresh your minds and help my story if I read it.

"Resolved, That these united colonies *are*, and of right, ought to be free and Independent States; that they are absolved from all allegiance to the British Crown; and that all political connection between them and the State of Great Britain *is*, and ought to be, dissolved."

Citizens, your fathers made good that resolution. They succeeded; and to-day you reap the fruits of their success. The freedom gained is yours; and you, therefore, may properly celebrate this anniversary. The 4th of July is the first great fact in your nation's history—the very ring-bolt in the chain of your yet undeveloped destiny.

Pride and patriotism, not less than gratitude, prompt you to celebrate and to hold it in perpetual remembrance. I have said that the Declaration of Independence is the RING-BOLT to the chain of your nation's destiny; so, indeed, I regard it. The principles contained in that instrument are saving principles. Stand by those principles, be true to them on all occasions, in all places, against all foes, and at whatever cost.

From the round top of your ship of state, dark and threatening clouds may be seen. Heavy billows, like mountains in the distance, disclose to the leeward huge forms of flinty rocks! That *bolt* drawn, that *chain* broken, and all is lost. *Cling to this day—cling to it*, and to its principles, with the grasp of a storm-tossed mariner to a spar at midnight.

The coming into being of a nation, in any circumstances, is an interesting event. But, besides general considerations, there were peculiar circumstances which make the advent of this republic an event of special attractiveness.

The whole scene, as I look back to it, was simple, dignified and sublime.

The population of the country, at the time, stood at the insignificant number of three millions. The country was poor in the munitions of war. The population was weak and scattered, and the country a wilderness unsubdued. There were then no means of concert and combination, such as exist now. Neither steam nor lightning had then been reduced to order and discipline. From the Potomac to the Delaware was a journey of many days. Under these, and innumerable other disadvantages, your fathers declared for liberty and independence and triumphed.

Fellow Citizens, I am not wanting in respect for the fathers of this republic. The signers of the Declaration of Independence were brave men. They were great men too—great enough to give fame to a great age. It does not often happen to a nation to raise, at one time, such a number of truly great men. The point from which I am compelled to view them is not, certainly, the most favorable; and yet I cannot contemplate their great deeds with less than admiration. They were statesmen, patriots and heroes, and for the good they did, and the principles they contended for, I will unite with you to honor their memory.

They loved their country better than their own private interests; and, though this is not the highest form of human excellence, all will concede that it is a rare virtue, and that when it is exhibited, it ought to command respect. He who will, intelligently, lay down his life for his country, is a man whom it is not in human nature to despise. Your fathers staked their lives, their fortunes, and their sacred honor, on the cause of their country. In their admiration of liberty, they lost sight of all other interests.

They were peace men; but they preferred revolution to peaceful submission to bondage. They were quiet men; but they did not shrink from agitating against oppression. They showed forbearance; but that they knew its limits. They believed in order; but not in the order of tyranny. With them, nothing was "*settled*" that was not right. With them, justice, liberty and humanity were "*final*;" not slavery and oppression. You may well cherish the memory of such men. They were great in their day and generation. Their solid manhood stands out the more as we contrast it with these degenerate times.

How circumspect, exact and proportionate were all their movements! How unlike the politicians of an hour! Their statesmanship looked beyond the passing moment, and stretched away in strength into the distant future. They seized upon eternal principles, and set a glorious example in their defence. Mark them!

Fully appreciating the hardship to be encountered, firmly believing in the right of their cause, honorably inviting the scrutiny of an on-looking world, reverently appealing to heaven to attest their sincerity, soundly comprehending the solemn responsibility they were about to assume, wisely measuring the terrible odds against them, your fathers, the fathers of this republic, did, most deliberately, under the inspiration of a glorious patriotism, and with a sublime faith in the great principles of justice and freedom, lay deep the corner-stone of the national superstructure, which has risen and still rises in grandeur around you.

Of this fundamental work, this day is the anniversary. Our eyes are met with demonstrations of joyous enthusiasm. Banners and pennants wave exultingly on the breeze. The din of business, too, is hushed. Even Mammon seems to have quitted his grasp on this day. The ear-piercing fife and the stirring drum unite their accents with the ascending peal of a thousand church bells. Prayers are made, hymns are sung, and sermons are preached in honor of this day; while the quick martial tramp of a great and multitudinous nation, echoed back by all the hills, valleys and mountains of a vast continent, bespeak the occasion one of thrilling and universal interest—a nation's jubilee.

Friends and citizens, I need not enter further into the causes which led to this anniversary. Many of you understand them better than I do. You could instruct me in regard to them. That is a branch of knowledge in which you feel, perhaps, a much deeper interest than your speaker. The causes which led to the separation of the colonies from the British crown have never lacked for a tongue. They have all been taught in your common schools, narrated at your firesides, unfolded from your pulpits, and thundered from your legislative halls, and are as familiar to you as household words. They form the staple of your national poetry and eloquence.

I remember, also, that, as a people, Americans are remarkably familiar with all facts which make in their own favor. This is esteemed by some as a national trait—perhaps a national weakness. It is a fact, that whatever makes for the wealth or for the reputation of Americans, and can be had *cheap!* will be found by Americans. I shall not be charged with slandering Americans, if I say I think the American side of any question may be safely left in American hands.

I leave, therefore, the great deeds of your fathers to other gentlemen whose claim to have been regularly descended will be less likely to be disputed than mine!

THE PRESENT.

My business, if I have any here to-day, is with the present. The accepted time with God and his cause is the ever-living now.

> "Trust no future, however pleasant,
>   Let the dead past bury its dead;
> Act, act in the living present,
>   Heart within, and God overhead."

We have to do with the past only as we can make it useful to the present and to the future. To all inspiring motives, to noble deeds which can be gained from the past, we are welcome. But now is the time, the important time. Your fathers have lived, died, and have done their work, and have done much of it well. You live and must die, and you must do your work. You have no right to enjoy a child's share in the labor of your fathers, unless your children are to be blest by your labors. You have no right to wear out and waste the hard-earned fame of your fathers to cover your indolence. Sydney Smith tells us that men seldom eulogize the wisdom and virtues of their fathers, but to excuse some folly or wickedness of their own. This truth is not a doubtful one. There are illustrations of it near and remote, ancient and modern. It was fashionable, hundreds of years ago, for the children of Jacob to boast, we have "Abraham to our father," when they had long lost Abraham's faith and spirit. That people contented themselves under the shadow of Abraham's great name, while they repudiated the deeds which made his name great. Need I remind you that a similar thing is being done all over this country to-day? Need I tell you that the Jews are not the only people who built the tombs of the prophets, and garnished the sepulchres of the righteous? Washington could not die till he had broken the chains of his slaves. Yet his monument is built up by the price of human blood, and the traders in the bodies and souls of men, shout—"We have Washington to *our father*." Alas! that it should be so; yet so it is.

> "The evil that men do, lives after them,
>   The good is oft' interred with their bones."

Fellow-citizens, pardon me, allow me to ask, why am I called upon to speak here to-day? What have I, or those I represent, to do with your national independence? Are the great principles of political freedom and of natural justice, embodied in that Declaration of Independence, extended to us? and am I, therefore, called upon to bring our humble offering to the national altar, and to confess the benefits and express devout gratitude for the blessings resulting from your independence to us?

Would to God, both for your sakes and ours, that an affirmative answer could be truthfully returned to these questions! Then would my task be light, and my burden easy and delightful. For *who* is there so cold, that a nation's sympathy could not warm him? Who so obdurate and dead to the claims of gratitude, that would not thankfully acknowledge such priceless benefits? Who so stolid and selfish, that would not give his voice to swell the hallelujahs of a nation's jubilee, when the chains of servitude had been torn from his limbs? I am not that man. In a case like that, the dumb might eloquently speak, and the "lame man leap as an hart."

But, such is not the state of the case. I say it with a sad sense of the disparity between us. I am not included within the pale of this glorious anniversary! Your high independence only reveals the immeasurable distance between us. The blessings in which you, this day, rejoice, are not enjoyed in common. The rich inheritance of justice, liberty, prosperity and independence, bequeathed by your fathers, is shared by you, not by me. The sunlight that brought life and healing to you, has brought stripes and death to me. This Fourth of July is *yours*, not *mine*. *You* may rejoice, *I* must mourn. To drag a man in fetters into the grand illuminated temple of liberty, and call upon him to join you in joyous anthems, were inhuman mockery and sacrilegious irony. Do you mean, citizens, to mock me, by asking me to speak to-day? If so, there is a parallel to your conduct. And let me warn you that it is dangerous to copy the example of a nation whose crimes, towering up to heaven, were thrown down by the breath of the Almighty, burying that nation in irrecoverable ruin! I can to-day take up the plaintive lament of a peeled and woe-smitten people!

"By the rivers of Babylon, there we sat down. Yea! we wept when we remembered Zion. We hanged our harps upon the willows in the midst thereof. For there, they that carried us away captive, required of us a song; and they who wasted us required of us mirth, saying, Sing us one of the songs of Zion. How can we sing the Lord's song in a strange land? If I forget thee, O Jerusalem, let my right hand forget her cunning. If I do not remember thee, let my tongue cleave to the roof of my mouth."

Fellow-citizens; above your national, tumultous joy, I hear the mournful wail of millions! whose chains, heavy and grievous yesterday, are, to-day, rendered more intolerable by the jubilee shouts that reach them. If I do forget, if I do not faithfully remember those bleeding children of sorrow this day, "may my right hand forget her cunning, and may my tongue cleave to the roof of my mouth!" To forget them, to pass lightly over their wrongs, and to chime in with the popular theme, would be treason most scandalous and shocking, and would make me a reproach before God and the world. My subject, then fellow-citizens, is AMERICAN SLAVERY. I shall see, this day, and its popular characteristics, from the slave's point of view. Standing, there, identified with the American bondman, making his wrongs mine, I do not hesitate to declare, with all my soul, that the character and conduct of this nation never looked blacker to me than on this 4th of July! Whether we turn to the declarations of the past, or to the professions of the present, the conduct of the nation seems equally hideous and revolting. America is false to the past, false to the present, and solemnly binds herself to be false to the future. Standing with God and the crushed and bleeding slave on this occasion, I will, in the name of humanity which is outraged, in the name of liberty which is fettered, in the name of the constitution and the Bible, which are disregarded and trampled upon, dare to call in question and to denounce, with all the emphasis I can command, everything that serves to perpetuate slavery—the great sin and shame of America! "I will not equivocate; I will not excuse;" I will use the severest language I can command; and yet not one word shall escape me that any man, whose judgement is not blinded by prejudice, or who is not at heart a slaveholder, shall not confess to be right and just.

But I fancy I hear some one of my audience say, it is just in this circumstance that you and your brother abolitionists fail to make a favorable impression on the public mind. Would you argue more, and denounce less, would you persuade more, and rebuke less, your cause would be much more likely to succeed. But, I submit, where all is plain there is nothing to be argued. What point in the anti-slavery creed would you have me argue? On what branch of the subject do the people of this country need light? Must I undertake to prove that the slave is a man? That point is conceded already. Nobody doubts it. The slaveholders themselves acknowledge it in the enactment of laws for their government. They acknowledge it when they punish disobedience on the part of the slave. There are seventy-two crimes in the State of Virginia, which, if committed by a black man, (no matter how ignorant he be), subject him to the punishment of death; while only two of the same crimes will subject a white man to the like punishment. What is this but the acknowledgement that the slave is a moral, intellectual and responsible being? The manhood of the slave is conceded. It is admitted in the fact that Southern statute books are covered with enactments forbidding, under severe fines and penalties, the teaching of the slave to read or to write. When you can point to any such laws, in reference to the beasts of the field, then I may consent to argue the manhood of the slave. When the dogs in your streets, when the fowls of the air, when the cattle on your hills, when the fish of the sea, and the reptiles that crawl, shall be unable to distinguish the slave from a brute, *then* will I argue with you that the slave is a man!

For the present, it is enough to affirm the equal manhood of the negro race. Is it not astonishing that, while we are ploughing, planting and reaping, using all kinds of mechanical tools, erecting houses, constructing bridges, building ships, working in metals of brass, iron, copper, silver and gold; that, while we are reading, writing and cyphering, acting as clerks, merchants and secretaries, having among us lawyers, doctors, ministers, poets, authors, editors, orators and teachers; that, while we are engaged in all manner of enterprises common to other men, digging gold in California, capturing the whale in the Pacific, feeding sheep and cattle on the hill-side, living, moving, acting, thinking, planning, living in families as husbands, wives and children, and, above all, confessing and worshipping the Christian's God, and looking hopefully for life and immortality beyond the grave, we are called upon to prove that we are men!

Would you have me argue that man is entitled to liberty? that he is the rightful owner of his own body? You have already declared it. Must I argue the wrongfulness of slavery? Is that a question for Republicans? Is it to be settled by the rules of logic and argumentation, as a matter beset with great difficulty, involving a doubtful application of the principle of justice, hard to be understood? How should I look to-day, in the presence of Americans, dividing, and subdividing a discourse, to show that men have a natural right to freedom? speaking of it relatively, and positively, negatively, and affirmatively. To do so, would be to make myself ridiculous, and to offer an insult to your understanding. There is not a man beneath the canopy of heaven, that does not know that slavery is wrong *for him*.

What, am I to argue that it is wrong to make men brutes, to rob them of their liberty, to work them without wages, to keep them ignorant of their relations to their fellow men, to beat them with sticks, to flay their flesh with the lash, to load their limbs with irons, to hunt them with dogs, to sell them at auction, to sunder their families, to knock out their teeth, to burn their flesh, to starve them into obedience and submission to their masters? Must I argue that a system thus marked with blood, and stained with pollution, is *wrong*? No! I will not. I have better employments for my time and strength, than such arguments would imply.

What, then, remains to be argued? Is it that slavery is not divine; that God did not establish it; that our doctors of divinity are mistaken? There is blasphemy in the thought. That which is inhuman, cannot be divine! *Who* can reason on such a proposition? They that can, may; I cannot. The time for such argument is past.

At a time like this, scorching irony, not convincing argument, is needed. O! had I the ability, and could I reach the nation's ear, I would, to-day, pour out a fiery stream of biting ridicule, blasting reproach, withering sarcasm, and stern rebuke. For it is not light that is needed, but fire; it is not the gentle shower, but thunder. We need the storm, the whirlwind, and the earthquake. The feeling of the nation must be quickened; the conscience of the nation must be roused; the propriety of the nation must be startled; the hypocrisy of the nation must be exposed; and its crimes against God and man must be proclaimed and denounced.

What, to the American slave, is your 4th of July? I answer: a day that reveals to him, more than all other days in the year, the gross injustice and cruelty to which he is the constant victim. To him, your celebration is a sham; your boasted liberty, an unholy license; your national greatness, swelling vanity; your sounds of rejoicing are empty and heartless; your denunciations of tyrants, brass fronted impudence; your shouts of liberty and equality, hollow mockery; your prayers and hymns, your sermons and thanksgivings, with all your religious parade, and solemnity, are, to him, mere bombast, fraud, deception, impiety, and hypocrisy—a thin veil to cover up crimes which would disgrace a nation of savages. There is not a nation on the earth guilty of practices, more shocking and bloody, than are the people of these United States, at this very hour.

Go where you may, search where you will, roam through all the monarchies and despotisms of the old world, travel through South America, search out every abuse, and when you have found the last, lay your facts by the side of the everyday practices of this nation, and you will say with me, that, for revolting barbarity and shameless hypocrisy, America reigns without a rival.

THE INTERNAL SLAVE TRADE.

Take the American slave-trade, which, we are told by the papers, is especially prosperous just now. Ex-Senator Benton tells us that the price of men was never higher than now. He mentions the fact to show that slavery is in no danger. This trade is one of the peculiarities of American institutions. It is carried on in all the large towns and cities in one-half of this confederacy; and millions are pocketed every year, by dealers in this horrid traffic. In several states, this trade is a chief source of wealth. It is called (in contradistinction to the foreign slave-trade) "*the internal slave-trade*." It is, probably, called so, too, in order to divert from it the horror with which the foreign slave-trade is contemplated. That trade has long since been denounced by this government, as piracy. It has been denounced with burning words, from the high places of the nation, as an execrable traffic. To arrest it, to put an end to it, this nation keeps a squadron, at immense cost, on the coast of Africa. Everywhere, in this country, it is safe to speak of this foreign slave-trade, as a most inhuman traffic, opposed alike to the laws of God and of man. The duty to extirpate and destroy it, is admitted even by our DOCTORS OF DIVINITY. In order to put an end to it, some of these last have consented that their colored brethren (nominally free) should leave this country, and establish themselves on the western coast of Africa! It is, however, a notable fact that, while so much execration is poured out by Americans upon those engaged in the foreign slave-trade, the men engaged in the slave-trade between the states pass without condemnation, and their business is deemed honorable.

Behold the practical operation of this internal slave-trade, the American slave-trade, sustained by American politics and American religion. Here you will see men and women reared like swine for the market. You know what is a swine-drover? I will show you a man-drover. They inhabit all our Southern States. They perambulate the country, and crowd the highways of the nation, with droves of human stock. You will see one of these human flesh-jobbers, armed with pistol, whip and bowie-knife, driving a company of a hundred men, women, and children, from the Potomac to the slave market at New Orleans. These wretched people are to be sold singly, or in lots, to suit purchasers. They are food for the cotton-field, and the deadly sugar-mill. Mark the sad procession, as it moves wearily along, and the inhuman wretch who drives them. Hear his savage yells and his blood-chilling oaths, as he hurries on his affrighted captives! There, see the old man, with locks thinned and gray. Cast one glance, if you please, upon that young mother, whose shoulders are bare to the scorching sun, her briny tears falling on the brow of the babe in her arms. See, too, that girl of thirteen, weeping, *yes!* weeping, as she thinks of the mother from whom she has been torn! The drove moves tardily. Heat and sorrow have nearly consumed their strength; suddenly you hear a quick snap, like the discharge of a rifle; the fetters clank, and the chain rattles simultaneously; your ears are saluted with a scream, that seems to have torn its way to the centre of your soul! The crack you heard, was the sound of the slave-whip; the scream you heard, was from the woman you saw with the babe. Her speed had faltered under the weight of her child and her chains! that gash on her shoulder tells her to move on. Follow this drove to New Orleans. Attend the auction; see men examined like horses; see the forms of women rudely and brutally exposed to the shocking gaze of American slave-buyers. See this drove sold and separated forever; and never forget the deep, sad sobs that arose from that scattered multitude. Tell me citizens, WHERE, under the sun, you can witness a spectacle more fiendish and shocking. Yet this is but a glance at the American slave-trade, as it exists, at this moment, in the ruling part of the United States.

I was born amid such sights and scenes. To me the American slave-trade is a terrible reality. When a child, my soul was often pierced with a sense of its horrors. I lived on Philpot Street, Fell's Point, Baltimore, and have watched from the wharves, the slave ships in the Basin, anchored from the shore, with their cargoes of human flesh, waiting for favorable winds to waft them down the Chesapeake. There was, at that time, a grand slave mart kept at the head of Pratt Street, by Austin Woldfolk. His agents were sent into every town and county in Maryland, announcing their arrival, through the papers, and on flaming "*hand-bills*," headed CASH FOR NEGROES. These men were generally well dressed men, and very captivating in their manners. Ever ready to drink, to treat, and to gamble. The fate of many a slave has depended upon the turn of a single card; and many a child has been snatched from the arms of its mother by bargains arranged in a state of brutal drunkenness.

The flesh-mongers gather up their victims by dozens, and

drive them, chained, to the general depot at Baltimore. When a sufficient number have been collected here, a ship is chartered, for the purpose of conveying the forlorn crew to Mobile, or to New Orleans. From the slave prison to the ship, they are usually driven in the darkness of night; for since the anti-slavery agitation, a certain caution is observed.

In the deep still darkness of midnight, I have been often aroused by the dead heavy footsteps, and the piteous cries of the chained gangs that passed our door. The anguish of my boyish heart was intense; and I was often consoled, when speaking to my mistress in the morning, to hear her say that the custom was very wicked; that she hated to hear the rattle of the chains, and the heart-rending cries. I was glad to find one who sympathized with me in my horror.

Fellow-citizens, this murderous traffic is, to-day, in active operation in this boasted republic. In the solitude of my spirit, I see clouds of dust raised on the highways of the South; I see the bleeding footsteps; I hear the doleful wail of fettered humanity, on the way to the slave-markets, where the victims are to be sold like *horses*, *sheep*, and *swine*, knocked off to the highest bidder. There I see the tenderest ties ruthlessly broken, to gratify the lust, caprice and rapacity of the buyers and sellers of men. My soul sickens at the sight.

> "Is this the land your Fathers loved.
>   The freedom which they toiled to win?
>   Is this the earth whereon they moved?
>   Are these the graves they slumber in?"

But a still more inhuman, disgraceful, and scandalous state of things remains to be presented.

By an act of the American Congress, not yet two years old, slavery has been nationalized in its most horrible and revolting form. By that act, Mason & Dixon's line has been obliterated; New York has become as Virginia; and the power to hold, hunt, and sell men, women, and children as slaves remains no longer a mere state institution, but is now an institution of the whole United States. The power is co-extensive with the star-spangled banner and American Christianity. Where these go, may also go the merciless slave-hunter. Where these are, man is not sacred. He is a bird for the sportsman's gun. By that most foul and fiendish of all human decrees, the liberty and person of every man are put in peril. Your broad republican domain is hunting ground for *men*. *Not* for thieves and robbers, enemies of society, merely, but for men guilty of no crime. Your law-makers have commanded all good citizens to engage in this hellish sport. Your President, your Secretary of State, your *lords, nobles,* and ecclesiastics, enforce, as a duty you owe to your free and glorious country, and to your God, that you do this accursed thing. Not fewer than forty Americans have, within the past two years, been hunted down and, without a moment's warning, hurried away in chains, and consigned to slavery and excruciating torture. Some of these have had wives and children, dependent on them for bread; but of this, no account was made. The right of the hunter to his prey stands superior to the right of marriage, and to *all* rights in this republic, the rights of God included! For black men there are neither law, justice, humanity, nor religion. The Fugitive Slave *Law* makes MERCY TO THEM, A CRIME; and bribes the judge who tries them. An American JUDGE GETS TEN DOLLARS FOR EVERY VICTIM HE CONSIGNS to slavery, and five, when he fails to do so. The oath of any two villains is sufficient, under this hell-black enactment, to send the most pious and exemplary black man into the remorseless jaws of slavery! His own testimony is nothing. He can bring no witnesses for himself. The minister of American justice is bound by the law to hear but *one* side; and *that* side, is the side of the oppressor. Let this damning fact be perpetually told. Let it be thundered around the world, that, in tyrant-killing, king-hating, people-loving, democratic, Christian America, the seats of justice are filled with judges, who hold their offices under an open and palpable *bribe*, and are bound, in deciding in the case of a man's liberty, *to hear only his accusers!*

In glaring violation of justice, in shameless disregard of the forms of administering law, in cunning arrangement to entrap the defenceless, and in diabolical intent, this Fugitive Slave Law stands alone in the annals of tyrannical legislation. I doubt if there be another nation on the globe, having the brass and the baseness to put such a law on the statute-book. If any man in this assembly thinks differently from me in this matter, and feels able to disprove my statements, I will gladly confront him at any suitable time and place he may select.

I take this law to be one of the grossest infringements of Christian Liberty, and, if the churches and ministers of our country were not stupidly blind, or most wickedly indifferent, they, too, would so regard it.

At the very moment that they are thanking God for the enjoyment of civil and religious liberty, and for the right to worship God according to the dictates of their own consciences, they are utterly silent in respect to a law which robs religion of its chief significance, and makes it utterly worthless to a world lying in wickedness. Did this law concern the "*mint, anise* and *cummin*"—abridge the right to sing psalms, to partake of the sacrament, or to engage in any of the ceremonies of religion, it would be smitten by the thunder of a thousand pulpits. A general shout would go up from the church, demanding *repeal, repeal, instant repeal!* And it would go hard with that politician who presumed to solicit the votes of the people without inscribing this motto on his banner. Further, if this demand were not complied with, another Scotland would be added to the history of religious liberty, and the stern old Covenanters would be thrown into the shade. A John Knox would be seen at every church door, and heard from every pulpit, and Fillmore would have no more quarter than was shown by Knox, to the beautiful, but treacherous Queen Mary of Scotland. The fact that the church of our country, (with fractional exceptions), does not esteem "the Fugitive Slave Law" as a declaration of war against religious liberty, implies that that church regards religion simply as a form of worship, an empty ceremony, and *not* a vital principle, requiring active benevolence, justice, love and good will towards man. It esteems sacrifice above mercy; psalm-singing above right doing; solemn meetings above practical righteousness. A worship that can be conducted by persons who refuse to give shelter to the houseless, to give bread to the hungry, clothing to the naked, and who enjoin obedience to a law forbidding these acts of mercy, is a curse, not a blessing to mankind. The Bible addresses all such persons as "scribes, pharisees, hypocrites, who pay tithe of *mint, anise, and cummin,* and have omitted the weighter matters of the law, judgement, mercy and faith."

THE CHURCH RESPONSIBLE.

But the church of this country is not only indifferent to the wrongs of the slave, it actually takes sides with the oppressors. It has made itself the bulwark of American slavery, and the shield of American slave-hunters. Many of its most eloquent Divines, who stand as the very lights of the church, have shamelessly given the sanction of religion and the Bible to the whole slave system. They have taught that man may, properly, be a slave; that the relation of master and slave is ordained of God; that to send back an escaped bondman to his master is clearly the duty of all the followers of the Lord Jesus Christ; and this horrible blasphemy is palmed off upon the world for Christianity.

For my part, I would say, welcome infidelity! welcome atheism! welcome anything! in preference to the gospel, *as preached by those Divines!* They convert the very name of religion into an engine of tyranny, and barbarous cruelty, and serve to confirm more infidels, in this age, than all the infidel writings of Thomas Paine, Voltaire, and Bolingbroke, put together, have done! These ministers make religion a cold and flinty-hearted thing, having neither principles of right action, nor bowels of compassion. They strip the love of God of its beauty, and leave the throne of religion a huge, horrible, repulsive form. It is a religion for oppressors, tyrants, man-stealers, and *thugs.* It is not that "*pure and undefiled religion*" which is from above, and which is "*first pure, then peaceable, easy to be entreated,* full of mercy and good fruits, *without partiality, and without hypocrisy.*" But a religion which favors the rich against the poor; which exalts the proud above the humble; which divides mankind into two classes, tyrants and slaves; which says to the man in chains, *stay there*; and to the oppressor, *oppress on*; it is a religion which may be professed and enjoyed by all the robbers and enslavers of mankind; it makes God a respecter of persons, denies his fatherhood of the race, and tramples in the dust the great truth of the brotherhood of man. All this we affirm to be true of the popular church, and the popular worship of our land and nation—a religion, a church, and a worship which, on the authority of inspired wisdom, we pronounce to be an abomination in the sight of God. In the language of Isaiah, the American church might be well addressed, "Bring no more vain oblations; incense is an abomination unto me: the new moons and Sabbaths, the calling of assemblies, I cannot away with; it is iniquity, even the solemn meeting. Your new moons and your appointed feasts my soul hateth. They are a trouble to me; I am weary to bear them; and when ye spread forth your hands I will hide mine eyes from you. Yea! when ye make many prayers, I will not hear. YOUR HANDS ARE FULL OF BLOOD; cease to do evil, learn to do well; seek judgement; relieve the oppressed; judge for the fatherless; plead for the widow."

The American church is guilty, when viewed in connection with what it is doing to uphold slavery; but it is superlatively guilty when viewed in connection with its ability to abolish slavery.

The sin of which it is guilty is one of omission as well as of commission. Albert Barnes but uttered what the common sense of every man at all observant of the actual state of the case will receive as truth, when he declared that "There is no power out of the church that could sustain slavery an hour, if it were not sustained in it."

Let the religious press, the pulpit, the Sunday school, the conference meeting, the great ecclesiastical, missionary, Bible and tract associations of the land array their immense powers against slavery and slave-holding; and the whole system of crime and blood would be scattered to the winds; and that they do not do this involves them in the most awful responsibility of which the mind can conceive.

In prosecuting the anti-slavery enterprise, we have been asked to spare the church, to spare the ministry; but *how*, we ask, could such a thing be done? We are met on the threshold of our efforts for the redemption of the slave, by the church and ministry of the country, in battle arrayed against us; and we are compelled to fight or flee. From what *quarter*, I beg to know, has proceeded a fire so deadly upon our ranks, during

the last two years, as from the Northern pulpit? As the champions of oppressors, the chosen men of American theology
have appeared—men, honored for their so-called piety, and
their real learning. The LORDS of Buffalo, the SPRINGS of New
York, the LATHROPS of Auburn, the COXES and SPENCERS of
Brooklyn, the GANNETS and SHARPS of Boston, the DEWEYS
of Washington, and other great religious lights of the land,
have, in utter denial of the authority of *Him*, by whom they
professed to be called to the ministry, deliberately taught us,
against the example of the Hebrews and against the remonstrance of the Apostles, they teach "*that we ought to obey man's
law before the law of God.*"

My spirit wearies of such blasphemy; and how such men can
be supported, as the "standing types and representatives of Jesus Christ," is a mystery which I leave others to penetrate. In
speaking of the American church, however, let it be distinctly
understood that I mean the *great mass* of the religious organizations of our land. There are exceptions, and I thank God that
there are. Noble men may be found, scattered all over these
Northern States, of whom Henry Ward Beecher of Brooklyn,
Samuel J. May of Syracuse, and my esteemed friend* on the
platform, are shining examples; and let me say further, that
upon these men lies the duty to inspire our ranks with high religious faith and zeal, and to cheer us on in the great mission
of the slave's redemption from his chains.

RELIGION IN ENGLAND AND
RELIGION IN AMERICA.

One is struck with the difference between the attitude of the
American church towards the anti-slavery movement, and that
occupied by the churches in England towards a similar movement in that country. There, the church, true to its mission of
ameliorating, elevating, and improving the condition of mankind, came forward promptly, bound up the wounds of the
West Indian slave, and restored him to his liberty. There, the
question of emancipation was a highly religious question. It
was demanded, in the name of humanity, and according to the

*Rev. R. R. Raymond.

law of the living God. The Sharps, the Clarksons, the Wilber-forces, the Buxtons, and Burchells and the Knibbs, were alike famous for their piety, and for their philanthropy. The anti-slavery movement *there* was not an anti-church movement, for the reason that the church took its full share in prosecuting that movement: and the anti-slavery movement in this country will cease to be an anti-church movement, when the church of this country shall assume a favorable, instead of a hostile posi-tion towards that movement.

Americans! your republican politics, not less than your re-publican religion, are flagrantly inconsistent. You boast of your love of liberty, your superior civilization, and your pure Chris-tianity, while the whole political power of the nation (as em-bodied in the two great political parties), is solemnly pledged to support and perpetuate the enslavement of three millions of your countrymen. You hurl your anathemas at the crowned headed tyrants of Russia and Austria, and pride yourselves on your Democratic institutions, while you yourselves consent to be the mere *tools* and *bodyguards* of the tyrants of Virginia and Carolina. You invite to your shores fugitives of oppression from abroad, honor them with banquets, greet them with ova-tions, cheer them, toast them, salute them, protect them, and pour out your money to them like water; but the fugitives from your own land you advertise, hunt, arrest, shoot and kill. You glory in your refinement and your universal education; yet you maintain a system as barbarous and dreadful as ever stained the character of a nation—a system begun in avarice, supported in pride, and perpetuated in cruelty. You shed tears over fallen Hungary, and make the sad story of her wrongs the theme of your poets, statesmen and orators, till your gallant sons are ready to fly to arms to vindicate her cause against her oppres-sors; but, in regard to the ten thousand wrongs of the Ameri-can slave, you would enforce the strictest silence, and would hail him as an enemy of the nation who dares to make those wrongs the subject of public discourse! You are all on fire at the mention of liberty for France or for Ireland; but are as cold as an iceberg at the thought of liberty for the enslaved of America. You discourse eloquently on the dignity of labor; yet, you sustain a system which, in its very essence, casts a stigma upon labor. You can bare your bosom to the storm of British artillery to throw off a threepenny tax on tea; and yet wring the last hard-earned farthing from the grasp of the black laborers of your country. You profess to believe "that, of one blood, God made all nations of men to dwell on the face of all the earth," and hath commanded all men, everywhere to love one another; yet you notoriously hate, (and glory in your hatred), all men whose skins are not colored like your own. You declare, before the world, and are understood by the world to declare, that you "*hold these truths to be self evident, that all men are created equal; and are endowed by their Creator with certain inalienable rights; and that, among these are, life, liberty, and the pursuit of happiness;*" and yet, you hold securely, in a bondage which, according to your own Thomas Jefferson, "*is worse than ages of that which your fathers rose in rebellion to oppose,*" *a seventh part* of the inhabitants of your country.

Fellow-citizens! I will not enlarge further on your national inconsistencies. The existence of slavery in this country brands your republicanism as a sham, your humanity as a base pretence, and your Christianity as a lie. It destroys your moral power abroad; it corrupts your politicians at home. It saps the foundation of religion; it makes your name a hissing, and a by-word to a mocking earth. It is the antagonistic force in your government, the only thing that seriously disturbs and endangers your *Union*. It fetters your progress; it is the enemy of improvement, the deadly foe of education; it fosters pride; it breeds insolence; it promotes vice; it shelters crime; it is a curse to the earth that supports it; and yet, you cling to it, as if it were the sheet anchor of all your hopes. Oh! be warned! be warned! a horrible reptile is coiled up in your nation's bosom; the venomous creature is nursing at the tender breast of your youthful republic; *for the love of God, tear away,* and fling from you the hideous monster, and *let the weight of twenty millions crush and destroy it forever!*

THE CONSTITUTION.

But it is answered in reply to all this, that precisely what I have now denounced is, in fact, guaranteed and sanctioned by the Constitution of the United States; that the right to hold and to hunt slaves is a part of that Constitution framed by the illustrious Fathers of this Republic.

Then, I dare to affirm, notwithstanding all I have said before, your fathers stooped, basely stooped

> "To palter with us in a double sense:
> And keep the word of promise to the ear,
> But break it to the heart."

And instead of being the honest men I have before declared them to be, they were the veriest imposters that ever practised on mankind. *This* is the inevitable conclusion, and from it there is no escape. But I differ from those who charge this baseness on the framers of the Constitution of the United States. *It is a slander upon their memory,* at least, so I believe. There is not time now to argue the constitutional question at length; nor have I the ability to discuss it as it ought to be discussed. The subject has been handled with masterly power by Lysander Spooner, Esq., by William Goodell, by Samuel E. Sewall, Esq., and last, though not least, by Gerritt Smith, Esq. These gentlemen have, as I think, fully and clearly vindicated the Constitution from any design to support slavery for an hour.

Fellow-citizens! there is no matter in respect to which, the people of the North have allowed themselves to be so ruinously imposed upon, as that of the pro-slavery character of the Constitution. In *that* instrument I hold there is neither warrant, license, nor sanction of the hateful thing; but, interpreted as it *ought* to be interpreted, the Constitution is a GLORIOUS LIBERTY DOCUMENT. Read its preamble, consider its purposes. Is slavery among them? Is it at the gateway? or is it in the temple? It is neither. While I do not intend to argue this question on the present occasion, let me ask, if it be not somewhat singular that, if the Constitution were intended to be, by its framers and adopters, a slave-holding instrument, why neither *slavery, slaveholding,* nor *slave* can anywhere be found in it. What would be thought of an instrument, drawn up, *legally* drawn up, for the purpose of entitling the city of Rochester to a tract of land, in which no mention of land was made? Now, there are certain rules of interpretation, for the proper understanding of all legal instruments. These rules are well established. They are plain, common-sense rules, such as you and I, and all of us, can understand and apply, without having passed years in the study of law. I scout the idea that the question of the constitutionality or unconstitutionality of slavery is not a question for the people. I hold that every American citizen has a right to form an opinion of the constitution, and to propagate that opinion, and to use all honorable means to make his opinion the prevailing one. Without this right, the liberty of an American citizen would be as insecure as that of a Frenchman. Ex-Vice-President Dallas tells us that the constitution is an object to which no American mind can be too attentive, and no American heart too devoted. He further says, the constitution, in its words, is plain and intelligible, and is meant for the home-bred, unsophisticated understandings of our fellow-citizens. Senator Berrien tells us that the Constitution is the fundamental law, that which controls all others. The charter of our liberties, which every citizen has a personal interest in understanding thoroughly. The testimony of Senator Breese, Lewis Cass, and many others that might be named, who are everywhere esteemed as sound lawyers, so regard the constitution. I take it, therefore, that it is not presumption in a private citizen to form an opinion of that instrument.

Now, take the constitution according to its plain reading, and I defy the presentation of a single pro-slavery clause in it. On the other hand it will be found to contain principles and purposes, entirely hostile to the existence of slavery.

I have detained my audience entirely too long already. At some future period I will gladly avail myself of an opportunity to give this subject a full and fair discussion.

Allow me to say, in conclusion, notwithstanding the dark picture I have this day presented of the state of the nation, I do not despair of this country. There are forces in operation, which must inevitably work the downfall of slavery. "*The arm of the Lord is not shortened*," and the doom of slavery is certain. I, therefore, leave off where I began, with *hope*. While drawing encouragement from the Declaration of Independence, the great principles it contains, and the genius of American Institutions, my spirit is also cheered by the obvious tendencies of the age. Nations do not now stand in the same relation to each other that they did ages ago. No nation can now shut itself up from the surrounding world, and trot round in the same old path of its fathers without interference. The time *was* when such could be done. Long established customs of hurtful character could formerly fence themselves in, and do their evil work with social impunity. Knowledge was then confined and enjoyed by the privileged few, and the multitude walked on in mental darkness. But a change has now come over the affairs of mankind. Walled cities and empires have become unfashionable. The arm of commerce has borne away the gates of the strong city. Intelligence is penetrating the darkest corners of the globe. It makes its pathway over and under the sea, as well as on the earth. Wind, steam, and lightning are its chartered agents. Oceans no longer divide, but link nations together. From Boston to London is now a holiday excursion. Space is comparatively annihilated. Thoughts expressed on one side of the Atlantic are distinctly heard on the other.

The far off and almost fabulous Pacific rolls in grandeur at our feet. The Celestial Empire, the mystery of ages, is being solved. The fiat of the Almighty, "*Let there be Light*," has not yet spent its force. No abuse, no outrage whether in taste, sport or avarice, can now hide itself from the all-pervading light. The iron shoe, and crippled foot of China must be seen, in contrast with nature. *Africa must rise and put on her yet unwoven garment.* "*Ethiopia shall stretch out her hand unto God.*" In the fervent aspirations of William Lloyd Garrison, I say, and let every heart join in saying it:

> God speed the year of jubilee
>   The wide world o'er!
> When from their galling chains set free,
> Th' oppress'd shall vilely bend the knee,
> And wear the yoke of tyranny
>   Like brutes no more.
> That year will come, and freedom's reign,
> To man his plundered rights again
>   Restore.
>
> God speed the day when human blood
>   Shall cease to flow!
> In every clime be understood,
> The claims of human brotherhood,
> And each return for evil, good,

Not blow for blow;
That day will come all feuds to end,
And change into a faithful friend
    Each foe.

God speed the hour, the glorious hour,
    When none on earth
Shall exercise a lordly power,
Nor in a tyrant's presence cower;
But all to manhood's stature tower,
    By equal birth!
THAT HOUR WILL COME, to each, to all,
And from his prison-house, the thrall
    Go forth.

Until that year, day, hour, arrive,
With head, and heart, and hand I'll strive,
To break the rod, and rend the gyve,
The spoiler of his prey deprive—
    So witness Heaven!
And never from my chosen post,
Whate'er the peril or the cost,
    Be driven.

CHARLES SUMNER

The Crime Against Kansas

Washington, D.C., May 19–20, 1856

M R. PRESIDENT, you are now called to redress a great
transgression. Seldom in the history of nations has such
a question been presented. Tariffs, Army bills, Navy bills, Land
bills, are important, and justly occupy your care; but these all
belong to the course of ordinary legislation. As means and instruments only, they are necessarily subordinate to the conser-
vation of Government itself. Grant them or deny them, in
greater or less degree, and you will inflict no shock. The machinery of Government will continue to move. The State will
not cease to exist. Far otherwise is it with the eminent question now before you, involving, as it does, Liberty in a broad
Territory, and also involving the peace of the whole country
with our good name in history for evermore.

Take down your map, sir, and you will find that the Territory of Kansas, more than any other region, occupies the middle spot of North America, equally distant from the Atlantic
on the east, and the Pacific on the west; from the frozen waters
of Hudson's Bay on the north, and the tepid Gulf Stream on
the south, constituting the precise territorial center of the
whole vast Continent. To such advantages of situation, on the
very highway between two oceans, are added a soil of unsurpassed richness, and a fascinating, undulating beauty of surface,
with a health-giving climate, calculated to nurture a powerful
and generous people, worthy to be a central pivot of American
Institutions. A few short months only have passed since this
spacious mediterranean country was open only to the savage,
who ran wild in its woods and prairies; and now it has already
drawn to its bosom a population of freemen larger than Athens
crowded within her historic gates, when her sons, under Miltiades, won Liberty for mankind on the field of Marathon; more
than Sparta contained when she ruled Greece, and sent forth

her devoted children, quickened by a mother's benediction, to return with their shields or on them; more than Rome gathered on her seven hills, when, under her kings, she commenced that sovereign sway, which afterwards embraced the whole earth; more than London held, when, on the fields of Crecy and Agincourt, the English banner was carried victoriously over the chivalrous hosts of France.

Against this Territory, thus fortunate in position and population, a Crime has been committed, which is without example in the records of the Past. Not in plundered provinces or in the cruelties of selfish governors will you find its parallel; and yet there is an ancient instance, which may show at least the path of justice. In the terrible impeachment by which the great Roman Orator has blasted through all time the name of Verres, amidst charges of robbery and sacrilege, the enormity which most aroused the indignant voice of his accuser, and which still stands forth with strongest distinctness, arresting the sympathetic indignation of all who read the story, is, that away in Sicily he had scourged a citizen of Rome—that the cry "I am a Roman citizen" had been interposed in vain against the lash of the tyrant governor. Other charges were, that he had carried away productions of art, and that he had violated the sacred shrines. It was in the presence of the Roman Senate that this arraignment proceeded; in a temple of the Forum; amidst crowds—such as no orator had ever before drawn together—thronging the porticos and colonnades, even clinging to the house-tops and neighboring slopes—and under the anxious gaze of witnesses summoned from the scene of crime. But an audience grander far—of higher dignity—of more various people and of wider intelligence—the countless multitude of succeeding generations, in every land, where eloquence has been studied or where the Roman name has been recognized—has listened to the accusation, and throbbed with condemnation of the criminal. Sir, speaking in an age of light and in a land of constitutional liberty, where the safeguards of elections are justly placed among the highest triumphs of civilization, I fearlessly assert that the wrongs of much-abused Sicily, thus memorable in history, were small by the side of the wrongs of Kansas, where the very shrines of popular institutions, more sacred than any heathen altar, have been desecrated; where the ballot-box, more precious than any work, in ivory or marble, from the cunning hand of art, has been plundered; and where the cry "I am an American citizen" has been interposed in vain against outrage of every kind, even upon life itself. Are you against sacrilege? I present it for your execration. Are you against robbery? I hold it up to your scorn. Are you for the protection of American citizens? I show you how their dearest rights have been cloven down, while a Tyrannical Usurpation has sought to install itself on their very necks!

But the wickedness which I now begin to expose is immeasurably aggravated by the motive which prompted it. Not in any common lust for power did this uncommon tragedy have its origin. It is the rape of a virgin Territory, compelling it to the hateful embrace of Slavery; and it may be clearly traced to a depraved longing for a new slave State, the hideous offspring of such a crime, in the hope of adding to the power of Slavery in the National Government. Yes, sir, when the whole world, alike Christian and Turk, is rising up to condemn this wrong, and to make it a hissing to the nations, here in our Republic, *force*—ay, sir, FORCE—has been openly employed in compelling Kansas to this pollution, and all for the sake of political power. There is the simple fact, which you will vainly attempt to deny, but which in itself presents an essential wickedness that makes other public crimes seem like public virtues.

But this, enormity, vast beyond comparison, swells to dimensions of wickedness which the imagination toils in vain to grasp, when it is understood, that for this purpose are hazarded the horrors of intestine feud, not only in this distant Territory, but everywhere throughout the country. Already the muster has begun. The strife is no longer local, but national. Even now, while I speak, portents hang on all the arches of the horizon, threatening to darken the broad land, which already yawns with the mutterings of civil war. The fury of the propagandists of Slavery, and the calm determination of their opponents, are now diffused from the distant Territory over wide-spread communities, and the whole country, in all its extent—marshaling hostile divisions, and foreshadowing a strife, which, unless happily averted by the triumph of Freedom, will become war—fratricidal, parricidal war—with an accumulated wickedness beyond the wickedness of any war in human annals; justly provoking the avenging judgment of Providence and the avenging pen of history, and constituting a strife, in the language of the ancient writer, more than *foreign*, more than *social*, more than *civil*; but something compounded of all these strifes, and in itself more than war; *sed potius commune quoddam ex omnibus, et plus quam bellum.*

Such is the Crime which you are to judge. But the criminal also must be dragged into day, that you may see and measure the power by which all this wrong is sustained. From no common source could it proceed. In its perpetration was needed a spirit of vaulting ambition which would hesitate at nothing; a hardihood of purpose which was insensible to the judgment of mankind; a madness for Slavery which should disregard the Constitution, the laws, and all the great examples of our history; also a consciousness of power such as comes from the habit of power; a combination of energies found only in a hundred arms directed by a hundred eyes; a control of Public Opinion, through venal pens and a prostituted press; an ability to subsidize crowds in every vocation of life—the politician with his local importance, the lawyer with his subtile tongue, and even the authority of the judge on the bench; and a familiar use of men in places high and low, so that none, from the President to the lowest border postmaster, should decline to be its tool; all these things and more were needed; and they were found in the Slave Power of our Republic. There, sir, stands the criminal—all unmasked before you—heartless, grasping, and tyrannical—with an audacity beyond that of Verres, a subtilety beyond that of Machiavel, a meanness beyond that of Bacon, and an ability beyond that of Hastings. Justice to Kansas can be secured only by the prostration of this influence; for this is the power behind—greater than any President—which succors and sustains the Crime. Nay, the proceedings I now arraign derive their fearful consequence only from this connection.

In now opening this great matter, I am not insensible to the austere demands of the occasion; but the dependence of the crime against Kansas upon the Slave Power is so peculiar and important, that I trust to be pardoned while I impress it by an illustration, which to some may seem trivial. It is related in Northern mythology, that the god of Force, visiting an enchanted region, was challenged by his royal entertainer to what seemed a humble feat of strength—merely, sir, to lift a cat from the ground. The god smiled at the challenge, and, calmly placing his hand under the belly of the animal, with superhuman strength, strove, while the back of the feline monster arched far upwards, even beyond reach, and one paw actually forsook the earth, until at last the discomfited divinity desisted; but he was little surprised at his defeat, when he learned that this creature, which seemed to be a cat, and nothing more, was not merely a cat, but that it belonged to and was a part of the great Terrestrial Serpent, which, in its innumerable folds, encircled the whole globe. Even so the creature, whose paws are now fastened upon Kansas, whatever it may seem to be, constitutes in reality a part of the Slave Power, which, with loathsome folds, is now coiled about the whole land. Thus do I expose the extent of the present contest, where we encounter not merely local resistance, but also the unconquered sustaining arm behind. But out of the vastness of the Crime attempted, with all its woe and shame, I derive a well-founded assurance of a commensurate vastness of effort against it, by the aroused masses of the country, determined not only to vindicate Right against Wrong, but to redeem the Republic from the thraldom of that Oligarchy, which prompts, directs, and concentrates, the distant wrong.

Such is the Crime, and such the criminal, which it is my duty in this debate to expose, and, by the blessing of God, this duty shall be done completely to the end. But this will not be enough. The Apologies, which, with strange hardihood, have been offered for the Crime, must be torn away, so that it shall stand forth, without a single rag, or fig-leaf, to cover its vileness. And, finally, the True Remedy must be shown. The subject is complex in its relations, as it is transcendent in importance; and yet, if I am honored by your attention, I hope to exhibit it clearly in all its parts, while I conduct you to the inevitable conclusion that Kansas must be admitted at once, with her present Constitution, as a State of this Union, and give a new star to the blue field of our National Flag. And here I derive satisfaction from the thought, that the cause is so strong in itself as to bear even the infirmities of its advocates; nor can it require anything beyond that simplicity of treatment and moderation of manner which I desire to cultivate. Its true character is such, that, like Hercules, it will conquer just so soon as it is recognized.

My task will be divided under three different heads; *first*, THE CRIME AGAINST KANSAS, in its origin and extent; *secondly*, THE APOLOGIES FOR THE CRIME; and *thirdly*, THE TRUE REMEDY.

But, before entering upon the argument, I must say something of a general character, particularly in response to what has fallen from Senators who have raised themselves to eminence on this floor in championship of human wrongs; I mean the Senator from South Carolina, [Mr. BUTLER,] and the Senator from Illinois, [Mr. DOUGLAS,] who, though unlike as Don Quixote and Sancho Panza, yet, like this couple, sally forth together in the same adventure. I regret much to miss the elder Senator from his seat; but the cause, against which he has run a tilt, with such activity of animosity, demands that the opportunity of exposing him should not be lost; and it is for the cause that I speak. The Senator from South Carolina has read many books of chivalry, and believes himself a chivalrous knight, with sentiments of honor and courage. Of course he has chosen a mistress to whom he has made his vows, and who, though ugly to others, is always lovely to him; though polluted in the sight of the world, is chaste in his sight—I mean the harlot, Slavery. For her, his tongue is always profuse in words. Let her be impeached in character, or any proposition made to shut her out from the extension of her wantonness, and no extravagance of manner or hardihood of assertion is then too great for this Senator. The frenzy of Don Quixote, in behalf of his wench, Dulcinea del Toboso, is all surpassed. The asserted rights of slavery, which shock equality of all kinds, are cloaked by a fantastic claim of equality. If the slave States cannot enjoy what, in mockery of the great fathers of the Republic, he misnames equality under the Constitution—in other words, the full power in the National Territories to compel fellow-men to unpaid toil, to separate husband and wife, and to sell little children at the auction block—then, sir, the chivalric Senator will conduct the State of South Carolina out of the Union! Heroic knight! Exalted Senator! A second Moses come for a second exodus!

But not content with this poor menace, which we have been twice told was "measured," the Senator, in the unrestrained chivalry of his nature, has undertaken to apply opprobrious words to those who differ from him on this floor. He calls them "sectional and fanatical;" and opposition to the usurpation in Kansas he denounces as "an uncalculating fanaticism." To be sure, these charges lack all grace of originality, and all sentiment of truth; but the adventurous Senator does not hesitate. He is the uncompromising, unblushing representative on this floor of a flagrant *sectionalism*, which now domineers over the Republic, and yet with a ludicrous ignorance of his own position—unable to see himself as others see him—or with an effrontery which even his white head ought not to protect from rebuke, he applies to those here who resist his *sectionalism* the very epithet which designates himself. The men who strive to bring back the Government to its original policy, when Freedom and not Slavery was national, while Slavery and not Freedom was sectional, he arraigns as *sectional*. This will not do. It involves too great a perversion of terms. I tell that Senator, that it is to himself, and to the "organization" of which he is the "committed advocate," that this epithet belongs. I now fasten it upon them. For myself, I care little for names; but since the question has been raised here, I affirm that the Republican party of the Union is in no just sense *sectional*, but, more than any other party, *national*; and that it now goes forth to dislodge from the high places of the Government the tyrannical sectionalism of which the Senator from South Carolina is one of the maddest zealots.

To the charge of fanaticism I also reply. Sir, fanaticism is found in an enthusiasm or exaggeration of opinions, particularly on religious subjects; but there may be a fanaticism for evil as well as for good. Now, I will not deny, that there are persons among us loving Liberty too well for their personal good, in a selfish generation. Such there may be, and, for the sake of their example, would that there were more! In calling them "fanatics," you cast contumely upon the noble army of martyrs, from the earliest day down to this hour; upon the great tribunes of human rights, by whom life, liberty, and happiness, on earth, have been secured; upon the long line of devoted patriots, who, throughout history, have truly loved their country; and, upon all, who, in noble aspirations for the general good and in forgetfulness of self, have stood out before their age, and gathered into their generous bosoms the shafts of tyranny and wrong, in order to make a pathway for Truth. You discredit Luther, when alone he nailed his articles to the door of the church at Wittenberg, and then, to the imperial demand that he should retract, firmly replied, "Here I stand; I cannot do otherwise, so help me God!" You discredit Hampden, when alone he refused to pay the few shillings of ship-money, and shook the throne of Charles I.; you discredit Milton, when, amidst the corruptions of a heartless Court, he lived on, the lofty friend of Liberty, above question or suspicion; you discredit Russell and Sidney, when, for the sake of their country, they calmly turned from family and friends, to tread the narrow steps of the scaffold; you discredit those early founders of American institutions, who preferred the hardships of a wilderness, surrounded by a savage foe, to injustice on beds of ease; you discredit our later fathers, who, few in numbers and weak in resources, yet strong in their cause, did not hesitate to brave the mighty power of England, already encircling the globe with her morning drum-beats. Yes, sir, of such are the fanatics of history, according to the Senator. But I tell that Senator, that there are characters badly eminent, of whose fanaticism there can be no question. Such were the ancient Egyptians, who worshipped divinities in brutish forms; the Druids, who darkened the forests of oak, in which they lived, by sacrifices of blood; the Mexicans, who surrendered countless victims to the propitiation of their obscene idols; the Spaniards, who, under Alva, sought to force the Inquisition upon Holland, by a tyranny kindred to that now employed to force Slavery upon Kansas; and such were the Algerines, when in solemn conclave, after listening to a speech not unlike that of the Senator from South Carolina, they resolved to continue the slavery of white Christians, and to extend it to the countrymen of Washington! Ay, sir, extend it! And in this same dreary catalogue faithful history must record all who now, in an enlightened age and in a land of boasted Freedom, stand up, in perversion of the Constitution and in denial of immortal truth, to fasten a new shackle upon their fellow-man. If the Senator wishes to see fanatics, let him look round among his own associates; let him look at himself.

But I have not done with the Senator. There is another matter regarded by him of such consequence, that he interpolated it into the speech of the Senator from New Hampshire, [Mr. HALE,] and also announced that he had prepared himself with it, to take in his pocket all the way to Boston, when he expected to address the people of that community. On this account, and for the sake of truth, I stop for one moment, and tread it to the earth. The North, according to the Senator, was engaged in the slave trade, and helped to introduce slaves into the Southern States; and this undeniable fact he proposed to establish by statistics, in stating which his errors surpassed his sentences in number. But I let these pass for the present, that I may deal with his argument. Pray, sir, is the acknowledged turpitude of a departed generation to become an example for us? And yet the suggestion of the Senator, if entitled to any consideration in this discussion, must have this extent. I join my friend from New Hampshire in thanking the Senator from South Carolina for adducing this instance; for it gives me an opportunity to say, that the Northern merchants, with homes in Boston, Bristol, Newport, New York, and Philadelphia, who catered for Slavery during the years of the slave trade, are the lineal progenitors of the Northern men, with homes in these places, who lend themselves to Slavery in our day; and especially that all, whether North or South, who take part, directly or indirectly, in the conspiracy against Kansas, do but continue the work of the slave-traders, which you condemn. It is true, too true, alas! that our fathers were engaged in this traffic; but that is no apology for it. And in repelling the authority of this example, I repel also the trite argument founded on the earlier example of England. It is true that our mother country, at the peace of Utrecht, extorted from Spain the Assiento Contract, securing the monopoly of the slave trade with the Spanish Colonies, as the whole price of all the blood of great victories; that she higgled at Aix-la-Chapelle for another lease of this exclusive traffic; and again, at the treaty of Madrid, clung to the wretched piracy. It is true, that in this spirit the power of the mother country was prostituted to the same base ends in her American Colonies, against indignant protests from our fathers.

All these things now rise up in judgment against her. Let us not follow the Senator from South Carolina to do the very evil to-day, which in another generation we condemn.

As the Senator from South Carolina is the Don Quixote, the Senator from Illinois [Mr. DOUGLAS] is the squire of Slavery, its very Sancho Panza, ready to do all its humiliating offices. This Senator, in his labored address, vindicating his labored report—piling one mass of elaborate error upon another mass —constrained himself, as you will remember, to unfamiliar decencies of speech. Of that address I have nothing to say at this moment, though before I sit down I shall show something of its fallacies. But I go back now to an earlier occasion, when, true to his native impulses, he threw into this discussion, "for a charm of powerful trouble," personalities most discreditable to this body. I will not stop to repel the imputations which he cast upon myself; but I mention them to remind you of the "sweltered venom sleeping got," which, with other poisoned ingredients, he cast into the caldron of this debate. Of other things I speak. Standing on this floor, the Senator issued his rescript, requiring submission to the Usurped Power of Kansas; and this was accompanied by a manner—all his own—such as befits the tyrannical threat. Very well. Let the Senator try. I tell him now that he cannot enforce any such submission. The Senator, with the Slave Power at his back, is strong; but he is not strong enough for this purpose. He is bold. He shrinks from nothing. Like Danton, he may cry, "*l'audace! l'audace! toujours l'audace!*" but even his audacity cannot compass this work. The Senator copies the British officer, who, with boastful swagger, said that with the hilt of his sword he would cram the "stamps" down the throats of the American people, and he will meet a similar failure. He may convulse this country with civil feud. Like the ancient madman, he may set fire to this Temple of Constitutional Liberty, grander than Ephesian dome; but he cannot enforce obedience to that tyrannical Usurpation.

The Senator dreams that he can subdue the North. He disclaims the open threat, but his conduct still implies it. How little that Senator knows himself or the strength of the cause which he persecutes! He is but a mortal man; against him is an immortal principle. With finite power he wrestles with the infinite, and he must fall. Against him are stonger battalions than any marshaled by mortal arm—the inborn, ineradicable, invincible sentiments of the human heart; against him is nature in all her subtile forces; against him is God. Let him try to subdue these.

But I pass from these things, which, though belonging to the very heart of the discussion, are yet preliminary in character, and press at once to the main question.

I. It belongs to me now, in the first place, to expose the CRIME AGAINST KANSAS, in its origin and extent. Logically, this is the beginning of the argument. I say Crime, and deliberately adopt this strongest term, as better than any other denoting the consummate transgression. I would go further, if language could further go. It is the *Crime of Crimes*—surpassing far the old *crimen majestatis*, pursued with vengeance by the laws of Rome, and containing all other crimes, as the greater contains the less. I do not go too far, when I call it the *Crime against Nature*, from which the soul recoils, and which language refuses to describe. To lay bare this enormity, I now proceed. The whole subject has already become a twice-told tale, and its renewed recital will be a renewal of its sorrow and shame; but I shall not hesitate to enter upon it. The occasion requires it from the beginning.

It has been well remarked by a distinguished historian of our country, that, at the Ithuriel touch of the Missouri discussion, the slave interest, hitherto hardly recognized as a distinct element in our system, started up portentous and dilated, with threats and assumptions, which are the origin of our existing national politics. This was in 1820. The discussion ended with the admission of Missouri as a slaveholding State, and the prohibition of Slavery in all the remaining territory west of the Mississippi, and north of 36° 30', leaving the condition of other territory south of this line, or subsequently acquired, untouched by the arrangement. Here was a solemn act of legislation, called at the time a compromise, a covenant, a compact, first brought forward in this body by a slaveholder—vindicated by slaveholders in debate—finally sanctioned by slaveholding votes—also upheld at the time by the essential approbation of a slaveholding President, James Monroe, and his Cabinet, of whom a majority were slaveholders, including Mr. Calhoun himself; and this compromise was made the condition of the admission of Missouri, without which that State could not have been received into the Union. The bargain was simple, and was applicable, of course, only to the territory named. Leaving all other territory to await the judgment of another generation, the South said to the North, Conquer your prejudices so far as to admit Missouri as a slave State, and, in consideration of this much-coveted boon, Slavery shall be prohibited forever in all the remaining Louisiana Territory above 36° 30'; and the North yielded.

In total disregard of history, the President, in his annual message, has told us that this compromise "was *reluctantly* acquiesced in by the Southern States." Just the contrary is true. It was the work of slaveholders, and was crowded by their concurring votes upon a reluctant North. At the time it was hailed by slaveholders as a victory. Charles Pinckney, of South Carolina, in an oft-quoted letter, written at three o'clock on the night of its passage, says, "It is considered here by the slave-holding States as a great triumph." At the North it was accepted as a defeat, and the friends of Freedom everywhere throughout the country bowed their heads with mortification. But little did they know the completeness of their disaster. Little did they dream that the prohibition of Slavery in the Territory, which was stipulated as the price of their fatal capitulation, would also at the very moment of its maturity be wrested from them.

Time passed, and it became necessary to provide for this Territory an organized Government. Suddenly, without notice in the public press, or the prayer of a single petition, or one word of open recommendation from the President—after an acquiescence of thirty-three years, and the irreclaimable possession by the South of its special share under this compromise— in violation of every obligation of honor, compact, and good neighborhood—and in contemptuous disregard of the out-gushing sentiments of an aroused North, this time-honored prohibition, in itself a Landmark of Freedom, was overturned, and the vast region now known as Kansas and Nebraska was opened to Slavery. It was natural that a measure thus repugnant in character should be pressed by arguments mutually repugnant. It was urged on two principal reasons, so opposite and inconsistent as to slap each other in the face—one being that, by the repeal of the prohibition, the Territory would be left open to the entry of slaveholders with their slaves, without hindrance; and the other being, that the people would be left absolutely free to determine the question for themselves, and to prohibit the entry of slaveholders with their slaves, if they should think best. With some, the apology was the alleged rights of slaveholders; with others, it was the alleged rights of the people. With some, it was openly the extension of Slavery; and with others, it was openly the establishment of Freedom, under the guise of Popular Sovereignty. Of course, the measure, thus upheld in defiance of reason, was carried through Congress in defiance of all the securities of legislation; and I mention these things that you may see in what foulness the present Crime was engendered.

It was carried, *first*, by *whipping in* to its support, through Executive influence and patronage, men who acted against their own declared judgment and the known will of their constituents. *Secondly*, by *foisting out of place*, both in the Senate and House of Representatives, important business, long pending, and usurping its room. *Thirdly*, by *trampling under foot* the rules of the House of Representatives, always before the safeguard of the minority. And *fourthly*, by *driving it to a close* during the very session in which it originated, so that it might not be arrested by the indignant voice of the People. Such are some of the means by which this snap judgment was obtained. If the clear will of the People had not been disregarded, it could not have passed. If the Government had not nefariously interposed its influence, it could not have passed. If it had been left to its natural place in the order of business, it could not have passed. If the rules of the House and the rights of the minority had not been violated, it could not have passed. If it had been allowed to go over to another Congress, when the People might be heard, it would have been ended; and then the Crime we now deplore, would have been without its first seminal life.

Mr. President, I mean to keep absolutely within the limits of parliamentary propriety. I make no personal imputations; but only with frankness, such as belongs to the occasion and my own character, describe a great historical act, which is now

enrolled in the Capitol. Sir, the Nebraska Bill was in every respect a swindle. It was a swindle by the South of the North. It
was, on the part of those who had already completely enjoyed
their share of the Missouri Compromise, a swindle of those
whose share was yet absolutely untouched; and the plea of
unconstitutionality set up—like the plea of usury after the borrowed money has been enjoyed—did not make it less a swindle. Urged as a Bill of Peace, it was a swindle of the whole
country. Urged as opening the doors to slave-masters with their
slaves, it was a swindle of the asserted doctrine of Popular Sovereignty. Urged as sanctioning Popular Sovereignty, it was a
swindle of the asserted rights of slave-masters. It was a swindle
of a broad territory, thus cheated of protection against Slavery.
It was a swindle of a great cause, early espoused by Washington, Franklin, and Jefferson, surrounded by the best fathers of
the Republic. Sir, it was a swindle of God-given inalienable
Rights. Turn it over; look at it on all sides, and it is everywhere
a swindle; and, if the word I now employ has not the authority
of classical usage, it has, on this occasion, the indubitable authority of fitness. No other word will adequately express the
mingled meanness and wickedness of the cheat.

Its character was still further apparent in the general structure of the bill. Amidst overflowing professions of regard for
the sovereignty of the people in the Territory, they were despoiled of every essential privilege of sovereignty. They were
not allowed to choose their Governor, Secretary, Chief Justice,
Associate Justices, Attorney, or Marshal—all of whom are sent
from Washington; nor were they allowed to regulate the salaries
of any of these functionaries, or the daily allowance of the legislative body, or even the pay of the clerks and doorkeepers;
but they were left free to adopt Slavery. And this was called
Popular Sovereignty! Time does not allow, nor does the occasion require, that I should stop to dwell on this transparent
device to cover a transcendent wrong. Suffice it to say that
Slavery is in itself an arrogant denial of Human Rights, and by
no human reason can the power to establish such a wrong be
placed among the attributes of any just sovereignty. In refusing
it such a place, I do not deny popular rights, but uphold them;
I do not restrain popular rights, but extend them. And, sir, to
this conclusion you must yet come, unless deaf, not only to the

admonitions of political justice, but also to the genius of our own Constitution, under which, when properly interpreted, no valid claim for Slavery can be set up anywhere in the National territory. The Senator from Michigan [Mr. CASS] may say, in response to the Senator from Mississippi, [Mr. BROWN,] that Slavery cannot go into the Territory under the Constitution, without legislative introduction; and permit me to add, in response to both, that Slavery cannot go there at all. *Nothing can come out of nothing;* and there is absolutely nothing in the Constitution out of which Slavery can be derived, while there are provisions, which, when properly interpreted, make its existence anywhere within the exclusive National jurisdiction impossible.

The offensive provision in the bill was in its form a legislative anomaly, utterly wanting the natural directness and simplicity of an honest transaction. It did not undertake openly to repeal the old Prohibition of Slavery, but seemed to mince the matter, as if conscious of the swindle. It is said that this Prohibition, "being inconsistent with the principle of non-intervention by Congress with Slavery in the States and Territories, as recognized by the legislation of 1850, commonly called the Compromise Measures, is hereby declared inoperative and void." Thus, with insidious ostentation, was it pretended that an act, violating the greatest compromise of our legislative history, and setting loose the foundations of all compromise, was derived out of a compromise. Then followed in the Bill the further declaration, which is entirely without precedent, and which has been aptly called "a stump speech in its belly," namely: "it being the true intent and meaning of this act, not to legislate Slavery into any Territory or State, nor to exclude it therefrom, but to leave the people thereof perfectly free to form and regulate their domestic institutions in their own way, subject only to the Constitution of the United States." Here were smooth words, such as belong to a cunning tongue enlisted in a bad cause. But whatever may have been their various hidden meanings, this at least was evident, that, by their effect, the Congressional Prohibition of Slavery, which had always been regarded as a seven-fold shield, covering the whole Louisiana Territory north of 36° 30′, was now removed, while a principle was declared, which would render the supplementary Prohibition of Slavery in Minnesota, Oregon, and Washington, "inoperative and void," and thus open to Slavery all these vast regions, now the rude cradles of mighty States. Here you see the magnitude of the mischief contemplated. But my purpose now is with the Crime against Kansas, and I shall not stop to expose the conspiracy beyond.

Mr. President, men are wisely presumed to intend the natural consequences of their conduct, and to seek what their acts seem to promote. Now, the Nebraska Bill, on its very face, openly cleared the way for Slavery, and it is not wrong to presume that its originators intended the natural consequences of such an act, and sought in this way to extend Slavery. Of course, they did. And this is the first stage in the Crime against Kansas.

But this was speedily followed by other developments. The bare-faced scheme was soon whispered, that Kansas must be a slave State. In conformity with this idea was the Government of this unhappy Territory organized in all its departments; and thus did the President, by whose complicity the Prohibition of Slavery had been overthrown, lend himself to a new complicity—giving to the conspirators a lease of connivance, amounting even to copartnership. The Governor, Secretary, Chief Justice, Associate Justices, Attorney, and Marshal, with a whole caucus of other stipendiaries, nominated by the President and confirmed by the Senate, were all commended as friendly to Slavery. No man, with the sentiments of Washington, or Jefferson, or Franklin, found any favor; nor is it too much to say, that, had these great patriots once more come among us, not one of them, with his recorded unretracted opinions on Slavery, could have been nominated by the President or confirmed by the Senate for any post in that Territory. With such auspices the conspiracy proceeded. Even in advance of the Nebraska Bill, secret societies were organized in Missouri, ostensibly to protect her institutions, and afterwards, under the name of "Self-Defensive Associations," and of "Blue Lodges," these were multiplied throughout the western counties of that State, *before any counter-movement from the North.* It was confidently anticipated, that, by the activity of these societies, and the interest of slaveholders everywhere, with the advantage derived from the neighborhood of Missouri, and the influence of the Territorial Government, Slavery might be introduced into Kansas, quietly but surely, without arousing a conflict—that the crocodile egg might be stealthily dropped in the sun-burnt soil, there to be hatched unobserved until it sent forth its reptile monster.

But the conspiracy was unexpectedly balked The debate, which convulsed Congress, had stirred the whole country. Attention from all sides was directed upon Kansas, which at once became the favorite goal of emigration. The Bill had loudly declared, that its object was "to leave the people perfectly free to form and regulate their domestic institutions in their own way;" and its supporters everywhere challenged the determination of the question between Freedom and Slavery by a competition of emigration. Thus, while opening the Territory to Slavery, the bill also opened it to emigrants from every quarter, who might by their votes redress the wrong. The populous North, stung by a sharp sense of outrage, and inspired by a noble cause, poured into the debatable land, and promised soon to establish a supremacy of numbers there, involving, of course, a just supremacy of Freedom.

Then was conceived the consummation of the Crime against Kansas. What could not be accomplished peaceably, was to be accomplished forcibly. The reptile monster, that could not be quietly and securely hatched there, was to be pushed full-grown into the Territory. All efforts were now given to the dismal work of forcing Slavery on Free Soil. In flagrant derogation of the very Popular Sovereignty, whose name helped to impose this Bill upon the country, the atrocious object was now distinctly avowed. And the avowal has been followed by the act. Slavery has been forcibly introduced into Kansas, and placed under the formal safeguards of pretended law. How this was done, belongs to the argument.

In depicting this consummation, the simplest outline, without one word of color, will be best. Whether regarded in its mass or its details, in its origin or its result, it is all blackness, illumined by nothing from itself, but only by the heroism of the undaunted men and women, whom it environed. A plain statement of facts will be a picture of fearful truth, which faithful history will preserve in its darkest gallery. In the foreground all will recognize a familiar character, in himself a connecting link between the President and the border ruffian—less

conspicuous for ability than for the exalted place he has occupied—who once sat in the seat where you now sit, sir; where
once sat John Adams and Thomas Jefferson; also, where once
sat Aaron Burr. I need not add the name of David R. Atchison.
You have not forgotten that, at the session of Congress immediately succeeding the Nebraska Bill, he came tardily to his
duty here, and then, after a short time, disappeared. The secret
has been long since disclosed. Like Catiline, he stalked into this
Chamber, reeking with conspiracy—*immo in Senatum venit*—
and then like Catiline he skulked away—*abiit, excessit, evasit,
erupit*—to join and provoke the conspirators, who at a distance awaited their congenial chief. Under the influence of his
malign presence the Crime ripened to its fatal fruits, while the
similitude with Catiline was again renewed in the sympathy,
not even concealed, which he found in the very Senate itself,
where, beyond even the Roman example, a Senator has not
hesitated to appear as his open compurgator.

And now, as I proceed to show the way in which this Territory was overrun and finally subjugated to Slavery, I desire to
remove in advance all question with regard to the authority on
which I rely. The evidence is secondary; but it is the best which,
in the nature of the case, can be had, and it is not less clear, direct, and peremptory, than any by which we are assured of the
campaigns in the Crimea or the fall of Sebastopol. In its manifold mass, I confidently assert, that it is such a body of evidence as the human mind is not able to resist. It is found in the
concurring reports of the public press; in the letters of corre-
spondents; in the testimony of travelers; and in the unaffected
story to which I have listened from leading citizens, who,
during this winter, have "come flocking" here from that distant
Territory. It breaks forth in the irrepressible outcry, reaching
us from Kansas, in truthful tones, which leave no ground of
mistake. It addresses us in formal complaints, instinct with the
indignation of a people determined to be free, and unim-
peachable as the declarations of a murdered man on his dying
bed against his murderer. And let me add, that all this testimony finds an echo in the very statute-book of the conspirators, and also in language dropped from the President of the
United States.

I begin with an admission from the President himself, in

whose sight the people of Kansas have little favor. And yet, after arraigning the innocent emigrants from the North, he was constrained to declare that their conduct was "far from justifying the *illegal* and *reprehensible* counter-movement which ensued." Then, by the reluctant admission of the Chief Magistrate, there was a counter-movement, at once *illegal* and *reprehensible*. I thank thee, President, for teaching me these words; and I now put them in the front of this exposition, as in themselves a confession. Sir, this "illegal and reprehensible counter-movement" is none other than the dreadful Crime—under an apologetic *alias*—by which, through successive invasions, Slavery has been forcibly planted in this Territory.

Next to this Presidential admission must be placed the details of the invasions, which I now present as not only "illegal and reprehensible," but also unquestionable evidence of the resulting Crime.

The violence, for some time threatened, broke forth on the 29th November, 1854, at the first election of a Delegate to Congress, when companies from Missouri, amounting to upwards of one thousand, crossed into Kansas, and, with force of arms, proceeded to vote for Mr. Whitfield, the candidate of Slavery. An eye-witness, General Pomeroy, of superior intelligence and perfect integrity, thus describes this scene:

"The first ballot-box that was opened upon our virgin soil was closed to us by overpowering numbers and impending force. So bold and reckless were our invaders, that they cared not to conceal their attack. They came upon us not in the guise of voters, to steal away our franchise, but boldly and openly, to snatch it with a strong hand. They came directly from their own homes, and in compact and organized bands, with arms in hand and provisions for the expedition, marched to our polls, and when their work was done, returned whence they came."

Here was an outrage at which the coolest blood of patriotism boils. Though, for various reasons unnecessary to develop, the busy settlers allowed the election to pass uncontested, still the means employed were none the less "illegal and reprehensible."

This infliction was a significant prelude to the grand invasion of the 30th March, 1855, at the election of the first Territorial Legislature under the organic law, when an armed multitude from Missouri entered the Territory, in larger numbers than General Taylor commanded at Buena Vista, or than General Jackson had within his lines at New Orleans—larger far than our fathers rallied on Bunker Hill. On they came as an "army with banners," organized in companies, with officers, munitions, tents, and provisions, as though marching upon a foreign foe, and breathing loud-mouthed threats that they would carry their purpose, if need be, by the bowie-knife and revolver. Among them, according to his own confession, was David R. Atchison, belted with the vulgar arms of his vulgar comrades. Arrived at their several destinations on the night before the election, the invaders pitched their tents, placed their sentries, and waited for the coming day. The same trustworthy eye-witness, whom I have already quoted, says, of one locality:

"Baggage-wagons were there, with arms and ammunition enough for a protracted fight, and among them two brass field-pieces, ready charged. They came with drums beating and flags flying, and their leaders were of the most prominent and conspicuous men of their State."

Of another locality he says:

"The invaders came together in one armed and organized body, with trains of fifty wagons, besides horsemen, and, the night before election, pitched their camp in the vicinity of the polls; and, having appointed their own judges in place of those who, from intimidation or otherwise, failed to attend, they voted without any proof of residence."

With this force they were able, on the succeeding day, in some places, to intimidate the judges of elections; in others, to substitute judges of their own appointment; in others, to wrest the ballot-boxes from their rightful possessors, and everywhere to exercise a complete control of the election, and thus, by a preternatural audacity of usurpation, impose a Legislature upon the free people of Kansas. Thus was conquered the Sevastopol of that Territory!

But it was not enough to secure the Legislature. The election of a member of Congress recurred on the 2d October, 1855, and the same foreigners, who had learned their strength, again manifested it. Another invasion, in controlling numbers, came from Missouri, and once more forcibly exercised the electoral franchise in Kansas.

At last, in the latter days of November, 1855, a storm, long brewing, burst upon the heads of the devoted people. The ballot-boxes had been violated, and a Legislature installed, which had proceeded to carry out the conspiracy of the invaders; but the good people of the Territory, born to freedom, and educated as American citizens, showed no signs of submission. Slavery, though recognized by pretended law, was in many places practically an outlaw. To the lawless borderers, this was hard to bear; and, like the Heathen of old, they raged, particularly against the town of Lawrence, already known, by the firmness of its principles and the character of its citizens, as the citadel of the good cause. On this account they threatened, in their peculiar language, to "wipe it out." Soon the hostile power was gathered for this purpose. The wickedness of this invasion was enhanced by the way in which it began. A citizen of Kansas, by the name of Dow, was murdered by one of the partisans of Slavery, under the name of "law and order." Such an outrage naturally aroused indignation and provoked threats. The professors of "law and order" allowed the murderer to escape; and, still further to illustrate the irony of the name they assumed, seized the friend of the murdered man, whose few neighbors soon rallied for his rescue. This transaction, though totally disregarded in its chief front of wickedness, became the excuse for unprecedented excitement. The weak Governor, with no faculty higher than servility to Slavery—whom the President, in his official delinquency, had appointed to a trust worthy only of a well-balanced character—was frightened from his propriety. By proclamation he invoked the Territory. By telegraph he invoked the President. The Territory would not respond to his senseless appeal. The President was dumb; but the proclamation was circulated throughout the border counties of Missouri; and Platte, Clay, Carlisle, Sabine, Howard, and Jefferson, each of them, contributed a volunteer company, recruited from the road sides, and armed with weapons which chance afforded—known as the "shot-gun militia"—with a Missouri officer as commissary general, dispensing rations, and another Missouri officer as general-in-chief; with two wagon loads of rifles, belonging to Missouri, drawn by six mules, from its arsenal at Jefferson City; with seven pieces of cannon, belonging to the United States, from its arsenal at Liberty; and this formidable force, amounting to at least 1,800 men, terrible with threats, with oaths, and with whisky, crossed the borders, and encamped in larger part at Wacherusa, over against the doomed town of Lawrence, which was now threatened with destruction. With these invaders was the Governor, who by this act levied war upon the people he was sent to protect. In camp with him was the original Catiline of the conspiracy, while by his side was the docile Chief Justice and the docile Judges. But this is not the first instance in which an unjust Governor has found tools where he ought to have found justice. In the great impeachment of Warren Hastings, the British orator, by whom it was conducted, exclaims, in words strictly applicable to the misdeed I now arraign, "Had he not the Chief Justice, the tamed and domesticated Chief Justice, who waited on him like a familiar spirit?" Thus was this invasion countenanced by those who should have stood in the breach against it. For more than a week it continued, while deadly conflict seemed imminent. I do not dwell on the heroism by which it was encountered, or the mean retreat to which it was compelled; for that is not necessary to exhibit the crime which you are to judge. But I cannot forbear to add other additional features, furnished in the letter of a clergyman, written at the time, who saw and was a part of what he describes:

"Our citizens have been shot at, *and in two instances murdered*, our houses invaded, hay-ricks burnt, corn and other provisions plundered, cattle driven off, all communication cut off between us and the States, wagons on the way to us with provisions stopped and plundered, and the drivers taken prisoners, and we in hourly expectation of an attack. *Nearly every man has been in arms in the village.* Fortifications have been thrown up, by incessant labor night and day. The sound of the drum and the tramp of armed men resounded through our streets, *families fleeing with their household goods for safety.* Day before yesterday, the report of cannon was heard at our house, from the direction of Lecompton. Last Thursday, one of our neighbors— one of the most peaceable and excellent of men, from Ohio—on his way home, was set upon by a gang of twelve men on horseback, and shot down. Over eight hundred men are gathered under arms at Lawrence. As yet, no act of violence has been perpetrated by those on our side. *No blood of retaliation stains our hands. We stand and are ready to act purely in the defense of our homes and lives.*"

But the catalogue is not yet complete. On the 15th of December, when the people assembled to vote on the Constitution then submitted for adoption—only a few days after the Treaty of Peace between the Governor on the one side and the town of Lawrence on the other—another and fifth irruption was made. But I leave all this untold. Enough of these details has been given.

Five several times and more have these invaders entered Kansas in armed array, and thus five several times and more have they trampled upon the organic law of the Territory. But these extraordinary expeditions are simply the extraordinary witnesses to successive uninterrupted violence. They stand out conspicuous, but not alone. The spirit of evil, in which they had their origin, was wakeful and incessant. From the beginning, it hung upon the skirts of this interesting Territory, harrowing its peace, disturbing its prosperity, and keeping its inhabitants under the painful alarms of war. Thus was all security of person, of property, and of labor, overthrown; and when I urge this incontrovertible fact, I set forth a wrong which is small only by the side of the giant wrong, for the consummation of which all this was done. Sir, what is man—what is government—without security; in the absence of which, nor man nor government can proceed in development or enjoy the fruits of existence? Without security, Civilization is cramped and dwarfed. Without security, there can be no true Freedom. Nor shall I say too much, when I declare that security, guarded of course by its offspring, Freedom, is the true end and aim of government. Of this indispensable boon the people of Kansas have thus far been despoiled—absolutely, totally. All this is aggravated by the nature of their pursuits, rendering them peculiarly sensitive to interruption, and at the same time attesting their innocence. They are for the most part engaged in the cultivation of the soil, which from time immemorial has been the sweet employment of undisturbed industry. Contented in the returns of bounteous nature and the shade of his own trees, the husbandman is not aggressive; accustomed to produce, and not to destroy, he is essentially peaceful, unless his home is invaded, when his arm derives vigor from the soil he treads, and his soul inspiration from the heavens beneath whose canopy he daily toils. And such are the people of Kansas, whose security has been overthrown. Scenes from which civilization averts her countenance have been a part of their daily life. The border incursions, which, in barbarous ages or barbarous lands, have fretted and "harried" an exposed people, have been here renewed, with this peculiarity, that our border robbers do not simply levy black mail and drive off a few cattle, like those who acted under the inspiration of the Douglas of other days; that they do not seize a few persons, and sweep them away into captivity, like the African slave-traders whom we brand as pirates; but that they commit a succession of acts, in which all border sorrows and all African wrongs are revived together on American soil, and which for the time being annuls all protection of all kinds, and enslaves the whole Territory.

Private griefs mingle their poignancy with public wrongs. I do not dwell on the anxieties which families have undergone, exposed to sudden assault, and obliged to lie down to rest with the alarms of war ringing in their ears, not knowing that another day might be spared to them. Throughout this bitter winter, with the thermometer at thirty degrees below zero the citizens of Lawrence have been constrained to sleep under arms, with sentinels treading their constant watch against surprise. But our souls are wrung by individual instances. In vain do we condemn the cruelties of another age—the refinements of torture to which men have been doomed—the rack and thumb-screw of the Inquisition, the last agonies of the regicide Ravaillac—"Luke's iron crown, and Damien's bed of steel"— for kindred outrages have disgraced these borders. Murder has stalked—assassination has skulked in the tall grass of the prairie, and the vindictiveness of man has assumed unwonted forms. A preacher of the Gospel of the Saviour has been ridden on a rail, and then thrown into the Missouri, fastened to a log, and left to drift down its muddy, tortuous current. And lately we have had the tidings of that enormity without precedent—a deed without a name—where a candidate for the Legislature was most brutally gashed with knives and hatchets, and then, after weltering in blood on the snow-clad earth, was trundled along with gaping wounds, to fall dead in the face of his wife. It is

common to drop a tear of sympathy over the trembling solicitudes of our early fathers, exposed to the stealthy assault of the
savage foe; and an eminent American artist has pictured this
scene in a marble group of rare beauty, on the front of the National Capitol, where the uplifted tomahawk is arrested by the
strong arm and generous countenance of the pioneer; while
his wife and children find shelter at his feet; but now the tear
must be dropped over the trembling solicitudes of fellow-
citizens, seeking to build a new State in Kansas, and exposed
to the perpetual assault of murderous robbers from Missouri.
Hirelings, picked from the drunken spew and vomit of an uneasy civilization—in the form of men—

> "Ay, in the catalogue ye go for men;
> As hounds and gray-hounds, mongrels, spaniels, curs,
> Shoughs, water-rugs, and demi-wolves, are called
> All by the name of dogs:"

leashed together by secret signs and lodges, have renewed the
incredible atrocities of the Assassins and of the Thugs; showing
the blind submission of the Assassins to the Old Man of the
Mountain, in robbing Christians on the road to Jerusalem, and
showing the heartlessness of the Thugs, who, avowing that
murder was their religion, waylaid travelers on the great road
from Agra to Delhi; with the more deadly bowie-knife for
the dagger of the Assassin, and the more deadly revolver for the
noose of the Thug.

In these invasions, attended by the entire subversion of all
security in this Territory, with the plunder of the ballot-box,
and the pollution of the electoral franchise, I show simply the
process in unprecedented Crime. If that be the best Government, where an injury to a single citizen is resented as an injury to the whole State, then must our Government forfeit all
claim to any such eminence, while it leaves its citizens thus exposed. In the outrage upon the ballot-box, even without the
illicit fruits which I shall soon exhibit, there is a peculiar crime
of the deepest dye, though subordinate to the final Crime,
which should be promptly avenged. In countries where royalty
is upheld, it is a special offense to rob the crown jewels, which
are the emblems of that sovereignty before which the loyal
subject bows, and it is treason to be found in adultery with the

Queen, for in this way may a false heir be imposed upon the State; but in our Republic the ballot-box is the single priceless jewel of that sovereignty which we respect, and the electoral franchise, out of which are born the rulers of a free people, is the Queen whom we are to guard against pollution. In this plain presentment, whether as regards Security, or as regards Elections, there is enough, surely, without proceeding further, to justify the intervention of Congress, most promptly and completely, to throw over this oppressed people the impenetrable shield of the Constitution and laws. But the half is not yet told.

As every point in a wide-spread horizon radiates from a common center, so everything said or done in this vast circle of Crime radiates from the *One Idea*, that Kansas, at all hazards, must be made a slave State. In all the manifold wickednesses that have occurred, and in every successive invasion, this *One Idea* has been ever present, as the Satanic tempter—the motive power—the *causing cause.*

To accomplish this result, three things were attempted: *first*, by outrages of all kinds to drive the friends of Freedom already there out of the Territory; *secondly*, to deter others from coming; and *thirdly*, to obtain the complete control of the Government. The process of driving out, and also of deterring, has failed. On the contrary, the friends of Freedom there became more fixed in their resolves to stay and fight the battle, which they had never sought, but from which they disdained to retreat; while the friends of Freedom elsewhere were more aroused to the duty of timely succors, by men and munitions of just self-defense.

But, while defeated in the first two processes proposed, the conspirators succeeded in the last. By the violence already portrayed at the election of the 30th March, when the polls were occupied by the armed hordes from Missouri, they imposed a Legislature upon the Territory, and thus, under the iron mask of law, established a Usurpation not less complete than any in history. That this was done, I proceed to prove. Here is the evidence:

1. Only in this way can this extraordinary expedition be adequately explained. In the words of Moliere, once employed by John Quincy Adams in the other House, *Que diable alliaent-*

ils faire dans cette galere? What did they go into the Territory for? If their purposes were peaceful, as has been suggested, why cannons, arms, flags, numbers, and all this violence? As simple citizens, proceeding to the honest exercise of the electoral franchise, they might have gone with nothing more than a pilgrim's staff. Philosophy always seeks a *sufficient cause*, and only in the *One Idea*, already presented, can a cause be found in any degree commensurate with this Crime; and this becomes so only when we consider the mad fanaticism of Slavery.

2. Public notoriety steps forward to confirm the suggestion of reason. In every place where Truth can freely travel, it has been asserted and understood, that the Legislature was imposed upon Kansas by foreigners from Missouri; and this universal voice is now received as undeniable verity.

3. It is also attested by the harangues of the conspirators. Here is what Stringfellow said *before* the invasion:

"To those who have qualms of conscience as to violating laws, State or National, the time has come when such impositions must be disregarded, as your rights and property are in danger; *and I advise you, one and all, to enter every election district in Kansas, in defiance of Reeder and his vile myrmidons, and vote at the point of the bowie-knife and revolver.* Neither give nor take quarter, as our case demands it. It is enough that the slaveholding interest wills it, from which there is no appeal. What right has Governor Reeder to rule Missourians in Kansas! His proclamation and prescribed oath must be repudiated. It is your interest to do so. Mind that Slavery is established where it is not prohibited."

Here is what Atchison said *after* the invasion:

"Well what next? Why an election for members of the Legislature to organize the Territory must be held. What did I advise you to do then? Why, meet them on their own ground, and beat them at their own game again; and cool and inclement as the weather was, I went over with a company of men. My object in going was not to vote. I had no right to vote, unless I had disfranchised myself in Missouri. I was not within two miles of a voting place. My object in going was not to vote, but to settle a difficulty between two of our candidates; and the Abolitionists of the North said, *and published it abroad, that Atchison was there with bowie-knives and revolvers, and by God 'twas true. I never did go into that Territory—I never intended to go into that Territory—without being prepared for all such kind of cattle.* Well, we beat them, and Governor Reeder gave certificates to a majority of all the members of both Houses, and then, after they were organized, as everybody will admit, they were the only competent persons to say who were, and who were not, members of the same."

4. It is confirmed by the cotemporaneous admission of the *Squatter Sovereign*, a paper published at Atchison, and at once the organ of the President and of these Borderers, which, under date of 1st April, thus recounts the victory:

"INDEPENDENCE, [MISSOURI,] *March 31, 1855*.

"Several hundred emigrants from Kansas have just entered our city. They were preceded by the Westport and Independence brass bands. They came in at the west side of the public square, and proceeded entirely around it, the bands cheering us with fine music, and the emigrants with good news. Immediately following the bands were about two hundred horsemen in regular order; following these were one hundred and fifty wagons, carriages, &c. They gave repeated cheers for Kansas and Missouri. They reported that not an Anti-Slavery man will be in the Legislature of Kansas. *We have made a clean sweep.*"

5. It is also confirmed by the cotemporaneous testimony of another paper, always faithful to Slavery, the New York *Herald*, in the letter of a correspondent from Brunswick, in Missouri, under date of 20th April, 1855:

"From five to seven thousand men started from Missouri to attend the election, some to remove, but the most to return to their families, with an intention, if they liked the Territory, to make it their permanent abode at the earliest moment practicable. But they intended to vote. The Missourians were, many of them, Douglas men. There were one hundred and fifty voters from this county, one hundred and seventy-five from Howard, one hundred from Cooper. Indeed, every county furnished its quota; and when they set out it looked like an army." * * * "They were armed." * * * "And, as there were no houses in the Territory, they carried tents. Their mission was a peaceable one—to vote, and to drive down stakes for their future homes. After the election, some one thousand five hundred of the voters sent a committee to Mr. Reeder, to ascertain if it was his purpose to ratify the election. He answered that it was, and said the majority at an election must carry the day. But it is not to be denied that the one thousand five hundred, apprehending that the Governor might attempt to play the tyrant—since his conduct had already been insidious and unjust—wore on their hats bunches of hemp. They were resolved, if a tyrant attempted to trample upon the rights of the sovereign people, to hang him."

6. It is again confirmed by the testimony of a lady, who for five years has lived in Western Missouri, and thus writes in a letter published in the *New Haven Register*:

"MIAMI, SALINE CO., *November 26, 1855.*
"You ask me to tell you something about the Kansas and Missouri troubles. Of course you know in what they have originated. *There is no denying that the Missourians have determined to control the elections, if possible;* and I don't know that their measures would be justifiable, except upon the principle of self-preservation; and that, you know, is the first law of nature."

7. And it is confirmed still further by the Circular of the Emigration Society of Lafayette, in Missouri, dated as late as 25th March, 1856, in which the efforts of Missourians are openly confessed:

"The Western counties of Missouri have for the last two years been heavily taxed, both in money and time, in fighting the battles of the South. *Lafayette county alone has expended more than one hundred thousand dollars in money, and as much or more in time. Up to this time, the border counties of Missouri have upheld and maintained the rights and interests of the South in this struggle, unassisted, and not unsuccessfully.* But the Abolitionists, staking their all upon the Kansas issue, and hesitating at no means, fair or foul, are moving heaven and earth to render that beautiful Territory a *Free State*."

8. Here, also, is complete admission of the Usurpation, by the *Intelligencer*, a leading paper of St. Louis, Missouri, made in the ensuing summer:

"Atchison and Stringfellow, with their Missouri followers, overwhelmed the settlers in Kansas, browbeat and bullied them, and took the Government from their hands. Missouri votes elected the present body of men who insult public intelligence and popular rights by styling themselves 'the Legislature of Kansas.' This body of men are helping themselves to fat speculations by locating the 'seat of Government' and getting town lots for their votes. They are passing laws disfranchising all the citizens of Kansas who do not believe Negro Slavery to be a Christian institution and a national blessing. They are proposing to punish with imprisonment the utterance of views inconsistent with their own. And they are trying to perpetuate their preposterous and infernal tyranny by appointing *for a term of years* creatures of their own, as commissioners in every county, to lay and collect taxes, and see that the laws they are passing are faithfully executed. Has this age anything to compare with these acts in audacity?"

9. In harmony with all these is the authoritative declaration of Governor Reeder, in a speech addressed to his neighbors, at Easton, Pennsylvania, at the end of April, 1855, and immediately afterwards published in the Washington *Union*. Here it is:

"It was indeed too true that Kansas had been invaded, conquered, subjugated, by an armed force from beyond her borders, led on by a fanatical spirit, trampling under foot the principles of the Kansas bill and the right of suffrage."

10. And in similar harmony is the complaint of the people of Kansas, in a public meeting at Big Springs, on the 5th September, 1855, embodied in these words:

"*Resolved*, That the body of men who for the last two months have been passing laws for the people of our Territory, moved, counseled, and dictated to by the demagogues of Missouri, are to us a foreign body, representing only the lawless invaders who elected them, and not the people of the Territory—that we repudiate their action, as the monstrous consummation of an act of violence, usurpation, and fraud unparalleled in the history of the Union, and worthy only of men unfitted for the duties and regardless of the responsibilities of Republicans."

11. And finally, by the official minutes, which have been laid on our table by the President, the invasion, which ended in the Usurpation, is clearly established; but the effect of this testimony has been so amply exposed by the Senator from Vermont, [Mr. COLLAMER,] in his able and indefatigable argument, that I content myself with simply referring to it.

On this cumulative, irresistible evidence, in concurrence with the antecedent history, I rest. And yet Senators here have argued that this cannot be so—precisely as the conspiracy of Catiline was doubted in the Roman Senate. *Non nulli sunt in hoc ordine, qui aut ea, quæ imminent non videant; aut ea, quæ vident, dissimulent; qui spem Catilinæ mollibus sententiis aluerunt, conjurationemque nascentem non credendo corroboraverunt.* As I listened to the Senator from Illinois, while he painfully strove to show that there was no Usurpation, I was reminded of the effort by a distinguished logician, in a much-admired argument, to prove that Napoleon Bonaparte never existed. And permit me to say, that the fact of his existence is not placed more completely above doubt than the fact of this Usurpation. This I assert on the proofs already presented. But confirmation comes almost while I speak. The columns of the public press are now daily filled with testimony, solemnly taken before the Committee of Congress in Kansas, which shows, in awful light, the violence ending in the Usurpation. Of this I may speak on some other occasion. Meanwhile, I proceed with the development of the Crime.

The usurping Legislature assembled at the appointed place in the interior, and then at once, in opposition to the veto of the Governor, by a majority of two thirds, removed to the Shawnee Mission, a place in most convenient proximity to the Missouri borderers, by whom it had been constituted, and whose tyrannical agent it was. The statutes of Missouri, in all their text, with their divisions and subdivisions, were adopted bodily, and with such little local adaptation that the word "State" in the original is not even changed to "Territory," but is left to be corrected by an explanatory act. But, all this general legislation was entirely subordinate to the special act, entitled "An Act to punish offenses against Slave Property," in which the One Idea, that provoked this whole conspiracy, is at last embodied in legislative form, and Human Slavery openly recognized on Free Soil, under the sanction of pretended law. This act of thirteen sections is in itself a *Dance of Death*. But its complex completeness of wickedness, without a parallel, may be partially conceived, when it is understood that in three sections only of it is the penalty of death denounced no less than forty-eight different times, by as many changes of language, against the heinous offense, described in forty-eight different ways, of interfering with what does not exist in that Territory—and under the Constitution cannot exist there—I mean property in human flesh. Thus is Liberty sacrificed to Slavery, and Death summoned to sit at the gates as guardian of the Wrong.

But the work of Usurpation was not perfected even yet. It had already cost too much to be left at any hazard.

> ———"To be thus was nothing;
> But to be safely thus!"

Such was the object. And this could not be, except by the entire prostration of all the safeguards of Human Rights. The liberty of speech, which is the very breath of a Republic; the press, which is the terror of wrong-doers; the bar, through which the oppressed beards the arrogance of law; the jury, by which right is vindicated; all these must be struck down, while officers are provided, in all places, ready to be the tools of this tyranny; and then, to obtain final assurance that their crime was secure, the whole Usurpation, stretching over the Territory, must be fastened and riveted by legislative bolts, spikes, and screws, *so as to defy all effort at change through the ordinary forms of law.* To this work, in its various parts, were bent the subtlest energies; and never, from Tubal Cain to this hour, was any fabric forged with more desperate skill and completeness.

Mark, sir, three different legislative enactments, which constitute part of this work. *First,* according to one act, all who deny, by spoken or written word, "the right of persons to hold slaves in this Territory," are denounced as felons, to be punished by imprisonment at hard labor, for a term not less than two years; it may be for life. And to show the extravagance of this injustice, it has been well put by the Senator from Vermont, [Mr. COLLAMER,] that should the Senator from Michigan, [Mr. CASS,] who believes that slavery cannot exist in a Territory, unless introduced by express legislative acts, venture there with his moderate opinions, his doom must be that of a felon! To this extent are the great liberties of speech and of the press subverted. *Secondly,* by another act, entitled "An act concerning Attorneys-at-Law," no person can practice as an attorney, unless he *shall obtain a license* from the Territorial courts, which, of course, a tyrannical discretion will be free to deny; and after obtaining such license, he is constrained to take an oath, not only "to support" the Constitution of the United States, but also "to support and sustain"—mark here the reduplication—the Territorial act, and the Fugitive Slave Bill, thus erecting a test for the function of the bar, calculated to exclude citizens who honestly regard that latter legislative enormity as unfit to be obeyed. And, *thirdly,* by another act, entitled "An act concerning Jurors," all persons "conscientiously opposed to holding slaves," or "not admitting the right to hold slaves in the Territory," are excluded from the jury on every question, civil or criminal, arising out of asserted slave property; while, in all cases, the summoning of the jury is left without one word of restraint to "the marshal, sheriff, or other officer," who are thus free to pack it according to their tyrannical discretion.

For the ready enforcement of all statutes against Human Freedom, the President had already furnished a powerful quota of officers, in the Governor, Chief Justice, Judges, Secretary, Attorney, and Marshal. The Legislature completed this part of the work, by constituting, in each county, a *Board of Commissioners*, composed of two persons, associated with the Probate Judge, whose duty it is "to appoint a county treasurer, coroner, justices of the peace, constables, and *all* other officers provided for by law," and then proceeded to the choice of this very Board; thus delegating and diffusing their usurped power, and tyrannically imposing upon the Territory a crowd of officers, in whose appointment the people have had no voice, directly or indirectly.

And still the final inexorable work remained. A Legislature, renovated in both branches, could not assemble until 1858, so that, during this long intermediate period, this whole system must continue in the likeness of law, unless overturned by the Federal Government, or, in default of such interposition, by a generous uprising of an oppressed people. But it was necessary to guard against the possibility of change, even tardily, at a future election; and this was done by two different acts; under the *first* of which, all who will not take the oath to support the Fugitive Slave Bill are excluded from the elective franchise; and under the *second* of which, all others are entitled to vote who shall tender a tax of one dollar to the Sheriff on the day of election; thus, by provision of Territorial law disfranchising all opposed to Slavery, and at the same time opening the door to the votes of the invaders; by an unconstitutional shibboleth, excluding from the polls the mass of actual settlers, and by making the franchise depend upon a petty tax only, admitting to the polls the mass of borderers from Missouri. Thus, by tyrannical forethought, the Usurpation not only fortified all that it did, but assumed a *self-perpetuating* energy.

Thus was the Crime consummated. Slavery now stands erect, clanking its chains on the Territory of Kansas, surrounded by a code of death, and trampling upon all cherished liberties, whether of speech, the press, the bar, the trial by jury, or the electoral franchise. And, sir, all this has been done, not merely to introduce a wrong which in itself is a denial of all rights, and in dread of which a mother has lately taken the life of her off-spring; not merely, as has been sometimes said, to protect Slavery in Missouri, since it is futile for this State to complain of Freedom on the side of Kansas, when Freedom exists without complaint on the side of Iowa and also on the side of Illinois; but it has been done for the sake of political power, in order to bring two new slaveholding Senators upon this floor, and thus to fortify in the National Government the desperate chances of a waning Oligarchy. As the ship, voyaging on pleasant summer seas, is assailed by a pirate crew, and robbed for the sake of its doubloons and dollars—so is this beautiful Territory now assailed in its peace and prosperity, and robbed, in order to wrest its political power to the side of Slavery. Even now the black flag of the land pirates from Missouri waves at the mast head; in their laws you hear the pirate yell, and see the flash of the pirate knife; while, incredible to relate! the President, gathering the Slave Power at his back, testifies a pirate sympathy.

Sir, all this was done in the name of Popular Sovereignty. And this is the close of the tragedy. Popular Sovereignty, which, when truly understood, is a fountain of just power, has ended in Popular Slavery; not merely in the subjection of the unhappy African race, but of this proud Caucasian blood, which you boast. The profession with which you began, of *All by the People*, has been lost in the wretched reality of *Nothing for the People*. Popular Sovereignty, in whose deceitful name plighted faith was broken, and an ancient Landmark of Freedom was overturned, now lifts itself before us, like Sin, in the terrible picture of Milton,

> "That seem'd a woman to the waist, and fair;
> But ended foul in many a scaly fold,
> Voluminous and vast! a serpent arm'd
> With mortal sting: about her middle round
> A cry of hell-hounds never ceasing bark'd

With wide Cerberian mouths full loud, and rung
A hideous peal: yet, when they list, would creep,
If aught disturb'd their noise, into her womb,
And kennel there; yet there still bark'd, and howl'd
Within, unseen."

The image is complete at all points; and, with this exposure, I take my leave of the Crime against Kansas.

II. Emerging from all the blackness of this Crime, in which we seem to have been lost, as in a savage wood, and turning our backs upon it, as upon desolation and death, from which, while others have suffered, we have escaped, I come now to THE APOLOGIES which the Crime has found. Sir, well may you start at the suggestion that such a series of wrongs, so clearly proved by various testimony, so openly confessed by the wrong-doers, and so widely recognized throughout the country, should find Apologies. But the partisan spirit, now, as in other days, hesitates at nothing. The great Crimes of history have never been without Apologies. The massacre of St. Bartholomew, which you now instinctively condemn, was, at the time, applauded in high quarters, and even commemorated by a Papal medal, which may still be procured at Rome; as the Crime against Kansas, which is hardly less conspicuous in dreadful eminence, has been shielded on this floor by extenuating words, and even by a Presidential message, which, like the Papal medal, can never be forgotten in considering the madness and perversity of men.

Sir, the Crime cannot be denied. The President himself has admitted "illegal and reprehensible" conduct. To such conclusion he was compelled by irresistible evidence; but what he mildly describes I openly arraign. Senators may affect to put it aside by a sneer; or to reason it away by figures; or to explain it by a theory, such as desperate invention has produced on this floor, that the Assassins and Thugs of Missouri were in reality citizens of Kansas; but all these efforts, so far as made, are only tokens of the weakness of the cause, while to the original Crime they add another offense of false testimony against innocent and suffering men. But the Apologies for the Crime are worse than the efforts at denial. In cruelty and heartlessness they identify their authors with the great transgression.

They are four in number, and four-fold in character. The first is the Apology *Tyrannical*; the second, the Apology *Imbecile*; the third the Apology *Absurd*; and the fourth, the Apology *Infamous*. This is all. Tyranny, imbecility, absurdity, and infamy, all unite to dance, like the weird sisters, about this Crime.

The Apology *Tyrannical* is founded on the mistaken act of Governor Reeder, in authenticating the Usurping Legislature, by which it is asserted that whatever may have been the actual force or fraud in its election, the people of Kansas are effectually concluded, and the whole proceeding is placed under the formal sanction of law. According to this assumption, complaint is now in vain, and it only remains that Congress should sit and hearken to it, without correcting the wrong, as the ancient tyrant listened and granted no redress to the human moans that issued from the heated brazen bull, which subtle cruelty had devised. This I call the Apology of technicality inspired by tyranny.

The facts on this head are few and plain. Governor Reeder, after allowing only five days for objections to the returns—a space of time unreasonably brief in that extensive Territory—declared a majority of the members of the Council and of the House of Representatives "duly elected," withheld certificates from certain others because of satisfactory proof that they were not duly elected, and appointed a day for new elections to supply these vacancies. Afterwards, by formal message, he recognized the Legislature as a legal body, and when he vetoed their act of adjournment to the neighborhood of Missouri, he did it simply on the ground of the illegality of such an adjournment under the organic law. Now, to every assumption founded on these facts, there are two satisfactory replies: *first*, that no certificate of the Governor can do more than authenticate a subsisting legal act, without of itself infusing legality where the essence of legality is not already; and *secondly*, that violence or fraud, wherever disclosed, vitiates completely every proceeding. In denying these principles, you place the certificate above the thing certified, and a perpetual lease to violence and fraud, merely because at an ephemeral moment they were unquestioned. This will not do.

In other matters, no such ostentatious imbecility appears. Only lately, a vessel of war in the Pacific has chastised the cannibals of the Fejee Islands, for alleged outrages on American citizens. But no person of ordinary intelligence will pretend that American citizens in the Pacific have received wrongs from these cannibals comparable in atrocity to those received by American citizens in Kansas. Ah, sir, the interests of Slavery are not touched by any chastisement of the Fejees!

Constantly we are informed of efforts at New York, through the agency of the Government, and sometimes only on the breath of suspicion, to arrest vessels about to sail on foreign voyages in violation of our neutrality laws or treaty stipulations. Now, no man familiar with the cases will presume to suggest that the urgency for these arrests was equal to the urgency for interposition against these successive invasions from Missouri. But the Slave Power is not disturbed by such arrests at New York!

At this moment, the President exults in the vigilance with which he has prevented the enlistment of a few soldiers, to be carried off to Halifax, in violation of our territorial sovereignty, and England is bravely threatened, even to the extent of a rupture of diplomatic relations, for her endeavor, though unsuccessful, and at once abandoned. Surely, no man in his senses will urge that this act was anything but trivial by the side of the Crime against Kansas. But the Slave Power is not concerned in this controversy.

Sir, I am no apologist for Governor Reeder. There is sad reason to believe that he went to Kansas originally as the tool of the President; but his simple nature, nurtured in the atmosphere of Pennsylvania, revolted at the service required, and he turned from his patron to duty. Grievously did he err in yielding to the Legislature any act of authentication; but he has in some measure answered for this error by determined efforts since to expose the utter illegality of that body, which he now repudiates entirely. It was said of certain Roman Emperors, who did infinite mischief in their beginnings, and infinite good towards their ends, that they should never have been born, or never died; and I would apply the same to the official life of this Kansas Governor. At all events, I dismiss the Apology founded on his acts, as the utterance of tyranny by the voice of law, transcending the declaration of the pedantic judge, in the British Parliament, on the eve of our Revolution, that our fathers, notwithstanding their complaints, were in reality represented in Parliament, inasmuch as their lands, under the original charters, were held "in common socage, as of the manor of Greenwich in Kent," which, being duly represented, carried with it all the Colonies. Thus in other ages has tyranny assumed the voice of law.

Next comes the Apology *Imbecile*, which is founded on the alleged want of power in the President to arrest this Crime. It is openly asserted, that, under the existing laws of the United States, the Chief Magistrate had no authority to interfere in Kansas for this purpose. Such is the broad statement, which, even if correct, furnishes no Apology for any proposed ratification of the Crime, but which is in reality untrue; and this, I call the Apology of imbecility.

Thus, where the Slave Power is indifferent, the President will see that the laws are faithfully executed; but, in other cases, where the interests of Slavery are at stake, he is controlled absolutely by this tyranny, ready at all times to do, or not to do, precisely as it dictates. Therefore it is, that Kansas is left a prey to the Propagandists of Slavery, while the whole Treasury, the Army and Navy of the United States, are lavished to hunt a single slave through the streets of Boston. You have not forgotten the latter instance; but I choose to refresh it in your minds.

As long ago as 1851, the War Department and Navy Department concurred in placing the forces of the United States, near Boston, at the command of the Marshal, if needed, for the enforcement of an Act of Congress, which had no support in the public conscience, as I believe it has no support in the Constitution; and thus these forces were degraded to the loathsome work of slave-hunters. More than three years afterwards, an occasion arose for their intervention. A fugitive from Virginia, who for some days had trod the streets of Boston as a freeman, was seized as a slave. The whole community was aroused, while Bunker Hill and Faneuil Hall quaked with responsive indignation. Then, sir, the President, anxious that no tittle of Slavery should suffer, was curiously eager in the enforcement of the statute. The dispatches between him and his agents in Boston attest his zeal. Here are some of them:

BOSTON, *May 27, 1854.*

To the President of the United States:
   In consequence of an attack upon the Court-house, last night, for the purpose of rescuing a fugitive slave, under arrest, and in which one of my own guards was killed, *I have availed myself of the resources of the United States, placed under my control by letter from the War and Navy Departments in 1851,* and now have two companies of troops, from Fort Independence, stationed in the Court-house. Everything is now quiet. The attack was repulsed by my own guard.

WATSON FREEMAN,
United States Marshal, Boston, Mass.

—

WASHINGTON, *May 27, 1854.*

TO WATSON FREEMAN,
   United States Marshal, Boston, Mass.:
   Your conduct is approved. The law must be executed.

FRANKLIN PIERCE.

—

WASHINGTON, *May 30, 1854.*

To Hon. B. F. HALLETT, *Boston, Mass.:*
   What is the state of the case of Burns?

SIDNEY WEBSTER.
[*Private Secretary of the President.*]

—

WASHINGTON, *May 31, 1854.*

To B. F. HALLETT,
   United States Attorney, Boston, Mass.:
   Incur any expense deemed necessary by the Marshal and yourself, for City Military, or otherwise, to insure the execution of the law.

FRANKLIN PIERCE.

   But the President was not content with such forces as were then on hand in the neighborhood. Other posts also were put under requisition. Two companies of National troops, stationed at New York, were kept under arms, ready at any moment to proceed to Boston; and the Adjutant General of the Army was directed to repair to the scene, there to superintend the execution of the statute. All this was done for the sake of Slavery; but during the long months of menace suspended over the Free Soil of Kansas, breaking forth in successive invasions, the President has folded his hands in complete listlessness, or, if he has moved at all, it has been only to encourage the robber propagandists.

And now the intelligence of the country is insulted by the Apology, that the President had no power to interfere. Why, sir, to make this confession is to confess our Government to be a practical failure—which I will never do, except, indeed, as it is administered now. No, sir, the imbecility of the Chief Magistrate shall not be charged upon our American Institutions. Where there is a will, there is a way; and, in his case, had the will existed, there would have been a way, easy and triumphant, to guard against the Crime we now deplore. His powers were in every respect ample; and this I will prove by the statute-book. By the Act of Congress of 28th February, 1795, it is enacted, "that whenever the laws of the United States shall be opposed, *or the execution thereof obstructed*, in any State, by combinations too powerful to be suppressed by the ordinary course of judicial proceedings, or by the powers vested in the marshals," the President "may call forth the militia." By the supplementary Act of 3d March, 1807, in all cases where he is authorized to call forth the militia "for the purpose of causing the laws to be duly executed," the President is further empowered, in any State *or Territory*, "to employ for the same purposes such part of the land or naval force of the United States as shall be judged necessary." There is the letter of the law, and you will please to mark the power conferred. In no case where the *laws of the United States* are *opposed*, or their execution *obstructed*, is the President constrained to wait for the requisition of a Governor, or even the petition of a citizen. Just so soon as he learns the fact, no matter by what channel, he is invested by law with full power to counteract it. True it is, that when the *laws of a State* are obstructed, he can interfere only on the application of the Legislature of such State, or of the Executive, when the Legislature cannot be convened; but when the Federal laws are obstructed, no such preliminary application is necessary. It is his high duty, under his oath of office, to see that they are executed, and, if need be, by the Federal forces.

And, sir, this is the precise exigency that has arisen in Kansas—precisely this; nor more, nor less. The Act of Congress, constituting the very *organic law* of the Territory, which, in peculiar phrase, as if to avoid ambiguity, declares, as "its true intent and meaning," that the people thereof "shall be left perfectly free to form and regulate their domestic institutions in their own way," has been from the beginning *opposed* and *ob-structed* in its execution. If the President had power to employ the Federal forces in Boston, when he supposed the Fugitive Slave Bill was obstructed, and merely in anticipation of such obstruction, it is absurd to say that he had not power in Kansas, when, in the face of the whole country, the very *organic law* of the Territory was trampled under foot by successive invasions, and the freedom of the people there overthrown. To assert ignorance of this obstruction—premeditated, long-continued, and stretching through months—attributes to him not merely imbecility, but idiocy. And thus do I dispose of this Apology.

Next comes the Apology *Absurd*, which is, indeed, in the nature of a pretext. It is alleged that a small printed pamphlet, containing the "Constitution and Ritual of the Grand Encampment and Regiments of the Kansas Legion," was taken from the person of one George F. Warren, who attempted to avoid detection by chewing it. The oaths and grandiose titles of the pretended Legion have all been set forth, and this poor mummery of a secret society, which existed only on paper, has been gravely introduced on this floor, in order to extenuate the Crime against Kansas. It has been paraded in more than one speech, and even stuffed into the report of the committee.

A part of the obligations assumed by the members of this Legion shows why it has been thus pursued, and also attests its innocence. It is as follows:

"I will never knowingly propose a person for membership in this order *who is not in favor of making Kansas a free State*, and whom I feel satisfied will exert his entire influence to bring about this result. I will support, maintain, and abide by any honorable movement made by the organization to secure this great end, *which will not conflict with the laws of the country and the Constitution of the United States.*"

Kansas is to be made a free State, by an honorable movement, which will not conflict with the laws and the Constitution. That is the object of the organization, declared in the very words of the initiatory obligation. Where is the wrong in this? What is there here, which can cast reproach, or even suspicion, upon the people of Kansas? Grant that the Legion was constituted, can you extract from it any Apology for the original Crime, or for its present ratification? Secret societies, with their extravagant oaths, are justly offensive; but who can find, in this mistaken machinery, any excuse for the denial of all rights to the people of Kansas? All this, I say, on the supposition that the society was a reality, which it was not. Existing in the fantastic brains of a few persons only, it never had any practical life. It was never organized. The whole tale, with the mode of obtaining the copy of the Constitution, is at once a cock-and-bull story, and a mare's nest; trivial as the former; absurd as the latter, and to be dismissed, with the Apology founded upon it, to the derision which triviality and absurdity justly receive.

It only remains, under this head, that I should speak of the Apology *Infamous*, founded on false testimony against the Emigrant Aid Company, and assumptions of duty more false than the testimony. Defying Truth and mocking Decency, this Apology excels all others in futility and audacity, while, from its utter hollowness, it proves the utter impotence of the conspirators to defend their Crime. Falsehood, always *infamous*, in this case arouses peculiar scorn. An association of sincere benevolence, faithful to the Constitution and laws, whose only fortifications are hotels, school-houses, and churches; whose only weapons are saw-mills, tools, and books; whose mission is peace and good will, has been falsely assailed on this floor, and an errand of blameless virtue has been made the pretext for an unpardonable Crime. Nay, more—the innocent are sacrificed, and the guilty set at liberty. They who seek to do the mission of the Savior are scourged and crucified, while the murderer, Barabbas, with the sympathy of the chief priests, goes at large.

Were I to take counsel of my own feelings, I should dismiss this whole Apology to the ineffable contempt which it deserves; but it has been made to play such a part in this conspiracy, that I feel it a duty to expose it completely.

Sir, from the earliest times, men have recognized the advantages of organization, as an effective agency in promoting works of peace or war. Especially at this moment, there is no interest, public or private, high or low, of charity or trade, of luxury or convenience, which does not seek its aid. Men organize to rear churches and to sell thread; to build schools and to sail ships; to construct roads and to manufacture toys; to spin cotton and to print books; to weave cloths and to quicken harvests; to provide food and to distribute light; to influence Public Opinion and to secure votes; to guard infancy in its weakness, old age in it decrepitude, and womanhood in its wretchedness; and now, in all large towns, when death has come, they are buried by organized societies, and, emigrants to another world, they lie down in pleasant places, adorned by organized skill. To complain that this prevailing principle has been applied to living emigration is to complain of Providence and the irresistible tendencies implanted in man.

But this application of the principle is no recent invention, brought forth for an existing emergency. It has the best stamp of Antiquity. It showed itself in the brightest days of Greece, where colonists moved in organized bands. It became a part of the mature policy of Rome, where bodies of men were constituted expressly for this purpose, *triumviri ad colonos deducendos.*—(Livy, XXXVII, § 46.) Naturally it has been accepted in modern times by every civilized State. With the sanction of Spain, an association of Genoese merchants first introduced slaves to this continent. With the sanction of France, the Society of Jesuits stretched their labors over Canada and the Great Lakes to the Mississippi. It was under the auspices of Emigrant Aid Companies, that our country was originally settled by the Pilgrim Fathers of Plymouth, by the adventurers of Virginia, and by the philanthropic Oglethorpe, whose "benevolence of soul," commemorated by Pope, sought to plant a Free State in Georgia. At this day, such associations, of an humbler character, are found in Europe, with offices in the great capitals, through whose activity emigrants are directed here.

For a long time, emigration to the West, from the Northern and Middle States, but particularly from New England, has been of marked significance. In quest of better homes, annually it has pressed to the unsettled lands, in numbers to be counted by tens of thousands; but this has been done heretofore with little knowledge, and without guide or counsel. Finally, when, by the establishment of a Government in Kansas, the tempting fields of that central region were opened to the competition of peaceful colonization, and especially when it was declared that the question of Freedom or Slavery there was to be determined by the votes of actual settlers, then at once was organization enlisted as an effective agency in quickening and conducting the emigration impelled thither, and, more than all, in providing homes for it on arrival there.

The Company was first constituted under an act of the Legislature of Massachusetts, 4th of May, 1854, some weeks prior to the passage of the Nebraska bill. The original act of incorporation was subsequently abandoned, and a new charter received in February, 1855, in which the objects of the Society are thus declared:

"For the purposes of directing emigration Westward, and *aiding in providing accommodations for the emigrants after arriving at their places of destination.*"

At any other moment, an association for these purposes would have taken its place, by general consent, among the philanthropic experiments of the age; but Crime is always suspicious, and shakes, like a sick man, merely at the pointing of a finger. The conspirators against Freedom in Kansas now shook with tremor, real or affected. Their wicked plot was about to fail. To help themselves, they denounced the Emigrant Aid Company; and their denunciations, after finding an echo in the President, have been repeated, with much particularity, on this floor, in the formal report of your committee.

The falsehood of the whole accusation will appear in illustrative specimens.

A charter is set out, section by section, which, though originally granted, was subsequently abandoned, and is not in reality the charter of the Company, but is materially unlike it.

The Company is represented as "a powerful corporation, with a capital of five millions;" when, by its actual charter, it is not allowed to hold property above one million, and, in point of fact, its capital has not exceeded one hundred thousand dollars.

Then, again, it is suggested, if not alleged, that this enormous capital, which I have already said does not exist, is invested in "cannon and rifles, in powder and lead, and implements of war"—all of which, whether alleged or suggested, is absolutely false. The officers of the Company authorize me to give to this whole pretension a point-blank denial.

All these allegations are of small importance, and I mention them only because they show the character of the report, and also something of the quicksand on which the Senator from Illinois has chosen to plant himself. But these are all capped by the unblushing assertion that the proceedings of the Company were "in perversion of the plain provisions of an Act of Congress;" and also, another unblushing assertion, as "certain and undeniable," that the Company was formed to promote certain objects, "regardless of the rights and wishes of the people, as guarantied by the Constitution of the United States, and secured by their organic law;" when it is certain and undeniable that the Company has done nothing in perversion of any Act of Congress, while to the extent of its power it has sought to protect the rights and wishes of the actual people in the Territory.

Sir, this Company has violated in no respect the Constitution or laws of the land; not in the severest letter or the slightest spirit. But every other imputation is equally baseless. It is not true, as the Senator from Illinois has alleged, in order in some way to compromise the Company, that it was informed before the public of the date fixed for the election of the Legislature. This statement is pronounced by the Secretary, in a letter now before me, "an unqualified falsehood, not having even the shadow of a shade of truth for its basis," It is not true that men have been hired by the Company to go to Kansas; for every emigrant, who has gone under its direction, has himself provided the means for his journey. Of course, sir, it is not true, as has been complained by the Senator from South Carolina, with that proclivity to error which marks all his utterances, that men have been sent by the Company "with one uniform gun, Sharpe's rifle;" for it has supplied no arms of any kind to anybody. It is not true that the Company has encouraged any fanatical aggression upon the people of Missouri; for it has counseled order, peace, forbearance. It is not true that the Company has chosen its emigrants on account of their political opinions; for it has asked no questions with regard to the opinions of any whom it aids, and at this moment stands ready to forward those from the South as well as the North, while, in the Territory, all, from whatever quarter, are admitted to an equal enjoyment of its tempting advantages. It is not true that the Company has sent persons merely to control elections, and not to remain in the Territory; for its whole action, and all its anticipation of pecuniary profits, are founded on the hope to stock the country with permanent settlers, by whose labor the capital of the Company shall be made to yield its increase, and by whose fixed interest in the soil the welfare of all shall be promoted.

Sir, it has not the honor of being an Abolition Society, or of numbering among its officers Abolitionists. Its President is a retired citizen, of ample means and charitable life, who has taken no part in the conflicts on Slavery, and has never allowed his sympathies to be felt by Abolitionists. One of its Vice Presidents is a gentleman from Virginia, with family and friends there, who has always opposed the Abolitionists. Its generous Treasurer, who is now justly absorbed by the objects of the Company, has always been understood as ranging with his extensive connections, by blood and marriage, on the side of that quietism which submits to all the tyranny of the Slave Power. Its Directors are more conspicuous for wealth and science, than for any activity against Slavery. Among these is an eminent lawyer of Massachusetts, Mr. Chapman—personally known, doubtless, to some who hear me—who has distinguished himself by an austere conservatism, too natural to the atmosphere of courts, which does not flinch even from the support of the Fugitive Slave Bill. In a recent address at a public meeting in Springfield, this gentleman thus speaks for himself and his associates:

"I have been a Director of the society from the first, and have kept myself well informed in regard to its proceedings. I am not aware that any one in this community ever suspected me of being an Abolitionist; but I have been accused of being Pro-Slavery; and I believe many good people think I am quite too conservative on that subject. I take this occasion to say that all the plans and proceedings of the Society have met my approbation; and I assert that it has never done a single act with which any political party or the people of any section of the country can justly find fault. The name of its President, Mr. Brown, of Provdence, and of its Treasurer, Mr. Lawrence, of Boston, are a sufficient guarantee in the estimation of intelligent men against its being engaged in any fanatical enterprise. Its stockholders are composed of men of all political parties except Abolitionists. I am not aware that it has received the patronage of that class of our fellow-citizens, and I am informed that some of them disapprove of its proceedings."

The acts of the Company have been such as might be expected from auspices thus severely careful at all points. The secret, through which, with small means, it has been able to accomplish so much, is, that, *as an inducement to emigration, it has gone forward and planted capital in advance of population.* According to the old immethodical system, this rule is reversed; and population has been left to grope blindly, without the advantage of fixed centers, with mills, schools, and churches—all calculated to soften the hardships of pioneer life—such as have been established beforehand in Kansas. Here, sir, is the secret of the Emigrant Aid Company. By this single principle, which is now practically applied for the first time in history, and which has the simplicity of genius, a business association at a distance, without a large capital, has become a beneficent instrument of civilization, exercising the functions of various Societies, and in itself being a Missionary Society, a Bible Society, a Tract Society, an Education Society, and a Society for the Diffusion of the Mechanic Arts. I would not claim too much for this Company; but I doubt if, at this moment, there is any Society, which is so completely philanthropic; and since its leading idea, like the light of a candle from which other candles are lighted without number, may be applied indefinitely, it promises to be an important aid to Human Progress. The lesson it teaches cannot be forgotten, and hereafter, wherever unsettled lands exist, intelligent capital will lead the way, anticipating the wants of the pioneer—nay, doing the very work of the original pioneer—while, amidst well-arranged harmonies, a new community will arise, to become, by its example, a more eloquent preacher than any solitary missionary. In subordination to this essential idea, is its humbler machinery for the aid of emigrants on their way, by combining parties, so that friends and neighbors might journey together; by purchasing tickets at wholesale, and furnishing them to individuals at the actual cost; by providing for each party a conductor familiar with the road, and, through these simple means, promoting the economy, safety, and comfort, of the expedition. The number of emigrants it has directly aided, even thus slightly, in their journey, has been infinitely exaggerated. From the beginning of its operations down to the close of the last autumn, all its detachments from Massachusetts contained only thirteen hundred and twelve persons.

Such is the simple tale of the Emigrant Aid Company. Sir, not even suspicion can justly touch it. But it must be made a scapegoat. This is the decree which has gone forth. I was hardly surprised at this outrage, when it proceeded from the President, for, like Macbeth, he is stepped so far in, that returning were as tedious as go on; but I did not expect it from the Senator from Missouri, [Mr. GEYER,] whom I had learned to respect for the general moderation of his views, and the name he has won in an honorable profession. Listening to him, I was saddened by the spectacle of the extent to which Slavery will sway a candid mind to do injustice. Had any other interest been in question, that Senator would have scorned to join in impeachment of such an association. His instincts as a lawyer, as a man of honor, and as a Senator, would have forbidden; but the Slave Power, in enforcing its behests, allows no hesitation, and the Senator surrendered.

In this vindication, I content myself with a statement of facts, rather than an argument. It might be urged that Missouri had organized a propagandist emigration long before any from Massachusetts, and you might be reminded of the wolf in the fable, which complained of the lamb for disturbing the waters, when in fact the alleged offender was lower down on the stream. It might be urged, also, that South Carolina has lately entered upon a similar system—while one of her chieftains, in rallying recruits, has unconsciously attested to the cause in which he was engaged, by exclaiming, in the words of Satan, addressed to his wicked forces,

"Awake! arise! or be forever fallen!"

Mr. EVANS. I should be glad to have the gentleman state where he got that information. I know something about South Carolina, and I never heard of any such thing, and I do not think it exists.

Mr. SUMNER. I beg the Senator's pardon; it was in a speech or letter of one of the gentlemen enlisted in obtaining emigrants in South Carolina. But the occasion needs no such defenses. I put them aside. Not on the example of Missouri, or the example of South Carolina, but on inherent rights, which no man, whether Senator or President, can justly assail, do I plant this impregnable justification. It will not do, in specious phrases, to allege the right of every State to be free in its domestic policy from foreign interference, and then to assume such wrongful interference by this Company. By the law and Constitution, we stand or fall; and that law and Constitution we have in no respect offended.

To cloak the overthrow of all law in Kansas, an assumption is now set up, which utterly denies one of the plainest rights of the people everywhere. Sir, I beg Senators to understand that this is a Government of laws; and that, under these laws, the people have an incontestable right to settle any portion of our broad territory, and, if they choose, to propagate any opinions there, not openly forbidden by the laws. If this were not so, pray, sir, by what title is the Senator from Illinois, who is an emigrant from Vermont, propagating his disastrous opinions in another State? Surely he has no monopoly of this right. Others may do what he is doing; nor can the right be in any way restrained. It is as broad as the people; and it matters not whether they go in numbers small or great, with assistance or without assistance, under the auspices of societies or not under such auspices. If this were not so, then, by what title are so many foreigners annually naturalized, under Democratic auspices, in order to secure their votes for misnamed Democratic principles? And if capital as well as combination cannot be employed, by what title do venerable associations exist, of ampler means and longer duration than any Emigrant Aid Company, around which cluster the regard and confidence of the country—the Tract Society, a powerful corporation, which scatters its publications freely in every corner of the land—the Bible Society, an incorporated body, with large resources, which seeks to carry the Book of Life alike into Territories and States—the Missionary Society, also an incorporated body, with large resources, which sends its agents everywhere, at home and in foreign lands? By what title do all these exist? Nay, sir, by what title does an Insurance Company in New York send its agent to open an office in New Orleans, and by what title does Massachusetts capital contribute to the Hannibal and St. Joseph Railroad in Missouri, and also to the copper mines of Michigan? The Senator inveighs against the Native American party;

but his own principle is narrower than any attributed to them. They object to the influence of emigrants from abroad; he objects to the influence of American citizens at home, when exerted in States or Territories where they were not born! The whole assumption is too audacious for respectful argument. But since a great right has been denied, the children of the Free States, over whose cradles has shone the North Star, owe it to themselves, to their ancestors, and to Freedom itself, that this right should now be asserted to the fullest extent. By the blessing of God, and under the continued protection of the laws, they will go to Kansas, there to plant their homes, in the hope of elevating this Territory soon into the sisterhood of Free States; and to such end they will not hesitate, in the employment of all legitimate means, whether by companies of men or contributions of money, to swell a virtuous emigration, and they will justly scout any attempt to question this unquestionable right. Sir, if they failed to do this, they would be fit only for slaves themselves.

God be praised! Massachusetts, honored Commonwealth that gives me the privilege to plead for Kansas on this floor, knows her rights, and will maintain them firmly to the end. This is not the first time in history, that her public acts have been arraigned, and that her public men have been exposed to contumely. Thus was it when, in the olden time, she began the great battle whose fruits you all enjoy. But never yet has she occupied a position so lofty as at this hour. By the intelligence of her population—by the resources of her industry—by her commerce, cleaving every wave—by her manufactures, various as human skill—by her institutions of education, various as human knowledge—by her institutions of benevolence, various as human suffering—by the pages of her scholars and historians—by the voices of her poets and orators, she is now exerting an influence more subtile and commanding than ever before—shooting her far-darting rays wherever ignorance, wretchedness, or wrong, prevail, and flashing light even upon those who travel far to persecute her. Such is Massachusetts, and I am proud to believe that you may as well attempt, with puny arm, to topple down the earth-rooted, heaven-kissing granite which crowns the historic sod of Bunker Hill, as to change her fixed resolves for Freedom everywhere, and especially now for Freedom in Kansas. I exult, too, that in this battle, which surpasses far in moral grandeur the whole war of the Revolution, she is able to preserve her just eminence. To the first she contributed a larger number of troops than any other State in the Union, and larger than all the Slave States together; and now to the second, which is not of contending armies, but of contending opinions, on whose issue hangs trembling the advancing civilization of the country, she contributes, through the manifold and endless intellectual activity of her children, more of that divine spark by which opinions are quickened into life, than is contributed by any other State, or by all the Slave States together, while her annual productive industry excels in value three times the whole vaunted cotton crop of the whole South.

Sir, to men on earth it belongs only to deserve success; not to secure it; and I know not how soon the efforts of Massachusetts will wear the crown of triumph. But it cannot be that she acts wrong for herself or children, when in this cause she thus encounters reproach. No; by the generous souls who were exposed at Lexington; by those who stood arrayed at Bunker Hill; by the many from her bosom who, on all the fields of the first great struggle, lent their vigorous arms to the cause of all; by the children she has borne, whose names alone are national trophies, is Massachusetts now vowed irrevocably to this work. What belongs to the faithful servant she will do in all things, and Providence shall determine the result.

And here ends what I have to say of the four Apologies for the Crime against Kansas.

Having spoken three hours, he yielded to a motion to adjourn.

———

TUESDAY, *May 20, 1856.*

To-day Mr. SUMNER concluded thus:

III. From this ample survey, where one obstruction after another has been removed, I now pass, in the third place, to the consideration of the *various remedies proposed*, ending with the TRUE REMEDY.

The Remedy should be coextensive with the original Wrong; and since, by the passage of the Nebraska Bill, not only Kansas, but also Nebraska, Minnesota, Washington, and even Oregon, have been opened to Slavery, the original Prohibition should be restored to its complete activity throughout these various Territories. By such a happy restoration, made in good faith, the whole country would be replaced in the condition which it enjoyed before the introduction of that dishonest measure. Here is the Alpha and the Omega of our aim in this immediate controversy. But no such extensive measure is now in question. The Crime against Kansas has been special, and all else is absorbed in the special remedies for it. Of these I shall now speak.

As the Apologies were four-fold, so are the Remedies proposed four-fold, and they range themselves in natural order, under designations which so truly disclose their character as even to supersede argument. First, we have the Remedy of Tyranny; next the Remedy of Folly; next the Remedy of Injustice and Civil War; and fourthly the Remedy of Justice and Peace. There are the four caskets; and you are to determine which shall be opened by Senatorial votes.

There is the *Remedy of Tyranny*, which, like its complement, the Apology of Tyranny—though espoused on this floor, especially by the Senator from Illinois—proceeds from the President, and is embodied in a special message. It proposes to enforce obedience to the existing laws of Kansas, "whether Federal or *local*," when, in fact, Kansas has no "local" laws except those imposed by the Usurpation from Missouri, and it calls for additional appropriations to complete this work of tyranny.

I shall not follow the President in his elaborate endeavor to prejudge the contested election now pending in the House of Representatives; for this whole matter belongs to the privileges of that body, and neither the President nor the Senate has a right to intermeddle therewith. I do not touch it. But now, while dismissing it, I should not pardon myself, if I failed to add, that any person who founds his claim to a seat in Congress on the pretended votes of hirelings from another State, with no home on the soil of Kansas, plays the part of Anacharsis Clootz, who, at the bar of the French Convention, undertook to represent nations that knew him not, or, if they knew him, scorned him; with this difference, that in our American case, the excessive farce of the transaction cannot cover its tragedy. But all this I put aside—to deal only with what is legitimately before the Senate.

I expose simply the Tyranny which upholds the existing Usurpation, and asks for additional appropriations. Let it be judged by an example, from which in this country there can be no appeal. Here is the speech of George III., made from the Throne to Parliament, in response to the complaints of the Province of Massachusetts Bay, which, though smarting under laws passed by usurped power, had yet avoided all armed opposition, while Lexington and Bunker Hill still slumbered in rural solitude, unconscious of the historic kindred which they were soon to claim. Instead of Massachuetts Bay, in the Royal speech, substitute Kansas, and the message of the President will be found fresh on the lips of the British King. Listen now to the words, which, in opening Parliament, 30th of November, 1774, his Majesty, according to the official report, was pleased to speak:

"My Lords and Gentlemen:

"It gives me much concern that I am obliged, at the opening of this Parliament, to inform you that a most daring *spirit of resistance and disobedience to the law* still unhappily prevails in the Province of the *Massachusetts Bay*, and has in divers parts of it broke forth in fresh violences of a very criminal nature. *These proceedings have been countenanced in other of my Colonies*, and *unwarrantable attempts have been made to obstruct the Commerce of this Kingdom, by unlawful combinations.* I have taken such measures and given such orders as I have judged most proper and effectual *for carrying into execution the laws which were passed, in the last session of the late Parliament*, for the protection and security of the Commerce of my subjects, and for the restoring and preserving peace, order, and good government, in the Province of the *Massachusetts Bay.*"—*American Archives*, 4th Series, Vol. I, p. 1465.

The King complained of a "daring spirit of resistance and disobedience to the law;" so also does the President. The King adds, that it has "broke forth in fresh violences of a very criminal nature;" so also does the President. The King declares that these proceedings have been "countenanced and encouraged in other of my Colonies;" even so the President declares that Kansas has found sympathy in "remote States." The King inveighs against "unwarrantable measures" and "unlawful combinations;" even so inveighs the President. The King proclaims that he has taken the necessary steps "for carrying into execution the laws," passed in defiance of the constitutional rights of the colonies; even so the President proclaims that he shall "exert the whole power of the Federal Executive" to support the Usurpation in Kansas. The parallel is complete. The Message, if not copied from the Speech of the King, has been fashioned on the same original block, and must be dismissed to the same limbo. I dismiss its tyrannical assumptions in favor of the Usurpation. I dismiss also its petition for additional appropriations in the affected desire to maintain order in Kansas. It is not money or troops that you need there; but simply the good will of the President. That is all, absolutely. Let his complicity with the Crime cease, and peace will be restored. For myself, I will not consent to wad the National artillery with fresh appropriation bills, when its murderous hail is to be directed against the constitutional rights of my fellow-citizens.

Next comes the *Remedy of Folly*, which, indeed, is also a Remedy of Tyranny; but its Folly is so surpassing as to eclipse even its Tyranny. It does not proceed from the President. With this proposition he is not in any way chargeable. It comes from the Senator from South Carolina, who, at the close of a long speech, offered it as his single contribution to the adjustment of this question, and who thus far stands alone in its support. It might, therefore, fitly bear his name; but that which I now give to it is a more suggestive synonim.

This proposition, nakedly expressed, is that the people of Kansas should be deprived of their arms. That I may not do the least injustice to the Senator, I quote his precise words:

"The President of the United States is under the highest and most solemn obligations to interpose; and if I were to indicate the manner in which he should interpose in Kansas, I would point out the old common-law process. I would serve a warrant on Sharpe's rifles, and if Sharpe's rifles did not answer the summons, and come into court on a day certain, or if they resisted the sheriff, I would summon the *posse comitatus*, and would have Colonel Sumner's regiment to be a part of that *posse comitatus*."

Really, sir, has it come to this? The rifle has ever been the companion of the pioneer, and, under God, his tutelary protector against the red man and the beast of the forest. Never was this efficient weapon more needed in just self-defense, than now in Kansas, and at least one article in our National Constitution must be blotted out, before the complete right to it can in any way be impeached. And yet such is the madness of the hour, that, in defiance of the solemn guarantee, embodied in the Amendments to the Constitution, that "the right of the people to keep and bear arms shall not be infringed," the people of Kansas have been arraigned for keeping and bearing them, and the Senator from South Carolina has had the face to say openly, on this floor, that they should be disarmed—of course, that the fanatics of Slavery, his allies and constituents, may meet no impediment. Sir, the Senator is venerable with years; he is reputed also to have worn at home, in the State which he represents, judicial honors; and he is placed here at the head of an important committee occupied particularly with questions of law; but neither his years nor his position, past or present, can give respectability to the demand he has made, or save him from indignant condemnation, when, to compass the wretched purposes of a wretched cause, he thus proposes to trample on one of the plainest provisions of constitutional liberty.

Next comes the *Remedy of Injustice and Civil War*—organized by Act of Congress. This proposition, which is also an offshoot of the original Remedy of Tyranny, proceeds from the Senator from Illinois, [MR. DOUGLAS,] with the sanction of the Committee on Territories, and is embodied in the Bill which is now pressed to a vote.

By this Bill it is proposed as follows:

"That whenever it shall appear, by a census to be taken under the direction of the Governor, by the authority of the Legislature, that there shall be 93,420 inhabitants (that being the number required by the present ratio of representation for a member of Congress) within the limits hereafter described as the Territory of Kansas, *the Legislature of said Territory shall be, and is hereby, authorized to provide by law for the election of delegates*, by the people of said Territory, to assemble in Convention and form a Constitution and State Government, preparatory to their admission into the Union on an equal footing with the original States in all respects whatsoever, by the name of the State of Kansas."

Now, sir, consider these words carefully, and you will see that, however plausible and velvet-pawed they may seem, yet in reality they are most unjust and cruel. While affecting to initiate honest proceedings for the formation of a State, they furnish to this Territory no redress for the Crime under which it suffers; nay, they recognize the very Usurpation, in which the Crime ended, and proceed to endow it with new prerogatives. It is *by the authority of the Legislature* that the census is to be taken, which is the first step in the work. It is also *by the authority of the Legislature* that a Convention is to be called for the formation of a Constitution, which is the second step. But the Legislature is not obliged to take either of these steps. To its absolute willfulness is it left to act or not to act in the premises. And since, in the ordinary course of business, there can be no action of the Legislature till January of the next year, all these steps, which are preliminary in their character, are postponed till after that distant day—thus keeping this great question open, to distract and irritate the country. Clearly this is not what is required. The country desires peace at once, and is determined to have it. But this objection is slight by the side of the glaring Tyranny, that, in recognizing the Legislature, and conferring upon it these new powers, the Bill recognizes the existing Usurpation, not only as the authentic Government of the Territory for the time being, but also as possessing a creative power to reproduce itself in the new State. Pass this Bill, and you enlist Congress in the conspiracy, not only to keep the people of Kansas in their present subjugation, throughout their Territorial existence, but also to protract this subjugation into their existence as a State, while you legalize and perpetuate the very *force* by which Slavery has been already planted there.

I know that there is another deceptive clause, which seems to throw certain safeguards around the election of delegates to the Convention, *when that Convention shall be ordered by the Legislature*; but out of this very clause do I draw a condemnation of the Usurpation which the Bill recognizes. It provides that the tests, coupled with the electoral franchise, shall not prevail in the election of delegates, and thus impliedly condemns them. But if they are not to prevail on this occasion, why are they permitted at the election of the Legislature? If they are unjust in the one case, they are unjust in the other. If annulled at the election of delegates, they should be annulled at the election of the Legislature; *whereas the bill of the Senator leaves all these offensive tests in full activity at the election of the very Legislature out of which this whole proceeding is to come*, and it leaves the polls at both elections in the control of the officers appointed by the Usurpation. Consider well the facts. By an existing statute, establishing the Fugitive Slave Bill as a shibboleth, a large portion of the honest citizens are excluded from voting for the Legislature, while, by another statute, all who present themselves with the fee of one dollar, whether from Missouri or not, and who can utter this shibboleth, are entitled to vote. And it is a Legislature thus chosen, under the auspices of officers appointed by the Usurpation, that you now propose to invest with parental powers to rear the Territory into a State. You recognize and confirm the Usurpation, which you ought to annul without delay. You put the infant State, now preparing to take a place in our sisterhood, to suckle with the wolf, which you ought at once to kill. The improbable story of Baron Münchausen is verified. The bear, which thrust itself into the harness of the horse it had devoured, and then whirled the sledge according to mere brutal bent, is recognized by this bill, and kept in its usurped place, when the safety of all requires that it should be shot.

In characterizing this Bill as the Remedy of Injustice and Civil War, I give it a plain, self-evident title. It is a continuation of the Crime against Kansas, and as such deserves the same condemnation. It can only be defended by those who defend the Crime. Sir, you cannot expect that the people of Kansas will submit to the Usurpation which this bill sets up, and bids them bow before—as the Austrian tyrant set up his cap in the Swiss market-place. If you madly persevere, Kansas will not be without her William Tell, who will refuse at all hazards to recognize the tyrannical edict; and this will be the beginning of civil war.

Next, and lastly, comes the *Remedy of Justice and Peace*, proposed by the Senator from New York, [Mr. SEWARD,] and embodied in his Bill for the immediate admission of Kansas as a State of this Union, now pending as a substitute for the bill of the Senator from Illinois. This is sustained by the prayer of the people of the Territory, setting forth a Constitution formed by a spontaneous movement, in which all there had opportunity to participate, without distinction of party. Rarely has any proposition, so simple in character, so entirely practicable, so absolutely within your power, been presented, which promised at once such beneficent results. In its adoption, the Crime against Kansas will be all happily absolved, the Usurpation which it established will be peacefully suppressed, and order will be permanently secured. By a joyful metamorphosis, this fair Territory may be saved from outrage.

> "Oh help," she cries, "in this extremest need,
> If you who hear are Deities indeed;
> Gape earth, and make for this dread foe a tomb.
> *Or change my form, whence all my sorrows come.*"

In offering this proposition, the Senator from New York has entitled himself to the gratitude of the country. He has, throughout a life of unsurpassed industry, and of eminent ability, done much for Freedom, which the world will not let die; but he has done nothing more opportune than this, and he has uttered no words more effective than the speech, so masterly and ingenious, by which he has vindicated it.

Kansas now presents herself for admission with a Constitution republican in form. And, independent of the great necessity of the case, three considerations of fact concur in commending her. First. She thus testifies her willingness to relieve the Federal Government of the considerable pecuniary responsibility to which it is now exposed on account of the pretended Territorial Government. Secondly. She has by her recent conduct, particularly in repelling the invasion at Wakarusa, evinced an ability to defend her Government. And, thirdly, by the pecuniary credit, which she now enjoys, she shows an undoubted ability to support it. What now can stand in her way?

The power of Congress to admit Kansas at once is explicit. It is found in a single clause of the Constitution, which, standing by itself, without any qualification applicable to the present case, and without doubtful words, requires no commentary. Here it is:

"New States *may* be admitted by Congress into this Union; but no new State shall be formed or erected within the jurisdiction of any other State, nor any State be formed by the junction of two or more States or parts of States, without the consent of the Legislatures of the States concerned, as well as of the Congress."

New States MAY be admitted. Out of that little word, *may*, comes the power, broadly and fully—without any limitation founded on population or preliminary forms—provided the State is not within the jurisdiction of another State, nor formed by the junction of two or more States or parts of States, without the consent of the Legislatures of the States. Kansas is not within the *legal* jurisdiction of another State, although the laws of Missouri have been tyrannically extended over her; nor is Kansas formed by the junction of two or more States; and, therefore, Kansas *may* be admitted by Congress into the Union, without regard to population or preliminary forms. You cannot deny the power, without obliterating this clause of the Constitution. The Senator from New York was right in rejecting all appeal to precedents, as entirely irrelevant; for the power invoked is clear and express in the Constitution, which is above all precedent. But, since precedent has been enlisted, let us look at precedent.

It is objected that the *population* of Kansas is not sufficient for a State; and this objection is sustained by under-reckoning the numbers there, and exaggerating the numbers required by precedent. In the absence of any recent census, it is impossible to do more than approximate to the actual population; but, from careful inquiry of the best sources, I am led to place it now at fifty thousand, though I observe that a prudent authority, the *Boston Daily Advertiser*, puts it as high as sixty thousand, and, while I speak, this remarkable population, fed by fresh emigration, is outstripping even these calculations. Nor can there be a doubt, that, before the assent of Congress can be perfected in the ordinary course of legislation, this population will swell to the large number of ninety-three thousand four hundred and twenty, required in the Bill of the Senator from Illinois. *But, in making this number the condition of the admission of Kansas, you set up an extraordinary standard.* There is nothing out of which it can be derived, from the beginning to the end of the precedents. Going back to the days of the Continental Congress, you will find that, in 1784, it was

declared that twenty thousand freemen in a Territory might
"establish a permanent Constitution and Government for
themselves," (Journals of Congress, Vol. 4, p. 379;) and,
though this number was afterwards, in the Ordinance of 1787
for the Northwestern Territory, raised to sixty thousand, yet
the power was left in Congress, and subsequently exercised in
more than one instance, to constitute a State with a smaller
number. Out of all the new States, only Maine, Wisconsin, and
Texas, contained, at the time of their admission into the Union,
so large a population as it is proposed to require in Kansas;
while no less than *fourteen* new States have been admitted with
a smaller population; as will appear in the following list, which
is the result of research, showing the number of "free inhabitants" in these States at the time of the proceedings which
ended in their admission:

Vermont 85,416	Illinois 45,000
Kentucky 61,103	Missouri 56,586
Tennessee 66,649	Arkansas 41,000
Ohio 50,000	Michigan 92,673
Louisiana 41,890	Florida 27,091
Indiana 60,000	Iowa 81,921
Mississippi 35,000	California 92,597
Alabama 50,000	

But this is not all. At the adoption of the Federal Constitution, there were three of the old Thirteen States whose respective populations did not reach the amount now required for
Kansas. These were Delaware, with a population of 59,096;
Rhode Island with a population of 64,689; and Georgia with a
population of 82,548. And even now, while I speak, there are at
least two States, with Senators on this floor, which, according
to the last census, do not contain the population now required
of Kansas. I refer to Delaware, with a population of 91,635, and
Florida, with a population of freemen amounting only to
47,203. So much for precedents of population.

But in sustaining this objection, it is not uncommon to depart from the strict rule of numerical precedent, by suggesting
that the population required in a new State has always been, in
point of fact, above the existing ratio of representation for a
member of the House of Representatives. But this is not true;

for at least one State, Florida, was admitted with a population below this ratio, which at the time was 70,680. So much, again, for precedents. But even if this coincidence were complete, it would be impossible to press it into a binding precedent. The rule seems reasonable, and, in ordinary cases, would not be questioned; but it cannot be drawn or implied from the Constitution. Besides, this ratio is, in itself, a sliding scale. At first, it was 33,000, and thus continued till 1811, when it was put at 35,000. In 1822, it was 40,000; in 1832, it was 47,700; in 1842, it was 70,680; and now, it is 93,420. If any ratio is to be made the foundation of a binding rule, it should be that which prevailed at the adoption of the Constitution, and which still continued, when Kansas, as a part of Louisiana, was acquired from France, under solemn stipulation that it should "be incorporated into the Union of the United States *as soon as* may be consistent with the principles of the Federal Constitution." But this whole objection is met by the memorial of the people of Florida, which, if good for that State, is also good for Kansas. Here is a passage:

"But the people of Florida respectfully insist that their right to be admitted into the Federal Union as a State is not dependent upon the fact of their having a population equal to such ratio. Their right to admission, it is conceived, is guarantied by the express pledge in the sixth article of the treaty before quoted; and if any rule as to the number of the population is to govern, it should be that in existence at the time of the cession, which was thirty-five thousand. They submit, however, that any ratio of representation, dependent upon legislative action, based solely on convenience and expediency, shifting and vacillating as the opinion of a majority of Congress may make it, now greater than at a previous apportionment, but which a future Congress may prescribe to be less, cannot be one of the *constitutional* 'PRINCIPLES' referred to in the treaty, consistency with which, by its terms, is required. It is, in truth, but a mere regulation, not founded on principle. No specified number of population is required by any recognized principle as necessary in the establishment of a free Government.

"It is in nowise '*inconsistent with the principles of the Federal Constitution*,' that the population of a State should be less than the ratio of Congressional representation. The very case is provided for in the Constitution. With such deficient population, she would be entitled to one Representative. If any event should cause a decrease of the population of one of the States even to a number below the *minimum* ratio of representation prescribed by the Constitution, she would still remain a member of the Confederacy, and be entitled to such Representatives. It is respectfully urged, that a rule or principle which would not justify the *expulsion* of a State with a deficient population, on the ground of inconsistency with the Constitution, should not exclude or prohibit *admission*."—*Ex. Doc., 27th Cong., 2d sess.*, Vol. 4, No. 206.

Thus, sir, do the people of Florida plead for the people of Kansas.

Distrusting the objection from inadequacy of population, it is said that the *proceedings for the formation of a new State are fatally defective in form*. It is not asserted that a previous enabling Act of Congress is indispensable; for there are notorious precedents the other way, among which are Kentucky in 1791; Tennessee in 1796; Maine in 1820; and Arkansas and Michigan in 1836. But it is urged that in no instance has a State been admitted, whose Constitution was formed without such enabling Act, or without the authority of the Territorial Legislature. This is not true; for California came into the Union with a Constitution formed not only without any previous enabling Act, but also without any sanction from a Territorial Legislature. The proceedings which ended in this Constitution were initiated by the military Governor there, acting under the exigency of the hour. This instance may not be identical in all respects with that of Kansas; but it displaces completely one of the assumptions which Kansas now encounters, and it also shows completely the disposition to relax all rule, under the exigency of the hour, in order to do substantial justice.

But there is a memorable instance, which contains in itself every element of irregularity which you denounce in the proceedings of Kansas. Michigan, now cherished with such pride as a sister State, achieved admission into the Union in persistent defiance of all rule. Do you ask for precedents? Here is a precedent for the largest latitude, which you, who profess a deference to precedent, cannot disown. Mark now the stages of this case. The first proceedings of Michigan were without any previous enabling Act of Congress; and she presented herself at your door with a Constitution thus formed, and with Senators chosen under that Constitution—precisely as Kansas now.

This was in December, 1835, while Andrew Jackson was President. By the leaders of the Democracy at that time, all objection for alleged defects of form was scouted, and language was employed which is strictly applicable to Kansas. There is nothing new under the sun; and the very objection of the President, that the application of Kansas proceeds from "persons acting against authorities duly constituted by Act of Congress," was hurled against the application of Michigan, in debate on this floor, by Mr. Hendricks, of Indiana. This was his language:

"But the people of Michigan, in presenting their Senate and House of Representatives as the legislative power existing there, *showed that they had trampled upon and violated the laws of the United States establishing a Territorial Government in Michigan.* These laws were, or ought to be, in full force there; but, by the character and position assumed, they had set up a Government antagonist to that of the United States."—*Congress. Deb., 24th Cong., 1st sess.*, Vol. 12, p. 288.

To this impeachment Mr. Benton replied in these effective words:

"Conventions were original acts of the people. They depended upon inherent and inalienable rights. The people of any State may at any time meet in Convention, without a law of their Legislature, and without any provision, or against any provision in their Constitution, and may alter or abolish the whole frame of Government as they please. The sovereign power to govern themselves was in the majority, and they could not be divested of it."—*Ibid.*, p. 1036.

Mr. Buchanan vied with Mr. Benton in vindicating the new State:

"The precedent in the case of Tennessee has completely silenced all opposition in regard to the necessity of a previous act of Congress to enable the people of Michigan to form a State Constitution. It now seems to be conceded that our subsequent approbation is equivalent to our previous action. This can no longer be doubted. *We have the unquestionable power of waiving any irregularities in the mode of framing the Constitution, had any such existed.*"—*Ibid.*, p. 1041.

"He did hope that by this bill all objections would be removed; and that this State, so ready to rush into our arms, would not be repulsed, *because of the absence of some formalities which perhaps were very proper, but certainly not indispensable.*"—*Ibid.*, p. 1015.

After an animated contest in the Senate, the Bill for the

admission of Michigan, *on her assent to certain conditions*, was passed, by 23 yeas to 8 nays. But you find weight, as well as numbers, on the side of the new State. Among the yeas were Thomas H. Benton of Missouri, James Buchanan of Pennsylvania, Silas Wright of New York, W. R. King of Alabama. (Cong. Globe, Vol. 3, p. 276, 1st session 24th Cong.) Subsequently, on motion of Mr. Buchanan, the two gentlemen sent as Senators by the new State received the regular compensation for attendance throughout the very session in which their seats had been so acrimoniously assailed. (Ibid., p. 448.)

In the House of Representatives, the application was equally successful. The Committee on the Judiciary, in an elaborate report, reviewed the objections, and, among other things, said:

"That the people of Michigan have, without due authority, formed a State Government, but, nevertheless, *that Congress has power to waive any objection which might, on that account, be entertained*, to the ratification of the Constitution which they have adopted, and to admit their Senators and Representatives to take their seats in the Congress of the United States."—*Ex. Doc., 1st sess. 24th Cong.*, Vol. 2, No. 380.

The House sustained this view by a vote of 153 yeas to 45 nays. In this large majority, by which the title of Michigan was then recognized, will be found the name of Franklin Pierce, at that time a Representative from New Hampshire.

But the case was not ended. The fiercest trial and the greatest irregularity remained. The Act providing for the admission of the new State contained a modification of its boundaries, and proceeded to require, as a *fundamental condition*, that these should "receive the assent of a convention of delegates, elected by the people of the said State, for the sole purpose of giving the assent herein required." (Statutes at Large, Vol. 5, p. 50, Act of June 5, 1836.) Such a Convention, duly elected under a call from the Legislature, met in pursuance of law, and, after consideration, declined to come into the Union on the condition proposed. But the action of this Convention was not universally satisfactory; and in order to effect an admission into the Union, another Convention was called *professedly* by the people, in their sovereign capacity, without any authority from State or Territorial Legislature; nay, sir, according to the language of the present President, "against authorities duly con-stituted by Act of Congress;" at least as much as the recent Convention in Kansas. The irregularity of this Convention was increased by the circumstance, that two of the oldest counties of the State comprising a population of some twenty-five thou-sand souls, refused to take any part in it, even to the extent of not opening the polls for the election of delegates, claiming that it was held without warrant of law, and in defiance of the legal Convention. This popular Convention, though wanting a popular support coextensive with the State, yet proceeded, by formal act, to give the assent of the people of Michigan to the fundamental condition proposed by Congress.

The proceedings of the two Conventions were transmitted to President Jackson, who, by message, dated 27th December, 1836, laid them both before Congress, indicating very clearly his desire to ascertain the will of the people, without regard to form. The origin of the popular Convention he thus describes:

"This Convention was not held or elected by virtue of any act of the Territorial or State Legislature. It originated from the People themselves, and was chosen by them in pursuance of resolutions adopted in primary assemblies held in the respective counties."—*Sen. Doc., 2d sess. 24th Cong.*, Vol. 1, No. 36.

And he then declares that, had these proceedings come to him during the recess of Congress, he should have felt it his duty, on being satisfied that they emanated from a Convention of delegates elected *in point of fact by the People of the State*, to is-sue his proclamation for the admission of the State.

The Committee on the Judiciary in the Senate, of which Fe-lix Grundy was Chairman, after inquiry, recognized the com-petency of the popular Convention, as "elected by the People of the State of Michigan," and reported a Bill, responsive to their assent of the proposed condition, for the admission of the State without further condition. (Statutes at Large, Vol. 5, p. 144, Act of 26th Jan., 1837.) Then, sir, appeared the very ob-jections which are now directed against Kansas. It was com-plained that the movement for immediate admission was the work of a "minority," and that "a great majority of the State feel otherwise." (Sen. Doc., 2d sess. 24th Cong., Vol. 1, No. 37.) And a leading Senator, of great ability and integrity, Mr. Ewing, of Ohio, broke forth in a catechism which would do for the present hour. He exclaimed:

"What evidence had the Senate of the organization of the Convention? Of the organization of the popular assemblies who appointed their delegates to that Convention? None on earth. Who they were that met and voted, we had no information. Who gave the notice? And for what did the People receive the notice? To meet and elect? What evidence was there that the Convention acted according to law? Were the delegates sworn? And, if so, they were extra-judicial oaths, and not binding upon them. Were the votes counted? In fact, it was not a proceeding under the forms of the law, for they were totally disregarded."—*Cong. Globe, 2d sess., 24th Cong., Vol. 4, p. 60.*

And the same able Senator, on another occasion, after exposing the imperfect evidence with regard to the action of the Convention, existing only in letters and in an article from a Detroit newspaper, again exclaimed:

"This, sir, is the evidence to support an organic law of a new State about to enter into the Union? Yes, of an organic law, the very highest act a community of men can perform. Letters referring to other letters and a scrap of a newspaper."—*Cong. Debates,* Vol. 13, part I., p. 233.

It was Mr. Calhoun, however, who pressed the opposition with the most persevering intensity. In his sight, the admission of Michigan, under the circumstances, "would be the most monstrous proceeding under our Constitution that can be conceived, the most repugnant to its principles, and dangerous in its consequences." (Cong. Debates, Vol. 13, p. 210.) "There is not," he exclaimed, "one particle of official evidence before us. We have nothing but the private letters of individuals, who do not know even the numbers that voted on either occasion. They know nothing of the qualifications of voters, nor how their votes were received, nor by whom counted." (Ibid.) And he proceeded to characterize the popular Convention as "not only a party caucus, for party purpose, but a criminal meeting—a meeting to subvert the authority of the State and to assume its sovereignty"—adding "that the actors in that meeting might be indicted, tried, and punished"—and he expressed astonishment that "a self-created meeting, convened for a criminal object, had dared to present to this Government an act of theirs, and to expect that we are to receive this irregular and criminal act as a fullfillment of the condition which we had presented for the admission of the State!" (Ibid., p. 299.) No stronger words have been employed against Kansas.

But the single question on which all the proceedings then hinged, and which is as pertinent in the case of Kansas as in the case of Michigan, was thus put by Mr. Morris, of Ohio—(Ibid. p. 215)—"*Will Congress recognize as valid, constitutional, and obligatory, without the color of a law of Michigan to sustain it, an act done by the People of that State in their primary assemblies, and acknowledge that act as obligatory on the constituted authorities and Legislature of the State?*" This question, thus distinctly presented, was answered in debate by able Senators, among whom were Mr. Benton and Mr. King. But there was one person, who has since enjoyed much public confidence, and has left many memorials of an industrious career in the Senate and in diplomatic life, James Buchanan, who rendered himself conspicuous by the ability and ardor with which, against all assaults, he upheld the cause of the popular Convention, which was so strongly denounced, and the entire conformity of its proceedings with the genius of American Institutions. His speeches on that occasion contain an unanswerable argument, at all points, *mutato nomine*, for the immediate admission of Kansas under her present Constitution; nor is there anything by which he is now distinguished than will redound so truly to his fame—if he only continues true to them. But the question was emphatically answered in the Senate by the final vote on the passage of the Bill, where we find twenty-five yeas to only ten nays. In the House of Representatives, after debate, the question was answered in the same way, by a vote of one hundred and forty-eight yeas to fifty-eight nays; and among the yeas is again the name of Franklin Pierce, a Representative from New Hampshire.

Thus, in that day, by such triumphant votes, did the cause of Kansas prevail in the name of Michigan. A popular Convention—called absolutely without authority, and containing delegates from a portion only of the population—called, too, in opposition to constituted authorities, and in derogation of another Convention assembled under the forms of law—stigmatized as a caucus and a criminal meeting, whose authors were liable to indictment, trial, and punishment—was, after ample debate, recognized by Congress as valid, and Michigan now holds her place in the Union, and her Senators sit on this floor, by virtue of that act. Sir, if Michigan is legitimate, Kansas cannot be illegitimate. You bastardize Michigan when you refuse to recognize Kansas.

But this is not all. The precedent is still more clinching. Thus far I have followed exclusively the public documents laid before Congress, and illustrated by the debates of that body; but well-authenticated facts, not of record here, make the case stronger still. It is sometimes said that the proceedings in Kansas are defective, because they originated in a party. This is not true; but even if it were true, then would they still find support in the example of Michigan, where all the proceedings, stretching through successive years, began and ended in party. The proposed State Government was pressed by the Democrats as a *party test;* and all who did not embark in it were denounced. Of the Legislative Council, which called the first Constitutional Convention in 1835, all were Democrats; and in the Convention itself, composed of eighty-seven members, only seven were Whigs. The Convention of 1836, which gave the final assent, originated in a Democratic Convention on the 29th October, in the county of Wayne, composed of one hundred and twenty-four delegates, all Democrats, who preceeded to resolve—

"That the delegates of the *Democratic party* of Wayne, solemnly impressed with the spreading evils and dangers which a refusal to go into the Union has brought upon the people of Michigan, earnestly recommend meetings to be immediately convened by their fellow-citizens in every county of the State, with a view to the expression of their sentiments in favor of the election and call of another Convention, in time to secure our admission into the Union before the first of January next."

Shortly afterwards, a committee of five, appointed by this Convention, all leading Democrats, issued a circular, "under the authority of the delegates of the county of Wayne," recommending that the voters throughout Michigan should meet and elect delegates to a Convention to give the necessary assent to the Act of Congress. In pursuance of this call, the Convention met; and, as it originated in an exclusively party recommendation, so it was of an exclusively party character. And it was the action of this Convention that was submitted to Congress, and, after discussion in both bodies, on solemn votes, approved.

But the precedent of Michigan has another feature, which is entitled to the gravest attention, especially at this moment, when citizens engaged in the effort to establish a State Government in Kansas are openly arrested on the charge of treason, and we are startled by tidings of the maddest efforts to press this procedure of preposterous Tyranny. No such madness prevailed under Andrew Jackson; although, during the long pendency of the Michigan proceedings, for more than fourteen months, the Territorial Government was entirely ousted, and the State Government organized in all its departments. One hundred and thirty different legislative acts were passed, providing for elections, imposing taxes, erecting corporations, and establishing courts of justice; including a Supreme Court and a Court of Chancery. All process was issued in the name of the people of the State of Michigan. And yet no attempt was made to question the legal validity of these proceedings, whether legislative or judicial. Least of all did any menial Governor, dressed in a little brief authority, play the fantastic tricks which we now witness in Kansas; nor did any person, wearing the robes of justice, shock high Heaven with the mockery of injustice now enacted by emissaries of the President in that Territory. No, sir; nothing of this kind then occurred. Andrew Jackson was President.

Again, I say, do you require a precedent? I give it to you. But I will not stake this cause on any precedent. I plant it firmly on the fundamental principle of American Institutions, so embodied in the Declaration of Independence, by which Government is recognized as deriving its just powers only *from the consent of the governed*, who may alter or abolish it when it becomes destructive of their rights. In the debate on the Nebraska Bill, at the overthrow of the Prohibition of Slavery, the Declaration of Independence was denounced as a "self-evident lie." It is only by a similar audacity that the fundamental principle, which sustains the proceedings in Kansas, can be assailed. Nay, more; you must disown the Declaration of Independence, and adopt the Circular of the Holy Alliance, which declares that "useful and necessary changes in legislation and in the administration of States *ought only to emanate from the free will and the intelligent and well-weighed conviction of those whom God has rendered responsible for power.*" Face to face, I put the principle of the Declaration of Independence and the principle of the Holy Alliance, and bid them grapple! "The one places the remedy in the hands which *feel* the disorder; the other places the remedy in the hands which *cause* the disorder;" and when I thus truthfully characterize them, I but adopt a sententious phrase from the Debates in the Virginia Convention on the adoption of the Federal Constitution. (3 Elliot's Debates, 107—Mr. Corbin.) And now these two principles, embodied in the rival propositions of the Senator from New York and the Senator from Illinois, must grapple on this floor.

Statesmen and judges, publicists and authors, with names of authority in American history, espouse and vindicate the American principle. Hand in hand, they now stand around Kansas, and feel this new State lean on them for support. Of these I content myself with adducing two only, both from slaveholding Virginia, in days when Human Rights were not without support in that State. Listen to the language of St. George Tucker, the distinguished commentator upon Blackstone, uttered from the bench in a judicial opinion:

"The power of convening the legal Assemblies, or the ordinary constitutional Legislature, *resided solely in the Executive.* They could neither be chosen without writs issued by its authority, nor assemble, when chosen, but under the same authority. The Conventions, on the contrary, were chosen and assembled, either in pursuance of recommendations from Congress, or from their own bodies, *or by the discretion and common consent of the people.* They were held even whilst a legal Assembly existed. Witness the Convention held at Richmond, in March, 1775; after which period, the legal constitutional Assembly was convened in Williamsburg, by the Governor, Lord Dunmore." * * * "*Yet a constitutional dependence on the British Government was never denied until the succeeding May.*" * * "The Convention, then, was not the ordinary Legislature of Virginia. It was the body of the people, impelled to assemble from a sense of common danger, consulting for the common good, and acting in all things for the common safety."—*Virginia Cases*, 70, 71, *Kamper vs. Hawkins.*

Listen also to the language of James Madison:

"That in all great changes of established government, forms ought to give way to substance; that a rigid adherence in such cases to the forms would render nominal and nugatory the transcendent and precious right of the people 'to abolish or alter their Government, as to them shall seem most likely to effect their safety and happiness.'"
*   *   *   "Nor can it have been forgotten *that no little ill-timed scruples, no zeal for adhering to ordinary forms, were anywhere seen, except in those who wished to indulge under these masks their secret enmity to the substance contended for.*"—*The Federalist*, No. 40.

Proceedings thus sustained, I am unwilling to call *revolutionary*, although this term has the sanction of the Senator from New York. They are founded on an unquestionable American right, declared with Independence, confirmed by the blood of the fathers, and expounded by patriots, which cannot be impeached without impairing the liberties of all. On this head the language of Mr. Buchanan, in reply to Mr. Calhoun, is explicit:

"Does the Senator [Mr. Calhoun] contend, then, that if, in one of the States of this Union, the Government be so organized as to utterly destroy the right of equal representation, there is no mode of obtaining redress, but by an act of the Legislature authorizing a Convention, or by open rebellion? Must the people step at once from oppression to open war? Must it be either absolute submission or absolute revolution? *Is there no middle course?* I cannot agree with the Senator. I say that the whole history of our Government establishes the principle that the people are sovereign, and that a majority of them can alter or change their fundamental laws at pleasure. *I deny that this is either rebellion or revolution. It is an essential and a recognized principle in all our forms of government.*"—*Congress. Debates, 24th Cong., 2d sess., Vol. 13, p. 313.*

Surely, sir, if ever there was occasion for the exercise of this right, the time had come in Kansas. The people there had been subjugated by a horde of foreign invaders, and brought under a tyrannical code of revolting barbarity, while property and life among them were left exposed to audacious assaults which flaunted at noonday, and to reptile abuses which crawled in the darkness of night. *Self-defense is the first law of nature*; and unless this law is temporarily silenced—as all other law has been silenced there—you cannot condemn the proceedings in Kansas. Here, sir, is an unquestionable authority—*in itself an overwhelming law*—which belongs to all countries and times—which is the same in Kansas as at Athens and Rome—which is now, and will be hereafter, as it was in other days—in presence of which Acts of Congress and Constitutions are powerless, as the voice of man against the thunder which rolls through the sky—which whispers itself coeval with life—whose very breath is life itself; and now, in the last resort, do I place all these proceedings under this supreme safeguard, which you will assail in vain. Any opposition must be founded on a fundamental perversion of facts, or a perversion of fundamental principles, which no speeches can uphold, though surpassing in numbers the nine hundred thousand piles driven into the mud in order to sustain the Dutch Stadt-house at Amsterdam!

Thus, on every ground of precedent, whether as regards population, or forms of proceeding; also, on the vital principle of American Institutions; and, lastly, on the absolute law of self-defense, do I now invoke the power of Congress to admit Kansas at once and without hesitation into the Union. "New States *may* be admitted by the Congress into the Union;" such are the words of the Constitution. If you hesitate for want of precedent, then do I appeal to the great principle of American Institutions. If, forgetting the origin of the Republic, you turn away from this principle, then, in the name of human nature, trampled down and oppressed, but aroused to a just self-defense, do I plead for the exercise of this power. Do not hearken, I pray you, to the propositions of Tyranny and Folly; do not be ensnared by that other proposition of the Senator from Illinois, [Mr. DOUGLAS,] in which is the horrid root of Injustice and Civil War. But apply gladly, and at once, the True Remedy, wherein are Justice and Peace.

Mr. President, an immense space has been traversed, and I now stand at the goal. The argument in its various parts is here closed. The Crime against Kansas has been displayed in its origin and extent, beginning with the overthrow of the Prohibition of Slavery; next cropping out in conspiracy on the borders of Missouri, then hardening into a continuity of outrage, through organized invasions and miscellaneous assaults, in which all security was destroyed, and ending at last in the perfect subjugation of a generous people to an unprecedented Usurpation. Turning aghast from the Crime, which, like murder, seemed to confess itself "with most miraculous organ," we have looked with mingled shame and indignation upon the four Apologies, whether of Tyranny, Imbecility, Absurdity, or Infamy, in which it has been wrapped, marking especially the false testimony, congenial with the original Crime, against the Emigrant Aid Company. Then were noted, in succession, the four Remedies, whether of Tyranny—Folly—Injustice and Civil War—or Justice and Peace, which last bids Kansas, in conformity with past precedents and under the exigencies of the hour, in order to redeem her from Usurpation, to take a place as a sovereign State of the Union; and this is the True Remedy. If in this argument I have not unworthily vindicated Truth, then have I spoken according to my desires; if imperfectly, then only according to my powers. But there are other things, not belonging to the argument, which still pass for utterance.

Sir, the people of Kansas, bone of your bone and flesh of your flesh, with the education of freemen and the rights of American citizens, now stand at your door. Will you send them away, or bid them enter? Will you push them back to renew their struggles with a deadly foe, or will you preserve them in security and peace? Will you cast them again into the den of Tyranny, or will you help their despairing efforts to escape? These questions I put with no common solicitude; for I feel that on their just determination depend all the most precious interests of the Republic; and I perceive too clearly the prejudices in the way, and the accumulating bitterness against this distant people, now claiming their simple birthright, while I am bowed with mortification, as I recognize the President of the United States, who should have been a staff to the weak and a shield to the innocent, at the head of this strange oppression.

At every stage, the similitude between the wrongs of Kansas, and those other wrongs against which our fathers rose, becomes more apparent. Read the Declaration of Independence, and there is hardly an accusation which is there directed against the British Monarch, which may not now be directed with increased force against the American President. The parallel has a fearful particularity. Our fathers complained that the King had "sent hither swarms of officers, to harass our people, and eat out their substance;" that he "had combined, with others, to subject us to a jurisdiction foreign to our Constitution, *giving his assent to their acts of pretended legislation*;" that "he had abdicated government here, by declaring us out of his protection, and *waging war against us*;" that "he had excited domestic insurrection among us, and *endeavored to bring on the inhabitants of our frontier the merciless, savages*;" that "our repeated petitions have been answered only by repeated injury." And this arraignment was aptly followed by the damning words, that "a Prince, whose character is thus marked by every act which may define a tyrant, is unfit to be the ruler of a free people." And surely, a President who has done all these things, cannot be less unfit than a Prince. At every stage, the responsibility is brought directly to him. His offense has been both of commission and omission. He has done that which he ought not to have done, and he has left undone that which he ought to have done. By his activity the Prohibition of Slavery was overturned. By his failure to act, the honest emigrants in Kansas have been left a prey to wrong of all kinds. *Nullum flagitium extitit, nisi per te; nullum flagitium sine te*. And now he stands forth the most conspicuous enemy of that unhappy Territory.

As the tyranny of the British King is all renewed in the President, so on this floor have the old indignities been renewed, which embittered and fomented the troubles of our Fathers. The early petition of the American Congress to Parliament, long before any suggestion of independence, was opposed—like the petitions of Kansas—because that body "was assembled without any requisition on the part of the Supreme Power." Another petition from New York, presented by Edmund Burke, was flatly rejected, as claiming rights derogatory to Parliament. And still another petition from Massachusetts Bay was dismissed as "vexatious and scandalous," while the patriot philosopher who bore it was exposed to peculiar contumely. Throughout the debates, our fathers were made the butt of sorry jests and supercilious assumptions. And now these scenes, with these precise objections, have been renewed in the American Senate.

With regret, I come again upon the Senator from South Carolina, [Mr. BUTLER,] who, omnipresent in this debate, overflowed with rage at the simple suggestion that Kansas had applied for admission as a State; and, with incoherent phrases, discharged the loose expectoration of his speech, now upon her representative, and then upon her people. There was no extravagance of the ancient Parliamentary debate which he did not repeat; nor was there any possible deviation from truth which he did not make, with so much of passion, I am glad to add, as to save him from the suspicion of intentional aberration. But the Senator touches nothing which he does not disfigure—with error, sometimes of principle, sometimes of fact. He shows an incapacity of accuracy, whether in stating the Constitution or in stating the law, whether in the details of statistics or the diversions of scholarship. He cannot ope his mouth, but out there flies a blunder. Surely he ought to be familiar with the life of Franklin; and yet he referred to this household character, while acting as agent of our fathers in England, as above suspicion; and this was done that he might give point to a false contrast with the agent of Kansas—not knowing that, however they may differ in genius and fame, in this experience they are alike: that Franklin, when intrusted with the petition of Massachusetts Bay, was assaulted by a foul-mouthed speaker, where he could not be heard in defense, and denounced as a "thief," even as the agent of Kansas has been assaulted on this floor, and denounced as a "forger." And let not the vanity of the Senator be inspired by the parallel with the British statesmen of that day; for it is only in hostility to Freedom that any parallel can be recognized.

But it is against the people of Kansas that the sensibilities of the Senator are particularly aroused. Coming, as he announces, "from a State"—ay, sir, from South Carolina—he turns with lordly disgust from this newly-formed community, which he will not recognize even as "a body-politic." Pray, sir, by what title does he indulge in this egotism? Has he read the history of "the State" which he represents? He cannot surely have forgotten its shameful imbecility from Slavery, confessed throughout the Revolution, followed by its more shameful assumptions for Slavery since. He cannot have forgotten its wretched persistence in the slave trade as the very apple of its eye, and the condition of its participation in the Union. He cannot have forgotten its Constitution, which is republican only in name, confirming power in the hands of the few, and founding the qualifications of its legislators on "a settled freehold estate and ten negroes." And yet the Senator, to whom that "State" has in part committed the guardianship of its good name, instead of moving, with backward treading steps, to cover its nakedness, rushes forward, in the very ecstasy of madness, to expose it by provoking a comparison with Kansas. South Carolina is old; Kansas is young. South Carolina counts by centuries; where Kansas counts by years. But a beneficent example may be born in a day; and I venture to say, that against the two centuries of the older "State," may be already set the two years of trial, evolving corresponding virtue, in the younger community. In the one, is the long wail of Slavery; in the other, the hymns of Freedom. And if we glance at special achievements, it will be difficult to find anything in the history of South Carolina which presents so much of heroic spirit in an heroic cause as appears in that repulse of the Missouri invaders by the beleaguered town of Lawrence, where even the women gave their effective efforts to Freedom. The matrons of Rome, who poured their jewels into the treasury for the public defense— the wives of Prussia, who, with delicate fingers, clothed their defenders against French invasion—the mothers of our own Revolution, who sent forth their sons, covered over with prayers and blessings, to combat for human rights, did nothing of self-sacrifice truer than did these women on this occasion. Were the whole history of South Carolina blotted out of existence, from its very beginning down to the day of the last election of the Senator to his present seat on this floor, civilization might lose—I do not say how little; but surely less than it has already gained by the example of Kansas, in its valiant struggle against oppression, and in the development of a new science of emigration. Already in Lawrence alone there are newspapers and schools, including a High School, and throughout this infant Territory there is more mature scholarship far, in proportion to its inhabitants, than in all South Carolina. Ah, sir, I tell the Senator that Kansas, welcomed as a free State, will be a "ministering angel" to the Republic, when South Carolina, in the cloak of darkness which she hugs, "lies howling."

The Senator from Illinois [Mr. DOUGLAS] naturally joins the Senator from South Carolina in this warfare, and gives to it the superior intensity of his nature. He thinks that the National Government has not completely proved its power, as it has never hanged a traitor; but, if the occasion requires, he hopes there will be no hesitation; and this threat is directed at Kansas, and even at the friends of Kansas throughout the country. Again occurs the parallel with the struggles of our Fathers, and I borrow the language of Patrick Henry, when, to the cry from the Senator, of "treason," "treason," I reply, "if this be treason, make the most of it." Sir, it is easy to call names; but I beg to tell the Senator that if the word "traitor" is in any way applicable to those who refuse submission to a tyrannical Usurpation, whether in Kansas or elsewhere, then must some new word, of deeper color, be invented, to designate those mad spirits who would endanger and degrade the Republic, while they betray all the cherished sentiments of the Fathers and the spirit of the Constitution, in order to give new spread to slavery. Let the Senator proceed. It will not be the first time in history, that a scaffold erected for punishment has become a pedestal of honor. Out of death comes life, and the "traitor" whom he blindly executes will live immortal in the cause.

"For Humanity sweeps onward; where to-day the martyr stands,
  On the morrow crouches Judas, with the silver in his hands;
  While the hooting mob of yesterday in silent awe return,
  To glean up the scattered ashes into History's golden urn."

Among these hostile Senators; there is yet another, with all the prejudice of the Senator from South Carolina, but without his generous impulses, who, on account of his character before the country, and the rancor of his opposition, deserves to be named. I mean the Senator from Virginia, [Mr. MASON,] who, as the author of the Fugitive Slave Bill, has associated himself with a special act of inhumanity and tyranny. Of him I shall say little, for he has said little in this debate, though within that little was compressed the bitterness of a life absorbed in the support of Slavery. He holds the commission of Virginia; but he does not represent that early Virginia, so dear to our hearts, which gave to us the pen of Jefferson, by which the equality of men was declared, and the sword of Washington, by which Independence was secured; but he represents that other Virginia, from which Washington and Jefferson now avert their faces, where human beings are bred as cattle for the shambles, and where a dungeon rewards the pious matron who teaches little children to relieve their bondage by reading the Book of Life. It is proper that such a Senator, representing such a State, should rail against Free Kansas.

Senators such as these are the natural enemies of Kansas, and I introduce them with reluctances simply that the country may understand the character of the hostility which must be overcome. Arrayed with them, of course, are all who unite, under any pretext or apology, in the propagandism of Human Slavery. To such, indeed, the time-honored safeguards of popular rights can be a name only, and nothing more. What are trial by jury, habeas corpus, the ballot-box, the right of petition, the liberty of Kansas, your liberty, sir, or mine, to one who lends himself, not merely to the support at home, but to the propagandism abroad, of that preposterous wrong, which denies even the right of a man to himself! Such a cause can be maintained only by a practical subversion of all rights. It is, therefore, merely according to reason that its partisans should uphold the Usurpation in Kansas.

To overthrow this Usurpation in now the special, importunate duty of Congress, admitting of no hesitation or postponement. To this end it must lift itself from the cabals of candidates, the machinations of party, and the low level of vulgar strife. It must turn from that Slave Oligarchy which now controls the Republic, and refuse to be its tool. Let its power be stretched forth towards this distant Territory, not to bind, but to unbind; not for the oppression of the weak, but for the subversion of the tyrannical; not for the prop and maintenance of a revolting Usurpation, but for the confirmation of Liberty.

"These are imperial arts, and worthy thee!"

Let it now take its stand between the living and dead, and cause this plague to be stayed. All this it can do; and if the interests of Slavery did not oppose, all this it would do at once, in reverent regard for justice, law, and order, driving far away all the alarms of war; nor would it dare to brave the shame and punishment of this Great Refusal. But the Slave Power dares anything; and it can be conquered only by the united masses of the People. From Congress to the People, I appeal.

Already Public Opinion gathers unwonted forces to scourge

the aggressors. In the press, in daily conversation, wherever two or three are gathered together, there the indignant utterance finds vent. And trade, by unerring indications, attests the growing energy. Public credit in Missouri droops. The six per cents of that State, which at par should be 102, have sunk to 84¼—thus at once completing the evidence of Crime, and attesting its punishment. Business is now turning from the Assassins and Thugs, that infest the Missouri River, on the way to Kansas, to seek some safer avenue. And this, though not unimportant in itself, is typical of greater changes. The political credit of the men who uphold the Usurpation, droops even more than the stocks; and the people are turning from all those through whom the Assassins and Thugs have derived their disgraceful immunity.

It was said of old, "Cursed be he that removeth his neighbor's Landmark. *And all the people shall say, Amen.*"—(Deut. xxvii., 17.) Cursed, it is said, in the city and in the field; cursed in basket and store; cursed when thou comest in, and cursed when thou goest out. These are terrible imprecations; but if ever any Landmark were sacred, it was that by which an immense territory was guarded *forever* against Slavery; and if ever such imprecations could justly descend upon any one, they must descend now upon all who, not content with the removal of this sacred Landmark, have since, with criminal complicity, fostered the incursions of the great Wrong against which it was intended to guard. But I utter no imprecations. These are not my words; nor is it my part to add to or subtract from them. But thanks be to God! they find a response in the hearts of an aroused People, making them turn from every man, whether President, or Senator, or Representative, who has been engaged in this Crime—especially from those who, cradled in free institutions, are without the apology of education or social prejudice—until of all such those other words of the prophet shall be fulfilled—"I will set my face against that man; and make him a sign and a proverb; and I will cut him off from the midst of my people."—(*Ezekiel* xiv., 8.) Turning thus from the authors of this Crime, the People will unite once more with the Fathers of the Republic, in a just condemnation of Slavery—determined especially that it shall find no home in the National Territories—while the Slave Power, in which the Crime had its beginning, and by which it is now sustained, will be swept into the charnel-house of defunct Tyrannies.

In this contest, Kansas bravely stands forth—the stripling leader, clad in the panoply of American institutions. In calmly meeting and adopting a frame of Government, her people have with intuitive promptitude performed the duties of freemen; and when I consider the difficulties by which she was beset, I find dignity in her attitude. *In offering herself for admission into the Union as a* FREE STATE, *she presents a single issue for the people to decide.* And since the Slave Power now stakes on this issue all its ill-gotten supremacy, the People, while vindicating Kansas, will at the same time overthrow this Tyranny. Thus does the contest which she now begins involve not only Liberty for herself, but for the whole country. God be praised, that she did not bend ignobly beneath the yoke! Far away on the prairies, she in now battling for the Liberty of all, against the President, who misrepresents all. Everywhere among those who are not insensible to Right, the generous struggle meets a generous response. From innumerable throbbing hearts go forth the very words of encouragement which, in the sorrowful days of our Fathers, were sent by Virginia, speaking by the pen of Richard Henry Lee, to Massachusetts, in the person of her popular tribune, Samuel Adams:

"CHANTILLY, (VA.,) *June 23, 1774.*

"I hope the good people of Boston will not lose their spirits under their present heavy oppression, for they will certainly be supported by the other Colonies; and the cause for which they suffer is so glorious and so deeply interesting to the present and future generations, that all America will owe, in a great measure, their political salvation to the present virtue of Massachusetts Bay."—*American Archives,* 4th Series, Vol. I, p. 446.

In all this sympathy there is strength. But in the cause itself there is angelic power. Unseen of men, the great spirits of History combat by the side of the people of Kansas, breathing a divine courage. Above all towers the majestic form of Washington once more, as on the bloody field, bidding them to remember those rights of Human Nature for which the War of Independence was waged. Such a cause, thus sustained, is invincible.

The contest, which, beginning in Kansas, has reached us, will soon be transferred from Congress to a broader stage, where every citizen will be not only spectator, but actor; and to their judgment I confidently appeal. To the People, now on the eve of exercising the electoral franchise, in choosing a Chief Magistrate of the Republic, I appeal, to vindicate the electoral franchise in Kansas. Let the ballot-box of the Union, with multitudinous might, protect the ballot-box in that Territory. Let the voters everywhere, while rejoicing in their own rights, help to guard the equal rights of distant fellow-citizens: that the shrines of popular institutions, now desecrated, may be sanctified anew; that the ballot-box, now plundered, may be restored; and that the cry, "I am an American citizen," may not be sent forth in vain against outrage of every kind. In just regard for free labor in that Territory, which it is sought to blast by unwelcome association with slave labor; in Christian sympathy with the slave, whom it is proposed to task and sell there; in stern condemnation of the Crime which has been consummated on that beautiful soil; in rescue of fellow-citizens, now subjugated to a tyrannical Usurpation; in dutiful respect for the early Fathers, whose aspirations are now ignobly thwarted; in the name of the Constitution, which has been outraged—of the Laws trampled down—of Justice banished—of Humanity degraded—of Peace destroyed—of Freedom crushed to earth; and, in the name of the Heavenly Father, whose service is perfect Freedom, I make this last appeal.

ABRAHAM LINCOLN

"House Divided" Speech

Springfield, Illinois, June 16, 1858

M R. PRESIDENT AND GENTLEMEN OF THE CONVENTION. If we could first know *where* we are, and *whither* we are tending, we could then better judge *what* to do, and *how* to do it.

We are now far into the *fifth* year, since a policy was initiated, with the *avowed* object, and *confident* promise, of putting an end to slavery agitation.

Under the operation of that policy, that agitation has not only, *not ceased*, but has *constantly augmented*.

In *my* opinion, it *will* not cease, until a *crisis* shall have been reached, and passed.

"A house divided against itself cannot stand."

I believe this government cannot endure, permanently half *slave* and half *free*.

I do not expect the Union to be *dissolved*—I do not expect the house to *fall*—but I *do* expect it will cease to be divided.

It will become *all* one thing, or *all* the other.

Either the *opponents* of slavery, will arrest the further spread of it, and place it where the public mind shall rest in the belief that it is in course of ultimate extinction; or its *advocates* will push it forward, till it shall become alike lawful in all the States, *old* as well as *new*—*North* as well as *South*.

Have we no *tendency* to the latter condition?

Let any one who doubts, carefully contemplate that now almost complete legal combination—piece of *machinery* so to speak—compounded of the Nebraska doctrine, and the Dred Scott decision. Let him consider not only *what work* the machinery is adapted to do, and *how well* adapted; but also, let him study the *history* of its construction, and trace, if he can, or rather *fail*, if he can, to trace the evidences of design, and concert of action, among its chief bosses, from the beginning.

The new year of 1854 found slavery excluded from more than half the States by State Constitutions, and from most of the national territory by Congressional prohibition.

Four days later, commenced the struggle, which ended in repealing that Congressional prohibition.

This opened all the national territory to slavery; and was the first point gained.

But, so far, *Congress* only, had acted; and an *indorsement* by the people, *real* or apparent, was indispensable, to *save* the point already gained, and give chance for more.

This necessity had not been overlooked; but had been provided for, as well as might be, in the notable argument of "*squatter sovereignty*," otherwise called "*sacred right of self government*," which latter phrase, though expressive of the only rightful basis of any government, was so perverted in this attempted use of it as to amount to just this: That if any *one* man, choose to enslave *another*, no *third* man shall be allowed to object.

That argument was incorporated into the Nebraska bill itself, in the language which follows: *"It being the true intent and meaning of this act not to legislate slavery into any Territory or state, nor to exclude it therefrom; but to leave the people thereof perfectly free to form and regulate their domestic institutions in their own way, subject only to the Constitution of the United States."*

Then opened the roar of loose declamation in favor of "Squatter Sovereignty," and "Sacred right of self government."

"But," said opposition members, "let us be more *specific*—let us *amend* the bill so as to expressly declare that the people of the territory *may* exclude slavery." "Not we," said the friends of the measure; and down they voted the amendment.

While the Nebraska bill was passing through congress, a *law case*, involving the question of a negroe's freedom, by reason of his owner having voluntarily taken him first into a free state and then a territory covered by the congressional prohibition, and held him as a slave, for a long time in each, was passing through the U.S. Circuit Court for the District of Missouri; and both Nebraska bill and law suit were brought to a decision in the same month of May, 1854. The negroe's name was "Dred Scott," which name now designates the decision finally made in the case.

Before the *then* next Presidential election, the law case came *to*, and was argued *in* the Supreme Court of the United States; but the *decision* of it was deferred until *after* the election. Still, *before* the election, Senator Trumbull, on the floor of the Senate, requests the leading advocate of the Nebraska bill to state *his opinion* whether the people of a territory can constitutionally exclude slavery from their limits; and the latter answers, "That is a question for the Supreme Court."

The election came. Mr. Buchanan was elected, and the *indorsement*, such as it was, secured. That was the *second* point gained. The indorsement, however, fell short of a clear popular majority by nearly four hundred thousand votes, and so, perhaps, was not overwhelmingly reliable and satisfactory.

The *outgoing* President, in his last annual message, as impressively as possible *echoed back* upon the people the *weight* and *authority* of the indorsement.

The Supreme Court met again; *did not* announce their decision, but ordered a re-argument.

The Presidential inauguration came, and still no decision of the court; but the *incoming* President, in his inaugural address, fervently exhorted the people to abide by the forthcoming decision, *whatever it might be*.

Then, in a few days, came the decision.

The reputed author of the Nebraska bill finds an early occasion to make a speech at this capitol indorsing the Dred Scott Decision, and vehemently denouncing all opposition to it.

The new President, too, seizes the early occasion of the Silliman letter to *indorse* and strongly *construe* that decision, and to express his *astonishment* that any different view had ever been entertained.

At length a squabble springs up between the President and the author of the Nebraska bill, on the *mere* question of *fact*, whether the Lecompton constitution was or was not, in any just sense, made by the people of Kansas; and in that squabble the latter declares that all he wants is a fair vote for the people, and that he *cares* not whether slavery be voted *down* or voted *up*. I do not understand his declaration that he cares not whether slavery be voted down or voted up, to be intended by him other than as an *apt definition* of the *policy* he would impress upon the public mind—the *principle* for which he declares he has suffered much, and is ready to suffer to the end.

And well may he cling to that principle. If he has any parental feeling, well may he cling to it. That principle, is the only *shred* left of his original Nebraska doctrine. Under the Dred Scott decision, "squatter sovereignty" squatted out of existence, tumbled down like temporary scaffolding—like the mould at the foundry served through one blast and fell back into loose sand—helped to carry an election, and then was kicked to the winds. His late *joint* struggle with the Republicans, against the Lecompton Constitution, involves nothing of the original Nebraska doctrine. That struggle was made on a point, the right of a people to make their own constitution, upon which he and the Republicans have never differed.

The several points of the Dred Scott decision, in connection with Senator Douglas' "care not" policy, constitute the piece of machinery, in its *present* state of advancement. This was the third point gained.

The *working* points of that machinery are:

First, that no negro slave, imported as such from Africa, and no descendant of such slave can ever be a *citizen* of any State, in the sense of that term as used in the Constitution of the United States.

This point is made in order to deprive the negro, in every possible event, of the benefit of this provision of the United States Constitution, which declares that—

"The citizens of each State shall be entitled to all privileges and immunities of citizens in the several States."

Secondly, that "subject to the Constitution of the United States," neither *Congress* nor a *Territorial Legislature* can exclude slavery from any United States territory.

This point is made in order that individual men may *fill up* the territories with slaves, without danger of losing them as property, and thus to enhance the chances of *permanency* to the institution through all the future.

Thirdly, that whether the holding a negro in actual slavery in a free State, makes him free, as against the holder, the United States courts will not decide, but will leave to be decided by the courts of any slave State the negro may be forced into by the master.

This point is made, not to be pressed *immediately*; but, if acquiesced in for a while, and apparently *indorsed* by the people at an election, *then* to sustain the logical conclusion that what Dred Scott's master might lawfully do with Dred Scott, in the free State of Illinois, every other master may lawfully do with any other *one*, or one *thousand* slaves, in Illinois, or in any other free State.

Auxiliary to all this, and working hand in hand with it, the Nebraska doctrine, or what is left of it, is to *educate* and *mould* public opinion, at least *Northern* public opinion, to not *care* whether slavery is voted *down* or voted *up*.

This shows exactly where we now *are*; and *partially* also, whither we are tending.

It will throw additional light on the latter, to go back, and run the mind over the string of historical facts already stated. Several things will *now* appear less *dark* and *mysterious* than they did *when* they were transpiring. The people were to be left "perfectly free" "subject only to the Constitution." What the *Constitution* had to do with it, outsiders could not *then* see. Plainly enough *now*, it was an exactly fitted *niche*, for the Dred Scott decision to afterwards come in, and declare the *perfect freedom* of the people, to be just no freedom at all.

Why was the amendment, expressly declaring the right of the people to exclude slavery, voted down? Plainly enough *now*, the adoption of it, would have spoiled the niche for the Dred Scott decision.

Why was the court decision held up? Why, even a Senator's individual opinion withheld, till *after* the Presidential election? Plainly enough *now*, the speaking out *then* would have damaged the "*perfectly free*" argument upon which the election was to be carried.

Why the *outgoing* President's felicitation on the indorsement? Why the delay of a reargument? Why the incoming President's *advance* exhortation in favor of the decision?

These things *look* like the cautious *patting* and *petting* a spirited horse, preparatory to mounting him, when it is dreaded that he may give the rider a fall.

And why the hasty after indorsements of the decision by the President and others?

We can not absolutely *know* that all these exact adaptations are the result of preconcert. But when we see a lot of framed timbers, different portions of which we know have been gotten out at different times and places and by different workmen— Stephen, Franklin, Roger and James, for instance—and when we see these timbers joined together, and see they exactly make the frame of a house or a mill, all the tenons and mortices exactly fitting, and all the lengths and proportions of the different pieces exactly adapted to their respective places, and not a piece too many or too few—not omitting even scaffolding— or, if a single piece be lacking, we can see the place in the frame exactly fitted and prepared to yet bring such piece in—in *such* a case, we find it impossible to not *believe* that Stephen and Franklin and Roger and James all understood one another from the beginning, and all worked upon a common *plan* or *draft* drawn up before the first lick was struck.

It should not be overlooked that, by the Nebraska bill, the people of a *State* as well as *Territory*, were to be left "*perfectly free*" "*subject only to the Constitution.*"

Why mention a *State*? They were legislating for *territories*, and not *for* or *about* States. Certainly the people of a State *are* and *ought to be* subject to the Constitution of the United States; but why is mention of this *lugged* into this merely *territorial* law? Why are the people of a *territory* and the people of a *state* therein *lumped* together, and their relation to the Constitution therein treated as being *precisely* the same?

While the opinion of *the Court*, by Chief Justice Taney, in the Dred Scott case, and the separate opinions of all the concurring Judges, expressly declare that the Constitution of the United States neither permits Congress nor a Territorial legislature to exclude slavery from any United States territory, they all *omit* to declare whether or not the same Constitution permits a *state*, or the people of a State, to exclude it.

Possibly, this was a mere *omission*; but who can be *quite* sure, if McLean or Curtis had sought to get into the opinion a declaration of unlimited power in the people of a *state* to exclude slavery from their limits, just as Chase and Macy sought to get such declaration, in behalf of the people of a territory, into the Nebraska bill—I ask, who can be quite *sure* that it would not have been voted down, in the one case, as it had been in the other.

The nearest approach to the point of declaring the power of a State over slavery, is made by Judge Nelson. He approaches it more than once, using the precise idea, and *almost* the language too, of the Nebraska act. On one occasion his exact language is, "except in cases where the power is restrained by the Constitution of the United States, the law of the State is supreme over the subject of slavery within its jurisdiction."

In what *cases* the power of the *states is* so restrained by the U.S. Constitution, is left an *open* question, precisely as the same question, as to the restraint on the power of the *territories* was left open in the Nebraska act. Put *that* and *that* together, and we have another nice little niche, which we may, ere long, see filled with another Supreme Court decision, declaring that the Constitution of the United States does not permit a *state* to exclude slavery from its limits.

And this may especially be expected if the doctrine of "care not whether slavery be voted *down* or voted *up*," shall gain upon the public mind sufficiently to give promise that such a decision can be maintained when made.

Such a decision is all that slavery now lacks of being alike lawful in all the States.

Welcome or unwelcome, such decision *is* probably coming, and will soon be upon us, unless the power of the present political dynasty shall be met and overthrown.

We shall *lie down* pleasantly dreaming that the people of *Missouri* are on the verge of making their State *free*; and we shall *awake* to the *reality*, instead, that the *Supreme* Court has made *Illinois* a *slave* State.

To meet and overthrow the power of that dynasty, is the work now before all those who would prevent that consummation.

That is *what* we have to do.

But *how* can we best do it?

There are those who denounce us *openly* to their *own* friends, and yet whisper *us softly*, that *Senator Douglas* is the *aptest* instrument there is, with which to effect that object. *They* do *not* tell us, nor has *he* told us, that he *wishes* any such object to be effected. They wish us to *infer* all, from the facts, that he now has a little quarrel with the present head of the dynasty; and that he has regularly voted with us, on a single point, upon which, he and we, have never differed.

They remind us that *he* is a very *great man*, and that the largest of *us* are very small ones. Let this be granted. But "a *living dog* is better than a *dead lion*." Judge Douglas, if not a *dead* lion *for this work*, is at least a *caged* and *toothless* one. How can he oppose the advances of slavery? He don't *care* anything about it. His avowed *mission is impressing* the "public heart" to *care* nothing about it.

A leading Douglas Democratic newspaper thinks Douglas' superior talent will be needed to resist the revival of the African slave trade.

Does Douglas believe an effort to revive that trade is approaching? He has not said so. Does he *really* think so? But if it is, how can he resist it? For years he has labored to prove it a *sacred right* of white men to take negro slaves into the new territories. Can he possibly show that it is *less* a sacred right to *buy* them where they can be bought cheapest? And, unquestionably they can be bought *cheaper in Africa* than in *Virginia*.

He has done all in his power to reduce the whole question of slavery to one of a mere *right of property*; and as such, how can *he* oppose the foreign slave trade—how can he refuse that trade in that "property" shall be "perfectly free"—unless he does it as a *protection* to the home production? And as the home *producers* will probably not *ask* the protection, he will be wholly without a ground of opposition.

Senator Douglas holds, we know, that a man may rightfully be *wiser to-day* than he was *yesterday*—that he may rightfully *change* when he finds himself wrong.

But, can we for that reason, run ahead, and *infer* that he *will* make any particular change, of which he, himself, has given no intimation? Can we *safely* base *our* action upon any such *vague* inference?

Now, as ever, I wish to not *misrepresent* Judge Douglas' *position*, question his *motives*, or do ought that can be personally offensive to him.

Whenever, *if ever*, he and we can come together on *principle* so that *our great cause* may have assistance from *his great ability*, I hope to have interposed no adventitious obstacle.

But clearly, he is not *now* with us—he does not *pretend* to be—he does not *promise* to *ever* be.

Our cause, then, must be intrusted to, and conducted by its

own undoubted friends—those whose hands are free, whose hearts are in the work—who *do care* for the result.

Two years ago the Republicans of the nation mustered over thirteen hundred thousand strong.

We did this under the single impulse of resistance to a common danger, with every external circumstance against us.

Of *strange, discordant,* and even, *hostile* elements, we gathered from the four winds, and *formed* and fought the battle through, under the constant hot fire of a disciplined, proud, and pampered enemy.

Did we brave all *then,* to *falter* now?—*now*—when that same enemy is *wavering,* dissevered and belligerent?

The result is not doubtful. We shall not fail—if we stand firm, we shall not fail.

Wise councils may *accelerate* or *mistakes delay* it, but, sooner or later the victory is *sure* to come.

WILLIAM SEWARD

The Irrepressible Conflict

Rochester, N.Y., October 25, 1858

T HE unmistakable outbreaks of zeal which occur all around me, show that you are earnest men—and such a man am I. Let us therefore, at least for a time, pass by all secondary and collateral questions, whether of a personal or of a general nature, and consider the main subject of the present canvass. The democratic party—or, to speak more accurately, the party which wears that attractive name—is in possession of the federal government. The republicans propose to dislodge that party, and dismiss it from its high trust.

The main subject, then, is, whether the democratic party deserves to retain the confidence of the American people. In attempting to prove it unworthy, I think that I am not actuated by prejudices against that party, or by prepossessions in favor of its adversary; for I have learned, by some experience, that virtue and patriotism, vice and selfishness, are found in all parties, and that they differ less in their motives than in the policies they pursue.

Our country is a theatre, which exhibits, in full operation, two radically different political systems; the one resting on the basis of servile or slave labor, the other on the basis of voluntary labor of freemen.

The laborers who are enslaved are all negroes, or persons more or less purely of African derivation. But this is only accidental. The principle of the system is, that labor in every society, by whomsoever performed, is necessarily unintellectual, groveling and base; and that the laborer, equally for his own good and for the welfare of the state, ought to be enslaved. The white laboring man, whether native or foreigner, is not enslaved, only because he cannot, as yet, be reduced to bondage.

You need not be told now that the slave system is the older of the two, and that once it was universal.

The emancipation of our own ancestors, Caucasians and Europeans as they were, hardly dates beyond a period of five hundred years. The great melioration of human society which modern times exhibit, is mainly due to the incomplete substitution of the system of voluntary labor for the old one of servile labor, which has already taken place. This African slave system is one which, in its origin and in its growth, has been altogether foreign from the habits of the races which colonized these states, and established civilization here. It was introduced on this new continent as an engine of conquest, and for the establishment of monarchical power, by the Portuguese and the Spaniards, and was rapidly extended by them all over South America, Central America, Louisiana and Mexico. Its legitimate fruits are seen in the poverty, imbecility, and anarchy, which now pervade all Portuguese and Spanish America. The free-labor system is of German extraction, and it was established in our country by emigrants from Sweden, Holland, Germany, Great Britain and Ireland.

We justly ascribe to its influences the strength, wealth, greatness, intelligence, and freedom, which the whole American people now enjoy. One of the chief elements of the value of human life is freedom in the pursuit of happiness. The slave system is not only intolerable, unjust, and inhuman, towards the laborer, whom, only because he is a laborer, it loads down with chains and converts into merchandise, but is scarcely less severe upon the freeman, to whom, only because he is a laborer from necessity, it denies facilities for employment, and whom it expels from the community because it cannot enslave and convert him into merchandise also. It is necessarily improvident and ruinous, because, as a general truth, communities prosper and flourish or droop and decline in just the degree that they practise or neglect to practise the primary duties of justice and humanity. The free-labor system conforms to the divine law of equality, which is written in the hearts and consciences of man, and therefore is always and everywhere beneficent.

The slave system is one of constant danger, distrust, suspicion, and watchfulness. It debases those whose toil alone can produce wealth and resources for defense, to the lowest degree of which human nature is capable, to guard against mutiny and insurrection, and thus wastes energies which otherwise might be employed in national development and aggrandizement.

The free-labor system educates all alike, and by opening all the fields of industrial employment, and all the departments of authority, to the unchecked and equal rivalry of all classes of men, at once secures universal contentment, and brings into the highest possible activity all the physical, moral and social energies of the whole state. In states where the slave system prevails, the masters, directly or indirectly, secure all political power, and constitute a ruling aristocracy. In states where the free-labor system prevails, universal suffrage necessarily obtains, and the state inevitably becomes, sooner or later, a republic or democracy.

Russia yet maintains slavery, and is a despotism. Most of the other European states have abolished slavery, and adopted the system of free labor. It was the antagonistic political tendencies of the two systems which the first Napoleon was contemplating when he predicted that Europe would ultimately be either all Cossack or all republican. Never did human sagacity utter a more pregnant truth. The two systems are at once perceived to be incongruous. But they are more than incongruous—they are incompatible. They never have permanently existed together in one country, and they never can. It would be easy to demonstrate this impossibility, from the irreconcilable contrast between their great principles and characteristics. But the experience of mankind has conclusively established it. Slavery, as I have already intimated, existed in every state in Europe. Free labor has supplanted it everywhere except in Russia and Turkey. State necessities developed in modern times, are now obliging even those two nations to encourage and employ free labor; and already, despotic as they are, we find them engaged in abolishing slavery. In the United States, slavery came into collision with free labor at the close of the last century, and fell before it in New England, New York, New Jersey and Pennsylvania, but triumphed over it effectually, and excluded it for a period yet undetermined, from Virginia, the Carolinas and Georgia. Indeed, so incompatible are the two systems, that every new state which is organized within our ever extending domain makes its first political act a choice of the one and the exclusion of the other, even at the cost of civil war, if necessary. The slave states, without law, at the last national election, successfully forbade, within their own limits, even the casting of votes for a candidate for president of the United States supposed to be favorable to the establishment of the free-labor system in new states.

Hitherto, the two systems have existed in different states, but side by side within the American Union. This has happened because the Union is a confederation of states. But in another aspect the United States constitute only one nation. Increase of population, which is filling the states out to their very borders, together with a new and extended net-work of railroads and other avenues, and an internal commerce which daily becomes more intimate, is rapidly bringing the states into a higher and more perfect social unity or consolidation. Thus, these antagonistic systems are continually coming into closer contact, and collision results.

Shall I tell you what this collision means? They who think that it is accidental, unnecessary, the work of interested or fanatical agitators, and therefore ephemeral, mistake the case altogether. It is an irrepressible conflict between opposing and enduring forces, and it means that the United States must and will, sooner or later, become either entirely a slaveholding nation, or entirely a free-labor nation. Either the cotton and rice-fields of South Carolina and the sugar plantations of Louisiana will ultimately be tilled by free labor, and Charleston and New Orleans become marts for legitimate merchandise alone, or else the rye-fields and wheat-fields of Massachusetts and New York must again be surrendered by their farmers to slave culture and to the production of slaves, and Boston and New York become once more markets for trade in the bodies and souls of men. It is the failure to apprehend this great truth that induces so many unsuccessful attempts at final compromise between the slave and free states, and it is the existence of this great fact that renders all such pretended compromises, when made, vain and ephemeral. Startling as this saying may appear to you, fellow citizens, it is by no means an original or even a moderate one. Our forefathers knew it to be true, and unanimously acted upon it when they framed the constitution of the United States. They regarded the existence of the servile system in so many of

the states with sorrow and shame, which they openly confessed, and they looked upon the collision between them,
which was then just revealing itself, and which we are now accustomed to deplore, with favor and hope. They knew that
either the one or the other system must exclusively prevail.

Unlike too many of those who in modern time invoke their
authority, they had a choice between the two. They preferred
the system of free labor, and they determined to organize the
government, and so to direct its activity, that that system
should surely and certainly prevail. For this purpose, and no
other, they based the whole structure of government broadly
on the principle that all men are created equal, and therefore
free—little dreaming that, within the short period of one hundred years, their descendants would bear to be told by any orator, however popular, that the utterance of that principle was
merely a rhetorical rhapsody; or by any judge, however vener-
ated, that it was attended by mental reservations, which rendered it hypocritical and false. By the ordinance of 1787, they
dedicated all of the national domain not yet polluted by slavery to free labor immediately, thenceforth and forever; while
by the new constitution and laws they invited foreign free labor from all lands under the sun, and interdicted the importation of African slave labor, at all times, in all places, and under
all circumstances whatsoever. It is true that they necessarily and
wisely modified this policy of freedom, by leaving it to the several states, affected as they were by differing circumstances, to
abolish slavery in their own way and at their own pleasure, instead of confiding that duty to congress; and that they secured
to the slave states, while yet retaining the system of slavery, a
three-fifths representation of slaves in the federal government,
until they should find themselves able to relinquish it with
safety. But the very nature of these modifications fortifies my
position that the fathers knew that the two systems could not
endure within the Union, and expected that within a short period slavery would disappear forever. Moreover, in order that
these modifications might not altogether defeat their grand design of a republic maintaining universal equality, they provided
that two-thirds of the states might amend the constitution.

It remains to say on this point only one word, to guard
against misapprehension. If these states are to again become

universally slaveholding, I do not pretend to say with what violations of the constitution that end shall be accomplished. On the other hand, while I do confidently believe and hope that my country will yet become a land of universal freedom, I do not expect that it will be made so otherwise than through the action of the several states coöperating with the federal government, and all acting in strict conformity with their respective constitutions.

The strife and contentions concerning slavery, which gently-disposed persons so habitually deprecate, are nothing more than the ripening of the conflict which the fathers themselves not only thus regarded with favor, but which they may be said to have instituted.

It is not to be denied, however, that thus far the course of that contest has not been according to their humane anticipations and wishes. In the field of federal politics, slavery, deriving unlooked-for advantages from commercial changes, and energies unforeseen from the facilities of combination between members of the slaveholding class and between that class and other property classes, early rallied, and has at length made a stand, not merely to retain its original defensive position, but to extend its sway throughout the whole Union. It is certain that the slaveholding class of American citizens indulge this high ambition, and that they derive encouragement for it from the rapid and effective political successes which they have already obtained. The plan of operation is this: By continued appliances of patronage and threats of disunion, they will keep a majority favorable to these designs in the senate, where each state has an equal representation. Through that majority they will defeat, as they best can, the admission of free states and secure the admission of slave states. Under the protection of the judiciary, they will, on the principle of the Dred Scott case, carry slavery into all the territories of the United States now existing and hereafter to be organized. By the action of the president and the senate, using the treaty-making power, they will annex foreign slaveholding states. In a favorable conjuncture they will induce congress to repeal the act of 1808, which prohibits the foreign slave trade, and so they will import from Africa, at the cost of only twenty dollars a head, slaves enough to fill up the interior of the continent. Thus relatively increasing the number of slave states, they will allow no amendment to the constitution prejudicial to their interest; and so, having permanently established their power, they expect the federal judiciary to nullify all state laws which shall interfere with internal or foreign commerce in slaves. When the free states shall be sufficiently demoralized to tolerate these designs, they reasonably conclude that slavery will be accepted by those states themselves. I shall not stop to show how speedy or how complete would be the ruin which the accomplishment of these slaveholding schemes would bring upon the country. For one, I should not remain in the country to test the sad experiment. Having spent my manhood, though not my whole life, in a free state, no aristocracy of any kind, much less an aristocracy of slaveholders, shall ever make the laws of the land in which I shall be content to live. Having seen the society around me universally engaged in agriculture, manufactures and trade, which were innocent and beneficent, I shall never be a denizen of a state where men and women are reared as cattle, and bought and sold as merchandise. When that evil day shall come, and all further effort at resistance shall be impossible, then, if there shall be no better hope for redemption than I can now foresee, I shall say with Franklin, while looking abroad over the whole earth for a new and more congenial home, "Where liberty dwells, there is my country."

You will tell me that these fears are extravagant and chimerical. I answer, they are so; but they are so only because the designs of the slaveholders must and can be defeated. But it is only the possibility of defeat that renders them so. They cannot be defeated by inactivity. There is no escape from them, compatible with non-resistance. How, then, and in what way, shall the necessary resistance be made. There is only one way. The democratic party must be permanently dislodged from the government. The reason is, that the democratic party is inextricably committed to the designs of the slaveholders, which I have described. Let me be well understood. I do not charge that the democratic candidates for public office now before the people are pledged to—much less that the democratic masses who support them really adopt—those atrocious and dangerous designs. Candidates may, and generally do, mean to act justly, wisely and patriotically, when they shall be elected; but they become the ministers and servants, not the dictators, of the power which elects them. The policy which a party shall pursue at a future period is only gradually developed, depending on the occurrence of events never fully foreknown. The motives of men, whether acting as electors or in any other capacity, are generally pure. Nevertheless, it is not more true that "hell is paved with good intentions," than it is that earth is covered with wrecks resulting from innocent and amiable motives.

The very constitution of the democratic party commits it to execute all the designs of the slaveholders, whatever they may be. It is not a party of the whole Union, of all the free states and of all the slave states; nor yet is it a party of the free states in the north and in the northwest; but it is a sectional and local party, having practically its seat within the slave states, and counting its constituency chiefly and almost exclusively there. Of all its representatives in congress and in the electoral colleges, two-thirds uniformly come from these states. Its great element of strength lies in the vote of the slaveholders, augmented by the representation of three-fifths of the slaves. Deprive the democratic party of this strength, and it would be a helpless and hopeless minority, incapable of continued organization. The democratic party, being thus local and sectional, acquires new strength from the admission of every new slave state, and loses relatively by the admission of every new free state into the Union.

A party is in one sense a joint stock association, in which those who contribute most direct the action and management of the concern. The slaveholders contributing in an overwhelming proportion to the capital strength of the democratic party, they necessarily dictate and prescribe its policy. The inevitable caucus system enables them to do so with a show of fairness and justice. If it were possible to conceive for a moment that the democratic party should disobey the behests of the slaveholders, we should then see a withdrawal of the slaveholders, which would leave the party to perish. The portion of the party which is found in the free states is a mere appendage, convenient to modify its sectional character, without impairing its sectional constitution, and is less effective in regulating its movement than the nebulous tail of the comet is in determining the appointed though apparently eccentric course of the fiery sphere from which it emanates.

To expect the democratic party to resist slavery and favor freedom, is as unreasonable as to look for protestant missionaries to the catholic propaganda of Rome. The history of the democratic party commits it to the policy of slavery. It has been the democratic party, and no other agency, which has carried that policy up to its present alarming culmination. Without stopping to ascertain, critically, the origin of the present democratic party, we may concede its claim to date from the era of good feeling which occurred under the administration of President Monroe. At that time, in this state, and about that time in many others of the free states, the democratic party deliberately disfranchised the free colored or African citizen, and it has pertinaciously continued this disfranchisement ever since. This was an effective aid to slavery; for, while the slaveholder votes for his slaves against freedom, the freed slave in the free states is prohibited from voting against slavery.

In 1824, the democracy resisted the election of John Quincy Adams—himself before that time an acceptable democrat—and in 1828 it expelled him from the presidency and put a slaveholder in his place, although the office had been filled by slaveholders thirty-two out of forty years.

In 1836, Martin Van Buren—the first non-slaveholding citizen of a free state to whose election the democratic party ever consented—signalized his inauguration into the presidency by a gratuitous announcement, that under no circumstances would he ever approve a bill for the abolition of slavery in the District of Columbia. From 1838 to 1844, the subject of abolishing slavery in the District of Columbia and in the national dock-yards and arsenals, was brought before congress by repeated popular appeals. The democratic party thereupon promptly denied the right of petition, and effectually suppressed the freedom of speech in congress, so far as the institution of slavery was concerned.

From 1840 to 1843, good and wise men counseled that Texas should remain outside the Union until she should consent to relinquish her self instituted slavery; but the democratic party precipitated her admission into the Union, not only without that condition, but even with a covenant that the state might be divided and reörganized so as to constitute four slave states instead of one.

In 1846, when the United States became involved in a war with Mexico, and it was apparent that the struggle would end in the dismemberment of that republic, which was a non-slaveholding power, the democratic party rejected a declaration that slavery should not be established within the territory to be acquired. When, in 1850, governments were to be instituted in the territories of California and New Mexico, the fruits of that war, the democratic party refused to admit New Mexico as a free state, and only consented to admit California as a free state on the condition, as it has since explained the transaction, of leaving all of New Mexico and Utah open to slavery, to which was also added the concession of perpetual slavery in the District of Columbia, and the passage of an unconstitutional, cruel and humiliating law, for the recapture of fugitive slaves, with a further stipulation that the subject of slavery should never again be agitated in either chamber of congress. When, in 1854, the slaveholders were contentedly reposing on these great advantages, then so recently won, the democratic party unnecessarily, officiously and with superserviceable liberality, awakened them from their slumber, to offer and force on their acceptance the abrogation of the law which declared that neither slavery nor involuntary servitude should ever exist within that part of the ancient territory of Louisiana which lay outside of the state of Missouri, and north of the parallel of 36° 30′ of north latitude—a law which, with the exception of one other, was the only statute of freedom then remaining in the federal code.

In 1856, when the people of Kansas had organized a new state within the region thus abandoned to slavery, and applied to be admitted as a free state into the Union, the democratic party contemptuously rejected their petition, and drove them with menaces and intimidations from the halls of congress, and armed the president with military power to enforce their submission to a slave code, established over them by fraud and usurpation. At every subsequent stage of the long contest which has since raged in Kansas, the democratic party has lent its sympathies, its aid, and all the powers of the government which it controlled, to enforce slavery upon that unwilling and injured people. And now, even at this day, while it mocks us with the assurance that Kansas is free, the democratic party keeps the state excluded from her just and proper place in the Union, under the hope that she may be dragooned into the acceptance of slavery.

The democratic party, finally, has procured from a supreme judiciary, fixed in its interest, a decree that slavery exists by force of the constitution in every territory of the United States, paramount to all legislative authority, either within the territory, or residing in congress.

Such is the democratic party. It has no policy, state or federal, for finance, or trade, or manufacture, or commerce, or education, or internal improvements, or for the protection or even the security of civil or religious liberty. It is positive and uncompromising in the interest of slavery—negative, compromising, and vacillating, in regard to everything else. It boasts its love of equality, and wastes its strength, and even its life, in fortifying the only aristocracy known in the land. It professes fraternity, and, so often as slavery requires, allies itself with proscription. It magnifies itself for conquests in foreign lands, but it sends the national eagle forth always with chains, and not the olive branch, in his fangs.

This dark record shows you, fellow citizens, what I was unwilling to announce at an earlier stage of this argument, that of the whole nefarious schedule of slaveholding designs which I have submitted to you, the democratic party has left only one yet to be consummated—the abrogation of the law which forbids the African slave trade.

Now, I know very well that the democratic party has, at every stage of these procceedings, disavowed the motive and the policy of fortifying and extending slavery, and has excused them on entirely different and more plausible grounds. But the inconsistency and frivolity of these pleas prove still more conclusively the guilt I charge upon that party. It must, indeed, try to excuse such guilt before mankind, and even to the consciences of its own adherents. There is an instinctive abhorrence of slavery, and an inborn and inhering love of freedom in the human heart, which render palliation of such gross misconduct indispensable. It disfranchised the free African on the ground of a fear that, if left to enjoy the right of suffrage, he might seduce the free white citizens into amalgamation with his wronged and despised race. The democratic party condemned and deposed John Quincy Adams, because he expended twelve millions a year, while it justifies his favored successor in spending seventy, eighty and even one hundred millions, a year. It denies emancipation in the District of Columbia, even with compensation to masters and the consent of the people, on the ground of an implied constitutional inhibition, although the constitution expressly confers upon congress sovereign legislative power in that district, and although the democratic party is tenacious of the principle of strict construction. It violated the express provisions of the constitution in suppressing petition and debate on the subject of slavery, through fear of disturbance of the public harmony, although it claims that the electors have a right to instruct their representatives, and even demand their resignation in cases of contumacy. It extended slavery over Texas, and connived at the attempt to spread it across the Mexican territories, even to the shores of the Pacific ocean, under a plea of enlarging the area of freedom. It abrogated the Mexican slave law and the Missouri compromise prohibition of slavery in Kansas, not to open the new territories to slavery, but to try therein the new and fascinating theories of non-intervention and popular sovereignty; and, finally, it overthrew both these new and elegant systems by the English Lecompton bill and the Dred Scott decision, on the ground that the free states ought not to enter the Union without a population equal to the representative basis of one member of congress, although slave states might come in without inspection as to their numbers.

Will any member of the democratic party now here claim that the authorities chosen by the suffrages of the party transcended their partisan platforms, and so misrepresented the party in the various transactions, I have recited? Then I ask him to name one democratic statesman or legislator, from Van Buren to Walker, who, either timidly or cautiously like them, or boldly and defiantly like Douglas, ever refused to execute a behest of the slaveholders and was not therefor, and for no other cause, immediately denounced, and deposed from his trust, and repudiated by the democratic party for that contumacy.

I think, fellow citizens, that I have shown you that it is high time for the friends of freedom to rush to the rescue of the constitution, and that their very first duty is to dismiss the democratic party from the administration of the government.

Why shall it not be done? All agree that it ought to be done. What, then, shall prevent its being done? Nothing but timidity or division of the opponents of the democratic party.

Some of these opponents start one objection, and some another. Let us notice these objections briefly. One class say that they cannot trust the republican party; that it has not avowed its hostility to slavery boldly enough, or its affection for freedom earnestly enough.

I ask, in reply, is there any other party which can be more safely trusted? Every one knows that it is the republican party, or none, that shall displace the democratic party. But I answer, further, that the character and fidelity of any party are determined, necessarily, not by its pledges, programmes, and platforms, but by the public exigencies, and the temper of the people when they call it into activity. Subserviency to slavery is a law written not only on the forehead of the democratic party, but also in its very soul—so resistance to slavery, and devotion to freedom, the popular elements now actively working for the republican party among the people, must and will be the resources for its ever-renewing strength and constant invigoration.

Others cannot support the republican party, because it has not sufficiently exposed its platform, and determined what it will do, and what it will not do, when triumphant. It may prove too progressive for some, and too conservative for others. As if any party ever foresaw so clearly the course of future events as to plan a universal scheme of future action, adapted to all possible emergencies. Who would ever have joined even the whig party of the revolution, if it had been obliged to answer, in 1775, whether it would declare for independence in 1776, and for this noble federal constitution of ours in 1787, and not a year earlier or later? The people will be as wise next year, and even ten years hence, as we are now. They will oblige the republican party to act as the public welfare and the interests of justice and humanity shall require, through all the stages of its career, whether of trial or triumph.

Others will not venture an effort, because they fear that the

Union would not endure the change. Will such objectors tell me how long a constitution can bear a strain directly along the fibres of which it is composed? This is a constitution of freedom. It is being converted into a constitution of slavery. It is a republican constitution. It is being made an aristocratic one. Others wish to wait until some collateral questions concerning temperance, or the exercise of the elective franchise are properly settled. Let me ask all such persons, whether time enough has not been wasted on these points already, without gaining any other than this single advantage, namely, the discovery that only one thing can be effectually done at one time, and that the one thing which must and will be done at any one time is just that thing which is most urgent, and will no longer admit of postponement or delay. Finally, we are told by faint-hearted men that they despond; the democratic party, they say is unconquerable, and the dominion of slavery is consequently inevitable. I reply that the complete and universal dominion of slavery would be intolerable enough, when it should have come, after the last possible effort to escape should have been made. There would then be left to us the consoling reflection of fidelity to duty.

But I reply further, that I know—few, I think, know better than I—the resources and energies of the democratic party, which is identical with the slave power. I do ample prestige to its traditional popularity. I know, further—few, I think, know better than I—the difficulties and disadvantages of organizing a new political force, like the republican party, and the obstacles it must encounter in laboring without prestige and without patronage. But, understanding all this, I know that the democratic party must go down, and that the republican party must rise into its place. The democratic party derived its strength, originally, from its adoption of the principles of equal and exact justice to all men. So long as it practised this principle faithfully, it was invulnerable. It became vulnerable when it renounced the principle, and since that time it has maintained itself, not by virtue of its own strength, or even of its traditional merits, but because there as yet had appeared in the political field no other party that had the conscience and the courage to take up, and avow, and practice the life-inspiring principle which the democratic party had surrendered. At last, the republican party has appeared. It avows, now, as the republican party of 1800 did, in one word, its faith and its works, "Equal and exact justice to all men." Even when it first entered the field, only half organized, it struck a blow which only just failed to secure complete and triumphant victory. In this, its second campaign, it has already won advantages which render that triumph now both easy and certain.

The secret of its assured success lies in that very characteristic which, in the mouth of scoffers, constitutes its great and lasting imbecility and reproach. It lies in the fact that it is a party of one idea; but that idea is a noble one—an idea that fills and expands all generous souls; the idea of equality—the equality of all men before human tribunals and human laws, as they all are equal before the Divine tribunal and Divine laws.

I know, and you know, that a revolution has begun. I know, and all the world knows, that revolutions never go backward. Twenty senators and a hundred representatives proclaim boldly in congress to-day sentiments and opinions and principles of freedom which hardly so many men, even in this free state, dared to utter in their own homes twenty years ago. While the government of the United States, under the conduct of the democratic party, has been all that time surrendering one plain and castle after another to slavery, the people of the United States have been no less steadily and perseveringly gathering together the forces with which to recover back again all the fields and all the castles which have been lost, and to confound and overthrow, by one decisive blow, the betrayers of the constitution and freedom forever.

CARL SCHURZ

True Americanism

Boston, April 18, 1859

M R. PRESIDENT AND GENTLEMEN:—
A few days ago I stood on the cupola of your State-house, and overlooked for the first time this venerable city and the country surrounding it. Then the streets, and hills, and waters around me began to teem with the life of historical recollections, recollections dear to all mankind, and a feeling of pride arose in my heart, and I said to myself, I, too, am an American citizen. [Applause.] There was Bunker Hill, there Charlestown, Lexington, and Dorchester Heights not far off; there the harbor into which the British tea was sunk; there the place where the old liberty-tree stood; there John Hancock's house; there Benjamin Franklin's birth-place—and now I stand in this grand old hall, which so often resounded with the noblest appeals that ever thrilled American hearts, and where I am almost afraid to hear the echo of my own feeble voice;— oh, sir, no man that loves liberty, wherever he may have first seen the light of day, can fail on this sacred spot to pay his tribute to Americanism. And here, with all these glorious memories crowding upon my heart, I will offer mine. I, born in a foreign land, pay my tribute to Americanism? Yes, for to me, the word Americanism, *true* Americanism, comprehends the noblest ideas which ever swelled a human heart with noble pride. [Applause.]

It is one of the earliest recollections of my boyhood, that one summer night our whole village was stirred up by an uncommon occurrence. I say our village, for I was born not far from that beautiful spot where the Rhine rolls his green waters out of the wonderful gate of the Seven Mountains, and then meanders with majestic tranquillity through one of the most glorious valleys of the world. That night our neighbors were pressing around a few wagons covered with linen sheets and loaded with household utensils and boxes and trunks to their utmost capacity. One of our neighboring families were moving far away across a great water, and it was said that they would never again return. And I saw silent tears trickling down weather-beaten cheeks, and the hands of rough peasants firmly pressing each other, and some of the men and women hardly able to speak when they nodded to one another a last farewell. At last the train started into motion, they gave three cheers for *America*, and then in the first gray dawn of the morning I saw them wending their way over the hill until they disappeared in the shadow of the forest. And I heard many a man say, how happy he would be if he could go with them to that great and free country, where a man could be himself. [Applause.]

That was the first time that I heard of America, and my childish imagination took possession of a land covered partly with majestic trees, partly with flowery prairies, immeasurable to the eye, and intersected with large rivers and broad lakes—a land where everybody could do what he thought best, and where nobody need be poor, because everybody was free.

And later, when I was old enough to read, and descriptions of this country and books on American history fell into my hands, the offspring of my imagination acquired the colors of reality, and I began to exercise my brain with the thought what man might be and become, when left perfectly free to himself. And still later, when ripening into manhood, I looked up from my school-books into the stir and bustle of the world, and the trumpet-tones of struggling humanity struck my ear and thrilled my heart, and I saw my nation shake her chains in order to burst them, and I heard a gigantic, universal shout for Liberty rising up to the skies; and at last, after having struggled manfully and drenched the earth of Fatherland with the blood of thousands of noble beings, I saw that nation crushed down again, not only by overwhelming armies, but by the dead weight of customs and institutions and notions and prejudices, which past centuries had heaped upon them, and which a moment of enthusiasm, however sublime, could not destroy; then I consoled an almost despondent heart with the idea of a youthful people and of original institutions clearing the way for an untrammeled development of the ideal nature of man. Then I turned my eyes instinctively across the Atlantic Ocean, and America and Americanism, as I fancied them, appeared to me as the last depositories of the hopes of all true friends of humanity. [Applause.]

I say all this, not as though I indulged in the presumptuous delusion that my personal feelings and experience would be of any interest to you, but in order to show you what America is to the thousands of thinking men in the old world, who, disappointed in their fondest hopes and depressed by the saddest experience, cling with their last remnant of confidence in human nature, to the last spot on earth where man is free to follow the road to attainable perfection, and where unbiassed by the disastrous influence of traditional notions, customs, and institutions, he acts on his own responsibility. They ask themselves: Was it but a wild delusion when we thought that man has the faculty to be free and to govern himself? Have we been fighting, were we ready to die, for a mere phantom, for a mere product of a morbid imagination? This question downtrodden humanity cries out into the world, and from this country it expects an answer.

As its advocate I speak to you. I will speak of Americanism as the great representative of the reformatory age, as the great champion of the dignity of human nature, as the great repository of the last hopes of suffering mankind. I will speak of the ideal mission of this country and of this people.

You may tell me that these views are visionary, that the destiny of this country is less exalted, that the American people are less great than I think they are or ought to be. I answer, ideals are like stars; you will not succeed in touching them with your hands. But like the seafaring man on the desert of waters, you choose them as your guides, and following them you will reach your destiny. I invite you to ascend with me the watchtower of history, overlooking the grand panorama of the development of human affairs, in which the American Republic stands in so bold and prominent relief.

He who reviews the past of this country in connection with the history of the world besides, cannot fail to discover a wonderful coincidence of great events and fortunate circumstances, which were destined to produce everlasting results, unless recklessly thrown away by imbecile generations.

Look back with me four or five centuries. The dark period of the middle ages is drawing near its close. The accidental explosion of that mysterious black powder, discovered by an obscure German monk, is the first flash of lightning preluding that gigantic thunder-storm which is to shatter the edifice of feudal society to pieces. The invention of gunpowder strips the feudal lord of his prestige as a *warrior*; another discovery is to strip him of his prestige as a *man*! Guttenberg, another obscure German, invents the printing-press, and as gunpowder blows the castles of the small feudal tyrants into the air, so the formidable artillery of printed letters batters down the citadels of ignorance and superstition. [Loud applause.] Soul and body take up arms and prepare themselves for the great battle of the Reformation. Now the mighty volcano of the German mind bursts the crust of indolence which has covered it. Luther's triumphant thunder rattles against the holy see of Rome. [Applause.] The world is ablaze, all the elements of society are rising up in boiling commotion—two ages are battling against each other.

This is the time, when the regeneration of the old world is to take place. But the old order of things, fortified in customs and prejudices and deeply-rooted institutions, does not surrender at the first blast of trumpets. The grand but fearful struggle of the reformatory movement plunges all Europe into endless confusion. The very wheel of progress seems to grind and crush one generation after another. The ideas which concerned the highest and most sacred relations of humanity, seem at the same time to call into their service the basest and most violent passions of the human heart, and in all Europe the wars of great principles degenerate into wars of general devastation.

But, meanwhile, a new country has opened its boundless fields to those great ideas, for the realization of which the old world seems no longer to be wide enough. It is as though the earth herself had taken part in the general revolution, and had thrown up from her sea-covered womb a new battle-ground for the spirit of the new era. That is America. Not only the invention of gunpowder and of the printing-press, but also the discovery of America, inaugurates the modern age.

There is the new and immense continent. The most restless and enterprising elements of European society direct their looks towards it. First, the greediness of the gold-hunting adventurer pounces upon the new conquest; but his inordinate appetites being disappointed, he gradually abandons the field to men in whose hearts the future of the new world is sleeping, unborn.

While the coast of Virginia is settled by a motley immigration, led and ruled by men of ideas and enterprise, the sturdiest champions of principle descend upon the stony shores of New England. [Applause.] While the southern colonies are settled under the auspices of lordly merchants and proprietaries, original democracy plants its stern banner upon Plymouth Rock. [Applause.] Mercantile speculation, aristocratic ambition, and stern virtue that seeks freedom and nothing but freedom, lead the most different classes of people, different in origin, habits and persuasion, upon the virgin soil, and entrust to them the task of realizing the great principles of the age. Nor is this privilege confined to one nationality alone. While the Anglo-Saxon takes possession of New England, Virginia and Pennsylvania, the Frenchman plants his colonies on the soil of French Florida and the interior of the continent; the Hollander locates New Netherlands on the banks of the Hudson; the Swede, led there by the great mind of Oxenstiern, occupies the banks of the Delaware; the Spaniard maintains himself in Peninsular Florida, and a numerous immigration of Germans, who follow the call of religious freedom, and of Irishmen, gradually flowing in, scatters itself all over this vast extent of country. Soon all the social and national elements of the civilized world are represented in the new land. Every people, every creed, every class of society has contributed its share to that wonderful mixture out of which is to grow the great nation of the new world. It is true, the Anglo-Saxon establishes and maintains his ascendancy, but without absolutely absorbing the other national elements. They modify each other, and their peculiar characteristics are to be blended together by the all-assimilating power of freedom. This is the origin of the American nationality, which did not spring from one family, one tribe, one country, but incorporates the vigorous elements of all civilized nations on earth. [Applause.]

This fact is not without great importance. It is an essential link in the chain of historical development. The student of history cannot fail to notice that when new periods of civilization break upon humanity, the people of the earth cannot maintain their national relations. New ideas are to be carried out by young nations. From time to time, violent, irresistible hurricanes sweep over the world, blowing the most different elements of the human family together, which by mingling reinvigorate each other, and the general confusion then becomes the starting-point of a new period of progress. Nations which have long subsisted exclusively on their own resources, will gradually lose their original vigor, and die the death of decrepitude. But mankind becomes young again by its different elements being shaken together, by race crossing race, and mind penetrating mind. [Applause.]

The oldest traditions of history speak of such great revulsions and general migrations, and if we could but lift the veil, which covers the remotest history of Asiatic tribes, we should discover the first scenes and acts of the drama, of which the downfall of the Roman empire is a portion. When that empire had exhausted its natural vitality, the dark forests of the North poured forth a barbarous but vigorous multitude, who trampled into ruins the decrepit civilization of the Roman world, but infused new blood into the veins of old Europe, grasping the great ideas of Christianity with a bloody but firm hand—and a new period of original progress sprang out of the seeming devastation. The German element took the helm of history. But, in the course of time, the development of things arrived at a new turning-point. The spirit of individualism took possession of the heart of civilized humanity, and the reformatory movement of the sixteenth century was its expression. But continental Europe appeared unable to incorporate the new and progressive ideas growing out of that spirit, in organic political institutions. While the heart of Europe was ravaged by a series of religious wars, the Anglo-Saxons of England attempted what other nations seemed unable to accomplish. But they also clung too fast to the traditions of past centuries; they failed in separating the Church from the State, and did not realize the cosmopolitan tendency of the new principle. Then the time of a new migration was at hand, and that migration rolled its waves towards America. [Applause.] The old process repeated itself under new forms, milder and more congenial to the humane ideas it represented. It is now not a barbarous multitude pouncing upon old and decrepit empires; not a violent concussion of tribes accompanied by all the horrors of general destruction; but we see the vigorous elements of all nations, we see the Anglo-Saxon, the leader in the practical movement, with his spirit of independence, of daring enterprise, and of indomitable perseverance; the German, the original leader in the movement of ideas, with his spirit of inquiry and his quiet and thoughtful application; the Celt, with the impulsive vivacity of his race; the Frenchman, the Scandinavian, the Scot, the Hollander, the Spaniard, and Italian—all these peaceably congregating and mingling together on virgin soil, where the backwoodsman's hatchet is the only battle-axe of civilization; led together by the irresistible attraction of free and broad principles; undertaking to commence a new era in the history of the world, without first destroying the results of the progress of past periods; undertaking to found a new cosmopolitan nation without marching over the dead bodies of slain millions. Thus was founded the *great colony of free humanity*, which has not old England alone, but the *world*, for its mother-country. [Cheers.]

This idea is, perhaps, not palatable to those who pride themselves on their unadulterated Anglo-Saxondom. To them I have to say, that the destinies of men are often greater than men themselves, and that a good many are swerving from the path of glory by not obeying the true instincts of their nature, and by sacrificing their mission to one-sided pride. [Applause.]

The Anglo-Saxon may justly be proud of the growth and development of this country, and if he ascribes most of it to the undaunted spirit of his race, we may not accuse him of overweening self-glorification. He possesses, in an eminent degree, the enviable talent of acting when others only think; of promptly executing his own ideas, and of appropriating the ideas of other people to his own use. [Applause.] There is, perhaps, no other race that, at so early a day, would have founded the stern democracy of the Plymouth settlement, no other race that would have defied the trials and hardships of the original settler's life so victoriously. No other race, perhaps, possesses in so high a degree not only the daring spirit of independent enterprise, but at the same time the stubborn steadfastness necessary to the final execution of great designs. The Anglo-Saxon spirit has been the locomotive of progress [applause];

but do not forget, that this locomotive would be of little use to the world, if it refused to draw its train over the iron highway, and carry its valuable freight towards its destination; that train consists of the vigorous elements of all nations; that freight is the vital ideas of our age; that destination is universal freedom and the ideal development of man. [Cheers.] That is the true greatness of the Anglo-Saxon race; that ought to be the source of Anglo-Saxon pride. I esteem the son who is proud of his father, if, at the same time, he is worthy of him.

Thus, I say, was founded the colony of free humanity on virgin soil. The youthful elements which constitute people of the new world, cannot submit to rules which are not of their own making; they must throw off the fetters which bind them to an old decrepit order of things. They resolve to enter the great family of nations as an independent member. And in the colony of free humanity, whose mother-country is the world, they establish *the Republic of equal rights, where the title of manhood is the title to citizenship.* [Applause.] My friends, if I had a thousand tongues, and a voice strong as the thunder of heaven, they would not be sufficient to impress upon your minds forcibly enough the greatness of this idea, the overshadowing glory of this result. This was the dream of the truest friends of man from the beginning; for this the noblest blood of martyrs has been shed; for this has mankind waded through seas of blood and tears. There it is now; there it stands, the noble fabric in all the splendor of reality.

They speak of the greatness of the Roman Republic! Oh, sir, if I could call the proudest of Romans from his grave, I would take him by the hand and say to him, Look at this picture, and at this! The greatness of thy Roman Republic consisted in its despotic rule over the world; the greatness of the American Republic consists in the secured right of man to govern himself. [Applause.] The dignity of the Roman citizen consisted in his exclusive privileges; the dignity of the American citizen consists in his holding the natural rights of his neighbor just as sacred as his own. [Continued applause.] The Roman Republic recognized and protected the *rights of the citizen*, at the same time disregarding and leaving unprotected the *rights of man*; Roman citizenship was founded upon monopoly, not upon the claims of human nature. What the citizen of Rome claimed for himself, he did not respect in others; his own greatness was his only object; his own liberty, as he regarded it, gave him the privilege to oppress his fellow-beings. His democracy, instead of elevating mankind to its own level, trampled the rights of man into the dust. The security of the Roman Republic, therefore, consisted in the power of the sword; the security of the American Republic rests in the equality of human rights! [Loud applause.] The Roman Republic perished by the sword; the American Republic will stand as long as the equality of human rights remains inviolate. [Cheers.] Which of the two Republics is the greater—the Republic of the Roman, or the Republic of *man*?

Sir, I wish the words of the Declaration of Independence, "that all men are created free and equal, and are endowed with certain inalienable rights," were inscribed upon every gate-post within the limits of this Republic. From this principle the Revolutionary Fathers derived their claim to independence; upon this they founded the institutions of this country, and the whole structure was to be the living incarnation of this idea. This principle contains the programme of our political existence. It is the most progressive, and at the same time the most conservative one; the most progressive, for it takes even the lowliest members of the human family out of their degradation, and inspires them with the elevating consciousness of equal human dignity; the most conservative, for it makes a common cause of individual rights. [Tumultuous applause.] From the equality of rights springs identity of our highest interests; you cannot subvert your neighbor's rights without striking a dangerous blow at your own. And when the rights of one cannot be infringed without finding a ready defence in all others who defend their own rights in defending his, then, and only then, are the rights of all safe against the usurpations of governmental authority.

This general identity of interests is the only thing that can guarantee the stability of democratic institutions. Equality of rights, embodied in general self-government, is the great moral element of true democracy; it is the only reliable safety-valve in the machinery of modern society. There is the solid foundation of our system of government; there is our mission; there is our greatness; there is our safety; there, and nowhere else! This is true Americanism, and to this I pay the tribute of my devotion. [Long and loud applause.]

Shall I point out to you the consequences of a deviation from this principle? Look at the Slave States. There is a class of men who are deprived of their natural rights. But this is not the only deplorable feature of that peculiar organization of society. Equally deplorable is it, that there is another class of men who keep the former in subjection. That there are slaves is bad; but almost worse is it, that there are masters. Are not the masters freemen? No, sir! Where is their liberty of the press? Where is their liberty of speech? Where is the man among them who dares to advocate openly principles not in strict accordance with the ruling system? They speak of a republican form of government—they speak of democracy, but the despotic spirit of slavery and mastership combined pervades their whole political life like a liquid poison. They do not dare to be free, lest the spirit of liberty become contagious. The system of slavery has enslaved them all, master as well as slave. [Applause; "true!"] What is the cause of all this? It is that you cannot deny one class of society the full measure of their natural rights without imposing restraints upon your own liberty. If you want to be free, there is but one way; it is to guarantee an equally full measure of liberty to all your neighbors. There is no other.

True, there are difficulties connected with an organization of society founded upon the basis of equal rights. Nobody denies it. A large number of those who come to you from foreign lands are not as capable of taking part in the administration of government as the man who was fortunate enough to drink the milk of liberty in his cradle. And certain religious denominations do, perhaps, nourish principles which are hardly in accordance with the doctrines of true democracy. There is a conglomeration on this continent of heterogeneous elements; there is a warfare of clashing interests and unruly aspirations; and with all this, our democratic system gives rights to the ignorant and power to the inexperienced. And the billows of passion will lash the sides of the ship, and the storm of party warfare will bend its masts, and the pusillanimous will cry out—"Master, master, we perish!" But the genius of true democracy will arise from his slumber, and rebuke the winds and the raging of the water, and say unto them—"Where is your faith?" Aye, where is the faith that led the fathers of this republic to invite the weary and burdened of all nations to the enjoyment of equal rights? Where is that broad and generous confidence in the efficiency of true democratic institutions? Has the present generation forgotten that true democracy bears in itself the remedy for all the difficulties that may grow out of it?

It is an old dodge of the advocates of despotism throughout the world, that the people who are not experienced in self-government, are not fit for the exercise of self-government, and must first be educated under the rule of a superior authority. But at the same time the advocates of despotism will never offer them an opportunity to acquire experience in self-government, lest they suddenly become fit for its independent exercise. To this treacherous sophistry the fathers of this republic opposed the noble doctrine, that liberty is the best school for liberty, and that self-government cannot be learned but by practising it. [Loud applause.] This, sir, is a truly American idea; this is true Americanism, and to this I pay the tribute of my devotion. [Cheers.]

You object that some people do not understand their own interests? There is nothing that, in the course of time, will make a man better understand his interests than the independent management of his own affairs on his own responsibility. You object that people are ignorant? There is no better schoolmaster in the world than self-government, independently exercised. You object that people have no just idea of their duties as citizens? There is no other source from which they can derive a just notion of their duties, than the enjoyment of the rights from which they arise. You object that people are misled by their religious prejudices, and by the intrigues of the Roman hierarchy? Since when have the enlightened citizens of this Republic lost their faith in the final invincibility of truth? Since when have they forgotten that if the Roman or any other church plants the seed of superstition, liberty sows broadcast the seed of enlightenment? [Applause.] Do they no longer believe in the invincible spirit of inquiry, which characterizes the reformatory age? If the struggle be fair, can the victory be doubtful? As to religious fanaticism, it will prosper under oppression; it will feed on persecution; it will grow strong by proscription; but it is powerless against genuine democracy. [Applause.] It may indulge in short-lived freaks of passion, or in wily intrigues, but it will die of itself, for its lungs are not adapted to breathe the atmosphere of liberty. [Prolonged applause.] It is like the shark of the sea; drag him into the air, and the monster will perhaps struggle fearfully and frighten timid people with the powerful blows of his tail, and the terrible array of his teeth, but leave him quietly to die and he will die. [Hearty applause.] But engage with him in a hand to hand struggle even then, and the last of his convulsions may fatally punish your rash attempt. Against fanaticism genuine democracy wields an irresistible weapon—it is *Toleration*. Toleration will not strike down the fanatic, but it will quietly and gently disarm him. But fight fanaticism *with* fanaticism, and you will restore it to its own congenial element. It is like Antæus, who gained strength when touching his native earth.

Whoever reads the history of this country calmly and thoroughly, cannot but discover that religious liberty is slowly but steadily rooting out the elements of superstition, and even of prejudice. It has dissolved the war of sects, of which persecution was characteristic, into a contest of abstract opinions, which creates convictions without oppressing men. By recognizing perfect freedom of inquiry, it will engender among men of different belief that mutual respect of true convictions, which makes inquiry earnest, and discussion fair. It will recognize as supremely inviolable, what Roger Williams, one of the most luminous stars of the American sky, called the sanctity of conscience. Read your history, and add the thousands and thousands of Romanists and their offspring together, who, from the first establishment of the colonies, gradually came to this country, and the sum will amount to many millions; compare that number with the number of Romanists who are now here, and you will find that millions are missing. Where are they? You did not kill them; you did not drive them away; they did not perish as the victims of persecution. But where are they? The peaceable working of the great principles which called this Republic into existence, has gradually and silently absorbed them. True Americanism, toleration, the equality of rights, has absorbed their prejudices, and will peaceably absorb everything that is not consistent with the victorious spirit of our institutions. [Cheers.]

Oh, sir, there is a wonderful vitality in true democracy, founded upon the equality of rights. There is an inexhaustible power of resistance in that system of government, which makes the protection of individual rights a matter of common interest. If preserved in its purity, there is no warfare of opinions which can endanger it—there is no conspiracy of despotic aspirations that can destroy it. But if not preserved in its purity! There are dangers which only blindness can not see, and which only stubborn party prejudice will not see.

I have already called your attention to the despotic tendency of the slaveholding system. I need not enlarge upon it; I need not describe how the existence of slavery in the South affected and demoralized even the political life of the Free States; how they attempted to press us, you and me, into the posse of the slave-catcher by that abominable act, which, worse than the "alien and sedition laws," still disgraces our statute-book; how the ruling party, which has devoted itself to the service of that despotic interest, shrinks from no violation of good faith, from no adulteration of the constitutional compact, from no encroachment upon natural right, from no treacherous abandonment of fundamental principles. And I do not hesitate to prophesy, that if the theories engendered by the institution of slavery be suffered to outgrow the equalizing tendency of true democracy, the American Republic will, at no distant day, crumble down under the burden of the laws and measures which the ruling interest will demand for its protection, and its name will be added to the sad catalogue of the broken hopes of humanity.

But the mischief does not come from that side alone; it is in things of small beginning, but fearful in their growth. One of these is the propensity of men *to lose sight of fundamental principles, when passing abuses are to be corrected.*

Is it not wonderful how nations who have won their liberty by the severest struggles, become so easily impatient of the small inconveniences and passing difficulties, which are almost inseparably connected with the practical working of general self-government? How they so easily forget that rights may be abused, and yet remain inalienable rights? Europe has witnessed many an attempt for the establishment of democratic institutions; some of them were at first successful, and the people were free, but the abuses and inconveniences connected with liberty became at once apparent. Then the ruling classes of society, in order to get rid of the abuses, restricted liberty; they did, indeed, get rid of the abuses, but they got rid of liberty at the same time. You heard liberal governments there speak of protecting and regulating the liberty of the press; and, in order to prevent that liberty from being abused, they adopted measures, apparently harmless at first, which ultimately resulted in an absolute censorship. Would it be much better if we, recognizing the right of man to the exercise of self-government, should, in order to protect the purity of the ballot-box, restrict the right of suffrage?

Liberty, sir, is like a spirited housewife; she will have her whims, she will be somewhat unruly sometimes, and, like so many husbands, you cannot always have it all your own way. She may spoil your favorite dish sometimes; but will you, therefore, at once smash her china, break her kettles, and shut her out from the kitchen? Let her practise, let her try again and again, and even when she makes a mistake, encourage her with a benignant smile, and your broth will be right after a while. [Laughter.] But meddle with her concerns, tease her, bore her, and your little squabbles, spirited as she is, will ultimately result in a divorce. What then? It is one of Jefferson's wisest words that "he would much rather be exposed to the inconveniences arising from too much liberty, than to those arising from too small a degree of it." [Immense applause.] It is a matter of historical experience, that nothing that is wrong in principle can be right in practice. [Sensation.] People are apt to delude themselves on that point; but the ultimate result will always prove the truth of the maxim. A violation of equal rights can never serve to maintain institutions which are founded upon equal rights. [Loud applause.] A contrary policy is not only pusillanimous and small, but it is senseless. It reminds me of the soldier who, for fear of being shot in battle, committed suicide on the march; or of the man who would cut off his foot, because he had a corn on his toe. [Laughter.] It is that ridiculous policy of premature despair, which commences to throw the freight overboard when there is a suspicious cloud in the sky.

Another danger for the safety of our institutions, and perhaps the most formidable one, arises from the general propensity of political parties and public men to act on a policy of mere expediency, and to sacrifice principle to local and temporary success. [Great sensation.] And here, sir, let me address a solemn appeal to the consciences of those with whom I am proud to struggle side by side against human thraldom.

You hate kingcraft, and you would sacrifice your fortunes and your lives in order to prevent its establishment on the soil of this Republic. But let me tell you that the rule of political parties which sacrifice principle to expediency, is no less dangerous, no less disastrous, no less aggressive, of no less despotic a nature, than the rule of monarchs. Do not indulge in the delusion, that in order to make a government fair and liberal, the only thing necessary is to make it elective. When a political party in power, however liberal their principles may be, have once adopted the policy of knocking down their opponents instead of voting them down, there is an end of justice and equal rights. [Applause.] The history of the world shows no example of a more arbitrary despotism, than that exercised by the party which ruled the National Assembly of France in the bloodiest days of the great French Revolution. I will not discuss here what might have been done, and what not, in those times of a fearful crisis; but I will say that they tried to establish liberty by means of despotism, and that in her gigantic struggle against the united monarchs of Europe, revolutionary France won the victory, but lost her liberty.

Remember the shout of indignation that went all over the Northern States when we heard that the border ruffians of Kansas had crowded the free-state men away from the polls and had not allowed them to vote. That indignation was just, not only because the men who were thus terrorized were free-state men and friends of liberty, but because they were deprived of their right of suffrage, and because the government of that territory was placed on the basis of force, instead of equal rights. Sir, if ever the party of liberty should use their local predominance for the purpose of disarming their opponents instead of convincing them, they will but follow the example set by the ruffians of Kansas, although legislative enactments may be a genteeler weapon than the revolver and bowie knife.

[Cheering.] They may perhaps achieve some petty local success, they may gain some small temporary advantage, but they will help to introduce a system of action into our politics which will gradually undermine the very foundations upon which our republican edifice rests. Of all the dangers and difficulties that beset us, there is none more horrible than the hideous monster, whose name is "Proscription for opinion's sake." [Cheers, and cries of "good."] I am an anti-slavery man, and I have a right to my opinion in South Carolina just as well as in Massachusetts. My neighbor is a pro-slavery man; I may be sorry for it, but I solemnly acknowledge his right to his opinion in Massachusetts as well as in South Carolina. You tell me, that for my opinion they would mob me in South Carolina? Sir, there is the difference between South Carolina and Massachusetts. [Prolonged cheering.] There is the difference between an anti-slavery man, who is a freeman, and a slaveholder, who is himself a slave. [Continued applause.]

Our present issues will pass away. The slavery question will be settled, liberty will be triumphant, and other matters of difference will divide the political parties of this country. What if we, in our struggle against slavery, had removed the solid basis of equal rights, on which such new matters of difference may be peaceably settled? What if we had based the institutions of this country upon a difference of rights between different classes of people? What if, in destroying the generality of natural rights, we had resolved them into privileges? There is a thing which stands above the command of the most ingenious of politicians: *it is the logic of things and events.* It cannot be turned and twisted by artificial arrangements and delusive settlements; it will go its own way with the steady step of fate. It will force you, with uncompromising severity, to choose between two social organizations, one of which is founded upon privilege, and the other upon the doctrine of equal rights.

Force instead of right, privilege instead of equality, expediency instead of principle, being once the leading motives of your policy, you will have no power to stem the current. There will be new abuses to be corrected, new inconveniences to be remedied, new supposed dangers to be obviated, new equally exacting ends to be subserved, and your encroachments upon the natural rights of your opponents now, will be used as welcome precedents for the mutual oppression of parties then. Having once knowingly disregarded the doctrine of equal rights, the ruling parties will soon accustom themselves to consult only their interests where fundamental principles are at stake. Those who lead us into this channel will be like the sorcerer who knew the art of making a giant snake. And when he had made it, he forgot the charm-word that would destroy it again. And the giant snake threw its horrid coils around him, and the unfortunate man was choked to death by the monster of his own creation.

On the evening of the 2d day of November, 1855, there stood on this very platform a man, known and loved by every true son of Massachusetts, who, unmoved by the whirlwind of proscriptive movement howling around him, spoke the following words:—

"It is proposed to attaint men for their religion, and also for their birth. If this object can prevail, vain are the triumphs of civil freedom in its many hard-fought fields; vain is that religious toleration which we all profess. The fires of Smithfield, the tortures of the inquisition, the proscription of the Nonconformists, may all be revived. Slowly among the struggling sects was evolved the great idea of the equality of all men before the law, without regard to religious belief; nor can any party now organize a proscription merely for religious (and I may add political) belief, without calling in question this unquestionable principle."

The man who said so was Charles Sumner. [Long-continued applause, and three hearty cheers "for Charles Sumner."] Then the day was not far off when suddenly the whole country was startled by the incredible news, that his noble head had drooped under the murderous blows of a Southern fanatic, and that his warm blood had covered the floor of the Senate Chamber, the noblest sprinkling that ever fertilized a barren soil. [Laughter and applause.] And now I tell you, when he lay on the lounge of the ante-chamber, his anxious friends busy around him, and his cowardly murderers slinking away like Cain—if at that solemn moment the first question addressed to his slowly returning senses had been: Shall those who support your dastardly assailants with their votes be deprived of their suffrage? he would have raised his bleeding head, and with the fire of indignation kindling in his dim eye, he would have answered: "No! In the name of my country, no! For the honor of Massachusetts, no! For the sake of the principles for which my blood is flowing, no! Let them kill me, but let the rights of man be safe!" [Tremendous applause.]

Sir, if you want to bestow a high praise upon man, you are apt to say he is an old Roman. But I know a higher epithet of praise; it is—He is a true American! Aye, Charles Sumner is a true American; he is a representative of the truest Americanism, and to him I pay the tribute of my enthusiastic admiration. [Enthusiastic cheering.]

Sir, I am coming to the close of my remarks. But I cannot refrain from alluding to a circumstance which concerns myself. I understand it has been said, that in speaking a few words on the principles of Jeffersonian democracy a few evenings since, I had attempted to interfere with the home affairs of this State, and to dictate to the Republicans their policy. Ah, sir, is there a man in Massachusetts, except he be a servant of the slave-power, who cannot hear me advocate the equal rights of man, without feeling serious pangs of conscience? [Laughter.] Is there a son of this glorious old Commonwealth who cannot hear me draw logical conclusions from the Declaration of Independence—who cannot hear me speak of the natural right of man to the exercise of self-government, without feeling a blush fluttering upon his cheeks? If so, sir, I am sorry for him; it is his fault, not mine. [Loud applause.]

Interfere with your local matters! How could I? What influence could I, an humble stranger among you, exercise on the action of Massachusetts? But one thing I must tell you. It ought never to be forgotten that this old Commonwealth occupies a representative position. Her history is familiar to the nation; even South Carolina knows it. [Laughter and applause.] The nation is so accustomed to admire her glorious deeds for freedom, that with this expectation their eyes are turned upon her. Massachusetts can do nothing in secret; Massachusetts can do nothing for herself alone; every one of her acts involves a hundred-fold responsibility. What Massachusetts does is felt from the Atlantic to the Pacific. But Massachusetts need only be herself, in order to be great. This is her position among the Free States, recognised by all. Can there be a more honorable one?

Sons of Massachusetts, you may be proud of it. Do not forget that from her greatness you cannot separate your responsibility.

No, I will not meddle with your home concerns. I will, however, say a word for the West. Strenuous advocate of individual rights and of local self-government as I am, if you ever hear of any movement in the West against the integrity of the fundamental principles underlying our system of government, I invite you, I entreat you, I conjure you, come one and all, and make our prairies resound and our forests shake, and our ears ring and tingle, with your appeals for the equal rights of man. [Loud and continued cheering.]

Sir, I was to speak on Republicanism at the West, and so I did. This *is* Western republicanism. These are its principles, and I am proud to say its principles are its policy. These are the ideas which have rallied around the banner of liberty not only the natives of the soil, but an innumerable host of Germans, Scandinavians, Scotchmen, Frenchmen, and a goodly number of Irishmen, also. And here I tell you, those are mistaken who believe that the Irish heart is devoid of those noble impulses which will lead him to the side of justice, where he sees his own rights respected and unendangered. [Applause.] Under this banner, all the languages of civilized mankind are spoken, every creed is protected, every right is sacred. There stands every element of Western society, with enthusiasm for a great cause, with confidence in each other, with honor to themselves. This is the banner floating over the glorious valley which stretches from the Western slope of the Alleghanies to the Rocky Mountains—that Valley of Jehoshaphat, where the nations of the world assemble to celebrate the resurrection of human freedom. [Tremendous applause.] The inscription on that banner is not "Opposition to the Democratic party for the sake of placing a new set of men into office;" for this battle-cry of speculators our hearts have no response. Nor is it "Restriction of slavery and restriction of the right of suffrage," for this—believe my words, I entreat you—this would be the signal of deserved, inevitable and disgraceful defeat. But the inscription is "Liberty and equal rights, common to all as the air of Heaven—Liberty and equal rights, one and inseparable!" [Enthusiastic cheers.]

With this banner we stand before the world. In this sign—in

this sign alone, and no other—there is victory. And thus sir, we mean to realize the great cosmopolitan idea, upon which the existence of the American nation rests. Thus we mean to fulfill the great mission of true Americanism—thus we mean to answer the anxious question of down-trodden humanity—"Has *man* the faculty to be free and to govern himself?" The answer is a triumphant "Aye," thundering into the ears of the despots of the old world that "a man is a man for all that;" proclaiming to the oppressed that they are held in subjection on false pretences; cheering the hearts of the despondent friends of man with consolation and renewed confidence.

This is true Americanism, clasping mankind to its great heart. Under its banner we march; let the world follow. [Loud applause, and three cheers for the champion of freedom in the West.]

JOHN BROWN

Speech to the Court

Charlestown, Virginia, November 2, 1859

I HAVE, may it please the Court, a few words to say. In the first place, I deny everything but what I have all along admitted, of a design on my part to free slaves. I intended certainly to have made a clean thing of that matter, as I did last winter when I went into Missouri, and there took slaves without the snapping of a gun on either side, moving them through the country, and finally leaving them in Canada. I designed to have done the same thing again on a larger scale. That was all I intended to do. I never did intend murder or treason, or the destruction of property, or to excite or incite the slaves to rebellion, or to make insurrection. I have another objection, and that is that it is unjust that I should suffer such a penalty. Had I interfered in the manner which I admit, and which I admit has been fairly proved—for I admire the truthfulness and candor of the greater portion of the witnesses who have testified in this case—had I so interfered in behalf of the rich, the powerful, the intelligent, the so-called great, or in behalf of any of their friends, either father, mother, brother, sister, wife, or children, or any of that class, and suffered and sacrificed what I have in this interference, it would have been all right, and every man in this Court would have deemed it an act worthy of reward rather than punishment. This Court acknowledges, too, as I suppose, the validity of the law of God. I see a book kissed, which I suppose to be the Bible, or at least the New Testament, which teaches me that all things whatsoever I would that men should do to me, I should do even so to them. It teaches me further to remember them that are in bonds as bound with them. I endeavored to act up to that instruction. I say I am yet too young to understand that God is any respecter of persons. I believe that to have interfered as I have done, as I have always freely admitted I have done in behalf of His despised poor, is

678

no wrong, but right. Now, if it is deemed necessary that I should forfeit my life for the furtherance of the ends of justice, and mingle my blood further with the blood of my children and with the blood of millions in this slave country whose rights are disregarded by wicked, cruel, and unjust enactments, I say let it be done. Let me say one word further. I feel entirely satisfied with the treatment I have received on my trial. Considering all the circumstances, it has been more generous than I expected. But I feel no consciousness of guilt. I have stated from the first what was my intention, and what was not. I never had any design against the liberty of any person, nor any disposition to commit treason or excite slaves to rebel or make any general insurrection. I never encouraged any man to do so, but always discouraged any idea of that kind. Let me say also in regard to the statements made by some of those who were connected with me, I fear it has been stated by some of them that I have induced them to join me, but the contrary is true. I do not say this to injure them, but as regretting their weakness. Not one but joined me of his own accord, and the greater part at their own expense. A number of them I never saw, and never had a word of conversation with till the day they came to me, and that was for the purpose I have stated. Now, I am done.

ABRAHAM LINCOLN

Address at Cooper Institute

New York City, February 27, 1860

M R. PRESIDENT AND FELLOW-CITIZENS OF NEW-YORK:—
The facts with which I shall deal this evening are mainly old and familiar; nor is there anything new in the general use I shall make of them. If there shall be any novelty, it will be in the mode of presenting the facts, and the inferences and observations following that presentation.

In his speech last autumn, at Columbus, Ohio, as reported in "The New-York Times," Senator Douglas said:

"Our fathers, when they framed the Government under which we live, understood this question just as well, and even better, than we do now."

I fully indorse this, and I adopt it as a text for this discourse. I so adopt it because it furnishes a precise and an agreed starting point for a discussion between Republicans and that wing of the Democracy headed by Senator Douglas. It simply leaves the inquiry: *"What was the understanding those fathers had of the question mentioned?"*

What is the frame of Government under which we live?

The answer must be: "The Constitution of the United States." That Constitution consists of the original, framed in 1787, (and under which the present government first went into operation,) and twelve subsequently framed amendments, the first ten of which were framed in 1789.

Who were our fathers that framed the Constitution? I suppose the "thirty-nine" who signed the original instrument may be fairly called our fathers who framed that part of the present Government. It is almost exactly true to say they framed it, and it is altogether true to say they fairly represented the opinion and sentiment of the whole nation at that time. Their names, being familiar to nearly all, and accessible to quite all, need not now be repeated.

I take these "thirty-nine" for the present, as being "our fathers who framed the Government under which we live."

What is the question which, according to the text, those fathers understood "just as well, and even better than we do now?"

It is this: Does the proper division of local from federal authority, or anything in the Constitution, forbid *our Federal Government* to control as to slavery in *our Federal Territories?*

Upon this, Senator Douglas holds the affirmative, and Republicans the negative. This affirmation and denial form an issue; and this issue—this question—is precisely what the text declares our fathers understood "better than we."

Let us now inquire whether the "thirty-nine," or any of them, ever acted upon this question; and if they did, how they acted upon it—how they expressed that better understanding?

In 1784, three years before the Constitution—the United States then owning the Northwestern Territory, and no other, the Congress of the Confederation had before them the question of prohibiting slavery in that Territory; and four of the "thirty-nine," who afterward framed the Constitution, were in that Congress, and voted on that question. Of these, Roger Sherman, Thomas Mifflin, and Hugh Williamson voted for the prohibition, thus showing that, in their understanding, no line dividing local from federal authority, nor anything else, properly forbade the Federal Government to control as to slavery in federal territory. The other of the four—James M'Henry—voted against the prohibition, showing that, for some cause, he thought it improper to vote for it.

In 1787, still before the Constitution, but while the Convention was in session framing it, and while the Northwestern Territory still was the only territory owned by the United States, the same question of prohibiting slavery in the territory again came before the Congress of the Confederation; and two more of the "thirty-nine" who afterward signed the Constitution, were in that Congress, and voted on the question. They were William Blount and William Few; and they both voted for the prohibition—thus showing that, in their understanding, no line dividing local from federal authority, nor anything else, properly forbade the Federal Government to control as to slavery in federal territory. This time the prohibition became a law, being part of what is now well known as the Ordinance of '87.

The question of federal control of slavery in the territories, seems not to have been directly before the Convention which framed the original Constitution; and hence it is not recorded that the "thirty-nine," or any of them, while engaged on that instrument, expressed any opinion of that precise question.

In 1789, by the first Congress which sat under the Constitution, an act was passed to enforce the Ordinance of '87, including the prohibition of slavery in the Northwestern Territory. The bill for this act was reported by one of the "thirty-nine," Thomas Fitzsimmons, then a member of the House of Representatives from Pennsylvania. It went through all its stages without a word of opposition, and finally passed both branches without yeas and nays, which is equivalent to an unanimous passage. In this Congress there were sixteen of the thirty-nine fathers who framed the original Constitution. They were John Langdon, Nicholas Gilman, Wm. S. Johnson, Roger Sherman, Robert Morris, Thos. Fitzsimmons, William Few, Abraham Baldwin, Rufus King, William Paterson, George Clymer, Richard Bassett, George Read, Pierce Butler, Daniel Carroll, James Madison.

This shows that, in their understanding, no line dividing local from federal authority, nor anything in the Constitution, properly forbade Congress to prohibit slavery in the federal territory; else both their fidelity to correct principle, and their oath to support the Constitution, would have constrained them to oppose the prohibition.

Again, George Washington, another of the "thirty-nine," was then President of the United States, and, as such, approved and signed the bill; thus completing its validity as a law, and thus showing that, in his understanding, no line dividing local from federal authority, nor anything in the Constitution, forbade the Federal Government, to control as to slavery in federal territory.

No great while after the adoption of the original Constitution, North Carolina ceded to the Federal Government the country now constituting the State of Tennessee; and a few years later Georgia ceded that which now constitutes the States of Mississippi and Alabama. In both deeds of cession it was made a condition by the ceding States that the Federal Government should not prohibit slavery in the ceded country. Besides this, slavery was then actually in the ceded country. Under these circumstances, Congress, on taking charge of these countries, did not absolutely prohibit slavery within them. But they did interfere with it—take control of it—even there, to a certain extent. In 1798, Congress organized the Territory of Mississippi. In the act of organization, they prohibited the bringing of slaves into the Territory, from any place without the United States, by fine, and giving freedom to slaves so brought. This act passed both branches of Congress without yeas and nays. In that Congress were three of the "thirty-nine" who framed the original Constitution. They were John Langdon, George Read and Abraham Baldwin. They all, probably, voted for it. Certainly they would have placed their opposition to it upon record, if, in their understanding, any line dividing local from federal authority, or anything in the Constitution, properly forbade the Federal Government to control as to slavery in federal territory.

In 1803, the Federal Government purchased the Louisiana country. Our former territorial acquisitions came from certain of our own States; but this Louisiana country was acquired from a foreign nation. In 1804, Congress gave a territorial organization to that part of it which now constitutes the State of Louisiana. New Orleans, lying within that part, was an old and comparatively large city. There were other considerable towns and settlements, and slavery was extensively and thoroughly intermingled with the people. Congress did not, in the Territorial Act, prohibit slavery; but they did interfere with it—take control of it—in a more marked and extensive way than they did in the case of Mississippi. The substance of the provision therein made, in relation to slaves, was:

First. That no slave should be imported into the territory from foreign parts.

Second. That no slave should be carried into it who had been imported into the United States since the first day of May, 1798.

Third. That no slave should be carried into it, except by the owner, and for his own use as a settler; the penalty in all the cases being a fine upon the violator of the law, and freedom to the slave.

This act also was passed without yeas and nays. In the Congress which passed it, there were two of the "thirty-nine." They were Abraham Baldwin and Jonathan Dayton. As stated in the case of Mississippi, it is probable they both voted for it. They would not have allowed it to pass without recording their opposition to it, if, in their understanding, it violated either the line properly dividing local from federal authority, or any provision of the Constitution.

In 1819–20, came and passed the Missouri question. Many votes were taken, by yeas and nays, in both branches of Congress, upon the various phases of the general question. Two of the "thirty-nine"—Rufus King and Charles Pinckney—were members of that Congress. Mr. King steadily voted for slavery prohibition and against all compromises, while Mr. Pinckney as steadily voted against slavery prohibition and against all compromises. By this, Mr. King showed that, in his understanding, no line dividing local from federal authority, nor anything in the Constitution, was violated by Congress prohibiting slavery in federal territory; while Mr. Pinckney, by his votes, showed that, in his understanding, there was some sufficient reason for opposing such prohibition in that case.

The cases I have mentioned are the only acts of the "thirty-nine," or of any of them, upon the direct issue, which I have been able to discover.

To enumerate the persons who thus acted, as being four in 1784, two in 1787, seventeen in 1789, three in 1798, two in 1804, and two in 1819–20—there would be thirty of them. But this would be counting John Langdon, Roger Sherman, William Few, Rufus King, and George Read, each twice, and Abraham Baldwin, three times. The true number of those of the "thirty-nine" whom I have shown to have acted upon the question, which, by the text, they understood better than we, is twenty-three, leaving sixteen not shown to have acted upon it in any way.

Here, then, we have twenty-three out of our thirty-nine fathers "who framed the Government under which we live," who have, upon their official responsibility and their corporal oaths, acted upon the very question which the text affirms they "understood just as well, and even better than we do now;" and twenty-one of them—a clear majority of the whole "thirty-nine"—so acting upon it as to make them guilty of gross political impropriety and wilful perjury, if, in their understanding, any proper division between local and federal authority, or anything in the Constitution they had made themselves, and sworn to support, forbade the Federal Government to control as to slavery in the federal territories. Thus the twenty-one acted; and, as actions speak louder than words, so actions, under such responsibility, speak still louder.

Two of the twenty-three voted against Congressional prohibition of slavery in the federal territories, in the instances in which they acted upon the question. But for what reasons they so voted is not known. They may have done so because they thought a proper division of local from federal authority, or some provision or principle of the Constitution, stood in the way; or they may, without any such question, have voted against the prohibition, on what appeared to them to be sufficient grounds of expediency. No one who has sworn to support the Constitution, can conscientiously vote for what he understands to be an unconstitutional measure, however expedient he may think it; but one may and ought to vote against a measure which he deems constitutional, if, at the same time, he deems it inexpedient. It, therefore, would be unsafe to set down even the two who voted against the prohibition, as having done so because, in their understanding, any proper division of local from federal authority, or anything in the Constitution, forbade the Federal Government to control as to slavery in federal territory.

The remaining sixteen of the "thirty-nine," so far as I have discovered, have left no record of their understanding upon the direct question of federal control of slavery in the federal territories. But there is much reason to believe that their understanding upon that question would not have appeared different from that of their twenty-three compeers, had it been manifested at all.

For the purpose of adhering rigidly to the text, I have purposely omitted whatever understanding may have been manifested by any person, however distinguished, other than the thirty-nine fathers who framed the original Constitution; and, for the same reason, I have also omitted whatever understanding may have been manifested by any of the "thirty-nine" even, on any other phase of the general question of slavery. If we should look into their acts and declarations on those other phases, as the foreign slave trade, and the morality and policy of slavery generally, it would appear to us that on the direct question of federal control of slavery in federal territories, the sixteen, if they had acted at all, would probably have acted just as the twenty-three did. Among that sixteen were several of the most noted anti-slavery men of those times—as Dr. Franklin, Alexander Hamilton and Gouverneur Morris—while there was not one now known to have been otherwise, unless it may be John Rutledge, of South Carolina.

The sum of the whole is, that of our thirty-nine fathers who framed the original Constitution, twenty-one—a clear majority of the whole—certainly understood that no proper division of local from federal authority, nor any part of the Constitution, forbade the Federal Government to control slavery in the federal territories; while all the rest probably had the same understanding. Such, unquestionably, was the understanding of our fathers who framed the original Constitution; and the text affirms that they understood the question "better than we."

But, so far, I have been considering the understanding of the question manifested by the framers of the original Constitution. In and by the original instrument, a mode was provided for amending it; and, as I have already stated, the present frame of "the Government under which we live" consists of that original, and twelve amendatory articles framed and adopted since. Those who now insist that federal control of slavery in federal territories violates the Constitution, point us to the provisions which they suppose it thus violates; and, as I understand, they all fix upon provisions in these amendatory articles, and not in the original instrument. The Supreme Court, in the Dred Scott case, plant themselves upon the fifth amendment, which provides that no person shall be deprived of "life, liberty or property without due process of law;" while Senator Douglas and his peculiar adherents plant themselves upon the tenth amendment, providing that "the powers not delegated to the United States by the Constitution," "are reserved to the States respectively, or to the people."

Now, it so happens that these amendments were framed by the first Congress which sat under the Constitution—the identical Congress which passed the act already mentioned, enforcing the prohibition of slavery in the Northwestern Territory. Not only was it the same Congress, but they were the identical, same individual men who, at the same session, and at the same time within the session, had under consideration, and in progress toward maturity, these Constitutional amendments, and this act prohibiting slavery in all the territory the nation then owned. The Constitutional amendments were introduced before, and passed after the act enforcing the Ordinance of '87; so that, during the whole pendency of the act to enforce the Ordinance, the Constitutional amendments were also pending.

The seventy-six members of that Congress, including sixteen of the framers of the original Constitution, as before stated, were preeminently our fathers who framed that part of "the Government under which we live," which is now claimed as forbidding the Federal Government to control slavery in the federal territories.

Is it not a little presumptuous in any one at this day to affirm that the two things which that Congress deliberately framed, and carried to maturity at the same time, are absolutely inconsistent with each other? And does not such affirmation become impudently absurd when coupled with the other affirmation from the same mouth, that those who did the two things, alleged to be inconsistent, understood whether they really were inconsistent better than we—better than he who affirms that they are inconsistent?

It is surely safe to assume that the thirty-nine framers of the original Constitution, and the seventy-six members of the Congress which framed the amendments thereto, taken together, do certainly include those who may be fairly called "our fathers who framed the Government under which we live." And so assuming, I defy any man to show that any one of them ever, in his whole life, declared that, in his understanding, any proper division of local from federal authority, or any part of the Constitution, forbade the Federal Government to control as to slavery in the federal territories. I go a step further. I defy any one to show that any living man in the whole world ever did, prior to the beginning of the present century, (and I might almost say prior to the beginning of the last half of the present century,) declare that, in his understanding, any proper division of local from federal authority, or any part of the Constitution, forbade the Federal Government to control as to slavery in the federal territories. To those who now so declare, I give, not only "our fathers who framed the Government under which we live," but with them all other living men within the century in which it was framed, among whom to search, and they shall not be able to find the evidence of a single man agreeing with them.

Now, and here, let me guard a little against being misunderstood. I do not mean to say we are bound to follow implicitly in whatever our fathers did. To do so, would be to discard all the lights of current experience—to reject all progress—all improvement. What I do say is, that if we would supplant the opinions and policy of our fathers in any case, we should do so upon evidence so conclusive, and argument so clear, that even their great authority, fairly considered and weighed, cannot stand; and most surely not in a case whereof we ourselves declare they understood the question better than we.

If any man at this day sincerely believes that a proper division of local from federal authority, or any part of the Constitution, forbids the Federal Government to control as to slavery in the federal territories, he is right to say so, and to enforce his position by all truthful evidence and fair argument which he can. But he has no right to mislead others, who have less access to history, and less leisure to study it, into the false belief that "our fathers, who framed the Government under which we live," were of the same opinion—thus substituting falsehood and deception for truthful evidence and fair argument. If any man at this day sincerely believes "our fathers who framed the Government under which we live," used and applied principles, in other cases, which ought to have led them to understand that a proper division of local from federal authority or some part of the Constitution, forbids the Federal Government to control as to slavery in the federal territories, he is right to say so. But he should, at the same time, brave the responsibility of declaring that, in his opinion, he understands their principles better than they did themselves; and especially should he not shirk that responsibility by asserting that they "understood the question just as well, and even better, than we do now."

But enough! *Let all who believe that "our fathers, who framed the Government under which we live, understood this question just as well, and even better, than we do now," speak as they spoke, and act as they acted upon it. This is all Republicans ask— all Republicans desire—in relation to slavery. As those fathers marked it, so let it be again marked, as an evil not to be extended, but to be tolerated and protected only because of and so far as its actual presence among us makes that toleration and protection a necessity. Let all the guaranties those fathers gave it, be, not grudgingly, but fully and fairly maintained.* For this Republicans contend, and with this, so far as I know or believe, they will be content.

And now, if they would listen—as I suppose they will not—I would address a few words to the Southern people.

I would say to them:—You consider yourselves a reasonable and a just people; and I consider that in the general qualities of reason and justice you are not inferior to any other people. Still, when you speak of us Republicans, you do so only to denounce us as reptiles, or, at the best, as no better than outlaws. You will grant a hearing to pirates or murderers, but nothing like it to "Black Republicans." In all your contentions with one another, each of you deems an unconditional condemnation of "Black Republicanism" as the first thing to be attended to. Indeed, such condemnation of us seems to be an indispensable prerequisite—license, so to speak—among you to be admitted or permitted to speak at all. Now, can you, or not, be prevailed upon to pause and to consider whether this is quite just to us, or even to yourselves? Bring forward your charges and specifications, and then be patient long enough to hear us deny or justify.

You say we are sectional. We deny it. That makes an issue; and the burden of proof is upon you. You produce your proof; and what is it? Why, that our party has no existence in your section—gets no votes in your section. The fact is substantially true; but does it prove the issue? If it does, then in case we should, without change of principle, begin to get votes in your section, we should thereby cease to be sectional. You cannot escape this conclusion; and yet, are you willing to abide by it? If you are, you will probably soon find that we have ceased to be sectional, for we shall get votes in your section this very year. You will then begin to discover, as the truth plainly is, that your proof does not touch the issue. The fact that we get no votes in your section, is a fact of your making, and not of ours. And if there be fault in that fact, that fault is primarily yours, and remains so until you show that we repel you by some wrong principle or practice. If we do repel you by any wrong principle or practice, the fault is ours; but this brings you to where you ought to have started—to a discussion of the right or wrong of our principle. If our principle, put in practice, would wrong your section for the benefit of ours, or for any other object, then our principle, and we with it, are sectional, and are justly opposed and denounced as such. Meet us, then, on the question of whether our principle, put in practice, would wrong your section; and so meet us as if it were possible that something may be said on our side. Do you accept the challenge? No! Then you really believe that the principle which "our fathers who framed the Government under which we live" thought so clearly right as to adopt it, and indorse it again and again, upon their official oaths, is in fact so clearly wrong as to demand your condemnation without a moment's consideration.

Some of you delight to flaunt in our faces the warning against sectional parties given by Washington in his Farewell Address. Less than eight years before Washington gave that warning, he had, as President of the United States, approved and signed an act of Congress, enforcing the prohibition of slavery in the Northwestern Territory, which act embodied the policy of the Government upon that subject up to and at the very moment he penned that warning; and about one year after he penned it, he wrote La Fayette that he considered that prohibition a wise measure, expressing in the same connection his hope that we should at some time have a confederacy of free States.

Bearing this in mind, and seeing that sectionalism has since arisen upon this same subject, is that warning a weapon in your hands against us, or in our hands against you? Could Washington himself speak, would he cast the blame of that sectionalism upon us, who sustain his policy, or upon you who repudiate it? We respect that warning of Washington, and we commend it to you, together with his example pointing to the right application of it.

But you say you are conservative—eminently conservative—

while we are revolutionary, destructive, or something of the sort. What is conservatism? Is it not adherence to the old and tried, against the new and untried? We stick to, contend for, the identical old policy on the point in controversy which was adopted by "our fathers who framed the Government under which we live;" while you with one accord reject, and scout, and spit upon that old policy, and insist upon substituting something new. True, you disagree among yourselves as to what that substitute shall be. You are divided on new propositions and plans, but you are unanimous in rejecting and denouncing the old policy of the fathers. Some of you are for reviving the foreign slave trade; some for a Congressional Slave-Code for the Territories; some for Congress forbidding the Territories to prohibit Slavery within their limits; some for maintaining Slavery in the Territories through the judiciary; some for the "gur-reat pur-rinciple" that "if one man would enslave another, no third man should object," fantastically called "Popular Sovereignty;" but never a man among you in favor of federal prohibition of slavery in federal territories, according to the practice of "our fathers who framed the Government under which we live." Not one of all your various plans can show a precedent or an advocate in the century within which our Government originated. Consider, then, whether your claim of conservatism for yourselves, and your charge of destructiveness against us, are based on the most clear and stable foundations.

Again, you say we have made the slavery question more prominent than it formerly was. We deny it. We admit that it is more prominent, but we deny that we made it so. It was not we, but you, who discarded the old policy of the fathers. We resisted, and still resist, your innovation; and thence comes the greater prominence of the question. Would you have that question reduced to its former proportions? Go back to that old policy. What has been will be again, under the same conditions. If you would have the peace of the old times, readopt the precepts and policy of the old times.

You charge that we stir up insurrections among your slaves. We deny it; and what is your proof? Harper's Ferry! John Brown!! John Brown was no Republican; and you have failed to implicate a single Republican in his Harper's Ferry enterprise.

If any member of our party is guilty in that matter, you know it or you do not know it. If you do know it, you are inexcusable for not designating the man and proving the fact. If you do not know it, you are inexcusable for asserting it, and especially for persisting in the assertion after you have tried and failed to make the proof. You need not be told that persisting in a charge which one does not know to be true, is simply malicious slander.

Some of you admit that no Republican designedly aided or encouraged the Harper's Ferry affair; but still insist that our doctrines and declarations necessarily lead to such results. We do not believe it. We know we hold to no doctrine, and make no declaration, which were not held to and made by "our fathers who framed the Government under which we live." You never dealt fairly by us in relation to this affair. When it occurred, some important State elections were near at hand, and you were in evident glee with the belief that, by charging the blame upon us, you could get an advantage of us in those elections. The elections came, and your expectations were not quite fulfilled. Every Republican man knew that, as to himself at least, your charge was a slander, and he was not much inclined by it to cast his vote in your favor. Republican doctrines and declarations are accompanied with a continual protest against any interference whatever with your slaves, or with you about your slaves. Surely, this does not encourage them to revolt. True, we do, in common with "our fathers, who framed the Government under which we live," declare our belief that slavery is wrong; but the slaves do not hear us declare even this. For anything we say or do, the slaves would scarcely know there is a Republican party. I believe they would not, in fact, generally know it but for your misrepresentations of us, in their hearing. In your political contests among yourselves, each faction charges the other with sympathy with Black Republicanism; and then, to give point to the charge, defines Black Republicanism to simply be insurrection, blood and thunder among the slaves.

Slave insurrections are no more common now than they were before the Republican party was organized. What induced the Southampton insurrection, twenty-eight years ago, in which, at least, three times as many lives were lost as at Harper's

Ferry? You can scarcely stretch your very elastic fancy to the conclusion that Southampton was "got up by Black Republicanism." In the present state of things in the United States, I do not think a general, or even a very extensive slave insurrection, is possible. The indispensable concert of action cannot be attained. The slaves have no means of rapid communication; nor can incendiary freemen, black or white, supply it. The explosive materials are everywhere in parcels; but there neither are, nor can be supplied, the indispensable connecting trains.

Much is said by Southern people about the affection of slaves for their masters and mistresses; and a part of it, at least, is true. A plot for an uprising could scarcely be devised and communicated to twenty individuals before some one of them, to save the life of a favorite master or mistress, would divulge it. This is the rule; and the slave revolution in Hayti was not an exception to it, but a case occurring under peculiar circumstances. The gunpowder plot of British history, though not connected with slaves, was more in point. In that case, only about twenty were admitted to the secret; and yet one of them, in his anxiety to save a friend, betrayed the plot to that friend, and, by consequence, averted the calamity. Occasional poisonings from the kitchen, and open or stealthy assassinations in the field, and local revolts extending to a score or so, will continue to occur as the natural results of slavery; but no general insurrection of slaves, as I think, can happen in this country for a long time. Whoever much fears, or much hopes for such an event, will be alike disappointed.

In the language of Mr. Jefferson, uttered many years ago, "It is still in our power to direct the process of emancipation, and deportation, peaceably, and in such slow degrees, as that the evil will wear off insensibly; and their places be, *pari passu*, filled up by free white laborers. If, on the contrary, it is left to force itself on, human nature must shudder at the prospect held up."

Mr. Jefferson did not mean to say, nor do I, that the power of emancipation is in the Federal Government. He spoke of Virginia; and, as to the power of emancipation, I speak of the slaveholding States only. The Federal Government, however, as we insist, has the power of restraining the extension of the institution—the power to insure that a slave insurrection shall never occur on any American soil which is now free from slavery.

John Brown's effort was peculiar. It was not a slave insurrection. It was an attempt by white men to get up a revolt among slaves, in which the slaves refused to participate. In fact, it was so absurd that the slaves, with all their ignorance, saw plainly enough it could not succeed. That affair, in its philosophy, corresponds with the many attempts, related in history, at the assassination of kings and emperors. An enthusiast broods over the oppression of a people till he fancies himself commissioned by Heaven to liberate them. He ventures the attempt, which ends in little else than his own execution. Orsini's attempt on Louis Napoleon, and John Brown's attempt at Harper's Ferry were, in their philosophy, precisely the same. The eagerness to cast blame on old England in the one case, and on New England in the other, does not disprove the sameness of the two things.

And how much would it avail you, if you could, by the use of John Brown, Helper's Book, and the like, break up the Republican organization? Human action can be modified to some extent, but human nature cannot be changed. There is a judgment and a feeling against slavery in this nation, which cast at least a million and a half of votes. You cannot destroy that judgment and feeling—that sentiment—by breaking up the political organization which rallies around it. You can scarcely scatter and disperse an army which has been formed into order in the face of your heaviest fire; but if you could, how much would you gain by forcing the sentiment which created it out of the peaceful channel of the ballot-box, into some other channel? What would that other channel probably be? Would the number of John Browns be lessened or enlarged by the operation?

But you will break up the Union rather than submit to a denial of your Constitutional rights.

That has a somewhat reckless sound; but it would be palliated, if not fully justified, were we proposing, by the mere force of numbers, to deprive you of some right, plainly written down in the Constitution. But we are proposing no such thing.

When you make these declarations, you have a specific and

well-understood allusion to an assumed Constitutional right of yours, to take slaves into the federal territories, and to hold them there as property. But no such right is specifically written in the Constitution. That instrument is literally silent about any such right. We, on the contrary, deny that such a right has any existence in the Constitution, even by implication.

Your purpose, then, plainly stated, is, that you will destroy the Government, unless you be allowed to construe and enforce the Constitution as you please, on all points in dispute between you and us. You will rule or ruin in all events.

This, plainly stated, is your language. Perhaps you will say the Supreme Court has decided the disputed Constitutional question in your favor. Not quite so. But waiving the lawyer's distinction between dictum and decision, the Court have decided the question for you in a sort of way. The Court have substantially said, it is your Constitutional right to take slaves into the federal territories, and to hold them there as property. When I say the decision was made in a sort of way, I mean it was made in a divided Court, by a bare majority of the Judges, and they not quite agreeing with one another in the reasons for making it; that it is so made as that its avowed supporters disagree with one another about its meaning, and that it was mainly based upon a mistaken statement of fact—the statement in the opinion that "the right of property in a slave is distinctly and expressly affirmed in the Constitution."

An inspection of the Constitution will show that the right of property in a slave is not "*distinctly* and *expressly* affirmed" in it. Bear in mind, the Judges do not pledge their judicial opinion that such right is *impliedly* affirmed in the Constitution; but they pledge their veracity that it is "*distinctly* and *expressly*" affirmed there—"distinctly," that is, not mingled with anything else—"expressly," that is, in words meaning just that, without the aid of any inference, and susceptible of no other meaning.

If they had only pledged their judicial opinion that such right is affirmed in the instrument by implication, it would be open to others to show that neither the word "slave" nor "slavery" is to be found in the Constitution, nor the word "property" even, in any connection with language alluding to the things slave, or slavery, and that wherever in that instrument the slave is alluded to, he is called a "person;"—and wherever his master's legal right in relation to him is alluded to, it is spoken of as "service or labor which may be due,"—as a debt payable in service or labor. Also, it would be open to show, by contemporaneous history, that this mode of alluding to slaves and slavery, instead of speaking of them, was employed on purpose to exclude from the Constitution the idea that there could be property in man.

To show all this, is easy and certain.

When this obvious mistake of the Judges shall be brought to their notice, is it not reasonable to expect that they will withdraw the mistaken statement, and reconsider the conclusion based upon it?

And then it is to be remembered that "our fathers, who framed the Government under which we live"—the men who made the Constitution—decided this same Constitutional question in our favor, long ago—decided it without division among themselves, when making the decision; without division among themselves about the meaning of it after it was made, and, so far as any evidence is left, without basing it upon any mistaken statement of facts.

Under all these circumstances, do you really feel yourselves justified to break up this Government, unless such a court decision as yours is, shall be at once submitted to as a conclusive and final rule of political action? But you will not abide the election of a Republican President! In that supposed event, you say, you will destroy the Union; and then, you say, the great crime of having destroyed it will be upon us! That is cool. A highwayman holds a pistol to my ear, and mutters through his teeth, "Stand and deliver, or I shall kill you, and then you will be a murderer!"

To be sure, what the robber demanded of me—my money—was my own; and I had a clear right to keep it; but it was no more my own than my vote is my own; and the threat of death to me, to extort my money, and the threat of destruction to the Union, to extort my vote, can scarcely be distinguished in principle.

A few words now to Republicans. *It is exceedingly desirable that all parts of this great Confederacy shall be at peace, and in harmony, one with another. Let us Republicans do our part to have it so. Even though much provoked, let us do nothing through passion and ill temper. Even though the southern people will not so much as listen to us, let us calmly consider their demands, and yield to them if, in our deliberate view of our duty, we possibly can.* Judging by all they say and do, and by the subject and nature of their controversy with us, let us determine, if we can, what will satisfy them.

Will they be satisfied if the Territories be unconditionally surrendered to them? We know they will not. In all their present complaints against us, the Territories are scarcely mentioned. Invasions and insurrections are the rage now. Will it satisfy them, if, in the future, we have nothing to do with invasions and insurrections? We know it will not. We so know, because we know we never had anything to do with invasions and insurrections; and yet this total abstaining does not exempt us from the charge and the denunciation.

The question recurs, what will satisfy them? Simply this: We must not only let them alone, but we must, somehow, convince them that we do let them alone. This, we know by experience, is no easy task. We have been so trying to convince them from the very beginning of our organization, but with no success. In all our platforms and speeches we have constantly protested our purpose to let them alone; but this has had no tendency to convince them. Alike unavailing to convince them, is the fact that they have never detected a man of us in any attempt to disturb them.

These natural, and apparently adequate means all failing, what will convince them? This, and this only: cease to call slavery *wrong*, and join them in calling it *right*. And this must be done thoroughly—done in *acts* as well as in *words*. Silence will not be tolerated—we must place ourselves avowedly with them. Senator Douglas's new sedition law must be enacted and enforced, suppressing all declarations that slavery is wrong, whether made in politics, in presses, in pulpits, or in private. We must arrest and return their fugitive slaves with greedy pleasure. We must pull down our Free State constitutions. The whole atmosphere must be disinfected from all taint of opposition to slavery, before they will cease to believe that all their troubles proceed from us.

I am quite aware they do not state their case precisely in this way. Most of them would probably say to us, "Let us alone, *do* nothing to us, and *say* what you please about slavery." But we do let them alone—have never disturbed them—so that, after all, it is what we say, which dissatisfies them. They will continue to accuse us of doing, until we cease saying.

I am also aware they have not, as yet, in terms, demanded the overthrow of our Free-State Constitutions. Yet those Constitutions declare the wrong of slavery, with more solemn emphasis, than do all other sayings against it; and when all these other sayings shall have been silenced, the overthrow of these Constitutions will be demanded, and nothing be left to resist the demand. It is nothing to the contrary, that they do not demand the whole of this just now. Demanding what they do, and for the reason they do, they can voluntarily stop nowhere short of this consummation. Holding, as they do, that slavery is morally right, and socially elevating, they cannot cease to demand a full national recognition of it, as a legal right, and a social blessing.

Nor can we justifiably withhold this, on any ground save our conviction that slavery is wrong. If slavery is right, all words, acts, laws, and constitutions against it, are themselves wrong, and should be silenced, and swept away. If it is right, we cannot justly object to its nationality—its universality; if it is wrong, they cannot justly insist upon its extension—its enlargement. All they ask, we could readily grant, if we thought slavery right; all we ask, they could as readily grant, if they thought it wrong. Their thinking it right, and our thinking it wrong, is the precise fact upon which depends the whole controversy. Thinking it right, as they do, they are not to blame for desiring its full recognition, as being right; but, thinking it wrong, as we do, can we yield to them? Can we cast our votes with their view, and against our own? In view of our moral, social, and political responsibilities, can we do this?

Wrong as we think slavery is, we can yet afford to let it alone where it is, because that much is due to the necessity arising from its actual presence in the nation; but can we, while our votes will prevent it, allow it to spread into the National Territories, and to overrun us here in these Free States? If our sense of duty forbids this, then let us stand by our duty, fearlessly and effectively. Let us be diverted by none of those sophistical contrivances wherewith we are so industriously plied and belabored—contrivances such as groping for some middle ground between the right and the wrong, vain as the search for a man who should be neither a living man nor a dead man—such as a policy of "don't care" on a question about which all true men do care—such as Union appeals beseeching true Union men to yield to Disunionists, reversing the divine rule, and calling, not the sinners, but the righteous to repentance—such as invocations to Washington, imploring men to unsay what Washington said, and undo what Washington did.

Neither let us be slandered from our duty by false accusations against us, nor frightened from it by menaces of destruction to the Government nor of dungeons to ourselves. LET US HAVE FAITH THAT RIGHT MAKES MIGHT, AND IN THAT FAITH, LET US, TO THE END, DARE TO DO OUR DUTY AS WE UNDERSTAND IT.

JEFFERSON DAVIS

Farewell Address in the Senate

Washington, D.C., January 21, 1861

I RISE, Mr. President, for the purpose of announcing to the Senate that I have satisfactory evidence that the State of Mississippi, by a solemn ordinance of her people in convention assembled, has declared her separation from the United States. Under these circumstances, of course my functions are terminated here. It has seemed to me proper, however, that I should appear in the Senate to announce that fact to my associates, and I will say but very little more. The occasion does not invite me to go into argument; and my physical condition would not permit me to do so if it were otherwise; and yet it seems to become me to say something on the part of the State I here represent, on an occasion so solemn as this.

It is known to Senators who have served with me here, that I have for many years advocated, as an essential attribute of State sovereignty, the right of a State to secede from the Union. Therefore, if I had not believed there was justifiable cause; if I had thought that Mississippi was acting without sufficient provocation, or without an existing necessity, I should still, under my theory of the Government, because of my allegiance to the State of which I am a citizen, have been bound by her action. I, however, may be permitted to say that I do think she has justifiable cause, and I approve of her act. I conferred with her people before that act was taken, counseled them then that if the state of things which they apprehended should exist when the convention met, they should take the action which they have now adopted.

I hope none who hear me will confound this expression of mine with the advocacy of the right of a State to remain in the Union, and to disregard its constitutional obligations by the nullification of the law. Such is not my theory. Nullification and secession, so often confounded, are indeed antagonistic principles. Nullification is a remedy which it is sought to apply within the Union, and against the agent of the States. It is only to be justified when the agent has violated his constitutional obligation, and a State, assuming to judge for itself, denies the right of the agent thus to act, and appeals to the other States of the Union for a decision; but when the States themselves, and when the people of the States, have so acted as to convince us that they will not regard our constitutional rights, then, and then for the first time, arises the doctrine of secession in its practical application.

A great man who now reposes with his fathers, and who has been often arraigned for a want of fealty to the Union, advocated the doctrine of nullification, because it preserved the Union. It was because of his deep-seated attachment to the Union, his determination to find some remedy for existing ills short of a severance of the ties which bound South Carolina to the other States, that Mr. Calhoun advocated the doctrine of nullification, which he proclaimed to be peaceful, to be within the limits of State power, not to disturb the Union, but only to be a means of bringing the agent before the tribunal of the States for their judgment.

Secession belongs to a different class of remedies. It is to be justified upon the basis that the States are sovereign. There was a time when none denied it. I hope the time may come again, when a better comprehension of the theory of our Government, and the inalienable rights of the people of the States, will prevent any one from denying that each State is a sovereign, and thus may reclaim the grants which it has made to any agent whomsoever.

I therefore say I concur in the action of the people of Mississippi, believing it to be necessary and proper, and should have been bound by their action if my belief had been otherwise; and this brings me to the important point which I wish on this last occasion to present to the Senate. It is by this confounding of nullification and secession that the name of a great man, whose ashes now mingle with his mother earth, has been invoked to justify coercion against a seceded State. The phrase "to execute the laws," was an expression which General Jackson applied to the case of a State refusing to obey the laws while yet a member of the Union. That is not the case which is now presented. The laws are to be executed over the United States, and upon the people of the United States. They have no relation to any foreign country. It is a perversion of terms, at least it is a great misapprehension of the case, which cites that expression for application to a State which has withdrawn from the Union. You may make war on a foreign State. If it be the purpose of gentlemen, they may make war against a State which has withdrawn from the Union; but there are no laws of the United States to be executed within the limits of a seceded State. A State finding herself in the condition in which Mississippi has judged she is, in which her safety requires that she should provide for the maintenance of her rights out of the Union, surrenders all the benefits, (and they are known to be many,) deprives herself of the advantages, (they are known to be great,) severs all the ties of affection, (and they are close and enduring,) which have bound her to the Union; and thus divesting herself of every benefit, taking upon herself every burden, she claims to be exempt from any power to execute the laws of the United States within her limits.

I well remember an occasion when Massachusetts was arraigned before the bar of the Senate, and when then the doctrine of coercion was rife and to be applied against her because of the rescue of a fugitive slave in Boston. My opinion then was the same that it is now. Not in a spirit of egotism, but to show that I am not influenced in my opinion because the case is my own, I refer to that time and that occasion as containing the opinion which I then entertained, and on which my present conduct is based. I then said, if Massachusetts, following her through a stated line of conduct, chooses to take the last step which separates her from the Union, it is her right to go, and I will neither vote one dollar nor one man to coerce her back; but will say to her, God speed, in memory of the kind associations which once existed between her and the other States.

It has been a conviction of pressing necessity, it has been a belief that we are to be deprived in the Union of the rights which our fathers bequeathed to us, which has brought Mississippi into her present decision. She has heard proclaimed the theory that all men are created free and equal, and this made the basis of an attack upon her social institutions; and the sacred Declaration of Independence has been invoked to maintain the position of the equality of the races. That Declaration of Independence is to be construed by the circumstances and purposes for which it was made. The communities were declaring their independence; the people of those communities were asserting that no man was born—to use the language of Mr. Jefferson—booted and spurred to ride over the rest of mankind; that men were created equal—meaning the men of the political community; that there was no divine right to rule; that no man inherited the right to govern; that there were no classes by which power and place descended to families, but that all stations were equally within the grasp of each member of the body-politic. These were the great principles they announced; these were the purposes for which they made their declaration; these were the ends to which their enunciation was directed. They have no reference to the slave; else, how happened it that among the items of arraignment made against George III was that he endeavored to do just what the North has been endeavoring of late to do—to stir up insurrection among our slaves? Had the Declaration announced that the negroes were free and equal, how was the Prince to be arraigned for stirring up insurrection among them? And how was this to be enumerated among the high crimes which caused the colonies to sever their connection with the mother country? When our Constitution was formed, the same idea was rendered more palpable, for there we find provision made for that very class of persons as property; they were not put upon the footing of equality with white men—not even upon that of paupers and convicts; but, so far as representation was concerned, were discriminated against as a lower caste, only to be represented in the numerical proportion of three fifths.

Then, Senators, we recur to the compact which binds us together; we recur to the principles upon which our Government was founded; and when you deny them, and when you deny to us the right to withdraw from a Government which thus perverted threatens to be destructive of our rights, we but tread in the path of our fathers when we proclaim our independence, and take the hazard. This is done not in hostility to others, not to injure any section of the country, not even for our own pecuniary benefit; but from the high and solemn motive of defending and protecting the rights we inherited, and which it is our sacred duty to transmit unshorn to our children.

I find in myself, perhaps, a type of the general feeling of my constituents towards yours. I am sure I feel no hostility to you, Senators from the North. I am sure there is not one of you, whatever sharp discussion there may have been between us, to whom I cannot now say, in the presence of my God, I wish you well; and such, I am sure, is the feeling of the people whom I represent towards those whom you represent. I therefore feel that I but express their desire when I say I hope, and they hope, for peaceful relations with you, though we must part. They may be mutually beneficial to us in the future, as they have been in the past, if you so will it. The reverse may bring disaster on every portion of the country; and if you will have it thus, we will invoke the God of our fathers, who delivered them from the power of the lion, to protect us from the ravages of the bear; and thus, putting our trust in God and in our own firm hearts and strong arms, we will vindicate the right as best we may.

In the course of my service here, associated at different times with a great variety of Senators, I see now around me some with whom I have served long; there have been points of collision; but whatever of offense there has been to me, I leave here; I carry with me no hostile remembrance. Whatever offense I have given which has not been redressed, or for which satisfaction has not been demanded, I have, Senators, in this hour of our parting, to offer you my apology for any pain which, in heat of discussion, I have inflicted. I go hence unencumbered of the remembrance of any injury received, and having discharged the duty of making the only reparation in my power for any injury offered.

Mr. President, and Senators, having made the announcement which the occasion seemed to me to require, it only remains to me to bid you a final adieu.

ABRAHAM LINCOLN

Speech at Independence Hall

Philadelphia, February 22, 1861

M R. CUYLER:—I am filled with deep emotion at finding myself standing here in the place where were collected together the wisdom, the patriotism, the devotion to principle, from which sprang the institutions under which we live. You have kindly suggested to me that in my hands is the task of restoring peace to our distracted country. I can say in return, sir, that all the political sentiments I entertain have been drawn, so far as I have been able to draw them, from the sentiments which originated, and were given to the world from this hall in which we stand. I have never had a feeling politically that did not spring from the sentiments embodied in the Declaration of Independence. (Great cheering.) I have often pondered over the dangers which were incurred by the men who assembled here and adopted that Declaration of Independence—I have pondered over the toils that were endured by the officers and soldiers of the army, who achieved that Independence. (Applause.) I have often inquired of myself, what great principle or idea it was that kept this Confederacy so long together. It was not the mere matter of the separation of the colonies from the mother land; but something in that Declaration giving liberty, not alone to the people of this country, but hope to the world for all future time. (Great applause.) It was that which gave promise that in due time the weights should be lifted from the shoulders of all men, and that *all* should have an equal chance. (Cheers.) This is the sentiment embodied in that Declaration of Independence.

Now, my friends, can this country be saved upon that basis? If it can, I will consider myself one of the happiest men in the world if I can help to save it. If it can't be saved upon that principle, it will be truly awful. But, if this country cannot be saved without giving up that principle—I was about to say I would rather be assassinated on this spot than to surrender it. (Applause.)

Now, in my view of the present aspect of affairs, there is no need of bloodshed and war. There is no necessity for it. I am not in favor of such a course, and I may say in advance, there will be no blood shed unless it be forced upon the Government. The Government will not use force unless force is used against it. (Prolonged applause and cries of "That's the proper sentiment.")

My friends, this is a wholly unprepared speech. I did not expect to be called upon to say a word when I came here—I supposed I was merely to do something towards raising a flag. I may, therefore, have said something indiscreet, (cries of "no, no"), but I have said nothing but what I am willing to live by, and, in the pleasure of Almighty God, die by.

ABRAHAM LINCOLN

First Inaugural Address

Washington, D.C., March 4, 1861

FELLOW CITIZENS OF THE UNITED STATES:

In compliance with a custom as old as the government itself, I appear before you to address you briefly, and to take, in your presence, the oath prescribed by the Constitution of the United States, to be taken by the President "before he enters on the execution of his office."

I do not consider it necessary, at present, for me to discuss those matters of administration about which there is no special anxiety, or excitement.

Apprehension seems to exist among the people of the Southern States, that by the accession of a Republican Administration, their property, and their peace, and personal security, are to be endangered. There has never been any reasonable cause for such apprehension. Indeed, the most ample evidence to the contrary has all the while existed, and been open to their inspection. It is found in nearly all the published speeches of him who now addresses you. I do but quote from one of those speeches when I declare that "I have no purpose, directly or indirectly, to interfere with the institution of slavery in the States where it exists. I believe I have no lawful right to do so, and I have no inclination to do so." Those who nominated and elected me did so with full knowledge that I had made this, and many similar declarations, and had never recanted them. And more than this, they placed in the platform, for my acceptance, and as a law to themselves, and to me, the clear and emphatic resolution which I now read:

"*Resolved*, That the maintenance inviolate of the rights of the States, and especially the right of each State to order and control its own domestic institutions according to its own judgment exclusively, is essential to that balance of power on which the perfection and endurance of our political fabric depend;

and we denounce the lawless invasion by armed force of the soil of any State or Territory, no matter under what pretext, as among the gravest of crimes."

I now reiterate these sentiments: and in doing so, I only press upon the public attention the most conclusive evidence of which the case is susceptible, that the property, peace and security of no section are to be in anywise endangered by the now incoming Administration. I add too, that all the protection which, consistently with the Constitution and the laws, can be given, will be cheerfully given to all the States when lawfully demanded, for whatever cause—as cheerfully to one section, as to another.

There is much controversy about the delivering up of fugitives from service or labor. The clause I now read is as plainly written in the Constitution as any other of its provisions:

"No person held to service or labor in one State, under the laws thereof, escaping into another, shall, in consequence of any law or regulation therein, be discharged from such service or labor, but shall be delivered up on claim of the party to whom such service or labor may be due."

It is scarcely questioned that this provision was intended by those who made it, for the reclaiming of what we call fugitive slaves; and the intention of the law-giver is the law. All members of Congress swear their support to the whole Constitution—to this provision as much as to any other. To the proposition, then, that slaves whose cases come within the terms of this clause, "shall be delivered up," their oaths are unanimous. Now, if they would make the effort in good temper, could they not, with nearly equal unanimity, frame and pass a law, by means of which to keep good that unanimous oath?

There is some difference of opinion whether this clause should be enforced by national or by state authority; but surely that difference is not a very material one. If the slave is to be surrendered, it can be of but little consequence to him, or to others, by which authority it is done. And should any one, in any case, be content that his oath shall go unkept, on a merely unsubstantial controversy as to *how* it shall be kept?

Again, in any law upon this subject, ought not all the safeguards of liberty known in civilized and humane jurisprudence to be introduced, so that a free man be not, in any case, surrendered as a slave? And might it not be well, at the same time, to provide by law for the enforcement of that clause in the Constitution which guarranties that "The citizens of each State shall be entitled to all previleges and immunities of citizens in the several States?"

I take the official oath to-day, with no mental reservations, and with no purpose to construe the Constitution or laws, by any hypercritical rules. And while I do not choose now to specify particular acts of Congress as proper to be enforced, I do suggest, that it will be much safer for all, both in official and private stations, to conform to, and abide by, all those acts which stand unrepealed, than to violate any of them, trusting to find impunity in having them held to be unconstitutional.

It is seventy-two years since the first inauguration of a President under our national Constitution. During that period fifteen different and greatly distinguished citizens, have, in succession, administered the executive branch of the government. They have conducted it through many perils; and, generally, with great success. Yet, with all this scope for precedent, I now enter upon the same task for the brief constitutional term of four years, under great and peculiar difficulty. A disruption of the Federal Union heretofore only menaced, is now formidably attempted.

I hold, that in contemplation of universal law, and of the Constitution, the Union of these States is perpetual. Perpetuity is implied, if not expressed, in the fundamental law of all national governments. It is safe to assert that no government proper, ever had a provision in its organic law for its own termination. Continue to execute all the express provisions of our national Constitution, and the Union will endure forever—it being impossible to destroy it, except by some action not provided for in the instrument itself.

Again, if the United States be not a government proper, but an association of States in the nature of contract merely, can it, as a contract, be peaceably unmade, by less than all the parties who made it? One party to a contract may violate it—break it, so to speak; but does it not require all to lawfully rescind it?

Descending from these general principles, we find the proposition that, in legal contemplation, the Union is perpetual, confirmed by the history of the Union itself. The Union is much older than the Constitution. It was formed in fact, by the Articles of Association in 1774. It was matured and continued by the Declaration of Independence in 1776. It was further matured and the faith of all the then thirteen States expressly plighted and engaged that it should be perpetual, by the Articles of Confederation in 1778. And finally, in 1787, one of the declared objects for ordaining and establishing the Constitution, was "*to form a more perfect union.*"

But if destruction of the Union, by one, or by a part only, of the States, be lawfully possible, the Union is *less* perfect than before the Constitution, having lost the vital element of perpetuity.

It follows from these views that no State, upon its own mere motion, can lawfully get out of the Union,—that *resolves* and *ordinances* to that effect are legally void; and that acts of violence, within any State or States, against the authority of the United States, are insurrectionary or revolutionary, according to circumstances.

I therefore consider that, in view of the Constitution and the laws, the Union is unbroken; and, to the extent of my ability, I shall take care, as the Constitution itself expressly enjoins upon me, that the laws of the Union be faithfully executed in all the States. Doing this I deem to be only a simple duty on my part; and I shall perform it, so far as practicable, unless my rightful masters, the American people, shall withhold the requisite means, or, in some authoritative manner, direct the contrary. I trust this will not be regarded as a menace, but only as the declared purpose of the Union that it *will* constitutionally defend, and maintain itself.

In doing this there needs to be no bloodshed or violence; and there shall be none, unless it be forced upon the national authority. The power confided to me, will be used to hold, occupy, and possess the property, and places belonging to the government, and to collect the duties and imposts; but beyond what may be necessary for these objects, there will be no invasion—no using of force against, or among the people anywhere. Where hostility to the United States, in any interior locality, shall be so great and so universal, as to prevent competent resident citizens from holding the Federal offices, there will be no attempt to force obnoxious strangers among the people for that object. While the strict legal right may exist in the government to enforce the exercise of these offices, the attempt to do so would be so irritating, and so nearly impracticable with all, that I deem it better to forego, for the time, the uses of such offices.

The mails, unless repelled, will continue to be furnished in all parts of the Union. So far as possible, the people everywhere shall have that sense of perfect security which is most favorable to calm thought and reflection. The course here indicated will be followed, unless current events, and experience, shall show a modification, or change, to be proper; and in every case and exigency, my best discretion will be exercised, according to circumstances actually existing, and with a view and a hope of a peaceful solution of the national troubles, and the restoration of fraternal sympathies and affections.

That there are persons in one section, or another who seek to destroy the Union at all events, and are glad of any pretext to do it, I will neither affirm or deny; but if there be such, I need address no word to them. To those, however, who really love the Union, may I not speak?

Before entering upon so grave a matter as the destruction of our national fabric, with all its benefits, its memories, and its hopes, would it not be wise to ascertain precisely why we do it? Will you hazard so desperate a step, while there is any possibility that any portion of the ills you fly from, have no real existence? Will you, while the certain ills you fly to, are greater than all the real ones you fly from? Will you risk the commission of so fearful a mistake?

All profess to be content in the Union, if all constitutional rights can be maintained. Is it true, then, that any right, plainly written in the Constitution, has been denied? I think not. Happily the human mind is so constituted, that no party can reach to the audacity of doing this. Think, if you can, of a single instance in which a plainly written provision of the Constitution has ever been denied. If, by the mere force of numbers, a majority should deprive a minority of any clearly written constitutional right, it might, in a moral point of view, justify revolution—certainly would, if such right were a vital one. But such is not our case. All the vital rights of minorities, and of individuals, are so plainly assured to them, by affirmations and negations, guarranties and prohibitions, in the Constitution, that controversies never arise concerning them. But no organic law can ever be framed with a provision specifically applicable to every question which may occur in practical administration. No foresight can anticipate, nor any document of reasonable length contain express provisions for all possible questions. Shall fugitives from labor be surrendered by national or by State authority? The Constitution does not expressly say. *May* Congress prohibit slavery in the territories? The Constitution does not expressly say. *Must* Congress protect slavery in the territories? The Constitution does not expressly say.

From questions of this class spring all our constitutional controversies, and we divide upon them into majorities and minorities. If the minority will not acquiesce, the majority must, or the government must cease. There is no other alternative; for continuing the government, is acquiescence on one side or the other. If a minority, in such case, will secede rather than acquiesce, they make a precedent which, in turn, will divide and ruin them; for a minority of their own will secede from them, whenever a majority refuses to be controlled by such minority. For instance, why may not any portion of a new confederacy, a year or two hence, arbitrarily secede again, precisely as portions of the present Union now claim to secede from it. All who cherish disunion sentiments, are now being educated to the exact temper of doing this. Is there such perfect identity of interests among the States to compose a new Union, as to produce harmony only, and prevent renewed secession?

Plainly, the central idea of secession, is the essence of anarchy. A majority, held in restraint by constitutional checks, and limitations, and always changing easily, with deliberate changes of popular opinions and sentiments, is the only true sovereign of a free people. Whoever rejects it, does, of necessity, fly to anarchy or to despotism. Unanimity is impossible; the rule of a minority, as a permanent arrangement, is wholly inadmissable; so that, rejecting the majority principle, anarchy, or despotism in some form, is all that is left.

I do not forget the position assumed by some, that constitutional questions are to be decided by the Supreme Court; nor do I deny that such decisions must be binding in any case, upon the parties to a suit, as to the object of that suit, while they are also entitled to very high respect and consideration, in all paralel cases, by all other departments of the government. And while it is obviously possible that such decision may be erroneous in any given case, still the evil effect following it, being limited to that particular case, with the chance that it may be over-ruled, and never become a precedent for other cases, can better be borne than could the evils of a different practice. At the same time the candid citizen must confess that if the policy of the government, upon vital questions, affecting the whole people, is to be irrevocably fixed by decisions of the Supreme Court, the instant they are made, in ordinary litigation between parties, in personal actions, the people will have ceased, to be their own rulers, having, to that extent, practically resigned their government, into the hands of that eminent tribunal. Nor is there, in this view, any assault upon the court, or the judges. It is a duty, from which they may not shrink, to decide cases properly brought before them; and it is no fault of theirs, if others seek to turn their decisions to political purposes.

One section of our country believes slavery is *right*, and ought to be extended, while the other believes it is *wrong*, and ought not to be extended. This is the only substantial dispute. The fugitive slave clause of the Constitution, and the law for the suppression of the foreign slave trade, are each as well enforced, perhaps, as any law can ever be in a community where the moral sense of the people imperfectly supports the law itself. The great body of the people abide by the dry legal obligation in both cases, and a few break over in each. This, I think, cannot be perfectly cured; and it would be worse in both cases *after* the separation of the sections, than before. The foreign slave trade, now imperfectly suppressed, would be ultimately revived without restriction, in one section; while fugitive slaves, now only partially surrendered, would not be surrendered at all, by the other.

Physically speaking, we cannot separate. We cannot remove our respective sections from each other, nor build an impassable wall between them. A husband and wife may be divorced, and go out of the presence, and beyond the reach of each other; but the different parts of our country cannot do this. They cannot but remain face to face; and intercourse, either amicable or hostile, must continue between them. Is it possible then to make that intercourse more advantageous, or more satisfactory, *after* separation than *before*? Can aliens make treaties easier than friends can make laws? Can treaties be more faithfully enforced between aliens, than laws can among friends? Suppose you go to war, you cannot fight always; and when, after much loss on both sides, and no gain on either, you cease fighting, the identical old questions, as to terms of intercourse, are again upon you.

This country, with its institutions, belongs to the people who inhabit it. Whenever they shall grow weary of the existing government, they can exercise their *constitutional* right of amending it, or their *revolutionary* right to dismember, or overthrow it. I can not be ignorant of the fact that many worthy, and patriotic citizens are desirous of having the national constitution amended. While I make no recommendation of amendments, I fully recognize the rightful authority of the people over the whole subject, to be exercised in either of the modes prescribed in the instrument itself; and I should, under existing circumstances, favor, rather than oppose, a fair oppertunity being afforded the people to act upon it.

I will venture to add that, to me, the convention mode seems preferable, in that it allows amendments to originate with the people themselves, instead of only permitting them to take, or reject, propositions, originated by others, not especially chosen for the purpose, and which might not be precisely such, as they would wish to either accept or refuse. I understand a proposed amendment to the Constitution—which amendment, however, I have not seen, has passed Congress, to the effect that the federal government, shall never interfere with the domestic institutions of the States, including that of persons held to service. To avoid misconstruction of what I have said, I depart from my purpose not to speak of particular amendments, so far as to say that, holding such a provision to now be implied constitutional law, I have no objection to its being made express, and irrevocable.

The Chief Magistrate derives all his authority from the people, and they have conferred none upon him to fix terms for the separation of the States. The people themselves can do this also if they choose; but the executive, as such, has nothing to do with it. His duty is to administer the present government, as it came to his hands, and to transmit it, unimpaired by him, to his successor.

Why should there not be a patient confidence in the ultimate justice of the people? Is there any better, or equal hope, in the world? In our present differences, is either party without faith of being in the right? If the Almighty Ruler of nations, with his eternal truth and justice, be on your side of the North, or on yours of the South, that truth, and that justice, will surely prevail, by the judgment of this great tribunal, the American people.

By the frame of the government under which we live, this same people have wisely given their public servants but little power for mischief; and have, with equal wisdom, provided for the return of that little to their own hands at very short intervals.

While the people retain their virtue, and vigilence, no administration, by any extreme of wickedness or folly, can very seriously injure the government, in the short space of four years.

My countrymen, one and all, think calmly and *well*, upon this whole subject. Nothing valuable can be lost by taking time. If there be an object to *hurry* any of you, in hot haste, to a step which you would never take *deliberately*, that object will be frustrated by taking time; but no good object can be frustrated by it. Such of you as are now dissatisfied, still have the old Constitution unimpaired, and, on the sensitive point, the laws of your own framing under it; while the new administration will have no immediate power, if it would, to change either. If it were admitted that you who are dissatisfied, hold the right side in the dispute, there still is no single good reason for precipitate action. Intelligence, patriotism, Christianity, and a firm reliance on Him, who has never yet forsaken this favored land, are still competent to adjust, in the best way, all our present difficulty.

In *your* hands, my dissatisfied fellow countrymen, and not in *mine*, is the momentous issue of civil war. The government will not assail *you*. You can have no conflict, without being yourselves the aggressors. *You* have no oath registered in Heaven to destroy the government, while *I* shall have the most solemn one to "preserve, protect and defend" it.

I am loth to close. We are not enemies, but friends. We must not be enemies. Though passion may have strained, it must not break our bonds of affection. The mystic chords of memory, streching from every battle-field, and patriot grave, to every living heart and hearthstone, all over this broad land, will yet swell the chorus of the Union, when again touched, as surely they will be, by the better angels of our nature.

ALEXANDER STEPHENS

"Corner-Stone" Speech

Savannah, Georgia, March 21, 1861

M R. MAYOR, AND GENTLEMEN OF THE COMMITTEE, AND
FELLOW CITIZENS:—For this reception you will please
accept most profound and sincere thanks. The compliment is
doubtless intended as much, or more, perhaps, in honor of the
occasion, and my public position, in connection with the great
events now crowding upon us, than to me personally and individually. It is however none the less appreciated by me on that
account. We are in the midst of one of the greatest epochs in
our history. The last ninety days will mark one of the most
memorable eras in the history of modern civilization.

[There was a general call from the outside of the building for
the speaker to go out, that there were more outside than in.]

The Mayor rose and requested silence at the doors, that Mr.
Stephens' health would not permit him to speak in the open
air.

Mr. STEPHENS said he would leave it to the audience whether
he should proceed indoors or out. There was a general cry indoors, as the ladies, a large number of whom were present,
could not hear outside.

Mr. STEPHENS said that the accommodation of the ladies
would determine the question, and he would proceed where
he was.

[At this point the uproar and clamor outside was greater still
for the speaker to go out on the steps. This was quieted by
Col. Lawton, Col. Freeman, Judge Jackson, and Mr. J. W.
Owens going out and stating the facts of the case to the dense
mass of men, women, and children who were outside, and entertaining them in brief speeches—Mr. Stephens all this while
quietly sitting down until the furor subsided.]

Mr. STEPHENS rose and said: When perfect quiet is restored,
I shall proceed. I cannot speak so long as there is any noise or

confusion. I shall take my time—I feel quite prepared to spend the night with you if necessary. [Loud applause.] I very much regret that every one who desires cannot hear what I have to say. Not that I have any display to make, or any thing very entertaining to present, but such views as I have to give, I wish *all*, not only in this city, but in this State, and throughout our Confederate Republic, could hear, who have a desire to hear them.

I was remarking, that we are passing through one of the greatest revolutions in the annals of the world. Seven States have within the last three months thrown off an old government and formed a new. This revolution has been signally marked, up to this time, by the fact of its having been accomplished without the loss of a single drop of blood. [Applause.]

This new constitution, or form of government, constitutes the subject to which your attention will be partly invited. In reference to it, I make this first general remark. It amply secures all our ancient rights, franchises, and liberties. All the great principles of Magna Charta are retained in it. No citizen is deprived of life, liberty, or property, but by the judgment of his peers under the laws of the land. The great principle of religious liberty, which was the honor and pride of the old constitution, is still maintained and secured. All the essentials of the old constitution, which have endeared it to the hearts of the American people, have been preserved and perpetuated. [Applause.] Some changes have been made. Of these I shall speak presently. Some of these I should have preferred not to have seen made; but these, perhaps, meet the cordial approbation of a majority of this audience, if not an overwhelming majority of the people of the Confederacy. Of them, therefore, I will not speak. But other important changes do meet my cordial approbation. They form great improvements upon the old constitution. So, taking the whole new constitution, I have no hesitancy in giving it as my judgment that it is decidedly better than the old. [Applause.]

Allow me briefly to allude to some of these improvements. The question of building up class interests, or fostering one branch of industry to the prejudice of another under the exercise of the revenue power, which gave us so much trouble under the old constitution, is put at rest forever under the new. We allow the imposition of no duty with a view of giving advantage to one class of persons, in any trade or business, over those of another. All, under our system, stand upon the same broad principles of perfect equality. Honest labor and enterprise are left free and unrestricted in whatever pursuit they may be engaged. This subject came well nigh causing a rupture of the old Union, under the lead of the gallant Palmetto State, which lies on our border, in 1833. This old thorn of the tariff, which was the cause of so much irritation in the old body politic, is removed forever from the new. [Applause.]

Again, the subject of internal improvements, under the power of Congress to regulate commerce, is put at rest under our system. The power claimed by construction under the old constitution, was at least a doubtful one—it rested solely upon construction. We of the South, generally apart from considerations of constitutional principles, opposed its exercise upon grounds of its inexpediency and injustice. Notwithstanding this opposition, millions of money, from the common treasury had been drawn for such purposes. Our opposition sprang from no hostility to commerce, or all necessary aids for facilitating it. With us it was simply a question, upon *whom* the burden should fall. In Georgia, for instance, we have done as much for the cause of internal improvements as any other portion of the country according to population and means. We have stretched out lines of railroads from the seaboard to the mountains; dug down the hills, and filled up the valleys at a cost of not less than twenty-five millions of dollars. All this was done to open an outlet for our products of the interior, and those to the west of us, to reach the marts of the world. No State was in greater need of such facilities than Georgia, but we did not ask that these works should be made by appropriations out of the common treasury. The cost of the grading, the superstructure, and equipments of our roads, was borne by those who entered on the enterprise. Nay, more—not only the cost of the iron, no small item in the aggregate cost, was borne in the same way—but we were compelled to pay into the common treasury several millions of dollars for the privilege of importing the iron, after the price was paid for it abroad. What justice was there in taking this money, which our people paid into the common treasury on the importation of our iron, and applying it to the improvement of rivers and harbors elsewhere?

The true principle is to subject the commerce of every locality, to whatever burdens may be necessary to facilitate it. If Charleston harbor needs improvement, let the commerce of Charleston bear the burden. If the mouth of the Savannah river has to be cleared out, let the sea-going navigation which is benefitted by it, bear the burden. So with the mouths of the Alabama and Mississippi river. Just as the products of the interior, our cotton, wheat, corn, and other articles, have to bear the necessary rates of freight over our railroads to reach the seas. This is again the broad principle of perfect equality and justice. [Applause.] And it is especially set forth and established in our new constitution.

Another feature to which I will allude, is that the new constitution provides that cabinet ministers and heads of departments may have the privilege of seats upon the floor of the Senate and House of Representatives—may have the right to participate in the debates and discussions upon the various subjects of administration. I should have preferred that this provision should have gone further, and required the President to select his constitutional advisers from the Senate and House of Representatives. That would have conformed entirely to the practice in the British Parliament, which, in my judgment, is one of the wisest provisions in the British constitution. It is the only feature that saves that government. It is that which gives it stability in its facility to change its administration. Ours, as it is, is a great approximation to the right principle.

Under the old constitution, a secretary of the treasury for instance, had no opportunity, save by his annual reports, of presenting any scheme or plan of finance or other matter. He had no opportunity of explaining, expounding, inforcing, or defending his views of policy; his only resort was through the medium of an organ. In the British parliament, the premier brings in his budget and stands before the nation responsible for its every item. If it is indefensible, he falls before the attacks upon it, as he ought to. This will now be the case to a limited extent under our system. In the new constitution, provision has been made by which our heads of departments can speak for themselves and the administration, in behalf of its entire policy, without resorting to the indirect and highly objectionable medium of a newspaper. It is to be greatly hoped that under our system we shall never have what is known as a government organ. [Rapturous applause.]

[A noise again arose from the clamor of the crowd outside, who wished to hear Mr. Stephens, and for some moments interrupted him. The mayor rose and called on the police to preserve order. Quiet being restored, Mr. S. proceeded.]

Another change in the constitution relates to the length of the tenure of the presidential office. In the new constitution it is six years instead of four, and the President rendered ineligible for a re-election. This is certainly a decidedly conservative change. It will remove from the incumbent all temptation to use his office or exert the powers confided to him for any objects of personal ambition. The only incentive to that higher ambition which should move and actuate one holding such high trusts in his hands, will be the good of the people, the advancement, prosperity, happiness, safety, honor, and true glory of the confederacy. [Applause.]

But not to be tedious in enumerating the numerous changes for the better, allow me to allude to one other—though last, not least. The new constitution has put at rest, *forever*, all the agitating questions relating to our peculiar institution—African slavery as it exists amongst us—the proper *status* of the negro in our form of civilization. This was the immediate cause of the late rupture and present revolution. Jefferson in his forecast, had anticipated this, as the "rock upon which the old Union would split." He was right. What was conjecture with him, is now a realized fact. But whether he fully comprehended the great truth upon which that rock *stood* and *stands*, may be doubted. The prevailing ideas entertained by him and most of the leading statesmen at the time of the formation of the old constitution, were that the enslavement of the African was in violation of the laws of nature; that it was wrong in *principle*, socially, morally, and politically. It was an evil they knew not well how to deal with, but the general opinion of the men of that day was that, somehow or other in the order of Providence, the institution would be evanescent and pass away. This idea, though not incorporated in the constitution, was the prevailing idea at that time. The constitution, it is true, secured every essential guarantee to the institution while it should last, and hence no argument can be justly urged against the constitutional guarantees thus secured, because of the common sentiment of the day. Those ideas, however, were fundamentally wrong. They rested upon the assumption of the equality of races. This was an error. It was a sandy foundation, and the government built upon it fell when the "storm came and the wind blew."

Our new government is founded upon exactly the opposite idea; its foundations are laid, its corner-stone rests upon the great truth, that the negro is not equal to the white man; that slavery—subordination to the superior race—is his natural and normal condition. [Applause.]

This, our new government, is the first, in the history of the world, based upon this great physical, philosophical, and moral truth. This truth has been slow in the process of its development, like all other truths in the various departments of science. It has been so even amongst us. Many who hear me, perhaps, can recollect well, that this truth was not generally admitted, even within their day. The errors of the past generation still clung to many as late as twenty years ago. Those at the North, who still cling to these errors, with a zeal above knowledge, we justly denominate fanatics. All fanaticism springs from an aberration of the mind—from a defect in reasoning. It is a species of insanity. One of the most striking characteristics of insanity, in many instances, is forming correct conclusions from fancied or erroneous premises; so with the anti-slavery fanatics; their conclusions are right if their premises were. They assume that the negro is equal, and hence conclude that he is entitled to equal privileges and rights with the white man. If their premises were correct, their conclusions would be logical and just—but their premise being wrong, their whole argument fails. I recollect once of having heard a gentleman from one of the northern States, of great power and ability, announce in the House of Representatives, with imposing effect, that we of the South would be compelled, ultimately, to yield upon this subject of slavery, that it was as impossible to war successfully against a principle in politics, as it was in physics or mechanics. That the principle would ultimately prevail. That we, in maintaining slavery as it exists with us, were warring against a principle, a principle founded in nature, the principle of the equality of men. The reply I made to him was, that upon his own grounds, we should, ultimately, succeed, and that he and his associates, in this crusade against our institutions, would ultimately fail. The truth announced, that it was as impossible to war successfully against a principle in politics as it was in physics and mechanics, I admitted; but told him that it was he, and those acting with him, who were warring against a principle. They were attempting to make things equal which the Creator had made unequal.

In the conflict thus far, success has been on our side, complete throughout the length and breadth of the Confederate States. It is upon this, as I have stated, our social fabric is firmly planted; and I cannot permit myself to doubt the ultimate success of a full recognition of this principle throughout the civilized and enlightened world.

As I have stated, the truth of this principle may be slow in development, as all truths are and ever have been, in the various branches of science. It was so with the principles announced by Galileo—it was so with Adam Smith and his principles of political economy. It was so with Harvey, and his theory of the circulation of the blood. It is stated that not a single one of the medical profession, living at the time of the announcement of the truths made by him, admitted them. Now, they are universally acknowledged. May we not, therefore, look with confidence to the ultimate universal acknowledgment of the truths upon which our system rests? It is the first government ever instituted upon the principles in strict conformity to nature, and the ordination of Providence, in furnishing the materials of human society. Many governments have been founded upon the principle of the subordination and serfdom of certain classes of the same race; such were and are in violation of the laws of nature. Our system commits no such violation of nature's laws. With us, all of the white race, however high or low, rich or poor, are equal in the eye of the law. Not so with the negro. Subordination is his place. He, by nature, or by the curse against Canaan, is fitted for that condition which he occupies in our system. The architect, in the construction of buildings, lays the foundation with the proper material—the granite;

then comes the brick or the marble. The substratum of our society is made of the material fitted by nature for it, and by experience we know that it is best, not only for the superior, but for the inferior race, that it should be so. It is, indeed, in conformity with the ordinance of the Creator. It is not for us to inquire into the wisdom of his ordinances, or to question them. For his own purposes, he has made one race to differ from another, as he has made "one star to differ from another star in glory."

The great objects of humanity are best attained when there is conformity to his laws and decrees, in the formation of governments as well as in all things else. Our confederacy is founded upon principles in strict conformity with these laws. This stone which was rejected by the first builders "is become the chief of the corner"—the real " corner-stone"—in our new edifice. [Applause.]

I have been asked, what of the future? It has been apprehended by some that we would have arrayed against us the civilized world. I care not who or how many they may be against us, when we stand upon the eternal principles of truth, *if we are true to ourselves and the principles for which we contend*, we are obliged to, and must triumph. [Immense applause.]

Thousands of people who begin to understand these truths are not yet completely out of the shell; they do not see them in their length and breadth. We hear much of the civilization and christianization of the barbarous tribes of Africa. In my judgment, those ends will never be attained, but by first teaching them the lesson taught to Adam, that "in the sweat of his brow he should eat his bread," [applause,] and teaching them to work, and feed, and clothe themselves.

But to pass on: Some have propounded the inquiry whether it is practicable for us to go on with the confederacy without further accessions? Have we the means and ability to maintain nationality among the powers of the earth? On this point I would barely say, that as anxiously as we all have been, and are, for the border States, with institutions similar to ours, to join us, still we are abundantly able to maintain our position, even if they should ultimately make up their minds not to cast their destiny with us. That they ultimately will join us—be compelled to do it—is my confident belief; but we can get on very well without them, even if they should not.

We have all the essential elements of a high national career. The idea has been given out at the North, and even in the border States, that we are too small and too weak to maintain a separate nationality. This is a great mistake. In extent of territory we embrace five hundred and sixty-four thousand square miles and upward. This is upward of two hundred thousand square miles more than was included within the limits of the original thirteen States. It is an area of country more than double the territory of France or the Austrian empire. France, in round numbers, has but two hundred and twelve thousand square miles. Austria, in round numbers, has two hundred and forty-eight thousand square miles. Ours is greater than both combined. It is greater than all France, Spain, Portugal, and Great Britain, including England, Ireland, and Scotland, together. In population we have upward of five millions, according to the census of 1860; this includes white and black. The entire population, including white and black, of the original thirteen States, was less than four millions in 1790, and still less in '76, when the independence of our fathers was achieved. If they, with a less population, dared maintain their independence against the greatest power on earth, shall we have any apprehension of maintaining ours now?

In point of material wealth and resources, we are greatly in advance of them. The taxable property of the Confederate States cannot be less than twenty-two hundred millions of dollars! This, I think I venture but little in saying, may be considered as five times more than the colonies possessed at the time they achieved their independence. Georgia, alone, possessed last year, according to the report of our comptroller-general, six hundred and seventy-two millions of taxable property. The debts of the seven confederate States sum up in the aggregate less than eighteen millions, while the existing debts of the other of the late United States sum up in the aggregate the enormous amount of one hundred and seventy-four millions of dollars. This is without taking into the account the heavy city debts, corporation debts, and railroad debts, which press, and will continue to press, as a heavy incubus upon the resources of those States. These debts, added to others, make a sum total not much under five hundred millions of dollars. With such an area of territory as we have—with such an amount of population—with a climate and soil unsurpassed by any on the face of the earth—with such resources already at our command —with productions which control the commerce of the world—who can entertain any apprehensions as to our ability to succeed, whether others join us or not?

It is true, I believe I state but the common sentiment, when I declare my earnest desire that the border States should join us. The differences of opinion that existed among us anterior to secession, related more to the policy in securing that result by co-operation than from any difference upon the ultimate security we all looked to in common.

These differences of opinion were more in reference to policy than principle, and as Mr. Jefferson said in his inaugural, in 1801, after the heated contest preceding his election, there might be differences of opinion without differences on principle, and that all, to some extent, had been federalists and all republicans; so it may now be said of us, that whatever differences of opinion as to the best policy in having a co-operation with our border sister slave States, if the worst came to the worst, that as we were all co-operationists, we are now all for independence, whether they come or not. [Continued applause.]

In this connection I take this occasion to state, that I was not without grave and serious apprehensions, that if the worst came to the worst, and cutting loose from the old government should be the only remedy for our safety and security, it would be attended with much more serious ills than it has been as yet. Thus far we have seen none of those incidents which usually attend revolutions. No such material as such convulsions usually throw up has been seen. Wisdom, prudence, and patriotism, have marked every step of our progress thus far. This augurs well for the future, and it is a matter of sincere gratification to me, that I am enabled to make the declaration. Of the men I met in the Congress at Montgomery, I may be pardoned for saying this, an abler, wiser, a more conservative, deliberate, determined, resolute, and patriotic body of men, I never met in my life. [Great applause.] Their works speak for them; the provisional government speaks for them; the constitution of the permanent government will be a lasting monument of their worth, merit, and statesmanship. [Applause.]

But to return to the question of the future. What is to be the result of this revolution?

Will every thing, commenced so well, continue as it has begun? In reply to this anxious inquiry, I can only say it all depends upon ourselves. A young man starting out in life on his majority, with health, talent, and ability, under a favoring Providence, may be said to be the architect of his own fortunes. His destinies are in his own hands. He may make for himself a name, of honor or dishonor, according to his own acts. If he plants himself upon truth, integrity, honor and uprightness, with industry, patience and energy, he cannot fail of success. So it is with us. We are a young republic, just entering upon the arena of nations; we will be the architects of our own fortunes. Our destiny, under Providence, is in our own hands. With wisdom, prudence, and statesmanship on the part of our public men, and intelligence, virtue and patriotism on the part of the people, success, to the full measures of our most sanguine hopes, may be looked for. But if unwise counsels prevail—if we become divided—if schisms arise—if dissensions spring up—if factions are engendered—if party spirit, nourished by unholy personal ambition shall rear its hydra head, I have no good to prophesy for you. Without intelligence, virtue, integrity, and patriotism on the part of the people, no republic or representative government can be durable or stable.

We have intelligence, and virtue, and patriotism. All that is required is to cultivate and perpetuate these. Intelligence will not do without virtue. France was a nation of philosophers. These philosophers become Jacobins. They lacked that virtue, that devotion to moral principle, and that patriotism which is essential to good government. Organized upon principles of perfect justice and right—seeking amity and friendship with all other powers—I see no obstacle in the way of our upward and onward progress. Our growth, by accessions from other States, will depend greatly upon whether we present to the world, as I trust we shall, a better government than that to which neighboring States belong. If we do this, North Carolina, Tennessee, and Arkansas cannot hesitate long; neither can Virginia, Kentucky, and Missouri. They will necessarily gravitate to us by an imperious law. We made ample provision in our constitution for the admission of other States; it is more guarded, and wisely so, I think, than the old constitution on the same subject, but not too guarded to receive them as fast as it may be proper. Looking to the distant future, and, perhaps, not very far distant either, it is not beyond the range of possibility, and even probability, that all the great States of the north-west will gravitate this way, as well as Tennessee, Kentucky, Missouri, Arkansas, etc. Should they do so, our doors are wide enough to receive them, but not until they are ready to assimilate with us in principle.

The process of disintegration in the old Union may be expected to go on with almost absolute certainty if we pursue the right course. We are now the nucleus of a growing power which, if we are true to ourselves, our destiny, and high mission, will become the controlling power on this continent. To what extent accessions will go on in the process of time, or where it will end, the future will determine. So far as it concerns States of the old Union, this process will be upon no such principles of *reconstruction* as now spoken of, but upon *reorganization* and new assimilation. [Loud applause.] Such are some of the glimpses of the future as I catch them.

But at first we must necessarily meet with the inconveniences and difficulties and embarrassments incident to all changes of government. These will be felt in our postal affairs and changes in the channel of trade. These inconveniences, it is to be hoped, will be but temporary, and must be borne with patience and forbearance.

As to whether we shall have war with our late confederates, or whether all matters of differences between us shall be amicably settled, I can only say that the prospect for a peaceful adjustment is better, so far as I am informed, than it has been.

The prospect of war is, at least, not so threatening as it has been. The idea of coercion, shadowed forth in President Lincoln's inaugural, seems not to be followed up thus far so vigorously as was expected. Fort Sumter, it is believed, will soon be evacuated. What course will be pursued toward Fort Pickens, and the other forts on the gulf, is not so well understood. It is to be greatly desired that all of them should be surrendered. Our object is *peace*, not only with the North, but with the world. All matters relating to the public property, public liabilities of the Union when we were members of it, we are ready and willing to adjust and settle upon the principles of right, equity, and good faith. War can be of no more benefit to the North than to us. Whether the intention of evacuating Fort Sumter is to be received as an evidence of a desire for a peaceful solution of our difficulties with the United States, or the result of necessity, I will not undertake to say. I would fain hope the former. Rumors are afloat, however, that it is the result of necessity. All I can say to you, therefore, on that point is, keep your armor bright and your powder dry. [Enthusiastic cheering.]

The surest way to secure peace, is to show your ability to maintain your rights. The principles and position of the present administration of the United States—the republican party—present some puzzling questions. While it is a fixed principle with them never to allow the increase of a foot of slave territory, they seem to be equally determined not to part with an inch "of the accursed soil." Notwithstanding their clamor against the institution, they seemed to be equally opposed to getting more, or letting go what they have got. They were ready to fight on the accession of Texas, and are equally ready to fight now on her secession. Why is this? How can this strange paradox be accounted for? There seems to be but one rational solution—and that is, notwithstanding their professions of humanity, they are disinclined to give up the benefits they derive from slave labor. Their philanthropy yields to their interest. The idea of enforcing the laws, has but one object, and that is a collection of the taxes, raised by slave labor to swell the fund, necessary to meet their heavy appropriations. The spoils is what they are after—though they come from the labor of the slave. [Continued applause.]

Mr. Stephens reviewed at some length, the extravagance and profligacy of appropriations by the Congress of the United States for several years past, and in this connection took occasion to allude to another one of the great improvements in our new constitution, which is a clause prohibiting Congress from appropriating any money from the treasury, except by a two-third vote, unless it be for some object which the executive may say is necessary to carry on the government.

When it is thus asked for, and estimated for, he continued, the majority may appropriate. This was a new feature.

Our fathers had guarded the assessment of taxes by insisting that representation and taxation should go together. This was inherited from the mother country, England. It was one of the principles upon which the revolution had been fought. Our fathers also provided in the old constitution, that all appropriation bills should originate in the representative branch of Congress, but our new constitution went a step further, and guarded not only the pockets of the people, but also the public money, after it was taken from their pockets.

He alluded to the difficulties and embarrassments which seemed to surround the question of a peaceful solution of the controversy with the old government. How can it be done? is perplexing many minds. The President seems to think that he cannot recognize our independence, nor can he, with and by the advice of the Senate, do so. The constitution makes no such provision. A general convention of all the States has been suggested by some.

Without proposing to solve the difficulty, he barely made the following suggestion:

"That as the admission of States by Congress under the constitution was an act of legislation, and in the nature of a contract or compact between the States admitted and the others admitting, why should not this contract or compact be regarded as of like character with all other civil contracts—liable to be rescinded by mutual agreement of both parties? The seceding States have rescinded it on their part, they have resumed their sovereignty. Why cannot the whole question be settled, if the north desire peace, simply by the Congress, in both branches, with the concurrence of the President, giving their consent to the separation, and a recognition of our independence?" This he merely offered as a suggestion, as one of the ways in which it might be done with much less violence by constructions to the constitution than many other acts of that government. [Applause.] The difficulty has to be solved in some way or other—this may be regarded as a fixed fact.

Several other points were alluded to by Mr. Stephens, particularly as to the policy of the new government toward foreign nations, and our commercial relations with them. Free trade, as far as practicable, would be the policy of this government. No higher duties would be imposed on foreign importations than would be necessary to support the government upon the strictest economy.

In olden times the olive branch was considered the emblem of peace; we will send to the nations of the earth another and far more potential emblem of the same, the cotton plant. The present duties were levied with a view of meeting the present necessities and exigencies, in preparation for war, if need be; but if we have peace, and he hoped we might, and trade should resume its proper course, a duty of ten per cent. upon foreign importations it was thought might be sufficient to meet the expenditures of the government. If some articles should be left on the free list, as they now are, such as breadstuffs, etc., then, of course, duties upon others would have to be higher—but in no event to an extent to embarrass trade and commerce. He concluded in an earnest appeal for union and harmony, on part of all the people in support of the common cause, in which we were all enlisted, and upon the issues of which such great consequences depend.

If, said he, we are true to ourselves, true to our cause, true to our destiny, true to our high mission, in presenting to the world the highest type of civilization ever exhibited by man— there will be found in our lexicon no such word as fail.

Mr. Stephens took his seat, amid a burst of enthusiasm and applause, such as the Athenæum has never had displayed within its walls, within "the recollection of the oldest inhabitant."

ABRAHAM LINCOLN

Address at Gettysburg, Pennsylvania

November 19, 1863

FOUR SCORE and seven years ago our fathers brought forth on this continent, a new nation, conceived in Liberty, and dedicated to the proposition that all men are created equal.

Now we are engaged in a great civil war, testing whether that nation, or any nation so conceived and so dedicated, can long endure. We are met on a great battle-field of that war. We have come to dedicate a portion of that field, as a final resting place for those who here gave their lives that that nation might live. It is altogether fitting and proper that we should do this.

But, in a larger sense, we can not dedicate—we can not consecrate—we can not hallow—this ground. The brave men, living and dead, who struggled here, have consecrated it, far above our poor power to add or detract. The world will little note, nor long remember what we say here, but it can never forget what they did here. It is for us the living, rather, to be dedicated here to the unfinished work which they who fought here have thus far so nobly advanced. It is rather for us to be here dedicated to the great task remaining before us—that from these honored dead we take increased devotion to that cause for which they gave the last full measure of devotion— that we here highly resolve that these dead shall not have died in vain—that this nation, under God, shall have a new birth of freedom—and that government of the people, by the people, for the people, shall not perish from the earth.

ABRAHAM LINCOLN

Second Inaugural Address

Washington, D.C., March 4, 1865

F ELLOW COUNTRYMEN:
    At this second appearing to take the oath of the presidential office, there is less occasion for an extended address than there was at the first. Then a statement, somewhat in detail, of a course to be pursued, seemed fitting and proper. Now, at the expiration of four years, during which public declarations have been constantly called forth on every point and phase of the great contest which still absorbs the attention, and engrosses the energies of the nation, little that is new could be presented. The progress of our arms, upon which all else chiefly depends, is as well known to the public as to myself; and it is, I trust, reasonably satisfactory and encouraging to all. With high hope for the future, no prediction in regard to it is ventured.

On the occasion corresponding to this four years ago, all thoughts were anxiously directed to an impending civil-war. All dreaded it—all sought to avert it. While the inaugeral address was being delivered from this place, devoted altogether to *saving* the Union without war, insurgent agents were in the city seeking to *destroy* it without war—seeking to dissolve the Union, and divide effects, by negotiation. Both parties deprecated war; but one of them would *make* war rather than let the nation survive; and the other would *accept* war rather than let it perish. And the war came.

One eighth of the whole population were colored slaves, not distributed generally over the Union, but localized in the Southern part of it. These slaves constituted a peculiar and powerful interest. All knew that this interest was, somehow, the cause of the war. To strengthen, perpetuate, and extend this interest was the object for which the insurgents would rend the Union, even by war; while the government claimed no right to do more than to restrict the territorial enlargement of it. Neither party expected for the war, the magnitude, or the duration, which it has already attained. Neither anticipated that the *cause* of the conflict might cease with, or even before, the conflict itself should cease. Each looked for an easier triumph, and a result less fundamental and astounding. Both read the same Bible, and pray to the same God; and each invokes His aid against the other. It may seem strange that any men should dare to ask a just God's assistance in wringing their bread from the sweat of other men's faces; but let us judge not that we be not judged. The prayers of both could not be answered; that of neither has been answered fully. The Almighty has His own purposes. "Woe unto the world because of offences! for it must needs be that offences come; but woe to that man by whom the offence cometh!" If we shall suppose that American Slavery is one of those offences which, in the providence of God, must needs come, but which, having continued through His appointed time, He now wills to remove, and that He gives to both North and South, this terrible war, as the woe due to those by whom the offence came, shall we discern therein any departure from those divine attributes which the believers in a Living God always ascribe to Him? Fondly do we hope—fervently do we pray—that this mighty scourge of war may speedily pass away. Yet, if God wills that it continue, until all the wealth piled by the bond-man's two hundred and fifty years of unrequited toil shall be sunk, and until every drop of blood drawn with the lash, shall be paid by another drawn with the sword, as was said three thousand years ago, so still it must be said "the judgments of the Lord, are true and righteous altogether"

With malice toward none; with charity for all; with firmness in the right, as God gives us to see the right, let us strive on to finish the work we are in; to bind up the nation's wounds; to care for him who shall have borne the battle, and for his widow, and his orphan—to do all which may achieve and cherish a just, and a lasting peace, among ourselves, and with all nations.

BIOGRAPHICAL NOTES

NOTE ON THE TEXTS

NOTES

INDEX

Biographical Notes

Thomas Hart Benton (March 14, 1782–April 10, 1858) Born in Harts Mill, near Hillsboro, North Carolina, the son of a lawyer. Admitted to the bar in Nashville, Tennessee, in 1806. Served in the Tennessee senate, 1809–11. Became an aide-de-camp to Andrew Jackson in 1812. Quarrel between Benton and Jackson resulted in gunfight in September 1813 in which Jackson was seriously wounded by Benton's brother Jesse. Served as an officer through the War of 1812, then moved to St. Louis in 1815 to practice law. Killed Charles Lucas, a fellow attorney, in a duel fought in 1817. Edited the St. Louis *Enquirer*, 1818–20. Elected to the U.S. Senate as a Democratic Republican (later as a Democrat) and served from 1821 to 1851. Reconciled with Jackson and joined him in opposing the Bank of the United States. Defeated for reelection after opposing the Compromise of 1850 for being too favorable to proslavery interests. Served in Congress, 1853–55, but was defeated for reelection because of his opposition to the Kansas-Nebraska Act; was also defeated in the 1856 Missouri gubernatorial election. Died in Washington, D.C.

John Brown (May 9, 1800–December 2, 1859) Born in West Torrington, Connecticut, the son of a farmer. Lived in Ohio, Pennsylvania, Massachusetts, and New York; worked as a cattle drover, tanner, sheep raiser, and wool merchant. Helped fugitive slaves. Went to Kansas in 1855 and joined a free-state militia. Led four of his sons and three other followers in a raid along Pottawatomie Creek, May 24, 1856, during which five proslavery settlers were murdered. Began planning slave uprising in the Virginia mountains. Led raid into Missouri in December 1858 that freed 11 slaves. Seized federal armory at Harpers Ferry, Virginia, with a small band of followers on October 16, 1858, but was captured when troops stormed the building on October 18. Tried, convicted, and hanged for murder and treason at Charlestown, Virginia.

John C. Calhoun (March 18, 1782–March 31, 1850) Born near Mount Carmel, South Carolina, the son of a farmer who served in the state legislature. Graduated from Yale College in 1804 and admitted to the bar in 1807. Member of the South Carolina house of representatives, 1808–9. Elected to Congress as a Democratic Republican and served from 1811 to 1817. Secretary of War in the cabinet of

James Monroe, 1817–25. Elected vice-president in 1824 after being nominated on both the John Quincy Adams and Andrew Jackson tickets, and was reelected in 1828 on the Jackson ticket. Resigned as vice-president on December 28, 1832, after being elected to the Senate, where he served until his resignation in 1843. Secretary of State in the cabinet of John Tyler, 1844–45. Elected again to the Senate and served from November 26, 1845, until his death in Washington, D.C. *A Disquisition on Government* and the unfinished *A Discourse on the Constitution and Government of the United States* published posthumously in 1851.

Henry Clay (April 12, 1777–June 29, 1852) Born in Hanover County, Virginia, the son of a Baptist minister and farmer. Admitted to the bar in 1797 and began practicing law in Lexington, Kentucky. Member of the Kentucky house of representatives, 1803–6. Elected as a Democratic Republican to fill the remainder of an unexpired term in the U.S. Senate, 1806–7. Member of the state house of representatives, 1807–10. Fought duel in 1809 with Humphrey Marshall in which both men were wounded. Filled another vacancy in the Senate, 1810–11. Elected to the U.S. House of Representatives and served as its Speaker from March 1811 to January 1814, when he resigned to join the peace commission sent to negotiate with Great Britain at Ghent. Returned to Congress and again served as speaker, 1815–21 and 1823–25. Finished fourth in the 1824 presidential election and supported John Quincy Adams when the election was decided in the House of Representatives. Served as Secretary of State in the Adams administration, 1825–29. Fought a bloodless duel with John Randolph in 1826. Elected to the Senate as a National Republican and served from 1831 until his resignation in 1842. Unsuccessfully ran for president against Andrew Jackson as the National Republican candidate in 1832 and against James Polk as the Whig candidate in 1844. Elected to the Senate as a Whig and served from 1849 until his death in Washington, D.C.

Jefferson Davis (June 3, 1808–December 6, 1889) Born in Todd County, Kentucky, the son of a farmer. Moved with his family to Mississippi. Graduated from the U.S. Military Academy in 1828 and served as an army officer until his resignation in 1835. Became a cotton planter in Warren County, Mississippi. Elected to Congress as a Democrat and served 1845–46, then resigned to command a Mississippi volunteer regiment in Mexico, 1846–47, where he fought at Monterrey and was wounded at Buena Vista. Elected to the Senate and served from 1847 to 1851, when he resigned to run unsuccessfully for governor. Secretary of War in the cabinet of Franklin Pierce,

1853–57. Elected to the Senate and served from 1857 to January 21, 1861, when he withdrew following the secession of Mississippi. Inaugurated as provisional president of the Confederate States of America on February 18, 1861. Elected without opposition to six-year term in November 1861 and inaugurated on February 22, 1862. Captured by Union cavalry near Irwinville, Georgia, on May 10, 1865. Imprisoned at Fort Monroe, Virginia, and indicted for treason. Released on bail on May 13, 1867; the indictment was dropped in 1869 without trial. Published *The Rise and Fall of the Confederate Government* in 1881. Died in New Orleans.

Frederick Douglass (February 1818–February 20, 1895) Born Frederick Bailey in Talbot County, Maryland, the son of a slave mother and an unknown white man. Escaped to Philadelphia in 1838 and settled in New Bedford, Massachusetts, where he took the name Douglass. Became a lecturer for the American Anti-Slavery Society, led by William Lloyd Garrison, in 1841. Published *Narrative of the Life of Frederick Douglass, An American Slave* in 1845. Made successful lecture tour in Great Britain and Ireland, 1845–47, during which a group of English supporters purchased his manumission. Began publishing an antislavery newspaper, *North Star*, in Rochester, New York, in 1847. Attended the woman's rights convention held at Seneca Falls, New York, in 1848. Broke with Garrison and became an ally of Gerrit Smith, who advocated an antislavery interpretation of the Constitution and participation in electoral politics. Published *My Bondage and My Freedom* in 1855. Advocated emancipation and the enlistment of black soldiers at the outbreak of the Civil War and eventually became a supporter of Abraham Lincoln. Continued his advocacy of racial equality and woman's rights after the Civil War. Served as U.S. marshal, 1877–81, and recorder of deeds, 1877–86, for the District of Columbia. Published *Life and Times of Frederick Douglass* in 1881. Served as minister to Haiti, 1889–91. Died in Washington, D.C.

Benjamin Franklin (January 17, 1706–April 17, 1790) Born in Boston, the son of a candle and soap maker. Learned printing trade in Boston and London. Settled in Philadelphia in 1726 and bought *The Pennsylvania Gazette* in 1729. Published *Poor Richard's Almanack*, 1732–57. Founded American Philosophical Society in 1743. Member of the Pennsylvania assembly, 1751–64. Proposed plan for colonial union in 1754. Elected to the Royal Society in 1756 after conducting series of experiments with electricity. Represented Pennsylvania assembly in London, 1757–62. Went to London as agent for Pennsylvania in 1764, and by 1770 was also representing Georgia, New Jersey, and Massachusetts. Returned to Philadelphia on May 5,

1775, and served as delegate to the Second Continental Congress, 1775–76. Appointed diplomatic commissioner by Congress on September 26, 1776, and arrived in France in December. Negotiated treaty of alliance with France, 1778, and peace treaty with Britain, 1782. Returned to United States in September 1785. Served as president of the Pennsylvania supreme executive council, 1785–88. Delegate to the Constitutional Convention, 1787. Died in Philadelphia.

Henry Highland Garnet (December 23, 1815–February 13, 1882) Born in Kent County, Maryland, the son of slaves. Family escaped in 1824 and settled in New York City, taking the name Garnet. Graduated from the Oneida Institute in Whitesboro, New York, in 1839. Served as pastor of the Liberty Street Presbyterian Church in Troy, New York, 1840–48. Underwent leg amputation in 1840 as the result of an earlier injury. Became active in the antislavery Liberty Party and a leading advocate of abolishing the property qualification that prevented most black men from voting in New York State. Attended National Negro Convention held in Buffalo in 1843, where his call for violent resistance to slavery was opposed by Frederick Douglass. Taught school in Geneva, New York, 1848–49. Toured Great Britain and Ireland as an antislavery speaker, 1850–53. Served as a Presbyterian missionary in Jamaica, 1853–56, and as pastor of the Shiloh Presbyterian Church in New York City, 1856–64. Founded African Civilization Society in 1858 to promote cotton cultivation by African-American colonists in the Niger valley. Helped recruit black troops and aided victims of the New York draft riots in 1863. Became pastor of the Fifteenth Street Presbyterian Church in Washington, D.C., in 1864. Delivered sermon in the House of Representatives in 1865 to celebrate congressional approval of the Thirteenth Amendment. President of Avery College in Allegheny, Pennsylvania, 1868–70, then returned to Shiloh Church. Appointed minister to Liberia in 1881 and died there shortly after his arrival.

Alexander Hamilton (January 11, 1755–July 12, 1804) Born in Nevis, in the West Indies. Moved to St. Croix in 1765 and worked as clerk for trading firm, 1766–72. Immigrated to America in 1772 and entered King's College (now Columbia) in 1773. Appointed captain of artillery by New York provincial congress in March 1776. Fought at Long Island, Harlem Heights, White Plains, Trenton, and Princeton. Became aide to George Washington on March 1, 1777, and served on his staff with rank of lieutenant colonel until April 1781. Commanded light infantry battalion at Yorktown. Admitted to New York bar in 1782. Served as delegate to the Continental Congress, 1782–83, and in New York assembly, 1786–87. Delegate to the Constitutional Convention, 1787, and the New York ratifying convention, 1788; wrote most of the *Federalist* essays advocating ratification of the Constitution, 1787–88. Appointed Secretary of the Treasury by George Washington in September 1789 and served until January 1795. Continued to advise Washington after returning to his law practice in New York City. Appointed major general and inspector general of the army in July 1798 during Franco-American crisis and served until June 1800. Died in New York City after being mortally wounded in duel with Vice-President Aaron Burr.

John Hancock (January 12, 1737–October 8, 1793) Born in Quincy, Massachusetts, the son of a Congregational minister. Graduated from Harvard in 1754. Entered his uncle's successful Boston mercantile firm, which he inherited in 1764. Served in the provincial house of representatives, 1766–72. President of the Massachusetts provincial congress, 1774–75. Delegate to the Second Continental Congress, 1775–80, and served as its president, May 24, 1775–October 30, 1777. Member of Massachusetts state constitutional convention, 1780. Governor of Massachusetts, 1780–85 and 1787–93. Member of the Massachusetts ratifying convention in 1788. Died in Quincy while serving as governor.

Patrick Henry (May 29, 1736–June 6, 1799) Born in Hanover County, Virginia, the son of a tobacco planter. Admitted to the bar in 1760. Served in the Virginia House of Burgesses, 1765–70, where he led opposition to the Stamp Act. Participated in the Revolutionary conventions in Virginia, 1774–76, and attended the Continental Congress, 1774–75. Helped draft the Virginia state constitution in 1776. First governor of Virginia, 1776–79. Member of the Virginia house of delegates, 1780–84. Governor of Virginia, 1784–86. Member of the House of Delegates, 1787–90. Leading opponent of the Constitution at the Virginia ratifying convention in 1788. Died at his home near Brookneal, Virginia.

Andrew Jackson (March 15, 1767–June 8, 1845) Born in the Waxhaw Settlements, South Carolina, the son of a farmer. Wounded by a British officer in 1781. Admitted to the bar in North Carolina in 1787. Moved to Nashville in 1788. Attended the Tennessee constitutional convention in 1796. Served in Congress, 1796–97, and in the Senate, 1797–98. Judge of the Tennessee superior court, 1798–1804. Killed Charles Dickson in a duel in 1806. Wounded in gunfight with Jesse and Thomas Hart Benton in 1813. As major general of the Tennessee militia, commanded successful campaign against the Creek Indians in 1814; appointed major general in the U.S. Army. Defeated British at the Battle of New Orleans in 1815. Invaded Spanish Florida in 1818 during campaign against the Seminoles. Served as governor of Florida Territory in 1821; resigned from the army. Served in the Senate, 1823–25. Won plurality of the electoral vote in the 1824 presidential election, but lost in the House of Representatives to John Quincy Adams. Defeated Adams in 1828 and served as president, 1829–33. Won reelection in 1832 by defeating Henry Clay and served second term, 1833–37. Died at the Hermitage, his estate near Nashville.

Thomas Jefferson (April 13, 1743–July 4, 1826) Born in Goochland (now Albemarle) County, Virginia, son of a landowner and surveyor. Educated at the College of William and Mary. Admitted to the Virginia bar in 1767. Served in Virginia assembly, 1769–74. Published *A Summary View of the Rights of British America* in 1774. Delegate to the Continental Congress, 1775–76; drafted the Declaration of Independence. Served in Virginia assembly, 1776–79, and as governor of Virginia, 1779–81. Delegate to the Continental Congress, 1783–84. Served as American minister to France, 1785–89. Appointed Secretary of State by George Washington and held office from March 1790 until December 1793. Republican candidate for president in 1796; finished second in the electoral voting and served as vice-president, 1797–1801. Tied with fellow Republican Aaron Burr in the electoral voting in 1800 and was elected president by the House of Representatives; defeated Federalist Charles Cotesworth Pinckney in 1804 and served as President of the United States, 1801–9. Founded University of Virginia. Died at Monticello, his estate near Charlottesville.

Henry Lee (July 29, 1756–March 25, 1818) Born at Leesylvania, near Dumfries, Prince William County, Virginia, the son of a plantation owner. Graduated from the College of New Jersey (now Princeton) in 1773. Joined Continental army as a captain in 1777 and was promoted to lieutenant colonel in 1780. Became known as "Light-Horse Harry" for his successful command of cavalry in both the northern and southern theaters. Served as a delegate to the Continental Congress, 1785–89. Supported ratification of the Constitution at the Virginia convention in 1788. Governor of Virginia, 1792–94. Elected to Congress as a Federalist and served 1799–1801. Father of Robert E. Lee. Imprisoned for debt, 1808–9, after engaging in land speculation. Seriously injured by a Baltimore mob in 1812 while attempting to help a friend who published an anti-administration newspaper. Died on Cumberland Island, Georgia.

Abraham Lincoln (February 12, 1809–April 15, 1865) Born near Hodgenville, Kentucky, the son of a farmer and carpenter. Family moved to Indiana in 1816 and to Illinois in 1830. Settled in New Salem, Illinois, and worked as a storekeeper, surveyor, and postmaster. Served as a Whig in the state legislature, 1834–41. Began law practice in 1836 and moved to Springfield in 1837. Elected to Congress as a Whig and served from 1847 to 1849. Became a public opponent of the extension of slavery after the passage of the Kansas-Nebraska Act in 1854. Helped found the Republican Party of Illinois in 1856. Campaigned in 1858 for Senate seat held by Stephen Douglas and debated him seven times on the slavery issue; although the Illinois legislature reelected Douglas, the campaign brought Lincoln national prominence. Received Republican presidential nomination in 1860 and won election in a four-way contest; his victory led to the secession of seven Southern states. Responded to the Confederate bombardment of Fort Sumter by calling up militia, proclaiming the blockade of Southern ports, and suspending habeas corpus. Issued preliminary and final emancipation proclamations on September 22w, 1862, and January 1, 1863. After long series of command changes, appointed Ulysses S. Grant commander of all Union forces in March 1864. Won reelection in 1864 by defeating Democrat George B. McClellan. Died in Washington, D.C., after being shot by John Wilkes Booth.

Ely Moore (July 4, 1798–January 27, 1860) Born near Belvidere, New Jersey. Practiced medicine in New York City before becoming a printer there. Elected president of the General Trades' Union of New York in 1833 and edited its journal, the *National Trades' Union*. Ran for Congress as a Jacksonian Democrat and served in the House of Representatives from 1835 to 1839. Surveyor of the port of New York, 1839–45. Appointed U.S. marshal for the southern district of New York in 1845. Returned to Belvidere and published the *Warren Journal*, then moved to Kansas, where he was appointed an Indian agent in 1853. Served as registrar of the federal land office in Lecompton, Kansas, 1855–60. Died in Lecompton.

James Otis (February 5, 1725–May 23, 1783) Born in West Barnstable, Massachusetts, the son of a lawyer. Graduated from Harvard in 1743 and was admitted to the bar in 1748. Began successful law practice and was appointed crown advocate general of the Boston vice-admiralty court in 1756. Resigned position to argue case before the Massachusetts superior court challenging the legality of writs of assistance (general search warrants) issued to royal customs officers; after hearing the case in February 1761 the court upheld the writs. Served in the Massachusetts house of representatives, 1761–70. Published a series pamphlets, 1762–65, defending colonial rights and protesting the Sugar and Stamp acts. Helped organize the Stamp Act Congress in 1765 and the non-importation movement launched in response to the Townshend Acts in 1767. Suffered from mental instability that worsened after he was struck on the head by an English customs officer during a brawl in 1769. Won election to the legislature in 1771, but was soon declared mentally incompetent and placed in the care of his family. Killed by lightning in Andover, Massachusetts.

Theodore Parker (August 24, 1810–May 10, 1860) Born in Lexington, Massachusetts, the son of a farmer and mechanic. Passed entrance examination to Harvard College but was too poor to enroll. Graduated from Harvard Divinity School in 1836 and became pastor of the Unitarian Church in West Roxbury in 1837. Created controversy with his unorthodox sermon *The Transient and Permanent in Christianity* (1841), and lecture series *A Discourse of Matters Pertaining to Religion* (1842). Traveled in Europe, 1843–44. Resigned his West Roxbury pastorate in 1846 and became minister of the new 28th Congregational Society of Boston, which met in the Melodeon (the society moved to the Music Hall in 1852). Became a popular lecturer and an advocate for abolitionism, temperance, prison reform, and other social causes. Helped organize and lead the Boston Vigilance Committee formed in 1850 to resist the new Fugitive Slave Act, and was indicted in 1854 for his role in the attempted rescue of Anthony Burns from the Boston federal courthouse (the charges were later dismissed). Raised money to purchase arms for free-state settlers in Kansas and secretly supported John Brown's plan for an uprising in the South; publicly defended Brown after his raid on Harpers Ferry. Retired from lecturing and preaching in 1859 because of worsening tuberculosis. Died in Florence, Italy.

Wendell Phillips (November 29, 1811–February 2, 1884) Born in Boston, the son of a wealthy lawyer and state senator. Graduated from Harvard College in 1831 and from Harvard Law School in 1834. Began making antislavery speeches in 1837 and became an ally of William Lloyd Garrison. Advocated abolitionism, prohibition, woman's rights, prison reform, and peaceful relations with American Indians while also giving popular lectures on non-political subjects. Criticized President Lincoln as lacking commitment to emancipation and equal rights, and broke with Garrison to oppose Lincoln's reelection in 1864. Succeeded Garrison as president of the American Anti-Slavery Society in 1865 and led the society until 1870, when it dissolved itself following the adoption of the Fifteenth Amendment. Ran for governor of Massachusetts in 1870 as the Labor Reform and

Prohibition candidate. Continued speaking in favor of an eight-hour workday and worker's cooperatives while opposing large corporations. Died in Boston.

John Randolph (June 2, 1773–May 24, 1833) Born in Prince George County, Virginia, the son of a plantation owner. Studied at the College of New Jersey, Columbia, and the College of William and Mary. Elected to Congress as a Republican and served from 1799 to 1813. Added "of Roanoke" to his name about 1810. Defeated for reelection in 1813 because of his opposition to the War of 1812. Returned to Congress and served 1815–17 and 1819–25. Filled the remainder of a term in the Senate, 1825–27. Fought a bloodless duel with Secretary of State Henry Clay in 1826. Defeated for reelection to the Senate, but served another term in the House, 1827–29. Delegate to the convention that revised the Virginia state constitution, 1829–30. Briefly served as minister to Russia in 1830. Died in Philadelphia.

Red Jacket (c. 1758–January 20, 1830) Born in the Finger Lakes region of New York, a member of the Wolf Clan of the Seneca. Named Otetiani (Always Ready) at age 10. Fought against the Americans during the Revolutionary War, 1777–80. Settled along Buffalo Creek near Lake Erie. Given name Sagoyewatha (He Who Keeps Them Awake), and became known to British and American officials as Red Jacket. Negotiated with Timothy Pickering and other American envoys, 1790–91. Met with President Washington in Philadelphia, 1792. Represented the Six Nations of the Iroquois in meetings with Ohio Indians and British and American emissaries. Helped negotiate the treaty between the United States and the Six Nations signed at Canandaigua in 1794, and agreed to the sale of a large portion of Seneca land at Genesco in 1797. Defended Seneca religious beliefs in his speeches to the Rev. Cram, 1805, and the Rev. Alexander, 1811. Supported the United States during the War of 1812. Became a leader of the Seneca "Pagan Party" opposed to Christian missionary activity and further land sales. Met President John Quincy Adams in 1828 and President Jackson in 1829. Died at Buffalo Creek.

Carl Schurz (March 2, 1829–May 14, 1906) Born in Liblar, near Cologne, Germany, the son of a schoolmaster. Participated in the 1848 Revolution while a student at the University of Bonn, then fled to Switzerland in 1849. Returned to Germany in 1850 to help a former professor escape from prison. Immigrated to the United States in 1852 and settled in Philadelphia. Moved to Watertown, Wisconsin, in 1855. Began campaigning for Republican candidates among both German- and English-speaking voters. Unsuccessful candidate for lieutenant governor of Wisconsin in 1857. U.S. minister to Spain, 1861–62. Served as a general in the Union army, 1862–65, commanding a division at Second Bull Run, Chancellorsville, Gettysburg, and Chattanooga. Edited newspapers in Detroit and St. Louis after the war. Elected to the Senate from Missouri as a Republican and served from 1869 to 1875. Helped lead the Liberal Republican movement opposed to Grant's reelection in 1872. Secretary of the Interior in the cabinet of Rutherford B. Hayes, 1877–81. Editor of the New York *Evening Post*, 1881–83. President of the National Civil Service Reform League, 1892–1901. Died in New York City.

William Seward (May 16, 1801–October 10, 1872) Born in Florida, New York, the son of a doctor. Graduated from Union College in 1820 and was admitted to the bar in 1822. Elected to the New York senate as an Anti-Masonic candidate and served until 1834. Unsuccessful Whig candidate for governor in 1834. Elected governor in 1838 and served until 1842. Elected to the U.S. Senate as a Whig and reelected as a Republican, serving from 1849 to 1861. Unsuccessful candidate for the Republican presidential nomination in 1860. Secretary of State in the cabinet of Abraham Lincoln, 1861–65. Wounded by a co-conspirator of John Wilkes Booth on April 14, 1865, but recovered and served as Secretary of State under Andrew Johnson, 1865–69. Negotiated the purchase of Alaska in 1867. Died in Auburn, New York.

Elizabeth Cady Stanton (November 12, 1815–October 26, 1902) Born Elizabeth Cady in Johnstown, New York, the daughter of a wealthy lawyer and landowner. Graduated from the Troy Female Seminary in 1833. Married Henry Stanton, an agent for the American Anti-Slavery Society who later became a lawyer, in 1840; they had seven children. Moved to Seneca Falls, New York, in 1847. Helped organize the woman's rights convention held in Seneca Falls in July 1848 and drafted its "Declaration of Rights and Sentiments." Began friendship with Susan B. Anthony in 1851. President of the Woman's State Temperance Society, 1852–53. Advocated woman's rights in appearances before the New York legislature in 1854 and 1860. Moved to New York City in 1862. Organized petition drive with Anthony in support of the Thirteenth Amendment, 1863–64. First vice-president of the American Equal Rights Association, 1866–68; opposed the Fourteenth and Fifteenth amendments because they did not enfranchise women. Edited weekly newspaper *Revolution*, 1868–70. President of the National Woman Suffrage Association, 1869–70 and 1877–90, and of its successor, the National American Woman Suffrage Association, 1890–92. Toured as a lyceum lecturer, 1870–79. Edited

History of Woman Suffrage (3 vols., 1881–86) with Anthony and Matilda Joslyn Gage. Formed "Revising Committee" to annotate and publish *The Woman's Bible* (2 vols., 1895–98). Died in New York City.

Alexander Stephens (February 11, 1812–March 4, 1883) Born in Taliaferro County, Georgia, the son of a farmer. Graduated from the University of Georgia in 1832. Admitted to the bar in 1834. Served in the Georgia house of representatives, 1836–41, and the Georgia senate, 1842. Elected to Congress as a Whig and then as a Democrat and served from 1843 to 1859. Member of the Georgia secession convention in 1861. Vice-president of the Confederate States of America, 1861–65. Held unsuccessful peace conference with Abraham Lincoln and William Seward at Hampton Roads, Virginia, on February 3, 1865. Arrested by Union troops on May 11, 1865, and imprisoned for five months in Boston. Published *A Constitutional View of the Late War Between the States* (2 vols., 1868–70). Elected to Congress as a Democrat and served from 1873 to 1882. Governor of Georgia from 1882 until his death in Atlanta.

Charles Sumner (January 6, 1811–March 11, 1874) Born in Boston, Massachusetts, the son of a lawyer. Graduated from Harvard College in 1830 and from Harvard Law School in 1833. Practiced law in Boston. Unsuccessful Free Soil candidate for Congress in 1848. Elected to the U.S. Senate as a Free Soiler in 1851. Badly beaten with a cane on the Senate floor by South Carolina congressman Preston Brooks on May 22, 1856, two days after delivering his speech "The Crime Against Kansas." Reelected as a Republican in 1857, but did not regularly return to his seat in the Senate until December 1859. Reelected in 1863 and 1869. Joined Liberal Republicans in opposing the reelection of President Grant in 1872. Died in Washington, D.C.

Sojourner Truth (c. 1797–November 26, 1883) Born Isabella in Hurley, Ulster County, New York, the child of Dutch-speaking slaves. Worked as a field hand and milkmaid on a farm in New Paltz, New York. Emancipated on July 4, 1827, by the law that ended slavery in New York State. Moved in 1829 to New York City, where she worked as a domestic. Member of the "Kingdom of Matthias," a utopian religious commune, from 1832 to 1834. Renamed herself Sojourner Truth in 1843 and became an itinerant preacher. Settled in 1844 in Northampton, Massachusetts, where she met William Lloyd Garrison, Frederick Douglass, and other antislavery and woman's rights activists. *Narrative of Sojourner Truth,* written by Olive Gilbert, a white abolitionist to whom Truth had told her story, published in

1850. Became a traveling speaker for antislavery and woman's rights. Moved to Battle Creek, Michigan, in 1857. Helped with relief efforts for freed slaves during the Civil War, campaigned for President Lincoln's reelection, and participated in the desegregation of the streetcars in Washington, D.C. Campaigned for western land grants for African-Americans and supported temperance while continuing to speak for woman's rights. Published an expanded edition of her *Narrative* in 1875 with the aid of her friend Frances Titus. Died in Battle Creek.

George Washington (February 22, 1732–December 14, 1799) Born on family plantation in Westmoreland County, Virginia. Worked as surveyor in western Virginia. Appointed major in Virginia militia; traveled to Ohio in 1753 to deliver British ultimatum to the French. Commanded militia in first skirmish of the French and Indian War, May 28, 1754. Served as aide to General Edward Braddock during British expedition against Fort Duquesne at the Forks of the Ohio in 1755 and helped command retreat after Braddock's defeat near the Monongahela River. Commissioned as colonel and commander of Virginia militia in August 1755. Served with successful expedition against Fort Duquesne in 1758, then resigned his commission. Elected to Virginia House of Burgesses in 1758 and served until 1774. Inherited Mount Vernon estate in 1761. Delegate to First Continental Congress, 1774, and Second Continental Congress, 1775. Chosen by Congress to be commander in chief of the Continental army on June 15, 1775, and served until December 23, 1783, when he resigned his commission and returned to Mount Vernon. Attended Constitutional Convention in 1787 and was unanimously elected its president. Elected first President of the United States in 1789 and served until 1797, twice receiving the unanimous vote of the electors. Commissioned lieutenant general and commander in chief of the army on July 4, 1798, during crisis in relations with France. Died at Mount Vernon.

Daniel Webster (January 18, 1782–October 24, 1852) Born in Salisbury, New Hampshire, the son of a farmer. Graduated from Dartmouth College in 1801. Admitted to the bar in 1805 and began to practice law in Portsmouth, New Hampshire, in 1807. Elected to Congress as a Federalist and served from 1813 to 1817. Moved to Boston in 1816. Appeared before the U.S. Supreme Court in numerous cases, including the Dartmouth College case, *McCulloch* v. *Maryland*, and *Gibbons* v. *Ogden*. Delegate to the convention that revised the Massachusetts state constitution, 1820–21. Began long career as a public orator with commemorative address at Plymouth, Massachusetts, in

1820. Served in Congress, 1823–27, and in the Senate, 1827–41. Won electoral vote of Massachusetts in 1836 as one of three Whig candidates for the presidency. Secretary of State in the cabinets of William Henry Harrison and John Tyler, 1841–43. Elected to the Senate as a Whig and served from 1845 to 1850. Secretary of State in the cabinet of Millard Fillmore from July 1850 until his death in Marshfield, Massachusetts.

Angelina Grimké Weld (February 20, 1805–October 26, 1879) Born in Charleston, South Carolina, the daughter of a wealthy landowner and judge. Joined her older sister Sarah in Philadelphia in 1829 and became a member of the Society of Friends. Publicly endorsed abolitionism in 1835, and published antislavery pamphlet *Appeal to the Christian Women of the South* in 1836. Along with Sarah, began giving lectures for the American Anti-Slavery Society in 1837, appearing before female, and then mixed, audiences. Married Theodore Weld, a Presbyterian minister and prominent abolitionist, on May 14, 1838, and soon retired from lecturing. Helped research *Slavery As It Is*, widely circulated pamphlet published by Theodore Weld in 1839. Taught school in Belleville, New Jersey, 1848–54; in Perth Amboy, New Jersey, 1854–63; and in Lexington, Massachusetts, 1863–67. Attended woman's rights conventions held in Rochester, 1851, and New York City, 1863, and became a member of the Massachusetts Woman Suffrage Association in 1868. Died in Hyde Park, Massachusetts (now part of Boston).

William Wirt (November 8, 1772–February 18, 1834) Born in Bladensburg, Maryland, the son of tavern keepers. Admitted to the bar in Culpeper County, Virginia, in 1792. Moved to Richmond in 1799. Helped defend James Callender at his trial under the Sedition Act in 1800 and was one of the prosecutors at the treason trial of Aaron Burr in 1807. Appointed U.S. attorney for the Richmond district in 1816. Attorney General in the cabinets of James Monroe and John Quincy Adams, 1817–29. Published *Sketches of the Life and Character of Patrick Henry* in 1817. Continued his private practice while Attorney General and appeared before the Supreme Court in the Dartmouth College case, *McCulloch* v. *Maryland*, and *Gibbons* v. *Ogden*. Won seven electoral votes as the Anti-Masonic candidate for president in 1832. Died in Washington, D.C.

Frances Wright (September 6, 1795–December 13, 1852) Born in Dundee, Scotland, the daughter of a wealthy linen manufacturer. Visited the United States, 1818–20. Published *Views of Society and Manners in America* (1821) and philosophical essay *A Few Days in*

Athens (1822). Became friends with Jeremy Bentham and the Marquis de Lafayette. Returned to the United States in 1824. Discussed slavery with Thomas Jefferson and James Madison. Purchased slaves and land in western Tennessee and in 1826 founded Nashoba, experimental community using cooperative labor intended to serve as a model for widespread emancipation. Visited England in 1827 and then returned to Nashoba accompanied by Frances Trollope. Published "Explanatory Notes" on Nashoba in which she criticized marriage and praised miscegenation. Left Nashoba in June 1828 and went to New Harmony, Indiana, cooperative community established by Robert Owen. Became co-editor of weekly *New Harmony Gazette* (later renamed *Free Enquirer*). Began lecturing to audiences of both men and women, becoming known as the "High Priestess of Infidelity" for her criticism of religion. Moved to New York City in 1829. Chartered brig in 1830 to carry former slaves from Nashoba to Haiti, then went to France and gave birth to a daughter. Married William Phiquepal D'Arusmont, the father of her child, in 1831. Returned to the United States in 1835. Gave speeches in support of Martin Van Buren and attacking the Bank of the United States, 1836–38. Became involved in prolonged property dispute with D'Arusmont while living in France, England, and the United States. Died in Cincinnati.

Note on the Texts

This volume collects the texts of 45 speeches on political subjects given by 32 American public figures between 1761 and 1865 and presents them in the chronological order of their delivery. Although some of these speeches were first published posthumously, most of them were printed during the lifetime of the speaker, and some were revised by the speaker after initial delivery. The texts presented in this volume are taken from the best printed sources available. Where there is more than one printed source, the text printed in this volume comes from the source that contains the fewest editorial alterations in spelling, capitalization, paragraphing, and punctuation.

This volume prints texts as they appear in the sources listed below, but with a few alterations in editorial procedure. In cases where earlier editors supplied in brackets words that were omitted from a source text by an obvious printer's error, this volume removes the brackets and accepts the editorial emendation. Bracketed identifications of persons that appeared in the original printed texts have been retained in this volume, but bracketed insertions used by subsequent editors to expand abbreviations, identify persons, or clarify meaning have been deleted. In cases where an obvious printer's error was marked by earlier editors with "[*sic*]," the present volume omits the "[*sic*]" and corrects the error. (Two editorial emendations that have not been accepted in the present volume are mentioned in the notes; see notes 296.2 and 296.16 in this volume.)

The following is a list of the speeches included in this volume, in the order of their appearance, giving the source of each text.

James Otis: Argument Against Writs of Assistance, Boston, February 24, 1761. *Legal Papers of John Adams*, vol. 2, ed. L. Kinvin Wroth and Hiller B. Zobel (Cambridge: The Belknap Press of Harvard University Press, 1965), pp. 139–44. © 1965 Massachusetts Historical Society. Reprinted by permission of the publishers.

John Hancock: Oration on the Boston Massacre, Boston, March 5, 1774. *An Oration; delivered March 5, 1774, at the Request of the Inhabitants of the Town of Boston: to Commemorate the Bloody Tragedy of the Fifth of March 1770, by the Honorable John Hancock, Esq.* (Boston: Edes and Gill, 1774), 5–20.

Patrick Henry: Speech in the Virginia Convention, Richmond, March 23, 1775. William Wirt, *Sketches of the Life and Character of Patrick Henry* (Philadelphia: James Webster, 1817), 119–23.

George Washington: Speech to Officers of the Continental Army, Newburgh, N.Y., March 15, 1783. *George Washington: Writings*, ed. John Rhodehamel (New York: Library of America, 1997), 496–500.

Benjamin Franklin: Speech at the Conclusion of the Constitutional Convention, Philadelphia, September 17, 1787. *The Debate on the Constitution, Part One*, ed. Bernard Bailyn (New York: Library of America, 1993), 3–5. Reprinted with permission of the Wisconsin Historical Society.

Patrick Henry: Speech in Virginia Ratifying Convention, Richmond, June 4, 1788. *The Debate on the Constitution, Part Two*, ed. Bernard Bailyn (New York: Library of America, 1993), 595–97.

George Washington: First Inaugural Address, New York City, April 30, 1789. *George Washington: Writings*, ed. John Rhodehamel (New York: Library of America, 1997), 730–34. Copyright © 1987 by the Rectors and Visitors of the University of Virginia. Reprinted with permission of the University of Virginia Press.

Red Jacket: Reply to President Washington, Philadelphia, March 31, 1792. William L. Stone, *The Life and Times of Red-Jacket, or Sa-go-ye-wat-ha* (New York: Wiley and Putnam, 1841), 74–80.

Henry Lee: Eulogy on George Washington, Philadelphia, December 26, 1799. Henry Lee, *A Funeral Oration on the Death of General Washington* (Philadelphia: 1800), 5–17.

Thomas Jefferson: First Inaugural Address, Washington, D.C., March 4, 1801. *Thomas Jefferson: Writings*, ed. Merrill D. Peterson (New York: Library of America, 1984), 492–96.

Alexander Hamilton: Remarks on the Repeal of the Judiciary Act, New York City, February 11, 1802. *Alexander Hamilton: Writings*, ed. Joanne B. Freeman (New York: Library of America, 2001), 983–85. Copyright © 1977 Columbia University Press. Reprinted with permission of Columbia University Press.

John Randolph: Speech in Congress Against Non-Importation, Washington, D.C., March 5, 1806. *The Debates and Proceedings in the Congress of the United States*, Ninth Congress, First Session (Washington: Gales and Seaton, 1852), 555–74.

Henry Clay: Speech in Congress on the War of 1812, Washington, D.C., January 8–9, 1813. *The Papers of Henry Clay*, vol. I, ed. James F. Hopkins, associate editor Mary W. M. Hargreaves (Lexington: University of Kentucky Press, 1959), 754–73. Copyright © 1959 by the University of Kentucky Press. Reprinted with permission.

Daniel Webster: Address at the Laying of the Cornerstone of the Bunker Hill Monument, Boston, June 17, 1825. Daniel Webster, *An Address Delivered at the Laying of the Corner Stone of the Bunker Hill Monument* (Boston: Cummings, Hilliard, and Company, 1825), 3–40.

William Wirt: Eulogy on John Adams and Thomas Jefferson, Washington, D.C., October 19, 1826. *A Selection of Eulogies, Pronounced in the Several States, in Honor of those Illustrious Patriots and Statesmen, John Adams and Thomas Jefferson* (Hartford: D.F. Robinson & Co. and Norton & Russell, 1826), 379–426.

Frances Wright: Fourth of July Address, New Harmony, Indiana, July 4, 1828. *Course of Popular Lectures, as delivered by Frances Wright* (New York: The Free Inquirer, 1829), 171–82.

Andrew Jackson: First Inaugural Address, Washington, D.C., March 4, 1829. *A Compilation of the Messages and Papers of the Presidents, 1789–1907*, vol. 2, ed. James D. Richardson (New York: Bureau of National Literature and Art, 1908), 436–38.

Daniel Webster: Second Reply to Hayne, Washington, January 26–27, 1830. *The Papers of Daniel Webster: Speeches and Formal Writings*, vol. I, ed. Charles M. Wiltse (Hanover, N.H.: University Press of New England, 1986), 287–348. Copyright © 1986 by Trustees of Dartmouth College. Reprinted by permission of University Press of New England, Hanover, N. H.

Andrew Jackson: Second Inaugural Address, Washington, D.C., March 4, 1833. *A Compilation of the Messages and Papers of the Presidents, 1789–1907*, vol. 3, ed. James D. Richardson (New York: Bureau of National Literature and Art, 1908), 3–5.

Ely Moore: Address to the General Trades' Union, New York City, December 2, 1833. Ely Moore, *Address delivered before the General Trades' Union of the City of New-York, at the Chatham-street Chapel, December 2, 1833* (New York: James Ormond, 1833), 7–32.

Thomas Hart Benton: Speech in the Senate on Expunging the Censure of President Jackson, Washington, D.C., January 12, 1837. *Gales and Seaton's Register of Debates in Congress*, Debates in the Senate, 24th Congress, Second Session, 382–391.

John C. Calhoun: Speech in the Senate on Antislavery Petitions, Washington, D.C., February 6, 1837. *The Papers of John C. Calhoun*, vol. 13, ed. Clyde N. Wilson (Columbia: University of South Carolina Press, 1980), pp. 391–98. Copyright © 1980 by the University of South Carolina. Reprinted with permission.

Wendell Phillips: The Murder of Lovejoy, Boston, December 8, 1837. Wendell Phillips, *Speeches, Lectures, and Letters* (Boston: Lee and Shepard, 1872), 2–10.

Angelina Grimké Weld: Antislavery Speech at Pennsylvania Hall, Philadelphia, May 16, 1838. *The Public Years of Sarah and Angelina Grimké: Selected Writings 1835–1839*, ed. Larry Ceplair (New York: Columbia University Press, 1989), 318–23. Copyright © 1989 by Columbia University Press. Reprinted with permission of Columbia University Press.

Henry Highland Garnet: Address to the Slaves of the United States of America, Buffalo, N.Y., August 21, 1843. *A Memorial Discourse by Rev. Henry Highland Garnet* (Philadelphia: Joseph M. Wilson, 1865), 44–51.

Abraham Lincoln: Speech in Congress on the War with Mexico, Washington, D.C., January 12, 1848. *Abraham Lincoln: Speeches and Writings, 1832–1858*, ed. Don E. Fehrenbacher (New York: Library of America, 1989), 161–71. Copyright © 1953 by The Abraham Lincoln Association.

Elizabeth Cady Stanton: Address to the Woman's Rights Convention, Seneca
Falls, N.Y., July 19, 1848. *Address of Mrs. Elizabeth Cady Stanton, Delivered
at Seneca Falls & Rochester, N.Y., July 19th & August 2, 1848* (New York:
Robert J. Johnston, 1870), 3–19.

Theodore Parker: The Political Destination of America and the Signs of the
Times, 1848. Theodore Parker, *Speeches, Addresses, and Occasional Sermons*,
vol. 2 (Boston: Horace B. Fuller, 1867), 198–251.

Henry Clay: Speech in the Senate on Compromise Resolutions, Washington,
D.C., February 5–6, 1850. *Congressional Globe*, 31st Congress, First Session,
appendix, 115–27.

John C. Calhoun: Speech in the Senate on Compromise Resolutions,
Washington, D.C., March 4, 1850. *The Papers of John C. Calhoun*, vol. 27,
ed. Clyde N. Wilson and Shirley Bright Cook (Columbia: University of
South Carolina Press, 2003), 187–212. Copyright © 2003 by the University
of South Carolina. Reprinted with permission.

Daniel Webster: Speech in the Senate on Compromise Resolutions,
Washington, D.C., March 7, 1850. *Congressional Globe*, 31st Congress,
First Session, appendix, 269–76.

Sojourner Truth: Speech to Woman's Rights Convention, Akron, Ohio,
May 29, 1851. *National Anti-Slavery Standard*, May 2, 1863.

Frederick Douglass: What to the Slave Is the Fourth of July?, Rochester,
N.Y., July 5, 1852. *The Frederick Douglass Papers*, Series One, Volume 2, ed.
John W. Blassingame (New Haven: Yale University Press, 1982), 359–88.
Copyright © 1982 by Yale University. Reprinted with permission of Yale
University Press.

Charles Sumner: The Crime Against Kansas, Washington, D.C., May 19–20,
1856. *Congressional Globe*, 34th Congress, First Session, appendix, 529–44.

Abraham Lincoln: "House Divided" Speech, Springfield, Illinois, June 16,
1858. *Abraham Lincoln: Speeches and Writings, 1832–1858*, ed. Don E.
Fehrenbacher (New York: Library of America, 1989), 426–34. Copyright ©
1953 by The Abraham Lincoln Association.

William Seward: The Irrepressible Conflict, Rochester, N.Y., October 25,
1858. *The Works of William H. Seward*, vol. IV, ed. George E. Baker
(Boston: Houghton, Mifflin and Company, 1884), 289–302.

Carl Schurz: True Americanism, Boston, Massachusetts, April 18, 1859. Carl
Schurz, *Speeches of Carl Schurz* (Phil.: J. B. Lippincott & Co., 1865), 51–75.

John Brown: Speech to the Court, Charlestown, Virginia, November 2, 1859.
*The Life, Trial and Execution of Captain John Brown, known as 'Old Brown
of Ossawatomie,' with a full account of the attempted insurrection at
Harper's Ferry* (New York: Robert M. De Witt, 1859), 94–95.

Abraham Lincoln: Address at Cooper Institute, New York City, February 27,
1860. *Abraham Lincoln: Speeches and Writings, 1859–1865*, ed. Don E.
Fehrenbacher (New York: Library of America, 1989), 111–30. Copyright ©
1953 by The Abraham Lincoln Association.

Jefferson Davis: Farewell Address in the Senate, Washington, D.C., January
21, 1861. *The Papers of Jefferson Davis*, Volume 7, ed. Lynda Laswell Crist

and Mary Seaton Dix (Baton Rouge: Louisiana State University Press, 1992), 18–23. Copyright © 1992 by Louisiana State University Press. Reprinted by permission of Louisiana State University Press.

Abraham Lincoln: Speech at Independence Hall, Philadelphia, February 22, 1861. *Abraham Lincoln: Speeches and Writings, 1859–1865*, ed. Don E. Fehrenbacher (New York: Library of America, 1989), 213–14. Copyright © 1953 by The Abraham Lincoln Association.

Abraham Lincoln: First Inaugural Address, Washington, D.C., March 4, 1861. *Abraham Lincoln: Speeches and Writings, 1859–1865*, ed. Don E. Fehrenbacher (New York: Library of America, 1989), 215–24. Copyright © 1953 by The Abraham Lincoln Association.

Alexander Stephens: "Corner-Stone" Speech, Savannah, Georgia, March 21, 1861. Henry Cleveland, *Alexander H. Stephens in Public and Private* (Philadelphia: National Publishing Company, 1866), 717–29.

Abraham Lincoln: Address at Gettysburg, Pennsylvania, November 19, 1863. *Abraham Lincoln: Speeches and Writings, 1859–1865*, ed. Don E. Fehrenbacher (New York: Library of America, 1989), 536. Copyright © 1953 by The Abraham Lincoln Association.

Abraham Lincoln: Second Inaugural Address, Washington, D.C., March 4, 1865. *Abraham Lincoln: Speeches and Writings, 1859–1865*, ed. Don E. Fehrenbacher (New York: Library of America, 1989), 686–87. Copyright © 1953 by The Abraham Lincoln Association.

This volume presents the texts of the printings chosen as sources here but does not attempt to reproduce features of their typographic design, or characteristics of 18th-century typography such as the long "s." The use of quotation marks has been modernized: only beginning and ending quotation marks are provided here, instead of placing a quotation mark at the beginning of every line of a quoted passage. The texts are printed without alteration except for the changes previously discussed and for the correction of typographical errors. Spelling, punctuation, and capitalization are often expressive features, and they are not altered, even when inconsistent or irregular. The following is a list of typographical errors corrected, cited by page and line number: 10.5, Massachusett's; 23.27, or; 73.4, connterpoise; 73.35, rooms.; 85.9, wihch; 98.9, struck."; 138.7, liberties the; 143.17, Jefferso'n; 145.20, thens aid; 151.36, anxius; 162.5, Thereeeas; 163.1 oft b lloquial; 163.34, letterswh ich; 167.16, strugling; 187.39, shaven; 266.14, difference; 268.27, occupatian; 269.23, Ithica; 308.13, slavery?"'; 339.9, come,; 340.22, superiority,; 345.20, come; 347.15, sad-ooking; 395.4, resolution; 403.22, edequate; 408.29, sctual; 423.21, that that; 463.34, converted in,; 490.30, indignation,; 502.3, Upsher; 505.17, polical; 549.36, track; 556.5–6, *quaddam*; 604.7, controversy-.; 620.13, proceedinga; 621.19, in. the; 625.15, pess; 659.36, enthusiam; 723.7, successfuly.

Notes

In the notes below, the reference numbers denote page and line of this volume (the line count includes headings). No note is made for material included in the eleventh edition of *Merriam-Webster's Collegiate Dictionary*. Biblical quotations are keyed to the King James Version. Quotations from Shakespeare are keyed to *The Riverside Shakespeare*, ed. G. Blakemore Evans (Boston: Houghton Mifflin, 1974).

1.2   *Argument Against Writs of Assistance*]   Writs of assistance were general warrants issued to customs officers that authorized them to search any ship or building they suspected contained contraband goods, and to call upon the assistance of justices of the peace, sheriffs, and constables in conducting searches. After the death of George II in 1760 Massachusetts customs officials petitioned the superior court to have their writs renewed (the writs expired six months after the death of the sovereign in whose name they were issued). James Otis, the crown advocate-general of the Boston vice-admiralty court, resigned his position in order to appear before the superior court on behalf of Boston merchants challenging the petition. In November 1761 the court ruled that general writs of assistance were lawful. The version of Otis's speech printed here was written in the spring of 1761 by John Adams, who attended the court. In a letter written in 1817, Adams described Otis as a "flame of fire" during his argument, and then wrote: "Then and there the child Independence was born."

2.4–5   cost one King . . . another his throne.]   Charles I was beheaded in 1649; James II was deposed in 1688.

2.28   Act of 14th Car. II. which Mr. Gridley]   An act passed in the 14th year of the reign of Charles II (his reign was measured from his father's death in 1649, not the Restoration in 1660). Jeremiah Gridley (1702–1767) represented the customs officials seeking new writs.

3.22   curse of Canaan]   See Genesis 9:25.

4.33   Vid. Viner]   Charles Viner (1678–1756), English jurist and legal commentator.

7.33   house of Brunswick]   The Hanoverian dynasty that began with George I (1714–1727).

8.7–8   The troops . . . arrival]   British troops landed in Boston on October 1, 1768.

9.19   Hillsborough]   Wills Hill, the Earl of Hillsborough (1718–1793), was Secretary of State for the Colonies from 1768 to 1772.

9.21   Preston]   Captain Thomas Preston was the commander of the soldiers who fired upon the crowd on March 5, 1770. Defended by John Adams, Preston was tried for murder in October 1770 and was acquitted.

10.9   unbiass'd pen of a Robinson]   Customs commissioner John Robinson sailed for London on March 16, 1770, carrying military depositions that blamed the Boston crowd for the shootings on March 5. The depositions were used in *A Fair Account of the Late Disturbances at Boston*, a pamphlet published in England later in the year. In 1769 Robinson had beaten James Otis during a coffeehouse brawl.

10.25–26 Maverick . . . Carr]   Samuel Maverick, an apprentice, Samuel Gray, a ropemaker, James Caldwell, a sailor, and Crispus Attucks, another sailor, were shot and killed on March 5, 1770; Patrick Carr, a leatherworker, died of his wounds on March 14.

10.31   the miserable Monk]   Christopher Monk, aged 17, was shot in the back and badly wounded.

17.4–9   *"Although the . . . our Salvation."*]   Habbakuk 3:17.

18.2   *Speech in the Virginia Convention*]   The second Virginia Convention was an extralegal session of the colonial assembly that met in Richmond from March 20 to 27, 1775. Henry spoke in support of a successful resolution calling for the colony to "be immediately put into a posture of Defence." The text printed here is the reconstruction of his speech published in 1817 by William Wirt in *Sketches of the Life and Character of Patrick Henry*.

19.7–8   our petition]   The First Continental Congress sent a petition to George III on October 26, 1774, seeking redress for colonial grievances.

22.2   *Speech . . . the Continental Army*]   An anonymous address written by Major John Armstrong (1758–1843), later Secretary of War, 1813–14, under President James Madison, was circulated on March 10, 1783, among the Continental Army officers camped at Newburgh, New York. The address condemned Congress for failing to pay the officers and incited the army to rebel if their demands were not met. Washington responded by calling for the officers to assemble on March 15. A second anonymous address, also written by Armstrong, was circulated on March 12, claiming that Washington sympathized with the aims and methods of the disaffected officers.

At the assembly held on March 15 Washington first read this speech and then began to read a letter from Joseph Jones, a Virginia delegate to Congress, promising just treatment for the army. Washington paused, produced a pair of spectacles, and said: "Gentlemen, you must pardon me. I have grown gray in your service and now find myself growing blind." (Another report of this remark is: "Gentlemen, you will permit me to put on my spectacles, for

I have not only grown gray, but almost blind, in the service of my country.")
His remark brought some of the formerly mutinous officers to tears. Washington then left the building and major generals Henry Knox and Israel Putnam introduced and carried a resolution condemning the address of March
10 and pledging obedience to civil authority.

23.39–40   Some Emissary . . . New York]   From the British high command in New York City (the city remained under British occupation until
November 1783).

27.2–3   *Speech . . . Constitutional Convention*]   This speech was read for
the 82-year-old Franklin by James Wilson, a fellow Pennsylvania delegate, on
the final day of the convention. The version printed here is taken from the
manuscript Franklin subsequently sent to Daniel Carroll, a Maryland delegate
to the convention.

27.15–19   Steele . . . in the Wrong.]   The mock dedication to Pope
Clement XI in Urbano Cerri, *An Account of the state of the Roman-Catholick
Religion* (1715), was attributed to Richard Steele, but was actually written by
Bishop Benjamin Hoadly (1676–1761). It includes the passage: "You are Infal-
lible, and We are always in the Right."

27.27–28   *Form* of Government . . . administred]   Cf. Alexander Pope,
An Essay on Man (1733–34), Epistle III, 303–4: "For Forms of Government
let fools contest; / Whate'er is best administered is best."

28.34–37   every Member . . . put his Name]   Despite Franklin's plea,
Massachusetts delegate Elbridge Gerry and Virginia delegates George Mason
and Edmund Randolph refused to sign the final document.

28.39   Consent &c]   "Consent of the States present."

29.2   *Virginia Ratifying Convention*]   The convention met from June 2
to 27, 1788, and on June 25 voted 89–79 to ratify the Constitution and recommended the subsequent adoption of a series of amendments.

34.34–35   Fifth article of the Constitution]   The article providing for
amendments.

35.18–24   I must decline . . . actual expenditures]   Despite Washington's request that he receive no compensation other than the reimbursement
of his expenses, Congress voted him an annual salary of $25,000.

36.5   Colonel Pickering]   Timothy Pickering (1745–1829), a former Continental Army officer who served as an emissary to the Seneca. He was
Postmaster-General, 1791–95; Secretary of War, 1795; Secretary of State, 1795–
1800; a Federalist senator from Massachusetts, 1803–11; and a Federalist congressman, 1813–17.

36.7   General Knox]   Henry Knox (1750–1806), a former major general in
the Continental Army, was Secretary of War, 1789–94.

36.25   CON-NEH-SAUTY]   Timothy Pickering.

37.33   treaty at Muskingum]   Under the terms of the Treaty of Fort Har-
mar, signed at the junction of the Muskingum and Ohio rivers on January 9,
1789, the Wyandot, Delaware, Ottawa, Chippewa, Sauk, and Potawatomi
nations ceded their claim to much of present-day Ohio.

40.1–2   an ambassador . . . England]   George Hammond, the first official British minister to the United States, arrived in Philadelphia on October
20, 1791.

44.8–10   a Chief . . . Abraham]   Sir William Howe (1729–1814), commander-in-chief of the British army in America, 1775–78, led light infantry in
the British victory at Quebec City in 1759.

44.11   Montgomery]   Brigadier General Richard Montgomery (1738–
1775) was killed leading an unsuccessful attack on Quebec City.

44.35–36   conqueror of India]   Charles Cornwallis (1738–1805) served as
governor general of India from 1786 to 1793 and defeated Tipu Sultan in 1792.

45.2–3   hushed . . . growing sedition]   The potential mutiny by Continental Army officers in 1783; see pp. 22–26 in this volume.

47.3   "O fortunatos . . . norint!"]   Virgil, *Georgics*, II, 458: "Oh happy,
if they knew their happy state!"

47.23   terrible conflict deluging Europe]   War began between revolutionary France and Great Britain in 1793.

47.24–25   the gallant Wayne]   Major General Anthony Wayne (1745–1796)
defeated a coalition of western Indians at the Battle of Fallen Timbers on
August 20, 1794.

48.1–4   "Justum . . . solida."]   Horace, *Odes*, III, iii: "Neither the passion of the citizenry demanding wrong, nor the face of a threatening tyrant,
shakes from firm resolve the man who is just and steadfast in his purpose."
(trans. Debra Hecht)

55.2   *Remarks on . . . Judiciary Act*]   The text of Hamilton's remarks
are taken from the New York *Commercial Advertiser*, February 26, 1802. The
Judiciary Act of 1801, signed by President John Adams on February 13, relieved Supreme Court justices from circuit duty and created five new district
court and 16 new circuit court judgeships. When the Republicans in Congress
moved on January 6, 1802, to repeal the act and abolish the new judgeships,
Federalists protested that removing judges already in office would violate the
independence of the judiciary. The repeal measure became law on March 8,
1802.

56.9–10   'sleep . . . eye-lids,']   Cf. Psalm 132:4, Proverbs 6:4.

58.2   *Speech . . . Non-Importation*]   The House of Representatives was debating a resolution to ban the importation of all British goods in retaliation for seizures of American ships trading with the French West Indies. On March 17, 1806, the House approved, 87–35, a different resolution that prohibited the importation of a specific list of British manufactures, including goods made of silk, flax, hemp, glass, paper, silver, brass, tin, leather, and some woolens.

58.12–13   gentleman from Pennsylvania]   Andrew Gregg (1755–1835), a Republican, served in Congress, 1791–1807, and in the Senate, 1807–13.

58.17–18   our lips . . . foreign relations]   Despite Randolph's objections, the House had voted 76–54 on January 16, 1806, to appropriate $2 million for the purchase of West Florida from Spain. The measure was debated and approved in secret session, and the appropriation did not become public until March 13, 1806.

58.32   Mr. J. CLAY]   Joseph Clay (1769–1811), a Republican, served in Congress from 1803 to 1808.

58.33   situation . . . in 1793]   When war began between revolutionary France and Great Britain.

59.8   Rodney's victory]   Admiral Sir George Rodney (1719–1792) defeated the French fleet off Dominica on April 12, 1782.

59.28–29   Mr. CROWNINSHIELD]   Jacob Crowninshield (1770–1808), a Republican, served in Congress from 1803 until his death.

59.34–35   North . . . Sandwich]   Lord North (1732–1792) was prime minister, 1770–82; the Earl of Sandwich (1718–1792) was first lord of the admiralty, 1771–82.

59.38   Suffrein]   Admiral Pierre André de Suffren (1729–1788) commanded the French fleet off India and Ceylon, 1782–83.

60.4   Count De Grasse]   French admiral whose victory at the Chesapeake Capes on September 5, 1781, prevented the evacuation of the British army at Yorktown.

60.5–6   Admiral Gravina, or Admiral Villeneuve]   The Spanish and French commanders of the combined fleet destroyed by the British under Nelson at the battle of Trafalgar on October 21, 1805.

61.2   Sir Robert Walpole]   Walpole (1676–1745) served as first lord of the treasury, 1721–42, and is generally regarded as the first prime minister of Great Britain.

63.3–4   naval war . . . Administration]   The undeclared naval war with France fought under the Adams administration, 1798–1800.

63.32   battle of Actium]   Naval battle fought off Greece in 31 B.C. in which Octavian decisively defeated Mark Anthony.

65.22   *Ne sutor ultra crepidam.*]   Let the shoemaker stick to his last.

67.3–4   paid fifteen millions]   In 1803 the United States purchased Louisiana from France for $15 million.

67.7   Mr. Chairman]   The House was meeting as a Committee of the Whole.

68.4   the British treaty]   The Jay Treaty of 1794.

68.27   Treaty of San Lorenzo]   The treaty, negotiated by Thomas Pinckney, was signed in 1795.

70.27   Palinurus]   The helmsman of Aeneas.

71.2–3   a book . . . its father.]   *An Examination of the British Doctrine, Which Subjects to Capture a Neutral Trade, Not Open in Time of Peace,* published anonymously by Secretary of State James Madison.

71.20   "War in Disguise"]   *War in Disguise; or, The Frauds of the Neutral Flags* (1805), a pamphlet by the English barrister James Stephen (1758–1832) that advocated a stricter interpretation of the law of blockade.

72.4   *mare liberum*]   Open sea.

74.12–13   *Quem . . . dementat.*]   Whom God wishes to destroy, he first makes mad.

75.14–15   dismantling of Dunkirk . . . Pondicherry]   Under the terms of the Treaty of Utrecht, signed in 1713 at the end of the War of the Spanish Succession, the port of Dunkirk was demolished to prevent its further use by French privateers. Britain captured Quebec in 1759, and the province was ceded by France in 1763. Pondicherry, the capital of the French territory in India, was captured by the British in 1761, 1778, and 1793, but was restored to France by treaty in 1763, 1783, and 1802. In 1803 it was again captured by the British.

75.35   *peculium*]   Property held for private, personal use.

75.12–13   public treasure . . . Turks and infidels]   The United States paid tribute to the Barbary States until 1815.

76.17–18   greater unanimity . . . Presidential election]   In 1804 Thomas Jefferson received 162 out of 176 electoral votes.

77.11–12   the miserable Governor]   William C. C. Claiborne (1775–1817) was governor of the Territory of Orleans, 1804–12, and the state of Louisiana, 1812–16.

77.33   lets slip the dogs of war]   Cf. *Julius Caesar*, III, I, 273.

78.9   Eustatia]   St. Eustatius, an island in the Netherlands Antilles near St. Kitts.

78.10   a joe] A Portuguese gold coin.

78.35   Cowpens] The site of an American victory in South Carolina on January 17, 1781.

79.21   immortal author . . . Curtius] John Thomson (1776–1799), a lawyer active in Virginia Republican politics, published five letters in 1798 criticizing John Marshall's defense of the Alien and Sedition Acts.

80.32   Pharsalia] Julius Caesar decisively defeated his rival Pompey at the battle of Pharsalus, fought in northern Greece in 48 B.C.

81.3   Horne Tooke and Hardy] English radical leaders John Horne Tooke (1736–1812) and Thomas Hardy (1752–1832) were tried for high treason in 1794 and acquitted.

81.5   Duke d'Enghein] Louis Antoine Henri de Bourbon-Condé, duc d'Enghein (1772–1804), an exiled French aristocrat, was falsely suspected of plotting against Napoleon. On March 15, 1804, French gendarmes seized him at his home in Etterheim in Germany and brought him to France, where he was summarily court-martialed and shot at the fortress of Vincennes on March 21.

82.9   Marquis Yrujo] Don Carlos Martinez de Yrujo y Tacón (1763–1824) was Spanish minister to the United States from 1796 to 1807. In January 1806 he publicly refused to leave Washington after being asked to do so by Secretary of State Madison.

82.14   "Charles Maurice Talleyrand."] Talleyrand (1754–1838) served as foreign minister of France, 1797–99, 1799–1807, and 1814–15.

83.5   this bill] The bill authorized the additional enlistment of 20,000 men in the army for one year.

84.29–33   partial non-importation . . . general non-importation] Congress passed a partial non-importation act on April 18, 1806 (see note 58.2), that went into effect on November 15, 1806. At President Jefferson's request, Congress suspended its operation in December 1806 for one year to allow negotiations with Great Britain to proceed. In December 1807 Jefferson called for a total ban on overseas trade and signed the Embargo Act on December 22. The embargo was repealed by the Nonintercourse Act, signed on March 1, 1809, which reopened American foreign commerce with all nations except Britain and France while authorizing the president to renew trade with either country if it removed its restrictions on American shipping. In April 1809 President Madison ordered the resumption of commerce with Britain, but then reimposed nonintercourse in August. The Nonintercourse Act expired in 1810 and was succeeded by Macon's Bill No. 2, which reopened commerce with both Britain and France while authorizing the president to prohibit trade with one nation if the other removed its restrictions on American shipping. In November 1810 the administration issued a proclamation closing off commerce with Britain on February 2, 1811, and in March 1811 Congress endorsed the proclamation by passing a new Nonintercourse Act prohibiting imports from Britain.

84.37   Mr. Erskine]   David Erskine (1776–1855) was the British minister to the United States from 1806 to 1809. In April 1809 Erskine and President Madison reached an agreement on American neutral rights, but the British government soon disavowed it and recalled Erskine.

85.2–3   proffered reparation . . . national vessel]   In 1809 David Erskine (see note above) offered to make reparation for the *Chesapeake* incident of 1807, in which a British frigate had opened fire on an American warship while searching for deserters from the Royal Navy. President Madison accepted the offer and withdrew the previous American demand that the officer responsible be tried, while asserting that judicial punishment "would best comport with what is due from his Britannic Majesty to his own honor."

85.9   Mr. Jackson's correspondence]   Francis James Jackson (1770–1814) was appointed British minister to the United States in May 1809 and arrived in Washington in September. In a series of letters written during the fall to Secretary of State Robert Smith, Jackson accused the administration of improper dealings with his predecessor, David Erskine. The administration responded by breaking off relations with Jackson on November 8, 1809. Jackson returned to England in September 1810.

86.7   the lie direct]   A direct accusation of lying.

86.25   an honorable member of this House]   Richard Cutts (1771–1845), a Republican congressman from Massachusetts, 1801–13. Cutts was a brother-in-law of Dolley Payne Madison.

87.33   days of her Dewitts]   Dutch statesmen Cornelis de Witt (1623–1672) and Johan de Witt (1625–1672).

88.14   (Mr. Quincy)]   Josiah Quincy (1772–1864) was a Federalist congressman from Massachusetts, 1805–13, and later served as the president of Harvard, 1829–45.

88.31–32   the Essex kennel!]   The "Essex Junto" was the conservative faction of the Massachusetts Federalist party.

89.9–10   Henry the Great of France]   Henry IV (1553–1610), also known as Henry of Navarre, was king of France from 1589 until his assassination by François Ravaillac, a fanatical Roman Catholic opposed to toleration of Protestants.

89.19   surrender of Jonathan Robbins]   In 1799 President Adams granted a British request for the extradition of Thomas Nash, an Irish sailor wanted for murder and mutiny in the Royal Navy, despite Nash's claim that he was actually an American citizen named Jonathan Robbins. Nash was subsequently convicted and hanged.

90.15 'peaceably if . . . if we must;'] In a speech delivered on January 14, 1811, Quincy warned that the admission of Louisiana as a state would be "virtually a dissolution of this Union," and asserted that "it will be the right of all" to "prepare for a separation,—amicably if they can, violently if they must."

90.16 Henry's mission to Boston] In 1809 Sir James Craig, the governor-general of Lower Canada, sent John Henry, a Canadian businessman, to New England with instructions to report on whether New England Federalists would ally themselves with Britain in the event of an Anglo-American war. Henry sold his papers to the State Department in 1812 for $50,000, and Madison submitted them to Congress on March 9, 1812. Federalists protested that nothing in the papers implicated any American citizens in disloyalty.

91.15–17 (Mr. Pearson) . . . (Mr. Bleecker)] Joseph Pearson (1776–1834), a Federalist congressman from North Carolina, 1809–1815; Timothy Pitkin (1766–1847), a Federalist congressman from Connecticut, 1805–9; Harmanus Bleecker, a Federalist congressman from New York, 1811–13.

91.18–20 the duplicity . . . Berlin and Milan] Napoleon signed a decree in Berlin on November 21, 1806, imposing a complete blockade against Great Britain and Ireland and making all British property and exports subject to seizure. The British government responded by issuing orders-in-council prohibiting neutral commerce with ports closed to British shipping and requiring vessels trading with open European ports to make prior stops in British ports. Napoleon then signed a decree in Milan on November 17, 1807, making neutral ships complying with the orders-in-council subject to seizure. In the fall of 1810 President Madison received a letter from the Duc de Cadore, the French foreign minister, falsely stating that the Berlin and Milan decrees would be revoked. Madison responded by issuing a proclamation closing off commerce with Great Britain (see note 84.29–33).

91.21 revocation of the orders in council] The British cabinet revoked the orders-in-council that restricted American shipping on June 23, 1812, five days after Congress declared war.

91.40–92.1 gentleman from Boston . . . rule of decorum] In his speech on January 5, 1813, Josiah Quincy had described supporters of the administration as "sycophants, fawning reptiles, who crowded at the feet of the president, and left their filthy slime upon the carpet of the palace."

92.4 (Mr. Wheaton)] Laban Wheaton (1754–1846), a Federalist congressman from Massachusetts, 1809–17.

93.12 "Thus far . . . no farther"] Cf. Job 38:11.

93.31 (Mr. M'Kee)] Samuel McKee (1774–1826), a Republican congressman from Kentucky, 1809–17.

93.37–38 the document . . . May last] The British privy council announced on April 21, 1812, that it would revoke its orders restricting American shipping if the Berlin and Milan decrees were repealed. On May 20, 1812, the American chargé d'affaires gave the British government a copy of an order, allegedly signed by Napoleon on April 28, 1811, revoking the decrees.

94.11   Lord Castlereagh] Viscount Castlereagh (1769–1822) was the foreign secretary of Great Britain from February 1812 until his death.

94.19   Mr. Monroe] James Monroe served as Secretary of State, 1811–17.

95.31   in terrorem] As a warning.

98.7–9   Truxtun . . . Guerriere] Captain Thomas Truxtun (1755–1822) commanded the frigate *Constellation* when it captured the frigate *L'Insurgente* off Nevis on February 9, 1799, during the undeclared naval war with France. The U.S. Navy fought a series of engagements during the war with Tripoli, 1801–5. The frigate *Constitution* sank the British frigate *Guerrière* in the North Atlantic on August 19, 1812.

98.20   Mr. King] Rufus King (1755–1827) was the American minister to Great Britain, 1796–1803.

98.25   Lords Hawkesbury and St. Vincent] Lord Hawkesbury (1770–1828) was foreign secretary, 1801–4; as the Earl of Liverpool, he was prime minister, 1812–27. The Earl of St. Vincent (1735–1823) was the first lord of the admiralty, 1801–4.

98.27   *mare clausum*] Closed sea.

98.35   Mr. Russell] Jonathan Russell (1771–1832) was the U.S. chargé d'affaires in London, 1811–12.

99.18   Sir William Scott] Scott (1745–1836) was an influential judge of the high court of admiralty, 1798–1828.

100.13   gentleman from Delaware] Henry Ridgely (1779–1847) was a Federalist congressman, 1811–15.

100.36   butcher the garrison of Chicago] The garrison of Fort Dearborn, located at the mouth of the Chicago River, was ambushed by Potawatomi Indians while evacuating the post on August 15, 1812. More than 50 men, women, and children were killed in the attack.

100.38–39   remote American fort, Michilimackinac] The outpost on Mackinac (Michilimackinac) Island surrendered on July 17, 1812. Its garrison was released on parole.

101.20   Mr. Stephen] See note 71.20.

101.33   Brownstown . . . Queenstown] A party of militia attempting to secure the American supply line to Ohio was attacked by Indians along the Detroit River at Brownstown on August 5, 1812, and forced to retreat 25 miles back to Detroit. American troops crossed the Niagara River into Canada on

October 13, 1812, and captured the Queenston Heights, but were then forced to surrender when New York militia refused to reinforce them.

101.35   disgrace of Detroit]   Brigadier General William Hull (1753–1825) surrendered his army of 2,200 men at Detroit on August 16, 1812, without firing a shot.

102.15–16   the former Indian war]   The campaign in Indiana Territory in the autumn of 1811 that concluded with the American victory at Tippecanoe Creek.

102.17   Newnan's party from Georgia.]   Colonel Daniel Newnan (c. 1780–1851) led Georgia militia on a raid into Florida against the Seminole Indians, September–October 1812.

102.18–20   the Detroit . . . Lieutenant Elliott]   On October 9, 1812, a party of sailors and soldiers led by Lieutenant Jesse Elliott (1782–1845), a naval officer, raided a British anchorage on Lake Erie, burning H.M.S. *Detroit* and capturing H.M.S. *Caledonia*.

104.2   Admiral Warren]   Admiral Sir John Warren (1753–1822), commander of the Royal Navy in North America and the West Indies, 1812–14.

106.2–3   *Address . . . Bunker Hill Monument*]   Webster delivered this address to an audience of 20,000, including about 200 Revolutionary War veterans. He also gave the oration at the dedication of the completed monument on June 17, 1843.

107.38   The society]   The Bunker Hill Monument Association.

111.36–37   'another . . . mid-noon;']   John Milton, *Paradise Lost*, V, 310–11.

112.1   the first great Martyr]   Dr. Joseph Warren (1741–1775), a Boston physician and patriot leader who succeeded John Hancock as president of the Massachusetts provincial congress on April 23, 1775, and was appointed major general of militia on June 14, three days before the battle.

113.18–20   the Act . . . Port of Boston]   The Massachusetts Government Act received the royal assent on May 20, 1774, and the Boston Port Act was signed on March 31, 1774. Both acts were passed by Parliament in response to the Boston Tea Party of December 16, 1773.

114.34–35   'totamque infusa . . . miscet.']   Virgil, *Aeneid*, VI, 726–7: "Mind, infused through the limbs, drives in motion the whole mass and mingles itself with the great body" (trans. Debra Hecht).

115.6–11   Quincy . . . die free men.']   Josiah Quincy (1744–1775), *Observations on the Act of Parliament Commonly Called the Boston Port-Bill; with Thoughts on Civil Society and Standing Armies* (1774). Quincy, an attorney and patriot leader, died at sea on April 26, 1775, while returning from

England. He was the father of the Federalist congressman Josiah Quincy (see note 88.14).

115.12   four New England colonies] Massachusetts, New Hampshire, Rhode Island, and Connecticut.

116.6   one who now hears me] The Marquis de Lafayette (1757–1834) attended the ceremony as part of his 1824–25 tour of the United States.

117.9   *Serus in cælum redeas*] Horace, *Odes*, I, ii, 45: "May you return late to heaven."

121.8–9   'Dispel this . . . asks no more.'] *Iliad*, XVII, 730 (trans. Alexander Pope).

121.25   struggle of the Greeks] Greece began its war of independence against the Ottoman empire in 1821. Fighting continued until 1829, and the Turks did not recognize Greek independence until 1832.

125.2   *Eulogy . . . Jefferson*] Wirt, then attorney general, delivered this eulogy in the Hall of the U.S. House of Representatives at the request of Congress.

127.12–15   Cromwell . . . "mute and inglorious."] See Thomas Gray, "Elegy Written in a Country Church-Yard."

127.21   The hero . . . St. Helena] Napoleon Bonaparte was exiled on St. Helena from 1815 until his death in 1821.

127.27   "shot madly from their spheres"] *A Midsummer Night's Dream*, II, i, 153.

129.2–3   Isaiah . . . the sun;"] See Isaiah 41:25.

130.8   Curtius] According to legend, an earthquake opened a chasm in the Roman Forum in 362 B.C. After seers proclaimed that "the chief strength of the Roman people" must be offered up to ensure the endurance of the republic, Marcus Curtius, a young soldier, proclaimed that Rome had no greater strength than its arms and valor. He then leapt into the abyss on his horse; his sacrifice closed the chasm and restored the Forum.

130.13   Sidney] Algernon Sidney (1622–1683), an English republican executed for allegedly plotting to assassinate Charles II. His *Discourses concerning Government* was posthumously published in 1698.

130.27–30   Hooker . . . of the world."] Richard Hooker, *Of the Laws of Ecclesiastical Polity* (1594). Hooker (1554–1600) was an Anglican theologian.

131.16–17   celebrated passage . . . Bacon] Seneca (c. 4 B.C.–A.D. 65), *Medea*, II, 375–79: "There shall come a time when the bands of ocean shall be loosened, and the vast earth shall be laid open; another Tiphys shall disclose new worlds, and lands shall be seen beyond Thule." (In Greek mythology, Tiphys was the helmsman of the Argonauts.) Francis Bacon (1561–1626) cited this passage in his essay "Of Prophecies."

132.11–13   Præcipitemque . . . nec requies.]   Virgil, *Aeneid*, V, 456–58: "Furious he drives Dares headlong over the entire plain, redoubling blows now right, now left; no delay, no respite." (trans. Debra Hecht)

132.16   Mayhew . . . Thacher]   Jonathan Mayhew (1720–1766), a Congregational minister; Joseph Hawley (1723–1788), a lawyer and patriot leader in western Massachusetts; Oxenbridge Thacher Jr. (1719–1765), a lawyer who joined James Otis in opposing the renewal of writs of assistance in 1761.

133.12   *dira*]   Ill-boding signs.

136.18   Josiah Quincy]   See note 115.6–11.

137.2   Nemean lion]   In Greek mythology, a ferocious beast killed by Heracles.

137.11–12   Sewall, the Attorney General]   Jonathan Sewall (1728–1796), a Loyalist, was attorney general of Massachusetts from 1767 until the summer of 1775, when he went into exile in England.

138.39   *fæculum*]   Foul.

139.38   George Wythe]   Wythe (1726–1806) was a signer of the Declaration of Independence, a judge of the Virginia high court of chancery, 1778–1806, and professor of law at William and Mary College, 1779–89. His law students included Jefferson, John Marshall, and Henry Clay.

140.3   Briareus]   In Greek mythology, a giant with 100 hands and 50 heads.

140.8   Mr. Hammond]   George Hammond (1763–1853) was the British minister to the United States, 1791–95.

142.23   "Ab eo libertas, a quo spiritus,"]   "From where comes the spirit, from there comes liberty."

142.34–35   "with hearts of controversy,"]   *Julius Caesar*, I, ii, 109.

144.6   Lord Chatham]   William Pitt (1708–1778), first Earl of Chatham, directed British foreign and military policy as secretary of state for the southern department, 1757–61, and later served as prime minister, 1766–68.

144.21   General Ward]   Artemas Ward (1727–1800), a Massachusetts militia officer, commanded the troops besieging Boston until Washington assumed command on July 3, 1775.

145.17   "Shadows, clouds, and darkness"]   Joseph Addison (1672–1719), *Cato* (1713), V, i, 40.

145.23–24   "Come to me . . . of the field."]   1 Samuel 17:44.

147.8–10   Botta . . . Lee]   Carlo Botta (1766–1837), author of *History of the War of the Independence of the United States of America* (1820–21), first published in Italian in 1809. Richard Henry Lee (1732–1794), a delegate from Virginia, submitted a resolution to the Continental Congress on June 7, 1776, calling for an immediate declaration of independence. John Dickinson (1732–1808), a delegate from Pennsylvania, opposed the resolution.

148.14   Marengo and the Nile]   Napoleon Bonaparte defeated the Austrians at Marengo in northern Italy on June 14, 1800; Horatio Nelson destroyed the French fleet at the mouth of the Nile on August 1, 1798.

148.39   CHARLES CARROLL, of Carrollton]   Charles Carroll of Carrollton (1737–1832), a signer of the Declaration of Independence from Maryland.

149.39–40   patriot Laurens . . . Tower of London]   Henry Laurens (1724–1792) was a South Carolina delegate to the Continental Congress, 1777–80, and served as its president from November 1777 to December 1778. Appointed American minister to Holland, he was captured at sea in September 1780 and imprisoned in the Tower of London until December 1781.

150.26   Pendleton]   Edmund Pendleton (1721–1803), a prominent lawyer who later served on the Virginia supreme court of appeals, 1779–1803.

152.9   Rittenhouse]   David Rittenhouse (1732–1796), Pennsylvania astronomer and maker of astronomical instruments.

153.19–21   "The Defence . . . Price]   *A Defence of the Constitutions of Government of the United States of America* (3 vols., 1787–88), written in response to observations by the French economist and statesman Anne-Robert-Jacques Turgot (1727–1781), the French philosopher Gabriel Bonnot de Mably (1709–1785), and the British moral philosopher and Presbyterian minister Richard Price (1723–1791).

156.5   that able manual]   *A Manual of Parliamentary Practice*, published in February 1801.

158.7   "their history . . . eyes!"]   Thomas Gray, "Elegy Written in a Country Church-Yard."

158.25   most elegant writers]   Cicero.

161.17   Caracci]   Giuseppe Ceracchi (1751–1801).

164.29   Δεινὴ . . . βιοῖο]   *Iliad*, I, 49: "A terrible sound arose from the silver bow" (trans. Debra Hecht).

165.29   "save my country . . . died!"]   Alexander Pope, "On Dr. Francis Atterbury, Bishop of Rochester, who died in exile at Paris, 1732."

166.25   Pisgah's top]   See Deuteronomy 34:1.

168.3   *New Harmony, Indiana*]   New Harmony was established as an experimental utopian community in 1825 by the British manufacturer and social reformer Robert Owen (1771–1858). Although Owen declared the experiment a failure in 1827, many of the reformers who had moved to New Harmony still remained when Wright spoke there in 1828.

182.2   *Second Reply to Hayne*]   Robert Hayne (1791–1839) was a senator from South Carolina, 1823–32. In a speech delivered in the Senate on January 19, 1830, Hayne attacked federal land and tariff policies as an attempt by the eastern states to dominate the South and West and called for federal lands to be distributed to the states. Webster replied on January 20, defending federal land policies and praising the prohibition of slavery contained in the Northwest Ordinance of 1787. Hayne then responded with a lengthy speech, delivered on January 21 and 25, in which he defended slavery. The text of the "Second Reply" printed here was recorded in shorthand by Joseph Gales and then revised by Webster for newspaper and pamphlet publication. More than 40,000 pamphlet copies of the speech were printed within three months of its issue.

184.20   his friend from Missouri]   Thomas Hart Benton (1782–1858) served in the Senate from 1821 to 1851.

185.18   *modestiæ gratia*]   For the sake of modesty.

187.1   the Coalition!]   The alliance between John Quincy Adams and Henry Clay that led to Adams winning the 1825 presidential election in the House of Representatives and Clay becoming Secretary of State in the Adams administration.

187.39   the gory locks were shaken.]   See *Macbeth*, III, iv, 61–62.

188.5–6   "Pr'ythee . . . I saw him!"]   *Macbeth*, III, iv, 81 and 88.

188.12–13   "Thou canst . . . did it!"]   *Macbeth*, III, iv, 61.

188.17   "Avaunt! and quit our sight!"]   *Macbeth*, III, iv, 111.

188.27–28   "filed their mind"]   Cf. *Macbeth*, III, iv, 69.

188.31–33   "a barren sceptre . . . *succeeding.*"]   Cf. *Macbeth*, III, iv, 63–65.

189.5   Mr. Dane]   Nathan Dane (1752–1835) was a Massachusetts delegate to the Continental Congress, 1785–88.

191.8–9   *vulnus immedicabile*]   Incurable wound.

191.19   Governor Randolph]   Edmund Randolph (1753–1813) was governor of Virginia, 1786–88. Randolph attended the Constitutional Convention and refused to sign the final document, but then changed his position and supported ratification in the Virginia convention in 1788. He later served as Attorney General of the United States, 1789–94, and as Secretary of State, 1794–95.

194.37   Jefferson, Chase, and Howell]   Thomas Jefferson; Jeremiah Chase (1748–1828), a delegate from Maryland, 1783–84; David Howell (1747–1824), a delegate from Rhode Island, 1782–85.

195.33–34   the Hartford Convention]   Federalist delegates from New Hampshire, Vermont, Massachusetts, Rhode Island, and Connecticut met in Hartford from December 15, 1814, to January 5, 1815. The convention proposed the adoption of seven constitutional amendments designed to protect New England against southern and western domination of the federal government, but its recommendations failed to win support in the aftermath of the American victory at New Orleans and the signing of the peace treaty with Great Britain.

196.10   Colleton and Abbeville]   Districts in South Carolina where nullification meetings had been held.

196.26   speech of mine in the other house]   Webster spoke in the House of Representatives on January 18, 1825, in support of a measure extending the Cumberland Road from the Ohio River at Wheeling to Zanesville, Ohio.

197.3–4   "to sever . . . northwest side,"]   Cf. Samuel Butler (1612–1680), *Hudibras*, Part I (1663), ll. 67–68: "He could distinguish, and divide / A hair 'twixt south, and south-west side."

197.16–17   honorable member from Connecticut]   Samuel Foot (1780–1846), a senator from Connecticut, 1827–33.

197.25   honorable member from New Hampshire]   Levi Woodbury (1789–1851), a senator from New Hampshire, 1825–31 and 1841–45.

197.31   honorable member from Maine]   Peleg Sprague (1793–1880), a senator from Maine, 1829–35.

198.37–38   speech of Colonel Barre]   The speech on the Stamp Act given by Isaac Barré on February 13, 1765. Barré (1726–1802) was a Member of Parliament, 1761–90.

209.20   *Teucro duce*]   "Under the guidance of Teucer," an allusion to Horace, *Odes*, I, vii, 27: "Nil desperandum Teuro duce et auspice Teucro." (Never despair while under the guidance and auspices of Teucer.)

210.8–9   honorable gentleman from Georgia]   John Forsyth (1780–1841) served in the House of Representatives, 1813–18 and 1823–27, and in the Senate, 1818–19 and 1829–34.

210.20   *causa causans*]   Primary cause.

211.27–28   *et noscitur a sociis*]   And he is known by his companions.

211.29   "ON INTERNAL IMPROVEMENTS,"]   Webster quoted from a pamphlet published in 1824, *Speech of Mr. McDuffie on Internal Improvements, With a Few Introductory Remarks in Answer to a Pamphlet Entitled*

"Consolidation." George McDuffie (1790–1851) was a congressman from
South Carolina, 1821–34, and a senator, 1842–46.

211.35–36   pamphlet . . . "Consolidation"] The pamphlet was written
by Thomas Cooper (1759–1839), a chemist and political economist who served
as president of South Carolina College, 1821–34.

211.36–37   renewing the charter . . . United States] The First Bank of
the United States was incorporated in 1791. Its charter expired in 1811, but the
Second Bank was chartered in 1816.

211.38   Mr. Crawford] William Crawford (1772–1834) was a senator from
Georgia, 1807–13; Secretary of War, 1815–16; and Secretary of the Treasury,
1816–25.

212.3   Cumberland Road] A highway running from Cumberland, Maryland, to the Ohio River at Wheeling that was authorized by Congress in 1802
and constructed between 1811 and 1818.

212.23   *Lowndes, and Cheves,*]   William Lowndes (1782–1822) was a
congressman from South Carolina, 1811–22; Langdon Cheves (1776–1857) was
a congressman from South Carolina, 1810–15, and president of the Second
Bank of the United States, 1819–22.

214.15   the Vice-President] John C. Calhoun of South Carolina.

216.36   Faneuil Hall] A meeting hall in Boston.

217.3–4   Mr. Madison's publication] Two public letters by James Madison defending the constitutionality of protective tariffs were published in
December 1828.

224.22   *ad annum urbis conditæ*] To the year of the city's founding.

224.32   Ultras of France] The reactionary ultraroyalist faction in France
during the Bourbon Restoration, 1814–30.

224.33–34   adherents of Don Miguel!] The absolutist supporters of
Miguel (1802–1866), who seized the throne of Portugal and ruled until his
exile in 1834.

225.9   Essex Junto] See note 88.31–32.

228.10   Him whose honored name] Isaac Hayne (1745–1781), a South
Carolina militia colonel who was captured and summarily hanged by the
British as a spy, was a cousin of Robert Hayne's grandfather.

230.40–231.2   "The sovereignty . . . honorable justice."] From a toast
made by Thomas Cooper (see note 211.35–36) at a banquet held in Columbia,
South Carolina, on December 9, 1829.

231.5   the Virginia resolution] Drafted by James Madison and adopted
by the Virginia assembly on December 24, 1798, the resolutions condemned

the Alien and Sedition Acts as unconstitutional and called upon the states to resist them.

234.36–235.5   "the tariff . . . compact is violated."]   Webster quotes from a resolution adopted at a public meeting held in Abbeville, South Carolina, on September 25, 1828.

236.17–18   "all the concentrated . . . passion,"]   From a speech by Robert Barnwell Rhett (1800–1876) delivered at Walterborough, South Carolina, on June 12, 1828. Rhett (then known as Robert Barnwell Smith) later served in Congress, 1837–49, and in the Senate, 1850–52. He was a leading advocate of secession in 1860.

237.28–29   Resolutions . . . South Carolina.]   The resolutions called for the repeal of the protective tariff.

238.13   an honorable and venerable gentleman]   James Hillhouse (1754–1832), who served as a congressman from Connecticut, 1791–96, and as a senator, 1796–1810.

241.9   Samuel Dexter]   Dexter (1761–1816) was a congressman from Massachusetts, 1793–95; a senator, 1799–1800; Secretary of War, 1800–1; and Secretary of the Treasury, 1801.

242.4   *quoad*]   As regards.

249.26–27   "All the while, . . . sounds."]   John Milton, *Paradise Lost*, I, 539–40.

250.14   John Fries]   On March 7, 1799, John Fries (1750–1818) led an armed party that forced the release of 18 men arrested in eastern Pennsylvania for resisting the 1798 federal property tax. Fries was convicted of treason and sentenced to death, but was pardoned by President John Adams on May 23, 1800.

256.31–38   "accustom yourselves . . . various parts."]   From Washington's Farewell Address, published on September 19, 1796. (In the passage quoted, Jackson substitutes "the Union" for "it.")

257.14–15   event of the existing crisis]   A South Carolina convention passed a nullification ordinance on November 24, 1832, prohibiting the collection of the federal tariffs authorized in 1828 and 1832 and threatening secession if the federal government responded with force. Jackson issued a proclamation on December 10 asserting federal supremacy and denouncing nullification as illegal. On March 2, 1833, he signed a Force Bill, authorizing the military to enforce the revenue laws, as well as a compromise tariff law lowering rates. The South Carolina convention then met on March 11 and rescinded the nullification ordinance, ending the crisis.

259.2   *General Trades' Union*]   The General Trades' Union of New York City was founded in 1833 and by the end of the year included members from

14 different trades. The union collapsed during the economic depression of 1837.

260.26   allodial] Held in absolute ownership.

260.37–38   septennial reversion . . . Rome] The Torah commanded the people of Israel to remit all debts and let their cultivated land lie fallow every seven years; see Exodus 23:10–11, Leviticus 25:1–7, and Deuteronomy 15:1–6. Roman agrarian law allowed the wealthy to rent, and effectively own, large tracts of public land.

264.39–265.1   "laugh at your . . . cometh."] Proverbs 1:26.

266.21   La Mothe] French philosopher François de La Mothe Le Vayer (1588–1672).

269.24   PALINURUS] The helmsman of Aeneas.

274.3   Codrus] A legendary king of Athens, said to have reigned in the 11th century B.C.

274.8–9   "Tower on Shinar's Plain,"] The Tower of Babel; see Genesis 11:1–9.

274.18   Flavian] The imperial dynasty that ruled Rome, A.D. 69–96.

274.33   Pergamean] A Greek kingdom in Asia Minor, founded in 280 B.C., that came under Roman rule in 133 B.C.

275.26   ROGER SHERMAN] A signer of the Declaration of Independence, Sherman (1721–1793) was a delegate to the Continental Congress from Connecticut, 1774–81 and 1784. He later served in the Constitutional Convention of 1787; in Congress, 1789–91; and in the Senate, 1791–93.

275.27   WILLIAM GIFFORD] Gifford (1756–1826), an Englishman, was the author of the poetic satires *The Baviad* (1791) and *The Maeviad* (1795) and the editor of *Quarterly Review*, 1809–24.

275.29   GEORGE WALTON] A signer of the Declaration of Independence, Walton (1749?–1804) was a Georgia delegate to the Continental Congress, 1776–77 and 1780–81. As a colonel of militia Walton was wounded and captured at Savannah in 1778. He later served as chief justice of Georgia, 1783–89, and as a judge of the state superior court.

275.31   General KNOX] Henry Knox (1750–1806) was chief of artillery in the Continental Army during the Revolutionary War. He later served as Secretary of War under the Confederation, 1784–89, and in the Washington administration, 1789–94.

275.32   General GREENE] Nathanael Greene (1742–1786) was a general in the Continental Army, 1775–83, and the commander of the Southern Department, 1780–83.

275.34   FRAZEE]   John Frazee (1790–1852) opened a marble shop in New York City in 1818 and became the first successful American-born sculptor.

277.2–3   *Speech . . . President Jackson*]   In 1832 President Andrew Jackson vetoed a bill rechartering the Second Bank of the United States, and in 1833 he directed Secretary of the Treasury Roger B. Taney to withdraw government deposits from the Second Bank and deposit them in state banks. On March 28, 1834, the Senate adopted, 26–20, a resolution, introduced by Henry Clay and supported by Daniel Webster and John C. Calhoun, censuring Jackson for assuming "authority and power not conferred by the constitution and laws but in derogation of both." Benton's resolution revoking the censure was approved by the Senate, 24–19, on January 16, 1837.

277.33–278.34   The candidate]   Vice-President Martin Van Buren was elected president in 1836, receiving 170 of 294 electoral votes.

283.7–8   an American vessel]   The *Friendship* was attacked by pirates in Kuala Batu harbor in February 1831. Most of its crew were killed and its cargo was stolen.

283.11   Commodore Downes]   Under the command of John Downes (1784–1854), the frigate *Potomac* captured four forts at Kuala Batu in February 1832 and then destroyed much of the town. Two Americans and more than 150 Malays were killed during the attack.

285.2–3   argument of General Hamilton . . . Supreme Court]   At the request of President Washington, Secretary of the Treasury Alexander Hamilton submitted an opinion upholding the constitutionality of a national bank on February 23, 1791; Washington then signed the bill chartering the First Bank of the United States. In *McCulloch* v. *Maryland* (1819), the Supreme Court unanimously upheld the constitutionality of the Second Bank in an opinion written by Chief Justice John Marshall.

285.18–19   *audita querela defendentis*]   The complaint of the defendant has been heard.

287.7   Dr. LINN]   Lewis Linn (1796–1843) was a senator from Missouri, 1833–43.

287.39   The Treasury order]   Known as the Specie Circular, the order was issued on July 11, 1836, by Secretary of the Treasury Levi Woodbury.

288.22   The difficulty with France]   A treaty signed in 1831 required France to pay the United States $5 million for spoliation claims from the Napoleonic wars. After the chamber of deputies failed to appropriate the necessary funds, President Jackson called in December 1834 for French property to be seized if the indemnity was not paid. France then recalled its minister from the United States, and the dispute continued until February 1836, when Jackson accepted British assurances that France would pay the indemnity.

289.20–21   a military successor]   William Henry Harrison, one of three Whig presidential candidates in 1836, received 73 electoral votes. Harrison had defeated the Indians at Tippecanoe in 1811 and the British and Indians at the Thames in 1813.

293.2   *Speech . . . Antislavery Petitions*]   Calhoun spoke during a debate over receiving petitions calling for the abolition of slavery and the slave trade in the District of Columbia. The text printed here was revised by Calhoun for pamphlet publication, and omits remarks made by other senators.

294.14   (Mr. Buchanan)]   James Buchanan (1791–1868) was a congressman from Pennsylvania, 1821–31; minister to Russia, 1832–34; a senator, 1834–45; Secretary of State in the Polk administration, 1845–49; minister to Great Britain, 1853–56; and President of the United States, 1857–61.

295.16   proclamation and the force bill]   See note 257.14–15.

296.2   without a shout]   In *The Papers of John C. Calhoun* this appears as: "without a shout [*sic*; shock?]."

296.16   two people]   In *The Papers of John C. Calhoun* this appears as: "two people[s]."

299.14   British West India Islands]   The Abolition Act of 1833 abolished slavery in the British West Indies as of August 1, 1834, but bound slaves older than six to work as apprentices for between four and six years. Protests against the apprenticeship system resulted in its abolition in 1838, and West Indian emancipation became complete on August 1, 1838.

300.2   *Murder of Lovejoy*]   Elijah P. Lovejoy (1802–1837), a Presbyterian minister, was shot by a mob in Alton, Illinois, on November 7, 1837, while attempting to defend the press of his antislavery newspaper. Phillips spoke at a public meeting organized by the Unitarian theologian and social reformer William Ellery Channing (1780–1842).

300.8   the last speaker]   James T. Austin (1784–1870), attorney general of Massachusetts, 1832–43.

303.34–37   "the broad shield . . . catastrophe."]   Cf. Daniel Webster's closing speech to the Massachusetts Senate at the impeachment trial of probate judge James Prescott, April 24, 1821: "I hold up before him the broad shield of the constitution; if through that he be pierced and fall, he will be but one sufferer in a common catastrophe."

304.32   "died as the fool dieth."]   Cf. 2 Samuel 3:33.

304.33   a reverend clergyman of this city]   Hubbard Winslow (1799–1864) had defined "republican liberty" as "liberty to say and do what the prevailing voice and will of the brotherhood will allow and protect."

305.12   Hugh Peters and John Cotton]   Hugh Peter (1598–1660), also known as Peters, was an English clergyman who landed in Massachusetts in

1635 and helped found Harvard College. He returned to England in 1641, served as a chaplain with the parliamentary armies during the English Civil War, and was executed in 1660 as a regicide. John Cotton (1584–1652) immigrated to Massachusetts in 1633 and became one of the leading Puritan ministers in the colony.

305.16   Hampden]   John Hampden (1594–1643) was a leader of the parliamentary opposition to Charles I. He was killed in battle during the English Civil War.

306.17   Mayhews and Coopers]   Jonathan Mayhew (1720–1766) and Samuel Cooper (1725–1783), Boston clergymen who were active in the colonial cause.

306.21   Lovejoy had fled]   Lovejoy left St. Louis and moved to Alton in 1836 after a mob destroyed his press. Two more of his presses were destroyed in Alton before the confrontation that ended in his death.

306.27–28   "in the gristle, . . . manhood."]   From Edmund Burke's speech in Parliament on conciliation with America, March 22, 1775.

308.2   *Pennsylvania Hall]*   The hall, built as a site for antislavery meetings, opened on May 14, 1838, and was burned by a mob on May 17.

308.10   "they know not . . . do."]   Luke 23:34.

309.12–13   "let us eat . . . die."]   1 Corinthians 15:32.

309.21   "as bound with them,"]   Hebrews 13:3.

311.4–5   "Oh tell it not . . . Askelon."]   2 Samuel 1:20.

311.13–14   He that is not . . . abroad.]   Matthew 12:30.

311.32–33   "God has chosen . . . that are."]   Cf. 1 Corinthians 1:28.

312.5–6   "the living coals of truth"]   John Greenleaf Whittier (1807–1892), "Expostulation" (1834).

312.38   the apprenticeship]   See note 299.14.

314.2–3   *Address to the Slaves . . . America]*   Garnet delivered this address to the 1843 National Negro Convention, which then debated his call for violent resistance to slavery. Frederick Douglass, at the time an adherent of the nonviolent abolitionism advocated by William Lloyd Garrison, spoke in opposition to Garnet, and the convention eventually voted, 19–18, not to endorse Garnet's address.

315.25   "ferried o'er the wave"]   William Cowper (1731–1800), *The Task* (1785), Book II.

318.8–9   "if hereditary bondmen . . . the blow."]   Cf. Byron, *Childe Harold's Pilgrimage*, Canto II (1812), lxxvi.

320.10 Denmark Veazie] Denmark Vesey (1767?–1822), a former slave who had purchased his freedom, was executed along with 35 other African-Americans for allegedly plotting a mass slave uprising in Charleston.

320.28 Nathaniel Turner] Nat Turner (1800–1831) led a slave insurrection in Southampton County, Virginia, in 1831 during which 57 white people were killed. More than 100 African-Americans were killed without trial during and after the uprising, and Turner and 19 of his followers were hanged.

320.33 Joseph Cinque] Cinque (Sengbe Pieh) was an enslaved African who led the rebellion on the Spanish slave ship *Amistad* off Cuba in 1839. After seizing the ship the rebels sailed north and eventually reached eastern Long Island, where they were arrested and charged with murder and mutiny. In March 1841 the U.S. Supreme Court ordered the mutineers freed, and in November 1841 the surviving rebels sailed for Sierra Leone.

320.39–321.5 Madison Washington . . . Nassau] Madison Washington led the revolt onboard the *Creole* on November 7, 1841. After the ship reached Nassau on November 9, the British imprisoned Washington and 18 other rebels while freeing the remaining slaves. Washington and the 16 other surviving mutineers (two had died in prison) were released in April 1842 after the British government ruled that the seizure of the ship was not an act of piracy. His subsequent fate is unknown.

322.2 *Speech . . . War with Mexico*] The text printed here follows Lincoln's handwritten manuscript. Variants that appeared in the *Congressional Globe Appendix* are indicated in the notes below.

322.10 the President] James K. Polk.

323.7 (Mr. Richardson)] William A. Richardson (1811–1875), a Democrat, served in Congress, 1847–56 and 1861–63, and in the Senate, 1863–65.

325.7 equally incomprehensible.] In the *Congressional Globe Appendix*, this was followed by: "The outrage upon common *right*, of seizing as our own what we have once sold, merely because it *was* ours *before* we sold it, is only equalled by the outrage on common sense of any attempt to justify it."

327.34–35 This strange . . . by design.] In the *Congressional Globe Appendix*, this appeared as: "In this strange omission chiefly consists the deception of the President's evidence—an omission which, it does seem to me, could scarely have occurred but by design."

327.39–40 point arising in the case] This appeared in the *Congressional Globe Appendix* as: "position pressed upon him by the prosecution."

329.28–29 Heaven against him] In the *Congressional Globe Appendix*, this was followed by: "; that he ordered General Taylor into the midst of a peaceful Mexican settlement, purposely to bring on a war;".

333.2 *Address to Woman's Rights Convention*] The text printed here is taken from *Address of Mrs. Elizabeth Cady Stanton, Delivered at Seneca Falls & Rochester, N.Y., July 19th & August 2, 1848*, a pamphlet issued in 1870 by Robert J. Johnston, who at the time was the printer of Stanton's newspaper *Revolution*. The editors of *The Selected Papers of Elizabeth Cady Stanton and Susan B. Anthony* print a variant text, based on a manuscript in the Library of Congress, in their volume *In the School of Anti-Slavery, 1840 to 1866* (New Brunswick, N.J.: 1997), and indicate that Stanton first delivered the speech in Waterloo, New York, in September 1848.

335.1–2   I am a . . . very blest]   Cf. Byron, *The Corsair* (1814), II, xiv.

335.3–6   When weary . . . frets away?]   Cf. Byron, *The Corsair* (1814), III, viii.

335.30–31   Caroline Herschel and Mary Somerville]   Herschel (1750–1848) was an English astronomer; Somerville (1780–1872) was a Scottish science writer. In 1835 they became the first female members of the Royal Astronomical Society.

340.2   Daniel Lambert]   Lambert (1770–1809) was an Englishman famous for his girth who exhibited himself as a natural curiosity, 1806–9. At the time of his death he weighed 739 pounds.

340.33–36   Some say . . . grows with using.]   Cf. Alfred Lord Tennyson, *The Princess* (1847), Canto II.

341.37–38   To uplift . . . with man's.]   Cf. Alfred Lord Tennyson, *The Princess* (1847), Canto III.

342.17   Gerrit Smith]   Smith (1797–1874) was a philanthropist and social reformer who helped found the antislavery Liberty Party in 1840. He and Stanton were first cousins.

343.5–6   "resist not evil," . . . saith the Lord."]   Matthew 5:39; Romans 12:19.

344.13   Miss Martineau . . . in the East,"]   Harriet Martineau (1802–1876), *Eastern Life, Present and Past* (1848).

344.31–32   Barren verbiage, . . . compliment.]   Alfred Lord Tennyson, *The Princess* (1847), Canto II.

344.34–38   Two heads . . . of the mind.]   Alfred Lord Tennyson, *The Princess* (1847), Canto II.

345.25–26   "Wives, obey . . . the Lord."]   Cf. Ephesians 5:22.

346.21–22   "weaker vessels"]   1 Peter 3:7.

348.29   book of the immortal Caudle]   *Mrs. Caudle's Curtain Lectures* (1845) by Douglas Jerrold (1803–1857), a contributor to *Punch*.

349.18–19   Margaret . . . Semiramis]   Margaret (1353–1412) was the ruler of Denmark, 1376–1412; of Norway, 1380–1412; and of Sweden, 1389–1412. Semiramis (Sammu-ramet) was an Assyrian queen of the 9th century B.C. and the legendary builder of Babylon.

349.30–34   "The fair negotiators . . . reconciliation."] William H. Prescott (1796–1859), *History of the Reign of Ferdinand and Isabella, the Catholic* (1837). The passage Stanton quotes describes the negotiations in 1479 between Isabella and her aunt Doña Beatriz, sister-in-law of Afonso V of Portugal, that resulted in the Treaty of Alcáçovas.

350.3   Tinga . . . Blanche] Nzinga (c. 1582–1663), or Njinga, resisted Portuguese expansion as ruler of the Ngongo and Mbanda kingdoms in present-day Angola, 1624–63. Blanche of Castile (1188–1252) was regent of France during the minority of Louis IX, 1226–34, and during his absence on crusade, 1248–52.

350.5–6   Caroline of England] Caroline of Ansbach (1683–1737) served as regent during George II's visits to Hanover, 1727–37.

350.16–23   Hannah Moore . . . Will Chip] Hannah More (1745–1833) was an English playwright, essayist, and philanthropist. She wrote *Village Politics, Addressed to All the Mechanics, Journeymen, and Day Labourers, in Great Britain* (1792) as "Will Chip" in response to the popularity of Thomas Paine's *Rights of Man*.

353.11–20   Then fear not . . . King and Queen] From *Woman in the Nineteenth Century* (1845) by Margaret Fuller.

354.2–3   *The Political Destination . . . the Times*] The text printed here is taken from *Speeches, Addresses, and Occasional Sermons* (1867), where a note describes this work as "An Address delivered before several literary Societies in 1848."

355.4   Augustulus] Romulus Augustulus, who reigned 475–76, was the last Roman emperor in the west.

355.12–13   "monument . . . brass,"] Horace, *Odes*, III, xxx.

357.34–35   *Non omnia possumus omnes*] Virgil, Eclogue VIII, 63: "We cannot all do all things."

362.3–4   the Fiddlers and the Trollopes] The Rev. Isaac Fidler, author of *Observations on Professions, Literature, Manners, and Emigration, in the United States and Canada, made during a residence there in 1832* (1833); Frances Trollope (1780–1863), author of *Domestic Manners of the Americans* (1832).

362.6–7   "the freest . . . the world"] Alexis de Tocqueville, *Democracy in America*, volume I (1835), chapter XVII.

364.39–40   La Place . . . office in Salem!] The astronomer and mathematician Nathaniel Bowditch (1773–1838) prepared an annotated translation, published 1829–39, of the first four volumes (1798–1805) of Laplace's *Traité de mécanique céleste*. Bowditch did much of the work on his Laplace edition while he was employed by the Essex Fire and Marine Insurance Company in Salem, Massachusetts, 1804–23.

367.1   Ramus] Petrus Ramus (Pierre de La Ramée, 1515–1572), French philosopher and logician.

367.6   Hingham] Hingham, Massachusetts.

367.23   Euripus] The narrow strait separating the center of the island of Évvoia (Euboea) from the Greek mainland.

369.2–3   only sixteen dissenting voices] The declaration of war with Mexico was approved in May 1846 by the House of Representatives, 174–14, and by the Senate, 40–2.

369.27–30   A great politician . . . to elect him.] Daniel Webster was absent from the Senate when war with Mexico was declared. He subsequently denounced the war as unjust and illegal, but voted for military supplies. Webster also opposed the nomination of General Zachary Taylor by the Whigs, but then endorsed Taylor's candidacy in a speech delivered at his home in Marshfield, Massachusetts, on September 1, 1848.

371.9–10   ready for a "buffalo hunt,"] In the late summer of 1848 a large party of Mexican War veterans gathered in southern Texas to take part in a filibustering expedition aimed at creating an independent Republic of the Sierra Madre in northern Mexico. The venture, which became known in the press as the "Buffalo Hunt," was abandoned during the fall.

374.29   Spurzheim] Johann Spurzheim (1776–1832) was a German physician and neuroanatomist and a founder of phrenology.

376.20   Leland or Francis] Thomas Leland (1722–1785), an Irish clergymen and historian, translated Demosthenes into English in three volumes, 1754–70; Philip Francis (1708?–1773), an Irish clergyman, translated Demosthenes in two volumes, 1753–55.

377.21–22   Cowpens . . . the Ilyssus] Cowpens was the site of an American victory in South Carolina on January 17, 1781. British and American troops fought a costly drawn battle at Lundy's Lane, near the Canadian side of Niagara Falls, on July 25, 1814. The American victories at Bemis Heights on September 19 and October 7, 1777, led to the surrender of the British army at Saratoga, New York, on October 19. The Ilissós is a river that flows through Athens.

377.23   "smooth-sliding . . . reeds,"] John Milton, *Lycidas* (1637), line 86.

378.3   Gil Blas] A picaresque novel by Alain-René Lesage (4 vols., 1715–35), first translated into English by Tobias Smollett in 1749.

378.11–12   "curious, . . . but nice."]   Alexander Pope, *An Essay on Criticism* (1711), II, 286.

387.2–3   *Speech . . . Compromise Resolutions*]   On January 29, 1850, Clay introduced eight resolutions concerning slavery and the territories won during the war with Mexico. Although the "Omnibus Bill" containing most of Clay's measures was defeated in the Senate on July 31, Congress passed several separate acts in September that later became known as "the compromise of 1850." The legislation admitted California into the Union as a free state, organized territorial governments for New Mexico and Utah without a congressional prohibition of slavery in those territories, settled the Texas–New Mexico boundary dispute, assumed $10 million of the debt of the Texas republic, abolished the slave trade in the District of Columbia, and replaced the 1793 Fugitive Slave Act with a stronger law.

387.31–32   Mr. HALE and Mr. PHELPS]   John Hale (1806–1873) served in Congress as a Democrat from New Hampshire, 1843–45, and in the Senate as a Free-Soiler, 1847–53, and as a Republican, 1855–65. Samuel Phelps (1793–1855) was a Whig senator from Vermont, 1839–51.

388.14   Mr. CASS]   Lewis Cass (1782–1866) was a Democratic senator from Michigan, 1845–48 and 1849–57. He was the Democratic presidential nominee in 1848 and later served as Secretary of State, 1857–60, in the Buchanan administration.

388.16   The VICE PRESIDENT]   Millard Fillmore (1800–1874) was vice-president of the United States from 1849 to July 10, 1850, when he became president following the death of Zachary Taylor. He served as president until 1853, and in 1856 was the presidential candidate of the American (Know-Nothing) Party.

388.20   Mr. FOOTE]   Henry Foote (1804–1880) was a Democratic senator from Mississippi, 1847–52.

388.21   Mr. BADGER]   George Badger (1795–1866) was a Whig senator from North Carolina, 1846–55.

392.38   the Wilmot proviso]   The proviso, introduced by David Wilmot (1814–1868), a Democratic congressman from Pennsylvania, would have prohibited slavery in any territory acquired from Mexico. It was adopted by the House on August 8, 1846, but failed to pass the Senate before Congress adjourned. A similar measure was approved by the House in February 1847 but again failed to pass the Senate.

395.31   Mr. Trist]   Nicholas P. Trist (1800–1874) was the special envoy who negotiated the peace treaty with Mexico signed at Guadalupe Hidalgo on February 2, 1848.

396.35   *eo instanti*]   At that moment.

401.27   Mr. CORWIN]   Thomas Corwin (1794–1865) was a Whig congressman from Ohio, 1831–40, and a senator, 1845–50. He served as Secretary of the Treasury in the Fillmore administration, 1850–53, and as a Republican congressman, 1859–61.

407.12   Mr. RUSK]   Thomas Rusk (1803–1857) was a Democratic senator from Texas, 1846–57.

407.35   Mr. UNDERWOOD]   Joseph Underwood (1791–1876), a Whig, was a congressman from Kentucky, 1835–43, and a senator, 1847–53.

415.28   Mr. MANGUM]   Willie Mangum (1792–1861), a Whig, was a congressman from North Carolina, 1823–26, and a senator, 1831–36 and 1840–53.

419.13–14   retrocession . . . Potomac]   The land was retroceded to Virginia in 1846.

424.30–31   famous Convention, . . . Nashville]   In October 1849 a public meeting in Jackson, Mississippi, called for delegates from the slaveholding states to meet in Nashville and "devise and adopt some mode of resistance" to Northern encroachments. Delegates from nine states met in June 1850 and adopted resolutions rejecting the power of Congress to exclude slavery from the territories while expressing a willingness to extend the Missouri Compromise line to the Pacific.

425.1   Mr. KING]   William R. King (1786–1853), a Democrat, was a congressman from North Carolina, 1811–16, and a senator from Alabama, 1819–44 and 1848–52. He briefly served as Vice-President of the United States in 1853.

427.33–34   recent decision of the Supreme Court]   In *Prigg* v. *Pennsylvania* (1842), a case involving the rendition of a fugitive slave from Pennsylvania to Maryland, the Supreme Court upheld the constitutionality of the 1793 Fugitive Slave Act and declared that state laws impeding the enforcement of the act were unconstitutional, but also ruled that Congress could not compel state officials to help return fugitive slaves.

430.31   Mr. DAYTON]   William Dayton (1807–1864) was a Whig senator from New Jersey, 1842–51, and the Republican vice-presidential candidate in 1856.

432.19–20   Mr. Hoar]   Samuel Hoar (1778–1856) was a prominent Massachusetts lawyer who served in Congress as a Whig, 1835–37.

433.8–9   passage of the laws by Massachusetts]   Massachusetts passed a law in 1843 forbidding the participation of state officials and the use of state courtrooms and jails in the rendition of fugitive slaves.

433.25   Mr. DAVIS]   John Davis (1787–1854), a Whig, was a congressman from Massachusetts, 1825–34, and a senator, 1835–41 and 1845–53.

435.14   decision of the Supreme Court]   In *Groves* v. *Slaughter* (1841), a case involving the sale of slaves imported into Mississippi, three of the seven justices who participated in the case wrote opinions denying that Congress had the power under the commerce clause to prohibit the interstate slave trade. The remaining four justices did not address the question.

436.29   Mr. BENTON]   See the Biographical Notes in this volume.

437.22   Mr. Thomas]   Jesse Thomas (1777–1853) was a senator from Illinois, 1818–29.

437.36   Mr. Pinkney]   William Pinkney (1764–1822) was a senator from Maryland, 1819–22.

437.39   Mr. Lowndes]   See note 212.23.

438.30–31   Mr. Randolph . . . Mr. Burton]   For John Randolph of Roanoke (1773–1833), see the Biographical Notes in this volume. Weldon Edwards (1788–1873) was a congressman from North Carolina, 1816–27; Hutchins Burton (1782–1836) was a congressman from North Carolina, 1819–24.

439.4   Curtius's and Leonidas's]   For Marcus Curtius, see note 130.8. Leonidas was the Spartan king killed fighting the Persians at Thermopylae in 480 B.C.

439.14   Mr. Taylor]   John Taylor (1784–1854) was a congressman from New York, 1813–33.

439.30   Mr. Livermore]   Arthur Livermore (1766–1853) was a congressman from New Hampshire, 1817–21 and 1823–25.

440.17–18   Mr. Holmes]   John Holmes (1773–1843) was a congressman from Massachusetts, 1817–20, and a senator from Maine, 1820–27 and 1829–33.

443.20   Mr. DAVIS]   Jefferson Davis; see Biographical Notes in this volume.

446.25   the one in command]   Zachary Taylor.

446.32–33   portion of the Mexican war . . . Scott]   General Winfield Scott landed his army near Veracruz on March 9, 1847, and, after a series of battles, captured Mexico City on September 14.

450.1–2   resolutions from North Carolina]   The resolutions, adopted by a meeting in Wilmington, endorsed sending delegates to the Nashville Convention, criticized the "fanaticism and political dishonesty" in the North regarding slavery, and asserted that the Union should be dissolved if necessary to preserve "honor and principle." Their submission by Senator Willie Mangum of North Carolina was objected to by Senator John Hale of New Hampshire, but the Senate eventually voted to receive them.

455.5   As much indisposed as I have been]   Calhoun had been absent from the Senate for six weeks in January and February 1850. He died on March 31, 1850.

455.22   MR. MASON]   James Mason (1798–1871), a Democrat, was a congressman from Virginia, 1837–39, and a senator, 1847–61. He served as a Confederate envoy to Britain during the Civil War.

468.35   Methodist Episcopal Church]   Founded in 1784, the church underwent a split in 1844.

469.3   the Baptists]   The Baptists divided along sectional lines in 1845.

472.30   plan of the Administration]   President Taylor had recommended the immediate admission of California as a free state in his special message to the Senate of January 23, 1850.

473.40   General Houston]   Sam Houston (1793–1863) was a congressman from Tennessee, 1823–27; president of the Texas republic, 1836–38 and 1841–44; a senator from Texas, 1846–59; and governor of Texas, 1859–61.

475.36   General Riley]   Bennet Riley (1787–1853) served as military governor of California, April 12–December 20, 1849.

476.25–26   the time that Michigan was admitted,]   Michigan was admitted to the Union in 1837.

479.6   Senators . . . the Chamber]   The Whig senators.

483.2–3   *Speech . . . Compromise Resolutions*]   The text printed here was revised and corrected by Webster for publication in the *Congressional Globe Appendix*.

483.29   "Hear me for my cause."]   *Julius Caesar*, III, ii, 13.

488.21–22   "let the oppressed go free."]   Isaiah 58:6.

489.6–8   Senator . . . Methodist Episcopal Church]   See pp. 468.34–469.2 and note 468.35 in this volume.

490.21–22   "that we . . . may come"]   Cf. Romans 3:8.

495.1–2   an honorable member of this body]   Senator James Mason of Virginia was a grandson of George Mason (1725–1792), a Virginia delegate to the Constitutional Convention.

498.8   Mr. Walker]   Robert Walker (1801–1869) was a Democratic senator from Mississppi, 1835–45, and Secretary of the Treasury in the Polk administration, 1845–49.

499.2   Mr. BELL]   John Bell (1797–1869), a Whig, was a congressman from Tennessee, 1827–41, and a senator, 1847–59. He was the Constitutional Union presidential candidate in 1860.

500.15   Mr. HAMLIN]   Hannibal Hamlin (1809–1891) served in Congress as a Democrat from Maine, 1843–47; in the Senate as a Democrat, 1848–57, and then as a Republican, 1857–61 and 1869–81; and as Vice-President of the United States, 1861–65.

500.19–20   the district . . . defeated the choice]   John G. Palfrey (1796–1881), an antislavery Whig, served in Congress, 1847–49, as the representative of the Fourth District (Middlesex County). In November 1848 Palfrey ran for reelection on the Free Soil ticket but fell short of winning the required majority. After 13 runoff elections failed to produce a result, the Massachusetts legislature passed a law enabling the election to be decided by a plurality, and in May 1851 Benjamin Thompson (1798–1852), a Conservative Whig, defeated Palfrey by 87 votes.

500.30   My honorable friend from Georgia]   John Berrien (1781–1856), a Whig, served in the Senate, 1825–29 and 1841–52.

501.3–4   Mr. Dix . . . Mr. Niles]   John Dix (1798–1879) was a Democratic senator from New York, 1845–49; John Niles (1787–1856) was a Democratic senator from Connecticut, 1835–39 and 1843–49.

501.24   *rectus*]   Right.

502.3   Mr. Upshur]   Abel Upshur (1791–1844) was Secretary of State, 1843–44, in the Tyler administration. Upshur, a former Secretary of the Navy, was killed by the explosion of a cannon onboard the steamship U.S.S. *Princeton.*

502.13–14   to the Greek Kalends]   To a date that does not exist, i.e., indefinitely.

502.30   *flagrante bello*]   While war is blazing.

503.30   Gen. Hamilton]   James Hamilton Jr. (1786–1857) was a congressman from South Carolina, 1822–29; governor of South Carolina, 1830–32; and a financial and political supporter of Texas independence.

504.2–3   Niblo's Garden]   A theater at Broadway and Prince Street in New York City.

504.4   Mr. GREENE]   Albert Greene (1792–1863) was a Whig senator from Rhode Island, 1845–51.

506.34   three million loan bill]   A bill, passed in March 1847, appropriating money for acquiring territory from Mexico.

511.31–32   my friend . . . Judiciary Committee]   Senator Andrew Butler of South Carolina.

513.11   Mr. Hilliard]   George Stillman Hilliard (1808–1879), a Whig lawyer and orator, later served as U.S. attorney for Massachusetts, 1866–71.

514.16   Mr. Randolph]   Thomas Jefferson Randolph (1792–1875), a grandson of Thomas Jefferson and the chief executor of his estate.

514.38   Gov. McDowell]   James McDowell (1795–1851) served in the Virginia House of Delegates, 1831–35 and in 1838. He was later governor of Virginia, 1843–46, and a congressman, 1846–51.

516.31   An honorable member from Louisiana] Solomon Downs (1801–1854) was a Democratic senator from Louisiana, 1847–53.

517.27   Mr. Hoar's mission] See p. 432.14–37 and note 432.19–20 in this volume.

520.14   Convention held at Nashville] See note 424.30–31.

520.29–30   Mr. Windham] William Windham (1750–1810), a Member of Parliament, 1784–1810, made the remark in the House of Commons on November 4, 1801.

521.16–17   great man . . . New York] Rufus King (1755–1827) was a senator from New York, 1789–96 and 1813–25.

523.3–6   "Now the broad . . . the whole."] *Iliad*, XVIII, 701–4 (trans. Alexander Pope).

524.2   *Speech to Woman's Rights Convention*] The text printed here is taken from "Sojourner Truth," an article by Frances Dana Gage that appeared in the *National Anti-Slavery Standard* on May 2, 1863. Gage (1808–1884), a white lecturer and writer who had presided at the Akron Convention, described her account as "but a faint sketch" of Truth's speech. There are four contemporary reports of her speech; the fullest appeared in the Salem, Ohio, *Anti-Slavery Bugle* on June 21, 1851, and is printed below.

One of the most unique and interesting speeches of the Convention was made by Sojourner Truth, an emancipated slave. It is impossible to transfer it to paper, or convey any adequate idea of the effect it produced upon the audience. Those only can appreciate it who saw her powerful form, her whole-souled, earnest gesture, and listened to her strong and truthful tones. She came forward to the platform and addressing the President said with great simplicity:

May I say a few words? Receiving an affirmative answer, she proceeded; I want to say a few words about this matter. I am a woman's rights. I have as much muscle as any man, and can do as much work as any man. I have plowed and reaped and husked and chopped and mowed, and can any man do more than that? I have heard much about the sexes being equal; I can carry as much as any man, and can eat as much too, if I can get it. I am as strong as any man that is now.

As for intellect, all I can say is, if woman have a pint and man a quart—why can't she have her little pint full? You need not be afraid to give us our rights for fear we will take too much—for we won't take more than our pint'll hold.

The poor men seem to be all in confusion and don't know what to do. Why children, if you have woman's rights give it to her and you will feel better. You will have your own rights, and they won't be so much trouble.

I can't read, but I can hear. I have heard the Bible and have learned that Eve caused man to sin. Well if woman upset the world, do give her a chance to set it right side up again. The lady has spoken about Jesus, how he never spurned woman from him, and she was right. When Lazarus died, Mary and Martha came to him with faith and love and besought him to raise their brother. And Jesus wept—and Lazarus came forth. And how came Jesus into the world? Through God who created him and woman who bore him. Man, where is your part?

But the women are coming up blessed be God and a few of the men are coming up with them. But man is in a tight place, the poor slave is on him, woman is coming on him, and he is surely between a hawk and a buzzard.

524.19   I have . . . chillen,]   In *Narrative of Sojourner Truth* (1850), written by her amanuensis Olive Gilbert, Truth is said to have had five children.

526.2   *What to the . . . 4th of July?*]   The text printed here is taken from a pamphlet published by Douglass, who delivered this speech at the invitation of the Rochester Ladies' Anti-Slavery Society.

529.37–38   a more modern . . . euphonious term]   Possibly an allusion to "Hunker," the name for the conservative faction in the New York Democratic Party opposed to the antislavery "Barnburners."

533.15–18   "Trust no future, . . . overhead."]   Henry Wadsworth Longfellow, "A Psalm of Life" (1838).

533.28   Sydney Smith]   Smith (1771–1845), an Anglican clergyman, was an English essayist, lecturer, and social reformer.

533.33–34   "Abraham to our father,"]   Luke 3:8.

534.3–4   Washington could not . . . his slaves.]   In July 1799, five months before his death, Washington drew up a will that resulted in the emancipation of 122 slaves.

534.8–9   "The evil . . . their bones."]   *Julius Caesar*, III, ii, 75–76.

534.29   "lame man . . . hart."]   Isaiah 35:6.

535.10–18   "By the rivers . . . mouth."]   Psalm 137:1–6.

536.5–6   "I will not . . . excuse;"]   In the first issue of *The Liberator*, January 1, 1831, William Lloyd Garrison wrote: "I am in earnest—I will not equivocate—I will not excuse—I will not retreat a single inch—and *I will be heard.*"

538.38   Ex-Senator Benton]   Thomas Hart Benton; see Biographical Notes.

541.24–27   "Is this . . . slumber in?"]   Cf. John Greenleaf Whittier, "Stanzas for the Times" (1835).

542.6   your Secretary of State,]   Daniel Webster served as Secretary of State in the Fillmore administration from July 22, 1850, until his death on October 24, 1852.

543.13–14   "*mint, anise and cummin*"]   Matthew 23:23.

544.29   "*pure and undefiled religion*"]   Cf. James 1:27.

544.30–32   "*first pure, . . . without hypocrisy.*"]   Cf. James 3:17.

545.6–16   "Bring no more . . . for the widow."]   Cf. Isaiah 11:13–17.

545.22   Albert Barnes]   Barnes (1798–1870) was pastor of the First Presbyterian Church in Philadelphia, 1830–70, and author of *An Inquiry into the Scriptural Views of Slavery* (1846).

546.21   Samuel J. May of Syracuse]   May (1797–1871) was a Unitarian pastor, woman's rights and temperance advocate, and abolitionist who assisted slaves fleeing to Canada. He was indicted, but not convicted, for taking part in the "Jerry rescue" of a fugitive slave from a Syracuse police station on October 1, 1851.

547.28–29   fallen Hungary]   The Hungarian Revolution of 1848 was repressed in 1849 by Austrian and Russian troops.

548.3–5   "that, of one . . . the earth,"]   Cf. Acts 17:26.

548.14–15   "*is worse . . . to oppose*,"]   Douglass paraphrases a letter Jefferson wrote to Jean Nicholas Démeunier on June 26, 1786.

549.5–7   "To palter . . . the heart."]   Cf. *Macbeth*, V, viii, 20–23.

549.16–18   Lysander Spooner . . . Gerritt Smith]   Spooner (1808–1887) was the author of *The Unconstitutionality of Slavery* (1845). William Goodell (1792–1878) was the author of *Views of American Constitutional Law, Its Bearing upon American Slavery* (1844). Samuel Sewall (1799–1888) published *Remarks on Slavery in the United States* in 1827 and was the Liberty Party candidate for governor of Massachusetts in 1843. Gerrit Smith (1797–1874) was a founder of the Liberty Party, the author of several pamphlets attacking the constitutionality of slavery, and a financial supporter of *Frederick Douglass' Paper*.

550.9   Ex-Vice-President Dallas]   George Dallas (1792–1864) was a senator from Pennsylvania, 1831–33, and vice-president under Polk, 1845–49.

550.14   Senator Berrien]   See note 500.30.

550.17–18   Senator Breese, Lewis Cass]   Sidney Breese (1800–1878) was a Democratic senator from Illinois, 1843–49. For Lewis Cass, see note 388.14.

550.32–33   "*The arm . . . shortened*,"]   Cf. Isaiah 59:1.

551.23   "*Ethiopia . . . unto God.*"]   See Psalm 68:31.

551.26–552.21   "God speed . . . driven."]   William Lloyd Garrison, "The Triumph of Freedom" (1845).

553.2   *The Crime Against Kansas*]   Sumner delivered this speech during a debate that began on March 17, 1856, when Senator Stephen A. Douglas reported a bill for Kansas statehood that recognized the proslavery territorial government established in 1855. After Sumner finished his speech on May 20, Senator Lewis Cass called it "un-American and unpatriotic," Douglas denounced its "malignity" and "lasciviousness and obscenity," and Senator James Mason described it as "depravity, vice in its most odious form uncoiled." Two days later, while seated at his desk on the Senate floor, Sumner was approached by South Carolina congressman Preston Brooks (1819–1857), a cousin of Senator Andrew Butler, who said: "I have read your speech twice over carefully. It is a libel on South Carolina, and Mr. Butler, who is a relative of mine—" Brooks then beat Sumner with his cane until the Senator lost consciousness. After a measure to expel him from the House failed to win the necessary two-thirds majority, Brooks resigned his seat and was reelected by his district. Sumner did not return regularly to the Senate until December 1859.

553.33   field of Marathon]   Site of the Greek victory over the invading Persian army in 490 B.C.

554.5–6   fields of Crecy and Agincourt]   The battles of Crécy (1346) and Agincourt (1415) were English victories during the Hundred Years War.

554.13–14   great Roman Orator . . . Verres]   In 70 B.C. Cicero prosecuted Gaius Verres, the former governor of Sicily, for corruption. The trial ended when Verres agreed to go into exile.

556.5–6   *sed potius . . . quam bellum*]   Florus, *Epitome of the Histories of Titus Livy*, II, xiii. The quotation can be translated as Sumner's "but something compounded of all these strifes, and in itself more than war," or as "but it was rather a war consisting of all of these, or even something more than a war."

556.29   Bacon . . . Hastings]   Francis Bacon (1561–1626), lord chancellor of England from 1618 until 1621, was removed from office for accepting bribes. Warren Hastings (1732–1818) was governor of Bengal, 1772–85. His impeachment on charges of corruption and cruelty in 1788 resulted, after prolonged proceedings, in his acquittal in 1795.

558.11   Mr. BUTLER]   Andrew Butler (1796–1857) was a Democratic senator from South Carolina, 1846–57.

558.12   Mr. DOUGLAS]   Stephen A. Douglas (1813–1861) was a Democratic congressman from Illinois, 1843–47, a senator, 1847–61, and the Northern Democratic candidate for president in 1860.

560.9   Hampden]   See note 305.16.

560.14   Russell and Sidney]   William Russell (1639–1683) and Algernon Sidney (1622–1683), political opponents of Charles II who were executed for allegedly plotting his assassination.

561.6   Mr. HALE] See note 387.31–32.

561.33–37   peace of Utrecht . . . treaty of Madrid] The treaty of Utrecht (1713) ended the War of the Spanish Succession (1702–13); the treaty of Aix-la-Chapelle, (1748) ended the War of the Austrian Succession (1740–48); the treaty of Madrid, signed by Britain and Spain in 1817, allowed Spain to continue the slave trade until 1820.

562.7–8   labored address . . . labored report] The Committee on Territories, which Douglas chaired, submitted a report on Kansas to the Senate on March 12, 1856, and Douglas spoke on March 20 in support of his bill for Kansas statehood.

562.13–14   "for a charm . . . trouble,"] *Macbeth*, IV, i, 18.

562.17   "sweltered venom sleeping got,"] *Macbeth*, IV, i, 8.

562.26   Like Danton] In his speech to the Legislative Assembly on September 2, 1792, urging resistance to the Prussian invasion.

562.32–34   ancient madman . . . Ephesian dome] Herostratus burned the Temple of Artemis at Ephesus in 356 B.C. in a bid to gain immortal fame.

563.15   *crimen majestatis,*] Crimes against the Roman state.

563.24   distinguished historian] Richard Hildreth (1809–1865), author of *History of the United States of America* (6 vols., 1849–52).

563.25   Ithuriel touch] In *Paradise Lost*, IV, 799–813, Satan reveals his true form in the Garden of Eden after being touched by the spear of the angel Ithuriel.

564.11   the President,] Franklin Pierce.

564.16   Charles Pinckney] Pinckney (1757–1824) served as a senator from South Carolina, 1798–1801, and as a congressman, 1819–21.

567.4   Mr. CASS] See note 388.14.

567.5   Mr. BROWN] Albert Gallatin Brown (1813–1880) was a Democratic congressman from Mississippi, 1839–41 and 1847–53, and a senator, 1854–61.

570.4   David R. Atchison] Atchison (1807–1886) was a Democratic senator from Missouri, 1843–56, and a leader of the Missouri "border ruffians" attempting to make Kansas a slave state. He had presided over the Senate as president pro tem on several occasions.

570.9   *immo in Senatum venit*] Cicero, *Oratio in Catilinam*, I, ii: "immo vero etiam in senatum venit" ("Yes, he even comes into the Senate").

570.10–11   *abiit, excessit, evasit, erupit*] Cicero, *Oratio in Catilinam*, II, i: "He has left, absconded, escaped, disappeared."

571.3–5 to declare . . . ensued."] In his special message on Kansas, January 24, 1856, Pierce condemned the convention that met at Topeka in the fall of 1855 and adopted a free-state constitution prohibiting slavery.

571.21 Mr. Whitfield] John W. Whitfield (1818–1879) served as the territorial delegate from Kansas from December 20, 1854, until August 1, 1856, when his seat was declared vacant.

571.22 General Pomeroy] Samuel C. Pomeroy (1818–1879) was a financial agent for the New England Emigrant Aid Company. He later served as a Republican senator from Kansas, 1861–73. The origin of his title "general" is not known.

573.26 The weak Governor,] Wilson Shannon (1802–1877), a former governor of Ohio, was appointed territorial governor of Kansas in August 1855 and served until his resignation in August 1856.

574.13 the British orator,] Edmund Burke.

576.10 the Douglas of other days] James, Lord Douglas (1286?–1330) and James, Earl of Douglas (1358?–1388) were Scottish nobles celebrated for their border raids into northern England.

576.28–29 regicide Ravaillac . . . bed of steel"] François Ravaillac was tortured to death in 1610 after he assassinated Henry IV of France. The quotation is from "The Traveller" (1764) by Oliver Goldsmith (1730–1774).

577.3 an eminent American artist] The sculptor Horatio Greenough (1805–1852).

577.13–16 "Ay, in . . . of dogs:"] *Macbeth*, III, i, 91–94.

578.40–579.1 *Que diable . . . galere?*] Molière, *Les Fourberies de Scapin* (1671), II, vii: "What the devil was he doing in that galley?"

579.16 Stringfellow] Benjamin F. Stringfellow (1816–1891), a Missouri lawyer, was the leader of an armed proslavery group in Kansas Territory.

579.21 *Reeder*] Andrew H. Reeder (1807–1864), the first territorial governor of Kansas, was appointed by Pierce in June 1854 and dismissed in July 1855 for supporting the free-soil settlers.

582.28 Mr. COLLAMER,] Jacob Collamer (1791–1865) was a Whig congressman from Vermont, 1843–49, and a Republican senator, 1855–65.

582.33–37 *Non nulli . . . corroboraverunt.*] Cicero, *Oratio in Catilinam*, I, xii: "There are some men in this body who either do not see what threatens, or dissemble what they do see; who have fed the hope of Catiline by mild sentiments, and have strengthened the rising conspiracy by not believing it" (trans. C. D. Yonge).

584.13 Tubal Cain] See Genesis 4:22.

586.35–587.5 "That seem'd . . . unseen."] *Paradise Lost*, II, 650–59.

587.18 massacre of St. Bartholomew] A series of massacres of French Protestants in 1572 began in Paris on August 24, St. Bartholomew's Day.

590.32–33 A fugitive from Virginia,] Anthony Burns (1834–1862) was arrested in Boston on May 24, 1854, and taken onboard a federal revenue cutter on June 2. In 1855 his freedom was purchased by a group of Massachusetts supporters.

595.15–16 *triumviri ad . . . deducendos*] A triumvirate to lead the colonists.

597.29–30 the Company . . . supplied no arms] Although the Emigrant Aid Company did not officially send weapons to Kansas, officers of the company purchased hundreds of rifles and shipped them to company agents in Kansas for distribution to free-state settlers.

598.8 Its President] John Carter Brown (1797–1874), a Rhode Island philanthropist and book collector.

598.13 Its generous Treasurer] Amos A. Lawrence (1814–1886), a wealthy Massachusetts textile manufacturer and philanthropist.

600.7–8 Macbeth . . . go on;] Cf. *Macbeth*, III, iv, 135–37.

600.9 Mr. GEYER,] Henry Geyer (1790–1859) was a Whig senator from Missouri, 1851–57.

600.30 "Awake! . . . fallen!"] *Paradise Lost*, I, 330.

600.31 Mr. EVANS] Josiah Evans (1786–1858) was a Democratic senator from South Carolina, 1853–58.

601.15–16 Senator from Illinois . . . Vermont] Stephen A. Douglas was born in Vermont and moved to Illinois in 1833.

601.40 Native American party] The anti-immigrant Know-Nothings.

604.27 contested election] The election of the territorial delegate from Kansas; see note 571.21.

604.34–35 Anacharsis Clootz] Anacharsis Cloots (1755–1794), a Prussian noble of Dutch ancestry, appeared before the National Assembly in 1790 as the "orator of the human race." He received French citizenship in 1792 and was elected to the Convention, but was expelled in December 1793 and guillotined by the Jacobins on March 24, 1794.

606.34 Colonel Sumner's regiment] Edwin Sumner (1797–1863) was assigned in March 1855 to command the 1st Cavalry Regiment at Fort Leavenworth, Kansas. (Edwin Sumner and Charles Sumner were both descended from William Sumner, who immigrated to Massachusetts in 1635.)

607.13–14   judicial honor . . . important committee]   Butler had served on the South Carolina court of common pleas, 1835–46, and was chairman of the Senate judiciary committee.

609.35   Mr. SEWARD]   See Biographical Notes.

610.9–12   "Oh help," . . . *sorrows come.*"]   Ovid, *Metamorphoses*, I.

610.27–28   invasion at Wakarusa]   In late 1855 a large party of Missouri "border ruffians" gathered along the Wakasura River near Lawrence, but dispersed when they learned that free-state settlers were preparing to defend the town.

615.9   Mr. Hendricks, of Indiana]   William Hendricks was a congressman, 1816–22, and a senator, 1825–37.

615.26   Mr. Buchanan]   See note 294.14.

617.28–29   Felix Grundy]   Grundy (1777–1840) was a congressman from Tennessee, 1811–14, and a senator, 1829–38 and 1839–40.

617.39   Mr. Ewing]   Thomas Ewing (1789–1871) was a senator from Ohio, 1831–37 and 1850–51.

619.6   Mr. Morris, of Ohio]   Thomas Morris (1776–1844) was a senator from Ohio, 1833–39.

619.22   *mutato nomine*]   Under a changed name.

621.36–37   "self-evident lie"]   The remark was made by John Pettit (1807–1877), a Democratic congressman from Indiana, 1843–49, and a senator, 1853–55.

621.40   the Holy Alliance]   An alliance formed in 1815 by Russia, Austria, and Prussia to suppress revolutionary movements in Europe.

621.21   St. George Tucker]   Tucker (1752–1827) was a judge of the Virginia court of appeals, 1804–13, and a federal district judge, 1813–25. He published a five-volume annotated edition of Blackstone's *Commentaries* in 1803.

623.16   Mr. Buchanan, in reply]   During the debate in the Senate on the admission of Michigan, January 5, 1837.

625.1   "with most miraculous organ,"]   *Hamlet*, II, ii, 594.

626.17–18   *Nullum flagitium . . . sine te.*]   His activity and inactivity are alike fatal.

626.30–31   the patriot philosopher]   Benjamin Franklin was accused of being a thief before the Privy Council in London by Solicitor General Alexander Wedderburn in January 1774.

629.5   language of Patrick Henry]   In his speech on the Stamp Act to the Virginia House of Burgesses in 1765.

629.19–22   "For Humanity . . . golden urn."] James Russell Lowell, "The Present Crisis" (1844).

629.27   Mr. MASON,] See note 455.22.

629.39   a dungeon rewards the pious matron] In January 1854 Margaret Douglas, a white woman, was sentenced to a month in jail in Norfolk, Virginia, for teaching African-American children to read.

630.29   "These are . . . thee!"] *Aeneid*, VI, 853.

630.35   Great Refusal] Cf. Dante, *Inferno*, III, 60.

634.2   *"House Divided" Speech*] Lincoln delivered this speech to the Republican state convention after it had endorsed him as its "first and only choice" for the Senate seat held by Stephen A. Douglas.

634.15   "A house . . . cannot stand."] Cf. Matthew 12:25; Mark 3:25.

636.4   Senator Trumbull] Lyman Trumbull (1813–1896) was a senator from Illinois, 1855–73. Initially elected as a Democrat opposed to the Nebraska Act, Trumbull later joined the Republicans.

636.5   leading advocate of the Nebraska bill] Stephen A. Douglas.

636.28–29   the Silliman letter] A public letter written by President Buchanan on August 15, 1857, in response to a protest against administration policy in Kansas signed by 40 Connecticut clergymen and educators.

636.34   the Lecompton constitution] A constitution adopted by a proslavery convention in Kansas on November 7, 1857. It was supported by Buchanan and opposed by Douglas.

639.4   Stephen, Franklin, Roger, and James] Senator Stephen A. Douglas, President Franklin Pierce, Chief Justice Roger B. Taney, and President James Buchanan.

639.34   McLean or Curtis] John McLean (1785–1861) and Benjamin R. Curtis (1809–1874), the two dissenting justices in the Dred Scott case.

639.36   Chase and Macy] Salmon P. Chase (1808–1873) was a Free Soil senator from Ohio, 1849–55. He later served as Secretary of the Treasury, 1861–64, and Chief Justice of the Supreme Court, 1864–73. John Macy (1799–1856) was a Democratic congressman from Wisconsin, 1853–55.

640.2   Judge Nelson] In the Dred Scott case, Justice Samuel Nelson (1792–1873) had written a separate decision, originally intended to be the opinion of the Court, ruling against Scott on narrower grounds than those given by Chief Justice Taney.

641.2–3   "a *living dog* . . . *lion*."] Ecclesiastes 9:4.

643.2   *The Irrepressible Conflict*] Seward made this speech while campaigning for the Republican ticket in the New York State election.

646.4   candidate for president] John C. Frémont, the Republican presidential candidate in 1856.

649.12–13   my manhood, . . . free state,] Seward was born in 1801; slavery was not finally abolished in New York State until 1827.

653.2–4   Kansas . . . the Union,] In March 1858 the Senate approved admitting Kansas as a state under the proslavery Lecompton constitution, but the House voted to have the constitution resubmitted to the voters. Congress then passed the English Bill, a compromise measure submitting the constitution under the guise of a land-grant referendum. The Lecompton constitution was rejected by the voters on August 2, 1858, and Kansas did not enter the Union until January 29, 1861, when it was admitted as a free state.

654.35   Walker] Robert J. Walker (see note 498.8). Walker was appointed as territorial governor of Kansas in April 1857, but resigned in December in protest over the fraudulent methods used to frame and adopt the Lecompton constitution.

658.2   *True Americanism*] Schurz delivered this speech at the request of Massachusetts Republicans opposed to an amendment to the state constitution prohibiting foreign-born citizens from voting until two years after their naturalization. The amendment was approved by the voters in May 1859 and repealed in 1863.

667.39   "Master, master, we perish!"] Luke 8:24.

668.2   "Where is your faith?"] Luke 8:25.

669.16   Antæus] A giant in Greek mythology who was defeated by Heracles.

671.26–28   "he would . . . degree of it."] From a letter to Archibald Stuart, December 23, 1791.

674.19   Smithfield] Area in London where heretics were burned in the 16th and early 17th centuries.

674.36   cowardly murderers] Virginia congressman George Edmundson and South Carolina congressman Laurence Keitt accompanied Preston Brooks when he entered the Senate chamber and assaulted Sumner on May 22, 1856.

675.14–15   speaking a few words . . . evenings since,] Schurz spoke at a Republican dinner held at the Parker House in Boston on April 13, 1859.

676.28   Valley of Jehoshaphat] Joel 3:2.

678.2   *Speech to the Court*] Brown spoke after being convicted in a Virginia court of conspiracy, murder, and treason following his failed raid on the federal armory at Harpers Ferry, October 16–18, 1859. He was hanged on December 2, 1859.

680.2   *Address at Cooper Institute*]   Lincoln delivered this address to an audience of 1,500 people. The text is taken from a pamphlet prepared under his supervision.

692.39–693.1   Southampton insurrection . . . Harper's Ferry?]   For the Southampton insurrection led by Nat Turner, see note 320.28. Fifteen people were killed during the raid on Harpers Ferry, and Brown and four of his followers had been hanged by the time of Lincoln's speech.

693.29–34   "It is still . . . held up."]   From the *Autobiography*, written in 1821 but not published until after Jefferson's death.

694.12–13   Orsini's . . . Napoleon]   Felice Orsini (1819–1858), an Italian revolutionary, attempted to assassinate Napoleon III on January 14, 1858. Eight people were killed in the attack, and Orsini was captured and executed.

694.19   Helper's Book]   *The Impending Crisis of the South: How to Meet It* (1857), by Hinton R. Helper (1829–1909) of North Carolina. Helper attacked slavery as harmful to the social and economic interests of nonslaveholding Southern whites. The publication in the North of an abridged version, and its endorsement by 68 Republican congressmen, created a sectional controversy.

700.6–7   Mississippi . . . separation]   The secession ordinance was passed on January 9, 1861.

702.23   rescue of a fugitive slave]   Frederick "Shadrach" Minkins was rescued from the Boston courthouse by a group of African-Americans on February 15, 1851, and later escaped to Canada.

703.6–7   language of Mr. Jefferson]   Jefferson wrote to Roger C. Weightman on June 24, 1826: "The general spread of the light of science has already laid open the palpable truth, that the mass of mankind has not been born with saddles on their backs, nor a favored few booted and spurred, ready to ride them legitimately, by the grace of God."

705.2   *Speech at Independence Hall*]   Lincoln made this speech while traveling from Springfield, Illinois, to Washington, D.C., for his inauguration.

706.1   assassinated on this spot]   Lincoln had been told the night before of a plot to assassinate him as he traveled through Baltimore.

710.1–2   Articles of Association in 1774.]   The articles were adopted by the First Continental Congress.

715.39–716.5   I am loth . . . our nature.]   This paragraph was proposed and drafted by William H. Seward as follows: "I close. We are not we must not be aliens or enemies but ~~countrm~~ fellow countrymen and brethren. Although passion has strained our bonds of affection too hardly they must not ~~be broken they will not~~, I am sure they will not be broken. The mystic chords which proceeding from ~~every ba~~ so many battle fields and ~~patriot~~ so many patriot graves ~~bind~~ pass through all the hearts and ~~hearths~~ all the hearths in this broad continent of ours will yet ~~harmon~~ again harmonize in their ancient music when ~~touched as they surely~~ breathed upon ~~again~~ by the ~~better angel~~ guardian angel of the nation."

717.2   *"Corner-Stone" Speech*]   Stephens gave this speech in the Savannah Atheneum. The text printed here first appeared in the Savannah *Republican* and was accompanied by a reporter's note stating that it was not "a perfect report, but only such a sketch of the address" as embraced the most important points.

718.10   Seven States]   South Carolina, Mississippi, Florida, Alabama, Georgia, Louisiana, and Texas.

719.8–9   Palmetto State, . . . in 1833.]   See note 257.14–15.

723.37–38   curse against Canaan,]   See Genesis 9:25.

724.8–9   "one star . . . glory."]   Cf. 1 Corinthians 15:41.

724.28–29   "in the sweat . . . bread,"]   Cf. Genesis 3:19.

726.12–13   the policy . . . co-operation]   In 1860–61 "co-operationists" opposed immediate secession and advocated having a united South present its demands to the North.

728.37–38   Fort Pickens]   The fort, which guarded the entrance to Pensacola Bay, was held by the Union throughout the Civil War.

732.2   *Address at Gettysburg, Pennsylvania*]   The text printed here is Lincoln's final version, prepared in the spring of 1864 for facsimile reproduction in *Autograph Leaves of Our Country's Authors*, a book published by the Baltimore Sanitary Fair. The Associated Press report printed below, based upon shorthand notes, may be closer to what Lincoln actually said at Gettysburg, but a comparison with other newspaper reports and with Lincoln's autograph drafts indicates that it probably contains several errors:

> Four score and seven years ago our fathers brought forth upon this continent a new Nation, conceived in Liberty, and dedicated to the proposition that all men are created equal. [Applause.] Now we are engaged in a great civil war, testing whether that Nation or any Nation so conceived and so dedicated can long endure. We are met on a great battle-field of that war. We are met to dedicate a portion of it as the final resting-place of those who gave their lives that that nation might live. It is altogether fitting and proper that we should do this. But in a larger sense we cannot dedicate, we cannot consecrate, we cannot hallow this ground. The brave men living and dead who struggled here have consecrated it far above our power to add or detract. [Applause.] The world will little note or long remember what we say here, but it can never forget what they did here. [Applause.] It is for us, the living, rather to be dedicated here to the refinished work that

they have thus far so nobly carried on. [Applause.] It is rather for us to be here dedicated to the great task remaining before us, that from these honored dead we take increased devotion to the cause for which they here gave the last full measure of devotion; that we here highly resolve that the dead shall not have died in vain [applause]; that the nation shall, under God, have a new birth of freedom; and that Governments of the people, by the people, and for the people, shall not perish from the earth. [Long-continued applause.]

734.9–10   let us . . . not judged.]   Cf. Matthew 7:1; Luke 6:37.

734.12–14   "Woe . . . cometh!"]   Matthew 18:7.

734.27–28   "the judgments . . . altogether"]   Psalm 19:9.

Index

Library of Congress Cataloging-in-Publication Data:

American speeches.
      p. cm. — (The Library of America ; 166–167)
      Contents: pt. 1. Political oratory from the Revolution to the
Civil War—pt. 2. Political oratory from Abraham Lincoln to Bill
Clinton.
    ISBN 1–931082–97–9 (v. 1 : alk. paper)—ISBN 1–931082–98–7
(v. 2 : alk. paper)
    1. United States—Politics and government—Sources.
2. United States—History—Sources. 3. Speeches, addresses, etc.,
American. 4. Political oratory—United States. I. Series: Library
of America (Series) ; 166–167.

E183.A498 2006
973—dc22   2006040928

THE LIBRARY OF AMERICA SERIES

The Library of America fosters appreciation and pride in America's literary heritage by publishing, and keeping permanently in print, authoritative editions of America's best and most significant writing. An independent nonprofit organization, it was founded in 1979 with seed money from the National Endowment for the Humanities and the Ford Foundation.

1. Herman Melville, *Typee, Omoo, Mardi* (1982)
2. Nathaniel Hawthorne, *Tales and Sketches* (1982)
3. Walt Whitman, *Poetry and Prose* (1982)
4. Harriet Beecher Stowe, *Three Novels* (1982)
5. Mark Twain, *Mississippi Writings* (1982)
6. Jack London, *Novels and Stories* (1982)
7. Jack London, *Novels and Social Writings* (1982)
8. William Dean Howells, *Novels 1875–1886* (1982)
9. Herman Melville, *Redburn, White-Jacket, Moby-Dick* (1983)
10. Nathaniel Hawthorne, *Collected Novels* (1983)
11. Francis Parkman, *France and England in North America*, vol. I (1983)
12. Francis Parkman, *France and England in North America*, vol. II (1983)
13. Henry James, *Novels 1871–1880* (1983)
14. Henry Adams, *Novels, Mont Saint Michel, The Education* (1983)
15. Ralph Waldo Emerson, *Essays and Lectures* (1983)
16. Washington Irving, *History, Tales and Sketches* (1983)
17. Thomas Jefferson, *Writings* (1984)
18. Stephen Crane, *Prose and Poetry* (1984)
19. Edgar Allan Poe, *Poetry and Tales* (1984)
20. Edgar Allan Poe, *Essays and Reviews* (1984)
21. Mark Twain, *The Innocents Abroad, Roughing It* (1984)
22. Henry James, *Literary Criticism: Essays, American & English Writers* (1984)
23. Henry James, *Literary Criticism: European Writers & The Prefaces* (1984)
24. Herman Melville, *Pierre, Israel Potter, The Confidence-Man, Tales & Billy Budd* (1985)
25. William Faulkner, *Novels 1930–1935* (1985)
26. James Fenimore Cooper, *The Leatherstocking Tales*, vol. I (1985)
27. James Fenimore Cooper, *The Leatherstocking Tales*, vol. II (1985)
28. Henry David Thoreau, *A Week, Walden, The Maine Woods, Cape Cod* (1985)
29. Henry James, *Novels 1881–1886* (1985)
30. Edith Wharton, *Novels* (1986)
31. Henry Adams, *History of the U.S. during the Administrations of Jefferson* (1986)
32. Henry Adams, *History of the U.S. during the Administrations of Madison* (1986)
33. Frank Norris, *Novels and Essays* (1986)
34. W.E.B. Du Bois, *Writings* (1986)
35. Willa Cather, *Early Novels and Stories* (1987)
36. Theodore Dreiser, *Sister Carrie, Jennie Gerhardt, Twelve Men* (1987)
37A. Benjamin Franklin, *Silence Dogood, The Busy-Body, & Early Writings* (1987)
37B. Benjamin Franklin, *Autobiography, Poor Richard, & Later Writings* (1987)
38. William James, *Writings 1902–1910* (1987)
39. Flannery O'Connor, *Collected Works* (1988)
40. Eugene O'Neill, *Complete Plays 1913–1920* (1988)
41. Eugene O'Neill, *Complete Plays 1920–1931* (1988)
42. Eugene O'Neill, *Complete Plays 1932–1943* (1988)
43. Henry James, *Novels 1886–1890* (1989)
44. William Dean Howells, *Novels 1886–1888* (1989)
45. Abraham Lincoln, *Speeches and Writings 1832–1858* (1989)
46. Abraham Lincoln, *Speeches and Writings 1859–1865* (1989)
47. Edith Wharton, *Novellas and Other Writings* (1990)
48. William Faulkner, *Novels 1936–1940* (1990)
49. Willa Cather, *Later Novels* (1990)

*This book is set in 10 point Linotron Galliard,
a face designed for photocomposition by Matthew Carter
and based on the sixteenth-century face Granjon. The paper
is acid-free lightweight opaque and meets the requirements
for permanence of the American National Standards Institute.
The binding material is Brillianta, a woven rayon cloth made
by Van Heek-Scholco Textielfabrieken, Holland. Composition by Dedicated Business Services. Printing by
Malloy Incorporated. Binding by Dekker Book-
binding. Designed by Bruce Campbell.*